Operations Management

An Integrated Approach

Operations Management: An Integrated Approach provides a state-of-the-art account of the systems, processes, people and technology that determine an organisation's strategy and success. With contributions from leading experts internationally, the text takes a comprehensive, comparative, and best-practice approach and applies this specifically to the Asia-Pacific region.

Rigorous in scholarship yet eminently accessible in style, *Operations Management* is replete with pedagogical features – figures and tables, discussion exercises, 'Learnings from the Internet', and a diversity of long and short case studies from around the world. Students are taken on a seamless journey from the fundamentals of operations management, through to the multiple approaches, the various innovations, challenges and risks, and ultimately to models of sustainability and evaluative tools and techniques.

The text effectively prepares future managers across every sector of the economy – whether in services, manufacturing, profit or non-profit environments – to lead, organise, plan and control a set of resources, in pursuit of identified goals.

Danny Samson is Professor of Management at the University of Melbourne.

Prakash J. Singh is Senior Lecturer in Management at the University of Melbourne.

Operations Management

An integrated approach

Edited by Danny Samson
and Prakash J. Singh

CAMBRIDGE
UNIVERSITY PRESS

CAMBRIDGE UNIVERSITY PRESS
Cambridge, New York, Melbourne, Madrid, Cape Town, Singapore, São Paulo

Cambridge University Press
477 Williamstown Road, Port Melbourne, VIC 3207, Australia

Published in the United States of America by Cambridge University Press, New York

www.cambridge.org
Information on this title: www.cambridge.org/9780521700771

© Danny Samson and Prakash J. Singh 2008

First published 2008

Printed in Australia by Ligare

A catalogue record for this publication is available from the British Library

National Library of Australia Cataloguing in Publication data
   Samson, Danny.
Operations management : an integrated approach / authors, Daniel Samson; Prakash J. Singh.
   Port Melbourne, Vic: Cambridge University Press, 2008.
   9780-521-70077-1 (pbk.)
   Management – Pacific Area.
   Production management – Pacific Area.
   Singh, Prakash J.
658.5

ISBN 978-0-521-70077-1

Contents

Part III Moving Forward with OM – Creating Competitive Advantage

Contributors

Brett M. Allen

Brett M. Allen is Purchasing Manager, Ford Australia, Brunswick West, Victoria.

Ron Beckett

Ron Beckett is Professor in the College of Business at the University of Western Sydney.

Tom Bevington

Tom Bevington is Director, Bevington Process Management Tools, Melbourne.

Kevin Burgess

Kevin Burgess is General Manager – Supply, at Queensland Rail, Brisbane.

Ross Chapman

Ross Chapman is Professor in the College of Business at the University of Western Sydney.

Lawrie Corbett

Lawrie Corbett is Associate Professor in the Victoria Management School at the Victoria University of Wellington.

Suzy Goldsmith

Suzy Goldsmith is Senior Research Fellow in the Department of Civil and Environmental Engineering at the University of Melbourne.

Victoria Hanna

Victoria Hanna is Lecturer in the Department of Management and Marketing at the University of Melbourne.

Z. Husain

Z. Husain is Professor in the Department of Business Administration at the

College of Business and Economics, United Arab Emirates University, Al-Ain, UAE.

Paul Hyland

Paul Hyland is Professorial Research Fellow in the School of Natural and Rural Systems Management at the University of Queensland.

Phillip Irvine

Phillip Irvine is Chief Operating Officer, Bartter Enterprises.

Bin Jiang

Bin Jiang is Assistant Professor in the Kellstadt Graduate School of Business, DePaul University, Chicago.

Senevi Kiridena

Senevi Kiridena is a PhD candidate in the School of Mechanical and Manufacturing Engineering at the University of New South Wales.

Richard Lane

Richard Lane is Professor in the UQ Business School at the University of Queensland.

John Morgan

John Morgan is Research Fellow in the Department of Management and Marketing at the University of Melbourne.

Patrick J. Murphy

Patrick J. Murphy is Assistant Professor in the Kellstadt Graduate School of Business, DePaul University, Chicago.

David Parker

David Parker is Senior Lecturer in the UQ Business School at the University of Queensland.

R. D. Pathak

R. D. Pathak is Professor in the School of Management and Public Administration at the University of the South Pacific, Suva.

Damien Power

Damien Power is Associate Professor in the Department of Management and Marketing at the University of Melbourne.

Daniel Prajogo

Daniel Prajogo is Senior Lecturer in the Department of Management at Monash University.

Danny Samson

Danny Samson is Professor in the Department of Management and Marketing at the University of Melbourne.

Jay Sankaran
Jay Sankaran is Associate Professor in the Department of Information Systems & Operations Management, at the University of Auckland.

Willem Selen
Willem Selen is Professor in the Middle East Technical University, Northern Cyprus Campus, Kalkanli – Guzelyurt, Mersin 10, Turkey.

Kannan Sethuraman
Kannan Sethuraman is Associate Professor in the Melbourne Business School at the University of Melbourne.

Dayna Simpson
Dayna Simpson is Lecturer in the Department of Marketing, Monash University.

Prakash J. Singh
Prakash J. Singh is Senior Lecturer in the Department of Management and Marketing at the University of Melbourne.

Terry Sloan
Terry Sloan is Associate Professor in the College of Business at the University of Western Sydney.

Claudine Soosay
Claudine Soosay is Lecturer in the School of Management at the University of South Australia.

Sum Chee Chuong
Sum Chee Chuong is Associate Professor in the Decisions Science Department, NUS Business School, National University of Singapore.

Sushil
Sushil is Professor in the Department of Management Studies at the Indian Institute of Technology, Delhi.

Clay Whybark
Clay Whybark is Professor in the Kenan-Flagler Business School at the University of North Carolina.

Preface

We edited and wrote this book, using a large team of contributors from around Asia Pacific, with a focus on the 'what' and 'how' of operations management. The field has matured strongly in the past decade in Australia, New Zealand and other countries in the region. It now is fully seen in most industries and organisations as a key management function and as a challenging and interesting career stream for professional managers.

Put simply, operations management is concerned with most effectively designing, conducting and improving the organisation's production processes, whatever the sector or industry, and whatever the product or service. Operations management delivers the outcomes that are specified within the organisation's overall strategy, and according to the market needs that the organisation is responding to. At its best, effective operations management creates more than just a great response to the business strategy, in that it can do more than just deliver the business strategy with effective and competitive outcomes. It can create competitive advantages which themselves provide new potential business strategies and capabilities which can be further exploited when correctly aimed at a market.

The operations function is where the goods and services are made. Most of the organisation's assets and people are deployed in its operations. Operations is where the outcomes that are critical to the organisation's survival and prosperity are decided, namely cost and productivity outcomes, as well as quality, delivery performance, flexibility, innovativeness and others.

Operations managers can have challenging and rewarding careers, in any and every industry, because all organisations exist to add value and to create goods and/or services for the consumption of other parties in the economy. Operations managers are a necessary and indeed key resource in all organisations, be it in mining operations, agriculture and farming, manufacturing, creating the built environment, services or government. Virtually everything we buy and consume, including all goods or services, was made under the supervision of an operations manager.

Operations managers are concerned with deciding and managing both 'hard' assets such as equipment and materials being transformed from inputs to outputs, and also 'soft' assets such as the workforce. Hence, they have a high variety of interesting breadth in their work, from making strategic decisions about assets such as designing a new facility or choosing a process technology, through to the daily management of staff and production processes, sometimes called line management.

Globalisation has increasingly meant that most of the operations in Asia Pacific are under pressure, to be as good as or better than the best competitor, which may be located anywhere in the world. If operations and the business which contain them are not competitive, they will not survive intact for long at all in most industries. Hence the term 'world's best practice' has arisen. It is no longer good enough to be doing things as well as the local industry practice; but operations must be as good as the best in the world, including in countries where cost structures are much lower than in Australia and New Zealand. If one cannot be competitive, then the threat with closure or outsourcing or 'offshoring' is ever present and very real. This has applied very much to manufactured goods for some forty years as a result of containerisation that made global shipping relatively inexpensive. In the past decade, a very similar thing has happened to many service sector operations as a result of the rapidly reducing costs of global information and telecommunications. Many companies have moved their factories to China or closed down and outsourced or subcontracted their manufacturing operations, and India has increasingly emerged as a powerhouse in service operations such as software development and maintenance, call centres and transaction processing. Australia and New Zealand have recently benefited from their operational efficiencies and competitive advantages in mining and in some farming and agricultural sectors. For example, mining operations across Australia, dairy farming and processing operations in New Zealand, and the wine industries and tourism sectors in both places are world class in operational effectiveness terms.

Relatively new developments in the lively and developing field of operations management have included the Operational Excellence field and Supply Chain Management. These are thoroughly covered in this book. Another strong trend has been to outsource those aspects and processes of an operation that someone else can do better, in order to not pay a competitive advantage price. Accomplishing outsourcing successfully requires a great deal of skill in itself on behalf of the operations manager.

Whatever the industry, and regardless of whether it is a huge company such as Australia's biggest employer with over 150,000 staff (the Woolworths group), or a one person business where that person is working from home, the core ideas of doing a good job on designing, conducting and improving the value-adding operations of the organisation can be applied. Indeed, the value adding processes of the organisation are much of its reason for existence, and clearly there is no such basis for existence if they are not present and operating effectively.

This is of course not to deny the importance of other functions and activities of the organisation. Outside the operation, critically important activities such as new product and service development, marketing and selling and numerous other tasks must also be done well. Doing those things well means that they are not done well separately from operations. Rather, they should complement and be integrated with the priorities and activities of the operations. Hence it is important for operations managers to understand the rest of the business, especially its overall strategy and market position. This is so that operations can deliver to that overall strategy in a precise and focused manner, and drive it to high standards of effective outcomes and competitiveness.

A book like this is a joint effort from many people. We are grateful to the many academics and professional managers who have contributed the work from which we have created and assembled the chapters and case studies in this book. We are also grateful to the many professional operations managers and students from whom we have learned over the years.

Thanks also go to our home institution, the University of Melbourne, for providing the supporting environment in which we produced this book. Finally, thanks to the team at Cambridge University Press for the fine job they have done in taking the manuscript through to publication.

We hope that for readers, our focus on Australia, New Zealand and Asia Pacific regional issues and examples will make this a useful and relevant volume for learning about the wonderful challenges and opportunities of operations management.

Danny Samson and Prakash J. Singh

Acknowledgements

We would like to acknowledge and thank many people who have directly or indirectly made the creation of this book possible.

First, we are grateful to our many colleagues who have contributed chapters and case studies. When we decided to produce an edited volume rather than write all of it ourselves, we chose leading academics and industry practitioners, and we thank you all most sincerely for your contributions. It was a pleasure to edit and add examples etc to your works.

Second, we want to thank the operations managers who we have interacted with over the past many years, who have taught us so much about what works, and what sometimes doesn't work in designing, conducting and improving operations of all types. We hope that the knowledge that we have gained from you will be effectively passed on to future generations of operations managers through this book and the courses and programs that make use of it.

We are also grateful to the University of Melbourne, our employer, for providing the infrastructure through which we have produced this book.

We gratefully acknowledge those who have given permission to reproduce copyright material used in this book: World Scientific Publishing and National University of Singapore (Box 8.2: Radical innovation – Skype, taken from Tan, L. L. 2007, 'Spotlight: Engaging callers globally.' *Innovation Magazine*, 6(3)); Australian Government, Attorney-General's Department (Box 8.3: Continuous innovation – Bega Cheese, Australia, taken from Thorburn, L. J. and Langdale, J. 2003, Embracing change – Case Study Illustrating How Australian Firms use Incremental Innovation to Support Growth: A report for the S&T Mapping Study (Dept Education Science and Training and Dept Industry Tourism and Resources), December 2003, copyright Commonwealth of Australia, reproduced by permission, and Box cs3.1: Productivity Commission review report excerpt, taken from Productivity Commission, *Review of TCF Assistance Inquiry Report*, Report no 26, 31 July 2003, p. 9, copyright Commonwealth of Australia, reproduced by permission); Starhub (Box 8.6: Market position innovation – Starhub

(Singapore), taken from StarHub (2007), StarHub corporate mile-stones, viewed 30 July at http://www.starhub.com/corporate/aboutus/milestones.html); the United Nations (Box 8.9: Technology licensing: Siam United Hi-Tech Ltd, Thailand, taken from United Nations 2005, Transfer of Technology for Successful Integration into the Global Economy: A Case Study of the Electronics Industry in Thailand, viewed 30 July 2007 at http://www.unctad.org/en/docs/iteipc20056_en.pdf); SAI Global (Figure 10.1: The Australian Business Excellence Framework, Table 10.1: Principles underpinning the Australian Business Excellence Framework and Table 10.2: Categories and associated items in the Australian Business Excellence Framework, all taken from the Australian Business Excellence Framework, reproduced with permission from SAI Global Ltd – the Australian Business Excellence Framework may be purchased online at http://www.saiglobal.com); the Singaporean Standards, Productivity and Innovation Board (Table 10.3: The Singapore Business Excellence Framework Criteria and Assessment Weightings, taken from the Singapore Quality Award and Business Excellence Framework – information available from the SPRING website http://www.spring.gov.sg/ – accessed on 25 July 2007); the New Zealand Business Excellence Foundation (Figure 10.3: Comparison between business improvement models as presented by the NZBEF, Figure 10.4: New Zealand Criteria for Performance Excellence and Table 10.4: Categories and associated items in the 2007 New Zealand Criteria for Performance Excellence – Business Category, taken from the New Zealand Business Excellence Foundation (NZBEF) – information available on the Criteria for Performance Excellence and Award categories from the NZBEF website http://www.nzbef.org.nz/ – accessed on 31 July 2007).

Thanks also to the whole team at Cambridge University Press for their diligent and disciplined approach to turning our vision and ideas into a delivered outcome.

Finally we want to thank our families for their support we have had in producing this volume.

Danny Samson and Prakash J. Singh

PART I

Operations within Organisations – Building Blocks

What is Operations Management and Why is it Important?

Prakash J. Singh

Learning objectives

After reading this chapter, you should be able to:

- define the meaning of 'operations management'
- explain the role of operations management within organisations, including how it relates to other functional areas
- describe the differences and similarities between goods and services, and show how these affect our understanding of operations management
- describe the decisions that fall within the field of operations management;
- discuss the trends that are encouraging organisations to focus on their operations
- trace the historical evolution of the field
- describe typical careers that can be developed within the operations management area.

Box 1.1: Management challenge: Woolworths Limited

Woolworths Limited is the largest retailer in Australia, collecting about 18 cents in every dollar spent in the retail industry. With a nominal capital of 25,000 pounds (approximately $A70,000 today), Woolworths opened its first store in Sydney in 1924. The company posted annual revenue of close to $38 billion, and net operating profit of over $1 billion in 2006. Along with its flagship Woolworths and Safeway supermarkets (which has close to 40 per cent market share in that industry sub-sector), it also owns Dick Smith Electronics, Tandy Electronics, Big W discount store chain, and Dan Murphy's liquor stores, among others. It has also formed alliances with companies such as Caltex to retail petrol. Currently, it operates close to 3,000 stores, petrol stations and hotels in Australia and New Zealand. The company employs more than 140,000 people. It has made massive investments in recent years in new technologies, refreshing its stores and new distribution centres, which are expected to fuel its next decade of competitiveness and operational capacity and capability.

So, how did Woolworths become so successful?

Introduction

Unlike other functional areas within organisations, many people find it hard to clearly and easily understand what activities come under the field of Operations. Finance, for example, deals with the use (and sometimes abuse) of funds. Marketing is primarily responsible for positioning, pricing, selling and liaison with customers. However, when it comes to Operations, it is not so clear-cut. This is because the word 'operations' is sometimes (wrongly) used interchangeably with 'operational', a word that is the opposite of strategic, and connotes detailed, localised, short-term, day-to-day activities.[1] Further complicating the situation is the use of context dependent labels in place of the generic word. For example, in manufacturing companies, production is frequently used in place of operations; in logistics firms, fleet management is typically used; and in a large restaurant, the title of duty manager is common instead of operations manager.

The purpose of this chapter is to remove the ambiguity associated with the term operations management. First, we explain what it means. In defining the term, we find that it is relevant to explain what role it plays within organisations and how it relates to other functional areas. Further, it is necessary to understand how the definition is affected by the apparent differences and similarities between goods and services. Second, we describe the typical and emergent decisions that fall within the field of operations management. The performance outcomes related to these decisions, in terms of productivity, efficiency and effectiveness, are described. Third, in order to understand the drivers of contemporary practices relating to operations management, it is necessary to have some understanding of how they have evolved over time. As such, a brief history of the field is provided. The chapter concludes with a description of typical career opportunities available to operations management practitioners.

What is operations management?

Although we may not consciously think about it in these terms, life for most of us without the goods and services we consume would be a lot different to what it is today. Consider these examples. Banks process billions of transactions every year. Telephone companies switch billions of phone calls and data packets around the globe every day. Most of us take the supply of electricity, water and gas for granted most days, but it is worth noting that these utilities are created and supplied to our homes and businesses through massive operations and supply networks. Car companies are able to assemble seven to ten thousand individual parts into a complete car in about four days, and have them rolling off the production line every ninety seconds or so. Government agencies such as Centrelink in Australia make hundreds of thousands of social security benefit payments every week.

How are all these things possible? The answer is quite simple: they all depend ultimately on operations management. The whole built environment and all the services we consume, are deliberately produced, and the design, conduct and continual improvement of these systems of production is the province of operations management. A sound operations management system leads to timely, reliable and accurate provision of goods and services to end-users. In this sense, one could think of operations management as being the productive heart of the organisation.

To define the term operations management, let us consider the two words separately. Operations, at the most general level, are all about the conversion or transformation of inputs into outputs. Inputs can be traditional resources such as labour, equipment, facilities, raw materials, processed components, time, and non-traditional resources in the form of knowledge, skills, customer relationships and reputation.[2] The outputs can be products, services, information and experiences. The transformation of inputs into outputs can be physical conversion or alteration, transportation, storage or inspection when dealing with goods.[3] For services, the change would be more at a personal or even psychological level. From a value perspective, value is created when the value of the outputs is greater than the sum total of the value of inputs.

As for the word 'management', there has been long debate about its meaning. For our purpose, we take the perspective of the functions that managers perform. The five traditional functions that managers perform are planning, organising, coordinating and controlling of resources.

Combining these separate definitions into one, *operations management* can therefore be defined as the *planning, organising, coordinating and controlling of transformation of inputs to outputs*. These aspects can be represented in the form of a simple model as shown in Figure 1.1.

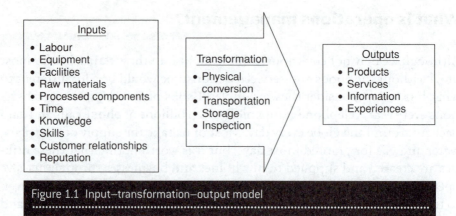

Inputs
- Labour
- Equipment
- Facilities
- Raw materials
- Processed components
- Time
- Knowledge
- Skills
- Customer relationships
- Reputation

Transformation
- Physical conversion
- Transportation
- Storage
- Inspection

Outputs
- Products
- Services
- Information
- Experiences

Figure 1.1 Input–transformation–output model

Box 1.2: Toyota Australia

Toyota Australia produces motor vehicles for domestic and export markets. Its parent company, Toyota Motor Corporation, is the largest automotive company in the world.

The Toyota Group was established in Japan in 1937. It manufactures automobiles in 26 countries and regions throughout the world. Its vehicles are sold in more than 140 countries and regions under the Toyota, Lexus, Daihatsu and Hino brands. It employs more than 260,000 people worldwide, including approximately 4500 people in Australia.

Toyota Australia operates its manufacturing activities in Melbourne and sales and marketing activities in Sydney. Starting with importing Land Cruisers in 1958, it assembled Corona and Corolla in the late 1960s. Toyota Australia began building engines and body panels during 1970s to 1980s. By 2005, Toyota had built 10 million Camrys. The new Aurion is also built locally.

So, how are cars built? An average car consists of anything between seven to ten thousand parts and components. In Toyota Australia's case, some of these are produced in-house, whilst many are made by suppliers. The production rate in Toyota Australia's plant is an average of 400 vehicles each day. It is easy to imagine that chaos would reign if a good system is not present for coordinating the production and receipt of various parts and their subsequent assembly!

Most car companies break the process for building a car into discrete and manageable sections. Toyota Australia's website (www.toyota.com.au) provides a summary of each stage of its production process:

- Building the engine. The Engine Plant is where the engines for the cars are built. It uses Toyota's latest technology, which enables improved fuel economy, lower emissions and improved performance. This is the first Australian-built engine with an aluminium block using high-pressure die casting. Many of the engine components are also manufactured in-house, including, pistons, cylinder head covers, exhaust manifolds, intake manifolds and bearing caps. Once completed, the engines head straight for the final assembly line.

- Producing body panels and parts. The Press Plant produces steel panels and parts for the cars. The largest press has a stamping force sufficient to produce an entire body side of a car. Having a single panel for the side of the car, from windscreen pillar to tail-light, brings greater strength and quality while reducing weight and manufacturing complexity. The Press Shop also builds a number of small components for Toyota vehicles. The body panels and parts are taken to the neighbouring weld shop.

- Welding the car shell. The welding process is not simply attaching the top, two sides, base, four doors, bonnet and boot lid. The welding to make each car shell involves 250 processes and 526 parts. Robots do 105 of the welding jobs with the remainder being done by some 145 people each of the two shifts per day. Maintenance of the welding equipment is carried out by 38 people. The shell or body of the car then moves to the neighbouring paint shop.

- Painting. Employees wearing lint-free overalls are air-scrubbed before entering the dust-free world of the paint shop. The car shells are immersed in water with cleaning fluids, in a phosphate dip to prepare the metal to accept the paint, and in the rust-proofing fluid. A spray bell turning at 35,000 revolutions per minute then applies the primer and two coats of water-based paint with a fine mist. The painted car shells are moved to the neighbouring assembly shop.

- Assembling. The painted car shells wind their way through seven assembly lines of about 250 metres each, travelling at a similar pace to a car in a car wash facility. Bumper bars, door trims, fuel tanks and trim fabrications, produced at another plant, are brought to the main plant for assembly of the vehicles. Within three hours, the car goes from a shell to a fully-tested finished product driven out of the assembly shop. Of the 182 functions, robots only perform the engine chassis and tyre fitments. One of the last functions before testing is reuniting each car with its doors.

- Although profitability data is unreliable, there is little doubt that Toyota Australia is by far the most profitable and successful automotive producer in the country. Consider the following:

- In 2006, it produced more than 111,000 vehicles in a plant that was built for a capacity of 100,000 vehicles per year.

- Nearly three quarters of the total production were exported.

- The Australian produced vehicles are some of the highest quality vehicles in comparison to those produced in other Toyota factories around the world, including Japan (personal communication).

- The three other local manufacturers (GM Holden, Ford and Mitsubishi) have seen rapidly declining market share in the last few years. This has led to financial stress and consequent plant closures and layoff of employees. Only Toyota has been able to increase its market share relative to others.

The natural question that emerges is: How has Toyota Australia managed to achieve such success when its competitors are struggling?

There is no doubt that the key factor for this outcome is the overall philosophy under which all parts of Toyota globally operate under. Known as the Toyota

Production System, or TPS for short, it defines how Toyota employees conduct themselves, how work is designed and executed, how Toyota relates to suppliers, etc. Many of the buzzwords in the operations management area such as 'lean operations', 'just-in-time' (JIT), 'kaizen' (continuous improvement), etc., were initially developed under the aegis of TPS. The key elements of TPS are discussed in detail in Chapter 2 and elsewhere in this book, so a full exposition on these will not be provided here.

Another factor that has contributed to the success of Toyota Australia is its heavy investment in plant and equipment. Since 2004, it has spent more that $800 million in Australian manufacturing facilities. This is at a time when many manufacturers are relocating to countries considered to be cheaper for production.

Source
www.toyota.com.au

Role of operations management in organisations

The above definition of operations management covers all aspects of an organisation that is involved in the creation and delivery of products and services to customers. As such, operations management plays a critical role in the success of organisations. The exact role of operations management can be viewed from multiple perspectives. One could look at it as a standalone unitary function within an organisation. It is also possible to look at operations management as it is practiced across all functional areas in the organisation. Further still, since outside parties such as suppliers and customers are inherently involved, there is a logical reason to view operations management from this extended perspective that is described as supply chain management. Aside from the functional role, operations management can be analysed for the strategic role it plays in organisations. In this section, all these roles are described.

Operations management as a standalone function

At the most basic level, operations is frequently seen as a distinct functional area alongside other key areas such as finance and marketing. In this context, the role of the operations management function is limited to simply producing goods and services.

As examples: in manufacturing firms, the operations area would be dealing with the production and assembly tasks that takes place on the factory-floor; in the school education context, operations is what happens in the classroom; in the hospital, operations would be what happens in the surgical theatres and wards; and in the hospitality industry, operations is about what happens

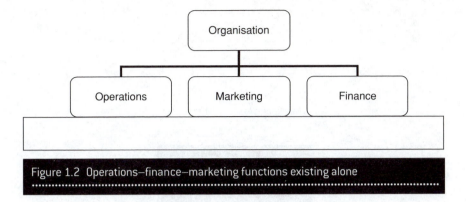

in the kitchens and bars. Figure 1.2 provides a general description of this view of operations management.

The standalone approach to operations management has many weaknesses. Many organisations that face stiff competition in their industries find that this structure makes them slow, cumbersome, bureaucratic, and generally unresponsive to customers. These organisations have largely abandoned this form of organisational structure in favour of one where there is a high level of inter-functional interaction. A strong feature of these organisations is the presence of teams in which members are drawn from different functional groups. This approach has proven to be a boon particularly at the design stage of new products. For example, Japanese car manufacturers have used this approach to design totally new cars and associated production facilities in less than eighteen months. Their competitors, who have long used the sequential approach to design, which used to take at least three years, have only now caught up with modern practices.

Operations management as a ubiquitous function

As opposed to a separate function, it is possible to view operations management as a ubiquitous concept that has a pervasive presence and permeates all aspects of the organisation. For example, operations management in a hospital would involve determining the size of the facility, deciding which types and quantities of equipment to acquire, arranging these facilities and equipments so the hospital is run efficiently, determining staffing levels and schedules to provide quality care, managing inventories of food and bedding, all in addition to the activities that clinical and medical work that takes place in the theatres and wards.

When viewed from this wider perspective, it is evident that operations are not confined to a specific area. The broader role can be difficult to deal with as the traditional functional boundaries are blurred, and members of the organisation need to develop strong understanding of what happens within

Figure 1.3 Overlapping roles for operations, marketing and finance functions

other functional groups as well as their own. Further, all functional groups need to be able to practise effective operations management. Figure 1.3 represents this view of operations management and shows the strong overlapping of functions, with operations management acting as the foundation upon which all other functions have an input.

Operations management within supply chains and networks

As competition in many industries has intensified, many firms have responded by attempting to develop stronger and deeper relationships with their key trading partners. This is an attempt to share market intelligence, collaborative arrangements for product development, and facilitate transactions efficiently. The idea is to ultimately develop seamless streams across the full length of supply chains so that final end-users of goods and services receive them in a timely fashion. (More about this perspective in Chapter 7.)

The entities exchanged between trading partners in supply chains and networks include physical goods, information and funds. If the operations management functions of the individual firms within the chains and the networks are not effectively integrated with others, then the transfer of these entities between the partners is not smooth. As a result, the experience of the final customers suffers and can be unsatisfactory. This adversely affects the performance of all members of the supply chain or network.

Operations management from a strategic perspective

Does operations management have a strategic role in organisations? If an organisation believes that the efficient and timely delivery of quality products or services to their customers leads them to generate profits, which then leads to them developing a sustainable competitive advantage over their rivals, then the answer to the question is an emphatic 'yes'.

Operations strategy involves firms competing with others along several dimensions. These include competition based on price, focus on quality, speed of delivery, dependability, flexibility and innovation. The conventional view has been that organisations need to choose one of these dimensions because there are mutually exclusive of each other. However, many firms, particularly Japanese multi-national corporations, have shown that it is possible to compete successfully along multiple dimensions. (More about Operations Strategy in Chapter 5.)

Whichever option is chosen, it is clear that all dimensions of competition require an operations management focus. For example, price based competition involves strong cost minimisation efforts. It has been estimated that on average, more than half of all workers in a typical organisation are involved in the operations function, and over three-fourths of a typical organisation's material and equipment costs are incurred by the operations function.[4] This means that relatively small reductions in operations costs (say one to two percent) can produce large increase in net profit (in the order of five to twenty percent). Likewise, improvements in quality, speed of delivery, flexibility and innovation all require adjustments to the way the operations function is carried out.

An operational perspective

While operations management has a strong long-term strategic role to play in organisations, it has an equally strong short-term, daily operational role as well. A large part of operations management deals with the planning, organising, controlling, leading and monitoring of day-to-day use of resources. Somebody has to run and oversee the daily activities of the organisation's production of its goods and services, and this is indeed a key part of operations management.

In support of these operational activities, a plethora of tools and techniques have been developed over time to assist in the detailed and localised decision-making and management processes. Many of these are quantitative models, whilst others are more conceptual in nature. Many of these are discussed throughout this book.

Integrated role of operations management

The above points make clear that the role of operations management can vary depending on how organisations view it, and decide to use it. These multiple roles can be classed into two general categories. The first category involves a functional view, consisting of a continuum that has the standalone, ubiquitous and supply chain perspectives involved. The second category involves

		Time/level of detail involved	
		Operational	Strategic
	Standalone		
	Ubiquitous		
	Supply chain		

Figure 1.4 Summary of roles of operations management

a time and level of detail aspect to it, with the continuum that involves strategic and operational as the two endpoints. These different roles can be summarised in matrix form as shown in Figure 1.4.

This matrix can be used to assess the overall view of an organisation relating to its operations management function. Firms that take an operational view and treat it as a standalone function could be considered to be taking a narrow approach to operations. On the other hand, if a firm takes a strategic perspective and sees it as a supply chain management functional area, then this is also a narrow perspective, albeit a different one to that presented above. We contend that good organisations would be thinking of operations management along all the perspectives described in Figure 1.4. This view covers all the cells of the matrix. We describe this as an integrated role of operations management. This integrated approach is reflected in the title of this book.

Box 1.3: Apple iPod

When the charismatic Steve Jobs retook the reins as CEO of Apple in 1997, the computer maker was struggling for survival. Despite the technical superiority of the flagship product, the Macintosh, Apple was still very much a niche product with about three per cent of the computer market share. Steve's job was simple but difficult: reinvigorate the Apple culture back to one that enabled it to once again produce products that performed brilliantly and customers loved. As an answer to this challenge, the revamped Macintosh, called the iMac, was relatively successful. But the real success story for Apple has been the iPod.

The iPod (i standing for internet) started life as an accessory for the iMac. However, during its development period, Jobs and his colleagues quickly realised that this device, whilst not unique – portal players of various types had been around for some time – represented an opportunity for Apple to overcome past mistakes and produce a product that had mass market appeal. From its launch in October 2001 to April 2007, more than one hundred million iPod units have been sold. This has generated billions of dollars of revenue, and made Apple one of the most successful consumer electronics product producers in history.

Even before the iPod, Apple has had long influence on the music industry. By making CD-burners available on Macs, it encouraged consumers to create their own music CDs. Apple took this philosophy several steps further with the iPod.

The iPod is basically a portable media player that is capable of playing MP3 and some other encoded audio formats of music. The original and most popular full size version, which now comes with video capability, is a unit that stores data on an internal hard drive. Over the years, Apple has produced smaller versions such as iPod mini (since discontinued), iPod nano and iPod shuffle, in order to cover price-sensitive segments of the market. These smaller iPods use flash memory for data storage. The iPods all have very elegant and sleek designs, with all (except the shuffle) using a central click wheel for navigation.

Apple's iTunes software is used to transfer music files to the iPod devices. iTunes stores the entire music collection on the user's computer. The music can be sourced from CDs. It can also be downloaded off the internet. Here, the Apple iTunes Music Store is an online service that lets consumers legally buy, download and use music at a relatively cheap price, and with far fewer rules and restrictions than any other service. It is fair to say that the iPod and the iTunes system is the first really easy-to-use portable music player. This hardware-software integration is slicker than any other system available. The strategy being pursued here is the reverse of the 'razor and blade' strategy, where Apple sells the music cheaply, but makes hefty profits on the music players.

While the success of the iPod as a consumer electronic product is an interesting story, perhaps even more interesting is how the iPods are made. Val Varian recently addressed this in the *New York Times*:

'Who makes the Apple iPod? Here's a hint: It is not Apple. The company out-sources the entire manufacture of the device to a number of Asian enterprises, among them ASUSTeK Inventec Appliances and Foxconn. But this list of compa-nies isn't a satisfactory answer either: They only do final assembly. What about the 451 parts that go into the iPod? Where are they made and by whom?'

Finding out the full details of how the iPods are made and by whom is not easy as Apple has always been tight lipped about backroom matters relating to design and manufacturing. However, through reverse engineering of the products (i.e., basi-cally pulling the iPods apart) and public discussions within the electronics industry, enough information is available to piece together details of Apple's development and manufacturing arrangements. What emerges is a fascinating story about how the modern world economy operates: globalisation, outsourcing, interconnection, and complexity!

Apple designed the iPod the way it has all of its other products – 'outside in'. The company had a vision of what the player should look like. This then dictated all the subsequent design parameters. The three main components – battery, hard drive and circuit board – are layered one on top of the other. All other components are squeezed into whatever little space that remains.

In a break from tradition, Apple has completely outsourced the design and production of the iPod. The brain of the iPod, the controller microchip that enables the player to function, was developed by a Silicon Valley firm called PortalPlayer.

This small firm was set up in 1999 and specialised in audio systems. Operating around the clock with teams of engineers in India and design specialists in the USA, PortalPlayer designed the chip and accompanying software. Both the chip design and software were Herculean tasks and represent the only truly unique intellectual properties in the devices. The software, called firmware because it is embedded directly onto the chip, consists of over one million lines of code that make songs on the iPod sound good and the device easy to use. Further, creating the chip, which is a piece of silicon with millions of transistors arranged in intricate and interconnecting patterns and layers, was a complicated process. Instead of creating one from scratch, PortalPlayer decided to modify an existing microprocessor owned by a UK-based firm. Verification of changes was also a painstaking process, and this was outsourced to two specialist companies in the Silicon Valley. For each new version and type of iPod launched on the market, PortalPlayer has improved the design of the chip and software in terms of cost, speed, features and power consumption.

Once the final design is accepted by Apple, then PortalPlayer engages two different made-to-order chip producers headquartered in Taiwan. These foundries, costing about $3 billion to set up, produce thousands of wafers, each of which is imprinted with hundreds of chips. The chopping of these wafers into individual chips, testing, plastic-coating and packaging is done by two other firms based in Taiwan and Korea. These are then shipped to a warehouse in Hong Kong, and then moved to Taiwanese-owned assembly plants in China where final assembly takes place. The final step is the delivery of the iPods by FedEx and others to the doors of the users!

The iPod controlling chip and the associated software are the only components that have been developed specifically for the device. All other components are standard off-the-self components produced by major electronics firms. For example, the batteries are produced by Sony, the hard-drives by Toshiba and the flash memory by Sharp Electronics. Texas Instruments and Wolfson Microelectronics also supply critical components.

Since virtually every aspect of the design, manufacture, assembly and delivery of the iPod is outsourced, what role does Apple play? And, will it lose out in the future? Industry insiders claim that Apple is very much in control of every aspect. It accrues value for itself by intelligently coordinating the myriad of suppliers and integrating their products such that the overall design is optimised, and the best audio performance is derived. It also has a very successful marketing track record, a clout that it has used to great effect with the iPod.

As successful as the product has been, there have been problems with the iPod. Some users have complained about battery performance, quality of sound reproduction, reliability and durability of the units, and allegations of worker exploitation in some of the Chinese assembly plants. From an overall business perspective, there have been some troublesome issues. For example, Apple has had to deal with several patent disputes. Looking into the future, there are concerns about the restrictive use of iPods and iTunes music and the highly integrated system that this is. Nonetheless, Apple seems to have learnt valuable lessons from its past mistakes and learnt new lessons from the iPod. It would be interesting to see how Steve Jobs and the rest of the team at Apple fare with the new products such as iPhone and iTV that they have launched.

Sources
www.apple.com
www.wikipedia.com
Articles published in several online forums, including: www.designchain.com; www.salon.com; www.businessweek.com; www.milestone-group.com; and www.forbes.com

Differences and similarities between goods and services

Earlier in this chapter, we stated that operations management deals with the transformation of inputs into outputs. While we discussed the nature of inputs, we left outputs in its non-specific form. Here, we intend to elaborate on the exact nature of these outputs.

Outputs are frequently classified into two groups: goods (also often called products) and services. There are two main differences between goods and services. The first key difference is that goods are tangible while services are intangible in nature. Goods can be physically felt, seen, and if necessary, can be smelt or tasted. Services, on the other hand, cannot be sensed in a physical manner. Instead, one experiences services. The second key difference is that goods can be stored, whereas services cannot. Stemming from these differences are a host of other secondary differences. These differences are summarised in Table 1.1.

Based on these differences, one could conclude that the production of goods is inherently different to provision of services. The resources required, skills involved, and transformation processes used, could all be different for the two types of outputs. Indeed, many organisations declare themselves as being either in the manufacturing industry or service industry based on these differing characteristics. Further, governments and data collection agencies use these to classify activities as services or goods. Activities within the sectors of transportation, utilities, lodging, entertainment, health care, legal services, education, communications, wholesale and retail trade, banking and finance, public administration, insurance, real estate, and others are classed as services. On the other hand, goods are defined as articles of trade, merchandise, or wares.

This goods – services classification system is convenient but it is also excessively simplistic and does not adequately reflect real world complexities. The outputs of an organisation are usually a combination of products and services. For example, a restaurant not only produces food, but it provides a

Table 1.1 Differences between goods and services

Goods	Services
Goods are tangible	Services are intangible
Goods can be stored	Services cannot be stored
Delayed consumption	Immediate consumption
Goods can be produced in the absence of the customer's physical presence	Services have to be produced in the customer's physical presence
Production of goods requires minimal involvement of customer	Production of services requires extensive involvement of customer
Goods are easy to measure	Services are difficult to measure
Goods can be checked for quality before customers receive them	Services cannot be checked before customers receive them
Defective goods can be repaired or scrapped	Defective services cannot be repaired and scrapped
Goods require equipment/capital intensive production	Services require labour intensive production
Ownership of goods is transferred when sold	Ownership of services is not generally transferred when sold
Goods can be resold	Services cannot be resold

venue and waiting staff. In this case, food is the good while the ambience of the venue and demeanour of the staff are the service component. These two components are intricately related.

Even if one could justify separating goods from services, the reality is that this may not be practically possible. For example, a supermarket sells products (goods) using facilities and staff (services). Likewise, a transport and logistics firm uses drivers, trucks (tangible elements), technology and acumen (intangible elements) to deliver (a service activity) parcels and packages (products) to customers. In both these examples, it is not clear where the product and service elements start and finish.

One approach for resolving the goods – services confusion would be not to think of outputs as goods or services! Instead, the outputs should be called *bundles of benefits*.[5] If a tangible and physical product is associated with the bundles of benefits, then it would be a *facilitating good*. Otherwise, the output would be a *pure service*. This way of viewing outputs blurs the artificial distinctions between goods and services. It allows organisations to be holistic in their assessment of how outputs are produced. Also, functional areas outside of operations can be more easily included. Finally, an external orientation focused on meeting the needs of customers can be more easily developed.

Typical decision areas within operations management

In one of the earliest textbooks in Operations Management, Bowman and Fetter,[6] listed the following decision areas of concern to the discipline:
1. inventory
2. production scheduling and control
3. equipment selection and replacement
4. maintenance
5. size and location of plants
6. plant layout and structure
7. quality control and inspection
8. traffic and materials handling
9. (work) methods

While this list was presented over forty years ago, these decision areas still remain largely relevant today. Most operations managers' work involves one or more of these aspects. In the past, the focus was on the short-term operational view where the application of tools and techniques took precedence, whereas nowadays this view is balanced by a clear recognition that a medium to long term strategic view is just as important.

Table 1.2 shows a list of typical operations management decision areas that we feel take up the most time, effort and energy of operations managers. Also shown are the key questions that are typically in need of resolution. It is highly unlikely that all operations managers will be dealing with all of these issues at one single time. More likely is that some issues will be more relevant at one point of time than others, depending on the situation facing the organisation. The important thing to recognise is that all of these decision areas have operational and strategic dimensions, and that they apply not only to within organisation contexts, but frequently expand out to partners within supply chains.

A number of observations can be made from the information presented in Table 1.2. Firstly, the range of decisions that operations managers need to make is enormous. Secondly, based on their nature, the decision areas listed in Table 1.2 can be clustered into three groups: strategic, supporting role, and operational. It is obvious that the first few items of Table 1.2 are strong on strategic aspects. For example, decisions relating to the bundles of benefits that the organisation chooses to offer, the location of its facilities, the design of processes and selection of technologies have long-term implications that are not easy to reverse or change quickly without incurring significant costs.

Table 1.2 Critical decisions with the operations management field

Decision areas	Typical questions that need to be resolved
Bundles of benefits offered by organisation	What should be offered?
Facility location	Where should the facility be physically located?
Process design and choice of technologies	What types of process are required to be able to produce the bundles of benefits offered by organisation?
Make-or-buy decision	What should be made in-house versus bought-in?
Supplier selection practices	How should suppliers be selected?
Information exchange system	How should information be exchanged internally? How should information be exchanged with external trading partners?
Capacity planning	What capacity level is needed to produce the bundles of benefits?
Intermediate-term aggregate Planning of resources	What level of resources is required to meet demand?
Production planning and control	What quantities should be produced?
Materials management and inventory control	How much inventory of each item should be carried?
Distribution and logistics	How should outputs be delivered to customers?
Quality assurance and control	How is quality defined? What is the acceptable quality level of inputs and outputs? How is this measured?
Job/work design	What is a reasonable work environment? What is reasonable production output of employees?
Scheduling personnel, equipment, jobs	Which employees should do which particular jobs on which particular equipment?
Maintenance	When should maintenance be carried out?
Other areas, such as sustainability policies and practices, risk management practices	What should be done about environmental practices, community outcomes? What is the risk appetite of the organisation and how should operational decisions comply with this?

These decisions relate to the design of the operating system. Careful and extensive analysis is usually carried out before decisions are made. These decisions have far-reaching consequences, with the sphere of influence extending well beyond internal stakeholder, affecting external trading partners. As a result, these aspects are usually decided by senior managers. In contrast, the last few items are classically operational in nature.

The design of jobs and work, scheduling of personnel, equipment and jobs, and maintenance activities have a very localised effect, are usually routine in nature, and changes are reasonably easily accommodated. Supervisory level staff are usually competent at this level of decision making. In between the strategic and operational items are a set of decision areas that play a supportive role. These form an eclectic group, consisting of decisions relating to supplier selection practices, the type of information exchange system that is established, planning and control of capacity, production, materials and inventory, distribution and logistics system, and quality assurance and control activities. These typically consist of processes that are infrastructural in nature. A considerable amount of policy work is required to guide these decisions. These decisions have a medium-term time duration, with most of these decisions not easy to change in the short term, but all being candidates for change in the long term. Overall, they facilitate the smooth and effective management of the operations of the organisation, in support of the greater strategies of the organisation. Middle managers are generally in charge of executing these decisions, after senior managers set the parameters.

The decision areas listed in Table 1.2 are strongly related to each other. In well-run organisations, there is usually a great deal of consistency and synchronicity in the decisions that are made. For example, an operationally well-managed organisation would choose its product offerings based on a strategic vision. Then, it would ensure that all decisions such as location of facilities, choice of processes and technologies, whether to make the product offerings in house or to buy in, selecting suppliers and the nature of the information exchange system are all aligned to deliver on the initial choice of product offering made by the organisation. Further, more detailed decisions relating to planning, control, monitoring and utilisation of resources also would be integrated with the overall objectives of the organisation. Finally, the highly detailed operational aspects such as job/work design, scheduling of personnel, jobs and equipment, and maintenance type activities would all be designed to properly support the earlier higher order decisions. In other words, in well-run organisations, a clear 'line-of-sight' would be present from the highest to the lowest levels of decisions. Many organisations find that such a clear line-of-sight is not present. There can be many reasons for this, including the fact that most organisations have developed over long periods of time and some aspects of the operating system have changed relative to others, resulting in a misalignment. Also, the presence of functional silos and interests can sometimes lead to an irrationally excessive focus on certain decision areas leading to localised optimisation of these areas, but the total operating system could well be performing at a sub-optimised level.

The final point about the decision areas in Table 1.2 is that these are, both individually but more importantly as a collection, based on reasonably sound theoretical bases. They are definitely not an eclectic and esoteric bunch of ideas that operate in a theory-free zone! As Professors Schmenner and Swink[7] have elucidated, knowledge within the operations management can in fact be expressed in several theories and laws. These are:

- law of variability
- law of bottlenecks
- law of scientific methods
- law of quality
- law of factory focus
- the theory of swift, even flow
- the theory of performance frontiers.

These laws and theories are discussed in more detail in Chapter 13. As a result of these proposed theories and laws, knowledge development and practice are being guided by sound and rational logic, and not seemingly unrelated and independent actions.

Box 1.4: [y e l l o w t a i l] ® Wines

The [yellowtail] brand is the most successful launch of any wine label in the history of the industry. The brand is owned by Casella Wines, an Australian family owned company based in the Riverina area of New South Wales. Launched in 2001, the brand's target market was the US. The launch has been phenomenally successful – against a planned sales volume of 250,000 cases, it actually sold 820,000 cases in the first calendar year. By 2006, it produced 11 million cases, of which about 8.5 million cases were sold in the US, and the rest in continental Europe, Asia, the UK, and Canada. [yellowtail] accounts for one third of all Australian wines exported to the US, the world's largest wine market. Its exceptional exporting performance has been recognised with many awards, including the coveted Australian Exporter of the Year Award (agribusiness division) which it won three years in a row (2003, 2004 and 2005).

The story behind the success of [yellowtail] is one where a number of key factors have come together to produce outstanding results. These factors include the 'fire-in-the-belly' attitude that drive such families to succeed, careful research, hard work, luck, serendipity, good-timing, excellent business judgements, financial acumen, and strong belief in ethical practices. These factors have acted synergistically to create tremendous value for all stakeholders (including, as will be seen later, competitors).

To describe the story simply, Casella Wines captured a significantly profitable segment in the US wine-drinking market with the [yellowtail] brand. As its popularity grew (ten-fold increase in six years), it managed to put together the production and storage facilities, workers, suppliers, logistics providers, etc. to enable it to successful supply to this market segment. In doing so, this case aptly demonstrates the inextricable symbiotic relationship between marketing and operations functions.

It all began in 1951 when an Italian couple, Filipo and Maria Casella, immigrated to Australia. They worked as itinerant farm workers, travelling along the eastern seaboard of the continent. Coming from a family that had a long history of wine making, Filipo decided to purchase a small 16-hectre farm and grow grapes. These grapes were sold to other wineries in the area, and eventually he set up his own winery in 1969. His son John, after studying oenology at university and working for other wineries, joined the family operation in 1994. He had ambitious expansion plans in mind, but even he would not have predicted how successful the company has been in the past few years. Today, Casella Wines is still a family-owned business. While Filipo and Maria have retired, they still live in the same house. John has been joined by his brothers and other family members to manage the company. Soon after taking over the operations, John Casella hired John Soutter as general manager and person in charge of sales and marketing. Much of the success of the [yellow tail] brand is due to Soutter's initial work in developing the brand in the US.

Some of the defining events in the company's relatively short history are as follows:

- Casella Wines' first attempted to enter the lucrative US wine market with a label called 'Carramar Estate'. The strategy was based on the traditional approach – compete on quality and prestige at a particular price point. This involved adding 'complexity' to the wine, this being 'layered personality and characteristics that reflect the uniqueness of the soil, season, and winemaker's skills in tannin, oak and aging process'. The arbiters of this are a handful of reviewers, wine show judges and winemakers' profiles. In a crowded field of 6500 labels, this traditional approach to gaining market entry failed miserably.
- Casella Wines learnt many important, valuable and useful lessons from this failure. First, they found out that many potential wine-drinkers thought the industry was very snobbish and pretentious. Second, most would-be wine drinkers preferred light, fruity, oaky and sweetish wines that were easy on the palate. This was anathema to the connoisseurs, reviewers and judges who preferred complexity in wines. Third, Casella Wines discovered that most people found the wine culture a mysterious and complicated one, one that was difficult for them to understand, let alone partake in. Fourth, Casella Wines felt that if they could produce a 'fun' wine to be sold at a price point just above that for jug wine, there would be a chance that many beer and ready-mixed spirit drinkers would be converted to wine drinking.
- Armed with these understandings, hunches, knowledge and lessons, Casella Wines set about creating a product for this market. Through some experimentation, Casella Wines was able to produce white (Chardonnay) and red (Shiraz) varieties that met the key criteria for being fun and easy-to-drink wines. Further, they were able to produce these wines in a manner that did not require long

aging, thereby dramatically reducing the time span and associated processing and storage costs.

- The marketing concept of [yellowtail] was an 'off-the-self' concept that John Casella bought from an Adelaide-based firm. The package consisted of the catchy label, advertising material, in-store promotional designs, cartons, capsules, back label story, taglines, etc. John Casella bought three out of the six concepts that were shown to him at the Sydney International Airport lounge, while he was waiting to catch a flight overseas. Thus, the [yellow tail] marketing concept was not developed through expensive market research and testing, but selected by John Casella on an intuition about its fit with the product (wine) and the market segment that would be targeted.

- To incentivise the distribution joint venture partners, Casella Wines generously offered 50 per cent of sales to them. This worked a treat, for its partner, W. J. Deutsch, a leading distributor of wines with a network in forty-four states, has shown a strong commitment to ensuring that the product is given the attention that Casella Wines had hoped for.

- As the label became popular upon its introduction in the US – there are stories of [yellowtail] 'flying' off the shelves and customers 'demanding' [yellowtail]s – Casella Wines had to quickly scale up its production in Australia and logistics between the two countries. In the space of a few years, it invested hundreds of millions of dollars in new state-of-the-art wine production, storage and bottling facilities at the company's original site. Further, the number of employees at its winery has increased from five in 1995 to about 400 currently. As for transportation, in 2001 when sales was increasing exponentially, the company was forced to airfreight some of its wine. Now, it uses specialist third party logistics providers to manage this part of the operations. As for the all important grapes, Casella Wines is only able to produce a small proportion (4 per cent in 2003) itself. The rest comes from a network of about 300 small and large growers. Many of these growers have planted thousands of acres of grape vines at the behest of Casella Wines. Casella Wines is very conscious of its relationships with these growers and has vowed to 'look after' them in the future.

- The success of [yellowtail] has been phenomenal and unprecedented. Indeed, the experience of [yellowtail] is now described in textbooks of business strategy. The company is lauded for being able to overcome the orthodoxies of an industry and create opportunities for itself (and others) by finding new customers in an existing market. It therefore provides a roadmap for other small companies that hope to break into new markets. But, looking forward, there are a number of factors that Casella Wines needs to take care of if it is to continue to prosper. Some of these are:

- Competitors are gearing up to take advantage of the market segment that Casella has successfully identified and catered to. Based on the popularity of everything Australiana in overseas countries, local and overseas companies are launching wine labels such as 'Crocodile Rock', 'Little Penguin', 'Boxing Roo', 'Didgeridoo', 'Three Koalas' and 'Three Mile Creek'. Labels based on other countries are also in development (e. g., the 'French Red Bicyclette'). So, what should Casella do? It has broadened the range to include other grape varieties. It has also increased the depth of the brand by introducing a pricier label called 'Reserve'. But, competition is intensifying. Casella Wines has had first mover advantage in this market space, but how long this lasts is an open question.

- The Australian grape-growing industry is under a great deal of stress. This is due to the prolonged drought and large bushfires. Further, a situation of oversupply – for example, in 2003, an average of one winery per day was being opened – is in the process of correcting itself, whereby many non-competitive vineyards and wineries are closing down. This overall reduction of supply of good quality grapes and wines will result in increasing costs for Casella Wines. This will then affect its ability to profitably sell at its current price point. Given the sensitivity of this market segment to changes in price, there is not much room for Casella Wines to move. Further exacerbating this is the rising value of the Australian dollar. These issues have the potential to affect its relationships with other stakeholders, especially growers that supply to it.
- The management and ownership of the company will need to be resolved as the company continues to grow. The family has indicated its reluctance to sell or list itself on the stock market. However, for the company to continue to grow, it will need to access capital and other resources such as assistance for marketing. These are usually more forthcoming for publicly-owned companies where financial and operational details are transparently published. Therefore, the Casella family would need to address these ownership issues going forward into the future.

Trends encouraging focus on operations

When practitioners and researchers formally described the operations management field in the 1960s, life for the average operations manager was relatively straightforward. Most organisations were small to medium sized, serviced local and sometimes national markets, customers were relatively unsophisticated and would uncritically accept whatever was offered, competition was not intense, labour was relatively cheap, and ethics and environmental issues were not that important. Under these conditions, there was a high degree of predictability and stability within which operating systems could be created and run.

The operations manager of today faces a world that is highly dynamic and very uncertain and unpredictable. A number of key factors have contributed to this state of affairs. First is the rapid globalisation of trade. Second is the incredibly high speed with which ideas, information, products and funds gets transferred. Third is the red hot competition that is present in many industry sectors. All these, and more, require operations managers to respond in markedly different ways to how they have done traditionally. To illustrate, we outline some of the key challenges that directly impinge on the operations area.

Develop a global focus

Due to the advent of the Internet-based communications superhighway, bilateral and multilateral trade liberation, fast and efficient transportation systems, and increasing homogenisation of cultures, organisations that traditionally served local markets can now become global players. Indeed, many organisations are able to find suppliers in places that they would traditionally not consider. Many organisations are themselves able to supply to customers in far away places. This is becoming true for almost all organisations irrespective of their size.

Think beyond organisation boundaries

In the past, many organisations focused on internal improvements. Many of these efforts have plateaued, with little possibility of step increases in performance now available. This has forced many organisations to look beyond their organisational boundaries. Many of these organisations are realising that tremendous waste is generated due to poor inter-organisational relationships that are a feature of the supply chains and networks within which they partake. In search of accelerated rates of performance improvements, many organisations are assessing their roles and responsibilities from a supply chain perspective. This involves assessing how customers are serviced from an end-to-end supply chain perspective. In many cases, this is leading to radical changes to the way an organisation conducts its business.

Be more responsive to customers

In the past, many organisations were able to get away with 'pushing' mass-produced and highly standardised products to their customers. This is not the case now. Organisations that continue with this practice usually find that deep price discounts are required to sell their product offerings. Customers prefer unique products that are customised to their requirements, and organisations that are able to deliver on this are able to generate price premiums. Concepts such as 'mass customisation' have been proposed, but significant practical hurdles remain. Other methods such as rapid product development are equally useful.

Establish distinctive capabilities

The days of totally vertically integrated organisations seem to be over. It is virtually impossible for organisations to continue to exist and prosper if they do not specialise in some way. This specialisation is a distinct competence, and if safeguarded from competitors, can become a source of sustainable competitive advantage. So, it is now common practice for organisations to concentrate on what they do well, and outsource what they think others can do better. Operations managers need to be asking themselves what their organisations are particularly good at doing, and what others could do for them in a better way.

Operations-led excellence

Some of our better managed organisations like Toyota have shown some ways in which operations-led excellence can be achieved: rapid product development through use of cross-functional design teams; lean operating systems where the focus is on minimising setup times of machines and workstations such that small quantities of production are economically justified; just-in-time arrangements with suppliers so that excess inventory does not build up; obsessive focus on quality improvements; and using a 'pull' system of production where customer orders act as the trigger for the start of the operating system. These are some aspects of modern operating systems that provide better managed organisations with strong competitive leverage over others. It is quite clear that those organisations that are more operationally excellent outperform those that are not so good at it. Operations managers need to have the skills to implement suitable lean operations principles in their organisations.

Treat employees as partners

People now work differently to the past. Many jobs now require strong intellectual input, active thinking and a high degree of skills and competence. Traditional ways of organising that involve hierarchical and bureaucratic structures, highly prescriptive process-centred work and excessive control procedures are not particularly suitable now. Instead, employees need to be empowered and need the freedom to decide on processes for achieving specified outcomes. Operations managers need to realise that work and job design now involves as much human aspects as the technical specification of the work.

Be an ethical operator

In the past, many organisations were able to get away with what we would now consider to be unethical conduct. Today, there is no escape. Organisations need to ensure that they are not polluting the environment. In terms of legal and moral hazards, organisations need to ensure that they have enough preventative safeguards in place. Managers must act in the interest of all stakeholder groups. All these present additional elements of complexity when managers think that their only job is to produce ever increasing levels of financial profits.

Box 1.5: Deloitte

Deloitte, also known as Deloitte Touche Tomatsu, is a professional services multinational firm that is one of the 'Big Four' (the others being PriceWaterhouseCoopers, KPMG and Ernst & Young). It is the oldest of the big four, starting in 1845 when William Deloitte opened his accountancy practice outside the Bankruptcy Court in London. By 2006, through a long series of mergers and acquisitions, the firm operated in 140 countries, employed 135,000 people, and generated over $20.2 billion in revenue, this being second only to PriceWaterhouseCoopers. Deloitte is legally structured as partnerships, and generally called 'Deloitte member firms'.

So what does Deloitte do? Like all other accounting firms, Deloitte's main area of business is providing auditing services to other firms, particularly those that are publicly traded. This involves systematically examining financial and other transactions and records of a client company and arriving at a considered judgement about their accuracy and veracity. Over time, Deloitte has developed many other lines of business. These include tax advice, strategic and operational management consulting, and financial advisory services. In more recent times, the range of the services has continued to proliferate (see list).

Furthermore, Deloitte provides services to a large number of clients, varied in size and spanning an extensive range of industry sectors. To illustrate, Deloitte member firms provide services to 80 per cent of the companies from the Fortune 500 list. But big businesses are not their only clients – 50 per cent of Deloitte's revenues come from 'middle market' firms, the small and medium sized firms that dominate most economies. The industries that client organisations operate in are very diverse – aviation and transport service, consumer business, energy and resources, financial services, life science and health care, manufacturing, public sector, and technology, media and telecommunications – to list a few.

The sheer diversity of clients, industry sectors and types of services makes the operations within Deloitte a complex one to manage.

The key products that Deloitte offers to its clients are 'professional services' of various kinds. Most of these services require strong intellectual input. Indeed, the often used cliché 'people are our most important resource' strongly applies to Deloitte and its ability to provide high value services to its clients. What this means for people within the firm is that they are required to be highly innovative, creative and inventive with the solutions and advice they provide to clients. In addition, they are required to have strong problem-solving skills and 'can-do' attitudes. If people at Deloitte do not exhibit these attributes, it is fair to say that in the medium to long run, there is high risk of the firm losing its market competitiveness. Deloitte is aware of this, and has instituted numerous formal and informal programs, all designed to ensure that the organisation nurtures a culture of innovativeness. While some of these programs have been successful, others have not.

The issues that militate against Deloitte's ability to be innovative stem from several sources. First, the nature of work that Deloitte performs stifles innovativeness. Like other large accounting firms, Deloitte member companies frequently face large volumes of work that is often repetitive in nature. Further, Deloitte finds itself with increasing levels of regulatory requirements to comply with, especially after the spectacular and catastrophic failure of Arthur Anderson. As a result, Deloitte member firms are required to be task-focused, quick and efficient. At the same time, they are expected to be systematic, thorough, complete, and accurate. These expectations have put a lot of pressure on the firm to ensure that high quality work is produced for clients.

Second, the organisational structure that has evolved stultifies innovation. Deloitte's structure is classically pyramidal and hierarchical. A small number of partners preside over a large number of junior employees, with several intermediary layers of managers. This makes for high levels of bureaucracy. Also, the many hierarchical layers prevent quick and easy communication between leaders (partners) and the large numbers of junior staff.

Third, the manner in which work is done affects innovativeness. The bulk of the detail work is done by junior staff. To ensure that the work is done accurately and speedily, partners have developed sophisticated control and coordination systems. These involve staff working to internal and external standards, and the use of both peer-based review systems and technological tools for checking and monitoring purposes. This enforces discipline, conformity and control. Simultaneously, this acts against innovation, creativity and inventiveness.

The end result for Deloitte and other similar firms is that junior staff members spend inordinate amounts of time doing high volumes of repetitive and routine work. Intellectual stimulation is generally low. Further, the control and coordination systems prevent the development of collegial systems. Staff members who are able to survive these early stages frequently find that the acculturation process results in them becoming very closely aligned to the expected culture of the firm, and in the process, losing their capacity to be innovative. As a result, not unexpectedly, the staff turnover rate is very high. While it can be argued that this turnover can be good because the pyramidal structure means that there are relatively few 'senior' positions, the loss of intellectual capital and experience has a negative effect on the firm's ability to provide cutting-edge solutions to clients.

Deloitte, like all other similar firms in the industry, has traditionally dealt with this problem by using carefully designed recruitment programs. These programs are ostensibly designed to replace staff who leave, but considerable care is taken to ensure that staff who are hired fit well with the organisation. Jeppersen (2007) lists recruitment selection policies such as the exclusion of minority and working-class people (at least in certain cultures), ensuring that employees' personality type is robust to bureaucracies, and applying a mentoring and training system that instils a partner-centric worldview. However, during times of economic prosperity, this recruitment-based strategy has not worked well as supply of good quality staff is limited.

Going forward, there are a couple of big issues that Deloitte faces and needs to resolve. First, how can it effectively address the apparent contradiction it faces in having to nurture a culture that is highly innovative, creative and inventive, and at the same time, be able to do high volumes of repetitive and routine work in an accurate and timely way? Second, Deloitte needs to think about other organisational forms that may assist it to develop a culture of innovativeness and deal with the very high rates of 'brain-drain' from the firm.

In 2007, Deloitte Australia offered the services listed below (source: www.deloitte.com.au).

Actuarial services
- Banking
- General Insurance
- Health
- Wealth management and life insurance

Assurance services
- Accounting alerts
- Financial instruments advisory services (FIAS)
- Funds management investment services
- IFRS
- Model financial reports
- Regulatory consulting
- Statutory audit
- Superannuation services
- US GAAP
- US listing services

Computer services
- Resource links
- Software solutions
- Training

Consulting
- CFO Services
- E-business solutions
- Enterprise applications
- Human Capital
- RFID

- Strategy and operations
- Technology integration

Corporate finance
- Advisory
- Business modelling
- Public policy and corporate strategy
- Transaction services
- Valuations

Corporate reorganisation services
- Business insolvency solutions
- Businesses for sale
- Businesses under administration
- Corporate structure simplification
- Financial services breakfast series
- Lender solutions
- Restructuring services

Enterprise risk services
- Business continuity management (BCM)
- Capital markets/treasury
- Corporate governance
- Data privacy
- Environment and sustainability services
- Internal audit
- IT control assurance
- OHS and Workers Compensation

Regulatory
- Risk management
- Sarbanes-Oxley
- Security services

Forensic
- Anti-money laundering (AML) and counter terrorist financing (CTF)
- Dispute solutions
- Forensic technology
- Investigation
- Risk

Middle market
- Commercialisation of new ideas
- e-letters
- Government, agencies and not for profits
- International companies setting up in Australia

- Small to medium-sized publicly listed companies
- Small, medium and large private businesses
- Wealth/high net worth individuals, families, business owners and entrepreneurs

Tax services
- 2007/08 federal budget
- Asia Pacific Dbriefs webcasts
- Corporate tax
- Deloitte Lawyers
- Indirect tax
- International assignment services
- International tax
- Transfer pricing

Sources

www.deloitte.com and www.deloitte.com.au

Jeppesen, K. K. (2007). 'Organizational risk in large audit firms.' *Managerial Auditing Journal.* 22(6) 590–603.

Squires, S. E., Smith, C. J., McDougall, L. and Yeack, W. R. (2003). *Inside Arthur Anderson: Shifting values, unexpected consequences,* Englewood Cliffs, New Jersey: Prentice-Hall.

Toffler, B. L. (2003). *Final Accounting: Ambition, greed, and the fall of Arthur Anderson,* Broadway Books, New York: Broadway Books.

Historical evolution of the field

The field of operations management has had a long, eventful and enduring history. Considerable operations management acumen would have been required to build the Egyptian pyramids, China's Great Wall and the Roman aqueducts. However, our interest is in understanding how large quantities of high quality products and services can be produced and delivered to customers all around the world, that is, operations management in its modern form. We know that relatively few organisations are currently able to do this effectively. Most others struggle. To understand why this is the case, one really needs to understand the practices embodied within their operating systems. These operating systems have been strongly influenced by ideas of brilliant personalities, major inventions, and profound insights. For this reason, a brief description of the key events relating to the evolution of the operations management field is provided.

The development of the operations management field can be classified into several distinct periods. These are outlined in the following sections.

Craft production

Prior to the advent of the industrial revolution, goods and services were predominantly produced by artisans and their apprentices. These highly skilled craftspeople produced one-off items, usually customised to the needs of their local customers. They mostly operated from shops and studios located next to their homes. Although this form of production stills exist today, the very high prices means that these types of items are mostly available to the wealthier members of society.

Batch production

In the latter half of the 1700s, a number of groundbreaking discoveries, insights and developments ostensibly brought an end to large-scale craft-based production. The development of the steam engine replaced human and animal power, providing a reliable supply of energy. Around the same time, the economist Adam Smith realised the value of specialisation and division of labour – if work is broken down into logically divisible tasks, workers, through training and repetition, can be a lot more productive than they would if they had to do all the tasks themselves. The gunsmith Eli Whitney took this idea one step further and put forward the idea of interchangeable parts, where parts and components can be produced to exact specifications in isolation, then brought together and assembled into complete products. While it took some time to implement these ideas and discoveries, they heralded the dawn of the industrial revolution and led to the reasonably large-scale production of firearms, machines, clocks, and many other consumer items. These required specialised machines, precision production of interchangeable parts, and co-ordinated work sequences and material flows. To facilitate all these, factories were first created.

Mass production

Two further significant developments provided added impetus to the industrial revolution. First, the astute industrial engineer F. W. Taylor decided to apply scientific methods to design work and jobs. Using careful observations, measurements and analysis, he worked out the best way of doing any given job. Then, these job designs were standardised, workers were trained and given incentives to ensure that they did the work in the way prescribed. This approach became known as the scientific management method. Second, Henry Ford realised that automobiles could be produced much more efficiently if the assembly line moved and workers were stationary in their positions, instead of the other way around. When this idea was implemented in his factory, car assembly time was brought down from a high of 728 hours to one-and-a-half hours.[8] These two discoveries combined with the other elements of the industrial revolution led to a tremendous increase in the production of very large volumes of all sorts of goods and services, and sold relatively cheaply within mass markets. The mass production phenomena played a critical role in many nations achieving full industrial development status.

Lean operation

In the 1970s and 1980s, Japanese firms were able to win substantial slices of market share in many industries around the world. They were producing automobiles, white goods, consumer electronics, machine tools, and many other items – all of which were very reliable, of much higher quality and had far fewer defects, but sold at considerably cheaper prices than their competitors. Further, it emerged that the Japanese factories were twice as productive as their competitors.[9] For operations management practitioners and researchers, it took a while to understand how these firms were able to perform so much better than their competitors.

Slowly, the elements of this system have been identified. These elements include: an obsessive attitudes towards improvement of all aspects of the organisation, but principally quality of products and processes; reduction of all forms of waste; use of highly flexible production cells (instead of long production lines); use of just-in-time systems; strong relationships with suppliers; and, strong sense of corporate culture. These elements as a collective are described as lean operations. A key point to appreciate is that these elements are not related to mass production any more. While these elements (and others not listed here) individually are eminently sensible and can be found in many organisations, what is unique in Japanese organisations is the synergistic way in which all these elements interact to produce qualities that are very innate and not easy for others to emulate.

Companies such as Toyota, Matsushita, NEC and others are examples of leading Japanese firms that are master exponents of lean operations. Organisations from around the world have been attempting to emulate these Japanese firms with varying degrees of success.

Mass customisation

While it is impossible to be absolutely certain about what will happen in the future, it is becoming clear that success of organisations will largely depend on their ability to efficiently provide highly personalised and customised product offerings to their customers. Although it is not clear exactly which form mass customisation will eventually take, it is possible that the architecture will be built upon lean operations, and use the information infrastructure made available through the Internet.

In recent years, these capabilities are being demanded of firms and their operations in the context of globalisation. Whatever the focus of your business and its operations, you now need to operate competitively, with the best competitor in the world, in order to survive and prosper. The best of technologies and operations systems can now be placed in low cost countries, sources such as China, where, for example, most of the world's textiles, clothing and footwear are now manufactured. Efficient and effective telecommunications and the maturing of the Internet now means that information intense companies and industries can get their software developed, their call centres staffed and their transactions processed most efficiently in low wage countries such as India. So when considering whether to make or buy a good or service, sometimes now called in-source versus out-source, one must also consider whether to 'offshore' an operation or part of it to a country source that can bring a comparative advantage in terms of cost, quality, service or delivery performance.

Careers in operations management

There are tremendous career opportunities for graduates who specialise in operations management. A cursory review of job advertisements in employment websites and newspapers show that there are many interesting and challenging career possibilities. In fact, it is estimated that about 40 per cent of all jobs are in the operations management area.[10] The nature of these jobs can vary considerably – supply chain coordinators, quality controllers, transport and logistics managers, production/manufacturing specialists, projects/events managers – the list is long. The industry sectors that hire operations management specialists also vary significantly. Along with the traditional manufacturing sector, jobs are in the services, retail, transport and logistics, healthcare, military, public administration, education and construction sectors, among many others.

Graduates from areas such as accounting, finance, marketing, engineering, human resource management and information systems would benefit a lot from taking a course or two from the operations management area. This is because there is tremendous cross-functional overlap between these functions within organisations. Further, if one takes into account the integrated perspective used in this textbook, then the execution of the activities within all these functional areas involves operations management principle – some understanding of these would be a tremendous advantage.

As one looks at more senior positions within organisations, it is common to find the job title of 'Chief Operations Officer' (COO). Other titles that some organisations use are 'Vice-President of Operations', 'General Manager – Operations', and 'Director – Operations'.

In many progressive organisations, the highest ranked officer, the Chief Executive Officer (CEO), has an operations background. In some organisations where the focus is on more exciting strategic activities such as mergers and acquisitions, marketing, and financial engineering, executives with finance or marketing backgrounds may be in the ascendancy. However, one should realise that even the world's most clever corporate strategy is useless if it is not implemented well. Effectively bedding down strategy essentially requires operations management skills. Besides, these 'exciting' strategies are relatively few and far between. The most common strategy that most organisations pursue is organic growth – the focus on steady but sure improvements to the important aspects of the organisation such that things are done in a better way over time. Here, the focus is directly and squarely on the operations management practices.

Summary

In answer to the management challenge posed at the start of the chapter, one has to realise that there is no one single reason for Woolworths' success. The success of Woolworths is based on sound decision-making on sales forecasts, location, and supply chain efficiency. These are all core operations management issues. As the very successful former chief executive officer Roger Corbett often used to say, Woolworths could not offer the lowest prices unless it was the lowest cost operator. Woolworths manages its operations very astutely.

The purpose of this chapter was to attempt to remove the ambiguity associated with the term 'operations management'. We have explained what it means by using the input–transformation–output model, and have suggested that 'operations' relates to the transformation stage of the model. In defining the term, we have shown that it plays a multi-facetted role within organisations, and that it relates to other functional areas in complex and interesting ways. Further, we have found it necessary to provide a more generic definition of outputs (bundles of benefits), thereby reducing the complexities associated with apparent differences and similarities between goods and services.

We have also described the typical decisions that fall within the field of operations management. The performance outcomes related to these decisions, in terms of productivity, efficiency and effectiveness, were described.

In order to understand the drivers of contemporary practices relating to operations management, it is necessary to have some understanding of how they have evolved over time. Accordingly, a brief history of the field was provided. The chapter concluded with a description of typical career opportunities available to operations management practitioners.

DISCUSSION QUESTIONS

1. Define operations management as a field of study.
2. What are some key decisions that operations managers would make in terms of designing the operations activities in:
   a) food manufacturer?
   b) bank?
   c) university?
   d) major sporting stadium?
   e) mine?
3. What are the main issues that connect the operations-related competence of a firm with its marketing strategy? Further, what potential problems would you foresee if marketing and operations variables were considered and decided upon separately?
4. What is the nature and impact of operations management on the financial outcomes of a business? Illustrate this with an example of a farm and a mining operation?
5. Does it matter and if so why does it matter whether the nine typical decision areas listed in this chapter are taken separately or in an integrated manner? Illustrate your answer with an example.
6. Describe an example of mass customisation and discuss the operational complexities of achieving this state as opposed to adopting a mass production approach.
7. Discuss the concepts of push and pull production, give an example of each from the fast food industry, and discuss the benefits and costs of each approach.

Further readings and references

Bowman, E. H. and Fetter, R. B. 1967. *Analysis for Production and Operations Management. 3rd edn*. New York: McGraw Hill/Irwin.

Finch, B. J. 2006. *Operations Now: Profitability, processes, performance. 2nd edn*. Boston: McGraw-Hill.

Heizer, J. and Render, B. 2006. *Principles of Operations Management*. Upper Saddle River, NJ: Pearson. p. 7.

Martinich, J. S. 1997. *Production and Operations Management: An applied modern approach*. New York: John Wiley.

Meredith, J. and Shafer, S. M. 2007. *Operations Management for MBAs. 3rd edn*. New York: John Wiley.

Russell, R. S. and Taylor, B. W. 2006. *Operations Management: Quality and competitiveness in a global environment. 5th edn*. New York: John Wiley. p. 6.

Schmenner, R. W. and Swink, M. 1998. 'On Theory in Operations Management.' *Journal of Operations Management*, 17: 97–113.

Slack, N., Chambers, S., Johnston, R., and Betts, A. 2006. *Operations and Process Management: Principles and practice for strategic impact*. Harlow, England: Prentice Hall.

Womack, J. P., Jones, D. T., and Roos, D. 1990. *The Machine that Changed the World*. New York: Rawson Associates.

Internet resources

Lion Nathan Limited – a company that has interesting material on its operations: http://www.lion-nathan.com.au. Look particularly at the process flow diagram.

List of resources collated by University of South Australia: www.library.unisa.edu.au/resources/subject/opman.asp

Online encyclopedia Wikipedia: www.en.wikipedia.org/wiki/Operations_management

The Australasian Production and Inventory Control Society (APICS) homepage: http://www.apics.org.au

The Production and Operations Management Society (POMS) homepage: http://www.poms.org

Toyota Australia website: http://www.toyota.com.au

Woolworths Australia webpage: www.woolworths.com.au

Notes

1 Slack, N., Chambers, S., Johnston, R., and Betts, A. 2006. *Operations and Process Management: Principles and practice for strategic impact*. Harlow, England: Prentice Hall.

2 Finch, B. J. 2006. *Operations Now: Profitability, processes, performance*. 2nd edn. Boston: McGraw-Hill.

3 Meredith, J. and Shafer, S. M. 2007. *Operations Management for MBAs*. 3rd edn. New York: John Wiley.

4 Martinich, J. S. 1997. *Production and Operations Management: An applied modern approach*. New York: John Wiley.

5 Meredith, J. and Shafer, S. M. 2007. *Operations Management for MBAs*. 3rd edn. New York: John Wiley.

6 Bowman, E. H. and Fetter, R. B. 1967. *Analysis for Production and Operations Management*. 3rd edn. New York: McGraw Hill/Irwin.

7 Schmenner, R. W. and Swink, M. 1998. 'On Theory in Operations Management.' *Journal of Operations Management*, 17: 97–113.

8 Russell, R. S. and Taylor, B. W. 2006. *Operations Management: Quality and competitiveness in a global environment*. 5th edn. New York: John Wiley. p. 6.

9 Womack, J. P., Jones, D. T., and Roos, D. 1990. *The Machine that Changed the World*. New York: Rawson Associates.

10 Heizer, J. and Render, B. 2006. *Principles of Operations Management*. Upper Saddle River, NJ: Pearson. p. 7.

Operating System Models

David Parker

Learning objectives

After reading this chapter you should be able to:

- appreciate the various factors that have influenced the drive for change in the way that products and services are produced and systems are developed
- understand the methods of production and delivery of services that have been adopted by various industries in pursuit of efficiency and effectiveness
- describe the characteristics of organisations that have achieved operations excellence and those that have struggled
- evaluate the advantages and disadvantages of alternative operating system models under varying market conditions
- appreciate the operations management challenges in meeting customers' needs.

Box 2.1: Management challenge: Toyota/Honda vs General Motors/Ford

When one looks at the international car industry, two distinct groups of firms are noticeable. One group consists of firms such as General Motors and Ford. These firms have been around for a long time (really since the advent of cars). While very successful in the past, these firms now seem to be less so. They take longer

---

than some of their competitors to produce new models and their models seem less well matched with market requirements. The cars are rated lower on quality and value of money (Womack et al., 1990; Holweg and Pil, 2004). As a result, these companies have suffered an erosion of market share in many market segments in which they compete. So, their frequent announcements of ever-growing financial losses do not come as a surprise to many.

On the other end of the spectrum are firms such as Toyota and Honda. These firms appear to be able to produce cars that are responsive to the needs of car buyers. The cars are reliable and generally of high quality. Most buyers believe that these cars represent good value for money. Over a relatively short period of time, these firms have captured large slices of market share around the world, with Toyota recently becoming the world-wide market leader. These firms are also amongst the very few in the industry that have been able to generate profits over successive years.

What are the essential differences between firms such as Toyota/Honda and General Motors/Ford that has given rise to such differences in performance?

Sources
Womack, J. P., Jones, D. T. and Roos, D., 1990. *The Machine that Changed the World*, Rawson Associates, New York.
Holweg, M. and Pil, F. K., 2004. *The Second Century: Reconnecting Customer and Value Chain through Build-to-Order*, The MIT Press, London.

Introduction . . . and a brief look back in time

Imagine you were living way back in the early 1700s. What sort of price and quality would you expect if you needed to buy a new woollen jumper? It could well be, of course, that you would not have actually paid for the jumper with money, but rather you might have bartered using produce that you may have grown yourself or with a product made at home. The quality could be highly variable, and the choices would be very few. Undoubtedly the way we use the '*market*' today proves that we have come a long way since those days of the 1700s. What is more, today we would expect to purchase a new woollen jumper from one of the many retail stores close by or even via the Internet. Moreover, we would have far greater aspirations for product quality and value for money. But looking back to history allows us to reflect on *why* methods of production change over time and what forces prevail to drive such change. This brief retrospective glance will help us to understand the reasons why even today we are continually adopting different and improved ways of producing products and delivering services.

Historically speaking, undoubtedly, the turning point for the production of products and the supply of services to satisfy *mass markets* was the *industrial revolution* from 1750 onward. This period saw substantial capital investment by wealthy entrepreneurs who had made their wealth from global trading, to the new-found technology of steam-driven machinery. Thus *factories* were created. Of importance, however, were the newly introduced methods of working in these factories. No longer would it be possible for workers to produce the complete products from start to completion; now workers were members of a designed production sequence, where their activities were highly planned, repetitive, of a relatively short time-span and closely monitored. The use of steam-driven machines required tasks to be broken down into small operations. Such small repetitive tasks meant that workers (who were abundant) could be quickly trained in unskilled operations. This gave the opportunity to accurately measure the time that tasks took to complete, and to introduce *standard times* upon which *payment by results* and *incentive schemes* could be based. *Economies of scale* were now being achieved, whereby limited resources were able to be maximised through large volumes of very similar products being produced. Those early days of factory working is what we now recognise as the rudiments of the modern *mass-production system*.

Box 2.2: The farm cart wheel

The wheel on your horse-drawn cart has broken and you need to take it to the local blacksmith for several damaged spokes to be replaced, a new metal rim to be fitted and several timber sections to be repaired. Fortunately, the multi-skills of the artisan blacksmith, gained from a lengthy apprenticeship followed by many years of experience, mean he is up to the task. The methods used to repair the wheel have been passed down through the generations. He is able to manufacture the wooden spokes, hew the metal rim, assemble the repaired wheel and fit it to the cart. Your cart is back on the farm after only a few days.

What do you imagine might be the advantages and disadvantages of this type of system?

The late 1920s saw a period of heightened industrial activity. Rapid *standardisation* and *mass production* provided an environment in which operations management and development of new manufacturing systems flourished. One of the significant reports of the era was *Waste in Industry* (1921), and involved information from more than two hundred companies. It indicated that little real progress in the application of scientific management had been achieved and that most systems of producing products had low *productivity* and created much wastage of materials and loss of effort. Economic hardship in the 1930s made operations management extremely cost conscious and created an environment in which new operating systems were eagerly sought. The World War II years saw a vast enlargement of industrial activities. Many modern production systems had their genesis during the period 1940–1950.

In surveying the postwar period, we can observe many significant factors that have influenced today's operating systems. Not least is the application of computerised *information systems* to plan, monitor and execute manufacturing *processes* and *technologies*. A new era was born: that of *automation*. Computer-controlled machine tool processes came into being and the drive to reduce, or even eliminate, the need for human involvement was pursued (for example using *robotics*). Simultaneously, the move for *systems analysis* and *systems design* gained importance. This is based on the recognition that industrial activities are composed of *systems of activities* that are made up of *subsystems*. Therefore it is necessary to study these systems to eliminate problems and provide an *organisation structure* that will optimise operations. It is this concept that many of the following sections explore. However, as will be apparent from the previous discussion, much has changed in the world since the organisation of work moved from a cottage industry to organised mass production in factories.

In more recent times we have seen a shift in emphasis away from improving the efficiency of individual workers to greater attention to human relations and improved group processes in an organisational environment encompassing mass-production and automation. While operating systems had become increasingly complex, workers were experiencing diminishing demands on their intellect, initiative and creativity. Attempts to remedy the previously stultifying relationship between people and technologies saw the initiation of concepts such as *human engineering* and *job enrichment*. The 1970s and 1980s saw a shift in market demand from low-variety high-volume (ably suited to mass operating systems) to high-variety low-volumes. Operating systems adopted to accommodate these market forces included *unit production systems*, *group technology*, *cellular configurations* and *team-working methods*.

Since the 1990s we have been experiencing the most significant changes to the *operating characteristics* of organisations. We live in exciting times! Operations management is a fast moving and dynamic field of professional practice. It is to these specific changing features that the remainder of this chapter is devoted. The reasons underlying the adoption of these new systems and techniques include economic factors, customer aspirations and market dynamics, global competition, shrinking profit margins and the ubiquitous application of information technology. The up-take of out-sourcing non-core activities and the sourcing of products and services to rapidly industrialising economies such as China and India are major contributors for the need to change. The net result has seen organisations adopting operating systems that are lean, agile, responsive, part of a collaborative network of suppliers and support services, highly efficient in their use of resources, while being cognisant of the role and importance of people, combined with the application of technology. *Supply chain management* and the adoption of systems of working to bring about *just-in-time* deliveries of supplies and finished goods are fundamental to bringing about lean and agile systems.

As our historical discussion has previously stated, there have been several eras of transformation of systems: craft, mass production and the current lean systems. Each has had an influence on the types of facilities and layouts adopted. Moreover, each has had a direct bearing on the relationship between the customer and the source of the service or offering.

It is important to think of manufacturing *and* services as a total integrated offering to customers, in terms of being a 'bundle of benefits'. After all, what is the use of having excellent service if the product is poorly produced? Also, we are fast becoming a *knowledge-based economy* where service-based organisations, with no tangible product *per se*, are becoming the dominant source of employment for the majority of people. The retailing sector, finance and banking, healthcare, tourism and leisure to name but a few, are typical examples. Consequently, we are now seeing a transferring of operating systems that were once primarily adopted in manufacturing, now being used in the services and other sectors.

The next section describes the key differences between the traditional operating systems that are found in many organisations and those modern systems found in more progressive organisations. Then, an extensive discussion on lean systems is provided.

Box 2.3: The Tasty Nibbles Restaurant

Lack of space appears to be the biggest restriction for revenue growth for this restaurant. At the moment, there is simply no more room for extra tables or for accepting lucrative large-group bookings for weddings and similar celebratory events. At present, almost a third of the total building space is used for storing stock. Purchasing large quantities of various catering ingredients brings with it tempting discounts. Typically there is six months stock of such items as sugar, coffee, salt, paper napkins, tins of baked beans and spaghetti and soups to name but a few. Likewise, the chilled storage and walk-in freezers have at least three months stock. Much of the current practice has been established through working closely with its hundreds of suppliers who automatically send scheduled deliveries at predetermined calendar dates. However, the restaurant is now facing a serious financial situation that must soon be resolved. It needs to expand its floor space for more tables and to create greater revenue, while also reducing its operating costs.

What would you advise the Tasty Nibbles Restaurant to do?

Traditional and progressive operating systems

One of the biggest problems that organisations such as the Tasty Nibbles Restaurant face, is anticipating how much to produce to ensure customers' requirements are met, while simultaneously not producing too much. Resources such as labour, materials and space are all affected by *forecasting* of demand. In the Tasty Nibbles Restaurant, for example, underestimating the number of customers or their choice in food will result in shortages. Clearly though, an overestimation in numbers of customers will result in wastage. How then are the managers or owners to plan for holding stock and scheduling of staff and equipment if they cannot accurately predict demand? They could, perhaps, draw heavily on their experience or use historical information or compare their business industry with comparable sectors for insightful clues. The strategy for many organisations has been to use various forecasting techniques to estimate demand, taking into account numerous influential factors such as seasonality, disposable income, trends and so forth. They could then advertise and promote their services and products of the restaurant when demand is lower than expected to promote sales. This approach to forecasting, producing for stock and supplying to customers is conceptualised as a push system; as the restaurant is in essence pushing its services and products *to* the market and customers.

If, however, using an alternative system, the restaurant were quickly able to adapt flexibly to customer demands, then it would not need stock. If the restaurant were *agile* and responsive, had suppliers that supplied it with supplies 'just-in-time', had multi-skilled staff and the equipment were easily changed and cleaned, then it could operate in response to customers' demands.

This is a simple example of the difference between the 'push' and 'pull' principles, or philosophies, of operating systems. *Push* places the emphasis for inventory management decisions with the supplier, manufacturer or producer. *Pull* places the instigation of action and for inventory management decisions with the purchaser or customer. *Push* forecasts what demand will be in the future and aligns all the systems for producing or delivering the services to that estimate. *Pull* prepares to fulfil demand as quickly and efficiently as it can, then actually waits for the future demand to present itself.

In a traditional organisation, long *lead times* are the time to make decisions and the time needed to carry out the work. But in the lean enterprise, short lead times mean less complex, more accurate forecasting and scheduling. Short lead times are also seen as a competitive advantage in winning customers. Short lead times mean less time for things to go wrong or to be changed. In contrast to using MRP (materials requirement planning – discussed extensively in Chapter 4) techniques of 'pushing work through the organisation', lean-based pull systems are driven by customer pull. Hence, if we were to observe a push system in action, we would see workers busy making items for stock and producing lots of work-in-progress (WIP). In comparison, a pull system is a control-based system that signals (using *kanban* – see later for full discussion) the requirement for parts as they are needed; hence we would see minimal WIP.

However, there are ways to combine push and pull. The place where push gives way to pull is known as the push-pull boundarys. For example, in the Tasty Nibbles Restaurant, the majority of the circular tables seat up to four guests based on projected demand. But when it has to accommodate larger groups of, say, twelve, it could place on top of the smaller circular table a much larger one. A large wheel would simply have to be rolled out and becomes the table-top once secured to the smaller table. The push-pull boundary in this case is just before the guests arrive.

The success of pull systems, when compared with push, has attracted much attention since the Japanese automobile companies (Toyota in particular) from the 1970s onwards have gained significant improvements over their rivals. The application of various pull-techniques, for example *kanban*, operating within a lean and agile organisation structure, has been known collectively as *just-in-time* or *JIT*. More recently, lean and JIT methods have started to become widely adopted in the service sectors such as hospitals, airlines, hospitality, finance sectors, etc.

Although pull systems have gained popularity, there are a number of issues that still require further study. For example, in a (conventional) push system, the concept of customer service is well understood. If the time to complete the task is less than or equal to the planned time (*lead-time*), the work is considered to be on time. Delivery to customers is a function of the planned time. However, in a pull system, the very notion of 'customer' takes on a different meaning. Ohno (1988), generally credited with developing Kanban and JIT, got his ideas from observing American supermarkets; a place where customers can get: (i) what is needed (ii) at the time needed, and (iii) in the amount needed. At Toyota, each process became both a 'supermarket' for downstream processes *and* a customer to preceding processes. Consequently, the lead-time in a pull system is zero: either the item is available or it is not! Therefore, service measures for pull systems are the probability of stock-out, the expected time to fill demand, and expected backlog of orders. So, unlike push systems that control throughput and measure WIP, pull systems control WIP (using kanbans) and measure throughput. A fundamental reason for their success, therefore, is in the way they prevent WIP.

Delivering on the proposition

Intuitively, one would expect companies to want to accept all customers' needs and to accept all orders. Likewise, you may think it better to provide a large range of options from which customers might select their particular needs. However, such an expansive offering, with its increase in *complexity*, confuses the operating system and increases errors and costs. With lean systems, the target market needs to be filtered and well defined; and the range of options available also needs careful consideration. Some customer demands can cause a *dysfunctional* effect on the system. Thus, the overall priorities of lean organisations over traditional firms are different. This perspective is reflected in the way lean organisations design their product strategy and service offering. Their *mission* in competing in the marketplace is different from that of the traditional organisation; and this permeates their operating system design.

Traditional companies design extra capacities of all kinds into their system *just-in-case* a problem arises. For example, they may have additional people, extra equipment, more space than needed, etc. All, of course, cost extra money. Whereas in lean organisations, excess capacity is regarded as waste – not least, of course, WIP. In place of excess capacities, tighter controls and monitoring techniques are used so that additional capacity is not needed.

The sustainable gains that can be accrued by any organisation that successfully implements a lean operating system are enormous. There are clear competitive advantages of faster, dependable response to an individual customer's needs or to new markets.

Box 2.4: Advantages of rapid response

Meredith and Shafer (2007) suggest a number of prerequisites for, and advantages of rapid response:

- *Sharper focus on the customer*: Faster response for both standard and custom-designed items places the customer at the centre of attention.
- *Better management*: The attention changes to management's real job of improving infrastructure and systems.
- *Efficient processing*: This reduces inventories, eliminates non-value-adding processing steps, smooths flows, and eliminates bottlenecks.
- *Higher quality*: Since there is no time for rectifying work, the operating system must be sufficiently improved to produce accurately, reliably, consistently and correctly.
- *Improved focus*: A customer-based focus is provided for strategy, investment and general attention (instead of an internal focus on surrogate measures such as utilisation).
- *Reduced changes*: With less time to delivery, there is less time for changes, especially changes to the order by the customer.
- *Faster revenue generation*: With faster deliveries, orders can be billed faster, thereby improving cash flows and reducing the need for working capital.
- *Better communication*: More direct communication lines result in fewer mistakes and oversights.
- *Improved morale*: Reduced processing steps and overhead charges allow workers to see the results of their efforts, giving a feeling of working for a smaller more intimate organisation. Teamwork gives greater visibility to the business; and shares the responsibility of organisational success to all employees.

Work-in-progress and inventory issues

Just-in-time method was first used by the Ford Motor Company, as described in Henry Ford's *My Life and Work* (1922):

> We have found in buying materials that it is not worth while to buy for other than immediate needs. We buy only enough to fit into the plan of production, taking into consideration the state of transportation at the time. If transportation were perfect and an even flow of materials could be assured, it would not be necessary to carry any stock whatsoever. The carloads of raw materials would arrive on schedule and in the planned order and amounts, and go from the railway cars into production. That would save a great deal of money, for it would give a very rapid turnover and thus decrease the amount of money tied up in materials. With bad transportation one has to carry larger stocks.

Just-in-time inventory systems are not just a simple method that an organisation has to buy in to; it has a whole philosophy that the organisation must follow. The ideas in this philosophy come from many different disciplines including; statistics, industrial engineering, production management and behavioural science. In the JIT inventory philosophy, there are views with respect to how inventory is looked upon, what it says about the management within the organisation, and the main principle behind JIT.

It is often said that most operations have to hold levels of inventories and additional capacity. The typical reasons for this are (Walters, 2003: 7) that they:
- act as a buffer between different operations.
- allow for mismatches between supply and demand rates.
- allow for demands that are larger than expected.
- allow for deliveries that are delayed or too small.
- avoid delays in passing products to customers.
- take advantage of price discounts.
- buy items when the price is low and expected to rise.
- make full loads and reduce transport costs.
- provide cover for emergencies.

It might be argued, however, that the reasons listed above are excuses for poor operations management, unreliable processes or bad buyer–supplier relationships. Admittedly, there are industries that are seasonal or extremely unpredictable and where the threat of obsolescence is low; in which case holding some inventories would be a positive strategy. But such cases are rare. Just-in-time, on the other hand, is not solely concerned with inventory. It also considers capacity, and aspects of quality management such as continuous improvement.

Philosophy of lean systems

The ideas behind what is now termed *lean thinking* were originally developed in Toyota's manufacturing operations – known as the Toyota Production System – and spread through its supply base in the 1970s, and then to its distribution and sales operations in the 1980s. The term was popularised in the seminal book *The Machine that Changed the World* (Womack, Jones and Roos, 1990), which clearly illustrated at that time the significant *productivity*[1] gap of approximately 3:1 between the Japanese and Western automotive industries. It described the key elements accounting for this superior performance as *lean production*. The term 'lean' was used because Japanese business methods used less of everything: human effort, capital investment, facilities, inventories and time. Moreover, underpinning lean thinking is the concept of pursuing 'value' for a specific product or service from the end customer's perspective; and therefore all the non-value activities, or 'waste', can be targeted for removal.

There has been a significant shift from previous systems of service delivery and manufacturing methods. A *lean philosophy* requires the organisation to view itself as part of an extended supply chain. As a result, it needs to think strategically beyond its own corporate boundary. Also, because value streams flow across several departments and functions within an organisation, it needs to be structured around its *key value streams*. Therefore, considering beyond the single organisation, some form of collective agreement (a *partnership relationship*) is needed to manage the whole value stream; and thereby setting common improvement targets, rules for sharing the gains and effort and for taking waste out of future product and service generating operations. This collective group (network) of organisations is called a *lean enterprise* (Womack and Jones, 2003).

Lean thinking can be applied to any organisation in any sector, whether producing a tangible product or supplying a service, e.g., a hospital, an airline, a bank, a grocery store, etc. Although its origins are firmly founded in the automotive production environment, the principles and techniques are transferable, often with little adaptation – and we have a wealth of case study evidence that backs up this assertion (Womack and Jones, 1996). The concept, philosophy and application of lean thinking has showed how organisations in many industries in North America, Europe, Japan, Australia and many other countries have followed this path and have greatly improved their performance while reducing inventories, throughput times and those annoying, expensive errors that reach the final customer. These results are found in all kinds of activities, including order processing, product development, manufacturing, warehousing, distribution and retailing.

Box 2.5: Toyota's lean system

It is generally agreed that Toyota's original approach to lean systems was not in the application of the various tools and methods they used, but rather it was the processes used to make design decisions. Four basic driving principles are (Womack, Jones and Roos, 1990):

- *Work Rule*: All work shall be highly specified as to content, sequence, timing and outcome.
- *Connection Rule*: Every customer-supplier connection must be direct, and there must be an unambiguous yes-or-no way to send requests and receive responses.
- *Pathway Rule*: The pathway for every product and service must be simple and direct.
- *Improvement Rule*: Any improvement must be made in accordance with the scientific method, under the guidance of a 'teacher', at the lowest possible level of the organisation.

These four rules define processes, work flows, customer interaction, and improvement routines, all of which are vital to lean operating systems.

What is value and what is waste?

What does the term 'value' mean to you? For most of us, it simply means whether the price asked appears to be worth it. That is *value for money*. But how can we judge such a subjective term in the context of manufacturing or a service delivery system? The starting point is to recognise that only a small fraction of the total time and effort expended in any organisation actually adds value for the end customer. By clearly defining value for a specific product or service from an end customer's perspective, all the non-value activities therefore, by definition, are waste, and can be targeted for elimination step by step. For most production operations, only 5 per cent of activities add value, some 35 per cent are 'necessary' non-value-adding activities and 60 per cent add no value for the customer at all. Eliminating this waste is usually the greatest potential source of improvement in productivity and customer service. Few products or services are provided by one organisation alone, so that waste removal has to be pursued throughout the whole *value stream*, that is to say the entire set of activities across all the organisations involved in jointly delivering the product or service.

But removal of waste is not an easy task. New types of relationships are required to eliminate inter-organisation waste and to effectively manage the value stream as a whole. Instead of managing the workload through successive departments, processes are reorganised so that the product or design flows through all the value-adding steps without interruption, using the various lean thinking techniques (discussed below) to successively remove any impediment to *continuous flow*. Activities across each organisation are syn-chronised by *pulling* the product or service from upstream steps, just when required, in time to meet the demand from the end customer. In other words, a *just-in-time* operation is used.

Making value flow along the value stream

The concept of 'flow' can be defined as the progressive achievement of tasks along the value stream. These tasks could be operations in the manufacture of a product; or equally, they could be actions taken during the provision of a ser-vice. For example, imagine the actions taken when receiving a telephone order from a potential customer. The 'value stream' in this instance is the specific activities required to process the order, record customer details and provide a specific service or product. Removing wasted time and effort represents the biggest opportunity for creating continuous flow and pull. A well-organised lean system starts with radically reorganising individual process steps; but the gains become truly significant when all the steps in a *process* link smoothly together. As this happens, more and more layers of waste become visible and the process continues towards the theoretical end point of perfection, where every asset and every action adds value for the end customer. In this way, lean thinking represents a path of sustained performance improvement, and not merely a one-off enhancement.

The notion of *flow* is fundamental to lean systems. If you merely add value (for example, by giving an additional service), then you should add in the value quickly to enhance the flow as well as is possible. If this is not the case, then waste builds up in the form of inventory or transportation or extra steps or wasted motion. The idea that flow should be 'pulled' from demand is also fundamental to lean production. 'Pull' means that nothing is done unless, and until, a downstream process requires it. The effect of 'pull' is that activities are not based on forecast; but commitment and work effort are delayed until demand is present to indicate what the customer *really* wants.

The 'batch and queue' habit in conventional systems is very hard to break. It seems counterintuitive at first that doing a little bit at a time at the last possible moment will give faster, better, cheaper results. But anyone design-ing a control system knows that a short feedback loop is far more effective at maintaining control of a process than a long loop. The problem with batches and queues is that they hide problems and allow them to grow. The idea of lean activities is to expose problems as soon as they arise, so they can be corrected immediately. It may seem that lean systems are fragile, because they have no WIP (meaning inventory stored at intermediate steps in the system). But in fact, lean systems are quite robust, because they do not hide unknown, lurking problems and they do not pretend they can forecast the future. To achieve lean and agile systems, there are a number of techniques and concepts that we can adopt, that highlight and remove *inefficiency*[2] and *non-effectiveness*.[3] Such techniques are discussed more fully in the following section.

The components of lean practice

A lean system focuses on reducing waste (rejects and defective working, over-producing, movement and transporting, waiting, inventory, motion, over-processing, wasting skills, etc.). This serves to improve quality, shorten operating time and lower cost. Lean 'tools' include techniques for process analysis, the use of 'pull' production or service delivery and mistake-proofing. Lean, as a management philosophy, also focuses on creating a better workplace through the principle of *respect for humanity*.

Key lean principles

We might, therefore, summarise the key lean principles as being:
- perfect first-time quality – quest for zero defects, revealing and solving problems at the source;
- waste minimisation – eliminating all activities that do not add value, and safety nets ('just-in-case'), maximise use of scarce resources (capital, people and space);
- continuous improvement – reducing costs, improving quality, increasing productivity and information sharing;
- pull-processing – operations are 'pulled' from the consumer end, not pushed from the organisation end;
- flexibility – producing different mixes or greater diversity of services and products quickly, without sacrificing efficiency at lower volumes of activity; and
- building and maintaining a long-term relationship with suppliers through collaborative risk-sharing, cost sharing and information sharing arrangements.

Lean is basically all about getting the right things, to the right place, at the right time, in the right quantity while minimising waste and being flexible and open to change. The seminal book *Lean Thinking* by Womack and Jones (2003) introduced five core concepts that should underpin the use of lean systems:

1. Specify value through the eyes of the customer.
2. Identify the value stream and eliminate waste.
3. Make value flow by the pull of the customer.
4. Involve and empower employees.
5. Continuously improve in the pursuit of perfection.

Numerous methods, tools and techniques have been developed to support the lean philosophy, and to enable organisations to apply the ideas and implement change. Many of these techniques emerged from the Toyota production system – hence the large number of Japanese terms in the lean vocabulary (see the examples below), while others have since been developed by numerous research organisations. Consequently, there is now an extensive 'toolkit' to help the lean-thinking practitioner. We will now discuss in more detail some of the more popular techniques.

Box 2.6: Five Ss

(Adapted from Womack and Jones, 1996, 2003)

Seiri: This means *tidiness*. It refers to the practice of sorting through all the tools and materials in the work area and keeping only essential items. Everything else is stored or discarded. There are fewer hazards and less clutter to interfere with work.

Seiton: This translates to *orderliness*. Tools, equipment, and materials must be systematically arranged for the easiest and most efficient access. There must be a place for everything, and everything must be in its place.

Seiso: This means *cleanliness*. It underscores the need to keep the workplace clean as well as neat. Cleaning should be a daily activity. At the end of each shift, the work area should be cleaned and everything restored to its place.

Seiketsu: This is the development of *standards*. Such standards allow for monitoring, control and consistency. This helps everyone know exactly what his or her responsibilities are; and describes in detail processes and procedures to follow.

Shitsuke: This refers to the sustaining of *discipline* and keeping the working area in a safe and efficient order, day after day, year after year.

Often, we can lose sight of the daily realities when trying to improve systems. *Genchi Genbutsu* encapsulates the notion of 'going into the *real world*' and relying less on information supplied to us. Such first-hand knowledge often reveals practical improvements. For example, try the little exercise shown below, and then read the material that follows.

Box 2.7: *Genchi genbutsu*: posting envelopes

Your small group has been asked to design a process to mail out marketing material. The work requires three different sheets of paper (red, green and yellow) to be folded and placed in an envelope. An adhesive address label is then peeled and stuck to the front of the envelope. The envelope is then sealed. For certain post-codes, the red coloured paper is replaced by *either* a blue (code 4000s) or white (code 5000s). The high quality of the folding prior to insertion to the envelope is important. The alignment of the adhesive label is also important (for optical reading).

How would you design the process?

Invariably when groups are asked to carry out this exercise, they go about it as though mass-producing automobiles. In other words, they apply the classic *division of labour* approach by allocating individuals to operations; such as: one person folding red paper, another folding green paper and so on. Yet another person has the task of inserting the folded paper and applying the adhesive label. There may even have been a person allocated solely for inspecting. What is usually revealed is a great deal of work-in-progress (lots of folded coloured paper!).

Group members are then asked to apply the principle of *genchi genbutsu* – imagine that they *are* the completed envelope and consider how they would like to be treated. How would they prefer to be filled with paper? This more often shows that group members, rather than completing the task in a production-line fashion, choose team methods. By up-skilling group members, individuals are capable of completing the total task. The result is no work-in-progress, personal ownership of quality and a flexible system that can easily accommodate changes in coloured paper and other customer needs.

Heijunka is the creation of a 'level schedule' by sequencing orders in a repetitive pattern and smoothing the day-to-day orders to correspond to longer-term demand. For example, imagine our restaurant example where customers arrive at random intervals with no discernible pattern throughout the week. Imagine what problems that would cause with staffing and preparation of materials. How might we 'smooth' customer demand to reduce drastic peaks and troughs?

Hoshin kanri is often referred to as 'policy deployment'. Top management vision can be translated into a set of coherent, consistent, understandable and attainable policies and actions that can be applied at all levels and in all functions of the organisation. When these strategies are applied, they result in a vision becoming a reality. *Hoshin kanri* provides an opportunity to continually improve performance by disseminating and deploying the vision, direction, targets, and plans of corporate management to the next level of operations management and to all employees. Moreover, *hoshin kanri focuses resources* on the critical initiatives necessary to accomplish the business objectives of the organisation and fosters *managing for outcomes*.

Jidoka is sometimes also referred to as 'automation with human intelligence'. It describes the ability of equipment to recognise when things are wrong and to stop! However, its application in a non-automated system, say when in a service situation such as an administrative environment, is also relevant. The fundamental concept is that when something goes wrong, then the activity stops, the problem is made visible and a solution is sought. Putting the defect right may be comparatively easy or, alternatively, it might need a thorough investigation. The people closest to the problem may have the task of investigating and developing better methods of working.

Kaikaku involves radical, step-change, improvement of an activity to eliminate waste. Traditional *kaizen* (see below) or continuous improvement activities are, by definition, long term. A *kaizen blitz* (or *kaikaku*) is fast and furious. It is up to a week of very highly focused activity involving everyone in a specific section or department or business process working together to create radical and sudden change.

Box 2.8: *Kaikaku* in action

(Adapted from Womack and Jones, 1996, 2003)

There are a number of fundamentals that make up a successful blitz event:

- *Speak with data*: Decisions to make changes are made based on real hard data gained from the current state. This will almost certainly involve developing value stream or process maps and an analysis of where value is created.
- *Develop a vision of the future*: A future map is created that defines what should be happening if all things were perfect. Realistic but challenging elements are drawn out from this to create a vision for what life will be like by the end of the week.
- *Involve everyone*: For a blitz to work, everyone has to be involved. This may mean shutting down a production line or a service department for the duration of the event.
- *Prepare the group*: It is essential that everyone involved is trained in how to perform a blitz. There will be times during the event when people are challenged as they are expected to make radical changes. Unilateral belief from the organisation's leadership will be a strong indicator to people that, while it may be uncomfortable, it is important to stick with it.

Plan for success: Choosing the right target for a blitz is also critical. The event must be built for success. Choose something that will have a big impact on the people as well as the organisation. Too big a challenge and it will fail, too small and it will not have the required impact.

Kaizen is gradual incremental change that results in small improvements throughout the organisation. It might be thought of as '1000 things done 1 per cent better'. It requires an organisational culture that promotes continuous, incremental improvement of an activity to eliminate waste (that is, non-value-adding activities). For example, imagine if we were to ask every employee in our organisation to submit one improvement every week, just think of the benefits that would accrue over time. With continuous, albeit small improvements to the way we operate, there would be substantial benefits gained.

Kanban is a control and monitoring system to regulate the *pull* of products or service by signalling to upstream production and service delivery operations. An alternative to a pull-system is a push-system where, for example, we produce products (say, loaves of bread) and then push their sale through marketing activities. A push-system relies heavily on forecasting demand; and often has to resort to discounting because of over-supply. However, in a pull-system, the *kanban* is a 'signal card', a communication method used to indicate that the system is ready to receive the input. Most often, this is done using a simple card as the indicator but it could also be some other indicator.

Muda is waste or an activity that consumes resources and creates no value. Waste reduction, therefore, is an effective way to increase profitability. Waste occurs when more resources are consumed than are necessary to produce goods or provide the service. For example, the check-out points-of-sale in shops take up expensive floor space; they require people to operate, and long queues cause customers to complain. Hence, if we could reduce or eliminate this part of the purchasing process, it would improve both efficiency and effectiveness. How then might this be possible? Bar-code self-scanning by customers has been adopted in some grocery shops, but the use of radio frequency identification (RFID) tags built into packaging offers significant savings in all sorts of ways.

Box 2.9: Types of waste

(Adapted from Ohno, 1988)

Eight types of waste are prevalent in most organisations:

- *Defects*: Quality defects in products or poor service cause customer dissatisfaction.
- *Overproducing*: This could be as a result of having too many people delivering the service or over-production or acquisition of items before they are actually required.
- *Movement and transporting*: Aisles, gangways and corridors take up space. Moreover, the time and effort required to move between activities is not a value-adding activity.
- *Waiting*: This is the time spent by staff waiting for resources to arrive, and the capital sunk in goods, materials and services that are not yet delivered to the customer.
- *Inventory*: Stocks of materials, work-in-progress (WIP), and equipment not being used, represent capital outlay that has not yet produced an income either by the producer or by the consumer. Often, companies are under the illusion that if they purchase or produce large quantities of materials, then *economies of scale* can bring down the unit cost; however, this saving is usually not the full cost. When other considerations are fully costed, holding inventory may turn out to be a waste of capital expense.
- *Motion*: This is the movement of people when performing their operations. Ergonomics is the science of people and their environment, and we know that poor ergonomics can seriously damage health as well as contribute to poor productivity. This has significance to impacts on the damage of products, safety and fatigue. Excessive bending, lifting, stretching or working under inadequate lighting and ventilation are examples of poor *motion economy*.

- *Over-processing*: This type of waste results from using a more expensive or otherwise more valuable resource than what is needed for the task. One obvious example is where people may need to perform tasks that they are overqualified for.
- *Skill*: Organisations employ their staff for the specific skill-sets that they have. However, these employees have other skills. Therefore, it is wasteful to not take advantage of these skills as well.

Poka-yoke translates to 'mistake-proofing'. Special devices can be used during manufacturing to prevent a defect. An example is the use of simple measuring gauges. Likewise, in a service environment, for example during order-taking, techniques can be adopted to prevent mistakes (say, by repeating the order back to the customer to ensure details are correct). If we want to design our system to be *right first time*, then we need to eliminate any opportunity for mistakes to happen. Moreover, such mistake-proofing does not need to be expensive or elaborate; often the more simple the prevention, the more likely it will be used.

Value stream mapping is a charting method for recording activities. Its purposes are to help us to fully understand what is going on and then allow us to streamline and improve work processes. A value stream map (sometimes referred to as an end-to-end system map) takes into account not only the activities to produce a product or undertake a service, but also the management and information systems that support the basic process. This is especially helpful when you are attempting to reduce the time taken to complete activities, because you gain insight into the decision-making flow in addition to the process flow. The first stage is to construct a 'present state map' that shows work processes as they currently exist. This is vital both to understand the need for change and to understand where opportunities for improvements lie. While value stream maps appear complex, in fact their construction is easy when taken in logical steps. By using a series of symbols, it is possible to develop a value stream map using paper and pencil. The results will help you to see and understand the flow of material and information as a product or service makes its way through the value stream.

Building a lean organisation

One of the most important considerations that an organisation needs to address when designing an operating system is establishing the *volume* (quantity of people, information or components and products) and *variety* of outputs (different requirements). High volumes would indicate the use of mass-automated systems. High variety, on the other hand, implies the use of skilled labour and general purpose equipment and facilities. However, few organisations use simply one operating system, but combine two or more methods in a *hybrid* system. Even within a service environment such as McDonald's, we would see staff preparing batches of Big Macs, but they also accept individual orders of just one item.

Operations managers must decide on the processing system(s) most appropriate for the organisation, considering aspects of efficiency, effectiveness, lead-time, capacity, quality, flexibility and agility. Undoubtedly there will have to be trade-offs; but the consequences of such choices must be well understood. The net result of a poorly designed operating system will manifest itself in poor customer service.

From our previous sections, it would have become clear that the underpinning message is that lean operations systems endeavour to eliminate all types of waste; the most common being excessive delays, moving long distances, spending too long setting-up equipment, using excessive space and generating poor standards of work. In sum, we can consider waste as being actions and activities that do not add value for the customer. The customers' requirements are central to a lean operating system design.

Lean layouts and technology

An organisation's *process architecture*, that is to say, the interactions of its operating activities and use of its resources, has a significant impact on the flow of work through the processes and the functioning of the processes to align activities with demand. One of the most famous production layouts is the flow-line for *mass production*, epitomised by Henry Ford's automotive assembly lines. These and several other types of layouts are discussed more fully in other chapters of this text. However, it suffices to say that the major determinant when identifying what type of layout to be adopted is the *quantity* of product to be produced. An advantage of such functional layouts is that it maximises available capacity for each function, thereby achieving good utilisation of comparatively large quantities of products. Moreover, it benefits from *division of labour*, specialisation and standardisation of work within each function. However, process layouts have several drawbacks when compared with lean systems.

Invariably, WIP has to travel significant distances between the various work stations, so the flow-time is high. Moreover, because each worker is narrowly focused on performing only part of the total processing task, workers can become bored, frustrated with the work and alienated. The consequence is that improvements are usually directed towards technology-focused alternatives. However, an alternative to process-based functional layouts is the product-focused *cellular layout*, where different workstations are brought together in a group (a cell), normally placed in a horseshoe configuration, so

Table 2.1 Types of service (Adapted from Chase & Tansik, 1983)

	Customer contact intensity	
	Low	High
Capital intensive	**Service 'factory'** Airlines, postal service, hotels, recreation	**Service 'batch'** Hospitals, car repair, travel agencies
Labour intensive	**Mass service** Sporting events, retailing, fast food	**Professional service** Legal services, doctors, architects

that successive operations can be performed on the product. The positions of the workstations are laid out within the cell to allow a linear flow; thus, the activities are performed sequentially.

Team working among the different functions within the cell also encourages cross-functional skill development; which will lead to more satisfying jobs. As all team members are working on the same product simultaneously, workers can experience a sense of 'ownership' of the total product process. This builds morale and motivation levels and drives improved quality.

Another major advantage of a cellular layout is that it is focused on a narrow range of customer needs, and contains all resources required to complete all or most of the total task. The focus of the cell is on flexibility, and it produces low-volume work so the rest of the plant can focus on producing high-volume parts efficiently. Similarly, in a service environment, such as a hospital, there are cellular process layouts that specialise in emergency admittance, maternity, geriatrics, trauma etc. These specialist 'cells' are established to process patients (customers) with specific needs.

The disadvantages of cellular layouts can be quickly identified as being due to low equipment utilisation. Because resources (particularly machines) are dedicated to specific cells, when they are not in operation we lose the advantage of resource pooling of a functional layout. Arguably, team-based incentives used in cellular-based operations are less attractive than individual incentives. This negative perspective is based on the view that there may be individuals who 'do not pull their weight'.

Lean operating systems for services

Many of the operating considerations of manufacturing organisations are of equal importance to services. Chase and Tansik (1983) classify four discrete types of services; this gives us an insight on how best to design operating systems for services (see Table 2.1).

Each quadrant has a label and examples that capture the essence and represent a unique service operating system, with particular managerial challenges. Those services at the high contact side of the matrix have low volumes with high customisation; and must attain their operating sustainability through high prices. Conversely, services on the other side with low contact and little customisation attain profitability through high volumes. Clearly, the managerial challenge for the low contact left-end is making the service appear attractive so as to attract high volumes. Alternatively, if the service is labour intensive, the challenge is to optimise wages and time spent on each customer. Moreover, if an organisation wants to shift its operating system across quadrant, then there are several considerations. For example, if a lawyer wants to move toward a more automated service ('batch' system) through computer email contact with clients or on-line preparation of wills, then there is an opportunity to use less skilled staff. The implication to clients of such a strategic move, however, needs careful consideration.

Employee empowerment

Focusing on the people who add value means investing in upgrading the skills of staff through training. It means forming teams that design their own processes and solve problems. It means that team leaders and managers exist to support teams in their improvement work, not to instruct them what to do. For this to happen, lean organisations are usually structured around teams that maintain responsibility for overall business value, rather than intermediate measurements such as their ability to answer a set number of phone calls per hour. The underlying operating culture is one that fosters a keen awareness that the downstream department is a customer, and satisfying this internal customer is the ultimate performance measurement.

The paradigm shift that is required with lean thinking is often hindered if the organisation is not structured around the flow of value and focused on helping the customer pull value from the enterprise. For this reason, teams are best structured around delivering increments of business value, with all the necessary skills on the same team (e. g., customer understanding and communication, use of database or manufacture of components).

In many instances, conventional operating systems measure and value the *yield rate*, that is to say the total produced as a ratio to time available, as the ultimate performance measurement. As long as people are measured primarily on such productivity measures, they will produce inventory. This is what is known as a sub-optimising measurement, because it creates behaviour which creates local optimisation at the expense of overall optimisation. One of the biggest sub-optimising measurements in most departments occurs when individuals are measured on piecework schemes. These types of payment-by-results schemes (e.g., number of phone calls per hour completed in a call centre) are the basis of the cost initially estimated for the tasks. Just as excess inventory in manufacturing slows down production and degrades over time, the inventory of tasks required for services gets in the way of delivering true business value and also degrades over time.

Empowered employees are a necessity due to the knowledge explosion and the more technical workplace; staffs are required to be more competent and flexible to meet head-on the range of needs of the customer. Decision making is now being handed to the individual worker and teams. Empowered employees can bring their experience and involvement to bear on both routine daily activities as well as problem solving. Their *ownership* of activities and responsibility for quality is therefore vitally important in a lean operating environment. This means that those tasks that have traditionally been assigned to supervisors can move to empowered employees. Lean organisations train and cross-train, and also take full advantage of that investment by *enriching* tasks. Lean's philosophy of JIT and use of continuous improvement techniques, gives all staff the opportunity to enrich their work.

The challenges of JIT management

The underlying *ethos* of just-in-time is that materials, staff, equipment and space will be available exactly at the time required and, moreover, these resources will match demand; so eliminating any waste. For most organisations JIT presents a massive challenge to the way they undertake their operations. Both internal and external factors require radical changes to 'usual' ways of working; not least, the need to 'get things right first time', because JIT will not tolerate mistakes, re-working or scrap. There is little or no 'safety net'. One of the greatest challenges for organisations is their ability to eliminate waste that is not solely centred on costs. Considerations such as agility and flexibility, rapid response to customer requirements, innovation, delivery speed, dependability, reliability and trusting relationships are also important factors. Unless such matters are addressed, JIT will not work effectively. The effect of JIT can be described in Table 2.2 (adapted from Brown, 1996).

In all organisations, either manufacturing or service, when there is little 'buffer' of inventory, materials, people or space, there is usually evidence of several types of waste (*muda*). Holding inventory, at any stage, can serve to cover up poor operating performance. Moreover, reducing inventory will, in the first instance, cause these problems to surface. This will allow us to identify where we can make improvements.

Supply relationship management

Traditional buyer–supplier relationships are ones based on adversarial terms. This is to say, organisations are reluctant to work closely with a just a few

Table 2.2 Effects of just-in-time (Adapted from Brown, 1996)

	Traditional operations	Just-in-time operations
Quality	'Acceptable' levels of poor quality – an inevitability that failures will occur. A specialist needed for checking.	'Right first time'; ongoing pursuit of process improvement. Everybody responsible for ensuring acceptable quality.
Inventory	An asset, part of the balance sheet and therefore part of the value of the firm. Buffers needed to keep operations running.	A liability, masking the real operating performance by hiding the operations problems.
Work loads	An economic order can be determined to show the balance between starting the work (set-up) and overall operating time.	Operating activity times must be as small as possible. Aiming towards producing one product or looking after one customer.
Material ordering	Determined by the economic order quantity.	Supply exactly meets demand, no more, no less. Delivery or availability (people, materials etc) is exactly when required.
Bottlenecks	Inevitable; shows that capacity utilisation is high.	No queues – operation is at the rate which prevents delays and queues.
People	A cost which can be reduced through more automation.	A valuable asset, able to problem-solve.

suppliers, but would rather have a range of alternative supplier sources in case quality or delivery performance from one supplier is poor. It is also believed that competition would drive down prices. Although there are numerous organisations that remain committed to this approach, there is clear evidence that buyer–supplier relationships are changing in a number of ways.

The most evident change has been in the reduction of suppliers that organisations deal with. Moreover, the relationship is based not on a contract between the parties but rather on cooperation, risk-sharing, a full exchange of information, a commitment to improve quality (together), and recognition that prices can be reduced while giving a reasonable level of profit. This *partnership approach*, therefore, is based on the supplier having clear demands; but these are made achievable by the purchaser helping the supplier to improve its business in terms of lower cost and faster delivery.

In order for the buyer–supplier relationships to be workable and sustainable, there has to be considerable trust between the two parties. Typically, there are three principal types of trust: *contractual trust* – these are formal legal contracts; *competence trust* – either side is capable of providing what has been promised; and *goodwill trust* – based upon ethical behaviour and mutual trust. For JIT to operate successfully, it is essential for the partnerships to be underpinned by these types of trust. Unfortunately, however, sometimes operations management is not up to the task and as a consequence JIT fails.

We have seen that the management of inventory has now developed from solely a tactical activity to an operating system-level of strategic planning. JIT is far more than inventory management because it represents a fundamental strategic change in how organisations meet customers' needs using a pull system.

Summary

The management challenge set out at the start of the chapter asked the question: "What are the essential differences between firms such as Toyota/Honda and General Motors/Ford that has given rise to such differences?" The probable answer is that successful companies emphasise lean methods for minimising costs while enhancing customers' value-drivers. Lean systems operate just-in-time and draw on the strengths of people as well as technology. This is evident in what has been described as the five lean principles of: (1) identifying value from the customer's perspective; (2) focus on value-adding activities; (3) design sequences of activities so there is value-flow; (4) let the work load pull activities through the process rather than have control mechanisms that are required to push work along; and, (5) pursue zero defects and excellent quality. Such lean thinking is used to improve performance of the total supply chain in meeting end-customer demand with reduced waste and optimised use of resources.

In our discussion of alternative approaches to designing and developing operating systems, whether they have been adopted to produce products or services, it has been evident that many of the traditional approaches lack the necessary speed, dependability, flexibility and quality of output. Whereas, lean systems appear to deliver on many of the requirements of the current marketplace; one where the customer's needs must prevail, quality is paramount and value for money is usually the final arbiter of customer choice.

Lean thinking means taking customers' needs, in terms of what they regard as *value*, as the basis for designing and developing an operating system. It is far more than a set of functional activities; but rather, it is a philosophy for efficiently and effectively using the resources an organisation has at its disposal. For example, make an appointment for a routine hospital check-up and, in the past, the chances were you would have to wait several weeks. Today, there are examples of hospitals that schedule all patients within a day for just about any medical service. Such hospitals have worked off their backlogs by extending their hours, and then vary their hours from week to week to maintain the workload to approximately one day. While doctors do not have the reassuring week-long lists of scheduled patients, they see just as many patients. The patients are happier and doctors detect medical problems far earlier than before. Such examples are as a result of asking: 'How can processes be organised so that the activities do nothing but *add value*, and as rapidly as possible?'

Organisations that re-think the *value chain* and find ways to provide what their customers' actually value, using significantly fewer resources than their counterparts, can develop an unassailable competitive advantage. Sometimes competitors are simply not able to deliver the new *value proposition*. (Many have tried to emulate Toyota; few have succeeded). Once we understand what value *is* and what activities and resources are absolutely necessary to create value, then everything else is waste.

As this chapter has described, a lean operating system offers a range of benefits, specifically:

- Reduction in operations costs: Savings can be made from inventory reductions, less wasted work, fewer mistakes, less space, less direct costs (labour), reduced overheads and a stable customer base.
- Employee empowerment: People in lean enterprises are more satisfied with their work so this will reduce staff turnover. Most people prefer working in teams. They are better trained for the flexibility and skills needed for problem solving and decision making.
- Problem solving: One of the benefits that accrue as a result of JIT is the greater visibility of problems. By increasing the speed to complete activities, and having little WIP, all types of difficulties are uncovered. Most of these problems are various forms of waste.
- Supplier relationships: Greater collaboration with fewer suppliers, particularly when planning, leads to transparency and trust, and mutual risk-sharing. Through JIT, both parties will find improvements and economies; whilst enhancing quality.

DISCUSSION QUESTIONS

1. Describe the important characteristics of lean systems and organisational agility.

2. Look up the recent profits of Toyota and Ford and General Motors on the Internet. If possible also look up the share price history of these companies. How do operations management factors relate to the differences in these financial performance levels?
3. Typically, push production results in high amounts of work-in-progress inventories, which in turn cause higher operating costs. Where are these costs incurred?
4. What are the advantages of kanban over other types of control methods?
5. If just-in-time supplies of materials offer such advantages, why can't all organisations apply it?
6. List and illustrate the five lean principles in an applied setting.
7. Eliminating waste is far more than reducing work-in-progress. Where else is there waste in many operating systems?
8. What are the advantages of short setup times?
9. Just-in-time will not work effectively if quality can not be assured. Why not?
10. Why are people an extremely important component of lean philosophy?
11. Could the lean philosophy be applied to, say, a hotel or an airline booking system?
12. Why is it important that suppliers must deliver small quantities on a continuous basis and with excellent quality?

References

American Engineering Council. 1921. *Waste in Industry*. Federated American Engineering Societies. New York: McGraw-Hill.

Brown, S. 1996. *Strategic Manufacturing for Competitive Advantage*. Hemel Hempstead: Prentice Hall.

Chase, R. B. and Tansik, D. A. 1983. 'The customer contact model for organisation design.' *Management Science*, 29: 1037–50.

Ford, Henry, in collaboration with Crowther, S. 1922. *My Life and Work*. New York: Kessinger Publishing.

Meredith, J. R. and Shafer, S. M. 2007. *Operations Management for MBAs*. Indianapolis: Wiley.

Ohno, Taiichi. 1988. *Toyota Production System: Beyond large-scale production*, Productivity Press, 1988.

Walters, D. 2003. *Operations Management: Producing goods and services*. Harlow: Addison Wesley.

Womack, J. and Jones, D. 1996. *Lean Thinking: Banish waste and create wealth in your corporation*. New York: Simon & Schuster.

Womack, J. and Jones, D. 2003. *Lean Thinking: Banish waste and create wealth in your corporation*. New York: Simon & Schuster.

Womack, J., Jones, D. and Roos, D. 1990. *The Machine that Changed the World*. New York: Rawson Associates.

Further readings and bibliography

Carlisle, J. and Parker, L. 1991. *Beyond Negotiation*. Chichester: Wiley.

George, Michael L. 2003. *Lean Six Sigma for Service*. New York: McGraw-Hill.

Goldratt, E. M. 1990. *Theory of Constraints*. Croton-on-Hudson: North River Press.

Harrison, A. 1992 *Just-in-Time Manufacturing Perspective*. Hemel Hempstead: Prentice Hall.

Hutchins, D. 1999. *Just-in-Time*. 2nd edn. London: Gower Books.

Levinson, William A. *Henry Ford's Lean Vision: Enduring principles from the first Ford motor plant*. New York: Productivity Press.

Monden, Y. 1993. *Toyota production System*. 2nd edn. Atlanta, GA: Industrial Engineering and Management Press.

Schniederjans, M. 1993. *Topics in Just-in-Time Management*. Boston: Allyn & Bacon.

Schonberger, R. 1996. *World Class Manufacturing: The next decade; building power, strength and value*. New York: Free Press.

Schonberger, R. and Knod, E. 2001.*Operations Management: Improving customer service*. New York: Irwin.

Internet resources

www.lean.org

www.aim.com.au

www.segla.com.au/

http://en.wikipedia.org/wiki/Lean_manufacturing

Notes

1 *Productivity* is the ratio of *inputs* to *outputs*. Two companies might be producing the same number of products but one company may use less input (such as materials, time, space, energy etc.) so it has the better productivity.

2 Inefficiency occurs when an activity makes poor use of resources such as time, materials, space or people.

3 Non-effective activities are not achieving their aim (even though they might be efficient). For example, we may have a very efficient automated service but customers find it complicated to use.

Key Decisions in OM

Willem Selen and Danny Samson

Learning objectives

After reading this chapter you will:
- become familiar with the key decisions that affect operating systems.
- understand the factors affecting the decision of organisations to 'make' or 'buy' parts of their requirements, and how these then relate to decisions to outsource these
- understand the types and nature of decisions that are involved when making demand forecasts
- appreciate the factors driving facility location decisions made in order to maximise operating and business effectiveness
- understand how capacity is planned, built, offered and executed in order to deliver relevant operations and business goals
- understand the connections between these key decisions, other aspects of the organisation, and the performance impacts of these, in a variety of industries.

Box 3.1: Management challenge: new Woolworths distribution centre

Woolworths has recently invested in a very large distribution centre near Minchinbury in New South Wales, just near Sydney, through which it will receive, distribute and 'move to store' over 300,000 cases per day of many of its 20,000 items that it sells in some 700 stores. What happens at this distribution centre? In essence, thousands of pallets of groceries are delivered daily by dozens of large trucks from hundreds of suppliers, which must be stored (for as little time as possible), and sent in the right volumes in a timely manner to the stores that require them, in order to meet the demands of those stores' customers. The overall challenge is to get the goods supplied, sorted and sent to the right place at the right time, in excellent quality condition, such as to avoid stockouts at stores, and to do all this at the lowest overall cost. This includes the cost of setting up the facility (the capital cost), the cost of operating the facility (labour, energy, technology, stock equipment maintenance, etc.), the cost of transport, the cost at the stores of receiving the goods in certain ways and at certain times, the costs of overstocking versus understocking the distribution centre and the stores. And all this is being done every day and at massive scale. The idea is to ultimately achieve what operations managers call 'swift and even flow', meaning smooth running distribution operations, with goods being delivered, stored for a short time, and sent to stores efficiently and effectively.

Why did Woolworths decide to build this new massive distribution centre, instead of using its current distribution centres? Why did it not decide to lease such a facility from someone else? Why was Minchinbury chosen by Woolworths as the location for this facility? Should Woolworths have built the facility big enough for its present operations, or to be able to accommodate 10 per cent growth that it anticipates, or 20 per cent over the longer term?

Introduction

In today's business environment where organisations compete and operate in global supply networks, a number of strategic operations decisions need to be taken. In this chapter, we focus on some of these, while others are covered in forthcoming chapters. Consider the following decisions:

- How much of the supply network should the organisation own? This will depend on many factors. All these can be factored into the *make or buy* decision-making framework; it is also sometimes called the *insource–outsource* decision.
- Where should each part of the network owned by the organisation be located? For example, where does Coles in Australia choose a particular location for its supermarkets? This investment is strategic for Coles, meaning that it involves large stakes (indeed hundreds of millions of dollars), is difficult to reverse or change, and has very long lasting impacts on the organisation. In the case of a new manufacturing facility, should it be close to its suppliers or close to its customers, or somewhere in between? These decisions relate to *operations facility location*.
- What physical capacity should each part of the network owned by the organisation have at any point in time? How large should the

manufacturing, distribution or service facility be? If it expands, should it do so in large capacity steps or small ones? Should it make sure that it always has more capacity than anticipated demand or less? These decisions are called long-term *capacity management* decisions.

Note that all three of these decisions rely on assumptions regarding the level of future demand. This justifies the importance of good forecasting. Some of the key decisions in this chapter have long lasting consequences, so, given that future demand for goods and services cannot be known for sure into the future, it must be estimated with the most reasonable accuracy possible.

We now turn to the first strategic operations decision category, namely how much of the global supply network should the operation own? It is certainly the case that organisations do not need to make every good or service which they sell. So what should they make, and what should they buy in from others?

Make-or-buy, outsource, or off-shore?

The make-or-buy decision

The *make-or-buy* decision is not only critical in itself but it also governs the nature of the supply chain and the resulting management tasks. Whether an organisation makes or buys, the need to effectively manage the whole supply chain has increasingly been recognised as a key executive role and one that directly impacts an organisation's ability to compete in its chosen markets. The concept of a totally integrated supply chain – from material producer through to end-customer – is bringing great changes to the way businesses operate. To bring this about, organisations need responsive and adaptive systems and procedures. This requires meaningful coordination, collaboration and fuller relationships to provide the essential basis for cooperation and joint developments. Here are some of the principal reasons that may form the basis of make-or-buy decisions.

Retaining the core technologies of the business

Most organisations choose to keep in-house those processes that represent the core elements of their business. For example, many service organisations wish to retain the process that constitutes the ultimate link with customers. Or it might be a proprietary technology that organisations wish to keep in-house.

Strategic considerations

Make-or-buy decisions need to be made within the strategic context of a business. For example, Dell Computer Corporation developed the capability to assemble PCs quickly in response to customers' orders, but found that this potentially competitive dimension was constrained by component suppliers' long lead times. A key factor is how current and future positions on the make-or-buy continuum impact the ability of operations to support those market criteria for which it is responsible.

Buy rather than make

A company might decide to buy in the technology in the form of components or materials for products and the expertise in the form of customer or information processing for services. For example, no automotive company, big or small, manufactures its own tyres. They all choose to buy rather than make their own. This is because of the specialised technologies and processes required in making tyres, which are very different from those of designing and making whole cars. One important consideration is that when an organisation chooses to buy in rather than make part of its goods or services, it is difficult to achieve any significant competitive advantage from that bought component or service aspect. For example, automotive companies do not get competitive advantage over each other from the tyres they supply as part of their vehicles.

Service and product volumes

Organisations faced with sets of demands for services and products that have different volume levels may consider outsourcing the response to one set of demands for which they may not wish to develop the in-house process. For example, an up-market ladies' clothes outlet undertakes internally any minor garment change for a customer, whereas more complex modifications are sourced from outside specialists.

Globalisation of world trade

Trade barriers across much of the world have declined sharply in recent years. This has made global manufacturing more commercially feasible. One outcome is the reduced need for many local plants. Markets that previously demanded local production facilities because of high tariff levels can now be supplied by imports. A good example of this is the Australian automotive sector. In the eighteen years to 2005, tariffs on imported cars dropped from 57.5 to 10 per cent. During this time, the market share of imported cars rose from 15 to about 70 per cent. Domestic car plants (for example Nissan and Mitsubishi) have closed or reduced local production volume.

To summarise, an organisation may decide to make a product or component: if it believes that this is a core competence that needs to be preserved; lower production costs; if reliable suppliers cannot be found; it surplus labour and facilities are available and can be gainfully utilised; to ensure that the right level of quality is produced; to remove the risk of suppliers acting opportunistically; to protect employees from layoffs; to protect intellectual property associated with the product; and, to preserve/increase size of the organisation (Heizer and Render, 2005, p. 329). On the other hand, there are equally good reasons for an organisation to buy a product or component. These include: freeing the organisations to concentrate on its primary business; lowing acquisition costs; maintaining relationships with suppliers; obtaining capabilities that it may not have in-house; dealing with capacity constraints; reducing inventory costs; and having to buy because items are protected by patents or trade secrets (Heizer and Render, 2005, p. 329).

Outsourcing

One of the most important decisions an organisation can make about its supply chain is whether to vertically integrate or outsource key business processes and functions. *Vertical integration* refers to the process of acquiring and consolidating elements of a supply chain to achieve more control. Although such a strategy provides more control, it adds more complexity to managing the supply chain.

Decentralising supply chain activities lessens the control that an organisation has over cost, quality, and other important business metrics and often leads to higher levels of risk. These decisions depend on the economics associated with consolidation and outsourcing, the technological capabilities of the organisation and external suppliers, and oftentimes, the impact on the organisation's human resources. Decisions to vertically integrate often focus on acquiring suppliers and technological capability and bringing them within the walls of the organisation.

Outsourcing is the process of having suppliers provide goods and services that were previously produced internally. Outsourcing is the opposite of vertical integration in the sense that the organisation is shedding (not acquiring) a part of itself. The organisation that outsources does not have ownership of the outsourced process or function. Banks and airlines, such as Westpac and Qantas, have outsourced their telephone call service centres and maintenance services to third-party suppliers. Once outsourced, these organisations buy these services in. They have switched from ownership and control of these assets and processes to buying them in. In doing so, they have switched some fixed costs for more of a mix of variable costs. Along with the shift in assets, there is usually a contract for the provision of goods or services, and a shift of some of the risks inherent to the outsourced assets. Of course those who take on the outsourced assets and processes expect to make a profit margin commensurate with the risks they have assumed!

Outsourcing transfers some of what are traditional internal activities and resources of an organisation to outside vendors, making it slightly different to the traditional make-or-buy decision. Outsourcing is part of the continuing trend towards utilising the efficiency that comes with specialisation. The vendor performing the outsourced service is an expert in that particular specialty, and the outsourcing organisation can focus on its critical success factors – its core competencies. The resources transferred to the supplying organisation may include facilities, people, and equipment. Many organisations now outsource their information-technology requirements, accounting work, legal functions, and even product assembly.

Off-shoring

Let us first differentiate off-shoring from outsourcing. While outsourcing involves the migration of services to an external provider, in off-shoring these providers are located in another country. Success of off-shoring primarily depends on taking advantage of lower-cost labour in another country. Typical off-shoring encompasses manufacturing, IT, and back-office services.

While outsourced processes are handed off to third-party vendors, off-shored processes can be handed off to third-party vendors or remain in-house. Off-shoring is the building, acquiring, or moving of process capabilities from a domestic location to another country location. Off-shoring decisions involve determining what primary support, or management processes should move to other countries. The decision to off-shore or outsource involves a variety of economic and non-economic issues. Not all multinational organisations locate across the globe. For example, Lego, the Danish toy maker, made a strategic decision long ago to locate its factories only in Europe and the United States. While most other toy manufacturers moved production to low-cost countries such as China, Lego wanted to stay in countries with expertise in injection moulding and mould design. It also wanted to have immediate access to the latest innovations in plastic materials. Lego justified its strategic decisions more on non-economic grounds. Yet, from a purely economic standpoint, off-shoring can make a lot of sense because it generally lowers unit costs. Countries such as China, India, and Russia have many educated people who are eager to work at low wage rates.

Many Australian and New Zealand manufacturing organisations have off-shored activities to China, such as basic manufacturing. This includes massive amounts of clothing and footwear, and components and products such as hardwares and homewares. Reports of cost reductions of 20 per cent and above make these arrangements worthwhile.

Alternatives to the make-or-buy decision

The discussion so far has implied that the choices on offer to organisations must involve an ownership or non-ownership option – organisations either invest in operations capabilities or they outsource their requirements. However, where greater control is considered necessary, organisations could include alternatives such as joint ventures, co-sourcing and non-equity-based collaboration.

Organisations often have to exploit opportunities, particularly in areas such as applied technology and research. Where two or more organisations have similar needs and can benefit from combining, a *joint venture* is a sensible alternative. The costs and benefits are shared in some way, between the joint venture partners.

Similar to a joint venture, *co-sourcing* is where an organisation brings in one or more competitors together with a specialist outsourcing organisation. For example, most banks are reluctant to outsource due to concerns of handing their skills to rivals or specialist organisations that would sell them to rivals. Yet banks have been forced to respond to global competition and co-sourcing is one alternative. This is illustrated by the example where, in 2002, one of the largest deals saw Barclays and Lloyds TSB (the UK's third and fourth largest banks respectively) pool their cheque processing into a new company controlled by Unisys, the US consultancy. In this new company, each of the two banks had a 24.5 per cent stake.

Organisations unwilling or unable to cope with joint venture arrangements can resort to an appropriate form of non-equity-based collaboration to meet their needs. These collaborations provide the means of establishing cooperative working arrangements that need a long-term base if the collaboration is to yield meaningful and useful results. Such arrangements may, for example, include research and development consortia to enhance innovation and exploit results, or joint purchasing activities to enhance buying power. Buying groups exist in many industries, such as retail operators on hardware, chemist and grocery operations. They involve independent operators (indeed often competitors), joining together to collaborate and use their joint scale and power to improve their collective outcomes in buying in goods and services.

Forecasting decisions

A forecast is a statement about the future. While many variables are forecasted in a typical organisation, for operations management purposes, the most important variable is levels of future demand. Also sometimes called sales forecast, knowledge of future patterns of demand is used to plan the resources and systems required to be able to produce *right* levels of products and services that will meet the needs of customers.

Role of demand forecasting for products and services

Demand forecasts provide the information that top managers need to plan product and service development, long-term capacity decisions, and other strategic decisions. Qantas, for example, needs long-range forecasts of demand for air travel to plan their purchases of airplanes. It is also vital for day-to-day operational decisions on scheduling of flight and other services, inventory (examples include everything from meals to spare parts for planes) and staffing decisions that directly affect customer service levels and parts shortages. Qantas needs short-term forecasts to develop seasonal routes and schedules, because demand patterns vary on different days of the week and different weeks of the year. Likewise, restaurants need forecasts to be able to plan for food purchases. These demand or sales forecasts drive an organisation's production, capacity, and resource scheduling systems and serve as inputs to financial, marketing, and personnel planning.

Overall, shortening product and service life cycles, changing technology, frequent price wars, and incentives for customers to switch services make accurate forecasts difficult. Imagine a major telecommunications organisation such as Telstra, Singtel or Telecom NZ trying to 'see' into the future as to how many and what services will be required by customers. Technology and related products and services, prices and usage by customers changes daily in that industry, such that forecasting the future as a key ingredient to planning operations is far from simple. Hence, even with the best of such forecasts, contingency planning is advisable, which involves considering what 'we' would do if the forecast is wrong.

Accurate forecasts are needed throughout the supply chain, and are used by all functional areas of an organisation. A problem here is that forecasting systems may be driven by individual departmental needs and incentives, yielding multiple sets of data for similar customers, work orders, and process performance. This in turn may lead to conflicting forecasts and organisational inefficiencies. One way to avoid these problems is by having only one integrated database that comprehensively covers the whole supply chain and demand planning software systems, such as those popularly supplied by software companies SAP or Oracle. Such software systems include statistical forecasting tools, as well as collaborative demand planning.

Box 3.2: Collaborative demand planning

Collaborative demand planning enables planners to share demand plans among key players in the supply chain, which reduces the need for forecasting in the traditional sense. In the past, organisations conducted planning based on known customer orders or forecasts of future customer orders. By sharing information across the supply chain about customer order status, customer and supplier delivery schedules, backorders, and inventory status, organisations in the supply chain reduce their need for forecasts and also improve the accuracy of the forecasts they have to make. However, it should be noted that although they promise much, these systems are expensive and complex to introduce and implement.

When an organisation develops a demand forecast, it is most important to know its purpose. Here, the level of aggregation often dictates the appropriate forecasting method. For example, for the major global consumer products company, Proctor & Gamble, forecasting the total amount of soap to produce over the next planning period is quite different from forecasting the amount of each individual product to produce. Aggregate forecasts are generally much easier to develop, whereas detailed forecasts require more time and resources.

Which forecasting approach to use?

The choice of forecasting method depends on criteria such as the time span for which the forecast is being made, the frequency of forecast updating, data requirements and technology involved, and the level of accuracy desired. The time span is one of the most important criteria, and can be divided into *short-range, intermediate-range, and long-range* forecasts.

Short-range forecasts

These forecasts are generally for periods of less than three months, but sometimes go up to one year. They are used for planning purchasing, job scheduling, workforce levels, job assignments, and production levels. How much shampoo will Proctor and Gamble expect to sell, in every product line, in every region, country and city of the world, by week over the next three months? This information as a series of forecast estimates is key to the scheduling of production, staffing, raw material purchasing, etc. Another example is the estimation of demand in an accounting firm, which must plan for scheduling the number of accountants that it needs to have in place to service its clients on a daily, weekly and monthly basis.

Medium-range forecasts

A medium-range forecast generally spans from three months to three years. It is useful in sales planning, production planning and budgeting, cash budgeting, and analysing various operating plans. For manufacturing companies such as Toyota, Ford or Sony, there must be forecasts of demand in place so that suppliers can be informed about approximately how many parts are required.

Long-range forecasts

Generally three years or more in time span, long-range forecasts are used in planning for new products and technology intensive services, capital expenditures, facility location or expansion, and research and development. It takes about three or four years to plan the development of a new car model and even longer to develop a new pharmaceutical product. At universities, before deciding to start a new degree, such as a Masters degree in Operations Management, the professors must estimate the number of students who will enrol in such a degree over a multi-year period.

As the time horizon lengthens, it is likely that one's forecast accuracy will diminish.

Mainstream forecasting methodologies can be grouped into *qualitative and quantitative* methods. Qualitative methods are used more for unique or new circumstances, where there is little or no reliable data to be used in constructing the forecast. Quantitative methods often use numerical data and methods such as mathematical formulae to extrapolate past trends into the future.

A *qualitative* approach involves collecting and appraising judgements, options, even best guesses as well as past performance from domain experts to make a prediction.

Box 3.3: Qualitative forecasting methods

- *Panel approach.* The panel acts like a focus group allowing everyone to talk openly and freely. With this approach it may be difficult to reach a consensus, or sometimes the views of the loudest or highest status person may emerge (the 'bandwagon effect'). Of course, while the brainpower of a panel may be more reliable than one person's view, even the experts may get it wrong. An example was when the price of crude oil rose dramatically in recent years, experts in most of the world's oil companies were not expecting it.
- *Delphi method.* This method attempts to reduce the influences from procedures of face-to-face meetings. It employs a questionnaire, emailed or posted to the experts. The replies are analysed and summarised and returned, anonymously, to all the experts. The experts are then asked to re-consider their original response in view of the replies and arguments from the other experts. This process is repeated a few times until a consensus is reached or a narrow range of decisions remains. The structure of this process, which has many variants, is aimed at getting the best from the independent views of experts.
- *Scenario planning.* This qualitative forecasting method is usually applied to long-range situations with great uncertainty. A panel is asked to devise a range of future scenarios, which in turn are discussed and inherent risk assessed. Unlike the Delphi method, scenario planning is not necessarily concerned with reaching a consensus, but rather looks at the possible range of options. Bankers and economists in government policy and advisory positions often use scenario planning to consider the longer-term future of interest rates, economic growth and other parameters that they must deal with.

Managers can also rely on a whole spectrum of *quantitative* forecasting methodologies to support their decision making. As we are describing key decision areas in operations management across a wider spectrum, it is not our aim to describe any of these methodologies in detail, but rather summarise their main features. These *quantitative* methodologies can be divided into *time series* analysis or *causal* methods.

Box 3.4: Quantitative forecasting methods

- *Time series* analysis, when applied to demand forecasting, examines the pattern of past sales to predict future demand patterns. Techniques such as moving averages and exponential smoothing 'decompose' this time series into longer-term trend and cyclical components, and extract the seasonality of the time series, which can cause an item such as sales to vary significantly from quarter to quarter, but which is an assignable and predictable cause of variation. In other words, the main idea of time series analysis is to uncover the relative strength of assignable longer-term causes such as trend and cyclical movements vis-à-vis short-term predictable seasonal swings when making forecasts. For example, December sales may jump significantly, but this may merely be due to a short-lived Christmas seasonal effect. The key weakness of time series analysis is that this approach simply looks at past behaviour to predict the future, ignoring causal variables that may be responsible for changes in future behaviour. Time series forecasts are often used for sales data, such as the weekly sales forecasts of items sold in supermarkets.
- *Causal* methods employ techniques that try to understand the strength of the relationships among a set of variables and the impact they have on each other. Sales performance may be linked to demographic and economic variables such as disposable family income. Techniques such as regression analysis estimate the relationship between a dependent variable such as sales, and a number of 'explanatory' or independent variables. Here the association among variables is key, and the naming of a 'causal' relationship may be misleading. For example, it is not that, because a family has more disposable income, it 'will' purchase more. Rather, it 'may'.

Besides traditional quantitative and qualitative forecasting methods, new forecasting technologies based on artificial neural networks (Moore et al., 1995) and advanced data-mining techniques are in development. Unlike the more common statistical forecasting techniques such as time-series analysis and regression analysis, neural networks simulate human learning. Over time and with repeated use, neural networks can develop an understanding of the complex relationships that exist between inputs into a forecasting model and the outputs. For example, in a service operation these inputs might include such factors as historical sales data, weather, time of day, day of week, and month. The output would be the number of customers expected to arrive on a given day and in a given time period. In addition, neural networks perform computations much faster than traditional forecasting techniques.

Performance of forecasting methods

Forecast accuracy and frequency of updating are important issues to consider and monitor. The inherent difficulties of forecasting have led to many methods being developed, and different methods are based on different sets of assumptions. Understanding these assumptions, particularly those that may have an impact on operations, is an essential step. Key factors to better understand forecast outcomes include the following:

- The accuracy level of predictions sought and achieved and the trade-offs involved.
- The extent to which a method assumes that past behavioural patterns and relationships will continue in the future. A continuous check on presumed levels of stability between the past and future has to be embodied in the forecasting procedure in order to evaluate this feature of a method.
- Establishing the appropriate forecasting horizon that reflects the capacity lead time currently experienced.
- The need to establish a match between the selected forecasting method and the data patterns that are present in a particular business. The most common patterns are described as being constant, trend, seasonal and cyclical. A business needs to ascertain its own data patterns to ensure that the method chosen reflects them appropriately.

We now turn to the third important category of operations decisions, namely where each part of the global supply network owned by the organisation should be located.

Location decisions

Strategic importance of location

The construction of a major manufacturing facility like an automobile assembly plant, a computer chip fabrication facility, or a food processing plant requires long-term commitment by an organisation. Building such a facility involves several strategic decisions, including (a) how big to make it, (b) when to build it, (c) where to build it, and (d) what type(s) of processes to install in it.

For manufacturing companies and back-office service operations, management must address many issues when addressing location issues. These include: Should the existing facility be closed? Can the existing facility be expanded? Should the new facility have different processes and technologies from existing operations? For a back-office service operations facility, the primary criterion is to minimise costs since back-office service operations usually require large capital investments. On the other hand, the decision to locate a front-office service facility that interacts directly with the customer (such as a fast food outlet or a bank branch) is primarily driven by its revenue potential. The capital investment is usually much smaller for front-office operations. However, the risks associated with selecting sites for front-office operations tend to be much higher, as the success of an operation at a given location is affected not only by the customer demographics within its immediate area but also by the unique characteristics of the site, such as a restaurant's location. For example, McDonald's competitive advantage is said to come at least partly from its ability to locate its outlets in prime locations.

The globalisation of business further complicates the location decision. Local customs, tax rates, tax incentives, and laws must be considered along with infrastructure such as roads, telecommunications, and supporting businesses. India, for example, is attracting service organisations and nowadays also manufacturing operations because of its relatively low cost and its highly educated workforce. Many of New Zealand's and Australia's banks, telecommunications companies and other organisations are moving their back offices and service centres to India because of the low cost and high quality workforces available there. Engineering companies are increasingly getting their design work done in India, and the same applies to software development. Facilities are being reduced in size or closed in high-cost economies, and reopened in India and other low-cost countries.

An incorrect site location decision is very expensive for both manufacturing and service organisations. A decision to build in the wrong location, at the wrong time, with the wrong capacity or the wrong processes can significantly reduce profits. After recognising a bad location decision, if management elects to sell the facility, a substantial portion of the initial investment may not be recovered. Location decisions manifest themselves increasingly on a supply chain level, as global competition has shifted the key decision frame from company to supply chain level.

Location decisions in supply chains

The principal goal of a supply chain is to provide customers with accurate and quick responses to their orders at the lowest possible cost. This requires a network of facilities that are located strategically in the supply chain. For example, in locating Toyota's assembly plant in Melbourne Australia, operations managers needed to account for transport of inbound components and outbound vehicle products, ease of access and proximity of suppliers, cost of land and utilities, access to a large local workforce, and numerous other factors. Since the first assembly line was built at the Altona plant, there have been numerous expansions, made possible by the long-term thinking of those who ensured that the site purchased was big enough to cope with the long-term growth that has occurred.

The process for working out location of facilities within supply chains focuses on determining the best network structure and geographical locations for facilities to maximise service and revenue and to minimise costs. These decisions can become complex, especially for a global supply chain, which must consider shipping costs between all demand and supply points in the network, fixed operating costs of each distribution or retail facility, revenue generation per customer location, facility labour and operating costs, and construction costs.

Locating service operations

Location is also critical in service supply chains. Service facilities such as post offices, branch banks, dentist offices, and fire stations typically need to be in close proximity to the customer. In many cases, the customer travels to the service facility, whereas in others, such as mobile X-ray and imaging centres or 'on-call' computer repair services, the service travels to the customer. Criteria for locating these facilities may differ depending on the nature of the service, based upon the degree and type of contact each has with the customer.

Davis and Heineke (2005) discuss where to locate a service facility, depending on the specific type of service provided and how it is delivered to the customer. Facilities can be distinguished depending on whether there is direct interface with the customer such as restaurants, branch offices of banks, and hospitals; facilities with indirect customer contact, such as telephone call centres and virtual organisations that only link to the customer through a website; and facilities with no customer contact, such as cheque-processing operation of a bank or a customer billing operation for a retail chain or credit card company.

We note that technology is not specific to a location and, in that way, is redefining what makes a location feasible. Physical proximity to aspects such as customers and raw materials will invariably remain important factors. However, advances in technology and electronic communications may reduce the emphasis placed on such factors. For example, virtual teams and groups of engineers and draftsmen may work on design projects in the Asia Pacific region, and when they finish the work day and go home, pass on their work to colleagues in India or Europe, who work on it for another eight hours, subsequently passing it on to their colleagues in Canada, USA or Mexico. As such, the project can be worked on almost continuously around the clock as it moves around the world, which means faster completion, and this translates into faster overall completion.

Factors to consider when evaluating potential site locations

Managers in both manufacturing and service operations need to consider both *qualitative* and *quantitative* factors in evaluating potential sites (Davis and Heineke, 2005). *Qualitative factors* influencing location decisions include local infrastructure, worker education and skills, product content requirements, and political and economic stability. While these factors are self-explanatory, product content requirements deserve some further explanation. Content requirements state that a minimum percentage of a product must be produced within the borders of a country in order for that product to be sold in that country. This assures jobs in the local economy while reducing the amount of imports. For example, for a car to be sold in the Philippines, it must be assembled there. Consequently, major car manufacturers that want to sell cars in the Philippines must have an assembly plant there even though demand for cars in that country is sufficiently small to suggest that importing them would be more economical.

Being near to the customer may be another qualitative factor. Increasingly, customers, especially those requiring frequent deliveries of materials in a just-in-time (JIT) context, require suppliers to build plants close by. In this way deliveries can be made, sometimes several times a day, thus keeping inventories low. Also, being close to the customer signals commitment and provides reassurance.

Last, but not least, individual preferences may play an important role in the location decision. Senior executives within an organisation may prefer a new site to be in one region, country or city for their own convenience or preferences and this can have a substantial bearing on the eventual choice.

Quantitative factors to take into account when making strategic location decisions include labour costs, distribution costs, facility costs, exchange rates, and tax rates. Labour costs can vary dramatically with location. Labour costs, of course, must be considered in light of labour skills. As we become more global, distribution and transportation costs take on added importance. In addition to the cost of transportation, the time required to deliver the products also must be considered.

Developing countries often offer incentives in the form of low-cost manufacturing facilities to attract companies. For example, within the People's Republic of China (PRC), many special economic zones (SEZ) have been established that are exempt from tariffs and duties – provided that the products made there are sold outside the PRC. In some countries, the local government will enter into a partnership with a firm, with the government providing the land, the building, and perhaps the training of the workforce.

The volatility of the exchange rates between countries can have a significant impact on sales and profits, while tax rates can differ significantly between countries. To attract businesses, many countries offer significant tax incentives. For example, a country may exempt an organisation from paying income taxes during its first five or ten years of operation, after which normal tax rates will apply.

The first high-level consideration is whether to expand local region capacity or supply that region from another part of the world. Then, it is a case of searching locally in that region for the best state or city or town, and for possible sites there. And all the way through this process, operations managers and executives are looking for the best combination of the qualitative and quantitative factors listed above as the evaluation criteria for site location. When Toyota is considering the location of its next manufacturing plant, it must consider all these qualitative and quantitative factors. Toyota has been recently expanding its facilities and establishing new manufacturing facilities in Canada and the USA, to match growing sales and market share in that region. Interestingly, similar factors apply when an organisation is reducing its overall capacity. While Toyota has been on a long-term growth and facility expansion path, Ford, General Motors and others have been closing plants and, sadly, reducing employment levels. In those organisations that are getting smaller, facility location decisions mean: 'Which facilities do we close?' However, the factors to be considered are similar, regardless of whether an organisation is expending or reducing its capacity.

We now turn to the operations decision of what physical capacity each part of the supply network owned by the organisation should have at any point in time?

Capacity decisions

Capacity comprises the resources to serve customers, process information or make products and is a mix of the people, systems, equipment and facilities needed to meet the demand for services or products involved. A bank needs staff to serve customers, IT systems to process transactions and cash machines to enable customers to draw out cash from their accounts. Similarly, a manufacturing company needs people and processes to make the products it sells. These elements constitute capacity. These capacity decisions relate to:

- delivery systems and process capability – to ensure that the technical specification of the service or product can be met
- volume – how many services to be processed or products to be made. Simple though it seems, this is a challenging task.

Issues in determining levels of capacity

Once created, plant and equipment capacity is usually an irreversible invest-ment decision. Further, staff capacity is an expensive decision to change. Not only are all these dimensions difficult in themselves but they also involve the interrelated aspects of market position and competitors' decisions on the size and timing of their capacity changes. To help manage capacity, organisations need to consider a range of demand and capacity issues.

Demand-related issues

An organisation usually focuses its planning efforts towards meeting the requirements of its customers. To do this, it needs to manage demand. This involves identifying the nature and size of demand and determining how it is best going to meet it. Although demand levels will vary, very often there are characteristics of sales from which patterns can be identified, enabling fluctuations to be more easily predicted. These include the seasonal nature of many services and products, predictable variations in demand (peaks during the day or week) and one-off demands, such as advertising sales at the Mel-bourne Cup day in Australia, the most famous horse-race of the year. Other demand characteristics are less predictable but still need to be managed. For example, to protect against 'no shows', airlines sometimes overbook on flights. The same policy is also adopted by hotel operators, particularly those in locations where the unpredictability of bookings or the frequency of late cancellations brings uncertainty in the pattern of demand and the resulting loss of revenue from having turned business away.

Capacity-related issues

As with demand, there are issues in the provision of capacity that increase the difficulty of this management task. Again, some of these are more predictable than others. The demands placed on capacity will vary to reflect the mix of services and products and the sales levels involved. For this reason, there are bottlenecks in the process where capacity is less than the demand placed on it. However, bottlenecks are short- to medium-term phenomena and so are predictable in terms of their position and extent. Knowing where they are is essential as this enables a business to manage capacity within this constraint, while directing attention and resources to increasing capacity in these parts of a process. As with demand, some aspects of capacity are less predictable and these introduce problems of a more ad hoc nature, for example absenteeism – people stay away from work for a number of reasons. In addition, short-term demand variations can often result in a temporary shortage of capacity, with the difficulties this presents in managing demand. For example, in some businesses, the first thing that an operations manager must do each day is to ascertain who has not come to work, then arrange to get casual workers in to ensure the tasks are done. This is often the case in call centres, warehouses, and some factories, where there are sizable unskilled or semiskilled workforces.

Capacity measurement

The main problem with measuring capacity is the complexity of most operations. Only when the operation is highly standardised and repetitive, is capacity easy to define unambiguously. The Australian Taxation Office may have the capacity to print and post 300,000 tax forms per week. A fast ride at DreamWorld might be designed to process batches of 60 people every three minutes – a capacity to convey 1200 people per hour. In each case, an output capacity measure is the most appropriate measure because the output from the operation does not vary in its nature. For many operations, however, the definition of capacity is not so obvious. For instance, when a wide range of outputs places varying demands on the process, output measures of capacity are not that useful. An example of this is a government department such as the Department of Human Services, which provides a complex mix of services, essentially from the same base of resources. Here, input capacity measures are frequently used to define capacity. Other examples include the number of seats in a plane, or the number of staff hours available on a project. Almost every type of operation could use a mixture of both input and output measures, but in practice most choose to use one or the other.

Impact of capacity planning and control

The decisions taken by operations managers in devising their capacity plans will affect several different aspects of performance:

- *Costs* will be affected by the balance between capacity and demand (or output level if that is different). Capacity levels in excess of demand could mean under-utilisation of capacity and therefore high unit cost. For example, the economics of processes with relatively high fixed costs are very clear: an empty or nearly empty airplane loses enormous amounts of money for its owner, whereas a full airplane makes money. This is because the costs are mostly fixed, and a definite break-even point exists, in which variable costs are covered and contribution to fixed costs and corporate overheads occurs. The load factor (percentage of seats occupied on a flight) usually considered for many airplanes to be approximately 'break-even' is around 60 to 75 per cent, depending on the cost of fuel, ticket prices, and numerous other factors.
- *Revenues* will also be affected by the balance between capacity and demand, but in the opposite way. Capacity levels equal to or higher

than demand at any point in time will ensure that all demand is satisfied and no revenue lost.

- *Working capital* will be affected if an operation decides to build up finished goods inventory prior to demand. This might allow demand to be satisfied, but the organisation will have to fund the inventory until it can be sold.
- *Quality* of goods or services might be affected by a capacity plan that involved large fluctuations in capacity levels, by hiring temporary staff for example. The new staff and the disruption to the routine working of the operation could increase the probability of errors being made.
- *Speed of response* to customer demand could be enhanced, either by the build-up of inventories (allowing customers to be satisfied directly from the inventory rather than having to wait for items to be manufactured) or by the deliberate provision of surplus capacity to avoid queuing.
- *Dependability of supply* will also be affected by how close demand levels are to capacity. The closer demand gets to the operation's capacity ceiling, the less able it is to cope with any unexpected disruptions and the less dependable its deliveries of goods and services could be.
- *Flexibility*, especially volume flexibility, will be enhanced by surplus capacity. If demand and capacity are in balance, the operation will not be able to respond to any unexpected increase in demand.
- *Capacity chunks* are step changes in capacity. For example, airline capacity changes in 'chucks' when aeroplanes are added or removed from fleets. Likewise, machine capacity is increased in 'chunks' when a new machine is commissioned. The step changes in capacity affects fixed costs of operations, and therefore the breakeven point for profitable operation changes as well.

The choices of capacity when a facility or group of facilities is set up, and the effective management of capacity in real time are critical to the success of any operation. Success can be measured in many ways, and indeed capacity choices often involve confronting tradeoffs between these measures. Building extra capacity generally adds flexibility, possibly responsiveness, and allows for higher service levels but certainly costs more!

Timing of capacity change and aggregate capacity strategies

Changing the capacity of an operation is not just a matter of deciding on the best size of a capacity increment. The organisation also needs to decide when to bring 'on-stream' new capacity. The organisation must choose a position somewhere between two extreme strategies:

- *capacity leads demand* – timing the introduction of capacity in such a way that there is always sufficient capacity to meet forecast demand; and
- *capacity lags demand* – timing the introduction of capacity so that demand is always equal to or greater than capacity.

There are arguments for and against using these two strategies. For capacity-leading demand strategies, the advantages are that: there will be always be sufficient capacity to meet demand; there will be a 'capacity cushion' which can absorb extra demand if forecasts are under-estimated; and, any critical start-up problems with new plants are less likely to affect supply to customers (Slack et al., 2004, p. 186). However, this strategy can lead to: under-utilisation of plants; high risks of over-capacity if demand does not reach forecast levels; and, early capital spending on plant (Slack et al., 2004, p. 186). For capacity-lagging strategies, the converse applies, that is, as advantages, there will always be sufficient demand to keep the plants working at full capacity; over-capacity problems are minimised; and, capital spending on the plants is delayed. The disadvantages of these strategies are: there are likely to be insufficient capacity to meet demand fully; no ability to exploit short-term increases in demand; and worsening position with inability to meet demand if there are start-up problems with the new plant (Slack et al., 2004, p. 186).

For some materials-processing and information-processing operations, the output from the operation that is not required in one period can be stored for use in the next period. As such, inventories can be used to obtain the advantages of both capacity leading and capacity lagging. Yet, this comes at a price, namely the cost of carrying inventory and the risks of obsolescence and deterioration of stock. However, for many services, sometimes considered as pure services, capacity simply cannot be stored for re-use. Consider someone running a haircutting and styling salon. The capacity of the chairs and staff cannot be stored and reused, and every idle chair and staff member's time, when they are idle is, simply, lost capacity. Such personal services as haircutting cannot be stored and must be produced and consumed at the same time and place exactly. The same applies to most medical services, where the 'items being processed' are people.

Balancing of capacity and safety capacity

Consider the challenge facing an operations manager in charge of a four-stage network of assembling air-conditioning units, consisting of manufacturing the parts from which they are made, assembling the products as such, moving them to a warehouse after assembling, where they are packed in cases, stored and loaded onto trucks as needed. The company's fleet of trucks then distributes them to its customers. In this case, parts manufacturing feeds assembly, which feeds the warehouse, which feeds the distribution operation. For the network to operate efficiently, all its stages must have the same capacity. If they have different capacities, the capacity of the network as a whole will be limited to the capacity of its slowest link, called the bottleneck in the supply network. Extra capacity in any stage is essentially wasted.

The actual utilisation rates at most facilities are not planned at 100 per cent full capacity. Unanticipated events such as equipment breakdowns, employee absences, materials shortages, or sudden short-term surges in demand will reduce the capability of planned capacity levels to meet demand and satisfy customers. This calls for some amount of safety capacity, defined as an amount of capacity reserved for unanticipated events to be planned into a process or facility. For most service industries, safety capacity may range from 10 to 50 per cent, as for example in hospitals and hotels. In 'lean' operations, the facility and processes run with very little spare capacity.

Capacity constraints

Many organisations operate at below their maximum processing capacity, either because there is insufficient demand to completely 'fill' their capacity, or as a deliberate policy so that the operation can respond quickly to every new order. Often, though, organisations find themselves with some parts of their operation operating below their capacity while other parts are at their capacity 'ceiling'.

It is the parts of the operation that are operating at their capacity ceiling that are the capacity constraint, or bottleneck, for the whole operation. Depending on the nature of demand, different parts of an operation might be pushed to their capacity ceiling and act as a constraint on the total operation. The Theory of Constraints (TOC), (Goldratt, 1990) is a set of principles that focuses on increasing total process throughput, net profits, and return on investment by maximising the utilisation of all bottleneck work activities and workstations. The philosophy and principles of TOC are valuable in understanding demand and capacity management.

The traditional operations management definition of throughput is the average number of goods or services completed per time period by a process. TOC views throughput differently. In TOC, throughput is the amount of money generated per time period through actual sales. For most business organisations, the goal is to maximise throughput, thereby maximising cash flow. Inherent in this definition is that it makes little sense to make goods or services until they can be sold and that excess inventory is wasteful. In TOC, a constraint is anything in an organisation that limits it from moving forward or achieving its goal. Constraints determine the throughput of a facility, because they limit production output to their own capacity.

TOC helps managers understand the relationship between demand, capacity, and resource utilisation. TOC is an important methodology, but quite involved in its implementation, and a detailed discussion is beyond our scope.

Service specific capacity issues

As mentioned earlier, service capacity is perishable. It cannot be put into inventory for use or sale in a future time period. A major task thus concerns adjusting capacity provision or influencing levels of demand in order to improve the trade-offs between the effective use of capacity and meeting the varying levels of customer demand.

Furthermore, within a service business, a distinction needs to be made between the two basic parts of the process – the back office and front office. A fundamental distinction between these two parts concerns the customer interface.

Front office

In the front office, customers are present (for example in person in a bank branch or on the telephone) and the service system has to manage customers in the delivery of the service. Service provision and consumption are simultaneous. Capacity provision needs to meet demand not only in terms of the range of services provided but also to reflect the differing levels of demand during the day, week or longer time periods.

When demand is greater than capacity, customers either wait or go elsewhere. Getting the balance right between capacity levels and queue lengths is an important decision affecting a business.

In a bank branch, demand fluctuates substantially during the day. For example, in any central business district, many people want to do their banking at lunchtime, so banks (and indeed almost all shops) need more service staff during this hour than at other times. Dealing with such peaks and indeed sometimes with instantaneous spikes in demand can be hard to arrange.

Even really well-organised systems such a McDonald's have difficulty dealing with spikes in demand. McDonald's is very good at meeting relatively smooth and steady demand with its supply and production processes, but what happens if one or even two full tour buses arrive? Can McDonald's rapidly raise its supply rate?

Back office

In the back office, customers are not present in the system and the pressure to respond immediately is not there. Consequently, tasks can be delayed until cumulated volumes are sufficiently large to secure the advantages of size or their completion better fits the overall schedule. This not only increases the opportunity to manage demand fluctuations more efficiently but cumulated volumes (often from more than one location) also justify investment in technology. Being able to cumulate volumes facilitates the use of the latter, which also improves productivity.

Summary

In this chapter, we explored some strategic operations decisions that have to be made for businesses to compete and operate efficiently and effectively in today's global supply networks. They are the key decisions that configure an operation, which set in place some aspects of its cost, quality flexibility and other outcomes.

First, the strategic operations decision of *how much of the supply network the operation should own* was addressed. This led to discussion of make-or-buy, outsource, and off-shore options, along with some other alternatives.

Second, *forecasting* was discussed. Its purpose is to give the organisation a good idea of customer demand in terms of volume and variability in order to be able to meet it. A number of forecasting approaches were discussed, along with the criteria that influence the *forecasting decision*.

Third, *location decisions* were discussed that addressed where each part of the supply network owned by the organisation should be located. Strategic considerations and supply chain location alternatives were discussed, leading into the service-specific issues of locating service operations.

The final strategic operations decision category relates to *medium-term to long-term capacity planning decisions*. What physical capacity should each part of the network owned by the organisation have at any point in time? How large should the facility be? If it expands, should it do so in large capacity steps or small ones? Should it make sure that it always has more capacity than anticipated demand or less? Demand and capacity-related issues, along with notions related to capacity measurement, balancing of capacity, and safety capacity were introduced. Subsequently, the impact of capacity planning and control on performance was further detailed. In medium-term and long-term capacity planning, the timing of capacity changes is important, leading to alternatives anywhere in between pure capacity leading and capacity lagging strategies. Capacity is constrained by bottlenecks, leading to the introduction of some theory-of-constraints concepts. Finally, service specific issues of capacity management relating to front-office and back-office operations, were highlighted.

At the beginning of this chapter we posed some questions about the management challenges that Woolworths faces as a result of its decision to build a new massive distribution centre, instead of using its current distribution centres. The decisions regarding the location and size of the new facility, and the processes and technologies to be used were seen as critical to the future competitiveness of the organisation. These decisions fix in stone the key aspects of cost, service levels, quality and delivery performance, so it is extremely important that such strategic decisions be made correctly.

Organisations very often build a first stage of a facility and since growth is never assured, they plan for the possibility of enlarging a facility by reserving additional land or other forms of capacity, perhaps nearby. In other words they must take these decisions one at a time, but also realise that they are part of a dynamic system, which can be considered as a multi-stage development of a system of operations networks. It is always possible to obtain extra capacity or services from a 'third party' service provider, rather than build, own, operate and maintain such facilities yourself; however, one way or the other, the costs must be borne and ultimately built in to the costs that are passed on to the consumer, so productivity and efficiency are the constant goal of the operations manager.

Why did Woolworths not decide to lease such a facility from someone else? Because this is a strategic part of Woolworths' business, and it needed to retain full control of it. Woolworths also has the capabilities and competencies to operate the facility, and these are aspects that Woolworths plans on further improving in the future. For a large retail group such as Woolworths, operating and managing an important distribution centre such as that at Minchinbury is too important to leave to others.

Why did Woolworths choose Minchinbury as the location for this facility? Clearly, transport costs and capacity from suppliers and to stores would have been a major consideration, including good freeways to the site, possibly rail infrastructure, as well as labour supply, cost of land and utilities and other cost factors.

Should Woolworths have built the facility big enough for its present operations, or to be able to accommodate 10 per cent growth that it anticipates, or 20 per cent over the longer term? As for the capacity of the facility, Woolworths, like most of other similar organisations, would have built with the present requirements in mind since growth is never assured. However, Woolworths would have planned for the possibility of enlarging the facility by reserving additional land or other forms of capacity, perhaps nearby. This applies to the capacity of its buildings, truck dock facilities, computers, conveyor systems, storage racking systems, offices for staff, indeed everything.

This is the case in every industry, whether the facility is conducting manufacturing, distribution or pure service operations. And these choices determine the cost, service and quality, agility or flexibility and other performance characteristics of the operation, so the decisions must be guided by the 'whole of business' objectives and competitive positioning of the investment decisions.

DISCUSSION QUESTIONS

1. Of the 10,000 or so components that go into a car, many are manufactured by the assembly company, but many are also bought in. Explain using factors such as cost and technological capability the reason why most automotive assemblers around the world choose to insource ('make') their assembly operations, but outsource ('buy') their tyres from suppliers such as Michelin, Goodyear or Bridgestone.

2. In a university, why is it important to try to forecast demand, meaning student numbers for the next year ahead? What key decisions does the forecast inform?

3. Explain why many service sector companies have moved their back office operations to India. What are the key advantages and what potential disadvantages and risk factors exist in this decision?

4. Many companies have chosen to outsource their information technology operations and development to third party specialists such as EDS. Look up the EDS website and consider their offering. Analyse the decision made by a major bank or insurance company to outsource its IT systems and operations in terms of cost, benefit and risk.

5. Mars Corporation, owner of Uncle Ben's pet food brand, deliberately locates its large manufacturing facilities in regional centres such as Wodonga and Ballarat. What are the key issues influencing this location decision, in terms of costs and benefits, relative to placing these factories near or within a major capital city?

6. Major airlines need to choose between using planes of various sizes, usually ranging from approximately 200 to nearly 400 passenger seating capacities. Recently, a much larger Airbus has been developed. If you were running Jetstar, and were expanding to offer flights from Sydney and Melbourne to Los Angeles, what factors would you consider in choosing the most effective plane size or capacity? How would this differ from your planes in flying the major east coast cities of Australia and why?

7. When trying to accurately forecast sales for products in retail organisations, it is often possible to forecast total sales for a category of product with reasonable accuracy, but much more difficult to forecast accurately the line item level, meaning the SKU (stock keeping unit) level. Why is this an important factor in forecasting, and what are the costs to a retailer of getting forecasts wrong at the SKU level?

8. When deciding whether to order a higher or relatively lower amount of stock, an automotive parts distributor wanted to consider the impact of profit of being wrong 'on the high side', versus being wrong 'on the low side' of demand. What are these cost drivers, and how would they impact the decision process?

9. When choosing the size of a call centre, and the level of staffing, how would you balance the factors involved? Identify these factors, and their impact on cost and service levels.

References

Davis M. and Heineke, J. 2005. *Operations Management-Integrating Manufacturing and Services*. 5th edn. New York: McGraw-Hill.

Goldratt, E. M. 1990. *The Theory of Constraints*. Croton-on-Hudson, N.Y.: North River Press.

Heizer, J. and Render, B. 2005. *Operations Management*. 7th edn. Upper-Saddle Rover, N.J.: Pearson-Prentice Hall.

Moore, K., Burbach, R. and Heeler, R. 1995. 'Using neural networks to analyze qualitative data.' *Marketing Research*, 7(1): 34–9.

Slack, N., Chambers S. and Johnston, R. 2004. *Operations Management*. 4th edn. Harlow: Prentice Hall.

Internet resources

Go to the Institute for Forecasting Education at:

http://www.forecastingeducation.com/forecastingsoftwarereviews.asp and source information on the quantitative forecasting techniques mentioned in this chapter, as well as software that supports these techniques.

Planning and Controlling the Use of Operating Assets and Resources

Sum Chee Chuong

Learning objectives

After reading this chapter you should be able to:

- understand the hierarchy of planning decisions that are involved in operations management
- understand the role of inventory and basic inventory management systems
- appreciate the need for the aggregation and disaggregation of operating plans
- be familiar with the different strategies for aggregate planning
- understand the process of developing a master schedule and materials plan
- know the workings of a material requirements planning (MRP) system and critical success factors for its implementation.

Box 4.1: Management challenge: managing quotations to customers

Sayon Nara Systems is an authorised distributor for electrical and electronics components and systems. It has 45 employees working in five sales offices in Asia – China, Indonesia, Singapore, the Philippines, and Vietnam. The company's headquarter is located in Thailand. It has an office space of more than 700 square metres inclusive of a warehouse to stock more than US$220 000 worth of products.

The company carries fifty product types and is also involved in the trading of semiconductor components. The product range includes electronic capacitors, connectors, and hardware for entire systems. Besides standard products, Sayon Nara also customises products to meet specific customer needs.

Different products have different sizes and weights. The company has to mark up on the cost prices to cover the freight, delivery and administrative costs and profits. With so many factors that have to be taken into consideration in costings, the mark-ups vary considerably across customers.

One problem that the company is facing is that it does not have a recording system to trace and monitor prices quoted to various customers. Sales personnel have to manually go through stacks of quotations printed in hard copies. This takes up a lot of time, thus leading to inefficiencies. Productivity improvements would lead to higher levels of profitability.

What can Sayon Nara do to better cope with the increasing complexity of its quotation processes?

Introduction

Imagine a scenario that when you step into a supermarket, all the shelves are empty and there is nothing left for you to buy. This could very well be an extreme case that only occurs when there is a crisis. But this could and does happen, albeit at a much lower level, due to malfunctioning in one or more of the following areas: planning, scheduling, coordination and inventory management. While supermarkets never stock out of everything, they very regularly run out of some items. The malfunction could manifest itself through inadequate planning, not having the required raw materials for production, not having sufficient capacity or equipment for production, or not having the facilities to store the finished goods after the production is completed. The topics covered in the chapter would assist in dealing with such types of problems.

Most organisations deal with some type of inventory, either physical or intangible. In Chapter 2, it was shown that organisations that have in place modern lean/JIT-based pull operating systems are able to deal with the myriad of problems associated with excessive levels of inventory, essentially by avoiding these problems from occurring. On the other hand, in organisations where the more traditional push-based approach to managing operations is practiced, there is a strong emphasis on planning and scheduling. As many organisations still have this traditional operating system, this chapter aims to provide an extensive discussion of the key elements to the 'planned approach' to managing operations.

Thus, the objective of this chapter is to introduce the concepts of planning and scheduling of operations in relation to the management of inventory. A

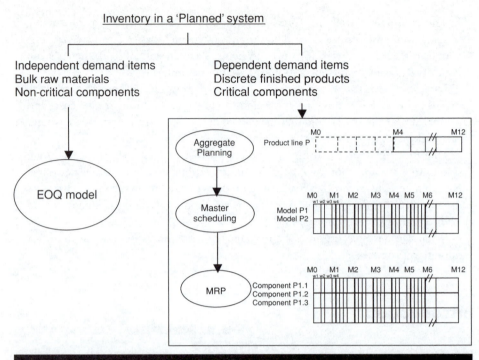

Figure 4.1 Overview of chapter

good inventory management system strikes a balance between providing sufficient materials to meet the needs of the operations section and customers, and minimising inventory costs. The concept of planning is discussed at length and at various levels of aggregation. The planning process starts with the establishment of an aggregate plan, followed by the development of the master schedule, and ends with material requirements planning.

The next section provides an overview of the key issues in effectively managing inventory. Various planning approaches are then presented, starting with the highest level of planning (aggregate planning). Following that, successively more detailed levels of planning will be discussed (master scheduling and materials requirements planning).

Figure 4.1 provides an overview of the topics covered in this chapter. While some of the terms in Figure 4.1 may appear new and complex, we hope that by the end of the chapter, all these will be clear.

Inventory management

Inventory is a stock of resources. These resources can be in physical or intangible forms. Intangible inventory are closely associated with services, and possesses many of the properties of services. An example of intangible inventory is the skills that workers possess. For simplicity, much of our discussion will be about physical inventory. Therefore, for our purposes, inventory is the physical stock of materials that is used to facilitate production or satisfy customer demand. Inventory is kept at various stages of production, from raw materials to work-in-process (WIP) to finished goods. As such, inventory management deals not only with customers but also with suppliers.

Box 4.2: Typical reasons for keeping inventory

- To meet anticipated changes in demand and supply
- To safeguard against uncertainties
- To decouple production processes
- To allow economic production and purchase
- To provide for product variety
- To ensure smooth production
- To enhance customer service.

Inventory costs

There are four basic types of inventory costs. They include holding (or carrying) cost, setup cost, ordering cost and shortage (or stock-out) cost. Some of these inventory costs exhibit trade-off relationships. For example, shortage cost can be reduced by carrying more inventory stocks and incurring higher holding cost. The objective of determining the optimal inventory level is to minimise the sum of the four types of inventory costs.

Box 4.3: Types of inventory costs

- Holding cost – the cost of keeping the items as inventory. There are three major components to this cost: capital cost, storage cost and obsolescence cost
- Setup cost – the cost of setting up a machine to produce a different product
- Ordering cost – the cost of preparing a purchase or production order
- Shortage cost – the cost of not meeting customer demand and includes late charges, loss of goodwill and lost sales.

Independent versus dependent demand

In inventory management, it is important to distinguish between independent and dependent demand. The nature of demand determines the kind of inventory management system to be used. An inappropriate inventory management system can lead to higher cost and poorer customer service.

When demand is influenced by conditions outside the control of operations, we say the demand is independent. Hence, end products are independent demand items since their demand comes from customers. When demand for an item is influenced by or derived from the demand for another item, we say that the item exhibits dependent demand. An example of dependent demand from the automotive manufacturing is the demand for tyres. The demand for tyres is dependent on the demand for the end product, that is, the automobile.

These two demand types tend to have different patterns. Since independent demand is subject to market conditions, its pattern tends to be random and uncertain. Independent demand is usually forecasted. On the other hand, for a dependent demand item, it is possible to compute its demand as it is derived. For example, a demand for 1000 automotives (end product) will translate to a demand of 4000 tyres (the dependent item), plus the spare tyres. Due to the manner in which dependent demand is computed, the demand pattern for dependent items tends to be more variable or lumpy compared to the end-item (independent item).

Inventory systems

An inventory management system spells out the operating policies for maintaining and controlling inventory. All inventory management systems should provide answers to two fundamental inventory questions:

1. What quantity needs to be purchased or produced?
2. When is the time to purchase or produce?

Inventory systems can be used to make decisions in single-period and multiple-period environments. In a single-period situation, the decision is one off and the item will not be reordered. An example of a one-time decision is the ordering of newspapers by a news-stand operator. The one-time production of T-shirts for a special event such as Olympics 2008 is another example. In a single-period situation, the optimal quantity is obtained when the marginal benefit is less than or equal to the marginal cost of ordering or producing that unit.

In a multiple-period situation, recurring purchase decisions are made and thus a balance between carrying inventory costs and ordering costs has to be made. There are two basic types of multiple-period inventory systems: reorder point systems and periodic review systems. A reorder point system tracks the inventory continuously and when the level of inventory falls to an inventory level called the reorder point, a fixed quantity is ordered. In a periodic review system, the inventory level is examined periodically and a quantity is ordered to bring the inventory level to a target level. Notice that both systems address the key questions of how much to order and when to order. Table 4.1 shows the differences between the two types of inventory systems.

Table 4.1 Differences between reorder point and periodic review systems

Reorder point system	Periodic review system
Continuous monitoring of inventory level is required	Inventory level is reviewed periodically at predetermined time intervals
When predetermined inventory level is reached, fixed quantity is ordered	Quantity is ordered to bring inventory to predetermined target level
Used for expensive or 'A' items because of greater effectiveness to avoid stock-out	Used for B and C (less critical) items
Requires more resources to maintain	Less record keeping

A reorder point system is relatively more effective in preventing stock-outs since inventory is monitored continuously. Whenever inventory is low, an order is placed to replenish inventory. However, reorder point systems are more costly to maintain as more inventory stock taking is required. A periodic review system has its advantages too. It requires less record keeping and the periodicity of review eases planning and implementation. In addition, periodic review systems allow for review of multiple items at the same time that could lead to economies of joint ordering and delivery.

In practice, a hybrid of the reorder point system and periodic review system could be used. For instance, inventory can be continuously reviewed and when the reorder point is reached, a quantity is ordered to bring the inventory level to a predetermined target level. Conceptually, the target level can represent the maximum limit of the warehouse or storage capacity.

Economic order quantity (EOQ) model

The economic order quantity (EOQ) model calculates the optimal order quantity under certain environmental assumptions and conditions. The EOQ model is commonly used to illustrate the fundamentals of inventory management such as the trade-offs between inventory cost categories and the relationship between order quantity and number of orders.

Box 4.4: Assumptions of EOQ model

- A single product
- Known and constant annual demand requirements
- Constant replenishment lead time
- No quantity discount
- Single delivery
- Inventory carrying and ordering/setup costs known and constant.

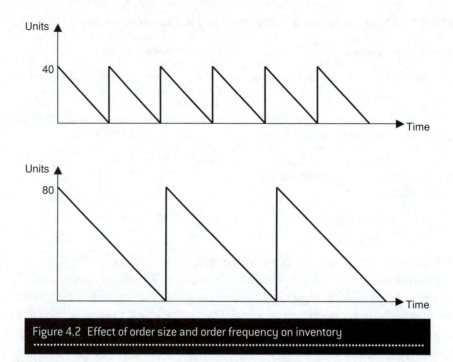

Figure 4.2 Effect of order size and order frequency on inventory

As can be seen in Figure 4.2, for the same demand and cost structure, the smaller the order quantity, the more frequently you have to order to replenish your inventory. The higher frequency of ordering increases your ordering cost. However, placing a larger order quantity will reduce the ordering cost, and increase the inventory carrying/holding cost accordingly. The goal of the EOQ model is to derive a quantity that minimises the sum of ordering and holding costs.

Mathematically, the total annual inventory cost can be expressed as:

$$\text{Total Annual Cost} = \text{Total Holding Cost} + \text{Total Ordering Cost}$$

$$= \frac{Q}{2}H + \frac{D}{Q}C \tag{1}$$

where D = Demand in units per year
      H = Holding cost per unit per year
      C = Ordering cost
      Q = Order quantity in units

The optimal order quantity, Q*, can be obtained using the following formula.

$$Q^* = \sqrt{\frac{2DC}{H}} \tag{2}$$

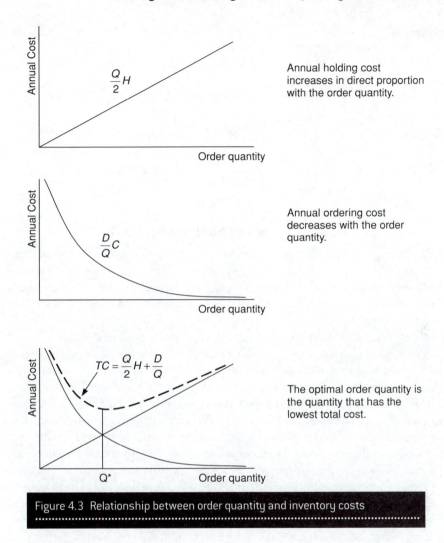

Annual holding cost increases in direct proportion with the order quantity.

Annual ordering cost decreases with the order quantity.

The optimal order quantity is the quantity that has the lowest total cost.

Figure 4.3 Relationship between order quantity and inventory costs

The minimum total annual cost can be found by substituting Q* into Equation (1).

Example

A soft drink plant requires 100,000 empty bottles each year to bottle its soft drink. Annual holding cost is $4 per bottle and ordering cost is $500. The plant operates 300 days a year.

1. What is the optimal order quantity, EOQ?
2. What is the annual total cost if the EOQ quantity is ordered?
3. What is the length of the order cycle?

Solution

$D = 100,000$ bottles, $H = \$4$, $C = \$500$

1. $Q^* = \sqrt{\dfrac{2 \times 100,000 \times 500}{4}} = 5,000 \; bottles$

2. $TC = \dfrac{5,000}{2} \times 4 + \dfrac{100,000}{5,000} \times 500 = \$20,000$

3. $Order\ Cycle\ Length = \dfrac{Q^*}{D} = \dfrac{5,000}{100,000} = 0.05 \times 300 \; days = 15 \; days$

Box 4.5: A more reliable way to fly

XYZ Cargo (not the real name) is one of the world's five largest international cargo airlines. XYZ Cargo is based in South East Asia. Currently, it operates a fleet of B747–400 freighters. With increasing competition from other airlines, there is tremendous pressure on XYZ Cargo to maximise revenue and minimise costs. One way to achieve this is to make sure that all the flights depart punctually. Aircraft downtime has to be minimised through prompt rectification of defects.

The engineering department in XYZ Cargo is in charge of the maintenance of the aircraft. The work has to be done in accordance with the international air navigation regulations and standards. The department has to ensure that all the aircraft are airworthy at all times. Any defect has to be rectified within a specific amount of time. The company has to meet a dispatch reliability target of 99 per cent. Any malfunction of aircraft during flights means that the aircraft have to be diverted to the nearest airports. As a safety precaution, fuel on the aircraft has to be dumped. All these actions are extremely costly and very disruptive to operations.

Most of the engineering functions of XYZ Cargo are outsourced. The spare parts are managed by its parent company. XYZ Cargo often faces a shortage of spare parts. Either the company filches the spare part from another aircraft or resorts to last minute sourcing. In some cases, the company may not even get hold of the required spare parts despite all the efforts. XYZ Cargo needs to improve the management of its supplier and inventory. Several solutions have been proposed. One of the ways is to set some real time notification system for the critical spare parts. When the stock of the spare parts falls below a certain level, the appropriate department will be notified. Another possible remedy is to set performance indicators for the supplier. If the supplier fails to meet the requirements, they will be penalised.

Aggregate planning

What is aggregate planning?

Aggregate planning is intermediate range capacity planning that usually covers a period of two to 18 months. Unless an organisation has only one product or service, aggregate planning focuses on a group of products or services. The purpose of aggregate planning is to specify the optimal or near-optimal combination of production output, workforce level and inventory needed to meet demand that could be fluctuating, uncertain or seasonal. An aggregate plan is not static; it is updated at regular intervals, often monthly, or when more up-to-date forecasts and other information become available. An appropriate aggregate measure of output has to be first defined when the organisation produces multiple products or services. Dollars (monetary value) of output is a common aggregate measure used by organisations.

Aggregate planning can seek to influence both demand and supply. It determines not only the output levels but also the appropriate resource input mix to be used. Although aggregate planning is primarily the responsibility of the operations function, other functional areas such as accounting, finance, human resources and marketing have to be brought in and included in the processes of formulating the aggregate plan. The relationship between financial budgeting and aggregate planning is especially strong. This is because most budgets are prepared based on the assumption of the aggregate output levels, which in turn are affected by the personnel level, inventory level, purchasing level and so forth.

Aggregate planning also has a notable influence on human resource planning as decisions on hiring, layoff, overtime, 'under-time' and subcontracting have to be made. Marketing is another functional area that is intimately involved in aggregate planning as marketing decisions such as pricing, advertising and product mix affect the aggregate plan. Therefore, aggregate planning is important because it helps to ensure smooth operations and production throughout the supply chain, which in turn, affects costs, equipment utilisation, employment levels and most important of all, customer satisfaction. The aggregate plan is translated subsequently into more detailed planning activities such as master scheduling and materials planning. Thus, aggregate planning can be considered as the central nervous system of the organisation by connecting all key elements of what makes the organisation tick. It is the key to effective coordination of a wide variety of activities across the organisation.

Planning options

Various decision options are available to an aggregate planner to modify demand and capacity. These options can be divided into two main groups: proactive and reactive. Proactive strategies involve the altering of demand so that planning can better match capacity or supply. Reactive strategies entail the altering of capacity to meet demand.

Proactive options that are available to aggregate planners to influence demand include pricing, advertising, promotion and backordering which refers to order fulfilment by delivering the orders after the specified or promised due date. Differential pricing is commonly used to shift demand from peak to off-peak periods. For example, movie tickets are cheaper on weekdays than on weekends. The effectiveness of differential pricing in shifting demand from peak to off-peak periods depends on the price elasticity of the product or service. The more price elastic the product or service, the more effective differential pricing will be in shifting demand. To the extent that differential pricing is effective, it comes with an opportunity cost. The profit margin is lower for off-peak sales. Sales could also be lost during the peak period.

Advertising and promotions can also be used to shift demand in order to match capacity more closely. However, the planner must have good knowledge of the customers' behaviours, requirements, needs, and their response patterns to achieve the desired results. Unlike differential pricing, the timing of demand is more difficult to control in such instances. There is a possibility that advertising and promotions could lead to unexpected demand at the wrong time, thus further stressing capacity.

Another option is to use backorders to shift demand. The effectiveness of using backorders to manage demand depends on how willing the customers are in accepting late delivery. In addition, it is difficult to accurately quantify the costs associated with using this option. The associated costs include loss of goodwill, bad-mouthing and lost sales that arise from unhappy and disappointed customers.

Reactive strategies involve the altering of capacity to match demand. Capacity adjustment options include hiring, retrenchment, overtime or slack time, hiring of part-time workers, inventories and subcontracting, or investing in new equipment to produce more output.

Although hiring and retrenchment can be used to modify the production capability of an organisation, factors such as costs, labour relations, productivity and worker morale have to be taken into consideration when using this option. The organisation's hiring and retrenchment practices can also be restricted by union contracts and organisation policies.

The use of overtime or slack time (i.e., undertime) is generally more acceptable than retrenchment. It can be implemented more quickly while at the same time allowing the organisation to maintain a steady base of employees. However, the use of overtime has its disadvantages. It could lead to lower productivity, poor quality, more accidents and increased payroll costs.

Part-time or casual workers can be used to augment capacity. Part-time workers are often employed in jobs that are seasonal in nature. The attractiveness of part-time workers is that they cost significantly less than full-time staff in pay and fringe benefits. However, quality control can be a concern when part-time or casual workers are used.

Inventories are employed by manufacturing organisations to plug the gap between supply and demand. To address the mismatch between demand and capacity, inventories are produced earlier and carried to fulfil demand in later time periods. The cost of holding inventories can be significant. These include storage and insurance costs, obsolescence, deterioration, spoilage, breakage and the opportunity cost of money tied up in inventory that could be invested elsewhere.

Subcontracting allows an organisation to acquire temporary capacity. The decision to subcontract depends on factors such as the expertise and reliability of the subcontractors, quality and costs. A potential compromise arising from the use of subcontracting is quality. In some circumstances, organisations can have less control over the quantity and timing of the output.

Aggregate planning strategies

Aggregate planners can choose from strategies ranging between a level-capacity strategy and a chase-demand strategy. A level-capacity strategy consists of a constant base of workforce and hence a constant level of output. Uneven demand is expected to be met by inventory and backorders. Lost sales, however, could occur if customers do not agree to backorders. In contrast, a chase-demand strategy stipulates that the output at any period is matched to the demand for that period. Hence demand is always met and there is no stock-out. The chase-demand strategy is usually achieved through the hiring or retrenchment of workers.

The two strategies (level production or demand-chase) have their advantages and disadvantages. The level-capacity strategy is less detrimental to the morale of the workers. However, the strategy does have its shortcomings. It can result in lower customer satisfaction, lower profits, higher inventory costs, and higher backordering costs. The strategy could also lead to inventoried products becoming obsolete. The chase-demand strategy has the advantage of keeping the inventory level low, but the human resources cost can be high due the more frequent hiring and retrenchment. Needless to say, the morale of the workers can be adversely affected. In addition, the strategy runs the risk of not having a sufficient pool of workers with the necessary skills when the need arises.

Two important factors, organisation policy and costs, affect the choice of strategy. Organisations can adopt a hybrid between the level-demand and chase-demand strategies. Organisation policy often sets restrictions on the available choices or on the extent to which they can be used. Within the limitations imposed, aggregate planners seek to match supply and demand at minimum cost.

Box 4.6: High level planning on a global scale at Toyota

Toyota's president, Katsuaki Watanabe, recently announced the global Toyota policy of global supply chain management and planning. In its factories outside Japan, Toyota will use a level production strategy, 'setting and forgetting' production levels. The aim is to contain costs, and operate factories using the principle of 'Swift and Even Flow'. This means that as far as possible, Toyota's plants in North America, Europe, Thailand, Australia, China, will run the same product mix and production volumes and schedules every day. These plants will therefore be shielded from the daily, weekly and monthly vagaries of the market place. They will be focused on continuous improvement to an essentially fixed production schedule.

So how does Toyota cope with changes to demand? Market forces are such that it is impossible to forecast demand exactly. In other words, even the mighty Toyota cannot know in advance exactly how many cars will be sold, by model, colour, features, etc., in any and every place that it offers its vehicles to the world. Toyota has decided to run its non-Japanese plants at constant levels and chase demand from its Japan-based plants. This means that the Japanese network of Toyota plants and the component supply industry there will supplement locally produced vehicles in all other regions of the world, reacting fast to changes in those regions. It means that Toyota in Japan must have enough production and assembly capacity and the organisational capability to react quickly and effectively to changes. The Toyota plants in Toyota city and other regions of Japan have a very impressive ability to 'flex', meaning they can be used to mix models and change volume. This allows Toyota's non-Japanese plants to produce in a relatively disturbance-free mode, reducing all sorts of costs in those plants that would be incurred if they were always trying to cope with the changes associated with chasing demand production strategies.

Toyota produces over 9 million vehicles globally per year. It exports many shiploads of these vehicles from Japan to the rest of the world to supplement local and regional plants. The plan of providing global flexibility and chasing global demand almost exclusively from its Japanese plants allows Toyota to optimise its cost and service levels globally, and makes it even harder for competitors to match its operational performance and high customer service levels. The bottom line profit of Toyota and its share price performance, especially relative to the other large assemblers in its market, Ford and GM, clearly show that Toyota is able to translate its operational excellence into marketplace and profit success. In recent years, Toyota has increased its profits regularly, while Ford and GM have mostly traded at a loss.

Techniques for aggregate planning

Aggregate planners employ numerous techniques to generate the aggregate plan. The techniques can be broadly classified into two categories: trial and error approaches and sophisticated mathematical techniques.

The simplest and most widely used aggregate planning technique is the trial and error approach. Aggregate planners compare projected demand requirements with existing capacity using simple tables or graphs. Aggregate planners can input the parameters (e. g., workforce level, overtime, subcontracting) into spreadsheets and tables, and evaluate the alternatives based on overall costs. The main shortcoming of the trial and error approach is that it does not necessarily lead to an optimal aggregate plan. It could lead to an acceptable plan, but not necessarily to the *best* plan that meets all customer requirements at the lowest cost.

Example

Planners of a bicycle manufacturing company are preparing an aggregate plan that will cover six periods. They have collected the following information.

Period	1	2	3	4	5	6	Total
Forecast	300	400	300	500	600	300	2,400

Costs	
Output	
Regular time	$80 per bicycle
Overtime	$100 per bicycle
Subcontract	$250 per bicycle
Inventory	$30 per bicycle per period on average inventory
Backorders	$120 per bicycle per period

Inventory and overtime are used to absorb uneven demand. Backorders are allowed. The maximum amount of overtime output per period is 40. Five of the workers are away for training on the third and fourth periods. Currently, the company has 100 bicycles in its inventory and is expected to maintain that level of inventory at the end of the sixth period. There are 20 workers and each can produce 20 bicycles per period. Since five workers are away for training, overtime was planned to increase output to meet the total demand over the planning horizon. There will be overtime production from periods 2 to 6 at 40 bicycles per period. Prepare an aggregate plan and determine its cost using the given information.

Solution

Period	1	2	3	4	5	6	Total
Forecast (bicycles)	300	400	300	500	600	300	2,400
Output							
Regular	400	400	300	300	400	400	2,200
Overtime	–	40	40	40	40	40	200
Subcontract	–	–	–	–	–	–	–
Output – Forecast	100	40	40	(160)	(160)	140	0
Inventory							
Beginning	100	200	240	280	120	0	
Ending	200	240	280	120	0	100	
Average	150	220	260	200	60	50	940
Backlog	0	0	0	0	40	0	40

Costs	1	2	3	4	5	6	Total
Output							
Regular	$32,000	$32,000	$24,000	$24,000	$32,000	$32,000	$176,000
Overtime	$0	$4,000	$4,000	$4,000	$4,000	$4,000	$20,000
Subcontract	–	–	–	–	–	–	–
Inventory	$4,500	$6,600	$7,800	$6,000	$1,800	$1,500	$28,200
Backorder	–	–	–	–	$4,800	–	$4,800
Total	$36,500	$42,600	$35,800	$34,000	$42,600	$37,500	$229,000

There are two parts to the aggregate planning worksheet. The upper portion shows the output in number of units (bicycles). The lower portion computes the costs. Ending inventory is the sum of the beginning inventory and the difference between output and forecast (i.e. output minus forecast). Average inventory equals beginning inventory plus ending inventory divided by 2. If there is insufficient inventory, a backlog occurs. The costs are computed using the relevant per unit cost information multiply by the output units in the upper portion of the table.

A number of mathematical techniques have been developed to perform aggregate planning. Linear programming models are used to obtain optimal solutions to problems involving the allocation of scarce resources. In linear programming, the aggregate planners seek to optimise an objective, often in the form of cost minimisation. There are several shortcomings in using linear programming. The relationships among variables are assumed to be linear (hence the term linear programming). Also, linear programming models only allow the optimisation of a single objective. This makes the technique restrictive.

Another mathematical technique is the linear decision rule. The rule seeks to minimise the overall costs using a set of cost approximating functions to obtain two linear equations. The two linear equations can be derived from the quadratic equation using calculus. The technique suffers from three limitations. First, we have to assume that the cost functions are quadratic. Second, a considerable amount of effort is spent to obtain the relevant cost data and develop the cost functions. Third, the technique may give infeasible or impractical solutions.

Simulation models, which are gaining popularity among organisations, are computerised models that test a variety of scenarios based on the parameters inputted by the planner. Though the simulation approach does not guarantee optimal plans, simulation modelling allows for fast evaluation of alternatives and produces reasonably acceptable aggregate plans.

Master scheduling

What is a master schedule?

After the aggregate plan has been developed for a set of products, we need to break down or disaggregate the information by individual end products and services. The objective of the disaggregating process is to develop detailed material and resource requirements for the end products for production purposes. The process of disaggregating the aggregate plan into production plans for the end products and services is called *master scheduling*. A master schedule shows the production quantity and timing of end products or services over a typical period of six to eight weeks.

The master schedule contains vital information for various groups of people. It contains information for marketing to make delivery commitments of specific end products to the final customers. The operations department can derive information from the master schedule to evaluate whether capacity is sufficient to produce the end products. The master schedule also provides useful information for operations and marketing to negotiate when customer requests cannot be met by normal capacity. In addition, it

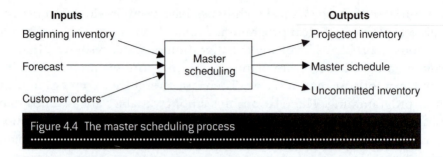

Figure 4.4 The master scheduling process

provides senior management with information on whether the business plan and its strategic objectives can be achieved. The master schedule also drives the planning process for the component parts and raw materials needed to make the end product. The planning process for component parts and raw materials is carried out by a software module called material requirements planning (MRP) and will be discussed in greater details later in this chapter.

Master scheduling process

Before the master schedule can be put into use, it has to be validated. Validation involves testing the feasibility of a tentative master schedule to ensure that there are no capacity violations that could render the master schedule unusable. Like the aggregate plan, the master schedule needs to be updated periodically, often monthly. Figure 4.4 shows the master scheduling process. Figure 4.4 shows that the master schedule has three primary inputs: beginning inventory, forecasts and customer orders.

One of the outputs of the master scheduling process is the *master schedule* (called *master production schedule* in manufacturing companies and *master operating schedule* in service organisations). The master schedule shows the quantity and timing of planned production, taking into account the customer orders and timing as well as the beginning inventory. The other two outputs of the master scheduling process are projected inventory and uncommitted inventory, also known as available-to-promise (ATP) inventory. Knowledge of the ATP inventory allows the marketing department to make realistic promises to customers regarding the deliveries of new orders. Table 4.2 shows what a master schedule looks like.

Changes, particularly those near to the current time period in the master schedule, can be highly disruptive. A decision tool that is frequently used to manage changes is 'time fencing'. Time fencing acts as a control mechanism for order promising and the entry of orders into the system. There are three types or categories of time fences: frozen, slushy and liquid. Within the frozen time fence, no changes to orders are accommodated or allowed. The length of the frozen time fence depends on the lead time to produce the

Table 4.2 Master schedule for an end item. Beginning inventory is 65 units

Week	1	2	3	4	5
Forecast	30	30	30	10	33
Customer order (Committed)	32	24	10	5	2
Projected on-hand inventory[a]	65 − 32 = 33	33 − 30 = 3	(50 − 27) = 23	(23 − 10) = 13	(50 − 20) = 30
Master Schedule (MS)[b]			50		50
Available-to-Promise inventory (uncommitted)[c]	65 − 32 − 24 = 9		50 − 10 − 5 = 35	. . .	

[a]Difference between previous week inventory and current week requirement. Current week requirement is the larger of forecast and customer order.
[b]Amount to be produced when projected inventory falls below specified limit (e.g., zero). In example, production lot size of 50 is used.
[c]Available inventory after fulfilling committed customer orders till next Master Schedule order.

product which includes the time taken to source for raw materials and the time required to make the product. Unlike the frozen time fence, changes to order quantities and due dates are allowed within the slushy time fence. However, these order changes have to be reviewed against available capacity and shop floor load conditions. The liquid time fence is by far the most flexible in terms of the types of changes allowed. New orders or cancellations can be made and accommodated by the system. The lengths of the frozen, slushy and liquid fences are different for different industries, and dependent on the production lead times, supplier delivery times and flexibility of the production systems.

Material requirements planning (MRP)

Is ERP the same as MRP?

Though Enterprise Resource Planning (ERP) and Material Requirements Planning (MRP) are closely related, the term ERP is by far more popular in industry. In essence, MRP is a term used to denote a software system for managing inventory, planning materials, priority scheduling of resources, and controlling shop floor operations. Advanced versions of an MRP system have an information technology platform that integrates operations/manufacturing with other functional areas such as finance and accounting, marketing and logistics. The first MRP system was developed in the 1950s, and since then, several generations of MRP systems have evolved, with the latest being ERP. Hence, ERP should be viewed as one of the versions or generations of an MRP system.

In the manufacturing context, an MRP system takes a master schedule and computes the quantity and timing of raw materials, component parts, assemblies and sub-assemblies required to produce the end products. It also links the inventory planning functions to the scheduling system by generating capacity requirements, triggering production and purchase orders, and assigning order priorities for shop floor operations. Given its wide functionality and features, MRP systems have also been adopted in many service organisations to integrate various departments and divisions, particularly in planning, coordination and performance tracking.

The major benefits of implementing an MRP system include minimising inventories to support production, effective planning of material requirements, and closing the loop by specifying capacity requirements and plans. All these and the integration of various functional areas enable an organisation to plan, organise, and control its activities more effectively, leading to better customer service and higher organisational performance. However, MRP requires the organisation to maintain up-to-date and accurate information on orders, inventory and capacity.

There are three types or generations of MRP systems: Type 1 MRP, Type 2 MRP and ERP systems. A Type 1 MRP system is basically an inventory planning system that generates a materials plan of planned order quantities and order start and due dates for all the items (i.e., raw materials, component parts, assemblies) needed to support production of the end products. Type 1 MRP releases manufacturing and purchase orders based on the materials plan. The system initiates orders to control work-in-progress and raw material inventories through proper timing of order placement and release. A Type 1 MRP system, however, does not have capacity planning and shop floor control features.

A Type 2 MRP system (also known as Manufacturing Resource Planning or MRPII) is a production and inventory control system. In addition to the features found in Type 1 MRP, a Type 2 MRP system has capacity planning and shop floor management capabilities. A Type 2 MRP system has a feedback loop between the materials planning function and capacity management where the planned order releases in the materials plan are translated into capacity requirements and checked against available capacity. The capacity requirements plan is then used by a planner to adjust capacity to fulfil the materials plan or modify the materials plan according to the capacity constraints. The ability of the planner in fine-tuning the material plan against available capacity is crucial in ensuring timely completion of the end products.

A Type 2 MRP system is also a management information system that facilitates the sharing of plans and production information with functional areas such as marketing and finance. The integration of production with other internal functional areas enhances the effectiveness and efficiency of an organisation to execute plans, coordinate resources, track performance and to serve its customers better.

The third type or generation of MRP system is ERP. An ERP system is an organisationwide planning system that has the ability to plan and control all resources such as cash, personnel, inventory and facilities. This is made possible by the fact the ERP system is integrated with all other information subsystems in the organisation through a common organisationwide database. The ERP system is discussed in greater details later in the chapter.

An MRP system can provide management with a wide range of outputs and controls. The outputs can be classified into primary reports and secondary reports. The primary reports provide information on planned orders, order releases and changes. The secondary reports include performance control reports, planning reports and exception reports.

Planning process and MRP module

The materials plan is a detailed schedule of planned order quantities, planned start dates and planned order due dates for all items needed to make the end product. This plan has great impact and implications on how resources, materials, and manpower are sourced and mobilised for implementation of the plan. As such, the generation of the materials plan is a core feature of an MRP system.

In a typical MRP system, the materials plan is generated by the Material Requirement Planning (MRP) module. The MRP module derives information from three major sources: the master schedule, bill-of-materials (BOM) file and inventory records file. The master schedule shows the quantity and timing of end products produced. It splits the planning horizon into blocks of time periods or time buckets. These time buckets need not be of equal length. The nearer-term portion of the master schedule can be expressed in weeks while those further away can be expressed in months or quarters. It is imperative that the master schedule covers far enough into the future so that managers and decision makers can have forward visibility of the market demand. The master schedule must also take into account the cumulative lead time for manufacturing a product. The cumulative lead time is the sum of all the lead times needed to manufacture the product, from ordering of raw

Table 4.3 A materials plan template

Item:						Week			
Lead time (LT): Gross requirements*	Beg. Inv.	1	2	3	4	5	6	7	8
Scheduled receipts									
On hand									
Net requirements									
Planned order receipts									
Planned order release									

* Gross requirements: Demand for the item at beginning of week
Scheduled receipts: Open production or purchase orders that are scheduled to arrive at beginning of week
On-hand: Inventory on-hand at end of week
Net requirements: Shortfall to meet gross requirements at beginning of week
Planned order receipts: Planned orders that are schedule to be completed at beginning of week
Planned order releases: Planned orders that will be released at beginning of week

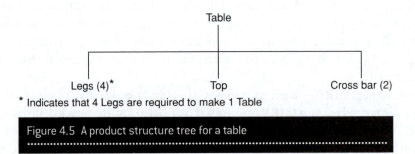

* Indicates that 4 Legs are required to make 1 Table

Figure 4.5 A product structure tree for a table

materials to final assembly of the product. Table 4.3 shows a Materials Plan template.

The bill-of-material (BOM) is a listing of all the materials or items or parts needed to produce one unit of the end product. The BOM is thus a recipe for making the end product. The BOM listing is hierarchical and depicted as a product structure tree. The product structure tree shows the quantities needed for each type of raw material to produce one unit of finished good. A product structure tree for a table is depicted in Figure 4.5. As products are being redesigned, BOMs have to be updated accordingly. Thus, there is a need for an effective engineering-change-order (ECO) system to keep the BOMs up-to-date. The importance of having an accurate BOM cannot be overemphasised. If there are errors in the BOMs, the right materials will not be acquired and the end product cannot be produced and delivered to the customer in a timely fashion. This is especially for the case where several levels of assembly are involved in the manufacturing of the product. The multi-level BOM will cause errors at one level, and this could be cascaded and 'magnified' in the MRP planning process. An incorrect BOM can have an adverse effect on production costs and customer service.

The third input for the MRP module is the inventory records file. The inventory records file contains information on the status of each item or part by time period. Like the BOM, the accuracy of the inventory records is paramount. Incorrect information on the amount-on-hand, for example, can cause confusion and lead to delay in delivery times.

Box 4.7: Information in inventory records file

- Gross requirements – total expected demand for an item/part for each time period.
- Scheduled receipts – open production or purchase orders scheduled to arrive.
- Expected amount-on-hand.
- Suppliers.
- Lead times.
- Lot size policy.
- Stock receipts and withdrawals.
- Cancelled orders.

The objective of the material planning process is to determine the net requirements of an item, that is, the actual quantity to be produced in each time period to meet customer demand. The net requirements of an item are computed from its demand (i.e., gross requirements), open orders that are scheduled to come into stock, and current inventory. Safety stock requirements can be incorporated in the planning process as a net requirement. The net requirements are then time-phased by their production lead times and batched into planned order releases. The computation of the net requirements (and hence the planned order releases) are carried out one item at a time, level by level, according to the BOM structure. The process of converting the master schedule into detailed material requirements for the items in the BOM is called 'explosion'.

Example

A plant has received two orders for tables: 70 and 80 tables due for delivery at the start of weeks 4 and 7 respectively. As shown in Figure 4.5, each table is assembled from four legs, one top and two cross bars. Except for the tabletop, which has a lead-time of two weeks, the lead-time for the other components is one week. Assembly of the tables requires one week. There is a scheduled receipt of 100 table legs at the beginning of Week 2. The Materials Plan for the end product table is shown below.

Master schedule: Table Week	Beg. Inv.	1	2	3	4	5	6	7	8
Quantity					70			80	

Item: Table					Week				
LT: 1 week	Beg. Inv.	1	2	3	4	5	6	7	8
Gross requirements					70			80	
Scheduled receipts									
On hand									
Net requirements					70			80	
Planned order receipts					70			80	
Planned order release				70			80		

Item: Legs (4)					Week				
LT: 1 week	Beg. Inv.	1	2	3	4	5	6	7	8
Gross requirements				280			320		
Scheduled receipts			100						
On hand			100						
Net requirements				180			320		
Planned order receipts				180			320		
Planned order release			180			320			

Item: Top (1)					Week				
LT: 2 week	Beg. Inv.	1	2	3	4	5	6	7	8
Gross requirements				70			80		
Scheduled receipts									
On hand									
Net requirements				70			80		
Planned order receipts				70			80		
Planned order release		70			80				

Item: Cross bar (2)					Week				
LT: 1 week	Beg. Inv.	1	2	3	4	5	6	7	8
Gross requirements				140			160		

Scheduled receipts		
On hand		
Net requirements	140	160
Planned order receipts	140	160
Planned order release	140	160

Managing change

One of the advantages of an MRP system is its ability to react to market and customer changes. These changes arise from new orders coming in or from customers altering their orders that are already being processed in the system. There are two basic approaches that are used to keep MRP records up-to-date: regenerative system and net-change system.

A regenerative system uses a batching approach that collates all the changes that occurred within a specific time interval and then updates the MRP system periodically. A regeneration of the system is typically carried out on a weekly basis.

On the other hand, a net-change system adopts a real-time approach to reflect changes as they occur. The MRP module is run daily, usually at the end of the day, to incorporate the changes. However, only those portions of the materials plan that are directly affected by the changes are re-computed. As a result, materials might not be properly synchronised for all the items in the BOM after a net-change has been executed. The discrepancies and inconsistencies can be resolved by carrying out a regenerative run, say, at the end of the week.

The regenerative and net-change approaches have their advantages and disadvantages. The regenerative approach favours a more stable operating environment. Changes that occur in a given time period can cancel each other thus reducing the need to modify and re-modify the materials plan. This leads to lower processing costs. The disadvantage of a regenerative system is that there is a time lag between when the information becomes available and when this information is actually incorporated into the MRP system. In contrast, the net-change approach is more suitable for an environment with frequent changes. The benefit of using a net-change approach is that decision makers have access to updated information for planning and control purposes, even though this comes at a higher cost due to a higher frequency of updating.

Other considerations

To maximise the benefits of an MRP system, managers must be familiar with other aspects of executing an MRP system. These include lot sizing and stability of the system.

Lot sizing

Lot sizing is an important aspect of the MRP planning process. Lot sizes are quantities of the items to be produced that are issued as planned order releases in the materials plan. These planned order releases are either production orders if the item is to be manufactured in-house or purchase orders if the item is procured from a supplier. Lot sizes are net requirements of an item that are batched over several periods. The number of periods of net requirements to be batched depends on the lot sizing method. Most lot sizing methods attempt to balance the setup or ordering costs and inventory carrying costs associated with batching of the net requirements over a number of time periods. The lot sizing method can be chosen by the MRP user. Lot sizing decisions are important because it affects efficiency and utilisation of production resources.

A number of lot sizing methods is available for determining lot sizes in an MRP system. Lot-for-lot is the simplest lot sizing method. Here, the lot size is set equal to the net requirement of the period. You might note that the example above on MRP computations used the lot-for-lot method. Although lot-for-lot minimises inventory carrying cost, this method can incur excessive setup or ordering cost.

In the fixed-period ordering method, the lot size is set equal to the net requirements over a predetermined number of periods. The number of periods can be set to match the production or purchase cycle or determined from the historical demand pattern.

Stability of the MRP system

The stability (or more appropriately the instability) of the MRP system is another important concern for MRP managers. MRP instability or 'nervousness' represents a situation when significant changes in the MRP plan are observed arising from minor changes in the master schedule. The significant changes in the MRP plan involve the quantity or timing of the planned release of orders. Due to the multi-level BOM structure, minor changes in the master schedule ripple and magnify significantly as the explosion process computes the planned order releases item by item, level by level, down the BOM structure. The use of some lot sizing techniques also contributes to the instability of the MRP system. The exaggerated changes in the MRP plan tend to distort priorities and cause unnecessary reactions at the shop floor.

There are several ways to reduce sensitivity or nervousness in an MRP system. First, potential causes of changes to the MRP plan should be avoided. Stability can be introduced into the master schedule by using mechanisms such as freezing and time fences that restrict only certain types of changes to be accepted by the system. The incidence of unplanned demand should also be avoided. Following the MRP plan strictly with regards to the timing and quantity of planned order releases helps to inject stability into the system. Last but not least, the introduction of parameter changes such as change in safety stock levels or planned lead times have to be controlled.

Lot sizing methods can influence the stability of the MRP system, and it is advisable to use different lot sizing methods at different levels of the BOM. For example, a fixed order quantity can be used at the higher levels of the BOM while lot-for-lot and economic order quantity can be used at the intermediate levels and bottom levels. Instability of the MRP system can be reduced by using firm planned orders. In other words, changes in the master schedule are ignored and insulated from the system. While this means that the MRP system is relatively more stable, such a 'de-coupling' between the master schedule and the MRP system could mean that the MRP plan might not be able to meet the production orders in the master schedule, and customer service might be compromised.

Successful MRP system

For an MRP system to be successful, a number of critical success factors must be present. Some of these are:

- implementation planning
- adequate computer support
- accurate data
- interdepartmental support
- user knowledge.

Implementation planning includes education of senior management, selection of project manager, appointment of an implementation team, clarity of adoption objectives, identification of expected costs and benefits, and a detailed action plan. This factor is crucial and the remaining four factors should only begin when this factor is done properly. Among the five factors, having an adequate computer system is relatively easy to implement. Instead of writing one's own MRP software, there are many software packages available in the market (e. g., SAP, Oracle, Baan).

Data accuracy is an important success factor as the plans produced by MRP are as good or bad as the integrity and quality of the data used to generate these plans. As the MRP system cuts across various functional areas and is used pervasively within an organisation, it is imperative that all departments support and accept the MRP system. The stakeholders in different departments must be actively involved in installing and embracing the MRP system. Finally, user knowledge is required to use the MRP system effectively. The employees must understand how their roles and responsibilities are affected by the MRP system, and adopt the plans produced by the MRP system.

Enterprise resource planning (ERP)

As mentioned earlier, ERP is the latest in the generations of MRP systems. Like manufacturing resource planning (MRPII), ERP possesses the operations logic to compute the materials plan and play the role of a management information system for the entire organisation. It differs from MRPII in that it has more advanced graphical user interfaces and sophisticated functionalities in integrating application programs and connecting with suppliers, business partners and customers. These additional functionalities include e-commerce and Internet applications.

As an integrated business solution, ERP facilitates the exchange and sharing of information, plans and data across all departments and functions in an organisation. These departments can be geographically located in different countries. As information does not have to re-entered at each step of a process in the ERP system, benefit is gained from the eradication of redundant processes, increased information accuracy and improved speed in responding to customers. Sometimes, a separate data warehouse is used to facilitate queries not built into the standard ERP system software. A data warehouse is a special program that is designed to automatically capture and process data for users that are outside the basic ERP system applications. The data warehouse software is set up so that users can access and analyse data without placing a burden on the ERP system.

Box 4.8: Characteristics of a standard ERP software system

- *Multifunctional in scope* – the software is able to accommodate the different nature of operations of various departments in an organisation. For instance, records in the finance department are denominated in monetary terms while those in purchasing department are in units of raw materials.
- *Integrated* – when data and information are entered into the system by one of the functions, records in related functions are updated concurrently.
- *Modular in structure* – although the software is meant to be a single expansive and integrated system, it is also able to function holistically at the departmental level.
- *Facilitate manufacturing planning and control activities* – this is the basic function of any MRP system which the ERP system is built upon.

How does ERP connect the functional areas?

An ERP system is made up of closely integrated modules that tap into a real-time, common database. Normally, the modules are focused on at least four major functional areas: finance, human resources, marketing and production. In finance, the ERP system provides a common platform to capture financial data. When a customer places an order, the transaction is automatically captured and triggers the accounts receivables to be updated once the order is shipped.

Similarly, the ERP system can provide the human resource department with the capabilities needed to manage, hire, pay and train its people. An ERP system has human resource functions such as payroll, employee scheduling and shift planning, workforce planning and benefits administration.

For marketing, the ERP system provides sales forecasting and customer management functions such as sales order management; credit checking configuration management; and distribution, shipping, and transportation management. The modules are increasingly implemented globally, allowing organisations to manage the sales process worldwide. Most ERP software today has CRM (Customer Relationship Management) capabilities or could act as an IT platform to support best-of-breed CRM applications.

An ERP system has many modules to support operations. Typical elements include sales and operations planning, materials requirements planning, capacity requirements planning, plant maintenance, quality management, production planning and control and project management.

Box 4.9: Factors to consider when choosing an ERP software system

Depending on the features and extent of customisation, an ERP system could cost from hundreds of thousands to millions of dollars. When evaluating ERP software, the following aspects should be carefully considered:

- The size and complexity of the business.
- The resources (e. g., financial, physical and personnel) available for implementing the system.
- The scalability, functionalities and features in the ERP system.
- The uniqueness of the organisation's processes and operations.
- The alignment of the organisation's needs with the manufacturing planning and control modules in the ERP system.
- Reputation and track record of customer service of the ERP vendor.

Box 4.10: Optimising raw material management

InnoFibres (not the real name) is a manufacturer of Lycra® fibre. Lycra is woven into fabrics at textile factories to improve the stretchable properties of the apparel. Every year, InnoFibres' plant produces more than 15,000 tons of Lycra. A total of nine major raw materials are used in the production of Lycra. Each raw material has a certain shelf life. For materials that have expired, the materials have to go through extensive tests and documentation. If the materials fail the tests or if there are doubts about the accuracy of the tests, materials are thrown away, wasting hundreds of dollars for each drum of materials. Therefore, raw material planning is an important and integral part of operation in the company. The raw material planner acts as a middleman among the various departments of the company such as production, logistics, finance and technical support. The responsibilities of the raw material planner include performing supplier qualifications, auditing vendors and suppliers, coordinating raw material tests, solving account payables problem, managing changes in production and materials expiry and quality issues. Thus, he gets many work requests from his upstream suppliers and downstream customers.

Raw material usage in the company does not vary greatly, as production volumes are fairly stable. Only when there are defects in the supplies or when the technical department calls for a raw material test, will there be drastic changes in the level of raw material inventory. Simple Excel spreadsheets are used to estimate when to bring in the next lots of deliveries. The sourcing department will process the purchase requisition put in by the raw material planner and issue the purchase order to the suppliers. When inventory arrives, the information is updated in the Excel spreadsheet by raw material planner.

Although the company is using SAP R3 (an ERP system) to link up the application programs of some of the departments in the company, there is no intention to expand the SAP usage to raw material planning due to its high costs.

Summary

The management challenge presented at the start of the chapter posed the question: 'What can the company Sayon Nara do to better cope with the increasing complexity of its quotation processes?' To solve the problem and hence increase productivity and profitability, an ERP system can be installed. Quotations are keyed into the computerised ERP system and can be used for reference subsequently. When the deals are closed, the quotation entries can be converted into sales and purchase orders. Furthermore, information on cost prices from suppliers, weights and sizes of the products can be retrieved to set the selling prices to different customers. Inventory levels can also be monitored with the software. Sales personnel can view the stock status of the products and provide customers with up-to-date information. The purchasing department can be alerted to replenish stock, taking into account the lead time of the products when the inventory level reaches the reorder level.

This chapter discussed planning in the context of inventory. Inventory is carried for a variety of reasons. How much inventory to order and when to order are key inventory decisions. Inventory decisions involve the trade-off between minimising inventory investment and maximising customer service. The two basic inventory systems are reorder point and periodic review.

Planning at various levels of aggregation was then discussed. Planning is first carried out at the aggregate level for a family of products or services. The objective of aggregate planning is to specify the optimal combination of production rates, workforce level and inventory to meet fluctuating, uncertain or seasonal demand over the medium term. At this level of planning, all functional areas are involved. Planners either use trial and error methods or mathematical techniques to develop an aggregate plan. The aggregate plan is then broken down into a master schedule of production requirements for specific end products. The master schedule is based on information on the beginning inventory, forecasts and customer orders.

MRP is a computerised system that creates detailed schedules showing the quantities and dates for the raw materials, components and assemblies required to make the end products. The MRP module derives its inputs from the master schedule, bills of materials and inventory data. The success of an MRP system depends on top management commitment, good project planning and implementation, data accuracy, and interdepartmental support and acceptance. ERP is the latest generation of MRP systems that provides an organisation with sophisticated planning and control functionalities and greater connectivity to its suppliers, business partners and customers.

DISCUSSION QUESTIONS

1. What are the functions of inventory?
2. Can one run a manufacturing enterprise without any inventory?
3. Compare and contrast the reorder point and periodic review systems. Which system is more effective in preventing stockouts?
4. What are the different types of plans? Describe each one.
5. Why do we need to have aggregation and disaggregation of plans?
6. What are the pros and cons of the level-capacity and chase-demand strategies?
7. What are the key inputs and outputs of master scheduling?
8. What information is provided in a materials plan?
9. What is the relationship between the MRP planning process and scheduling?
10. Having just bought a suburban newsagency, you must decide how many newspapers, magazines, greeting cards, etc., to order and keep. For each of these three items, describe the key drivers of the decisions about how many you would order.

Further readings and references

Brandimarte, Paolo and Villa, A. 1999. *Modeling Manufacturing Systems: From aggregate planning to real-time control.* Berlin: Springer-Verlag Telos.

Chase, Richard B., Jacobs, F. Robert and Aquilano, Nicholas J. 2006. *Operations Management for Competitive Advantage*. New York: McGraw-Hill Irwin.

Herrmann, Jeffrey W. 2006. *Handbook of Production Scheduling*. New York: Springer.

Pinedo, Michael L. 2005. *Planning and Scheduling in Manufacturing and Services*. New York: Springer.

Proud, John F. 2007. *Master Scheduling: A practical guide to competitive manufacturing*. Hoboken, N. J.: John Wiley & Sons Inc.

Schroeder, Roger, G. 2006. *Operations Management: Concepts and cases*. New York: McGraw-Hill Irwin.

Stevenson, William J. 2005. *Operations Management*. New York: McGraw-Hill Irwin, 2005

Vollmann, Thomas E., Berry, William L., Wybark, D. Clary and Jacobs, F. Robert. 2005. *Manufacturing Planning and Control for Supply Chain Management*. New York: McGraw-Hill Irwin.

Wallace, F. and Kremzar, Michael H. 2001. *ERP: Making it happen; the implementers' guide to success with enterprise resource planning*. New York: Wiley.

Zipkin, Paul H. 2000. *Foundations of Inventory Management*. New York: McGraw-Hill.

Internet resources

Association for Operations Management at www.apics.org/default.htm

A website developed by Penn State University and Boise State University students at www.freequality.org

A wonderful website on inventory management at www.cris.com/~kthill/inventry.htm

Information on inventory management at www.inventoryops.com

Oracle at www.oracle.com

SAP at www.sap.com

PART II

Approaches to Understanding OM

Strategic Approach to Operations Management

Senevi Kiridena and Prakash J. Singh

Learning objectives

After reading this chapter you should be able to:

- understand and interpret the concept of operations as part of organisational strategy and related analytical perspectives
- understand and interpret the notion of competitive advantage and the nature of generic competitive strategies pursued by organisations
- understand and appreciate the strategic role of the operations function and its contribution to the sustainable competitive advantage of the organisation
- understand and describe the role of competitive priorities in operationalising strategy
- discuss the concept of trade-offs as applied to key decisions and actions regarding the operations structure and infrastructure of an organisation
- demonstrate your ability to apply the conceptual understanding developed as above to support managerial decisions and actions.

Box 5.1: Management challenge: strategic operations options for Delta-tech

Delta-tech, a small privately owned company based in New South Wales (NSW), Australia, was founded in 1947 to supply speciality consumables to the local heavy manufacturing sector. Over the past ten years, after being bought by its current owner Ed Palmer, the company has grown from a small-scale maintenance service-provider/equipment and consumables supplier to a technology developer/small-scale manufacturer of equipment that exceeded the performance and quality standards of reputed international brands. It currently employs 22 staff (including Mr Palmer as MD and three other supervisory staff), with an annual sales revenue exceeding $5 million. Delta-tech is currently catering to a niche market segment within the heavy manufacturing and process industry in NSW and Queensland with limited exports, and operates from its Sydney facility. Its customer base consists of both small and large organisations, but mainly those with speciality needs.

Over the past ten years, the company's product-market decisions have reflected a focused self-paced growth in niche market segments. Its current competitive priorities appear to be superior quality and flexibility. Innovative new product development is an integral part of its operations. The entrepreneurial leadership and the creative and motivated workforce provide an environment conducive to generate and test new ideas on the shop-floor itself. (Mr Palmer says new ideas could come from anywhere in the company; from the cleaner to the MD, or even from outside such as from its customers.)

Delta-tech's product development and manufacturing capabilities have improved substantially over the past decade from simple reverse-engineering of competitor products to complete design, development and manufacturing of its own brands, which outperform major competitor offerings. The company uses advanced manufacturing technologies in order to keep pace with the latest developments in process (metal-cutting) technology, and continues to acquire and develop extra capacity and flexibility through upgrading of process technology and machine tools, etc.

In light of its continuing success, Mr Palmer is keen to expand the business. This would ideally involve upgrading existing facilities to support full-blown manufacturing and extending its services to cover all five major (mainland) states in Australia and some parts of South Africa. He is confident that the company has the technical capabilities to operate at this level but is not sure of the wider business implications of such a move.

The challenge facing the company is to explore the strategic operations implications of this business decision with a view to prudently choosing a course of action, being mindful of the potential benefits and possible pitfalls.

Introduction

In the first two chapters of this book, we emphasised the importance of operations in successfully running a business. Now, we turn to further exploring the strategic role and significance of operations. How does the operations function contribute to the long-term well-being of an organisation? As discussed in Chapters 3 and 4, operations managers are constantly engaged in making decisions and initiating actions. These could be about locating new facilities, adding new capacity, introducing new technology, upgrading existing plant and equipment, running a second shift, scheduling staff and jobs, improving skill levels of people, resolving workforce issues or looking after the welfare and safety of staff. Some of these undertakings could be tactical in nature and of a more routine type (for example, some of the activities discussed in Chapter 4). Others are substantial, with profound long-term impacts on the whole business – those of strategic significance (such as the topics covered in Chapter 3). These decisions and actions often revolve around identifying trade-offs, prioritising issues, and making informed judgements and choices.

Consider, as examples, the cases of a hospital looking to buy new diagnostic equipment, a retail chain introducing a new technology-based stock replenishment system, or a manufacturing organisation looking to acquire a new enterprise resource planning system. These initiatives seem all too familiar, but they are significant decisions that affect an organisation's capacity to serve its purpose, and if not made with due diligence, could have major consequences. Furthermore, the decisions and actions of operations managers are guided, influenced and constrained by a multitude of factors that are internal and external to the organisation. These include the annual budget of the business unit, marketing's goals, top management's expectations, the skill levels of staff and the organisational culture, to name a few internal factors, and then such external factors as changing customer needs, technological advancements, competitors' actions and regulatory requirements. These decisions and actions, collectively and cumulatively, shape the structure and character of the operations system as well as its capacity to respond to market needs which, in turn, determine the competitive success of the organisation. Therefore, it is imperative that current or aspiring managers develop a sound understanding of the dynamics of these managerial endeavours along with their outcomes and the organisational settings in which they take place.

The strategic approach to operations management takes on this challenge. It examines the role and contribution of operations in ensuring the long-term competitive success of the organisation. It also deals with the issues that affect and approaches that enhance its competitiveness. In summarising these ideas, consider the operations function as the 'heart of the organisation'. This is where most of the organisation's people work, where most of its financial assets are deployed, and where the outcomes of cost, quality, delivery performance, flexibility and other key outcomes are decided.

The connection between operations and business strategy can be summarised into two ideas. First is the idea that operations is the part of the organisation that primarily delivers the business strategy. This implies that operations outcomes are not an end in themselves, but are indeed nothing more nor less than a means towards an end: the end being organisational success in achieving its goals. Second, outstanding outcomes from operations, meaning 'being really good at operations management' can allow for new business strategies. Businesses that achieve 'operations excellence' can use this capability as a competitive weapon in the marketplace. For these reasons, it is clear that in order to be an effective operations manager, one must be able as part of that role to orient the operations decisions and priorities to both serve and drive the business strategy.

The notion of 'strategic approach' stems from the central concept of strategy, which will be briefly explored first in this chapter, along with other general perspectives of strategy. This is followed by a brief discussion of the notion of competitive advantage and associated concepts that form the foundation of contemporary strategy studies. The strategic approach to operations management is explored in the next section with some detailed discussions of the core concepts such as competitive priorities, strategic operations decision areas and trade-offs. The chapter then presents some significant findings of recent research into the practice of operations strategy highlighting the challenges faced by practising managers in operationalising the above concepts. It concludes with a summary accompanied by a brief response to the management challenge presented at the beginning of the chapter.

Box 5.2: Toll Holdings

Toll Holdings was founded in 1888 by one Albert F. Toll who used horse-drawn carts to transport coal in Newcastle, Australia. It languished as a trucking company until 1986 when a group of managers led by Paul Little bought it for $1.5 million. In the space of twenty years, Toll Holdings has become by far Australia's leading transport and logistics service providing company. It was listed on the Australian stock market in 1993. Today, it is worth about $9.5 billion, generating revenues of $7.6 billion, and healthy net profits.[1]

In terms of its operations, Toll Holdings employs more than 27,000 people, and operates a network of over 670 sites in over 17 countries across the Asia-Pacific region. Toll provides a range of services such as: transport via road, rail, sea and air; warehousing and distribution (it has a capacity of three million square metres of warehouse space); port management, port services, container and general stevedoring; and passenger and freight airline services. With its business heavily involved in the automotive, beverage, food and retail, ports, relocation and resources sectors, it has strategically put in place a logistics model to provide an integrated service. The model, aimed to achieve supply chain excellence for customers, involves ownership and management of transport and logistics assets such as ports, railways, warehousing, road fleets and air capacity; use of smart technology and operational expertise. As such, Toll has become a highly vertically integrated organisation that is able to provide complete transport and logistics service solutions to its customers.

So, how has Toll managed to grow so fast? An important element of Toll's growth has been through astute acquisitions. Since 1986, Toll has made 52 strategic acquisitions of transport and logistics businesses including TNT, BHP Stevedoring, BHP Transport and Logistics (NZ), Freight Australia, Patrick Corporation and Virginblue Airline. These acquisitions have mostly been in Australia, and some in New Zealand. In 2006, it acquired Singapore-based SembCorp Logistics, since rebadged as Toll Asia, in a concerted effort to expand its operations in the greater Asian region.

While a large proportion of the growth is due to acquisitions, the company has focused on organic growth as well. For example, for financial year 2006, organic growth contributed $382 million to revenue, while acquisitions accounted for $765 million.[2] Organic growth in Toll's case has been through providing additional value-added services to its existing customers, as well as vigorously pursuing new customers in the various industry sectors that it serves in.

Going forward, Toll faces many significant challenges. Some of these are:

- Consolidating its operations. As a result of the large number of acquisitions, up to 30 different business units form the structural basis of the company. It is in Toll's interest to ensure that all these business units benefit from centralised corporate resources and minimise unnecessary duplications. Given that the transport and logistics industry is capital intensive and technology driven, integrating these disparate systems from all the acquired entities has been a challenge. Given that some of Toll's recent acquisitions are very large, simply replacing Toll's systems in place of the acquired entities systems may not be a as simple and straightforward as it has been when smaller entities were acquired.

- Concerns about market concentration and reduction in competition. The transport and logistics sector has gone through radical rationalisation in the past 20 years or so. Indeed, Toll has been a major protagonist in this. As a result, competition has lessened and market share has become concentrated in the hands of a few powerful players. As a consequence, regulators, in this case the Australian Competition and Consumer Commission (ACCC), took a dim view of further rationalisation. This means that opportunities for Toll to continue to grow through aggressive acquisitions are likely to become limited. Indeed, Toll has had to restructure itself to meet some of the regulators' concerns that it was becoming too powerful a player in the industry. Toll will need to be able to deal with concerns of regulators as it becomes a 'big' player in the industry.

- Challenges of pursing organic growth. Given that growth through acquisitions may be limited, Toll will need to carefully think about other opportunities. Organic growth within the local market may be one solution to this problem. The Australian and New Zealand freight and logistics market is estimated at over $66 billion per annum, of which $33 billion currently remains in-house, providing opportunities for Toll.[3] Further, in Australia, it is anticipated that the size of the freight business will double in size over the next 15 years, creating opportunities for companies like Toll to be able to offer transport and logistics solutions. But, as is well known, organic growth can be a long, arduous and slow process. Toll would need to develop new skill and mind sets for this form of growth.

- Potential pitfalls in pursuing international expansion. Another obvious source for growth is to expand internationally. Many of Toll's existing customers import and export products. So far, Toll has used collaborative relationships with other transport and logistics providers that assist Toll in providing some of these functions. However, Toll is now expanding its operations to areas in this region. Its purchase of a Singaporean operator will give Toll market entry into Singapore, Thailand, Malaysia other several other countries in the region. Further, its network of 32 distribution centres in China will assist them to provide logistical support to Australian importers. But, the social, cultural, economic and political circumstances in these countries are unique and quite different to Australia. Many other firms have not been able to successful cope with these challenges. Toll will need to develop capacity in these aspects if it is to successfully expand internationally.

- Operational challenges. As with any corporation, Toll needs to ensure that its operations are as efficient as possible. So far, it appears to have successfully managed to do this. However, there are issues, especially macro-environmental ones, that could be significant challenges. First, the high fuel prices have emerged as a significant cost impost and risk factor. For the first time ever, fuel costs have exceeded labour costs in relation to long-haul road freight business.[4] Second, Australian industries are having to endure infrastructure-related capacity constraints. Also, there are skills shortages in many of the professional and trade skills areas. Finally, productivity improvements in many areas relevant to Toll have plateaued (e. g., container movement rates at major ports increased from about 26 containers per hour per ship in the late 1990s to about 45 in the early 2000s – this has not changed recently).[5] Toll will need to develop innovative ways of dealing with these issues, many of which are not under its direct control.

Paul Little (estimated personal worth close to one billion dollars)[6] and his colleagues have developed a fantastic business based mainly on a strategic model of rapid expansion through aggressive acquisitions, supported by organic growth. Now that Toll Holdings has become a 'big' business and market leader in its industry, it will be interesting to see how they go about dealing with the set of relatively new challenges that it faces.

Notes

1   'Snapshot of Toll', available from www.toll. com.au (accessed: 8 August 2007).
2   'Toll group profit announcement – June 2006'. Available from: www.toll.com.au
3   'Market environment', www.toll.com.au
4   M. Carter and D. Mariuz, 'Fast forward.' *Business Review Weekly*, 23–29 November 2006, pp. 36–39.
5   K. Chinnery, 'A stake on the waterfront.' *Business Review Weekly*, 18–24 January 2007, pp. 18–19.
6   '*The Bulletin* smart 100 – business and manufacturing.' *The Bulletin Magazine* (daily edition), 19 June 2007. http://bulletin.ninemsn.com.au

Strategy: general organisational perspectives

Strategy underpins virtually all managerial undertakings. Whether you are performing the role of a front-desk customer service supervisor, back-office accounts administrator, team leader on the production floor, departmental manager or a general manager, your decisions and actions are conditioned by and/or contributing to the strategic behaviour of the organisation in some way. When you join the workforce, you carry with you a certain set of skills, knowledge and experience, as well as some predispositions as to what the world around you is about. When you discharge your duties or engage in your day-to-day work, you make decisions, take actions, relate to your colleagues and perhaps interact with customers in a certain manner. Those engagements are guided by the expectations of your role (as a team leader, department manager or the chief executive officer) as well as your own understanding and interpretation of information and events. These undertakings, especially those of senior executives and those that affect what organisations do in terms of which markets they serve, how they compete in each market and the way they create or deliver products and services, will eventually determine the overall well-being (the survival, growth and returns) of an organisation. So, what is this concept of strategy all about?

The roots of 'strategic thought' can be traced far back into history to when people used a variety of approaches to succeed on military fronts, in politics and lately in sports. Over the years, the idea of and the perceptions about strategy have continued to evolve. The migration of the strategy concept into the business domain could be seen as a significant milestone in this progressive journey. The concept, as applied to organisations, has been greatly influenced and shaped by the ideas of the early management scholars and industrialists of the 20th century: Igor Ansoff (1965), Alfred Chandler (1962), Peter Drucker (1954), Edith Penrose (1959), Phillip Selznick (1957) and Alfred Sloan (1963).

Defining strategy: reconciling multiple view points

There have been numerous attempts to develop a widely acceptable definition of strategy. But some authors see those as futile efforts because of the sophisti-cated nature of the concept and the dynamic organisational settings in which it is applied. It is virtually impossible to arrive at a single universal definition of strategy that captures all viewpoints and fits all situations. Nonetheless, we witness a core set of characteristics resonating whenever the term is used and interpreted by scholars and practitioners alike. For example, aspects like long-term goals or purpose, pervasiveness, direction and guidance, resource allocation, coordination and control have been portrayed as the key elements that characterise the concept from its very inception. Therefore, we aim at a working definition that will serve the purpose of this chapter. Let us begin with a brief historical overview that captures the following three complementary, overlapping and, in some ways, competing schools of thought.

The early conceptualisations of business strategy and policy, which had their roots in the military practice and economic rationalism, emerged as a formal school of thought with the contributions of a number of writers, as acknowledged earlier. For the convenience of comparison, we call this the *classical school of thought*. The predominant long-standing consensus within this school is that strategy is a set of important decisions derived from a systematic decision-making process conducted at the highest level of an organisation. Accordingly, strategy fell within the responsibility of senior managers and the staff planners who provided analytical support to them. Within the classical school, profit maximising was the key objective of the organisation and it relied on long-term rational planning for achieving that objective through such means as the efficient allocation of resources and controlling through the structure of the organisation. As implied in these interpretations, the strategy process was also conceived as a top-down, controlled, and concerted exercise that resulted in executable strategies.

However, since the inception of a strategy concept within the business domain, numerous other propositions have appeared, both supplementing and challenging the doctrines of the classical school. These contributions emerged as alternative approaches to formal planning, and we shall call this the *traditional school of thought*. Notable aspects associated with this school of thought are a shift in emphasis from prescriptions towards descriptions of strategy (Mintzberg, 1978; Mintzberg and Waters, 1985) and viewing strategy as positioning of the organisation in a target market so as to avert or negate the threat of competitive forces (Porter, 1980). For example, Mintzberg (1978) suggested a definition of strategy emphasising the patterns in a stream of decisions: 'when a sequence of decisions in some area exhibits a consistency over time, a strategy will be considered to have formed' (p. 935).

The third, which we call the *contemporary school of thought*, consists of processual and evolutionary models of strategy as well as integrational frameworks. For instance, Farjoun (2002), by synthesising and extending the ideas of the previous schools of thought, defined strategy as the 'planned or actual coordination of the firm's major goals and actions, in time and space, that continuously co-align the firm with its environment' (p. 570). The central theme in scholarly discussions within this school appears to be the implicit or explicit integration of multiple perspectives, a notable movement away from the previously held fragmented (reductionist) views, towards more holistic frameworks. It also reflects a shift in thinking about the strategy process towards synthesising the prescriptive and descriptive approaches into organic forms that emphasise organisational culture and learning. Proponents of integrative and organic models point out the deficits of fragmented and mechanistic approaches to conceptualising strategy. These models, they argue, are not robust enough to reflect the highly complex and increasingly dynamic attributes and behaviour of the individuals, markets and organisations that form the basis of strategy.

All in all, the above developments represent a shifting identity, perception and treatment of the strategy concept from a science-like (mechanistic–prescriptive) through an art-like (emergent–descriptive) to a craft-like (integrative–organic) perspective.

As previously stated, we settle for a succinct *working definition* of strategy. Based on the works of Frery (2006), Hax (1990) and Hambrick (1980), we assert that:

Strategy is the coherent, unifying and integrative patterns of decisions and actions that determine and/or shape the course of an organisation in its pursuit of sustainable competitive advantage – particularly in terms of identifying and exploiting opportunities, anticipating and dealing with competitive forces and other relevant changes in the business environment, avoiding or minimising unnecessary risks as well as allocating resources and developing organisational competencies.

Thus, strategies could be proactive as well as reactive. They deal with the positioning of an organisation within a particular market and may reveal the desired future status of an organisation. They could exist in the more explicit forms of documented statements, plans, policies, procedures and so on, or implicitly reside in the heads (mental models) of those who make key decisions for the organisation. Similarly, the organisational processes through which strategies develop could also vary, depending on the type of business, the size of the organisation and a number of other factors that will be introduced later.

Strategy and the organisational hierarchy

Organisations evolve over time, for instance, from small, owner-operated start-up businesses to large global corporations. One way of dealing with the increasing level of sophistication that accompanies growth of an organisation is organising it based on formal structures that are usually built around the systems logic. Along a similar line of thought, strategies are also conceptualised in a hierarchical order. As such, strategies may exist at corporate, business unit and business function levels, depending on the size and type of an organisation. For example, for a large multinational corporation, strategies at corporate, strategic business unit and functional levels that deal with the key issues of varying scope can be conceptually organised as shown in Table 5.1.

Table 5.1 Strategy hierarchy based on organisational structure

Hierarchical level	Key questions	Key issues (examples)
Corporate	What business should we be in?	Investment/divestment (portfolio of businesses/investments). Resources acquisition/allocation.
Business unit	How should we compete in each business?	Scope of business activities. Positioning (product-market postures).
Business function (marketing, operations, finance etc.)	How can we contribute to competitive advantage?	Market intelligence/segmentation. System design/technology choice. Investment evaluation/budgeting.

Those organisations that exist as a single business unit may only depict business unit and business function level strategies. Even smaller enterprises that are usually not organised along strict functional specialisations would simply have strategies in the emergent form meaning that most of the time, they reside within the heads of the key decision-makers (for example, entrepreneurial owner-managers). Furthermore, strategies at upper echelons of the hierarchy are intended to serve as an umbrella that guides strategies at the lower echelons, in a cascading style.

Strategy: content, process and context

Strategy has traditionally been studied in terms of process, content and context (though, in reality, they are all intertwined). This means examining the ways in which strategies are formed, their outcomes in various forms and the organisational settings in which they form, along with the interactions among those elements.

In specific terms, the *content* of strategy covers three aspects: the overall goals of the organisation, the scope of strategy and the nature of specific strategies. The goals of the organisation, which can be formally expressed in the form of objective statements or revealed as part of unfolding strategic intent, may also imply desired performance levels. The scope of strategy indicates the span of control and the degree of pervasiveness of strategies pursued at each level. For example, studies of corporate level strategy have typically focused on such issues as diversification, strategic alliances and geographical expansion. The actual strategies formally agreed upon or emerged as patterns in decisions and actions may be studied in numerous forms, such as programs, action plans, strategic archetypes or stages of growth and evolution.

The *process* refers to the mechanisms through which strategies are formed, be they deliberate or emergent, and the way they are realised through implementation via structure, control and change or performance management etc., or as witnessed in the form of a more subtle and evolutionary progression of events.

The *context* of strategy or the organisational setting in which strategies are formed relates to the internal and external organisational contextual factors that shape the content and process of strategy. Anecdotal as well as empirical evidence suggest that strategy process is contingent upon such diverse contextual factors as the nature of the business (product-market aspects), level of competition, organisation size, stage of organisation development or maturity, organisational culture, as well as the personal profile or attributes and the leadership styles of the key decision-makers involved.

Finally, another important aspect that some authors consider the 'linchpin' of strategic management is *organisational performance*. The link between strategy and performance has been the subject of research over a long period of time, and the majority of findings support a strongly positive relationship between the two. It has also been found that the way strategies are formed under the influence of a multitude of internal and external contextual factors does affect the effectiveness of strategies in achieving superior organisation performance.

Box 5.3: Flight Centre Limited

Flight Centre Limited is Australia's largest travel agency business. It has over 1500 stores in nine different countries with about 8000 consultants and support staff.[1] Its sales revenue was about one billion dollars, and total transactions were close to eight billion dollars in 2006.[2] It is currently listed on the Australian Stock Exchange with a market capitalisation of about $1.8 billion.

The company was founded in 1981 by Graham Turner. Prior to this, he ran a successful budget bus travel company in Europe called 'Top Deck'. By 1990, Flight Centre had opened stores in New Zealand, the UK and the US. Operations in the latter two countries were closed in 1991 as a result of travel downturns associated with the first Gulf War. The company expanded to South Africa in 1994 and Canada in 1995. The UK and US operations recommenced in 1995 and 1999 respectively.[3] Further international opportunities in Hong Kong, India and China have been pursued in the last few years.

Flight Centre's business model has been described as follows:

'Flight Centre revolutionised the retailing of international air-travel in Australia by shifting to a model where profitability was driven by volume rather than margins. Initially they built a price advantage by bypassing ticketing wholesalers, seeking out less well-known airlines, and also by arbitraging price differentials across markets.'[4]

As the company grew rapidly, it established different brands to cater to different parts of the travel market. For example, FCm Travel Solutions caters to the corporate market. Similarly, Student Flights and Overseas Working Holidays target the student market. Campus Travel is aimed at the academic and university markets. Flight Centre also runs businesses in the discount holiday organiser segment with brands such as Escape Travel, travelthere.com and quickbeds.com. Other subsidiaries that make up the group include the luxury holiday company Travel Associates and retail cruise specialists Cruiseabout.

For each of these market segments, the subsidiaries provide highly customised services. For example, FCm Travel, which caters to the corporate travel market segment, claims to work closely with clients to manage all aspects of their travel needs, including account management, software configuration and pricing options. FCm works in partnership with travel-related service providers such as airlines, hotel chains and car hire companies nationally, regionally, and internationally so that every aspect of travel is covered fully.

After many successive years of strong growth in revenues and profits, Flight Centre suffered its first ever decline in annual profit in 2005. The stock market punished the company severely with the share price decreasing by 57 per cent from its peak in 2002. Flight Centre was the second worst performing stock in the Australian Stock Exchange's list of top 200 companies. The stock market was reflecting not only concerns about the company's management but also its long-term prospects.

The concern about management related to the confusing leadership of the company. Graham Turner, the founder and long-term CEO, stood down from his position in 2002 to take the position of Executive Chairman. He hoped to focus on long-term strategies. A senior manager from the group was appointed as CEO, with his main job being to take care of day-to-day operations. However, this did not pan out as planned. In 2005, Turner eventually resumed his previous role as the CEO.

From a strategic sense, the company faces some major challenges. Most of these challenges are a consequence of the disintermediation (i.e., the removal of intermediaries in a supply chain) occurring in the travel industry as a result of the Internet. Many travellers are organising their travel by dealing directly with suppliers by going through their websites instead of going through travel agents. In order to deal with this, Flight Centre has created several portals, including quickbeds.com, escapetravel.com.au, flightcentrehotels.com.au and studentflights.com.au. Its flagship website flightcentre.com has been one of the most popular Australian travel agency websites for several years. However, the Internet-based travel industry business is highly fragmented and Flight Centre has had difficulty gaining visibility and traction for its brands in this medium. Reflecting this trend, several airlines including Qantas have announced that they will drastically cut, and in some cases, pay no commissions to travel agents for sales of tickets. To make matters worse, the company has recently been preoccupied with attempts to take it out of the stock market and into private ownership. This attempt involves Turner, who retains 18 per cent of ownership and a private equity firm. So far, the attempt has been unsuccessful, leading to further decline in its stock price. At a time when the industry is undergoing considerable change, there is little doubt that these ownership-related issues are distractive to the running of the company. All these 'troubles' that the company is facing have caused considerable angst amongst shareholders of the firm, leading one financial analysts to put a sell recommendation on the stock in a report titled '*Flightless* Centre'.[5]

Sources
www.flightcentre.com.au
www.wikipedia.com

Notes
1 www.flightcentre.com.au
2 Flight Centre Annual Report 2006. Available from: www.flightcentre.com.au
3 André Sammartino 2007. 'Retail', in H. Dick. and D. Merrett (eds), *The Internationalisation Strategies of Small-Country Firms: The Australian experience of globalisation.* Cheltenham, UK: Edward Elgar, pp. 175–94.
4 Ibid.
5 J. Freed, 'Air agency founder back in hot seat.' *Sydney Morning Herald,* 2 September 2005, www.smh.com.au

Competitive advantage and generic strategies

Competitive advantage rests on an organisation's ability to outperform other similar product and/or service providers in a particular market through consistently offering better products and services in better ways than its competitors do. As the statement suggests, there are three major parties involved in this field of competition:

1. the organisation – its resources, capabilities and value systems, etc.
2. the market (customers) – its structure and needs
3. the competition – its make-up and intensity.

Manoeuvring the forces generated by the interests of these parties for the advantage of the organisation is a huge challenge and there is no one best way of dealing with it. The current practice suggests that different organisations with varying resource bases, capabilities and value systems may pursue different strategies to serve different markets and still be successful and remain competitive.

However, during the formative stages of strategic management as a field of study, it was believed that an organisation could enhance and sustain its competitiveness through the efficient deployment of resources alone. This view would have certainly been influenced by the mass production mentality prevailing at the time. The idea was that high volume or large batch production of standard goods resulted in lower costs or prices. Dramatic shifts later witnessed in the business environment showed that the challenge was much bigger than that. Organisations were now facing deregulated markets, changed customer preferences and increased competition (particularly against the backdrop of the post-World War II success of Japanese organisations).

Today, it is widely agreed that the competition is also about choosing the right markets and business activities, wisely exploiting new market opportunities, matching organisation capabilities with market needs as well as configuring business processes and mobilising resources in a way that averts or negates competitive threats. This contemporary view is informed by what were originally proposed as two quite contrasting perspectives on the sources of competitive advantage: market-based and resource-based views.

Market-based view of competition

The market-based view has its primary focus on the external environment (market/industry dynamics) and attempts to position the organisation so as to gain full advantage from market imperfections or heterogeneity. The essence of this approach is carefully choosing what to do and what not to do, and then supporting the chosen activities through appropriate investments and allocation of resources, etc. According to Michael Porter (1996), strategic positioning is 'performing different activities from rivals' or performing similar activities in different ways' (p. 62).

Porter (1980) identified five basic competitive forces that determine the attractiveness of an industry with respect to the profit-earning potential of an organisation located within that industry. He advocated that organisations should learn how to cope with and influence these forces in order to remain competitive. Despite other more recent advancements in the field of strategic management, Porter's five forces model (as depicted in Figure 5.1) is still considered to be a useful analytical tool for understanding positioning advantage and industry dynamics.

Resource-based view of competition

The resource-based view of competitive advantage is built on the premise that organisations' heterogeneous and relatively immobile resource endowments are the primary determinants of competitive advantage. The resource-based approach to competition involves identifying the organisation's internal resources and capabilities, assessing their profit-earning potential and exploiting those resources and capabilities for the sustainable advantage of the organisation. Market intelligence and technology foresight, customer interaction and strategic partnering, organisational culture and learning, internal resources and dynamic capabilities are all considered to be the key elements of the resource-based approach. The notion of core competencies as

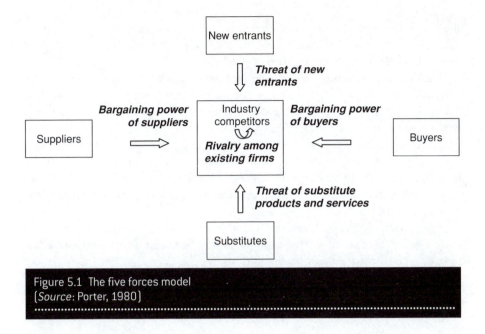

a key source of competitive advantage further reinforces the central argument of the resource-based view.

Thus, competitive advantage is more about being different than being on top of the productivity frontier, be it resource-based or market-based. If you can avoid head-on confrontation with your rivals and still win the customers to grow your market share, then that would often be considered the smartest way to outperform your competition. This may look hypothetical, but there are businesses, big and small, that thrive on this approach. For example, this is just what organisations are trying to achieve when they follow differentiation or focus strategies, as will be discussed later in this section.

Box 5.4: IKEA: different from the rest

IKEA makes both its tangible offering and the service experience for consumers different from others with whom it competes. IKEA operates a truly global supply chain, sourcing its products in low-cost countries and moving over 10,000 stock keeping units (often called 'SKUs' meaning items that it sells) around the world from over 40 source countries through a global set of warehouses to some 150 stores in most major regions of the world.

With only a small number of distinctive stores in even major cities, IKEA offers a unique shopping experience. IKEA is uniquely positioned, with inexpensive, yet modern design and styling built into its products. The supply chain is focused on efficiency and low cost in order to support the 'inexpensive' part of the value proposition. Even the flat-packed goods and the self-assembly are in-synch with the rest of the strategy. Communication with customers is the same the world over: catalogues, which are not usually seen by consumers as 'junk' mail to be thrown away, but rather to be kept and used as needed.

IKEA has a lean culture, and people are respected, rewarded and promoted for what they achieve, not what their job title is. The lean culture is symbolised and led by the global CEO, who even as one of the world's richest men, flies the world in economy class!

IKEA's stores are an experience themselves, not just a place to go and do a simple shopping transaction. Women in particular, who IKEA know are the most important people in those categories of goods, love the IKEA experience. IKEA does very extensive and detailed market research to support every one of its marketing moves, store design, etc.

In summary, IKEA's business strategy, operations and supply chain, culture and market orientation are all driving a unique point of strategic difference that has led to lasting market success and profitability.

See www.ikea.com

Market-driving vs market-driven organisations

The marketing and strategy literature captures two types of market orientation reflected in the strategic behaviour of organisations: market-driven and market-driving. Market-driven organisations seek to gain a competitive edge by understanding and best catering to current or future market needs. This is achieved through the careful analysis of markets and accommodating the voice of customers. Established multinational corporations like Nestlé, Proctor & Gamble and Unilever fall into this category (Kumar et al., 2000). However, the competitive behaviour of these organisations is driven by currently held best-practice models, implying that market-driven organisations rarely attempt to change the existing structure of markets or the competitive norms. This approach can be static, too reactive and inadequate in an increasingly competitive business environment. A more dynamic and innovative approach may be warranted.

In contrast, market-driving organisations seek to proactively influence the market and competitor behaviour by manipulating the existing norms to their advantage. Organisations like Amazon.com, IKEA and Starbucks have been hailed as prime examples of market-driving organisations (Kumar et al., 2000). These organisations often capitalise on opportunities created by shifting customer preferences and technological breakthroughs that redefine industry boundaries and existing patterns of competitor behaviour.

Informed by particular market orientations, organisations may pursue alternative approaches to competition and customer value creation, as well as the design of operations systems.

Generic competitive strategies

Porter (1980, 1985) originally proposed three generic competitive strategies that organisations should choose from for creating and sustaining
competitive advantage, namely, cost leadership, differentiation, and focus.
He warned of the perils of losing focus by being everything to everyone and
called it the 'stuck-in-the middle' situation.

Cost Leadership, the most common form of generic strategy, attempts to
outperform competition through offering the lowest price based on efficient
cost structures. Primarily, this can be achieved through structures and processes that reinforce economies of scale and steeper learning curves where
standardised products (with acceptable quality) in high volumes succeed in
large markets. Other sources of cost leadership may include low-cost material
and labour, efficient distribution networks and process technology. However,
if there is more than one organisation pursuing this strategy in an industry,
competition could be head-on and sometimes fierce, particularly when barriers to entry are relatively weak. But it is anticipated that organisations can still
earn above-average returns as long as there is a sizeable market to maintain
scale economies for each competitor. Wal-Mart is an example of a successful
competitor in this space, with Kmart being less successful. Coles and Woolworths supermarkets in Australia attempt to achieve low cost positioning.
We note that such organisations often communicate their positioning as
'everyday low prices'.

Differentiation, as a generic strategy, aims at winning customer loyalty
through the perceived uniqueness of product/service offerings. Within this
approach, the options or the bases for differentiation could be many and
varied depending on the capabilities of the organisation and the characteristics of the target markets. This strategy, which is primarily based on the
economies of scope, attempts to move away from competing based on price
by delivering a unique value proposition appealing to those customers who
are assumed to be less price sensitive compared to those catered to through
the previous approach. This allows the organisation to enjoy a higher margin of profit on those differentiated products/services. Within this approach,
head-on confrontation is minimal, because the competition is fought among
specific value propositions. BMW, Porsche, and Rolls Royce fit this category,
as does Chanel perfume.

Both of the above approaches rely on relatively large markets and treat
them rather indiscriminately, whereas the third generic strategy focuses on
small niche markets. The segmentation could be based on geographic, demographic or speciality needs and the aim is to cater to each small customer
base more efficiently and effectively than other competitors do. *Focus* strategies are quite popular among small organisations operating in geographically
isolated markets or those organisations serving market segments that large

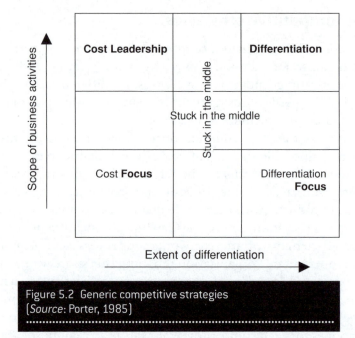

Figure 5.2 Generic competitive strategies
(*Source*: Porter, 1985)

organisations are unable to serve or not interested in catering to. Within this strategy, market penetration can be achieved through either low cost or differentiation. Focus is all about specialisation in some form. The essence of Porter's ideas is summarised in Figure 5.2.

There are many examples to illustrate the applications of generic strategies: no-frills airlines, budget motels and generic-brand products all follow cost leadership. Products and services that carry reputed brand names (could be as diverse as consumer electronics, clothing, footwear, personal care and industrial goods), leading consultancy, financial and law firms, business class air travel, up-market restaurants, luxury hotels, are all examples of organisations following differentiation strategies.

Your local professional or legal practice, hairdresser, as well as most small businesses serving niche markets may follow a focus strategy.

Although the exclusivity of the above strategies is no longer held strongly in practice, they still have significant implications for designing and managing operations systems, as will be revealed in the next section of this chapter.

The strategic approach to operations: key concepts

Earlier in the book, we introduced operations as one of the three main functional areas of an organisation. Now, we claim that it is, in fact, more than that; operations is the *critical mass* of any organisation – be it a profit-seeking enterprise, public sector agency or a not-for-profit entity. If business-level strategy is concerned with the ways of achieving and sustaining competitive advantage as acknowledged in the previous section, operations is *the* part of the business that can actually make it happen – by way of creating and delivering products or services that satisfy customer needs. Of course, people in the operations area would like to become aware of new market opportunities, information about competitors' product or service offerings and, more importantly, customer needs, when designing products and services. Similarly, customers would like to know what an organisation has to offer, particularly the utility and attributes of alternative product or service offerings available in the market when they make a purchase decision. Therefore, the dynamic role played by marketing in the whole process of linking customers and markets to operations is indispensable. So is the role of finance, which manages the all-important flow of funds. However, our attention in this chapter will be limited to the strategic role of operations.

As pointed out in Chapter 1, the operations function holds the ownership of the core transformation processes and manages the vast majority of the value-adding activities taking place within an organisation. It also accounts for the bulk of an organisation's resources, be they people, facilities, technology or knowledge and skills. It is through the diligent and skilful deployment of these resources and capabilities (as embedded in various organisational activities), guided and conditioned by strategy and organisational values, that an organisation creates and sustains its competitive advantage. However, historically, the role of operations in contributing to the competitive advantage had not been well-recognised at the corporate level. It was through the relentless efforts of Professor Wickham Skinner from the Harvard University, who pioneered the cause of manufacturing policy, later known as 'manufacturing strategy', that this issue was first brought to light. Skinner laid the foundation for the whole body of knowledge that we share today as 'operations strategy'. Skinner's work, elaborated and further refined by his colleagues Robert Hayes, Steven Wheelwright and Roger Schmenner (Hayes, 2002), articulated the link between operations decisions and corporate strategy, as well as the nature and the significance of strategic decisions and actions that fall within the domain of operations. Some of the concepts he introduced will be discussed in this chapter, along with other more recent developments in the area.

Strategic operations decision areas

Operations systems consisting of facilities, plant and equipment, as well as people and processes, could be classed as socio-technical systems. Business decisions regarding the design and operation of such systems deal with hardware-related issues such as the location of facilities, choice of technology and capacity of plants, as well as such soft issues as management and control

Table 5.2 Strategic Operations decision areas

Structural decisions	Infrastructural decisions
System capacity: planning, addition . . .	Operations planning and control: policies/procedures
Facilities: location, layout . . .	Organisation: structure, culture . . .
Process positioning/vertical integration	Workforce: attributes, skill levels . . .
System design/process selection	Quality: systems, practices . . .
Technology: choice, acquisition . . .	

of business processes, training and motivation of employees, development of capabilities, and implementation of new technology.

You might have already noticed that the scope of these decisions and actions is, in part, what sets apart a functional strategy from its business and corporate level counterparts. Skinner classified these decisions into two categories: structural and infrastructural, as listed in Table 5.2. Over time, these decisions, often conditioned by business-level strategy, current skill levels of employees, organisational values and managerial styles, etc., shape the character and capabilities of the operations system, which will eventually determine its ability to support the business-level strategy. In addition, most of these decisions are considered to be irreversible, meaning that it would be very costly to fix any problems caused by a poor decision at a later stage.

Operations' contribution to competitive advantage

Businesses may enhance their competitiveness, vis-à-vis competitors, in a number of ways: improving productivity, application of advanced technology, developing new knowledge and capabilities, through product and process innovation, and the list goes on. But most of the contemporary discussions revolve around the concept of *customer value creation*. Potential customers evaluate alternative products or services that are available in the market based on their *utility*, a term that comes from economics. Utility as a value determinant reflects the benefits derived from consuming or possessing a product or service. Customers (business or retail) all have their own particular utility functions, meaning their own sets of tastes, preferences and values, and their own position of a unique purchasing power, disposable income, etc.

For example, for some customers, it could be the superior quality of the product and customer service that matter most when making a purchase decision, whereas for others, it could be the quicker delivery of the product or service and convenience. Yet another group of customers would be happy with a reasonable level of functional value offered by a product, but make their purchase decision primarily based on the (lower) price and availability. This does not necessarily mean that customers who make their purchasing decision based on one or two key value determinants are ignoring all other attributes. They still expect other attributes of a product or service to be satisfactory. This is just a way of acknowledging that markets exist in a set of market segments, across which the dimensions that are valued by customers differ. We assume that within a market segment, consumer tastes (and hence utility functions) are similar, and between market segments, they are significantly different.

Hill (1989) coined the terms 'order qualifiers' and 'order winners' to illustrate this concept. *Order qualifiers* are the product or service characteristics that help them to go onto a customer's short-list, whereas *order winners* are those characteristics that are perceived by potential customers as superior to competitors' offerings and hence convince them to buy the product or service. Qualifying characteristics are necessary but not sufficient for a product or service to gain entry into a market and stay there. Both order qualifiers and order winners are market specific and do change over time. Therefore, Hill argued that organisations must identify order-winning and order-qualifying criteria for each market they target or serve and develop and sustain those product and service characteristics on an ongoing basis.

From an operations perspective, *customer value* is defined as a function of performance-related parameters of a product or service, such as quality, delivery speed, service level, etc., and the price at which they are delivered. For the benefit of those who are adept in quantitative analysis, the relationship between those parameters can be expressed using the following formulae (Melnyk and Denzler, 1996):

$$\text{Customer Value} = \frac{\text{Performance}}{\text{Price}}$$

$$\text{Customer Value} = \frac{f[\text{Quality, delivery, flexibility, service, etc.}]}{\text{Price}}$$

As such, organisations can enhance customer value by way of improving product or service performance in terms of one or more of the value determinants, reducing the cost of delivering a certain level of performance or some combinations of both. In Porter's (1996) terms:

> it [the organisation] must deliver greater value to customers or create comparable value at a lower cost, or do both . . . delivering greater value allows a company to charge higher average unit prices; greater efficiency results in lower average unit costs'. (p. 62)

This depicts the essence of operations' contribution to competitive advantage! Operations can greatly contribute to both the numerator and denominator of the above expression to drive value creation as will be further discussed in the next section.

In practice, customer value is created through various activities undertaken as part of the transformation process, which, in turn, is the core of any operations system. Therefore, an organisation's ability to deliver customer value in the forms discussed above depends, to a large degree, on the capabilities and other characteristics of its operations system.

Competitive priorities

In line with the generic competitive strategies discussed earlier and considering the concept of value creation introduced above, operations' contribution to competitive advantage can be ratified using the notion of competitive priorities. In essence, competitive priorities establish the conceptual link between business-level and business function-level strategies.

Building on Skinner's (1969) original work that defined manufacturing task and based on their own earlier work, Hayes and Wheelwright (1984) articulated four competitive priorities: cost, quality, delivery and flexibility, as strategic preferences or the ways in which an organisation chooses to compete in the market (you may readily recognise that these priorities relate to the key value determinants outlined earlier). Later contributions by a number of other authors have expanded this list, while some have adapted and interpreted the concept in slightly different formats. The widely cited competitive priorities, along with illustrative examples, are presented in Table 5.3.

If differentiation at the business-unit level is achieved through positioning, as discussed before, differentiation at the functional level is achieved through the operationalisation of those competitive priorities. This means, by choosing to configure the operations system to support a particular set of competitive priorities, an organisation can offer a customer value profile that is unique or rare within a target market. However, the appropriate set of priorities must be determined based on a sound understanding of the characteristics and needs of target markets and the profile and capabilities of operations processes.

The concept of trade-offs in operations

An organisation may not opt to or be able to maximise customer value along all of these dimensions simultaneously, due to a variety of reasons. This proposition is often explained using the concept of trade-offs. Most organisations have limited resources in terms of money, staff and time, etc., which they strive to utilise wisely so as to maximise the return on investment for the whole business. Thus, when it comes to investing in operations systems, it often becomes an issue of choosing between alternatives, for example, hiring extra tellers at the bank branch office and training existing staff or increasing the research and development budget and upgrading plant and

Table 5.3 Competitive priorities

Priority	Dimensions (sample only)	Examples
Price	Lowest price	No-frills airlines, generic-brand products
	Competitive Price	An order qualifier for most products/services
Quality	Consistent (conformance) quality	An order qualifier for most products/services
	Superior (high) quality	Prestige cars, up-market restaurants
Delivery (time)	Faster delivery (speed)	Courier service, express post
	On-time delivery (reliability)	Trade services, air-transport/travel
Flexibility	Volume flexibility (demand-based)	Contract manufacturing/packaging
	Variety flexibility/customisation	Auto-supermarkets/professional services
Service	Pre-/Post-sales service	Automobiles, white goods
	Convenience/availability	Service stations, ATMs, supermarkets

equipment – and all of these things add cost. These compromises are central to managerial decision-making, although most of the time, managers may commit to them intuitively. So, the general argument is that most organisations are not in a position to invest in improving all aspects of their operations so as to excel in all dimensions of quality, delivery, cost and flexibility, etc., simultaneously.

A deeper understanding of this trade-offs concept can be developed through examining the inherent technical limitations associated with the design of operations systems. For instance, an operations system designed for producing high-volume, low-cost products may not be able to offer the flexibility required to produce customised products. That explains, in part, why fast-food outlets like McDonald's cannot and do not offer the full menu services available at up-market restaurants (or vice-versa), even if they would like to do so. McDonald's does not generally customise to specific customer needs, (e. g., 'please cook it medium-rare'), which other restaurants do.

Box 5.5: Trade-offs in action

Let's examine the classic example of producing custom-made wooden furniture vs standard furniture. Customised furniture typically targets high-value markets and competes based on superior quality (craftsmanship) and flexibility (customisation). For such products, high quality and flexibility are order winners, while price could still be an order qualifier (competitive prices).

The production of customised furniture requires an operations process with sufficient flexibility, for example, consisting of general-purpose machines or tools, highly skilled workforce (craftspersons) and may use high-quality material (more expensive varieties of wood). In contrast, standard furniture usually caters to low-value markets where price and availability act as order winners and consistent quality would be an order qualifier. Therefore, to be able to offer the lowest possible price, standardised furniture is best produced in high volumes using machinery and equipment that provide the advantages of scale economies (mass production, semi-skilled labour, automation, etc.). This type of production allows for planning of resources ahead of time and standardised furniture-making processes so that a limited choice at the lowest possible price with a short, predictable delivery time can be offered.

Now, if one wants to produce both custom-made and standard furniture on the same system, would one be able to maintain the same level of performance with regard to price, quality and delivery time? The answer is probably not, and that is because the production system designed for one product type may not have the specific types of facilities, capabilities and resources demanded by the other, as well as the flexibility required to deal with the resultant patterns of demand. As a result, service levels may suffer, become more prone to missing delivery targets and find it difficult to maintain consistent quality. Perhaps, one might end up not doing anything exceptionally well – 'stuck in the middle'. This would likely result in wins in both segments of the furniture market to the specialists, who are only trying to do one thing particularly well.

This does not necessarily mean that one should give up one option altogether in favour of the other. Rather, it highlights the need to consider and address the trade-offs at the early stage of designing operations systems, so that one can come up with the most desirable product–process configuration – a plant within a plant?

In fact, much of the work of the early writers such as Skinner, Hayes and Wheelwright focused on this trade-off issue and their solution to it – the 'focused factory' concept. Skinner (1974) advocated a focused approach to capability development along one or two carefully selected priorities, based on their relative importance in supporting the desired business strategy. However, empirical evidence has since led a number of scholars to challenge this proposition. In particular, puzzled by the post-World War II success of Japanese manufacturing organisations on multiple dimensions, researchers looked for new ways of exploring and explaining the trade-offs concept. They also came up with a few alternative answers.

Technology and the trade-offs concept

One quite plausible explanation was the application of technology. It is widely agreed that technology helps to deliver customer value by positively influencing the determinants of quality, speed, flexibility and cost. But more convincingly, advanced process technologies such as flexible manufacturing systems (FMS) are known to have improved quality and flexibility, while at the same time driving down costs. Today, the applications of technology in the new product development area (rapid prototyping, engineering analysis, concurrent engineering, and other design concepts and technologies) and their contributions in the areas of quality, time-to-market, etc., are quite obvious. Improved decision-making, reduced inventory levels and quick response times achieved through the deployment of information technology and enterprise resource planning systems, etc., are other technology applications that have helped many organisations to achieve world-class or best-practice levels of performance on multiple frontiers. However, technology can easily become a management cop-out if not selected and introduced wisely.

If one takes a comprehensive contextual view of technology, it can be argued that products are, in fact, physical manifestations of technological capabilities which, when combined with other resources and organisation-specific routines, will generate the unique (core) competencies required to support a portfolio of products and services (with order-winning characteristics) that create a sustainable competitive advantage for the organisation.

Box 5.6: Value creation: a metaphorical analysis

Using a large tree as a metaphor, Prahalad and Hamel (1990) drew an interesting parallel between the roots of the tree and the core competencies of an organisation: the corporation, like the tree, grows from its roots; core products (trunk and major limbs) are nourished by competencies and engender business units, whose fruits are end products' (p. 81). Let's extend this analogy a little further in an attempt to paint a more complete picture of the value creation process at the organisation level.

First, if we look at the root system in terms of sub-roots and rootlets that draw nourishment from surrounding soil, we can also account for the capabilities and resources. If the main roots represent core competencies, then the sub-roots and rootlets would represent capabilities and resources. Then, we can draw a reasonable comparison between the plant-specific features of the root system; the size, spread, penetration capacity, etc. and the organisation-specific attributes of the core competencies; their ability to contribute to unique value propositions.

Second, we may treat the organisational activities that create products and services as equivalent to the organic or chemical processes such as photosynthesis that convert the nutrients and other intakes (such as water and energy from sunlight) into food that fuels growth and fertilisation that produces fruits.

However, it appears that a minor adjustment to the analogy is needed in order to fully appreciate the major contributors to the value creation process. Although it might not be the ideal metaphorical analysis, we would like to compare the leaves and other green parts to the productive elements of the business unit, ones like the operations system, where the actual value-adding takes place. This would perhaps help us to illustrate how different activities that use particular combinations of capabilities, resources and organisation-specific routines create value with varying degrees of success. Then we can see why organisations of different type located in different places, produce different types of products or services with different attributes and appeals to different groups of customers with varying tastes.

The 'sand cone' model

Taking a logical and cumulative approach to capability-building is considered to be another useful way of minimising or even eliminating the trade-offs effect in operations. This proposition, put forward by Ferdows and De Meyer (1990) as the 'sand-cone' model, explores the complementarities that exist among priorities, and argues that existing capabilities in one area can reinforce capability building in the other area if they are developed in a particular sequence. Comparing the operating practices of organisations in Europe, North America and Japan, Ferdows and De Meyer suggested that this order should be quality, dependability, speed or flexibility and cost as illustrated in Figure 5.3.

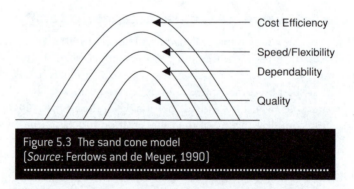

Cost Efficiency

Speed/Flexibility

Dependability

Quality

Figure 5.3 The sand cone model
(*Source*: Ferdows and de Meyer, 1990)

A number of other authors have further explored various aspects of this trade-offs model through both conceptual analysis and empirical studies, and have made valuable contributions to enhancing our understanding of the dynamics and limitations of the concept. Overall, though the findings do not appear to be conclusive, there is general consensus on and empirical support for the cumulative model. These insights are particularly useful for operations managers in their choice and prioritisation of improvement programs so as to build capabilities that support business-level strategies over time.

Defining operations strategy

We have already explored the role of operations and its contribution to competitive advantage. If the strategic role of operations is to contribute to the organisation's competitive advantage through creating superior customer value, then, operations strategy is about the ways the organisation develops and deploys its resources so as to create a unique customer value proposition. Now, let us consider some of the formal definitions and associated interpretations available in the literature towards carving a definition of operations strategy that is suitable for our purpose.

The early conceptualisations of operations strategy that drew upon the central ideas of Skinner (1969, 1971, 1974) were heavily biased toward the top-down planning approach to strategic management prevailing at the time. However, the potential pitfalls of adopting such a biased view were brought to light soon afterwards, and the subsequent work of a number of authors recognised the emergent aspects of operations strategy as well. For instance, Wheelwright (1984) emphasised that the 'pattern of structural decisions over time' constitutes 'the manufacturing strategy of a business unit' (p. 85) and 'not what is said or written in annual reports or planning documents' (p. 30).

Hayes and Wheelwright (1984), in their four-stage framework, clearly articulated the big-picture scenario for understanding the evolving strategic role of operations within an organisation. The framework identified four stages (Table 5.4) on a continuum starting with a 'most passive and least progressive' to a 'most aggressive and progressive' roles (p. 396).

While, for numerous reasons, the operations function of an organisation may occupy a particular position on this continuum at a given time, the most innovative and pioneering organisations have thrived on a stage-4 type contribution from operations. For example, most of the organisations mentioned earlier in this chapter as examples of market-driving organisations have developed their innovative business models based on operations' strengths; a stage-4 type contribution. By comparison, business models of leading market-driven organisations mentioned would, arguably, reflect a stage-3 type contribution from operations. This means that organisations, in general, should strive to move up the ladder towards achieving a stage-4 type contribution from operations.

While acknowledging the challenge of reconciling multiple perspectives and varying interests, we offer the following definition:

> *Operations strategy* is the conditional and consistent patterns of decisions and actions regarding the operations structure and infrastructure of an organisation that determine and/or shape the resources, capabilities and work routines of its operations system in supporting a set of competitive priorities (explicit and/or implicit) agreed upon at the business-unit level.

We propose this as a *working definition* that falls in line with the broader view of organisation-level strategy presented earlier in this chapter. Thus, the

Table 5.4 Stages in the evolution of operations' strategic role

Stage-4: Externally Supportive *pursue an operations-based* *competitive advantage*	Anticipate the potential of operations practices/technologies. Operations is involved in marketing/engineering decisions. Long-range programs to acquire capabilities ahead of needs.
Stage-3: Internally Supportive *provide credible support to the* *business strategy*	Operations investments are aligned with business strategy. Changes in business strategy are translated to operations. Longer-term operations issues are systematically addressed.
Stage-2: Externally Neutral *achieve parity with competitors*	Industry practice is followed. Planning horizons for operations fall in line with business cycles. Capital investments as the primary means of achieving competitive advantage.
Stage-1: Internally Neutral *minimise operations' negative* *potential*	Use of external experts to solve operations issues. Internal management controls as primary means of monitoring operations performance.

(*Source*: Hayes and Wheelwright, 1984)

emphasis on patterns of decisions and actions, as against programs and action plans, implies both deliberate and emergent perspectives of strategy. Also implied in this definition is the role and scope of operations strategy that establish its link to the business unit-level strategy. For instance, within a more formal and systematic approach to strategy, an agreement on competitive priorities is reached at the business unit-level. As part of this exercise, operations should articulate its strategic contribution to business unit-level strategy (preferably, in terms of the four-stages above) and garner the support of other functions for the same. This will then serve as the overarching framework for guiding decisions and actions within operations that support capability building as well as value creation based on agreed competitive priorities.

Box 5.7: Strategy as patterns in decisions and actions

Lexcon, a leading manufacturer of a certain building services product in Australia, with an annual turnover exceeding $A70 million, is currently undergoing healthy growth. Its products are competing against reputed brands, mainly those of the Southeast Asian manufacturing giants. The products are competing based on superior quality (including technical capabilities and product features) and customer service backed up by a strong after-sales product support and an extended warranty scheme.

In the absence of an explicit business strategy or an operations strategy in the documented form, its overall strategic direction is set by the Managing Director (MD) and other directors. In the past, senior managers' decisions and actions have been guided by the future business scenarios established and agreed upon at the monthly business development meetings (BDM). However, decisions and actions regarding structural and infrastructural aspects of operations could be initiated at any level of the business from the MD to the supervisors.

For example, the MD initiated a major decision to relocate and upgrade the company's facilities/plant and was personally involved in the execution of this over a period of 18 months. The Manufacturing Manager (MM) took the initiative to purchase a new production line after realising that manufacturing's capacity to fulfil future demand (as indicated by sales targets established at the BDM) was inadequate. This initiative then progressed in collaboration with the Research and Development Manager (RDM) to the stage where it was sanctioned by the MD after considering a formal capital expenditure proposal. Another decision to create a new staff position at the warehouse was initiated by the Logistics Supervisor (LS) and slowly progressed in an interactive fashion with support from the Logistics and Procurement Manager (LPM) until formal approval was granted by the MD. Yet another decision to change the inventory control policy was initiated by the LS and was actioned soon after the agreement of the LPM.

None of these initiatives appeared to have been informed by an explicit understanding of the role of competitive priorities or the concept of trade-offs discussed earlier in this chapter. But the company's strategic decisions and actions set out a clear pattern in which actions and decisions of varying scope and significance were progressed in a fairly orderly manner. The consistent success (performance) and continuing growth of the business also suggest that this approach has so far worked well for this company. Nonetheless, a few recent initiatives undertaken by the MD (hiring of three senior managers from outside to lead the finance, marketing and operations functions and engaging an external consultant to look into strategic issues) indicate that this company is moving towards embracing a formal planning approach to strategy.

Operations strategy: content, process and context

If operations strategy is defined as above, then we can conceptualise the content, process and context of it in the same way as we did with the organisation-level strategy. Operations strategy *content* is about the types of strategies (policies, choices, plans and actions) deployed by the operations function in supporting the competitive strategy of the business. Literature on operations strategy content deals with two key aspects: the choice of competitive priorities and the strategic decision areas as introduced earlier. However, compared to organisation-level strategy, operations strategy may be less explicit in that it often does not exist in documented form. Instead, operations strategies are often captured as consistent patterns in decisions and actions (such as improvement initiatives and capital investments) regarding the operations structure and infrastructure of an organisation.

The *process* aspect of operations strategy has traditionally been examined using the top-down rational planning model popularised by the business strategy scholars. This formulate-then-implement type approach starts with identifying operations objectives that support overall business goals and evaluation of current capabilities and resources, along with an assessment of their ability to meet those objectives. It then attempts to find ways of bridging any gaps between the current and expected levels of operations performance so as to meet the set objectives. This approach corresponds to the popular SWOT (strengths-weaknesses-opportunities-threats) analysis used in the development of business unit-level strategy. Strategies so developed are realised through the allocation of additional resources, improved practices and restructuring of the operations system so as to improve the fit and alignment with business as well as other functional strategies. Underlying this whole process is a series of interrelated decisions and actions that revolve around identifying trade-offs, setting priorities, making informed judgements and choices which form part of the core of managerial undertakings. An emergent view of strategy formation recognises the consistent patterns in these decisions and actions as operations strategy.

Operations managers make such decisions situated within the larger *context* of the organisation and its business environment. That means their decisions and actions are conditioned by what is happening within the business (for example, goals and expectations of other functional areas such as marketing and finance) as well as outside the business (for example, competitor initiatives and changing market needs). Therefore, it is important that operations decisions and actions are internally consistent and coherent on their own, as well as across other functional areas, and are aligned with the overall business strategy. Ideally, they also need to be congruent with and contingent upon the specific, but often evolving organisational settings. Further, compared to organisation-level strategy development, the scope of operations management decision-making is limited and the impact of some external forces would be less relevant, due to the expectation that they should have already been dealt with at the business-unit level.

Nonetheless, strategy formation in practice is not an orderly, logical and neatly hierarchical process. On the one hand, managers (operations, marketing or general) are always alert to what's happening outside the organisation – be it competitor moves, regulatory pressure or market opportunities. On the other hand, their work is constrained by a multitude of internal factors – be they budgetary provisions, top management's expectations and personalities, workforce character, organisational culture and so on. There is also the possibility that managers may act in self-interest. Moreover, managers act under pressure of sometimes conflicting demands. For instance, developing operations capabilities for the long haul is a noble goal of operations strategy, but this has to be weighed against increasing pressure to maximise the short-term bottom-line performance, and often against the backdrop of fierce competition. So, managers' decisions are either consciously or subconsciously affected by a large number of factors. In practice, it's a case of having an articulated and agreed operations strategy and 'chipping away' in real time, or as some operations managers have expressed it: 'In real time its one step forward, half a step backwards, maybe a step sideways and then hopefully another step forward . . .'

To fully benefit from having a concept of operations strategy, it needs to be widely discussed while it is being formulated, including by general managers and marketing managers, and then it needs to be widely disseminated or published so that all and sundry can commit to playing their part in implementing it.

Finally, like its business-level counterpart, *operations performance* is measured in terms of its ability to support an agreed set of competitive priorities. Typical measures include product or service quality, delivery speed and reliability, productivity, inventory turnover, new product development cycle time (time-to-market) and the number of order change requests accommodated. The strategic approach to operations management advocates the development of performance measures to reinforce both short-term and long-term objectives of operations, activity-based costing in place of traditional cost accounting as well as performance management systems that incorporate a whole enterprise perspective. One should clearly focus the measurement on what is important to the strategy, meaning particularly the order winners!

Operations strategy in practice

Despite all the intellectually compelling arguments supporting the concept of operations strategy and the prescriptive guidelines available for its formulation and implementation, it still appears that many operations managers are not adept at the operationalisation of these concepts. Possible reasons for this lack of adoption and diffusion of scholarly contributions among practitioners are many and varied.

Many operations management scholars identify the way operations systems have evolved over the past as a major cause of this problem. Deep-rooted issues covering aspects as diverse as people and their attitudes, operations structure and infrastructure and organisational practices have been comprehensively treated in the works of leading authors like Hill (1989), Skinner (1985) and Hayes and Wheelwright (1984). Another widely held view is that the currently available models of operations strategy and associated prescriptions do not adequately reflect what is happening in practice: they are too simplistic, too rational and highly abstract, and, therefore, not very useful to practising managers. With a view to providing some insights into the alternative forms of operations strategy in practice, we turn now to key findings of recent research in the area.

Major improvement programs as operations strategy

Many empirical studies have shown that a formal documented operations strategy is far from reality. A quite obvious trend evident in the recent past is that many organisations indiscriminately adopt major improvement programs (such as total quality management, just-in-time or lean operations, and six-sigma) rather than taking a comprehensive and systematic approach to formulating and implementing an operations strategy as advocated in many textbooks. Consequently, a new stream of research has begun to examine the choice of major improvement programs, or best practices and their contribution to operations performance. This is clearly a shift away from following the popular formal planning route or the tracking of consistent patterns in operations decisions and actions as the basis of operations strategy. The popular improvement programs that have proved their potential through the experiences of high-performing world-class organisations are assumed to be internally consistent, but the challenge still remains with the selection of those off-the-shelf type programs so as to align with the overall business-level strategy and to fit with the unique organisational settings. Moreover, authors like Hayes and Pisano (1994) and Skinner (1988) have questioned the whole notion of using the so-called best practices and techniques in place of a comprehensive operations strategy.

Specific organisational practices as operations strategy

Other empirical studies have examined the use of specific organisational practices such as benchmarking, continuous improvements or incremental innovations, outsourcing or off-shoring, quality function deployment, workforce empowerment, gain-sharing and the adoption of advanced technology as the basis for enhancing competitiveness. For instance, several publications reporting on the operations strategies of manufacturing organisations in Australia and New Zealand have focused on aspects like continuous improvement, specific operations practices and the adoption of new technology and their contribution to operations performance. Most of these specific organisational practices are too narrowly focused and do not appear to substantially address operations strategy in a wholistic and meaningful way.

Entrepreneurial initiatives as operations strategy

There are many organisations (particularly smaller firms) that are success-ful but have not shown themselves to have adopted major improvement programs, a coherent set of specific organisational practices or a rational planning approach to strategy. Most of the time, small organisations operat-ing in niche markets are rarely organised around functional specialisations and they do not usually have specialist staff and other resources required for formal planning. They are also not likely to embrace the off-the-shelf solution packages, given their financial capacity and the scale of operations. Their competitive success is best described by their innovative capacity and behaviour that is primarily driven by the entrepreneurial characteristics or culture and personal aspirations of their owners.

These observations reflect the alternative manifestations of what we called the 'content' of operations strategy, and the challenges associated with the development and deployment of a universal model of operations strategy. Therefore, it is imperative that our conceptual understanding of operations strategy is supplemented with an exposure to what is available in the form of empirical evidence in the area.

Operations strategy process in practice

Similar results have also been reported in some recent empirical studies into the process of operations strategy. Swamidass et al. (2001), captured three evolving alternatives to the popular top-down planning approach used in operations strategy development, namely, a coherent pattern of actions, major improvement programs and the pursuit of core operating capabilities. For instance, a consistent pattern of incremental decisions and actions repre-sented stepwise but focused investments in the operations system aimed at meeting specific competitive priorities. Barnes (2002) found that operations strategy is formed through a complex process of managerial interpretation under the influence of a range of individual, cultural and political factors. Kiridena (2005) developed a process model of operations strategy captur-ing four key phases and multiple modes of initiation and progression of strategic decisions and actions. The study revealed that strategic initiatives are triggered by factors as diverse as the personal aspirations of owners and managers, operational problems, market opportunities, and technological breakthroughs.

These findings provide useful insights into the complexities associated with the strategy formation process, highlight the pluralistic nature of the successful strategies pursued by different organisations and explore the influence of a range of internal and external contextual factors on the strategy process and its outcomes.

Summary

Strategies are consistent patterns in decisions and actions of those who assume leadership positions in organisations. They help steer an organisation towards achieving its long-term goals and, therefore, shape the future status and success of the organisation. They can be developed and implemented through formal (planning) efforts or emerge as consistent patterns in decisions and actions that are conditioned by a variety of internal and external organisational contextual factors.

The strategic approach to operations management recognises the pivotal role played by dynamic capabilities and the significance of organisation-specific combinations of organisational resources, work routines, value systems, etc., in delivering a unique value proposition that is perceived by customers as superior to competitor offerings. A normative approach to strategic management of operations advocates the identification, agreement and definition of competitive priorities based on target markets at the business-unit level. The heart of this hierarchical planning approach is developing and deploying operations capabilities for supporting the agreed competitive priorities. Underlying this approach are managerial decisions and actions regarding the operations structure and infrastructure of the organisation. Moreover, the dynamics of this approach are underpinned by the intricacies of the internal and external organisational context. Alternatively, an emergent view of strategy recognises the significance of consistent patterns in decisions and actions as the basis of studying operations strategy.

The current practice indicates that organisations successfully pursue alternatives to the formal planning approach, such as the choice of major improvement programs, pursuing specific organisational practices, consistent entrepreneurial behaviour of individuals, etc. Irrespective of the particular approach taken, there are some core themes that represent the strategic approach to operations management. It has a unifying objective: developing operations resources, capabilities and work routines that inform and support long-term organisational goals, it deals with decisions and actions regarding the operations structure and infrastructure of an organisation. The success or otherwise of these endeavours is reflected in operations performance: outcomes focused on short-term profit as well as long-term capabilities that ensure the sustainable competitive advantage of the organisation. Overall, they articulate the operations' strategic contribution to business-levels strategy.

With this knowledge and understanding, let us revisit the management challenge presented at the beginning of this chapter. Our aim is to identify the strategic operations implications of a key business decision. Moving from small-scale technology-based manufacturing to full-scale production poses a significant challenge for operations. Let us work out the new business scenario first. With this move, Delta-tech's target market would change, most probably, from the current niche markets to a differentiated (high-value) broader market. Obviously, given its innovative capacity and superior products and services, Delta-tech would not want to compete based on cost alone. Delta-tech's new business model will be substantially different from the current one and perhaps it will be competing against the multinationals that provide similar products and services. Can Delta-tech successfully launch and sustain this new business model? It depends, to a large degree, on how successfully operations can take on the challenge and marketing could lead it from the front.

The processes and systems for manufacturing in high volumes are quite different to the current low-volume system. For example, a full blown manufacturing facility would, most likely, consist of automated production lines run by semi-skilled operators aimed at high levels of outputs. So, would the current capabilities, resources and work practices that have worked so well so far for the company also ensure the success of the new venture? Perhaps more importantly, can (and should) Delta-tech duplicate the current creative and free-flowing organisation culture in the new venture? Should Delta-tech expand the current site or locate the new facility elsewhere? If Delta-tech happens to be competing against large multinationals, can the company still treat price as a low priority for winning orders. Would the new facility deliver the scale economies required to compete against new rivals? Do these mean a change in the current competitive priorities? There are many more questions, and we might not be able to answer all of them comprehensively here. However, the benefits, if the venture becomes successful, are quite obvious and some of the pitfalls are already apparent. Given the size of investment involved in this kind of a venture, we need to undertake a more systematic and detailed analysis of the issues presented above, before making a final commitment. We should also note that Mr Palmer has so far made most of the key decisions affecting this business based on his intuitive judgements. But this time he is a little unsure of what exactly he should be doing. The kind of material covered in chapter would hopefully help him make good decisions.

DISCUSSION QUESTIONS

1. Identify the core dimensions that characterise the concept of strategy and use them to arrive at your own definition/interpretation of strategy.
2. Identify the key strategic issues meant to be dealt with at each of the three levels of the organisational hierarchy and give examples for each.

3. Would the consistent patterns in strategic decisions and actions be considered as important determinants of organisational performance? Explain.
4. Compare and contrast the market-based and resource-based approaches to competitive advantage and explain why a combined approach would be beneficial.
5. If competitiveness reflects an organisation's relative position vis-à-vis its competitors, briefly describe the role of operations in enhancing organisation-level competitiveness.
6. Briefly describe how competitive priorities can be used to guide strategic operations decisions and actions in achieving and sustaining a competitive advantage.
7. Describe the notion of trade-offs as applied to strategic operations decisions and discuss the ways in which their (negative) impact on operations can be minimised.
8. Identify and briefly describe the three alternatives to the formal planning model of operations strategy. To what extent do you think they represent current practice?
9. Discuss the operational implications of the stakeholder approach to value creation.
10. Explore the web sites (or other available sources) of several leading local organisations and examine their business models to determine if they are pursuing a market-driven or a market-driving approach to competition.

Further readings and references

Anderson, J. C., Cleveland, G. Schroeder, R. G. 1989. 'Operations strategy: a literature review.' *Journal of Operations Management*, 8(2): 133–58.

Ansoff, H. I. 1965. *Corporate Strategy: An analytical approach to business policy for growth and expansion*. New York: McGraw-Hill.

Barnes, D. 2002. 'The complexities of the manufacturing strategy formation process in practice.' *International Journal of Operations & Production Management*, 22(10): 1090–1111.

Chandler, A. D. 1962. *Strategy and Structure*. Cambridge, MA: MIT Press.

Drucker, P. 1954. *The Practice of Management*. New York: Harper &; Row.

Farjoun, M. 2002. 'Towards an organic perspective on strategy.' *Strategic Management Journal*, 23(7): 561–94.

Ferdows, K. and De Meyer, A. 1990. 'Lasting improvements in manufacturing performance: in search of new theory.' *Production and Operations Management*, 9(2): 168–84.

Frery, F. 2006. 'The fundamental dimensions of strategy.' *Sloan Management Review*, 48(1): 70–75.

Hambrick, D. C. 1980. 'Operationalising the concept of business-level strategy in research.' *Academy of Management Review*, 5(4): 567–575.

Hax, A. C. 1990. 'Redefining the concept of strategy and the strategy formation process.' *Planning Review*, May/June: 34–40.

Hayes, R. H. 2002. 'Wick Skinner: a life sailing against the wind.' *Production and Operations Management*, 11(1): 1–8.

Hayes, R. H. and Pisano, G. P. 1994. 'Beyond world-class: the new manufacturing strategy,' *Harvard Business Review*, 72(1): 77–86.

Hayes, R. H. and Wheelwright, S. C. 1984. *Restoring Our Competitive Edge*. New York: The Free Press.

Hill, T. 1989. *Manufacturing Strategy: Text and cases*. UK: Richard D. Irwin Inc.

Kiridena, S. 2005. 'Beyond constructs and linkages: a grounded model of the manufacturing strategy formation process in practice.' Proceedings of the 3rd ANZAM Operations Management Symposium, Rockhampton, Australia.

Kumar, N., Scheer, L. and Kotler, P. 2000. 'From market driven to market driving.' *European Management Journal*, 18(2): 129–41.

Melnyk, S. A. and Denzler, D. R. 1996. *Operations Management: A value-driven approach*. Burr Ridge, IL: Irwin McGraw-Hill.

Mintzberg, H. 1978. 'Patterns of strategy formation.' *Management Science*, 24(9): 934–48.

Mintzberg, H. and Waters, J. A. 1985. 'Of strategies, deliberate and emergent.' *Strategic Management Journal*, 6(3): 257–72.

Penrose, E. T. 1959. *The Theory of the Growth of the Firm*. Oxford: Oxford University Press.

Porter, M. E. 1980. *Competitive Strategy: Techniques for analysing industries and competitors*. New York: The Free Press.

Porter, M. E. 1985. *Competitive Advantage: Creating and sustaining superior performance*. New York: The Free Press.

Porter, M. E. 1996. 'What is strategy?' *Harvard Business Review*, 74(6): 61–78.

Prahalad C. K. and Hamel, G. 1990. 'The core competence of corporation.' *Harvard Business Review*, May-June: 71–91.

Ramanathan, K. 1994. 'The polytrophic components of manufacturing technology.' *Technology Forecasting and Social Change*, 46(3): 221–258.

Selznick, P. 1957. *Leadership in Administration: A sociological interpretation*. New York: Harper & Row.

Skinner, W. 1969. 'Manufacturing-missing link in corporate strategy.' *Harvard Business Review*, 47(3): 136–45.

Skinner, W. 1971. 'The anachronistic factory.' *Harvard Business Review*, 49(1): 61–70.

Skinner, W. 1974. 'The focused factory.' *Harvard Business Review*, 52(3): 113–21.

Skinner, W. 1985. *Manufacturing: The Formidable Competitive Weapon*, John Wiley & Sons. New York.

Skinner, W. 1988. 'What matters to manufacturing.' *Harvard Business Review*, 66(1): 10–16.

Sloan A. P. 1963. *My Years with General Motors*. London: Sedgwick & Jackson.

Swamidass, P. M., Darlow, N. and Baines, T. 2001. 'Evolving forms of manufacturing strategy development: evidence and implications.' *International Journal of Operations and Production Management*, 21(10): 1289–1304.

Wheelwright, S. C. 1984. 'Manufacturing strategy: defining the missing link.' *Strategic Management Journal*, 5(1), 77–91.

Internet resources

http://www.ame.org
http://www.som.cranfield.ac.uk/som/groups/opsman/bfa/reports.asp
http://www.icmr.icfai.org
http://forecast.umkc.edu/vtours
http://www.auspost.com.au/
http://www.afrbiz.com.au/
http://www.visy.com.au
http://www.hardrock.com
http://www.macquarie.com.au
http://www.fedex.com

Processes and Systems in Operations Management

Daniel Prajogo, Prakash J. Singh and Danny Samson

Learning objectives

After reading this chapter, you should be able to:

- understand the meaning of processes and the role they play in organisations
- appreciate the characteristics of generic process types
- realise how various standard operating system layouts result from the generic process types
- understand how 'people management' and technology affect process design considerations
- understand how processes can be analysed and measured
- recognise the scheduling issues associated with different process types.

Box 6.1: Managerial challenge: call centre processes

Brisbane City Council is the largest local government in Australia. It provides traditional civic services to close to one million people. These services include water supply, sewerage treatment, refuse collection, pet registration, library facilities, public health services, public transportation, roads and parks maintenance, city planning, building services, etc. The council spends over $1.5 billion on these services and employs over 6000 workers.

At the insistence of then Lord Mayor Jim Soorley, who had become frustrated with the council's inability to respond in a timely manner to ratepayers needs,

---

a call centre was set up in 1996. The stated objectives of the call centre were: (1) to add value to the council's operational areas; (2) 90 per cent of all calls to be answered in 20 seconds; and (3) 90 per cent of all calls were to be handled at point of entry. The call centre started with 40 employees answering about 1200 calls daily for a handful of the council's departments. In 1997, 24-hour service was introduced. Today, the call centre is now part of the larger 'Contact Centre'. External customer contacts via the Contact Centre are now approximately 7400 per day (approximately 6000 via the call centre, 1300 via the Customer Service Centre network and 100 e-mails). These contacts can be on any one of more than 4000 topics. A breakdown of inquiry types is as follows: 68 per cent information; 21 per cent requests for service; 9 per cent payment transactions; and 2 per cent all other.

The performance of the centre has been stellar. It achieved 90 per cent customer satisfaction levels with call centre services. Independent ratings for three key performance indicators were: outcome of calls – score of 9 out of 10; the call centre integration with the organisation – 8 out of 10; and people management as reflected by hiring, training, career progression, staff involvement in process design, staff turnover and fulfilment – 8.5 out of 10. To put these performance levels into context, only a handful of other call centres around the world have similar or higher scores.

The obvious question is: How has Brisbane City Council managed to create such a successful centre? Further, considering the large variety of services that the council provides, how is the centre able to deal with this diversity? The answers to these questions invariably relate to the how processes are managed.

Sources
Brisbane City Council Annual Report 2006; Brisbane City Council Strategic Plan 2006–2026; http://callcentres.com.au/bbc1.htm

Introduction

How can one describe an organisation? If you ask an economist, you are likely to receive an answer that suggests that an organisation is essentially a 'bundle of transactions'. A strategist, on the other hand, would suggest that the same organisation is a 'collection of resources'. We in the operations management area are likely to suggest that an organisation is best characterised in terms of a 'network of processes'. None of these views are wrong; they are all simply different ways of describing and thinking about the same entity – that being an organisation. In the operations management world though, there is a strong tendency to think about organisations in terms of processes and systems that produce goods and services to achieve value creating goals.

Therefore, in this chapter, we are interested in developing a good understanding of what a process is. We are also interested in how this process-based view affects our understanding of what transpires in a typical organisation and how decisions relating to the provision of products and services to customers are affected. Further, we hope to develop an understanding of processes in terms of their generic characteristics, and from these, see how they lead to the classification of processes into generic archetypes. Along this vein, we are interested to see how processes affect and contribute to particular physical arrangements (topological layouts). In addition to this, we are interested in developing knowledge of how processes can be designed and managed – this requires the ability to do things such as study, map, analyse, improve, change and monitor processes. For this, mastery over process management tools and techniques is required. Finally, we recognise that scheduling plays a vital role in the production of goods and services by dealing with how jobs and orders are allocated and matched with capacity and production resources. The sequencing and prioritisation of jobs and orders influence the timing and quantity of output and thus have a potential impact on customer service.

We begin our discussion of the process view of an organisation by discussing its meaning in the next section. Then, generic process types and layouts are discussed. The effects of 'people' and technology issues are examined next. This is followed by a description of various process analysis and measurement methods. Last but not least is a discussion of scheduling processes in different operating environments. The chapter concludes with a summary of main points, and answers to the questions posed in the management challenge above.

What does 'process' mean?

So, what do we mean by the word 'process'? Unfortunately, the word is so widely used that it would appear to be almost impossible to find a definition that satisfies everyone. A meaningful discussion of this word would invariably require the context and situation to be considered.

Having stated this, let's consider a generic approach to defining processes. One way in which we could conceptualise a process is by placing it in the context of tasks or activities. In this case, a process is a string of related tasks or activities. In this way of thinking, tasks or activities are at a level of analysis that is uniquely describable and performable. Once these tasks or activities logically link up, we would call it a process. These processes would have identifiable starts and finishes. In most real situations, there is likely to be a multitude of similar and different processes. When grouped together, this network of processes would then be the system. This arrangement is illustrated graphically in Figure 6.1. The advantage of this way of thinking about processes is its inherent simplicity. Unfortunately, this simplicity is also its drawback: it is not so meaningful in a practical sense because it is not

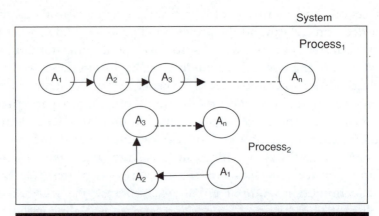

Figure 6.1 Process defined as set of related tasks or activities

so easy to identify tasks or activities, work out the linkages between them, and demonstrate how they interact in most real situations. Further, this approach can be confusing if the level of analysis is mixed, that is to say, if some activities and tasks are at a high level (perhaps strategic in nature) and others are at a more detailed level (operational level).

To deal with this 'problem', one could envisage processes as a multi-level phenomenon. Processes then could be described using activities or tasks and their inter-relationships that are at the same level of detail. These processes would then be arranged in a hierarchical system where there would be increasing level of detail as one goes from the top to the bottom levels. Depending on the level, these could be at high levels of abstraction and generality, or high degrees of specificity. At the higher levels, processes can cover a wide breadth of entities. It is not uncommon to find that end-to-end supply chains are modelled at this level. An example would be of potatoes, right from the farm, through the various manufacturing and transport processes until they appear in a red 'box' in a bag at McDonald's. At the other end of the spectrum, the lowest level of processes is limited to activities or tasks that cannot be further sub-divided. Figure 6.2 provides an illustration of this arrangement of processes. Under this scheme, a vast array of processes can be described while preserving clarity. Such an approach is widely utilised in many process mapping methodologies, some of which are discussed later in this chapter.

As stated earlier, defining processes require the context to be considered. So what sorts of context-related issues are relevant to operations management? In Chapter 1, operations management was presented as being about the transformation of inputs into outputs. Here, transformation is the process. We propose that the hierarchical approach described above can be used to describe and model the transformation process, which is at the heart of operations management.

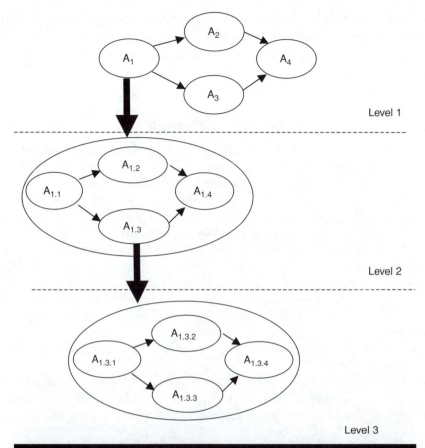

Level 1

Level 2

Level 3

Figure 6.2 Dealing with mixed levels of analysis by separating and organising processes according to level of detail

How would such an approach to defining processes relevant to operations management take practical effect? In the manufacturing area, the transformation process is applied on products with physical dimensions. The process is tangible, and is conceptually relatively straightforward and clearly defined. Transformation is concerned with the physical form which takes place in production of discrete products, in mining and minerals processing, or in 'flow' industries such as oil refining and petrochemicals. However, this straightforwardness does not apply to the services areas. For example, hospital services, retail services such as in grocery stores, haircutting services and automotive repair shops do not have significant physical transformation of the product; however, they do add value. Masses of customers value these services as evidenced by the prices paid for them. Education providers add value by transferring knowledge and skills to students. Banks add value by allowing customers to manage their financial transaction in a convenient way. Entertainment services provide customers with psychological and emotional benefits. Hence, they can be said to be adding value. This value-adding element is the equivalent of the transformation process in the services area.

Box 6.2: Centrelink

Centrelink was created in 1997 to be the 'public face' of the Australian government. Prior to this, federal government payments and social services were provided to the citizens (whom Centrelink calls 'customers') in a rather haphazard and uncoordinated manner. Centrelink was specifically created as a concerted effort by the incoming Howard government to simplify the way in which citizens engaged with government. This involved getting rid of the need for people to navigate and engage with highly dispersed and complex bureaucratic structures. Further, the new government was interested in creating a service delivery organisation that was highly responsive to implementing its policies. It also made a lot of sense from a scale and scope of services provision perspective – a 'one-stop-shop' organisational concept would break down barriers and remove duplication of effort among myriad departments, thereby generating cost savings.

So what does Centrelink do? Consider the following facts and figures from its recent annual report:[1]

'Centrelink is in the top one hundred of Australian companies in terms of size and turnover. Its recurrent budget is $2.3 billion and it distributes approximately $63 billion in social security payments on behalf of policy departments.

'Centrelink:

- has 6.5 million customers, or approximately one-third of the Australian population
- pays 10 million individual entitlements each year and records 5.2 billion electronic customer transactions each year
- administers more than 140 different products and services for 25 government agencies
- employs more than 25,000 staff
- has more than 1000 service delivery points ranging from large Customer Service Centres to small visiting services
- has reduced the number of letters sent to customers from more than 87 million (in 2004–2005) to 86.4 million per year (in 2005–2006)
- provides personalised services in over 80 languages
- receives more than 30.77 million telephone calls each year
- receives 47.2 million website page views each year
- grants more than 2.8 million new claims each year.'

Much of its services such as payment of old-age, disability, unemployment, family and childcare benefits are routine in nature for which there is reasonably long lead times to plan their delivery. However, from time to time, Centrelink has also had to provide highly tailored services at short notice. For example, it has had to be part of emergency response teams, providing financial and psychological assistance to Australians affected by recent events such as the Asian tsunami tragedy, the two Bali and London bombings, and floods in Katherine and Cyclone Larry. Since inception, there has been a proliferation of types of services that Centrelink provides to its customers.

In making payments and providing services to customers, Centrelink has to ensure that these are readily accessible, accurate, reliable and timely. Since there is a very high volume of services that Centrelink provides, it has developed standard processes and procedures for delivering these. These are well developed, extensive training is provided to staff, and a standard regime for continual improvement is in place. Much of these are supported by technology-based decision support systems. While volumes are large, Centrelink also finds itself with an ever-increasing variety of services that it provides. This service variety, when combined with the fact that the individual circumstances of each customer is reasonably unique, means that it is generally not possible for Centrelink to apply standardised processes and procedures that it uses to deal with most other customers and situations. Instead, Centrelink has to provide personalised services to its customers.

To be able to conduct its operations, whether routine or ad hoc, Centrelink depends heavily on its information management system. Centrelink staff spend inordinate amount of time collecting information from customers on their incomes, assets, employment situation, family status, etc. This information is analysed against stated government policy to determine if customers qualify for payments. While paper-based systems are still used, Centrelink has invested heavily in computerised systems for managing information. As part of this effort, it has recently introduced a web-based computer system which pre-populates forms that are up to 35 pages long.[2] This has led to significant time-savings, faster processing of claims and improved data quality.[3] Centrelink also uses software systems for managing the design and implementation of various projects. Over time, it has been able to improve the competency and skill levels of staff in project management.[4] While competency has improved, the integrity of the information system has come under the spotlight – recently, more than 100 staff were sacked or forced out for inappropriately accessing records of customers.[5] Effective and efficient information management is thus an important element of Centrelink's operations.

At the same time that it provides readily accessible and timely services, it also has to protect taxpayers from fraud. For these activities, Centrelink has developed sophisticated systems. To detect fraud, a multi-pronged system based on data-matching with other agencies such as the Tax Office, tip-offs from the general public, and selective reviews of customers with suspicious circumstances. During 2005/06, over four million reviews were carried out, which resulted in action being taken in over half a million cases. Where overpayments are made, Centrelink raises and recovers debts.

Given the sheer size and scope of activities, how well does Centrelink perform? Centrelink has invested significant resources in a range of customer feedback systems, and gathers large amounts of information regarding customer experience. The most important of these are the customer satisfaction surveys. Conducted annually and involving large numbers of customers (for example, 62,000 in 2003), Centrelink uses the results for reporting and monitoring purposes. In 2006, the top level result for customer satisfaction with Centrelink services was 87.1 per cent, a score that has been relatively stable for some years. This measure, which is a composite score that is reported to parliament and which gives an overall measure of customer satisfaction,[6] compares well with the pre-specified standard set at 85 per cent. However, there is lingering doubt about the validity and reliability of such a measure. For example, the Auditor General has highlighted weaknesses in sampling and data analysis procedures that violate statistical principles, and thus render the measure as potentially meaningless.[7] Also, a recent book written by a whistle-blowing former manager claims, *inter alia*, that Centrelink staff and managers frequently act in ways that result in improvements to performance measures, but not in actual customer experiences.[8] Indeed, if one takes into account that a large proportion of Centrelink's engagement with customers results in saying 'no' to various claims for payments, that a similarly measured staff satisfaction score is a lowly 66 per cent, and the various anecdotal reports of difficulties that customers have with Centrelink, one could plausibly conclude that the 87.1 per cent customer satisfaction score is not all that credible.

Going forward, there are many challenges that Centrelink faces. Some of these are:

- Given the ever-expanding range and complexity of services that it is being called upon to provide, how can Centrelink organise its operations so that it is able to provide the 'right' services to its customers? In other words, how can Centrelink become more efficient and effective in its service delivery operations?
- What are some of the lessons that Centrelink can learn from the experiences similar sized organisations in other industry sectors as it attempts to further develop and refine its operating system? Are there ideas that it can 'borrow' from these organisations? What are these, and will it be easy to implement them?
- What type of performance measurement system is required such that Centrelink is able to effectively balance the competing requirements of various stakeholders? For example, governments require Centrelink to be able to implement its social policies quickly and effectively; taxpayers who provide the funds for distribution require Centrelink to be efficient and to operate at the highest levels of probity; and, customers would value Centrelink to be sympathetic and responsive to their needs, resulting in a high variability in services that are provided. All the requirements can act against each other, and so simple performance measurement systems will not work well.

Notes

1   Centrelink Annual Report 2005–06. Available from: www.centrelink.gov.au
2   S. Bushell, 2005. 'Business rules boost to Centrelink', CIO.com.au, 25 October, 2005.
3   Centrelink Annual Report 2005–06 (chapter 7, pp. 119), available at www.centrelink.com.au

4   E. Cane, 'The public face of government.' *The Primavera Magazine.*

5   'Centrelink staff sacked for spying', *Sydney Morning Herald*, 23 August 2006. An internal Centrelink investigation revealed almost 600 cases of staff wrongfully accessing customer records in the past two years. In five cases, staff changed records. In most other cases, staff looked up the records of friends, neighbours and relatives.

6   This measure is obtained as the 'per cent of Family and Child Care; Seniors, Carers and Rural; and Working Age Participation customers surveyed who rate the overall quality of service received on their last visit to a Centrelink Customer Service Centre or phone call to a Call Centre as either "very good" or "good"' (Centrelink Annual Report 2005–06, p. 56).

7   Performance Audit: Centrelink's Customer Satisfaction Surveys, 2005. The Auditor-General Audit Report No.33 2004–05. The Commonwealth of Australia.

8   R. Whyte, 2005. *Australia's Artful Dodger: Centrelink exposed.* Canberra: Welfare Watchdog Publications.

Classification of processes into generic types

Factors affecting choice of process type

There are five basic process types that can be found in most organisations. These are: project process, job process, batch process, line process and continuous process. Indeed, these process types form a continuum. All these five process types will be described below, but at this stage, let's briefly consider the factors that lead to the choice of one process type over the others.

Professor Nigel Slack and his colleagues (2006) suggest that there are four key factors that invariably dictate the process type that an organisation chooses. Called the 'four Vs', these are:

- the *volume* of the products or services that are produced
- the *variety* of the different products or services that are produced
- the *variation* in the demand for the products or services
- the degree of *visibility* that customers have of the production of products or service.

Conventional wisdom is that high volume, low variety, low variation and low visibility all point towards batch, line or continuous processing systems. On the other hand, low volume, high variety, high variation and high visibility would suggest that a project or job shop process system would be suitable. But, this conventional wisdom is under challenge. With technological improvements and emergence of mass customisation, it is not inconceivable that high volumes of high variety items that have high variation in demand and that are highly visible to customers could be economically produced. The notion that there needs to be a trade-off between process type and the four Vs may not be applicable in the future!

Project process type

The project process type lies at the low-volume, high-variety, high-variation and high-visibility end of the four Vs spectra. The product or service is normally made to individual customer specifications. Since each individual product is unique or close to it, each requires different kinds of resources. Projects can also vary in scope, complexity, as well as sequence of steps used. Each project has a definite start and finish point, and because of the non-repetitive activities involved in each project, it could take a relatively long time to prepare and organise the resources required for each project. Also, efficiency in terms of high utilisation of resources is not a great concern in projects. Indeed, it is not unusual to see that one resource is acquired just for running one particular project (known as resource-to-order).

A feature of project-based processes is the absence of prior knowledge in making the particular product caused by the project's uniqueness. This presents managers with several operational challenges, including planning and scheduling of resources and activities. This is accompanied by another problem, namely that of accurately determining and controlling the cost of the processes. The high variety of products also makes it difficult to automate projects in a large scale. Therefore, projects are usually labour intensive and the required labour skills will be high in order to cope with the different nature of products produced.

Box 6.3: Examples of projects and project-based organisations

- Construction companies, such as those which organised the design and building of the Sydney Opera House, or more recently the Australian company which reconstructed Wembley stadium. These projects did not go according to plan. Both went well over budget and ran significantly late. They suffered from their uniqueness, and hence the lack of experience in the technical factors associated with them.
- Design engineering firms such as GHD, PB, Maunsells, Ove Arup, Hatch, Jacobs, Connell Wagner and SKM, all employ hundreds of engineers and other technical professionals designing the infrastructure (buildings, roads, dams, ports and docks, manufacturing plants, and mines) that lies at the heart of our economy. These firms pass their designs to construction and building contractors such as John Holland and Multiplex, which actually project manage their implementation.
- Consulting firms, such as Boston Consulting Group (BCG), Deloitte, Accenture, McKinsey and PwC, all organise to do customised projects for their clients and indeed they are run as fully project-based organisations.
- Publishers of text books, such as Cambridge University Press, Thomson, McGraw-Hill and Pearson, which treat each text as a project, requiring a series

of process steps, from specification, contracting, author drafting, editing, book design, production, and finally distribution for sale.

- Research organisations such as Australia's CSIRO, University research activities and commercial companies which conduct research and/or development work on new products or services. As an example, by its nature, new product development is somewhat to very different every time, and is best organised as a set of distinct projects. Consider the myriad of tasks which had to be accomplished in order to develop and commercialise the Apple iPod, or more recently Apple's iPhone, or the Sony PlayStation 3. There are unique technical works, marketing and manufacturing arrangements which each of these required, and the best way to organise such work is to use the wonderful disciplines and tools of project management.

Job process type

Job processes (also sometimes called job shops) are characterised by low volumes, high variety, high variation and high visibility. However, volume is not as low as for a project process as there is a small degree of repetitiveness by customers' orders. With high customisation, most jobs have different scope and sequence of steps, hence creating jumbled flow paths in the operations. However, unlike in project processes, there can be identical sub-processes in different jobs which create line flows with a limited degree of repetitiveness and less degree of complexity compared to projects. In terms of resources, there is still a high degree of flexibility to handle divergent tasks. However, due to similarities of sub-processes between different products, resources can be shared among them, hence, improving efficiency in terms of their utilisation. Organising resources is more pertinent in job process whereby resources (workers and equipment) which are required to perform similar types of works are located together (called work centres). Due to high customisation, in job process systems, each order is handled separately, and therefore organisations make products only after the orders are placed (Make-to-Order).

Box 6.4: Examples of job shop processes

- A general hospital has many sub-systems and processes within it. These include the operating theatres, wards, physiotherapy, X-ray department, intensive care, emergency department, and many others. Each patient has a unique diagnosis and set of needs for treatment in the hospital. Consider an emergency heart attack victim, a woman delivering a baby and a person with a broken leg from a sporting injury. They will need different treatments and from an operations and 'flow' perspective, these three patients will take very different paths through the hospital. The hospital must be flexible to accommodate this high variety of needs. It cannot be organised like a line flow process (e.g., assembly line). It has its resources organised as fixed work stations and departments that individual items (patients) visit as needed.

- A general metal processing factory is a type of organisation where it is possible to make to order, almost anything out of metal. These factories make to order by having workstations and departments that comprise cutting equipment, grinding, drilling, welding, painting and other process stations, which can produce metal structures to any specification. Like a general hospital, such a 'metal bashing' factory has a lot of flexibility, but not the efficiency that can come from repetition, because it is clearly making up to ordered 'jobs'.

Batch process type

Batch processing has moderate volume, variety, demand variability and visibility. All products belonging to one batch are produced repetitively before the operation is shifted into another batch. As such, the degree of repetitiveness which dictates the degree of volume is determined by the size of the batch. Small-sized batches will make batch process type not significantly different to job process type. However, when the batch size is large, the degree of repetitiveness is high and efficiencies are high. With the increased degree of repetitiveness, product variety is narrowed down. Nevertheless, by its very nature, batch processing is still a case of managing variety between batches, which makes it difficult for organisations to dedicate particular production lines for single products or product lines. The process still has a jumbled flow to some extent, as different parts can take different routes or paths throughout the process, but the paths are relatively more predictable than job process type. The activities performed at each stage of the process are also relatively standardised, creating a line flow in the sub-processes. Resources in terms of workers and equipment still need to be flexible to handle different batches. Still, it is difficult or at least complex to do production scheduling and therefore a make-to-order system is suitable for batch process.

Many factories are set up to produce batches of goods, where there is limited or no variety within a batch, but where the overall requirement is to produce a variety of similar items. Consider packaged food production, such as the canned pet food produced at Uncle Ben's pet food factory in Wodonga Victoria. This gigantic factory creates large batches of uncooked product from raw materials of the many varieties of dog and cat food that it makes, then sends these down line flow process to be cooked and packaged up for sale and delivery. Similarly, beer is brewed in batches, then normally bottled or canned in line flow processes that are downstream from the batch brewing.

Box 6.5: Examples of batch processes

- Universities use lecture and tutorial groups and similar *batches* to gain efficiencies in use of their critical resources, namely their lecture rooms, laboratories, and lecturers and professors. Imagine the costs of treating each student as an individual item and teaching all classes with only one student in them, as if each was a unique project. While this might increase quality (or it might not!), it would make the costs of university education completely prohibitive. Fortunately, students can be batched into groups that have similar requirements, such as becoming an engineer, or becoming an accountant, and members of these groups of individuals can be treated similarly in terms of attending the same lectures, etc. They are being batch processed! On the other hand some research degree students such as those doing PhDs are of course managed as 'projects', and assigned to an academic supervisor, because each one is doing a different study.
- A manufactured product we all commonly use that is produced in batch processing is a pen or a pencil. In such factories, the processing is actually done as a 'hybrid' of line and batch flow systems. The factory would produce a batch of say, black ink pens, possibly many thousands of these, then it would be changed over to produce blue pens, then red, etc.

Line or mass process type

Line or mass process type is characterised by high volume and low variety. This process type can also be seen in situations where variations in demand and production visibility are low. Products are standardised and so are the resources required to produce them. Product variety is still possible so long as it does not create disruption of the existing flow of the standard process. As such, resources are organised around the particular products, creating a line flow in the whole process with each step performing similar types of activities all the time. Therefore, it is easier to control and schedule. Each product line requires specific resources which are dedicated only to that line. Due to high volume, the need for equipment with large capacity (requiring large investment) is usual. Therefore, high utilisation of resources is an important issue in mass operations. By its very nature, high volume of operations indicates that products will be consumed regularly by the market, and therefore production is run without necessarily waiting for customer orders. Finished products are held in inventory and ready to be delivered once orders are placed (make-to-stock).

Most cars are made in assembly line flow processes as are many other consumer durable products, such as refrigerators and washing machines. Generally, line flow processes are lower in cost than other generic process types, but this efficiency comes with relative inflexibility. For example, it requires a lot of work and much planning to change the processing rate even a little bit of a car assembly line, and it is impossible to use such a process to do anything productive except produce assembled cars of a certain type!

Continuous process type

A continuous process type is characterised by high volume, standardised products, and rigid production flows. It is the extreme opposite of the project process. It is called continuous process because one kind of product flows in the production line without stopping and there is no interval between product's units, for example water, gas, oil refining and electricity supply. The process also operates continuously without any interruption of change-over or set-ups. The process usually uses capital-intensive technologies and therefore requires a very high utilisation and long time periods of operation. Oil refineries are very efficient, but completely inflexible in terms of processing anything except the grade of oil they were designed for. They cannot be redeployed for other purposes and they require massive initial capital investments in equipment. In such continuous flow processes, one cannot even identify discrete products because of the continuous nature of the products such as liquids or gases.

Process types in services

The four Vs (volume, variety, variation and visibility) can be applied to processes in the services sector. This results in three common process types that are reasonably unique to this sector. These are professional services, service shops and mass services.

Professional services are characterised by high-contact with customers. Professional service is usually more labour intensive than technology intensive. Highly skilled staff are required and normally empowered with discretion to adapt the service to meet individual needs of customers. Such tailored services can cause organisations to suffer from low efficiency in terms of cost and time. As a result, they pass on these cost burdens to customers by charging a premium price. Examples are management consulting and accounting firms such as Deloitte, PricewaterhouseCoopers (PwC), Ernst and Young, and many other such firms, small and large.

Mass services have preset specifications of the services offered to customers. An example we are all familiar with is that of the major banks, which process millions of customer service requests each day and must do so in quite standard ways. Airlines also conduct mass processing. Given that the services are normally built into the processes, there is quite limited scope for tailoring the service to meet individual customer needs. There is a limited degree of variability and customers may select from a limited range of options that suit their needs. For example, airline or railway services offer a range of destinations and schedules which customers can choose from. With such standardised services, customers can have clear expectations of what they will get in the service package along with time and costs incurred from purchasing the services. Also, similar to mass production, mass services can be automated due to their standardised outputs and processes. Mass services are commonly more technology intensive than labour intensive. Accordingly, providers of mass services can pursue economies of scale that allow them to offer services at a relatively low cost.

Box 6.6: Mass processing example: banks' data processing

Banks' financial data are processed automatically using a variety of information technologies. Imagine how many people would be needed to manually process Australia's bank transactions if not for computers! The Reserve Bank of Australia reports that this mass bank process service in 2006 comprised 68 million ATM transactions, 107 million uses of EFTPOS and 115 million credit card transactions per month, totalling some 290 million transactions monthly, nearly 10 million per day. Without computers we would need much of Australia's workforce to do these transactions in manual mode!

Service shops are positioned between the extremes of professional and mass services. The services offered are characterised by a fair degree of variety and volume, hence, similar to job shops in manufacturing sectors. There is a high degree of customer contact, so the role of people is important in performing the services. Examples are gymnasiums, hairdressing establishments or indeed most goods retailers, such as jewellery shops and department stores.

Process layout

The process type of an operation (described in the previous section) usually affects how facilities are physically arranged. This arrangement, when viewed from a topological perspective, is the *process layout*. Process layout deals with how machines, equipment, workstations, people, etc. are co-located in order to effectively accomplish the work tasks. While layouts are relatively easy to visualise if the entities are physical in nature, this may not be so if the entities are non-tangible, such as information or service. As was the case with process types, layouts can also be classed into groups. The four basic layout types covered here are fixed-position layout, process-focused layout, product-focused layout, and cell layout. Before looking at these layout types, let's consider the factors that contribute to the choice of a particular layout over others.

Layout decision

The layout decision is based on optimising flow. This could be reducing unnecessary movement of materials, information or workers in a manufacturing setting. Conversely, it could be about maximising movement of customers in a retail outlet. The objectives thus usually result in the general type of the arrangement of the physical resources and facilities of the operation. Consider how IKEA stores are laid out versus Bunnings Hardware stores. There are different purposes driving these different layouts.

Since changing layout can be difficult and expensive, even impossible in certain situations, companies need to attend to the layout decision as part of their long-term operations goals and strategy. Changing layout of an existing operation can cause disruptions, leading to customer dissatisfaction or lost production. Also, if the layout (with hindsight) is wrong, it can lead to overly long or confused flow patterns, build up of inventory of materials, customer queues building up in the operation, customers being inconvenienced, long processing times, inflexible operations, unpredictable flow and high cost. Poor layout can mean poor quality and service.

Fixed-position layout

Fixed-position layouts are typical of projects where product remains stationary for the entire production process. This is normally because the product is difficult to move because it is too large, too heavy or too fragile. It is the equipment, workers, material and other resources which are brought to the production site. Due to the one-off nature of these projects, many organisations decide to hire rather than purchase equipment to minimise their idleness. As a result, the fixed costs are low, but the variable costs are high.

The production of large items such as heavy machine tools, airplanes, buildings, locomotives, and ships is usually accomplished in a fixed-position layout. Consider a shipyard. Clearly it is a very specialised facility with activities arranged to produce a ship, then launch it and produce another. Service-providing organisations also use fixed-position layouts; examples include major hardware and software installations, and sporting and cultural events.

> **Box 6.7: Examples of fixed-position layout:**
>
> - Building constructions comprise several stages of production from foundation, erecting the wall (brick or concrete), installing doors and windows, installing bathroom and kitchen facilities and fitting electrical and/or gas equipments. All of these processes are carried out in the location where the building is located.
> - Fine dining restaurants serve full meals (from appetisers to dessert) to customers in a one location where the customer is seated.

Process-focused layout

By definition, process-focused layout means that production resources and facilities are arranged based on their functions or processes they perform. In this case, similar processes are located together, in departmental arrangement. This may be because it is convenient to group them together, or that the utilisation of transforming resources is improved. It means that when products, information or customers flow through the operation, they will take a route from activity to activity according to their needs. Different products or customers will have different needs and therefore take different routes. Usually this makes the flow pattern in the operation very complex.

Box 6.8: Examples of process-focused layouts

- Manufacturing of jet engines – since these products are highly specialised, process-focused layout is most suitable. Production of different parts will take different paths through the facility.
- Hospital – some processes (e.g. X-ray machines and laboratories) are required by several types of patient; some processes (e.g. general wards) can achieve high staff and bed utilisation.
- Supermarket – some products, such as tinned goods, are convenient to restock if grouped together. Some areas, such as those holding frozen vegetables, need the common technology of freezer cabinets. Others, such as the areas holding fresh vegetables, might be together because they can then be made to look attractive to customers.

Product-focused layout

Product-focused layout is the opposite of process-focused layout. In the product-focused layout, resources and facilities are arranged according to the sequence of activities required to produce one particular product. As materials consistently flow along a series of processes, this type of layout is often called a production, assembly or operating line. Also, because the flow of materials is highly predictable and easy to control, this layout is labelled as flow layout. All of these are based on the high volume and low variety of the products produced. In this layout type, fixed costs are high but variable costs are low and with high volume, organisations can benefit from economies of scale.

There are several disadvantages associated with product layouts. For instance, a breakdown of one piece of equipment can cause the entire process to shut down. In addition, since the layout is determined by the good or service, a change in product design or the introduction of new products may require major changes in the layout; thus flexibility can be limited. Therefore, product-focused layouts are less flexible and are expensive to change. Finally, and perhaps most important, people's jobs in a product-layout facility, such as those on a mass-production line, may provide little job satisfaction. This is primarily because of the high level of division of labour often required, which usually results in specialisation of tasks, repetition and monotony.

Box 6.9: Examples of product-focused layouts

- Automobile assembly (or any other form of flow or line assembly process) – almost all variants of the same model require the same sequence of processes, and move smoothly along the steps in the sequence.
- Mass-immunisation programme – all customers require the same sequence of clerical, medical and counselling activities.
- Self-service cafeteria – generally the sequence of customer requirements (starter, main course, dessert and drink) is common to all customers, but the 'flow' layout also helps control customer movement.

Cellular layout

A cell contains all processes needed to be performed as one part of an operation. In a cell layout, materials flow through one cell to another until completion. Cellular layout is sometimes called a hybrid layout since it reflects a combination between product-focused and process-focused layouts. This is because the layout within each cell is close to product-focused while the layout between cells resembles process-focused. Parts/processes are classified and coded and those with similar characteristics are grouped together into 'families'. Each family is typically made through a similar process flow using similar equipment. Therefore, equipment is arranged to form one cell. In effect, cell layout is an attempt to bring some order to the complexity of flow that characterises process layout. This is because similar parts are now processed in a closed loop rather than through scattered processes as found in process-focused layout. Also, due to the small differences among parts or processes in one cell, the set-up time for that cell can be reduced.

In implementing a cellular system, organisations seek to standardise as many part/process designs as possible to increase batch sizes produced in the cell. As the batch sizes become larger, the production process approaches high volume, process control becomes easier, and automation becomes more feasible. Many manufacturing facilities employ cells for production, consisting

After identifying the flow pattern of each product the processes are now reallocated

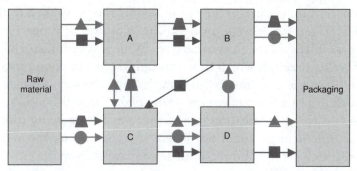

into four cells with each of them being dedicated into individual part. The cell layout is presented in figure below.

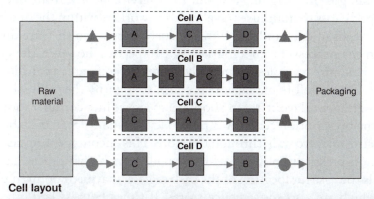

Cell layout

Figure 6.3 Example of cell layout
(Adapted from Jacobs and Chase 2008, p. 87)

of three to seven people who perform a series of related or sequential tasks, then pass their components or goods to the next cell.

Figure 6.3 is an example of a cell layout derived from a process layout. It shows how a cell can embrace both product and process layouts.

Layout in services sector organisations

Service industry organisations, just as their counter-parts in the manufacturing sector, also need to carefully consider their layouts. This is not only because a good layout will make the processes more efficient, but also the degree of visibility of processes to customers is higher in service. Indeed, there are many service facilities where services are performed as parts of the service itself.

Some principles in designing layout of manufacturing processes can also be applied to the service context. For example, minimising crossing points and non-adjacent moves in the flow of materials can be applied to the flow of customers in service delivery process. The adoption of process layout in services is dependent on the flow of services. While in manufacturing organisations, it is the materials which flow through the production processes, in services it is often the customers who flow through the service processes. An example of this is in a hospital where patients go through several stages of examination, surgery, medication, and treatment before being discharged. Another example is in an aquarium where customers walk through a 'one way' path through several showcases of sea creatures from the entry gate to the exit door, which replicates the product-focused layout in manufacturing process.

The overall goal in designing a layout for a service facility, from an operations perspective, is to minimise travel time for workers within the operation and to create an understandable flow for customers when they are directly involved in the process. From a marketing perspective, however, the goal is usually to maximise revenues. Frequently, these two goals are in conflict with each other. It is therefore management's task to identify the trade-offs that exist in designing the layout, taking both perspectives into consideration. For example, the prescription centre in a pharmacy is usually located at the rear, requiring customers to walk through the store. This encourages impulse purchases of non-prescription items, which usually have higher profit margins. The same is the case for location of the cash register/payment point in petrol stations, which are also convenience stores. If Coles Express laid out their stores so that the payment station was right at the front door or even outside the shop, would they sell as many pies, sandwiches, drinks, magazines and chocolate bars?

In designing facility layouts for service operations, additional, service-unique issues need to be considered. First, the cost per square metre for retail locations is usually very expensive. Service retail operations, therefore, must design their facilities to maximise the sales generated per square metre. To accomplish this, operations such as restaurants have reduced the percentage of area devoted to the back-of-the-house operations, like the kitchen, to allow more area for customers to be seated. Another approach is taken by Benihana's of Tokyo, a chain of Japanese steak houses. Benihana's strategy is to move the kitchen to the front of the house so customers can actually participate in the food preparation process.

Another service-unique factor that needs to be taken into consideration is the customer's presence in the transformation process. As a result, the decor package of the service operation plays an important role in determining the customer's overall satisfaction with the service encounter.

People and technology in processes

The role of people in processes

In the context of process design, the issue of people is focused on job design which designates the scope and the level of both work design and skills required to perform tasks. A narrow level of work specification normally requires a narrow and (usually) low level of skills. On the other hand, a wide 'scope of works' requires workers with a wide range of skills. In essence, the scope of works and the level of skills create a continuum ranging from specialisation at one end and flexibility on the other end. Specialisation is a concept that originated from the principles of scientific management developed by Frederick Taylor in the early 20th century. According to Taylor, organisations must attempt to break down tasks of the operations to the simplest level that can be performed by the lowest skilled workers in a repetitive manner. In this way, efficiency can be achieved through a fast pace of works, low wages and low training costs. However, specialisation has caused several major problems that can undermine the overall performance effectiveness of the process.

The most notable problem is poor employees' morale because of the monotonous and boring nature of such work. This problem often results in high turnover and low quality products, which is opposite to the original intent of specialisation. In response to these problems, several alternative strategies have been commonly adopted. These include job rotation, job enlargement and job enrichment.

Box 6.10: Some strategies for improving workplace morale

- Job rotation allows workers to periodically exchange their jobs with other jobs with an equal level of skills. Besides reducing boredom, this system provides an opportunity for workers to expand their skills, hence, increasing their flexibility. From a management perspective, this system helps in finding a replacement for absent workers with other workers from different work stations. It also helps workers to appreciate the internal customers' perspective, meaning that of their work colleagues, since they have gained an appreciation of various jobs in the organisation through doing them.
- Job enlargement expands a worker's job 'horizontally' by increasing the range of tasks at the same level to complete a larger proportion of the total work required for the service or product. Similar to job rotation, this system leads to expansion of skills, and with the increasing scope of the work, normally the wage also increases. Therefore, job enlargement has a greater potential to increase employee satisfaction as workers find themselves with a greater sense of responsibility, accomplishment, and well-being. Teamwork is an extension of this

concept, which builds morale and workplace commitment, and when correctly implemented can lead to many benefits for both the organisation's effectiveness and its workers' job satisfaction.

- <u>Job enrichment</u> expands workers' jobs vertically as they have greater control and responsibility for an entire process, not just a specific skill or operation. This approach supports the development of employee empowerment and self-managed teams, whereby employees make basic decisions about their jobs. Job enrichment generally increases job satisfaction because it gives workers a sense of achievement in mastering many tasks, recognition and direct feedback from users of the output and responsibility for the quality of the output.

The role of technology in processes

Process technologies are the machines and equipment that are used in the transformation processes in operations to produce products and services. These technologies are not only used widely in the manufacturing sector, but also for information-processing and customer-processing in the services sector. Organisations adopt process technologies to acquire several key benefits, most notably: speed, accuracy (precision), consistency, volume, and low cost. In the services sector, technology can also improve convenience for customers in purchasing services. For example, the use of ATM technology makes it easier for customers to withdraw or deposit money. In pursuing these benefits, organisations commonly implement automation of their processes where technology is installed as a replacement of human resources. The degree of automation in a process ranges from manual (no machines, full human effort) to complete automation (full use of technology). Organisations take many factors into account in making technical investment decisions, these principally being cost, quality, reliability, delivery, flexibility and other aspects of technical performance and customer requirements.

Despite the potential benefits of technology adoption, it is very important for managers to understand the whole gamut of issues in making decisions about technology. There is a real danger if we view technology as a solution for any problems in the production processes without understanding how the processes themselves work. This is because technology decisions often involve a large amount of investment and wrong decisions (mainly driven by the idea of matching competitors or following industry trends) can expose the organisation to unnecessary financial risks. The larger the investment in technology, the broader the aspects of the organisation that needs to be involved in making the decision. Systems thinking is paramount here and any changes in the operations must be directed at improving the overall performance of the whole system, not just the subsystem.

Management of technology is further discussed in Chapter 8.

Box 6.11: Woolworths Limited

When Roger Corbett became the CEO of Woolworths Limited in 1999, there were no high expectations – the share price of the company took a dive when his appointment was announced. However, Corbett, who had been with the company for his entire career and had previously had a successful long stint as head of Big-W discount stores (Woolworths' subsidiary), presided over radical supply chain and logistics reforms that have cut billions of dollars of costs associated with the processes in delivering products from factories to the supermarkets. In the process, Corbett, who retired in 2006, transformed the company from one which was complacent with its position at the head of a cosy duopoly and whose offerings were 'stable', to one that is very efficient and competitive, resulting in sharp increases in its market share and profitability.

What was the impetus for Woolworths' embarking on this transformation journey? Corbett made the following comments at an industry conference in 2000 where he made the observation that Australia had ultra-modern supermarkets ('24-hour, 21st century business') and outdated, decrepit supply chains ('19th century, 9 am to 5 pm, Monday to Friday supply chain'):

'In the store, we sell products every day to our customers and we replenish those products every day in the stores and, for some products, multiple times in the day. We also receive weekly and daily warehouse deliveries from vendors. Why then do we have more than 50 days of stock in the pipelines, an average service level of 90 per cent and an out-of-stock level at store between four and six per cent?'[1]

At that time, the world best practice for average inventory turnover rate was 20 days, so Woolworths' performance was very poor. Further, customer satisfaction rates were not good. A key cause of this was the high levels of out-of-stocks incidences. These incidences were occurring with suppliers and retailers, and it was difficult to pinpoint exactly where and how they were occurring. There were times when there would be no stocks of items on the retailers' shelves or stores, but plenty in the warehouses. The fault was with in-store processes and systems communications up and down the supply chains. Indeed, as White notes, 'The industry was struggling with the challenge of industry-wide collaborative supply chain management.'[2] As if these were not enough, large overseas players like Wal-Mart and Tesco, noticing poor operations of Woolworths and other local players, were looking into entering the Australian market. Corbett realised that 'something' needed to be done; otherwise, there was strong possibility that Woolworths would not survive for long.

So, what did Corbett and Woolworths do? Based on successful practices of Wal-Mart, Tesco and other successful international retailers, Woolworths has completely overhauled its organisational structure, supply chains and logistics systems. Called 'Project Refresh', it is an eight year plan that will cost more than a billion dollars to implement. The key elements of this plan, most of which are now in place, are:

- Centralisation of the buying function. Woolworths previously had a state-based structure where each state had different pallet load sizes, order cycles,

IT interfaces with suppliers, etc. Moving to a central buying structure means that decision-making processes are streamlined, suppliers deal with a single point of contact, opportunities for national marketing have been created, and duplication of efforts is removed.

- Implementation of shared services. With centralisation of the key buying function, it made sense to create and operate a shared services functional structure to take care of backroom processes.
- Redesign of distribution network. This involved consolidation of 31 distribution centres to 9 regional distribution centres (RDCs) and the introduction of two national distribution centres (NDCs) where goods are received directly from suppliers and distributed to regional distribution centres.
- Redesign of transportation system. The company implemented a transport management system (TMS) to reduce the volume of direct store deliveries and take control of inbound freight volumes to the distribution centres. This, as opposed to the previous practice where suppliers supplied goods directly to the regional distribution centres, is aimed at reducing the costs in supplying grocery products.
- Development and implementation of IT-based inventory replenishment systems. Specifically, forecast-based replenishment systems for distribution centres ('StockSmart') and stores (AutoStockR) have been installed in all the DCs and stores. In addition, point-of-sale data signalling systems have been integrated into the store and DC communication systems. These parts, some of which have been bought-in and others which have been built in-house, were the riskiest parts of Project Refresh.
- Establishing Electronic Data Interchange (EDI) connection with top suppliers. Woolworths' has established full two-way live electronic inter-connection with most of its 1,800 suppliers, thereby avoiding the need to process information manually.

What have been the outcomes of all these changes? There is little doubt that the project has been an overwhelming success. Consider the following:

- Project Refresh has delivered cost savings of 4.51 per cent of sales. This amounts to $5.3 billion in savings over seven years (remember that the cost of the project has been $1 billion).[3]
- The average inventory holding period has decreased dramatically. This was close to 50 days in 1999, was down to 34.1 days by 2003, and is now tracking in the 20s. Considering that reducing inventory holdings by two days represents about $100 million a year in free cash flow,[4] this dramatic and significant improvement in inventory turnover rate has generated at least a billion dollars of free cash flow.
- Woolworths has put most of the savings (80 per cent, it claims) to good use – reducing prices and improving in-store amenities. This has resulted in improvements in sales and profits. This 'sales up/costs down' approach, is a virtuous cycle that is propelling Woolworth's to gain further market share, and ultimately, higher profit margins and returns to equity.[5]

Going forward, there are some interesting challenges that Woolworths is likely to face. Some of these are:

- How will Woolworths consolidate the system that it has created? Not all parts of the system are operating smoothly. For example, there have been complaints from some members of the supplier community about the manner in which they were effectively 'forced' into developing EDI inter-connection with Woolworths.[6]
- Woolworths plans to extend Project Refresh to other parts of its business empire. These include its liquor businesses and overseas operations in New Zealand. There are expected to be different challenges that will be faced. What will these be, and how would they be best managed?
- As successful as Project Refresh been, more changes are taking place in the industry. These will necessitate changes to the way Woolworths operates. For example, there is a view that if Woolworths continues in its current trajectory, it will dominate the industry to such an extent that others would become niche market players. What would this mean to Woolworths, and how should it react to such an eventuality?

While Roger Corbett has departed Woolworths, the company still faces some interesting times ahead. It would be interesting to see how it reacts to the challenges. If its track record is any guide, it seems that Woolworths would react and cope better than any of its competitors.

Notes

1   As reported in L. White, 2007. 'Chain Reaction', www.insidertrading.com.au, Feb 02, 2007.
2   Ibid.
3   Woolworths Limited Annual Report 2006. Available from: www.woolworths.com.au[c]
4   F. Chong, 'Woolies to fix chain's weak links', *The Australian*, Wed 29 October 2003, p. 32.
5   'Gospel according to Corbett is good news to Woolworths', www.theage.com.au, August 26, 2003.
6   L. Colquhoun, 'Supply chain wars'. *MIS Asia*. www.misweb.com, 1 August 2003.

Process analysis and measurement

Process analysis and measurement is an important part of process management. As the old saying goes, 'If you can't measure it, you can't manage it'. Process analysis aims to understand how the process works through setting out its steps and understanding the relationships between these steps. Once a comprehensive analysis is conducted, then we can measure the performance of the process and its impact on operations and business performance. Therefore, the value of process measurement is not only to identify any improvement or degradation in the process, but also, in the context of competition, it can provide information on the competitive status of the company against its competitors, known as benchmarking.

There are several measurement units (metrics) that have been commonly used to gauge the performance of processes. We now turn to them.

Quality

This has been heralded as one of the key sources of competitive advantage. There are several ways to measure quality depending on the way it is defined. In the context of process analysis, the most commonly adopted definition is conformance to specification and the key metric to measure it is the percentage defect rate. The lower the defect rate, the higher the quality. More details on measuring quality can be found in Chapter 9.

Another useful way to measure the quality of processes is to examine the total cost of things that do not go right the first time, including rework, scrap and errors in work that get to the market place. In banking, quality is partially measured by the proportion of 'bad' loans that are made. In hotels and airlines, customer fill-out cards indicate levels of service quality.

Productivity

Also often called efficiency, productivity is the ratio between the output produced by the process and the input absorbed by the process in producing the output. The higher the ratio, the higher the productivity. Since input and output may not be measured in the same units or measures due to the transformation process changing the form of materials or service inputs, it is necessary to standardise or equalise the metrics between the two variables.

The most commonly used metric is of course the monetary unit. For example, a bank's most critical measure of efficiency is the *cost to income ratio*. This ratio measures the cost of goods sold (COGS) divided by the revenue of the organisation. Major banks benchmark themselves against each other on this key ratio, and set improvement targets on it, then set about implementing initiatives to achieve these operating goals. Executives in these banks are very familiar with ideas such as the notion of a cost to income ratio of under 40 per cent is very good, while a ratio of about 60 per cent means inefficiency.

Utilisation

This is the ratio between the actual use of the capacity of a resource and the potential or rated capacity of the resources. Metrics which can be used to measure utilisation are volume and time. The leftover or unused capacity in a system is called idle capacity. In process industries such as oil refining, 'uptime' capacity utilisation of the refining equipment is an extremely important measure because of the large investment made in the capital equipment.

Standard time

This is the amount of time required to perform a single activity that is part of a process. This metric is most suitable for repetitive works that are normally performed using low-level skilled labours or automatic machines. Standard time is the basic measure of the speed performance of a process.

Throughput time

This is the amount of time required to process one unit of product from the start until finish, or the time that the unit spends in the process. Throughput is important in understanding how quickly and efficiently a process runs. In measuring throughput time, it is important to segregate the kinds of activities and time components spent by the unit. For example, how much time was required to process the unit, and how much time was required for the unit to wait before being processed. This can be done by mapping the process and this is discussed later in this chapter.

Delivery-in-full-on-time-in-specification (DIFOTIS)

This is a powerful indicator of the whole operation or delivery system performance. It has practical meaning, in terms of the percentage of orders placed on a system that are delivered or filled: 'IN FULL', meaning everything in the order was supplied; 'ON TIME', meaning the delivery standard or expectation was achieved; and 'IN SPEC' (specification), meaning that those items or services delivered were made as required and expected, errorfree and with the right quality. DIFOTIS can be used to measure the effectiveness of a warehouse that supplies to orders from the stores that draw their goods from it, through to a fast food company, such as McDonald's, which thrives on its high levels of DIFOTIS.

Having introduced the metrics to measure process performance, it is necessary to emphasise once again the need for having systemwide thinking in mind. This is particularly so in processes which involve a series of processes rather than just a single process. Since these processes work as a system, they are interdependent on each other. In the end, it is the total performance of the system that matters. The point being made here is that any efforts at improving the performance of any parts of the process must be assessed against their impact on the performance of the system as a whole.

Flowchart or process mapping

A flowchart is a schematic drawing that identifies the key elements and show how various entities flow between them. There are many different types of flow charts that have been developed. Most of these have sophisticated software modelling packages associated with them.

In the operations area, a particular type of flow diagram – process map – has been popular. This map is the flow of material from the beginning until the end of the production process. The flow of the materials throughout a series of activities is mapped against two variables: workstations (functions) and their activities and time taken in the process. In this way, the role of each function in the production process can be identified.

The other purpose of flowcharts is to identify the value-added activities among a number of activities involved in the whole production process. As shown in the diagram, there are five different generic types of activities which can be found in a process: operation (usually meaning transformation), transportation, inspection, delay, and storage. Among these five activities, operation is the only truly value-adding activity. Delay, on

Step	Minutes	Chart Symbols	Process Description
1	03.00		Enter immigration area
2	10.00		Line up at immigration gates
3	02.00		Immigration check
4	03.00		Walk into baggage claim
5	10.00		Wait for baggage delivery
6	01.00		Pick up the baggage
7	02.00		Walk into customs area
8	10.00		Line up for customs inspection
9	05.00		Customs inspection
10	04.00		Walk into taxi area
11	10.00		Line up for taxi
12	01.00		Take a taxi and leave the airport
	61.00	2 4 2 4 -	

○ Operation   ⇨ Transport   ☐ Inspect   D Delay   ▽ Store

Figure 6.4 Example of process mapping of flow in an airport

the other hand, is the most non-value-adding activity and therefore needs to be reduced or eliminated to maximise the efficiency of the process. The other three activities are sometimes necessary although they are not value-adding, so, they should be minimised wherever possible. For example, transportation can be reduced by improving layout or combining several activities into one workstation. Inspection can be reduced by building in preventive quality mechanisms. Storage can be minimised by improving production planning and implementing just-time-time operating systems. Maximising the value-adding activities and minimising the non-value-adding activities will maximise both effectiveness and efficiency of the process.

Service blueprinting

The application of flow chart analyses in services sector has been given the label of 'service blueprinting'. The purpose of service blueprinting is, other than understanding the process's flow, to understand how customers and service providers interact at each activity step of the service delivery process. The stages of operations where contact with customers occur are called 'front-office' processes. The events where services are performed during contact with customers are also called 'moments of truth'. On the other hand, processes that are performed in the absence of customers are called 'back-office' processes. Managing the total cycle of service as well as the coordination between front office and back office activities is essential to providing excellent service and achieving customer satisfaction. For example, a good dining room and friendly staff are the front office of a restaurant, while the kitchen is the back office.

An example of a service blueprinting diagram is shown in Figure 6.5. Here, the processes used by a financial institution to process a credit card application from a customer is shown.

Scheduling

Scheduling plays an important role in the production of goods and services. Scheduling deals with how jobs are allocated to and matched with capacity and production resources. The sequencing and prioritisation of jobs/orders influences the timing and quantity of output and thus has a strong impact on customer service levels. The specific scheduling methods employed are different, depending on the types of processes and industry sectors. Some of these are discussed below.

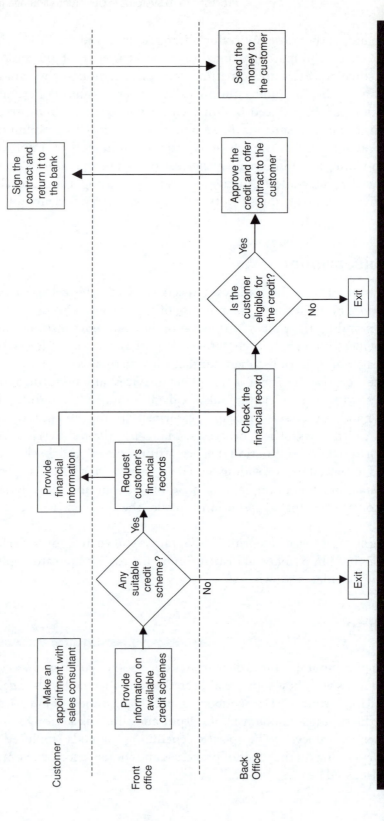

Figure 6.5 Example of service blueprint of processes used by a financial institution to process a credit card application

Scheduling in high volume systems

As explained earlier, operations systems with high volume, which are known as line or mass process type systems, are characterised by the use of standardised equipment to produce a single product or a set of very similar products. The goal is to utilise labour and equipment to the fullest to achieve specialisation and efficiency, and to attain a smooth production flow through the system. The equipment or work stations are arranged in a linear sequence (hence the term line) along the flow of materials.

In order to design a line process that is efficient, the designer needs to 'balance' the line so that materials flow smoothly. As we know, lines consist of sets of tasks. If individual tasks can be grouped together to form workstations, and the time spent at each of the workstations is roughly equal, then we would observe that there will be a reasonably smooth flow of materials through the line. This process of assigning tasks to the workstations to achieve balance is known as *line balancing*. When the line is not balanced, the output rate of the line will be determined by the slowest work station (or bottleneck).

The key objective in a line flow system is to produce high volumes of output at low cost. As materials move quickly and smoothly in the line flow system, work-in-process inventory is minimised. The cycle time of a line flow system is defined as the time between consecutive outputs. To maintain a specified cycle time and high volume production, the line must operate smoothly without disruptions as any disruption will result in less than the desired output. The following are factors that will determine the ability of line flow systems to avoid disruptions and operate successfully:

- balance of workload at stations
- preventive maintenance of equipment
- rapid repair when breakdowns occur
- quick identification and resolution of quality problems
- reliability of suppliers to feed line with raw materials.

Example of line balancing

The production line of product X is described in the table below. 720 units of product X must be produced daily with production time being 6 hours per day. Design a line that minimises the number of workstations based on the cycle time and the precedence of the tasks.

Task	Task time (in seconds)	Tasks that must precede
A	20	–
B	10	A
C	30	A

Task	Task time (in seconds)	Tasks that must precede
D	15	B
E	25	B
F	15	D, E
G	20	C
H	10	F, G
I	15	H
Total	160	

1. Start by drawing the precedence diagram.
2. Calculate the cycle time of the production line.

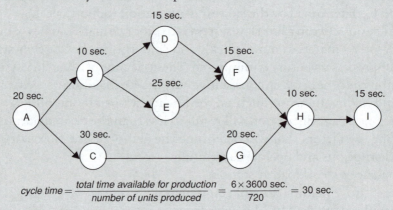

$$cycle\ time = \frac{total\ time\ available\ for\ production}{number\ of\ units\ produced} = \frac{6 \times 3600\ sec.}{720} = 30\ sec.$$

3. Calculate the minimum number of the workstations

$$number\ of\ work\ stations = \frac{total\ processing\ time}{cycle\ time}$$

$$= \frac{160\ sec}{30\ sec} = 5.33 \approx 6\ (rounded\ up)$$

4. Prioritise the assignment of each task into a workstation based on the number of following tasks as described below.

Based on the table below, task A must be assigned first. Since the time allocated for each workstation must not exceed the cycle time (i.e. 30 seconds), task A must be combined with task B as Work Station (WS) 1. The next task which needs to be assigned is either task C, D, or E. In this case, task C is selected because of its longest operation time. Since the operation time of task C is equal to the cycle time, it has to be considered as a stand alone workstation (WS2). This iteration continues until all tasks are assigned to workstations. The result is illustrated in the diagram below.

Task	Number of following tasks
A	8
B	5
C, D, or E	3
F or G	2
H	1
I	0

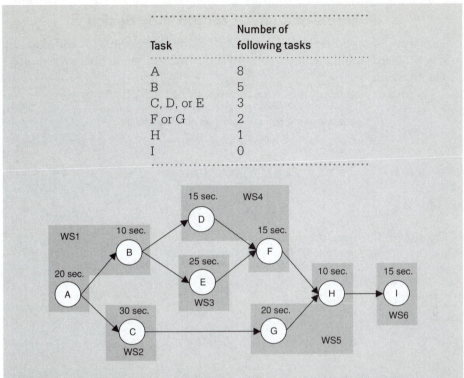

Having established the work stations, the efficiency of the work stations can be calculated as:

160/6 × 30 = 88%. This means that on average, the workstations are utilised 88 per cent of the time. An average of 12 per cent of the time is idle.

Scheduling in intermediate and low volume systems

When dealing with production of non-standard products (e.g., printing name cards, producing and serving restaurant food, operating machine tools) in relatively smaller volumes, job shop type process arrangements is most suitable because it is able to cater for a large number of different products are made in small batches. A batch process, which is an intermediate volume environment that makes a variety of products at relatively higher volume compared to a job shop, would also be suitable.

A key design issue in job and batch shops is the relative positioning of the work centres. If historical or forecast data on the volume of material flow across the work centres (due to the products) are available, then we can compute the total material flow cost of a particular layout. Iterative approaches can be used to improve the total material flow cost of a layout by exchanging pairs of work centres or three work centres at a time. Commercial computerised layout techniques (e.g., CRAFT) using such iterative approaches are available to aid in the layout design.

Example of analysis for job shop design

A facility consists of three rooms: A, B and C. Three departments (1, 2 and 3) need to be arranged within the three rooms such that the total transportation costs are minimised.

The average number of trips per day between the three departments are:

Department pairs	Average number of trips
1–2	20
2–3	200
1–3	100

The distances between the three rooms are:

Room pairs	Distance between rooms
A-B	50 metres
B-C	50 metres
A-C	100 metres

The 'problem' can be summarised pictorially as follows, with a decision being to choose one from the three possible options.

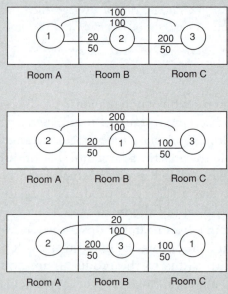

The total transportation costs for each departmental configuration, assuming the unit is $1 per trip per metre travelled, are:

Departmental configuration:	Sum of Load × Distance:
1–2–3	$20 \times 50 + 200 \times 50 + 100 \times 100 = 21{,}000$
2–1–3	$20 \times 50 + 100 \times 50 + 200 \times 100 = 26{,}000$
2–3–1	$200 \times 50 + 100 \times 50 + 20 \times 100 = 17{,}000$

Based on this analysis, least cost departmental arrangement would be:

Room:	Department:
A	2
B	3
C	1

The purpose of scheduling is twofold: to evaluate the workloads on work centres and to determine the priority of jobs to be processed. For intermediate and low volume systems, the assessment of work centre workloads is especially useful for planning capacity. The assignment of jobs to work centres is referred to as loading. Specifically, it involves the assignment of specific jobs to work centres and to various machines in the work centres. When a job can only be processed by a specific work centre, loading presents little difficulty. Challenges arise when there are two or more jobs that need to be processed and these jobs can be processed by several work centres. In such instances, the manager can choose to assign the jobs to the work centres based on different objectives: minimisation of processing and setup costs, minimisation of idle time among work centres or minimisation of job completion times.

Two approaches are used to load work centres, namely infinite loading and finite loading. Infinite loading involves the assigning of jobs to work centres assuming unlimited capacity at the work centres. In contrast, finite loading takes into account that the capacity of the work centres are limited and finite.

When a work centre or machine is available and there is queue of jobs waiting, a key decision is choosing which job to process next. Job prioritisation determines the sequence of jobs to be processed. This is pertinent in intermediate and low volume environments where jobs have different routings and have to contend with other jobs in queue for a work centre or machine to be available for processing.

Priority rules are used to determine the order in which jobs will be processed. There are two types of priority rules: global and local. Global rules take into account information from and on several work centres whereas

Table 6.1 Priority rules: advantages and disadvantages

Priority Rule	Description	Advantages	Disadvantages
First Come, First Served	Jobs that arrive at the work centre first are processed.	Simple and fair. Suitable for jobs with processing time that is difficult to estimate.	Long jobs will tend to delay other jobs.
Shortest Processing Time	Jobs with the shortest processing time are processed first.	Minimises in-process inventories. Less congestion in work centres. Minimises downstream idle time.	Does not incorporate due dates. Make long jobs wait.
Earliest Due Date	Jobs with the earliest due date are processed first.	Incorporate due dates. Minimises lateness.	Does not take into account the processing time. Result in some jobs waiting a long time.
Critical Ratio	Jobs with the smallest ratio of time remaining until due date to processing time remaining are processed first.	Minimises lateness.	
Slack per Operation	Jobs with the shortest average slack times are processed first.	Incorporate downstream information in arriving at a job sequence. Minimises lateness.	
Rush	Jobs that are urgent or belong to preferred customers are processed first.	–	–

local rules only consider information on a single work centre. Commonly used priority rules include: first come, first served; shortest processing time; earliest due date; critical ratio; slack per operation, and 'rush' jobs. Each of the priority rules serves to achieve certain objectives. These rules, and their advantage and disadvantages are presented in Table 6.1.

Scheduling services

Scheduling services is different from scheduling tangible products. Services cannot be stored, and in a service environment, customer requests often arrive randomly. The random arrivals of service customers are especially problematic. It makes the matching of the flow of customers and service capacity extremely difficult. The problem is exacerbated when there is great variability in service times. Thus services scheduling involves the scheduling of the workforce, capacity and equipment as well as customers. Consider for example the emergency department of a hospital. It is impossible to accurately know, forecast make appointments or 'take orders' in advance for these services. Planning and scheduling are done under uncertainty. What if there is an emergency near the hospital and a sudden pulse of arrivals comes in above and beyond the usual 'base load' of customer requirements? And even the base load varies unpredictably at any given time.

Scheduling customers often takes the form of appointment and reservation systems, where these are practicable. Appointment systems minimise waiting time of the customers by controlling their arrival time. Problems can still arise with appointment systems if the customers are late or fail to turn up for the appointment. The inability to fully control the length of service time can upset the appointment system. The problem can be mitigated by trying to match the time reserved for a customer with the time required to service the specific needs rather than by setting appointments at regular intervals. Consider a doctor's office. It's impossible, or at best not easy, to know in advance if any given patient will need 3 or 5 minutes of the doctor's time, or 30 or even 50 minutes.

Reservation systems aim, by formulating an accurate estimate of the demand for a given time period, to minimise excessive waiting by customers or customers' inability to obtain service. However, like appointment systems, late arrivals or failure to turn up can disrupt the system. Appointments or reservations can only partially increase the 'orderliness' and efficiency of service systems. Consider a popular restaurant, which only allows people in who make reservations. How long will people stay, before their table can be reused? How many people will book and not show up? Planning processes and capacity management needs to account for these 'unknowns', which can be estimated and factored in to decision-making, but vary in real time within any given time period.

Summary

We started off this chapter by suggesting that we in the operations management area like to think of organisations in terms of processes. After reading this chapter, we hope that you are convinced about the merits of such an approach!

The overarching purpose of this chapter was to provide an understanding of what a process is. We were also interested in showing how this process-based view affect the workings of a typical organisation and decisions relating to provision of products and services to customers. This was done by providing an explicit definition of a process, classifying processes into generic archetypes, and how these then result in standard topological layouts. We then discussed human and technological issues affecting processes. In addition, we explained how processes can be designed and managed with the aid of some process management tools and techniques. Finally, we showed how scheduling of jobs and orders can be done in several operating environments. Through all of these, we hope that the value of taking a process-based view of operations in particular, and enterprise more broadly, is self-evident.

The management challenge presented at the start of this chapter is about processes in call centres. Organisations in sectors such as financial services, utilities, hotels and travel have made extensive use of telephone-based service provision systems through call centre operations. The principle on which these are built is that customers telephone the centre. Either call centre staff or computer systems handle queries and requests in a (hopefully) fast and customised manner. In the case of Brisbane City Council, its call centre has been very successful in its operations because it has paid strong attention to processes. Indeed, this call centre's whole modus operandi is based on a very process-focused view. Its six key drivers are: (1) operating under the vision of 'customer comes first'; (2) identifying and mapping all customer contract processes; (3) establishing key performance indicators for every customer interaction process; (4) integrating the call centre with the rest of the organisation; (5) clearly defining outcome-based performance standards; and finally (6) translating improved service delivery into cost savings. This has required staff to have very good understanding of the council's processes and systems. Given that customer queries can be on as many as 4000 different topic areas, a system based on call centre employees 'remembering' what answers are found where would be futile. Instead, a process of navigation was created to identify what information is needed to do what. This essentially involved getting information and knowledge from heads and files into navigable systems. This required a tremendous amount of analysis of processes.

DISCUSSION QUESTIONS

1. Discuss a few differences of the practical meaning of processes between manufacturing and service operations.

2. Mass production and customisation have very different strategic goals in their operations with respect to the degree of volume and variety. Discuss these differences, then provide your view on the feasibility of an operation that is characterised with low volume and low variety.

3. Discuss the differences between job shop and flow shop with regards to the following:
   - labour skills
   - flow of the materials
   - work-in-progress (WIP)
   - fixed costs and variable costs of the outputs
   - production scheduling
   - utilisation of resources.

4. Discuss how a flowchart would help the design of the process layout, and how it would play a role in determining the effectiveness and the efficiency of the process.

5. One of the issues in process layout is determining the proximity between processes. Discuss the similarities and differences of proximity between different rooms in a hospital and different sections in a department store.

6. Discuss the roles of Advanced Manufacturing Technology (AMT) in enhancing the effectiveness and the efficiency of the process. Also discuss several key characteristics of processes which make them suitable for AMT to be used. Give some examples.

7. Discuss the roles of Information and Communication Technology (ICT) from two major aspects of the process: internal operations and links with customers or business partners. Illustrate your answer, providing examples of customers or industries in which ICT has had a very major impact on processes through to those which are relatively unchanged by ICT.

8. In analysing a process using service blue-printing, we need to be clear about the location of activities, whether they are performed in the back office or front office. Discuss the implication of the difference between these two sides of service operations. Use examples of banking and restaurants to illustrate your answer.

9. Discuss the purpose of line balancing and how to achieve it from theoretical perspectives. What is the purpose of line balancing?

10. In determining the sequence of the jobs, we have several methods for sequencing based on the quantitative information, namely due date and time of processing. Discuss the qualitative factors which might affect the sequencing decision.

References

Jacobs, F. R. and Chase, R. B. 2008. *Operations and Supply Management: The core.* New York: McGraw-Hill Inc.

Slack, N. et al. 2006. *Operations and Process Management: Principles and practice for strategic impact.* London: Prentice-Hall.

Internet resources

The following websites provide further details related to the process view of operations and organisations:

http://thequalityportal.com/q_patool.htm

http://en.wikipedia.org/wiki/Business_analysis

http://www.asq.org/learn-about-quality/process-analysis-tools/overview/overview.html

http://www.oracle.com/technologies/soa/bpa-suite.html

Supply Chain or Network Approach to Operations Management

Richard Lane

Learning objectives

After reading this chapter you should be able to:

- describe the scope and importance of Supply Chain Management
- understand the importance of supply chain management in coordinating inter-firm activities and improving overall effectiveness
- discuss the impact of the Internet and information technology on supply systems
- understand the role of supply chain strategy in linking corporate strategy and operations
- explain how the available infrastructure can affect supply chain options
- understand the role of third-party service providers in supply chains
- make suggestions for improvements to supply chains.

Box 7.1: Management challenge: Myer department stores

Myer is an iconic Australian business, part of Australian history. The story started in 1900 when Sidney and Elcon Myer opened a store in Bendigo. By the 1980s Myer had a chain of mid-market department stores across Australia and in August 1985, it merged with GJ Coles & Co. Ltd to form Coles Myer Ltd.

By 2005, the group management was facing concerns over the lack of profitability of the Myer chain as well as general issues of lack of fit between the operations and worries over the possible entry of retailing giants such as Tesco and Wal-Mart into the Australian market in the future. In March 2006, Coles Myer announced it would sell Myer to a consortium including the Myer family and the US private equity group Newbridge Capital, part of the Texas Pacific group. The group has interests in the UK department store Debenhams and the high-end US retailer Neiman Marcus. The de-merger took effect in November 2006.

The de-merger presents opportunities for Myer, in giving it ability to concentrate on its distinctive business. Suppose you recently joined a major consulting group that is talking to Myer about its supply systems. The principal consultant asks you for suggestions. What do you suggest?

Introduction

Supply chains are the strings that tie companies together. They link organisations such as miners, farmers, manufacturers and service firms to their suppliers and to their customers. They perform seeming miracles in providing consumers with an unparalleled range of products at ever lower real costs. But the products that the consumer sees and buys are really only the tip of the iceberg. Most business is transacted as business-to-business. The product the consumer picks up in the shop is usually only the final step in a long and complex supply chain.

There have always been supply chains but supply systems today have become vastly complex and sophisticated, in terms of the numbers of items involved, the geographical scope of the markets and their rate of change. Changes in supply chains have been partly an outcome of the changes in technology of products, manufacturing processes and information processing. Consumer expectations have risen, technology has become more complex, companies have become more interdependent, the pace of change has accelerated as the world's businesses globalise. At the same time, new developments in supply chain systems have opened up new possibilities for consumers and producers. The rapidity and extent of the changes have created new issues that companies are still trying to deal with.

This chapter provides an introduction to supply chain management. It points out the complexity of many of these operations. It outlines some ways in which supply chains can be improved. It discusses the Internet, and its role in supply chains. One question is whether the Internet simplifies the management of supply chains or makes the problems worse. Other issues that arise include the role of forecasting and inter-enterprise systems, the need for supply chain flexibility, and rapid adaptation to technical and consumer changes.

The next section introduces some of the fundamental concepts – what we mean by a supply chain, what the fundamental tradeoffs are in running supply chains and logistics systems, and some of the options for improving supply systems. We then turn to a glamour item – the Internet. These days we seemingly cannot live as consumers without e-mail and the Internet. We can order products online from around the world while sitting at home. But how do companies deal with the issues this raises? And what role does information technology play in supply chains? We then look at service providers – those companies that provide distribution services or infrastructure that supports modern supply systems. Much of this is so much taken for granted in advanced countries that it is difficult to image life without it. But what happens when we buy or sell things in less advanced countries? Wal-Mart, the world's biggest company by dollars of sales, discovered the answer when it set up in China. This is the topic of the following section. The final section returns to the question of what it means to have a good supply system. We look at some current challenges and measures of success.

Box 7.2: What's behind production of the things we consume?

Consider the supply chain behind a McDonald's meal, or the car that you drive or your bank account. For a hamburger, some fries and perhaps a soft drink, consider how many steps are involved in getting that product ready. Most of those steps are not conducted by the final producer, McDonald's! For a hamburger, the bread has to be baked and delivered, and this is usually done to McDonald's specification by a specialist, high-volume baking company. It had to buy in flour from a flour milling company, which in turn created that flour from wheat and other inputs in a flour mill. There are numerous other components of the bread, which could also be traced back to their original sources, which essentially come ultimately from the earth we live on, meaning either agricultural sources or minerals. Remember also the equipment, buildings, computers, even the stationary used in the supply chain companies, which are directly or indirectly used in the production systems involved in this chain. As well as the bread, McDonald's also sources beef, fish, chicken, sauces, salad and vegetable components, cheese from the dairy industry and numerous other elements of supply. And do not forget the packaging, which brings into the supply picture a series of other companies, from paper manufacturing, printing and related sectors. Then, there are the industries and companies needed to build and maintain McDonald's stores, the advertising industry, and the newspapers and TV industry in which the advertisements are placed, and so on. There is also a lot of transport involved, which means trucks, possibly ships or trains, and definitely oil as a supply component to fuel the vehicles, as well as the truck manufacturers and their supply chain. From all of this complexity, we normally consider the *primary* supply chain, not all of the secondary aspects, when we consider supply chain management issues and opportunities, where the primary supply chain is defined as those which produce components or materials, information or services that directly contribute to the material offering of the company that sells to the consumer. So McDonald's primary supply chain would include the beef producers, bakeries and flour mills, fishing operations, chicken and cheese suppliers and dairies, potato farmers, packaging producing companies, and many others who contribute to the actual products and services that are sold. However, to keep things simple and manageable, we would normally not consider the oil producer that produced the petrol for transport purposes, or the coal miner that obtained the coal for producing electricity that McDonald's buys, as these effects are too indirect. Nevertheless, we can see that McDonald's assembles its products and services from a long and complex series of operations that supply it in a number of 'tiers'.

How many components are in your car? Think about all the screws, nuts, bolts, plastic bits and pieces, body work and drive train parts. There are indeed up to 10,000 parts in most cars. These were mostly not actually produced by Nissan, Ford, Mitsubishi, GM Holden, Toyota, BMW, or whoever else assembled the car you drive. They were made within a complex yet very efficient supply chain of companies, which has many tiers, and can be traced all the way back to industries and companies making steel, raw plastics, glass, and other materials. As with McDonald's, there is a chain of suppliers, many of them indirect, supplying equipment, computer software, energy, and many other things that are necessary to this industry's operation.

For many companies, the extent of and the importance of effectively managing the supply network can be seen from analysing the total cost of goods sold (COGS) for that company. In the manufacturing sector, COGS often breaks down into the components of about 60 per cent bought-in materials, 10 per cent direct labour, with the rest being indirect labour and other overheads such as energy, office, equipment, managers, marketing, etc. In the service sector, whether it is mass producing services such as banks, or professional services such as law firms or management consultants, there tends to be less complexity in supply chains, because services are more often produced by direct human actions. However, in banks, the supply of technology, back-office processing (such as cheque clearing, credit card transaction processing) and many other services are often bought in and these days, they are often bought in from the best, possibly cheapest, place in the world they can be obtained. Call centre services are often bought-in items from suppliers. Software development may be similar. Service companies have a much lower proportion of their cost (COGS) in materials and are much higher, for example perhaps 50 per cent of COGS, in labour cost. However, this does not mean that supply chain management issues and opportunities do not exist or are not important in service companies: they certainly are so!

What is a supply chain?

The objective of Supply Chain Management is 'managing the entire flow of information, materials, and services from raw materials suppliers through factories and warehouses to the end customer' (Burt et al., 2003, p. 622).

Supply chain management therefore potentially involves many separate, independent organisations – suppliers, manufacturers, distributors, retailers, and service organisations – that are supposed to be 'managed' to facilitate the whole process. This in itself is a problem. What is not so clear from this short definition is some of the other dimensions. The companies may be handling hundreds of thousands of different items. They may be procured worldwide. They involve processes or materials that were still under development at the time the product was planned. There may be competitive pressures to get products to market at short notice. The product may only be saleable for a short time before it is replaced by a better product or a product for another season.

Companies and situations

We start by sketching some examples.

Woolworths (also branded as Safeway) supermarkets are a familiar sight throughout Australia. They handle more than 20,000 different items on a regular basis, with each item, package size or flavour being a separate stock keeping unit (SKU). In addition to this, there are large numbers of seasonal items and promotions. Customers are very price sensitive.

Caterpillar is a global manufacturer of bulldozers, excavators, dump trucks and other mining and earth moving equipment. It supplies mining companies and construction companies. Caterpillar has 86 facilities in 25 countries and ships 84 million lines of parts annually to over 200 countries.

Myer is our management challenge. It sells goods – up-market clothes, fashion goods, perfumes, shoes, furniture, crockery, hi-fi equipment, and other items – that present different challenges from the previous two examples. Many of the goods are seasonal or fashionable, so that on-time delivery and quick sale is important. Goods are sourced worldwide.

Operations like these are a familiar sight throughout most of the world. The objective of the chapter is to explore issues such as what we mean by 'good' supply chain management practice. How should we assess whether a particular system is 'good'? What options are available for improving systems?

Some obvious features of these examples are that they are all large-scale operations, handling thousands, or even hundreds of thousands, of different items and millions or billions of transactions. They involve multiple suppliers and partners, with links on a global scale.

Another feature is that cost is often only one of a number of criteria for measuring success. There are few companies or operations for which cost is not an important factor, but there are many for which this cost is not the only or key determinant of success. At Woolworths, mark-ups are small, making cost a critical factor, but even here customer service plays an important role. At Myer, the margins are bigger and cost control is not quite so paramount.

Style and product quality play greater roles, along with product availability of short-lived products sourced from around the world. Caterpillar deals in expensive equipment, for which unnecessary down-time is an unforgivable sin. Product quality, support and services overshadow cost control, but even here cost cannot be ignored.

Operating the supply chain

Our examples give a hint of what needs to happen in the background so that what we are looking for appears on the shelf of a retailer. But even more complexity lurks behind the scenes. The computer on sale in the store – one of thousands of items in the store – may have been made in Malaysia using chips made in Taiwan and other components from Japan. Not only do we have to procure computers, but the manufacturers have to procure components, as do their suppliers. Supply chains can be enormously complicated. Many of the choices are non-intuitive and depend on system-wide considerations. As an example, air freight is widely used even when it is not the cheapest means of transport.

Despite the complexity, we propose that many of the issues can be understood in terms of a couple of basic concepts. One is the need for economies (meaning low cost and efficiency) in transportation and handling. The other is the fact that forecasts are almost never right. There is an old saying in forecasting: 'Forecasting is hard, especially out into the future'. If only we knew exactly how many of that dress in pale gold, small size, style #3087, would sell in Melbourne in November! Then we could place the orders with the supplier in March, so he could order the materials in April, ship them in a full container going to Melbourne, so they arrive in Melbourne in time to go on the shelf.

The benefits of developments in transportation and handling are easy to see. Modern shipping and transportation is largely based around handling of large unit loads in the form of shipping containers and full truck loads. Full containers can be packed at factories and trucked or shipped to customers for unpacking on their premises. This results in highly efficient handling and low costs. Transport by truck gives one-day delivery almost anywhere within the continental USA, or within Australia, or within Europe. Sea transport has much longer lead times with delivery times between Europe, America and Asia running up to a couple of months after shipment, port handling and customs are taken into account.

Simply having good transport is not enough. The next layer of supply chain management is the design of a physical distribution system. A basic trend is to try to minimise stocks throughout the system, just as for *just-in-time* (JIT) approaches. Warehouses where goods are stored are re-designated as *distribution centres* to emphasise that their role is not to store goods 'just in case', but to ship them out to where they are needed as soon as possible. In many cases their role is to provide product mixing. For other products, the distribution centre will play a *break bulk* role. Bulk deliveries will be placed on racks in the warehouse and staff will go around to pick the quantities of each of the several thousand products needed by a store, and make up a load for local delivery. At the store, the delivered stock is then put directly on the shelves. Bar-codes at the cash registers can track sales item by item. Pre-planning can extend back through the supply chain. Goods can be delivered already labelled, priced, with bar-codes on individual items, pre-sorted by store location and rack, so as to minimise handling costs at the store.

An issue that is now receiving increased attention is the vulnerability of supply chains to unexpected events. Operating a system might be relatively straightforward if only there were perfect forecasts. Demand would be known, orders placed, materials obtained, production scheduled, and products shipped to stores. In practice this does not often happen. Despite the best market research, no-one really knows whether a new model of car is going to sell well or poorly, still less if a particular Christmas card will. Complicating factors are seasonal promotions, rapid product development, competitors' actions, economic conditions and the general fickleness of weather. An important aspect of supply systems is therefore their coping mechanisms. A range of strategies have been developed to increase the flexibility of such systems. Many come under the rubric of *quick response*. This is based on, and allied to, ideas of JIT in manufacturing. We will illustrate a few here.

One well-tried method is *form postponement*. The traditional example is paint. In the old days, a paint shop had rows of cans of different shades of paint pre-mixed at the factory. Now, a paint shop stocks only a few uncoloured paint bases, which can be tinted in the shop to any colour the customer wants. This largely solves the forecasting problem. The paint shop no longer has to forecast what colours need to be ordered and stocked. Another example is lounge furniture. If you order a lounge suite in a particular fabric and colour, it is not pulled out of a warehouse for you. You pay the store, the store orders a lounge suite to your specifications from the factory and a trucker delivers it to your front door. A more elaborate example of the same strategy is used by the Spanish clothing manufacturer Zara. If a particular line of jeans is not selling, Zara can design a new style, get the fabric woven and dyed, and the new item cut and sewn and into the stores within a week.

Another important aspect is flexibility to deal with volume changes and product changes. Here, the key concept is to keep the minimum stock in the system compatible with meeting service requirements. Ideally stock is delivered just in time. As with JIT, this requires appropriate system design, including flexible capacity, quality control, and reliable suppliers. Finally, in this section, we mention that despite all this forecasting, planning and design, there will still be cases where we run out of stock or do not have the right item on hand. If a store does not have the size and colour shoe you want, they should be able to tell you on the spot whether another store in the chain has it in stock, then reserve it for you, and have it delivered to your store for you to collect. This requires efficient communications and small-lot shipping not necessarily available in every country of the world. We discuss infrastructure and services later.

Sourcing and strategic issues

In a famous article in 1962, the noted management guru Peter Drucker described distribution as 'the economy's dark continent', adding that 'we know little more about distribution today than Napoleon's contemporaries knew about the interior of Africa'. The article itself discusses the problems of managing distribution, once a product is manufactured, and the converse, namely the problems in purchasing. While it is easy to focus on what happens inside the plant, what happens outside may be just as important.

This is still a major issue and a major opportunity for most businesses even today, and refers directly to supply chains and their management. Most companies have been striving for decades to make the operations within their organisational walls more efficient and effective, and only relatively recently has attention been given to these inter-company coordination opportunities.

Companies may outsource or purchase up to 50 to 75 per cent of the value of their sales. Some companies have thousands of suppliers. And many companies sell not to consumers but to other companies. Indeed, one common estimate is that 60 per cent of all business is *business-to-business* (B2B). There are though inherent conflicts. A supplier would like high prices, long-term contracts, predictable demand and long-production runs and long lead times so it can optimise production and shipping. The purchaser would like low prices, short-lead times, and flexibility to change volumes and specifications at short notice. So cooperation across a supply chain relationship, while attractive, is often accompanied with some tension and conflict.

The best companies have probably always recognised the value of reliable suppliers but the issue really came to prominence with the evolution of the just-in-time concept. The Japanese stunned the West in the 1960s by producing high-quality manufactured goods at low cost. Initially, people claimed this was dumping at uneconomic prices. Later, it was learnt that lean production involved unprecedented cooperation between suppliers and manufacturers. A popular view was then that this was a cultural phenomenon resulting from oriental traditions of trust and mutual respect, and so not really applicable in the West. The Western tradition was for customers, especially large powerful customers such as automotive assemblers (Ford, General Motors, Chrysler) to 'hammer' their suppliers down on prices. This often caused suppliers to cut corners on quality, which led to poor outcomes for all players involved.

Nishiguchi (1994) presents an interesting historical study of what really happened in Japan. Early in the twentieth century, burgeoning factories attracted unskilled workers from the land. Manufacturers were forced to train workers, and offered the incentive of automatic salary increases to those who stayed with the company in an attempt to retain the workers they had trained. This eventually evolved into the supposed Japanese tradition of life-time employment. Subcontracting evolved in the 1930s in response to a big build up of military demands. Subcontractors had no design capability and little quality control, and were treated with contempt. In 1953, the Japanese government was forced to pass legislation prohibiting unfair subcontract-ing practices. At that time any abuse you could imagine was being practised, although a few forward-looking companies such as Toyota had always appre-ciated the critical role of suppliers and worked hard to develop constructive relations.

The real changes in Japanese practice only came in the 1960s. Faced with major quality problems, Japanese manufacturers were forced to address the issue. The American experts Deming and Juran went to Japan to introduce quality control philosophies and techniques. The nature of subcontract-ing changed. Larger assemblies were contracted. Subcontractors developed design capabilities. Second and third tier subcontractors appeared. Collabo-rative subcontracting involved commitment to continued collaboration and support, even in recessions. Firms collaborated in inter-firm problem-solving to ensure high quality and low costs, with shared benefits. These concepts are today accepted as part of best practice, but are often still difficult to attain given the potential conflicts of interest inherent in the supplier–customer relationship. It seems that companies are still putting short-term profits ahead of long-term interests critical to survival.

Supplier relations are increasingly characterised and improved by col-laboration and sharing of information. Companies collaborate on prod-uct design. Automotive companies regularly provide suppliers with infor-mation about planned production, information that in earlier years was a tightly guarded secret. The choice of suppliers and partners is therefore crit-ical. It is necessary to understand the supplier's business and potential and get beyond short-term issue of lowest price. One company might use high labour and basic processes offering little opportunity for quality improve-ment or economies of scale with increasing purchases. Another company might offer the same price but may have made big investments in capi-tal equipment offering major opportunities for low marginal costs and big economies of scale with increased volume. One company may have exper-tise to support development of next generation equipment; another may not. In any case, a range of relationships are possible. Possibilities range from on-going repeated purchase, without any long-term contract, through to joint ventures and takeover. Companies can be involved in multiple relationships, collaborating in some areas while competing aggressively in others.

Designing success with SCOR®

SCOR® is a tool developed by The Supply-Chain Council to provide a practical link between the concepts outlined above and real implementation in a multi-organisational supply chain. The council is an industry group with close to 1000 corporate members worldwide. It was organised in 1996 with the aim of providing a common language in which members of a supply chain could 'address, improve, and communicate supply-chain management practices within and between all interested parties' (See SCC, 2006). The council developed SCOR, the Supply-Chain Operations Reference model, as a process reference model for supply-chain management, spanning from the supplier's supplier to the customer's customer. It incorporates concepts of business process reengineering, benchmarking, and best practices analysis. (See SCC, 2006).

The SCOR model involves several management processes which can be decomposed into further detail, as well as standard attributes and metrics which facilitate inter-organisation communication, linkage with corporate strategy, and the ability to re-configure information, source locations, and delivery channels. The five distinct management processes are: plan, source, make, deliver and return. These can be further specified. Deliver, for example, includes order, warehouse, transportation, and installation management for stocked, make-to-order, and engineer-to-order products (SCOR 2006: 4). The metrics incorporated provide 'calculations by which an implementing organisation can measure how successful they are in achieving their desired positioning within the competitive market space' (SCC 2006: 8). These again can be specified in more detail corresponding to more detailed levels of process disaggregation.

The model therefore fills an important role in linking concepts and strategies to practice. However, it is critical to note that ultimately, success depends on people. Team building is hard enough within an organisation. Successful supply chain management may require team building between different organisations scattered worldwide.

Box 7.3: Caterpillar®

Caterpillar is almost a household name in Australia even for those that do not buy heavy construction equipment. Caterpillar has been building the world's infrastructure and helping in development for 80 years. In 2005, it had sales revenue of US$36 billion. It is the leading manufacturer of construction and mining equipment, diesel and natural gas engines and industrial gas turbines. It is a US-based corporation but is a global supplier, with half of all sales to customers outside the United States.

Caterpillar has three primary strengths – product quality, superior customer service and world class parts distribution. The operating environment for the equipment is extremely harsh, leading to heavy emphasis on in-house manufacturing and quality control, unlike the situation in the automotive or PC industries where hundreds of suppliers are used and the emphasis in manufacturing is more on high volume assembly operations. Another key strength of the company is its dealer network. Komatsu, probably its main competitor for much of the period, experienced great difficulty in getting a toe-hold in the US market for this reason.

The other part of this equation is the world class parts distribution organisation. Caterpillar products are heavy-duty mining and construction equipment and large engines. Even the finest equipment is useless without instant availability of parts and service in even the most remote corners of the world, which is where much of the equipment is to be found. Caterpillar Logistics Services, Inc, offers world-wide support. It has 86 facilities in 25 countries; over 18 million square feet of warehouse space, and ships over 5 billion kilograms of freight annually to over 200 countries. It also trades on this expertise to offer third-party logistics services to more than 60 other companies.

In 2006, Caterpillar announced that it was moving its Asia Pacific Operations headquarters to Beijing, China. Caterpillar Vice President Rich Lavin relocated from Tokyo to Beijing. He has responsibility for manufacturing operations in China, India, Indonesia and Japan. For outside observers, the move to China is unsurprising. Manufacturers worldwide are being forced to move facilities to lower cost regions in China or Eastern Europe. For Caterpillar, there is the added incentive to participate in building, developing and modernising China's infrastructure and economy.

Sources
Company website and Company Annual Report.

The Internet and IT

Strategy and the Internet

At the beginning of this decade, Internet businesses were the rage. The stock market boomed. Companies appeared and overnight became worth millions of dollars on stock market all over the world. Students flocked to courses in e-business. There was a report of one company that was floated to sell dog food over the Internet. And what is more, people invested in it. In 1999, the top 17 Internet stocks were worth US$47 billion, six months later US$296 billion, and in March 2000, they were worth US$729 billion. By the following

January, they dropped to a quarter of this at US$164 billion. Many dot.com companies vanished. Students deserted the e-business courses and faculty moved on. It was a bubble! And it burst.

In the aftermath, the famous business strategist Michael Porter (2001) offered some interesting insights into the business realities underlying e-business and the Internet. The Internet boom resulted from a combination of the lack of real experience in how business could use the Internet and unrealistic estimates of actual growth of the Internet. The euphoric growth reported by early Internet companies could be explained in a number of ways. Many of the costs were hidden or distorted. Equipment was offered at subsidised prices or generous credit terms based on the expectations of future profits by the purchaser. The high publicity to the new technology inevitably resulted in curiosity sales from people willing to experiment with it, especially if offered at subsidised prices at or below those available through traditional channels. Why not order books online from Amazon or dog food from an online dog food store?

In the longer term though, business realities set in. There were often enormous up-front costs in establishing the online business and when sales were made, there was the problem of physically delivering the product, if it involved a physical product. Music can be downloaded online, pharmaceuticals are high value light in weight and can be posted, but dog food is more problematic.

During the boom period, conditions resulted in serious underestimation of the need for capital, demand for services and true costs of delivering on the sales. E-business did not take over the world. Many observers predict that the main beneficiaries of e-business may be established players that have the logistics in place to deliver on orders – the 'clicks and bricks' model. So after the 'irrational exuberance' was over, and reality set in, it became time to examine the real wealth creating opportunities presented by the Internet, of better trading conditions (meaning lower cost and more effective communications) in supply chains.

E-business offers both threats and opportunities to conventional business. Porter (2001) offers an analysis in terms of his well-known framework of rivalry among existing competitors: power of suppliers and buyers, barriers to entry and threats of substitute products or services. The Internet reduces barriers to entry as even small operators can become worldwide names on the Internet. It shifts bargaining power to end consumers, making them less dependent on traditional channels, and encourages price competition. Online procurement may increase competition between suppliers, but, on the other hand, widening of suppliers' opportunities online may give many companies access to the same inputs, leading eventually to standardised products with less differentiation.

Most of these influences are fairly negative for producers. However, the Internet can be used creatively. A company can use the Internet to create increased awareness of products, supplying technical information or other value-adding information. Purchasers may use the Internet to check product specifications and availability before ordering. Some purchasers order online but ask to pick up the product themselves to guarantee faster delivery. Other customers want delivery, which presupposes the availability of efficient low-cost package delivery services. These services are discussed below.

Internet and operations

Supply chains can involve billions of transactions a year with hundreds or thousands of suppliers and distributors, often geographically dispersed. For each transaction the companies must take orders, arrange payment, shipment and handling and record delivery. The companies must also deal with requests for information on specifications and availability, product queries, servicing and complaints. Apart from this, the companies may be engaged in negotiations on contracts, joint development of new products and services, exchange of technical information and designs and other non-transactional data.

The Internet now provides the communications backbone that supports these types of communications. In the early days of computers, companies had to develop proprietary computer-to-computer links to support inter-company data transfer, making systems expensive to develop and difficult to change if a company wanted to change suppliers or distributors. The Internet offers standard interfaces, greater flexibility and reduced costs, although this is not always in the strategic interests of the company (see above).

For the operations manager, the Internet enables many value-adding services. Porter (2001) classifies activities in terms of inbound and outbound logistics and operations, which together make up supply chain management, and marketing and sales, and after sales service. Applications include real-time integrated scheduling and online order and delivery information. Customers may also be able to configure products online themselves and obtain technical support and service information.

In terms of the supply chain structures we have discussed above, the Internet both supports and reduces costs of routine transactions and also facilitates quick-response programs, promoting supply chain flexibility to deal with contingencies. It is also a key tool for transportation and package delivery services, discussed in the next section. The two case studies attached to this section – Cathay Pacific and E-pharmacy – show the use of the Internet in an airline and in a genuine online business.

Box 7.4: Cathay Pacific Airways

Cathay Pacific Airways is one of the world's top-rated airlines. It was founded in Shanghai and commenced operations in 1946 with a flight from Hong Kong to Manila. It now operates passenger services to 102 destinations, offering First and Business Class passengers the use of personal TVs with movies on demand and fully adjustable seats that fold down into beds. It is a member of Oneworld and has code-sharing arrangements with British Airways, American Airlines and Qantas and other airlines. In 1990, Cathay Pacific acquired a shareholding in Dragonair and the cargo airline Air Hong Kong. It now runs freighter services to Beijing and Shanghai using Boeing 747 Freighters. Other freighter services serve Europe and America.

The passenger sees the glamour of the service, the luxury lounges and the courteous flight attendants. As in many services, this is only the tip of the iceberg. The airline operates over a hundred aircraft including Boeing 747s and every day is faced with keeping track of tens of thousands of items of luggage and cargo, supplies, fuel, and passengers. Aircraft maintenance is a high-tech business, with critical aircraft parts being individually numbered and certified. Operations are on a global scale and involve hundreds of suppliers. The entire operation depends on efficient global communications and IT systems.

In 2000, the airline announced a plan to invest US$256 million over three years in Internet systems to support its e-business. The plan included a new website, and projects in the areas of Passenger, Cargo and Procurement. The projects were expected to generate new revenue and achieve significant cost savings. Savings were expected to come particularly from online purchasing and substantial reduction in inventory. Total savings of US$30 million a year were expected.

A key part of the e-business plan was the development of efficient purchasing processes and capability in the industry. Before the project, the company had 750 suppliers but after review, this was reduced to 400 dealing in over 4,000 items. The new system, CXeBuy, standardised part and item definitions, automated paperwork for orders, and was integrated with other Cathay Pacific information and accounting systems.

Sources
Company website, Company Report, Farhoom and Ng, 2002.

Box 7.5: E-pharmacy

E-pharmacy is Australia's largest Internet pharmacy. It has a partnership with Chemist Warehouse, with stores around Australia. The group now employs over 500 staff generating in excess of $100 million in revenue a year. Patients can order goods online or collect them from one of the stores. Internet orders are normally delivered by Australia Post from dispatch centres in Brisbane, Townsville and Melbourne.

The pharmacy is run by qualified pharmacists operating under Australian Laws and Standards. Chemists have an obligation to check for potential drug, health or allergic reactions with pharmaceutical items. Prescription medications can only be supplied with written medication information. Prescriptions must be original written documents, but repeats can be ordered online. Some medications, deemed 'pharmacist only medication', require personal counselling by a pharmacist. For these items, the patient must supply a medical prescription or have a telephone consultation with the pharmacy. Prescriptions are normally packed and dispatched within 24 hours of placement.

Apart from prescription medications, the Internet pharmacy supplies the full range of normal products available in pharmacies. The list includes health products, beauty, medicines, personal care, veterinary and medical aids.

The e-pharmacy model offers advantages to the customer and makes business sense. It is attractive to patients and customers who do not have ready access to pharmacies, either because they do not live near a pharmacy or because they have mobility or access problems. It is also attractive because it offers lower prices over a large range of items. Patients can register medical information with the pharmacy. They also have free access to the pharmacy's own health and drug information, allowing them to search for relevant information from home.

The business model of the pharmacy offers several advantages over traditional pharmacies. Traditional pharmacies are often located in very expensive prime shopping centres, whereas the chemist warehouses and e-pharmacies can be located in more functional locations. The large size of the group puts it in a better position to negotiate prices. Prescription filling and order handling can be streamlined to reduce transaction costs.

Bullwhip and the Internet

The importance of inter-firm cooperation and coordination, as well as forecasting and flexibility, is well demonstrated by the so-called *bullwhip* effect. Many supply chains include many stages. The dress in the shop, for example, may start life with a manufacturer producing thread. This must be dyed and woven. The fabric must be cut and sewn. The dress may then go to a distributor, then a retailer, the final purchaser. Consider now what happens if demand is higher than forecast. The retailer will back-order from the distributor, who will back-order from the manufacturer, who will back-order fabric, who will back-order thread. Only then will increased production start through the pipeline. Given normal delays and ordering policies along the chain, not only may the production arrive at the retailer too late to be of value, but also the variations in production levels and orders gets magnified the further back in the chain we go. This potentially results in a highly unstable production chain, with inefficient utilisation of capacity, and overstocks and stock-outs.

The bullwhip effect is a matter of serious concern in some industries, with estimated costs running to billions of dollars. The basic tools discussed in this book, and in this chapter, provide remedies. One approach is to change the physical situation to speed up production and distribution times. For example, it may be possible to eliminate physical stages in the distribution chain. Quick response can reduce delays. Smaller orders can be placed more frequently. The other main approach is to speed up information flows, in many cases using Internet to link stages in the chain. Also, forecasts can be improved or distribution requirement planning (DRP) systems can be used to plan inventories downstream.

Infrastructure and services

Infrastructure

The supply chains we have discussed, using low-cost transportation of unit loads and quick-response services to deal with forecast uncertainties and other problems, depend on physical and business infrastructure. In most developed countries, it is difficult to imagine a world without interstate highways, overnight trucking, courier services, FedEx, online money transfers, long-distant telephone and the Internet. Also needed, and taken for granted, is soft infrastructure like a functioning legal system, a banking and financial system, transparent government regulation and intellectual property protection.

In developing countries, however, many or all of these facilities may be lacking. Nike experienced a slow start to sourcing in China due to the lack of infrastructure and mutual unfamiliarity with requirements by both sides. Similarly, Wal-Mart's early experiences in establishing operations in China were less than satisfactory (Huffman 2003). Difficulties encountered included regionalism, choice of appropriate technology levels, non-tariff trade barriers, lack of less-than-truckload (LTL) transportation and nationwide parcel delivery, and the error-prone reliance on hard-copy paper flow of documentation. These problems made it difficult to run effective operations in the vaunted Wal-Mart configuration. Wal-Mart, with exports of $10 billion and 31 retail stores across China, however, saw these difficulties as challenges and worked with local parties on closing these gaps. China today has programs in place for extensive modernisation and development of all aspects of infrastructure. Wal-Mart is rapidly expanding its sourcing in China and its local network of Chinese stores.

Lack of modern infrastructure can add to costs. Delays in shipping or clearance can lead to longer planning horizons and forecast periods, causing a reversion from lean or agile production to something like a 'just in case' model. There are real penalties in terms of costs and lack of flexibility.

Service providers

Supply chain management requires many organisations and intermediaries to provide efficient banking and financial services, transportation, reliable energy, telecommunications, and customs clearance. The most obvious need for supply chain management is an efficient transportation system, but it is important to appreciate that without the other parts of the infrastructure and services, even this would not be possible.

Transportation itself can be visualised as comprising two segments. Where possible, companies will make use of efficient large-scale transportation in unit loads, in the form of full shipping containers and full truck loads, to obtain low transportation costs. However, not all companies have scales of operation that justify frequent deliveries on this scale, and even those that do can find it necessary or cost-effective to use quick small-lot deliveries to meet unexpected requirements and avoid the necessity for large inventories. Indeed, the whole JIT and quick-response philosophy requires rapid movement of smaller lots at the time they are needed. Many service operations and retailers also depend on small-lot shipments.

There are many service providers that now offer effective small-lot delivery. One of the first and best known is FedEx. FedEx is credited with creating the concept of overnight delivery and setting the standards for online shipment tracking and other innovations. The company began operations in 1973 using a fleet of 14 aircraft connecting 25 US cities. It pioneered the *hub–spoke* distribution system for airfreight, enabling it to operate efficiently even while guaranteeing overnight delivery service within the mainland US. It now has revenues of US$32 billion and employs 275,000 employees. This massive company uses a fleet of 670 aircraft and 40,000 local delivery trucks to move packages for its overnight courier services. It also provides integrated services to corporate customers. Cisco is reported to be eliminating its self-operated warehouses, using instead *merge-in-transport* services from FedEx for direct shipment to end customers (Bowersox et al., 2002: 38).

The boundaries of logistics services are constantly expanding. Some companies have outsourced not only deliveries but even entire supply chain operations. Integrated logistics suppliers can consolidate deliveries, pick orders and arrange deliveries to factories needing frequent on-schedule deliveries for operating just-in-time production.

Box 7.6: Australia Post

The first Postmaster in Australia was an ex-convict who in Sydney in 1809 took on the job of collecting mail off the arriving ships. The first overland mail service was started in 1838 between Sydney and Melbourne. In 1930, the Postmaster-General's Department unveiled world-first mechanical mail handling equipment at the Sydney Mail Exchange. In 1931 'experimental' airmail flights between Australia and England were completed. Postcodes were created in 1967 when a giant new mail exchange building opened in Sydney, featuring the latest electronic equipment and technology. Australia Post is now a government business enterprise with the Commonwealth Government as its sole shareholder. Since the early 1990s, it has transformed its service culture and now competes on commercial terms for most of its business, although it still has a monopoly over standard letter delivery (addressed letters less than 250 grams).

The modern corporation runs three main types of business – letters, retail and agency services, and parcels and logistics. The traditional letter business continues to grow, but only slowly, as more and more personal and business communication moves online and mobile phones make letter writing an alien activity for many people. The letter business has undergone tremendous changes. The old monumental post office buildings have given way to small suburban offices. Mail is sorted in highly automated mail centres, where supervisors can track incoming mail online on a national basis enabling them to coordinate transport and workloads. Australia Post offers overnight delivery to capital cities, express mail services and corporate services for large mailing. For example, in 1999 it mailed 12.6 million pamphlets explaining the republic referendum.

The second major part of Australia Post's business is Retail and Agency Services, a non-traditional business, offered through its network of postal outlets. Services include bill payment services, banking services, money orders and services for travellers.

The fastest growing part of Australia Post's business is Parcels and Logistics, which exceeded the traditional letter business for the first time in 2006. It offers a whole range of services to business, both nationally and internationally. It has joint ventures with Sai Cheng Logistics International – a joint venture with China Post to provide supply chain management and logistics services between China and Australia and the rest of the world. It has joint ventures with Qantas to provide express air and line haul delivery and express business-to-business transport. It aims to provide a seamless logistics service between China and Australia. It also provides direct-to-consumer logistics services, including inventory management, order fulfilment and delivery of groceries, including frozen, chilled and fresh produce.

Source
2005/2006 Annual Report.

Current challenges and success

Supply chains face a bewildering array of options and problems. In this section we will sketch some accepted ideas on what constitutes good practice and some areas in which even good companies are still facing challenges. The description is necessarily in fairly generic terms. The challenge each company faces is to develop effective answers to its own unique problems and situation.

Burt et al. (2003) argue that for most companies, there is an evolution from internal company issues, through to supplier focus, and finally to the management of a network of enterprises including the customer as well as suppliers (Burt et al., pp. 622–37). In the first stage the company tries to get control of its own internal processes. For a manufacturing company this means focusing on things like materials management, purchasing, inventory control, warehousing, materials handling and shipping. MRP and ERP systems can be installed for linking functional areas.

The next level in this model emphasises the development of long-term, collaborative relationships with key suppliers. This has been something emphasised above. It may involve information systems on an Internet backbone, but is more concerned with collaboration than big systems. JIT, for example, is often presented as a breakthrough in simplifying systems and facilitating flexible cooperation. The final stage in the model emphasises a still wider view with attention to full-chain cooperation to meet the needs of the final paying customer.

The progression in this model is basically from internal processes and clerical compliance, through to mechanical implementation, to proactive management of supplier relationship, through to active full-chain management. Functions that we once regarded as low-level clerical functions are seen to have wider managerial significance, reaching the stage where sourcing and supply chain are viewed as strategic management issues. Table 7.1, adapted from Burt et al. (2003) gives a picture of how the focus changes. A few companies have reached world-class standards in all areas, and indeed define what is meant by world-class practice, but many companies still face challenges.

Summary

The formal definition of supply chain management is the 'management of the entire flow of information, materials and services from raw materials suppliers through factories and warehouses to the end consumer'. This definition carries with it many difficulties and even contradictions. It requires that companies think about what happens outside the company walls. It also requires companies to work with other companies, despite possible or actual conflicts of interest. It also implies that the whole system be 'managed', even though there may be no-one with ownership of the whole system.

Despite the difficulties, highly developed supply systems have emerged. Overall, successful performance is in everyone's best interests. Companies are driven by global pressures for cost reduction, pursuit of new markets and

Table 7.1 Selected demand and supply characteristics at different performance levels

Clerical	Mechanical	Proactive	World Class
Process paperwork	Transactional focus	Involved in developing master production schedules	Involved in strategic product decisions
Sales forecast is unchallenged	Involvement in developing master production schedule	Uses cross-functional teams to minimise conflicts	Integrates supply and planning strategies
Goal is schedule attainment	Inventory management as the product/family level	Attempts to balance customer satisfaction and inventory risk	Cross functional teams involving customers and suppliers
Adversarial relations with suppliers	Reports to Materials Management	Centralised real time data base systems	IT systems communicate requirements throughout the supply chain
Inbound and outbound transportation are organisationally separate	Function areas such as warehousing and materials handling are relatively independent	Improved customer satisfaction from proactive management	Comprehensive performance measurement with senior management overview
Lack of collaboration in the supply chain	Reports at low levels in the organisation	Report to middle levels of management	Real-time traceability of materials and products through the supply chain

(Adapted from: Burt, Dobler & Starling (2003), *World Class Supply Management*, McGraw-Hill, Figures 27.4 & 27.6)

the constant pressure for innovation of new and better products. These pressures lead to almost contradictory requirements for great efficiency while simultaneously developing great flexibility. It is no longer sufficient to process paperwork correctly or manage inventory at the component level only, or even at the product or family level. It is necessary to think in terms of concepts such as balancing customer satisfaction, inventory risk and investment and to work with suppliers and customers in meeting their requirements. It requires developing infrastructure and systems to make these things possible, selecting suppliers and partners, and reconfiguring value chains for better results. This chapter has given an overview of the area, discussed some of the ways in which these conflicting requirements can be addressed, and presented real cases as examples.

The management challenge we presented was the Australian icon, Myer. For twenty one years it had been part of the Coles Myer group. The problem for Myer was that it did not really fit in the high-volume low-margin framework of the rest of the group. As profitability of Coles slid, attention to Myer no doubt slid too.

Myer sources a wide variety of goods on a global scale and so faces a complex supply chain and distribution environment. Many of the ideas sketched in this chapter can be used. Goods sourced overseas may be sorted and re-packed in containers, pre-labelled and bar-coded, and delivered direct to stores in Australia. Internet systems can provide links to suppliers and shipments tracked on-line. Flexibility can be provided to relocate stock items to other stores in response to specific customer requests, utilising computer communications and small-lot delivery. Form postponement techniques such as custom finishing can be used for furniture. Consulting groups establish registers of consultants with experience in similar non-conflicting business, as well as databases of previous consulting assignments. These can be used to profile and benchmark best industry practices.

DISCUSSION QUESTIONS

1. Define supply chain management. What are the major issues?
2. Explain why airfreight can be attractive (and cheaper) even if airfreight is almost always the most expensive method of transportation.
3. Discuss the advantages and disadvantages of having a single supplier for an item.
4. Why might you decide *not* to accept the supplier offering the lowest cost?
5. Give three different ways of dealing with unexpected market demands.
6. Discuss the feasibility of 'demand management', that is, changing demand rather than attempting to meet demands. Give examples.
7. You reduced stocks and told your supplier to be ready to deliver at short notice. Will this reduce your total costs?
8. Why is it often to (almost) everyone's advantage to reduce lead times? Give three methods of reducing lead times in the supply chain?
9. Who does the Internet benefit most – the supplier or the customer? Why?
10. How can companies like FedEx or Australia Post help reduce total supply chain costs?
11. What do companies consider the biggest current issues in supply chain management?

12. Take a case study company from the chapter and try to identify the how the SCOR model would apply to it. (You will need to consult the SCC website or other sources.)

References

Bowersox, D. J. Closs, D. J. and Cooper, M. B. 2002. *Supply Chain Logistics Management.* New York: McGraw-Hill.

Burt, D. N., Dobler, D. W. and Starling, S. L. 2003. *World Class Supply Management.* New York: McGraw-Hill Irwin.

Drucker, P. 1962. 'The economy's dark continent.' *Fortune,* 72(April): 103, 265–70.

Farhoomand, A. and Ng, P. 2002. *E-procurement at Cathay Pacific Airways: e-business valuation.* Hong Kong: Centre for Asian Business Cases, The University of Hong Kong.

Huffman, T. P. 2003. 'Wal-Mart in China: challenges facing a foreign retailer's supply chain.' *The China Business Review,* September–October.

Nishiguchi, T. 1994. *Strategic Industrial Sourcing.* Oxford: Oxford University Press.

Porter, M. E. 2001. 'Strategy and the Internet.' *Harvard Business Review,* March: 63–77.

Supply-Chain Council. 2006. *Supply-Chain Operations Reference-model. SCOR® Overview.* Supply-Chain Council (at http://www.supply-chain.org/public/scor.asp/).

Internet resources

Australia Post at www.auspost.com.au

Federal Express at www.fedex.com

Stanford Supply Chain Forum at http://www.stanford.edu/group/scforum/Welcome/

Supply-Chain Council at http://www.supply-chain.org

Supply Chain Management (journal) at http://www.mcb.co.uk/scm.htm

Woolworths Limited at www.woolworthslimited.com.au

PART III

Moving Forward with OM – Creating Competitive Advantage

Innovation, Technology and Knowledge Management

Paul Hyland and Claudine Soosay

Learning objectives

After reading this chapter you should be able to:

- explain the meaning of innovation, in all the forms, states and rates that it takes place
- explain why innovation is important to an organisation's performance
- explain how innovation can be effectively managed
- understand the issues involved in managing technology in organisations
- understand how knowledge can be formally managed in organisations
- explain how concepts of innovation, technology and knowledge are related.

Box 8.1: Management challenge: hybrid energy drive technology

Consider the example of Toyota and General Motors and the development of the hybrid energy drive technology for powering automobiles and improving fuel efficiency. In the mid to late 1990s, Toyota and General Motors were both investigating such technology and were about at the same early stage of development. Toyota redoubled its efforts into this radical innovation, while General Motors abandoned it for a number of reasons. The rest is history. Toyota invested over $1 billion in the technology. It used it first in the Prius and has now migrated this successful

---

fuel efficient system into many of its other vehicles, from Lexus models to larger passenger vans. It is commercially producing this technology in Japan and more recently has been migrating it into the USA factories, in other words, scaling up the new technology and having it 'main-streamed'. In contrast, General Motors has no equivalent technology and is lumbering towards a different technology, and it has certainly lost any potential for many years to come to be a technological leader in this field.

The ability to make correct decisions about innovation and new technology is crucial to every organisation's future prospects. This includes the many steps from invention and early stage development of the concept to the scale up stages when operations managers must manage the introduction of the innovation into the organisation's value adding processes. What sorts of issues do managers need to consider when thinking about making their organisations innovative, in both technological and knowledge senses?

Introduction

In many countries, and especially those that are industrialised, rapid transition from the industrial age to the knowledge-based economy is taking place. As Peter Drucker (1969) suggested, manual workers (who work with their hands and produce 'stuff') are being replaced with knowledge workers (who work with their heads and produce ideas, knowledge and information). This system depends on, and levers off an economy that is dominated by services, has high degree of interconnectedness and is free to trade globally. Business success then depends on the ability of organisations to be highly innovative, create and use technologies and exploit knowledge. While one could argue that these requirements are not new and that organisations have had to do these for a long time, what is new is that under the knowledge-based economic system, these requirements have become increasingly important. Organisations that operate in this environment need to understand the 'rules' if they are to compete, survive and prosper.

From an operations management perspective, organisations operating in a knowledge-based economy require a range of skills and capabilities, many of which are different from what was needed in the past. These skills and capabilities frequently involve technological changes from both within and outside the organisation. One of the challenges is that technological solutions are often expensive and the results are unforeseeable. There is also risk involved in anything new. The adoption of technological solutions and innovation requires careful implementation and evaluation if real benefits are to be achieved and the risks minimised.

This chapter deals with operations-related issues affecting the management of innovation, technology and knowledge. In the next section, we examine the meaning of innovation. Then, the rates of innovation and how innovations affect core business processes and activities are dealt with. We then show the various forms of innovation – product, service, process and paradigm, and how innovation is associated with renewal and ongoing change in the organisation. We also highlight how the use of technology is inevitable in many aspects of business operations. Further, we show the importance of operations managers being able to evaluate the impact and importance of managing and implementing technological requirements to ensure survival and competitiveness of the organisations. The final section of this chapter highlights the importance of knowledge as the foundation of innovative activities, and how managers can embrace and facilitate knowledge to build capabilities in innovative and effective operations.

The challenges and benefits of innovation success

The challenges of successfully leading and managing innovation, and the benefits from doing it well, can be immense. Consider the benefits from creating a new consumer product or service that is a 'hit' in the world's markets. The Apple iPod is a fine recent example. Sales have been in the tens of millions of units for Apple, however even Apple, which has been successful with Macintosh, iPod and more recently iPhone, has had a number of failures. Consider the key challenges that a new product or service must face to be successful. There are six major areas of such challenges. We briefly outline each of them before turning to some successful innovators who have overcome these challenges.

The customer value proposition challenge

This means that the new product or service must be superior to existing and new competing products or services in appealing to customers. It needs to solve a human or a business requirement in delivering more value to clients than its competitors. When Sony pioneered the Discman, a portable compact disc player, its clearly superior offer to consumers was more convenient, higher quality portable music than previous technologies and products such as the cassette-playing Walkman. The Discman enjoyed some two decades of overwhelming success.

The channel to market challenge

This involves the capability to sell and mass-distribute the product to customers. An example of a product that failed this challenge was the robotic sheep shearer, invented in Australia, which was a technical success and offered an automated alternative to the strenuous and difficult work of shearing sheep. However, the large truck full of expensive equipment needed to support this technology could only be at one place at a time, and Australia's 100 million sheep are literally spread all over the country's outback, making a robotic sheep-shearing service difficult to sell and distribute economically.

The scale up and supply challenge

Meeting this challenge means being able to reliably and efficiently mass produce a new innovative product service or process. Imagine if McDonald's came up with a tasty new product offering in its research laboratory, but could not achieve consistent supplies of the necessary raw materials on a widespread basis, or could not devise or find a production process to deploy which would live up to this company's high standards of reliability and process control. This product could not be moved from the laboratory and prototype stage into McDonald's mainstream global menu unless these challenges were successfully solved.

This supply challenge, of being able to mass produce the offering efficiently and with consistency is clearly a major challenge facing operations managers, in implementing product and service innovations. Value is not created through the invention and production of prototypes only; it does not happen until the successful scale-up to full operational levels is successful. Hence operations managers must be skilled at the process of bringing new items into their production mix, while remaining efficient and effective in their existing production systems, which is quite a challenge! Imagine if Sony were able to make the Discman or more recently the Playstation 3 at low volume only in controlled laboratory conditions, but were unable to mass produce these. Without the operations management capability of efficient and effective mass production, invention normally does not develop into successful innovation and value creation.

The key people challenge

This means that to be successful at innovation management, an integrated approach is needed. Talented managers including operations managers, technology and marketing managers and even general managers have to be able to work together to achieve the many aspects required of successful commercialisation. When inventors go to banks to ask for funding to take their inventive new products or services forward towards the marketplace, the banks need to be convinced that the managerial skill base is in place to overcome the many challenges that will occur during the development process, before lending any money. Technological excellence in the invention process is clearly not enough to guarantee market success, nor is it the same capability as is required in the development and commercialisation process that follows invention and takes the idea through to commercial success. The broad range of human skills must be in place, well beyond those of technology.

The sustainable development challenge

This is the fifth challenge: to make the new market offering acceptable to a whole range of stakeholders and parties who have an interest in it or are affected by it. Communities of interest include those who will work on producing, selling, servicing and distributing it, and indeed it goes much further than that.

Environmental concerns must be satisfied: the product, service and its production process must satisfy environmental regulations, and also labour laws and standards as well as many other legal and ethical requirements. For manufactured products, this means even being responsible these days for disposing of the product once it has finished its useful life. A recycling plan may be required. This challenge acknowledges that new products, services and process technologies must increasingly take a fully responsible position in respect of *all* of its impacts on all members of society and the environment. Products and their production processes will be likely one day to have to prove themselves as 'carbon neutral' before they can be commercialised.

The return on financial investment

This challenge is measured in monetary terms. Those who fund the development, through taking positions in equity terms or providing debt funding, need to see that the risk is well justified through the projected returns, usually needing a solid business plan that sets this out. Imagine the risks and returns inherent in inventing and developing new pharmaceutical products, meaning medicines. It takes some ten plus years to bring a new prescription medicine from the earliest research expenditure stage to product launch, involving many stage-gate or 'go/no-go' decision points. Once a product is launched, its revenue stream must:

- create net profits that more than cover the full cost of production and distribution, marketing and selling it
- pay for the product development process on a discounted cash flow basis, where some of the invested dollars might have been from a decade earlier

- cover the costs invested in the many other trials of potential medicines that were stopped before being fully commercialised and launched.

Meeting the six challenges

These challenges may at first seem daunting, so much so that one is tempted to ask why anyone would take the risk of investing in innovative new products, services or processes at all. The answer comes from entrepreneurs and innovative company managers, who point out that the process of innovating, when it is done well, can indeed be personally very rewarding and satisfying, and can also create tremendous long-term wealth. Innovation can be exciting in every way!

Consider Fred Smith, who entrepreneurially built Federal Express from scratch into a huge business, first in the USA then globally. This business generated well over A$40 billion in revenue in 2007, generating a gross profit of over A$10 billion, financially successful in every way. Mr Smith had to overcome a variety of sceptics, who said this system of hub and spoke overnight parcel delivery, would never work. He had early difficulty in raising the money to finance such an operation. Mr Smith had to find ways to overcome all the six challenges listed above, from a standing start. He is reported as having first proposed his system in a university assignment, and having been criticised by his professor who said it would not work! However, he has prevailed in meeting each and every challenge put in front of him.

At its best, innovation is not about a single big breakthrough, and is also certainly not simply about luck or good fortune. Consider Toyota, which has in the past decade emerged as being not just an excellent quality manufacturer, but has shown itself to be systematically innovative, in both the *small* and the *large*. By small and large, we consider Toyota to be systematically innovative.

In *small step innovation*, Toyota has virtually all of its many thousands of employees, at all levels, conducting small step innovations in their work processes. These employees are both trained and motivated to constantly be questioning their work processes by striving to find ways to improve the efficiency, quality, safety, etc., of their activities. In some Toyota facilities, employees on average come up with almost one improvement suggestion per month.

At the *large* end of innovation, Toyota is leading the mass automotive market in its investment in new vehicle features, both through invention and deployment across its range. The hybrid synergy drive is clearly such an example, as is Toyota's automatic reverse parking capability and many other technical features that create value for consumers. Toyota invests a great deal in its technology centres around the world, including a large facility in Toyota City in Japan and also one in Melbourne, Australia. The key lesson from Toyota is that in order to achieve a consistent stream of innovations, one needs to be systematic and substantial in the amount invested, and focused and disciplined in overcoming the challenges described above.

3M is another company that is renowned for its systematic innovation and 'intrapreneurial' success within all its business units. From its high technology divisions to those making sandpaper and Postit Notes, 3M has had a global goal of 10 per cent each year of revenue coming from new products, and it invests heavily in the creation of new ideas for products services and processes, plus the systematic capability of bringing the best of those through to commercialisation and value creation.

Managing innovation

Innovation is a complex concept. For our purpose, innovation is the introduction of new and useful products, services, methods, practices or processes that add value to the organisation. It is critical for organisational growth and success, yet it is not easily managed. As competition intensifies, product life cycles shorten and technologies proliferate, the pressure on organisations to innovate has heightened.

Innovation is often confused with invention. An invention is only the first step in a long process of bringing a good idea to the marketplace. Many innovations are services and processes, and do not involve inventing a new product. Being a good inventor provides no guarantee of commercial success. For example, the electric vacuum cleaner was invented by J. Murray Spengler. But it was W. H. Hoover who took the idea and worked out how to market and sell the innovative product. At the organisation level, innovation also involves learning and unlearning, and it requires strategic direction to focus on this process. Innovation needs to alter market conditions either through increasing the competitiveness of an organisation in terms of price (or cost), quality, timeliness, delivery performance or in other ways by displacing a product or service from the market with a better offering. So, innovation can encompass any and all aspects of an organisation, from the nature and design of the goods and services it offers to the world, to its production processes and internal service processes, through to and including how it is organised and structured.

Innovation and its impact on operations management

The key task of an operations manager is to ensure that products and services are produced and delivered in an effective and efficient manner. In ensuring that resources are managed effectively, operations managers need to take into account the cost of producing a service or product and the level of quality required to meet the customers' needs. It is also the responsibility of the operations manager to ensure that there is sufficient flexibility in the system to meet variations in the customers' requirements and the reliability of products and services so that they are available and delivered when the customers wants them and on time.

At the same time, there is a need to keep pace with competition, technology improvements, customer needs and wants, and the marketplace. This is because businesses today operate in dynamic environments. Organisations managers are under pressure to continuously seek ways to improve customer satisfaction through their product and service offerings. Innovation is about change; including changing product and service specifications, changing process and systems requirements, changing markets and customers and changing the ways that the business operates.

So, while managing effectively and efficiently is concerned with reducing variation and standardising processes, products and services; innovation is about changing those very same things that the operations manager is attempting to standardise. In this sense, innovation is continually disrupting operations. These disruptions can be small or large scale changes to processes or additional features added to a product or a service that has to be delivered at a new time or in an entirely new location.

Balancing operational effectiveness and innovation capacity

Regardless of the change or the nature of the change, innovations will require investments of time and resources. These investments often mean resources are diverted from the effective and efficient operation of core activities. At the same time, it requires the operations manager to align or re-align existing resources to allow for innovation to take place.

Bessant (2002) argues that organisations need to manage within one setting to operate routines for 'doing what we do better' and at the same time allow space for another set of routines for 'doing things differently' – moving into new and uncharted territory. To do things better and do things differently require two different capacities, an *operational capacity* and an *innovation capacity*.

Organisations use their capabilities to add to their operational and innovation capacities. In most cases, businesses striving to be globally competitive and finish on or near the top emphasise *exploitation* strategies. Exploitation builds on existing ideas and technologies and focuses on incremental improvements. Often small and medium businesses emphasise *exploration* (March 1991). Exploration allows these businesses to find radically new ideas and technologies that can enable them to leap-frog existing players. So, the decision to explore or exploit is a strategic choice and depends on the strategy of an organisation. Many businesses try to both explore and exploit and this is a difficult balancing act.

Rates of innovation

Innovation can take place at different speeds or rates. These can be classified in many ways. For our purposes, we classify the rate of innovation into four types: radical, incremental, continuous and discontinuous innovation.

Radical innovation

Radical innovation emphasises a dramatic departure from existing product offerings and processes or their logical extensions. Radical innovation is high-risk and high-return. Uncertainty plagues radical innovation projects, whether this is technical, market, organisational or resource uncertainties. For example, the digital video disk (DVD) is a radically different technology to video tapes, and the DVD player has altered the market for video tapes and video cassette recorders. Video on disk was not new to the market and laser disk players had made inroads into the video market. However, the DVD player has virtually destroyed the market for laser disks and has dramatically decreased the market for videos and stand alone video cassette recorders.

Box 8.2: Radical innovation – Skype

Skype is without doubt one of the most effective innovations to hit the 21st century. The peer-to-peer (P2P) Internet communications company is turning the communications world on its head by offering consumers free, superior-quality computer to computer audio communications/calls worldwide.

Skype enables people to create the first user-driven, software-based, global Internet communications network that lets them speak to each other for free. It provides paid products that allow users to call traditional telephone numbers (SkypeOut), receive calls from traditional phones (SkypeIn), and receive voicemail messages. Skype also offers users the ability to make video calls, share information such as photos when online, send SMS messages, and develop new ways to express themselves such as personalising their ring tones and Skype profiles.

The technology behind Skype was designed by a group of engineers who have continued to develop their technology with the aim of making it incredibly easy to use. Co-founder, Niklas Zennstrom says:

'We listen to what our customers tell us – what they like and don't like – and this helps us to introduce new features that make using Skype even more enjoyable.'

'We are really focused on enabling the world's conversations. What this means is that today, when you make a call, it's not just about talking. It's about sharing information, for example, looking at photos or communicating in different ways by sending text messages . . .'

'We will never stop innovating. We are also currently previewing a new product called Skypecasts. These are the equivalent of real-time discussion groups on the Internet, for up to 100 people. They are free to set up and participate; we are already seeing amazing interest in them. We are also 100 per cent committed to keeping Skype really simple to use.'

Source
Innovation Magazine, 2007.

Incremental innovation

Not all innovation is large scale. Innovation can occur gradually and can involve small improvements to a process, product or service. Incremental innovation that is gradual and consists of small steps can have a significant impact on a business' competitive position in the market. For example, computers generally and the PC in particular have evolved and improved over the last sixty years. Manufacturers have reduced the size and improved functionality by incorporating new and improved technologies.

While some of the technologies such as transistors and micro-chips may have been radical innovations, the functions and structures of the PC have changed little externally yet the operational capacity and effectiveness have changed enormously. From a risk exposure perspective, organisations that focus only on incremental innovation are attempting to avoid risk. But, at the same time, they could be missing out on opportunities.

Continuous innovation

Organisations sometimes undertake both radical and incremental innovation activities. It should be realised though that to engage in radical innovation, small incremental improvements may sometimes be required. Continuous innovation is defined as 'the ongoing interaction between operations, incremental improvement, learning and radical innovation aimed at effectively combining operational effectiveness and strategic flexibility, exploitation and exploration' (Hyland and Boer, 2006, p. 390). It is an ongoing process, and the motive for continuous innovation is to improve performance and remain competitive.

It is not uncommon for organisations to have an integrated approach to innovation engaging in both radical and incremental innovations. Various departments, through cross-functional teams, will often converge ideas to improve products, services and processes in the organisation with capabilities from various fields. For example, engineers will provide input on designing new products, marketing personnel will advise on when the best time is to launch the product and logistics managers will recommend the best distribution methods. This integration of efforts comprises both radical and incremental improvements.

Box 8.3: Continuous innovation – Bega Cheese, Australia

Bega Cheese started in the Bega Valley in 1899 with the establishment of the Bega Co-operative Creamery Company. It is still structured as a cooperative, and Bega Cheese is now Australia's No. 1 selling single cheese brand. The organisation's mission is 'to make the best dairy product in Australia, in the most hygienic manner, using state-of-the-art equipment and techniques, while still retaining the traditional properties, experience and craft of its heritage.' More than fifty million Bega branded products are sold throughout Australia, split between natural cheddar cheese and processed cheddar cheese. Total output is 60,000 tonnes p. a. The firm employs 500 people, all of whom live within the Bega district in southern New South Wales. The co-op sells a range of cheese types in various packaging. The most recent product innovation is processed cheese in cans. This product is sold throughout Australia and is exported to the Middle East.

Bega Cheese's approach has always been to continuously improve production processes, but it also makes one-off investments to induce in-depth changes in operational efficiency. Facilities and equipment are essential to the innovative activities of the firm. The co-op believes it has the fastest and most technologically advanced cheese processing machines in Australia and it strives to be at the technical forefront in its chosen area of expertise. In the recent past, it has made a major investment in its IT and computer systems and a major investment in automating its processors. Its fundamental target is to develop a world competitive cost structure, which will enable it to compete with other cheese producers. Bega Cheese obtains ideas for innovation and change by examining world's best practices. This is largely the role of the CEO and the senior management team, but the firm also employs many consultants and specialists and relies on the advice of customers (distributors) and machinery suppliers.

Source
Thorburn and Langdale, 2003.

Discontinuous innovation

The concept of discontinuous or disruptive innovation is becoming an increasingly important issue for operations managers. Discontinuous innovation is about new market disruption where the focus is on unmet or unimagined needs in the market or a market segment. A new-market disruption is 'an innovation that enables a larger population of people who previously lacked the money or skill now to begin buying and using a product' (Christensen and Raynor, 2003, p. 102). Organisations need to have capabilities to deal with uncertainties arising from discontinuous shifts in technology, the market or regulation. Under discontinuous conditions, where the rules of the game shift in a disruptive way, the existing players in an industry tend to do badly.

There are cases where radical technological step-change has led to discontinuous conditions across industries. Examples include the shift from grinding to float glass production methods, the move from cable-actuated technology to hydraulic technology, the move from ice harvesting to refrigeration technology; and valves to solid state electronics (Utterback, 1994). One role of managers therefore is to ensure alternative innovation management routines (that the organisation is prepared for disruption and changes in technology, marketplace or regulation) and exploit the position in renewing the organisation's competitive position. This means being receptive in the organisation's mainstream production processes to the new opportunities that arise.

Forms of innovation

There are various forms of innovation. Bessant (2006), expanding on the work of Tidd et al. (2001), has classified them as product/service, process, market position and paradigm.

Product and service innovation

Product innovation consists of successful exploration and exploitation of new ideas and therefore implies the conditions of novelty and use. Product innovation is a process that includes the technical design, research and development (R&D), manufacturing, management and commercial activities involved in the marketing of a new (or improved) product. Consider the totality of what was required to successfully bring the Apple iPod from its initial idea stage to full market introduction.

Products in organisations face the issues of shorter life cycles, the compression of time to market, as well as production and distribution times. Product policies seem to be ever more directed towards scheduling product duration with a deliberate wind down. This increases the importance of developing new products and makes most competitive those companies able to shorten launch times with specific technical and organisational skills. There are many different types of new product development (e. g., improvements to existing products, cost reductions, repositioning, additions to existing product lines, style changes and new product lines).

In comparison to products, the specific characteristics of services make the innovation and development of new services in some ways more complex. Service innovation differs from product innovation in two important ways. First, for labour-intensive, interactive services, the actual providers – the service delivery staff – are part of the customer experience and thus part of the innovation. Second, service innovators usually may not have a tangible product to carry a brand name.

Box 8.4: Product innovation – the case of Mobicon (Australia)

Brisbane-based container handling specialist Mobicon Systems has designed an innovative and unique container handler called the Mobicon which is a cost-effective alternative to larger forklifts, swing lifts and trailers. Developed by Brisbane inventor Tom Schults, the Mobicon consists of two towers on wheels which sit at either end of the container to move it almost anywhere in the yard, even inside the warehouse. The ability to manoeuvre in smaller spaces than other container handling equipment means the Mobicon can handle all containers. The container handler costs less than most other comparable equipment available in the market, has the lowest axle loading and is lighter than any other container handler in the world. The Mobicon is ideally suited for companies handling between 5–400 containers per week, and is a cost effective solution for smaller companies.

The Mobicon is used by a variety of organisations, from Australian Customs which uses the Mobicon to lift containers in each of the major ports in Australia, to major transport specialists Toll, which has the largest supply of Mobicon to date. Sadleirs Transport, Smorgon Steel Reinforcing, Simon National Carriers are also Mobicon users, with some clients even reporting to have increased productivity by up to 20 per cent due to the Mobicon.

Ever since the Mobicon business was established, Tom Schults has taken advantage of the Department of State Development, Trade and Innovation's (DSDTI) Manufacturing Industries Pipeline (MIP) business resources and services. In addition to export and business planning support provided to Mobicon, Mr Schults took part in Mentoring for Growth (M4G) and Mentoring for Investment (M4I) panels. Today, Mobicon boasts an established dealer network in Africa, North America, Europe and New Zealand. The technical knowledge gained from undertaking product development helps Mobicon to research and develop its own modified version of the product to accommodate the logistics of delivering essential supplies such as food and fuel to developing countries and disaster zones.

Process innovation

Process innovation refers to efforts that are aimed at making improvements to how things are done. These efforts can be radical shifts to new process routes for the organisation and industry. Examples include the Bessemer process for steel-making replacing conventional charcoal smelting, and the Pilkington float glass process replacing grinding and polishing. Process innovation can also be incremental improvements in key performance parameters. For example, lean process and performance improvement focus on reducing any waste in a system or process and increasing reliability to enhance flexibility and achieve consistent results. Most businesses that engage in continuous improvement are looking at process innovations.

Box 8.5: Process innovation – Wotif.com (Australia)

Graeme Wood revolutionised the travel industry in Australia when he created the concept for, and co-founded, Wotif.com in 2000. From his simple and innovative idea, Graeme has grown Wotif.com into a global company with a team of over 130 employees worldwide. Graeme's background is in information technology, with more than 30 years' experience in the field of information systems and software development, beginning with NCR and later IBM. His career as an entrepreneur began in the early 1980s with the first of several technology start-ups. In 2004, Graeme's innovative management strategy saw Wotif.com announced as overall winner of the Premier of Queensland's SMART Awards, as well as receiving the award for Outstanding Achievement by an organisation in the services sector.

This great business idea has turned into a commercial reality, with sales doubling, staff levels increasing by 40 per cent, and offices opening world-wide in just four years. The great idea – matching vacant hotel rooms at cut-price rates with last-minute travellers – underpins a major process innovation. The process of booking a room or finding a room meant customers had to look at a range of websites or media outlets or use a travel agent. 'Using traditional media to advertise vacant rooms at short notice is too expensive and inflexible, while promotional discount offers can devalue a hotel's brand. This left the internet as a perfect solution.'

In the process, hotels can list available rooms at any time of the day and as their bookings increase a hotel can remove cheap rooms from the website. This process allows hotels to control on an hour-by-hour basis the number and price of rooms available. Before Wotif.com, this was very difficult. The fact that everybody from top hotel chains to budget accommodation providers quickly started using Wotif.com as a sales distribution channel for vacant rooms at the last minute has been the cornerstone of its success.

Market position innovation

Market position innovation involves redefining the perception of a product or service for customers. The product or service may have additional features or functions to gain a leading edge over competing products. For example, in mobile telephones a shift has taken place from a business tool to a leisure and recreation aid, with considerable associated incremental product and process development (ring tones, cartoon displays, text messaging, built-in camera) emerging as a result of such positional innovation.

Organisations may also target new markets with existing product base to gain positioning in the marketplace. This requires creating completely new markets rather than extending and deepening existing segments or incremental brand identity changes. For example, satellite navigation was originally developed for military use but is now used by sailors, motorists, surveyors and even postmen. Christensen's (1997) study of the rapid evolution of the hard disk drive industry highlights the ways in which unimagined markets can quickly become the key segment.

Box 8.6: Market position innovation – Starhub (Singapore)

Singapore's StarHub started in 1998 as a provider of telephony services. Today StarHub is Singapore's second largest info-communication company and the sole operator delivering a full range of information, communications and entertainment services over fixed, cable, mobile and Internet platforms. StarHub operates a 3G mobile network in addition to its GSM network and is the exclusive provider of i-mode mobile Internet service over its 2.5G and 3G networks. StarHub also operates its own nation-wide HFC network that delivers multi-channel cable TV services (including Digital Cable), voice and Internet access for both consumer and corporate markets. The table below depicts some of its position innovation through products and service offerings.

2000	StarHub introduced first-in-market features such as Per Second Billing and Free Incoming Calls
2003	StarHub established cable broadband open standard in Singapore, the first country in Asia and among the first in the world. This service allows other ISPs to provide their own cable broadband service via StarHub's cable network
	StarHub was the first in Singapore to commercially launch BlackBerry, the world's leading secure wireless email platform
2004	StarHub rolled out its 3G network and started customer trials of 3G services
	StarHub partnered EMI Music Singapore to launch the largest music download service on StarHub's music portal
	StarHub launched Digital Cable services
2005	StarHub launched i-mode mobile Internet service exclusively over its 2.5G and 3G networks, offering over 100 sites from more than 80 international and local content providers
	StarHub launched Demand TV, Singapore's first near video-on-demand service on television
	StarHub introduced Digital Terrestrial Television (DTTV) system which offers better quality service and a compelling selection of cable TV channels for corporate customers
	StarHub launched 3G services and introduced a broad portfolio of mobile video content over its 2G and 3G mobile platforms

2006	StarHub launched Smart TV, a digital recording service to allow customers to 'time shift' so that they have more control when TV programmes are viewed
	StarHub introduced first Nokia i-mode enabled phone in Singapore
2007	StarHub customers enjoy free wireless broadband access at various StarHub hotspots in Singapore
	StarHub launched Southeast Asia's first commercial High Definition Television service

Source
StarHub, 2007.

Paradigm innovation

Paradigm innovations occur when businesses discover significantly new ways of doing business. The major shift in the last twenty years in business has been the use of the Internet to deliver services to customers. In areas such as banking, customers can move money from accounts, pay bills, receive their wages and never physically see money as in cash. The banks' customers now provide the service themselves, which is called straight-through-self-service. This has saved enormous amounts of labour and costs to the banks.

There have been many other shifts in paradigm that have produced a flow on effect in innovation. The digital watch forced Swatch to move into watches as fashion accessories rather than luxury items. The mobile or cellular phone is not simply a communication device: it is a fashion accessory for many consumers, not only must it have the right features, it must look funky and be small enough to fit in a pocket or the smallest handbag. The advent of product-service bundles saw incremental changes to how cars and other consumer goods and industrial goods are sold. When you purchase a car, it comes with a service warranty included in the purchase price. Similarly, when aircraft manufacturers purchases engines, the price includes a contract to service these engines.

Managing technology

Technology as a source of competitive advantage is of vital importance for many organisations. Technology is the means by which we apply our understanding of the natural world to the solution of practical problems. It is a combination of hardware (buildings, plant and equipment), software (the way to operate hardware) and know-how (skills, knowledge and experience together with suitable organisational and institutional arrangement). Technology management encompasses all management activities associated with the procurement of technology, research, development, adaptation and accommodation of technologies in the enterprise, and the exploitation of technologies for the production of goods and services. Some of important issues are discussed below.

Hard and soft technologies

Technologies take different forms in business operations. Most people regard technology as hardware – the machines and tools such as computers and production lines that are used to produce a product or service. But other soft technologies (for example, information processing in service organisations) are important and can have a greater impact than hard technologies. Technologies such as software and process tools such as total quality management, project management tools and six-sigma can have very large impacts on the operational performance of businesses.

Measuring and managing the impact of technologies

There are very many examples of where advanced technologies have delivered wonderful benefits for those who invested in them, and probably about as many where the technology failed to deliver net operational and business benefits. Massive investments in software systems that failed in development or implementation are legendary in the finance sector, such that major banks, for example, have made investments of tens of millions of dollars, or sometimes even a hundred million dollars or more, that led to no effective outcome or benefit, and were 'thrown away'.

Similarly, many process technologies in manufacturing have worked, but many proved to not be technically feasible or economically feasible or both. There are examples from metal manufacturing and assembly processes where numerically controlled machines or robots have been brought in to replace labour-intensive work. Sometimes these have worked well. Often however, technology is bought and installed that is found to be not practical, and not at the leading edge, but at what can be called the *bleeding edge*, referring to the bleeding of company funds spent on getting it right, getting it working, etc. We have seen examples of advanced process technologies in which equipment was installed that replaced only two or three manual workers. The equipment was costly in terms of capital investment, and required two or three technicians to continually adjust it to keep it working. The net benefit of such technology is clearly negative, and can be significantly so.

This leads to the term, *correct level of technology*, meaning that we should seek the right level of technology that best delivers the organisation's operations strategy and hence the business strategy. Blindly pursuing advanced technology, sometimes known as the *toy train syndrome* (technology for its own sake) often leads to the 'bleeding edge' phenomenon we refer to above, or the corporate form of shedding tears (meaning wasting money).

Box 8.7: Assessing technology: issues to consider

- Investment and operating costs, including purchasing, installation and commissioning, and ongoing maintenance.
- Possible expansion of technology in the future which calls for compatibility among different technologies used in the operations.
- The level and type of skills required to operate the technology. Higher levels of automation usually require higher levels of operator and technical support skills, however there are exceptions.
- The extent to which technology will replace people or change existing jobs, hence, affecting the nature of work and employees' well-being.
- A thorough cost-benefit analysis is important not only in the view of short-term results but also long-term effects, including product life cycle which can make the technology obsolete.
- The impact of technology on the customer experience, customer satisfaction and perceptions of the organisation by all stakeholders, meaning the impact on marketing variables of the proposed new technology. For example, if a wine producing company brings in high levels of processing automation, does it negatively impact the 'romantic' notion of people making wine by hand, that might have been the positioning in the market of the company?

Harnessing information and communication technologies

In every industry to some extent, business today has been very strongly influenced by information and communication technology (ICT) related developments. The rapid spread of ICT has changed the way organisations are doing business today, including the means and speed of communication both internally and externally, wider access to information, and the global scope of business. Terms such as e-business, e-commerce, e-operations and the like have become hot topics since the end of last century. Massive investments and large gains and sometimes losses have occurred through attempts to implement new ICT and particularly in recent years, Internet related technologies.

ICT has played several key roles in business operations. First, it provides an effective means of communication and information between organisations and their customers. By using websites, organisations can provide information on its products or services that can be accessed by customers (business-to-customers – 'B2C') or other organisations (business-to-business – 'B2B') from any part of the world wherever the Internet is available. This opens up global competition where organisations are exposed to international markets. Second, the use of ICT for internal communication (intranet, ERP, data warehouse, etc.) allows the integration of information from various business functions (marketing, sales, distribution, purchasing, production, human resources, finance, etc.) that would otherwise be scattered in paper-based environments and less available for coordination and effective decision-making within organisations. Finally, ICT has allowed businesses to be physically fragmented to their benefit. In the past, market, materials, and production were usually located close to each other; now, thanks to the effectiveness of digital technologies and communications, market, materials and production can be separated.

Box 8.8: Changing business processes in banks

IT developments have changed the way banks conduct business. Most banks now have provided customers with the choice of doing transactions via the Internet. This provides customers with accessibility, speed, flexibility and convenience in using the bank's services compared to the past situation where all transactions had to be done on the physical site (bricks and mortar). ATMs are now the principal way of withdrawing cash from a bank account. Increasingly, automated branches are adding video disc and Internet displays selling insurance, providing details of loans and screens offering share quotations. In parts of Europe and the USA, fully automatic branches are replacing existing arrangements. These offer all the usual customer services but do not use bank tellers. These changes necessitate layouts that accommodate these new delivery systems. The space needs to provide for varying numbers of customers, informal queries, areas to complete paying-in slips and the like, sufficient space to allow secure transactions to take place, and a layout that allows limited forms of access when the branch is closed or not fully functioning. These changes have not only reduced costs and lead times within systems and procedures but have also enabled organisations to redesign many of these delivery systems.

New forms of organisational structures

Over the last few decades, many organisations have moved away from traditional vertical hierarchies to horizontal or matrix structures. Organisations may be assembled to meet specific needs or special technology and disbanded as the technology changes or the need disappears. This involves greater integration among and within organisations, especially those facilitated by ICT and the incorporation of Internet. Sometimes referred to as virtual organisations, these are emerging as powerful new forms of organisational structures. The ICT based connectivity allows for sharing of costs, skills and access to global markets. Operations managers will need to embrace new organisational forms, structures and relationships that rapid changes in technology are creating.

Technology transfer

Technology can sometimes be transferred among organisations such as between parent organisation and subsidiaries to streamline operations. In supply chains, it is not uncommon for technology to be shared among suppliers, manufacturers, retailers or customers on the basis of collaborative agreements. For example, electronic data interchange and vendor-managed inventory systems are sometimes used among trading partners. The process of technology acquisition is one of learning and improving their technological capability. This is a complex, long-term process with various levels of technological competence such as the ability to use the technology, adapt it, stretch it, and eventually to become more independent by developing, designing and selling it.

Box 8.9: Technology licensing: Siam United Hi-Tech Ltd, Thailand

Siam United Hi-Tech (SUH) Limited was formed in 1990 following the acquisition of the WN keyboard technology (101 keys) from US electronics company, Honeywell. Previously, SUH had manufactured plastic toys, but was not able to compete in the market owing to cheaper Chinese-made plastic toys. With the licensed technology, the company switched to the production of keyboards. Although this required more sophisticated technology than toys, they too are made of plastic. Therefore, only a modest technological upgrade of SUH's production facility was needed to switch from the manufacture of toys to keyboards.

During the first period (1990–1994), the company manufactured the WN keyboards under the 'SUH-Honeywell' brand name. In 1994, the licensing arrangement with Honeywell expired, and SUH had to develop its own brand name and technology. To meet these challenges, the company employed several foreign technicians and marketing experts who had previously worked with Honeywell. In 1994, SUH released its first originally designed keyboard and sold its entire production to one major customer. In 1996, it developed two new keyboards in addition to updating the product line to include the new Windows 95 keys on all keyboards.

In July 1996, SUH moved into a new state-of-the-art manufacturing facility to meet the increasing demand. Currently, SUH has four keyboard assembly lines with a production capacity of 300,000 keyboards per month with additional space for expansion. SUH uses either laser engraving or sublimation process technologies to print graphics on the key tops. Both methods produce durable characters on the key tops. All keyboards undergo functional testing of every key to ensure that they produce the right electrical signals. Testing is performed using an automatic functional tester that depresses each key. All plastic modelled parts are made in-house using injection moulding facilities adjacent to the final assembly lines.

Keyboards can be divided into low-end and high-end categories according to customers' needs. The low-end keyboards have a limited number of functions and use less sophisticated technology. They are made to complement personal computers. SUH aims to produce high-end products that require a higher level of technology, sophisticated designs and advanced functions.

The licensing of technology from a reputed international electronics company was just the first step for SUH. Much of its success is largely due to its ability to innovate and upgrade the acquired technology, and keep up with technological developments and the needs of its customers. It harnessed the extensive experience of Honeywell to build its brand name and customer base. For instance, the hiring of former Honeywell employees helped in the acquisition of technical, managerial and marketing capabilities. In addition, SUH sent some of its local technicians for training to Honeywell's headquarters in the United States.

Source
United Nations, 2005.

Managing knowledge

Innovation depends on the collective knowledge and capabilities in an organisation. Davenport et al. (1998) define knowledge as a combination of experience, interpretation and reflection. Knowledge is generated and utilised both inside and outside of organisations and is considered the building blocks for competences and capabilities. Organisational knowledge is individually created and collectively held (Brown and Duguid, 1998).

Absorptive capacity

The concept of absorptive capacity deals with the ability of an organisation to adopt new technologies and new business practices (Cohen and Levinthal, 1990). It consists of building the organisation's capability to access external and internal knowledge, which requires a knowledge-sharing culture, and the organisational ability to transform and implement knowledge within the organisation to enhance its core competencies. The absorptive capacities consist of capabilities to recognise the value of new information, assimilate it, and apply it to commercial ends or to evaluate and utilise internal and external knowledge (Cohen and Levinthal, 1990).

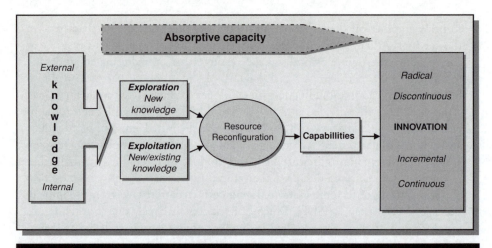

Figure 8.1 Role of knowledge in innovation (*Source*: Soosay and Hyland, 2008)

When there is a need to acquire knowledge that is different from the existing knowledge base, organisations need to explore for new knowledge. For example, Skype needs to continually generate new knowledge to maintain its market position. To do this, it accesses ideas from suppliers, customers and users who are sources of new knowledge to enhance its product and service offering.

Most organisations exploit existing knowledge by incrementally adding to their existing stock of knowledge, where they can innovate and continuously improve their products and services. For example, Bega Cheese improved its packaging and is selling processed cheese in cans. This enabled the company to sell its product in regions with little or no refrigeration. Incremental innovation such as this allows firms to exploit their existing knowledge and the existing knowledge held by their suppliers. In the case of Bega Cheese, the company can now enter new markets. In Figure 8.1, it can be seen that the absorptive capacity is underpinned by the exploration of new knowledge and the exploitation of new or existing knowledge.

Resource reconfiguration

To benefit from knowledge gained from exploration and exploitation, organisations need to configure their resources (see Figure 8.1) so that knowledge can be utilised. The critical resources for knowledge are people and technology. Managers need to ensure that they have their resources aligned in ways that ensures their effective and efficient operational performances. It could mean restructuring work processes and effectively utilising employees, machinery or equipment. For example, Wotif.com has configured its technology resources to allow its customers to use its technology in the most efficient manner. At the same time, Wotif.com's employees can focus on exploiting existing knowledge and technologies to improve the business and explore new knowledge to expand the business.

Knowledge therefore can be seen as a significant resource for various innovation activities in organisations. The acquired information and knowledge has to be converted into a transferable form involving a reconfiguration of resources (knowledge and assets). Capabilities are then formed through understanding and applying the knowledge combination for business activities. For example, through adopting cross-functional structures and empowerment, employees are able to combine knowledge and develop higher skills than before. This integration of knowledge and skills could enable better work processes, efficiencies and operational effectiveness – which form organisational capabilities – that could lead to improvements and innovative activities. As such, managers need to be committed to constant improvement and renewal. They not only have to understand the dynamic market environment and the specific knowledge relevant to business operations, but ensure the continual upgrade and revamp of capabilities within the organisation that will enable innovation activities and operational effectiveness.

Summary

Organisations that operate in the current knowledge-based economy realise that 'rules' for being players in this system are quite different to what they have been used to in the past. In this economic system, there is a heightened requirement for innovativeness, creativity and inventiveness. In the past, many organisations left these to chance, luck and serendipity. Nowadays, depending on these would not be prudent. Organisations need to be a lot more systematic and organised in the way that they go about being innovative. This calls for organisations to be a lot more technology-embracing and knowledge-intensive.

In response to this imperative, this chapter has dealt with salient operations-based issues relating to management of innovation, technology and knowledge. We began by examining the meaning of innovation. Then, the rates of innovation and how they affect core business processes and activities were described. We then showed how it can take various forms – product, service, process and paradigm, and how innovation is associated with renewal and change in organisations. We also highlighted how the use of technology is inevitable in many aspects of business operations. Further, we discussed the imperative for managers to be able to evaluate the impact and importance of managing and implementing technological requirements to ensure competitiveness and survival of organisations. The last section of this chapter highlighted the importance of knowledge as the foundation of innovative activities and showed how operations managers can embrace and facilitate knowledge for capabilities in innovative and effective operations.

At the start of the chapter, the management challenge presented the case of the hybrid energy drive technology for powering automobiles and improving fuel efficiency. Toyota and General Motors both considered this technology at around the same time, but only one of them (Toyota) decided that it was in its strategic interest to pursue this innovation, managed to fully resolve all the technical challenges and eventually bring this innovation to full commercial reality. Obviously, there are many issues that Toyota had to overcome to realise this successful innovation. The technical details involved in creating this drive technology are well described in the book *The Toyota Way* (Liker, 2004). For our purposes, perhaps the most important issues are: the long-term strategic decision that Toyota took; the tenacity it showed in pursuing this technology and resolving all the technical problems; the investment of resources (financial, human, technical); the supportive role of senior executives; and the careful project management of the whole process. Beyond this, the complex interplay between innovation-related practices that inherently require informality, intuition, creativity and spontaneity; and careful management processes that involve discipline, decisiveness, control and monitoring, were all managed in a way that eventually led to a successful outcome. It would seem that some organisations (like Toyota) have available to them all the required elements to be able to successfully deliver on innovations. The challenge is for others to develop similar systems, otherwise the same fate as that of General Motors awaits them!

DISCUSSION QUESTIONS

1. What are the major types of innovation, and how do they encompass the core business process and activities in organisations?
2. What are the factors that operations managers should consider when implementing an innovation strategy in new product development?
3. How can knowledge in various departments enable an operations strategy for the organisation?
4. What are the issues facing technology implementation in manufacturing and service organisations?
5. Explain how organisations need to develop capabilities to balance operational effectiveness and innovation capacity.
6. Explain the concept of Absorptive Capacity and how this enables innovation in organisations.
7. What is the importance of soft technologies to operations management and how do they lead to efficiencies and competitive advantage?
8. How can managers balance operational effectiveness and the demands of being innovative?

References

Bessant, J. 2002. 'Developing routines for innovation management within the firm.' In Sundbo, J. and Fuglsand, L. (eds), *Innovation as Strategic Reflexivity*. London: Routledge.

Bessant, J. 2006. Dealing with Discontinuous Innovation — The European Experience. Proceedings of Continuous Innovation – CI and sustainability: Designing the road ahead. The 7th International CINet Conference. Lucca, Italy, 8–12 September. pp. 115–26.

Brown, J. and Duguid, P. 1998. 'Organizing Knowledge.' *California Management Review*, 40(3): 90–111.

Christensen, C. M. 1997. *The Innovator's Dilemma: When new technologies cause great firms to fail*. New York: Harvard Business School Press.

Christensen, C. M. and Raynor, M. E. 2003. *The Innovator's Solution: Creating and sustaining successful growth*. New York: Harvard Business School Press.

Cohen, W. M. and Levinthal, D. A. 1990. 'Absorptive Capacity: A New Perspective on Learning and Innovation.' *Administrative Science Quarterly*, 35: 128–52.

Davenport, T. H. De, Long, W. D. and Beers, M. C. 1998. 'Successful knowledge management projects.' *Sloan Management Review*, 39(2):43–57.

Drucker, P. 1969. *The Age of Discontinuity: Guidelines to our changing society*. New York: Harper & Row.

Hyland P. and Boer, H. 2006. A Continuous Innovation Framework: some thoughts for consideration. Proceedings of Continuous Innovation – CI and sustainability: Designing the road ahead. The 7th International CINet Conference. Lucca, Italy, 8–12 September. pp. 389–400.

Liker, J. 2004. *The Toyota Way*. New York: McGraw-Hill.

March, J. G. 1991, 'Exploration and exploitation in organizational learning.' *Organization Science*, 2: 71–87.

Soosay, C. and Hyland, P. 2008. 'Exploration and exploitation: the interplay between knowledge and continuous innovation.' *International Journal of Technology Management*, forthcoming.

StarHub (2007). StarHub corporate milestones. Viewed 30 July. http://www.starhub.com/corporate/aboutus/milestones.html

Tan, L. L. 2007. 'Spotlight: Engaging callers globally.' *Innovation Magazine*, 6(3). World Scientific Publishing and National University of Singapore. Viewed 30 July. http://www.innovationmagazine.com/innovation/volumes/v6n3/spotlight1.shtml

Thorburn, L. J. and Langdale, J. 2003. Embracing change – Case Study Illustrating How Australian Firms use Incremental Innovation to Support Growth: A report for the S& T Mapping Study (Dept Education Science and Training and Dept Industry Tourism and Resources), December 2003.

Tidd, J., Bessant, J. and Pavitt, K. 2001. *Managing Innovation: Integrating Technological, Market and Organizational Change*. 2nd edn. UK: John Wiley & Sons Inc.

United Nations 2005. Transfer of Technology for Successful Integration into the Global Economy: A Case Study of the Electronics Industry in Thailand. Viewed 30 July 2007. http://www.unctad.org/en/docs/iteipc20056˙en.pdf

Utterback, J. 1994. *Mastering the Dynamics of Innovation*. Boston, MA: Harvard Business School Press.

Internet resources

http://www.innovation.gov.au/
http://www.ausicom.com/
http://www.aciic.org.au/
http://www.techhistory.co.nz/
http://www.irl.cri.nz/
http://www.med.govt.nz/
http://www.itc.gov.hk/en/welcome.htm

Quality Management in Operations

Lawrie Corbett

Learning objectives

After reading this chapter, you should be able to:
- understand the role of quality management in organisations
- know and appreciate the different definitions of quality
- be familiar with the main ideas of quality 'gurus' such as Deming and Juran
- understand the nature and use of ISO 9000 quality management system
- know how to use the seven basic quality control tools
- be able to apply the seven 'advanced' management and planning tools
- know of the challenges in implementation of quality improvement initiatives
- appreciate the role of teams in quality management.

Box 9.1: Management challenge: the Intercontinental Hotel

The Intercontinental Hotel in Wellington, New Zealand is particularly concerned with the impression that guests receive as they arrive. An employee quality improvement team has identified more than 100 possible events or instances that could affect their guests' impression of the hotel's service between the time they get out of the taxi and reach the front desk to check-in. These include such events as how they are greeted, smudges on door handles, and mishandling of luggage. There are many tangible and also some intangible factors that must be considered, in a hotel that wants to position itself in a market at the top end of service quality and price.

How can the operations managers at this hotel ensure that the highest level of quality is consistently given to customers?

Introduction

Quality is a key business driver. While quality and quality management have been around for a long time, it is only since the rise of Japanese companies such as Toyota, Honda, Sony and others in consumer markets that people have begun to realise the importance of quality in the production and delivery of goods and services. In New Zealand, after the economic deregulation of 1984, leading companies started putting emphasis on improving the quality of their goods and services as the basis of ensuring their survival. Similarly, in Australia, during the 1980s and subsequently, managers in most industries have been attempting to improve the quality of all their processes and their goods and services. This has also been the experience in many other countries.

The essence of the Japanese approach is that they did not believe in a trade off between cost and quality. The chapter on operations strategy (chapter 5) has discussed the trade-off model. Prior to the success of these Japanese companies, Western managers believed that if they wanted to produce high quality goods and services, they had to spend more money and more time to get it. The Japanese approach was that quality was the means and cost was the end, in other words, if they improved their processes and stopped producing waste, rework, scrap, then they would reduce the cost of production and in so doing, they could offer higher quality at lower or not increased cost and so gain market share. It's a compelling argument and has been proven to work, first by Japanese companies and more recently by leading companies all around the world.

In many sectors of the global manufacturing industry, those Japanese companies showed that such views and beliefs were not empty rhetoric, but indeed could be implemented and turned to market place advantage. During that period, industries from steel and ship building to consumer electronics and of course automobiles were led by Japanese companies. Their ascendancy in terms of competitive advantage in many of these industries still exists, and has been one of the most powerful and lasting sets of improvement initiatives seen in the business world in the past fifty years. Perhaps the best example is Toyota, which has founded its success on quality excellence, making it by far the most successful mass producer of cars in the world. Some forty years after the first Toyota cars were seen in Australia, New Zealand, USA and Europe, they have gained tremendous market share from previously entrenched players, at a profit, while most Western automotive companies have been losing money and contracting their volumes and market share. A key question is: 'How has this happened?' The short answer is superior quality of processes, the consequent reliability of their vehicles, and hence of the value proposition of Toyota's product offering to its customers.

Box 9.2: Made in China

At the time of writing, manufacturers in China are under intense scrutiny owing to a series of quality problems with their products. The Chinese Government is struggling to limit the negative fall-out of a series of recent scandals involving low-quality, shoddy and dangerous export products that are made in China. It has been reported that China has established a blacklist of companies that have violated rules on the quality of exports, the commerce ministry said amid growing global concern about the safety of China-made goods.[1] It appears many manufacturers are attempting to increase their profits by the deliberate and secret reduction in the quantity and quality of the materials they are using in their processes – known as 'quality fade'. This apparently also happened at end of 19th century in China when demand expanded for its silk products, competitors moved in and the Chinese began to use inferior quality material in their products. They lost their dominance of the market to Japan. As mentioned above, the Japanese managed to turn around the image that their products had after World War II, as being cheap and shoddy. It remains to be seen whether Chinese firms can do the same. As Paul Midler wrote recently:

'Chinese manufacturers that engage in quality fade unfortunately subscribe to the view that business is about increasing one's share of the pie rather than growing the pie over time. They often focus on extracting profit through short-term manoeuvres that inevitably militate against long-term development. This approach, it should be noted, contrasts sharply with the success strategies of such economies as Japan and Korea, which focus on building market share and developing strategic relationships.

'Some blame quality problems and product recalls on the relentless pursuit of lower prices. Importers most often go to the cheapest supplier, so the supplier who quotes low and quietly cuts corners on quality is the one who wins. Honest suppliers who prefer to quote higher and offer a better quality product lose out. The supplier who obfuscates catches orders first – and most often.

'China's quality situation is by no means hopeless. Japan was known decades ago for making inferior products, but that changed. The key to turning the situation around is to incorporate a habit of quality into the culture. China, however, has not shown that it has any interest in doing so. Recent accusations of unreliability in Chinese products are now being met with tit-for-tat claims that US products are faulty. This is an unfortunate strategy for China, and it means that we will continue to see quality problems. China will not be able to succeed so long as manufacturers are competing in a race to the bottom.'[2]

Notes

1   http://www.channelnewsasia.com/stories/afp_asiapacific_business/view/292234/1/.html (accessed 11 April 2007).

2   http://knowledge.wharton.upenn.edu/article.cfm?articleid=1776#(accessed 11 April 2007).

Quality management

As you will have discovered while reading earlier chapters of this book, the field of operations management is replete with acronyms. The field of quality management has also contributed its share of acronyms. In its early days people used the term *quality control* (QC). This term reflected the fact that the approach to quality at that time was all to do with control and typically companies employed a group of people called quality inspectors who came along as the product was about to go to the customer, and they decided whether or not the product met the customer's specification. The term 'QC' also reflected the origins of quality management in a manufacturing environment. It included a lot of inspection and rework as needed, and also some good works on building quality into the organisation's operational processes, in order to reduce errors.

When people realised the importance of services in the economies of the developed countries, *quality assurance* (QA) was developed to describe all the processes and procedures that organisations used to ensure that their products and services did meet customers' specifications or provided consumers with goods and services of appropriate quality. Since the 1970s the term *total quality management* (TQM) has been adopted. Fundamentally, TQM implies that quality is not solely a control or technical issue but quality must be addressed from the perspective of strategic management and the top levels in the organisation. In leading companies, it has been a company-wide approach and initiative. The principles embodied in total quality management include:

1. committing to continuous improvement
2. working to reduce variation within processes
3. aiming to 'get it right' for internal and external customers the first time
4. eliminating waste and all forms of errors in processes
5. setting appropriate objectives and measures for the output of processes
6. investing the necessary resources in training and development of staff who run processes
7. top management involved and committed to the company wide effort to provide high-quality goods and services.

This century, some people say that total quality management (TQM) has lost favour and is no longer a buzz-word. At some level this may appear true, but more likely the reason is that many organisations now have well-developed quality management systems and consequently no longer need to trumpet the use of the term 'TQM'. Also, it is important to note that the latest developments or extensions of TQM such as 'six-sigma' and 'business excellence' are both based on the fundamentals of total quality management. Six-sigma and business excellence are discussed in Chapter 10 of this book.

The meaning of quality

What do we mean by quality? What do you understand by the term 'quality'? There are probably as many different ideas about quality as there are organisations operating today. As a place to begin let us consider what quality means to you. Think about the following statements:

> 'Compared with gourmet French food, McDonald's is not high-quality food.'
> 'Doing things right is more difficult than deciding what the right thing to do is.'
> 'My boss is my most important customer.'
> 'If it ain't broken, don't fix it!'
> 'Quality will improve if people strive for continuous improvement in their interactions with one another.'

Do you agree or disagree with these statements? Can you say why you agree or disagree? Discuss the statements with some of your fellow students and see if you can come to an agreed position on each of them. Notice how many different views people hold on what quality means. There may or may not be one right answer for the statements, but by the time you reach the end of this chapter, hopefully you will have a clearer idea about the meaning of quality.

Defining quality

Over the years, many definitions have been proposed for the word 'quality'. In 1994, two researchers, C. Reeves and D. Bednar, summarised all the definitions they could find in the literature. The following list of four definitions is based on their classification of all the definitions that had been put forward.

Transcendent quality

Under this definition, quality is synonymous with superiority or innate excellence. Therefore quality is an absolute and universally recognisable. If we accept this view, quality is recognised only through experience. Quality is something subjective. In the cult novel of the 1970s, *Zen and the Art of Motorcycle Maintenance: An enquiry into values*, Pirsig (1974) described a journey across the United States punctuated by mechanical breakdowns and numerous philosophical discussions on the meaning of the concept 'quality'. Pirsig argued that this definition is the only or best definition of quality; in his view it means quality is in the eye of the beholder and you will know it when you see it. As you can imagine, this is not a useful operational definition, but if you can attach this definition to your product or service it can have substantial marketing benefits. For example, luxury goods may aim to use this definition. Works of art would also fit under this definition.

Product-based quality

Here, quality is a precise and measurable variable and this definition says that differences in quality reflect differences in the quantity of some product attribute. For example, Merino wool is high quality wool because it is finer than that from other sheep breeds. Also, a V8 car is higher quality than a car with four cylinders for people who are concerned with engine power. This definition also tends to imply that higher price items are higher quality.

Manufacturing-based quality

This definition suggests that high quality is achieved with conformance to specifications. Specifications are those targets and tolerances determined by the designers of the product or service or required by the customer. For example, a quality airline service might be one where all of its flights arrive within ten minutes of the scheduled arrival time. This is a key definition that will be used in the later discussion on process capability and in the context of the technical aspects of quality control in the section on statistical process control. A strength of this definition is that it is perhaps the most easy to operationalise, and it is the most precise.

Consider how well Toyota does on this aspect of quality, with the vast majority of its new cars being sold in pristine or virtually perfect conformance to specification. The same applies to McDonald's, which produces and sells millions of hamburgers each week that are exactly right on the specification, according to customer requirements.

Value-based quality

In this definition, a quality product or service is one that provides performance at an acceptable price or can perform at an acceptable cost. For example, items fitting this definition might include computer 'clones' (meaning non-branded computers), or generic pharmaceuticals. This definition can be difficult to apply in practice because it incorporates two distinct concepts, namely quality and price.

User-based quality

Here, quality is determined by what the customer wants and is willing to pay for. In other words quality is defined as 'fitness for use' and can be measured by how well the product performs its intended function. Using the example of automobiles again, a BMW and a Jeep can both qualify as high quality because they are fit for use (transport) but they simply serve different needs and different groups of customers. This definition is driven by the idea of customer satisfaction being very important and it has become one of the principal definitions of quality from a managerial perspective.

Quality as meeting or exceeding expectations

By the end of the 1980s, a related but fundamentally different definition emerged. Under this definition quality is 'meeting or exceeding customer expectations'. The customer can be the external customer who is the ultimate purchaser of the good or service, or could be an internal customer who is the person who performs the next operation in the process. This definition implies that understanding who your customers are and what their expectations are is fundamental to achieving customer satisfaction. This definition is applicable across all industries and is responsive to market changes. It is an all-encompassing definition, but perhaps the most complex definition. It may be difficult to measure quality under this definition. Also, customers may not know their expectations, or pre-purchase attitudes may affect subsequent judgements.

It is clear that different definitions of quality can exist within an organisation. Perspectives change at different points within an organisation as the product or service moves from the design stage to the market. For example, while the production staff will be interested in the manufacturing-based definition, the marketing staff may be interested in the transcendent definition. The customer will be interested in the user-based definition. Thus, all the different views are necessary and must be embodied in an overall company philosophy in order to produce a quality product or service. Deming, in his book *Out of the Crisis* (1986), called this an operational definition. A term is operationally-defined if the users of that term agree on a common definition. As he said: 'An operational definition is one that people can do business with. An operational definition of safe, round, reliable, or any other quality must be communicable, with the same meaning to vendor as to purchaser, same meaning yesterday and today to the production worker' (Deming, 1986, p. 277).

Quality and grade

An important distinction needs to be drawn between quality and 'grade' of a product or service. If quality is a measure of the conformance of the product or service to the users' needs, then a fundamental restriction of the users' ability to satisfy their needs is the price they can afford to pay. Hence, comparisons of quality are only realistic if they compare items of similar price. Quality in the sense of excellence without price constraints is a meaningless concept from the perspective of the purchasers who are attempting to satisfy their needs. However we all recognise that paying a higher price often provides a better product or service. In this situation, the item is said to be of a higher grade. For example, to compare the quality of a Toyota Corolla with a luxury vehicle such as a top end Jaguar or Ferrari makes little sense, simply because few customers would be choosing between these cars, which are in very different market segments. The Ferrari and the Jaguar cost many times more than the Corolla. By the way, it is worth noting in passing that the manufacturing-related process quality (measured as defects per car) of the Toyota Corolla may actually be better than that of the Jaguar or Ferrari.

Grade is defined as a category or rank given the two entities (products or services) having the same functional use but different requirements for quality. Grade reflects a planned or recognised difference in requirements for quality. The emphasis is on a functional use and cost relationship. For example, if we are staying in a five-star hotel, we expect it to be different from a stay in a two-star hotel. Both hotels offer the same functional use that is a bed to sleep in, but there is a different cost relationship. A five-star hotel has a planned difference from a two-star hotel. Quality is not the same as grade. In summary, quality is about achieving more value for the same money, not more value for more money.

This point is just to recognise that segments exist in markets and that we should not confuse the achievement of quality with different specifications or grades across market segments. As a further example, consider that most of us fly economy class when we fly in commercial airlines. As we look longingly at the increased comfort of the first class and business class seats on our way towards the back of the plane, are we comparing different quality of seat and service, or grade? Business class tickets generally cost about three times as much as economy tickets, so it is clearly a different grade of service, indeed very different market segments. In each of these market segments, it is possible to achieve a high standard of quality, meaning consistent service to the expected service specification, or not to do so.

Qantas and Air New Zealand compete with Singapore Airlines, Emirates, Malaysian Airlines, Cathay Pacific and others, in each of these segments, with customers who are in the market for one or other class of service comparing prices and service levels across airlines and within their desired market segment, more than across market segments.

Competing on quality

Many researchers and professional managers have attempted to understand the diversity of the above definitions of quality and to delve more deeply into what are the drivers of customer satisfaction. In other words, they have sought to examine how companies can compete on the various aspects of quality. They have carefully considered how customers evaluate quality and then become satisfied or dissatisfied to one extent or another, which impacts on repurchase decisions and 'word of mouth' recommendation.

David Garvin (1987) proposed eight principal product quality dimensions on which companies could compete. They are:

1. Performance – a product's primary operating characteristics, e.g., the size of a car's engine.
2. Features – the 'bells and whistles' of a product, e.g., a mobile phone that can send and receive video and also incorporates an MP3 player.
3. Reliability – the probability of a product surviving over a specified period of time under stated conditions of use.
4. Conformance – the degree to which the physical and performance characteristics of the product or service match the pre-established standards, e.g., the pizza arrives within the promised 30 minutes.
5. Durability – the amount of use one gets from the product before it physically deteriorates, e.g., a $200 chainsaw may have a life expectancy of 100 hours, whereas if you spend $800 on a chainsaw, you may expect it to last 600 hours.
6. Serviceability – the speed, courtesy, and competence of repair, e.g., the New Zealand home appliance company L. V. Martin had the advertising slogan 'It is the putting right that counts'.
7. Aesthetics – how a product looks, feels, tastes, sounds or smells, e.g., the sleek, thin body of the Apple iPod Nano.
8. Perceived quality – a subjective assessment resulting from the image, advertising or brand names, e.g., a Rolex watch or BMW vehicle.

Early research into operations management in service industries suggested that there were a number of distinct characteristics of services that meant the role of the operations manager in a service business was different from that of an operations manager in a manufacturing business (Sasser, Olsen and Wyckoff, 1978). These characteristics are:

1. The service delivery system was a process in which the customer participated.
2. Services are generally intangible.
3. Services are perishable, that is they cannot be stored.
4. Services outputs generally have a higher level of heterogeneity or variability. This is due to both the intangible nature of the service and the presence of the customer resulting in slightly different delivery each time despite the firm having standardised procedures and well-trained staff.

5. The simultaneous production and consumption of most services compounds the other characteristics. As services do not flow through distribution channels, customers must come to the service facility or the service provider must be brought to the customer, e.g., Starbucks has 7800 company-owned stores worldwide and has a long-term aim to increase that to 40,000 so people will not have to walk far to buy a coffee from them.

These characteristics led service operations managers to be dissatisfied with manufacturing-derived measures of quality and tended to favour the last-mentioned definition listed above, that is, meeting or exceeding customer's expectations. As we saw, this definition is hard to operationalise but a group of service industry researchers, studying customers in financial services markets, has identified five key dimensions of service quality that contribute to customer perceptions and expectations. Their model is known as the SERVQUAL model (Zeithaml, Parasuraman and Berry, 1990). The dimensions of the service quality are:

1. Reliability – the ability to provide what was promised, dependably and accurately, e.g., sending out error-free invoices.
2. Assurance – the knowledge and courtesy of employees, and their ability to convey trust and confidence, e.g., employees are polite and pleasant when dealing with customer transactions.
3. Tangibles – the physical facilities and equipment, and the appearance of personnel, e.g., employees are wearing the company uniform.
4. Empathy – the degree of caring and individual attention provided to customers, e.g., teller staff in a bank recognise regular customers by name.
5. Responsiveness – the willingness to help customers and provide prompt service, e.g., giving prompt credit for returned merchandise.

Consider a professional service provider such as a doctor, accountant or engineer. The perceived quality of their work as seen by their clients will likely be of more than just the technical quality of their work, but will be some combination of the five SERVQUAL factors above. If a doctor gives a technically correct diagnosis and treatment, but fails to give reasonable empathy and is unresponsive to follow up questions, patients will generally not be fully satisfied.

Box 9.3: Service quality at Tranz Metro, Wellington

A few years ago one, the SERVQUAL model was applied to the local commuter rail services in Wellington, New Zealand. In order to elicit customers' perceptions and expectations related to each of the five dimensions, the customers were asked questions like the following, and respondents circled a number that represented how they felt:

	My Minimum Service Level is:		My Desired Service Level is:		My Perception of Tranz Metro's Service Performance is:	
	Low	High	Low	High	Low	High
When it comes to . . .						
Staff on train						
1. Courtesy	1 2 3 4 5 6 7 8 9		1 2 3 4 5 6 7 8 9		1 2 3 4 5 6 7 8 9 N	
2. A neat, professional appearance	1 2 3 4 5 6 7 8 9		1 2 3 4 5 6 7 8 9		1 2 3 4 5 6 7 8 9 N	
Willingness to help you	1 2 3 4 5 6 7 8 9		1 2 3 4 5 6 7 8 9		1 2 3 4 5 6 7 8 9 N	

N = No opinion

In analysing the results from a large number of commuters, it was possible to work out the gap between expectations and perceptions and make recommendations to the management (Cavana, Corbett, and Lo, 2007). The company has since taken up this kind of service quality study on a regular basis using a market research company.

Another approach to competing on quality has been proposed by a Japanese researcher, Noriaki Kano. He suggested there are three classes of customer requirements that companies need to identify, and his work showed that there are further complexities in that the customer needs may be invisible to both the customer and the producer (Kano et al. 1984). The three classes of customer requirements are:

1. *Dissatisfiers.* These are requirements that are expected in a product or service but they are generally not stated by customers but assumed as given. Then, if these features are not present, the customer is dissatisfied. For example, when we go to the movies, it is not explicitly stated that the temperature will be in a reasonable range of comfort, but if it is too hot or cold, then customer dissatisfaction will result.

2. *Satisfiers.* These are requirements that customers say they want, and although these requirements are generally expected, by fulfilling them, the company creates customer satisfaction. For example, when the movie goer orders a cup of coffee with milk in the theatre café, it is not satisfactory to be given black coffee because the establishment has run out of milk. One expects what is reasonably asked for, and then is satisfied on getting it.

3. *Exciters/delighters.* These are new or innovative features that customers do not expect, and the presence of these unexpected features leads to high perceptions of quality. When the coffee is ordered in that theatre café, if it is served with a gourmet biscuit on the house, then many customers would see this as above their expectation and be delighted.

To further illustrate this model, the following example is adapted from the work of Mazur.[1] Imagine you are flying on an aeroplane from Sydney to Melbourne. If the plane takes off and lands safely, passengers take no notice. If you were to interview them as to the level of satisfaction, most would claim to be neutral. If, however, the plane did not take off and land safely, passengers would complain loudly (though perhaps briefly) about their dissatisfaction. In other words certain requirements are only visible when they unfulfilled.

Imagine that the flight service between Sydney and Melbourne included champagne and caviar, even in the economy cabin. Passengers would no doubt be excited, but if the service did not include champagne and caviar, they would not complain. Exciting requirements are those that satisfy when fulfilled but do not dissatisfy when left unfulfilled. They too are invisible since customers do not even know to ask.

Mazur suggests Kano's model is more complex. Let us say the plane landed safely and smoothly but it was during a raging storm. The passengers applauded the efforts of the crew. Thus, what was expected in safe weather becomes exciting in bad weather. So, the requirement and expectation changes depending on the environment. The expected requirements and exciting requirements provide the best opportunity for competitive advantage if you can find a way to make them visible and then deliver on them. To do this requires a strong link with the product or service design process, which is covered in another chapter.

Significant contributors

This section considers the main ideas, philosophies and frameworks proposed by two leading personalities that contributed to the development of the quality management field. They are W. Edwards Deming and Joseph Juran.

W. Edwards Deming

Dr Deming, a statistician by training, is credited with being a major influence in the revival of Japanese industry after World War II. He persuaded Japanese business people and government officials to use his methods despite their reservations. Japanese goods had had a reputation of being cheap and shoddy in the early post World War II days, but by using Deming's methods, the Japanese managed to improve the quality of their goods, and their productivity, and competitive position enormously over the following years.

For Deming, quality management meant a major cultural change in an organisation. He defined quality as a predictable degree of uniformity and dependability at low cost that also was suited to the market.

Deming developed a theory of management called the *system of profound knowledge*. Deming's theory of profound knowledge consists of four interdependent components: appreciation of the system; theory of variation; theory of knowledge; and psychology.

Appreciation of the system

Deming described the system as a collection of components that can direct resources towards a common purpose or aim. He stressed it was the job of top management to optimise the entire system towards its aim. It was important that everyone in the organisation understood the aim of the system. An example would be in a restaurant where the work of the cooks, cleaners, waiters, food buyers, and other staff all are aimed at giving the customers an enjoyable, safe, hygienic and tasty experience. Management must coordinate the various activities of these staff, set the standards and measure for adherence to these standards.

Theory of variation

Deming pointed out that variation is inherent in all processes. There are two types of variation – *special cause* and *common cause*. Special causes of variation are external to the system. Common causes of variation are due to the inherent variability of the system, meaning the natural variability within the system and they define a system's quality. For Deming, statistics is the common language in the organisation. Everyone should understand statistics, statistical thinking, and how to handle data in order to reduce uncertainty and variation in the system. Deming suggested there were two types of mistakes you can make in business: (1) act when you should not act, and (2) not act when you should act – in other words, treating a special cause of variation as a common cause of variation, or treating a common cause of variation as a special cause of variation. The latter is by far the more frequent of the two mistakes. It is called *tampering with the system* and will invariably increase the variability of that system. Deming insisted management needed knowledge about the directions between the components of a system and its environment in order to make the system more predictable or achieve the degree of predictability that he talked about in his definition of quality.

Theory of knowledge

This concerns the difference between information and knowledge. Knowledge is concerned with the ability to predict future events. We use a theory to predict the future outcome or to compare the observed outcome with the predicted outcome. Deming said that experience on its own teaches us nothing, meaning that experience is of no value without the aid of theory. Theory allows people to understand and interpret experience.

Psychology

For Deming, psychology was incorporated in his theory in order to help us understand people, interactions between people, and interactions between people and the system of which they are part. He stressed that management must understand the difference between the intrinsic motivation and extrinsic motivation of their employees, and how people needed different amounts of each kind of motivation. He noted people are different and they learn in different ways and at different speeds. He was therefore rather scathing of schemes that attempt to rank people or employees.

Profound knowledge and management

The system of profound knowledge led Deming to generate his 14 points for management (Deming, 1986). He claimed his 14 points provide guidelines, a kind of roadmap, for the changes in managerial thinking required for organisational success. For Deming, they formed a highly interactive system of management. He said no one point can be studied in isolation and they should not be treated as a menu for managers to pick and choose which point they would adopt.

Box 9.4: Deming's fourteen points (adapted from *Out of the Crisis*, 1986)

1. Create constancy of purpose towards improvement.
2. Adopt the new philosophy.
3. Cease dependence on inspection.
4. Move towards a single supplier for any one item.
5. Improve constantly and forever.
6. Institute training on the job.
7. Institute leadership instead of supervision.
8. Drive out fear.
9. Break down barriers between departments.
10. Eliminate slogans.
11. Eliminate management by objectives.
12. Remove barriers to pride of workmanship.
13. Institute education and self-improvement.
14. The transformation is everyone's job.

Deming Wheel

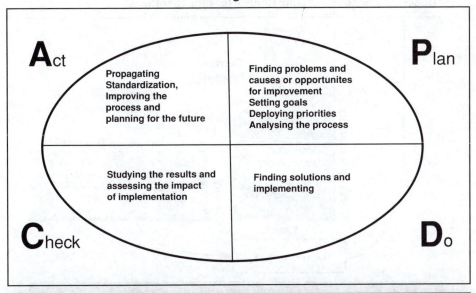

Figure 9.1 Deming Wheel

Deming's approach to continuous improvement was based on the 'plan-do-check-act' (PDCA) cycle of work group problem-solving. This has become known as the Deming Wheel (Figure 9.1). He believed processes could always be improved and variation reduced.

Deming also developed some experiments in order to demonstrate the futility of trying to improve a bad system. These are his famous 'Funnel experiment' and the 'Red Beads' experiment. For a complete discussion of these and his other contributions, go to the Deming website at www.Deming.org.

Joseph Juran

Joseph Juran also helped with the revival of Japanese industry in the 1950s. His approach was to improve quality by working within the existing cultural system in the organisation. His preferred definition for quality was 'fitness for use'.

Juran said that to obtain quality, it is well to begin by establishing the 'vision' for the organisation, along with policies and goals. Conversion of goals into results (making quality happen) is then done through managerial processes, that is, sequences of activities that produce the intended results. He proposed that 'managing for quality' should make extensive use

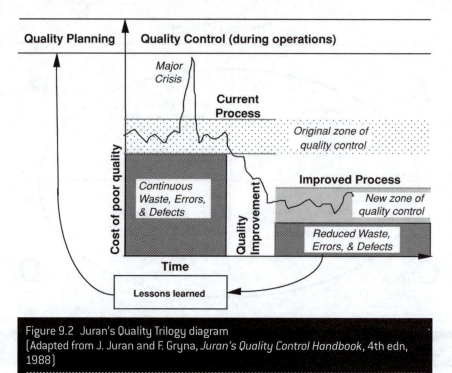

Figure 9.2 Juran's Quality Trilogy diagram
(Adapted from J. Juran and F. Gryna, *Juran's Quality Control Handbook*, 4th edn, 1988)

of three managerial processes:
- quality planning
- quality control
- quality improvement.

These processes have become known as the 'Juran trilogy' (see Figure 9.2). He suggested they parallel the processes used by organisations to manage their finances, such as financial planning, financial control and financial improvement. He believed that the financial analogy helped managers realise that they could manage for quality by using the same processes of planning, control, and improvement.

Juran also believed it was necessary for different languages to exist at different levels in the organisation. He believed that in order to attract the attention of top management to quality improvement, it needed to be expressed in monetary terms. He developed the idea of the cost of quality approach. Given that money is the basic language of senior management, he proposed the figures for the cost of poor quality provide senior managers with information showing the overall size of quality related costs, and the major areas for potential improvement. There are four categories of quality costs: internal failure costs; external failure costs; appraisal costs; and prevention costs.

Internal failure costs

These are costs of deficiencies discovered before delivery which are associated with failure of the process to meet explicit requirements or implicit needs of external or internal customers. For example, scrap, rework, lost or missing information, reinspection, retest, changing processes, redesign of software.

External failure costs

These are costs associated with deficiencies that are found after the product or service is received by the customer. Examples are warranty costs, cost of investigating complaints, cost of handling returned material, lost profits due to customers switching for reasons of quality.

Appraisal costs

These are the costs incurred to determine the degree of performance to quality requirements. Examples are incoming inspection and test, in-process inspection and testing, final inspection and testing.

Prevention costs

These are the costs incurred to keep failure and appraisal costs to a minimum. Examples are money spent on process planning studies, quality audits, supplier evaluation, and particularly training.

Chronic and sporadic waste

Juran also developed the ideas of chronic and sporadic waste. If the process is unable to produce 100 per cent good output as it proceeds, then it is producing a certain amount of waste. This waste is chronic – it goes on and on. The reason for the chronic waste is because the operating process was planned or at least was set up that way, Juran claims. If there is a sudden increase in the defect level of the process, this is called a *sporadic spike*. This has resulted from some unplanned event such as a power failure, process breakdown, or human error (Juran and Godfrey, 1998).

With the cost of quality approach, Juran believed it was not possible to achieve zero defects because the cost of chasing fewer and fewer defects would ultimately exceed the value of a lower defect rate.

Standards-based approach to quality management

ISO 9000 quality management system

The ISO 9000 standards were conceived as a way of giving firms reassurance that their suppliers had a sound quality management system in place.

ISO 9000 Framework

Basic aim is to reduce process variation throughout the organisation

ISO 9000: 2000 -   Quality Management Systems - Fundamentals and Vocabulary

ISO 9001: 2000 -   Quality Management Systems - Requirements

ISO 9004: 2000 -   Quality Management Systems - Guidelines for Performance Improvement

---

Figure 9.3 ISO 9000 Framework

This was particularly important with the rise in international trade from the 1970s. Prior to these standards being developed, there were various national and international quality system standards but they were not sufficiently consistent in terminology or content for widespread use in international trade.

Essentially, the ISO 9000 standards deal with management systems used by organisations to design, produce, deliver, and support their products and services. The standards are written in a way so they apply to all generic product categories: hardware, software, process materials, and services. The ISO 9000 quality system standard is not just one single comprehensive standard, but rather a series of individual standards. The initial series came out in 1987. The standards are under regular revision with an approximately seven year cycle between each series. Also, additional standards have been developed or are under development, e.g., ISO 14000 (Environmental management systems), ISO 22000 (Food safety management standards). The latest revision is shown in Figure 9.3. All of these relate to process standards, and not to product standards. The current ISO standards are more comprehensive than the initial standards. With each new series, these standards have become focused much more on the achievement of high performance through quality excellence than mere conformance to system standards.

A firm becomes entitled to claim ISO 9000 accreditation status when it has completed the preparation work specified in the standard and the firm's operations have been evaluated by a registrar or inspector. Registrars are a trained third party, independent of the company seeking ISO 9000 certification. The registrar is certified by an accrediting organisation. There are a number of different accrediting organisations in various countries. Once accredited, the company must undergo periodic audits by the independent registrars. In other words, accreditation is not given permanently, but is subject to suspension if the firm does not adhere to its certified process, procedures, and quality systems and products.

The way for the company to reach certification is as follows:

1. Determine the scope of activities that would be covered for registration by the standard. Note that not all activities of the organisation need to be covered.
2. Set up a committee or group representing all functions within the organisation, and assign responsibility and authority to drive and coordinate the project.
3. Set up a documentation hierarchy that cascades from one level to the next, meeting all traceability and control requirements. For example:
   - Level 1: quality manual – a policy document that should describe the basis of the company system with regard to all the elements defined by the appropriate standard. It is recommended to keep this as simple as possible.
   - Level 2: procedures – these describe the what, when, where, and who of the company's system.
   - Level 3: work instructions – these should be machine, task, and product specific and should be written by those people who know how to perform the tasks.
   - Level 4: records of process measurements and outputs.

The quality manual, procedures, and work instructions should be controlled documents that are numbered and kept up-to-date. An ISO 9000 certificate is not a once-and-for-all award, but must be renewed at regular intervals recommended by the certification body, usually around three years, with intervening visits from auditors about twice per year.

Current implementation and efficacy

In Australia and New Zealand, accreditation of certifying organisations and consultants is controlled by a body known as the Joint Accreditations System of Australia and New Zealand (JAS-ANZ). This organisation maintains a register of all certified organisations. In 2006, there were 10,015 ISO 9000 certified companies in Australia and 1,774 in New Zealand. Worldwide, up to the end of December 2005, at least 776,608 ISO 9001:2000 certificates had been issued in 161 countries and economies, an increase of 18 per cent over 2004, when the total was 660,132 in 154 countries and economies.[2] It is estimated that about 75 per cent of these certificates are firms in service businesses, including some very small businesses.

Despite its widespread adoption, ISO 9000 has attracted a considerable amount of criticism related to the cost/benefit of implementation, i.e., a large amount of money, paperwork and time are required for registration, and that it promotes procedures and control rather than process understanding and improvement. A rigorous empirical study of over 1000 firms in Australia and

New Zealand found that quality certification had no significant, positive relationship with business performance (Terziovski et al., 1997). The researchers noted that the principal motivation for pursuing quality certification was the ability of the certificate to open customers' doors that were previously closed, or would close, if quality certification were not achieved. The ISO organisation in Geneva aims to take into account such criticism by issuing revised standards approximately every seven years as mentioned above in order to keep up with best-practice management.

Process control and improvement

In this section, we examine the tools that are available for on-going quality management and process improvement. These are the tools that are used to work with the data that is collected while operating processes.

In his book *Right First Time* (1984), Frank Price has proposed these three rules for quality control: no inspection or measurement without proper recording; no recording without analysis; and, no analysis without action. In other words, if you are going to go to the expense of collecting data, then you must ensure that you record it properly (the back of an envelope is not recommended), analyse it using appropriate tools and techniques and then take action on the basis of your analysis. Otherwise why measure in the first place?

Data: variable, attribute, subjective

There are three kinds of data that we are interested in, and it is important to understand the differences between them:

1. Variable data use a continuous scale, e.g., length, weight (something you measure).
2. Attribute data can have only one of two states, e.g., yes/no, on/off, red/not red (something you count).
3. Subjective data are based on opinions and perceptions, data are usually collected on a five, six or seven point scale. Called the Likert scale, these can sometimes be turned into variable data.

Accuracy, precision and stability

We would generally like our organisational processes to be accurate, precise, and stable. It is important to understand the distinctions between these three.

Accuracy is the ability to produce an average measured value that agrees with the true value or standard being used. Precision, on the other hand, is the ability to measure repeatedly the same product or service and obtain the same results. A high degree of precision means lower variance, which usually means higher customer satisfaction. Finally, stability is the ability to achieve and measure repeatedly the same product or service over time and obtain the same average measured value. Examples are the standard way in which staff at the Intercontinental hotel in Wellington greet guests, or the way that McDonald's achieves the same taste and look in its French fries, day after day, and even year after year in thousands of its restaurants.

Process control and inspection

Process control happens during the production of the good or service. If things are going wrong, they are detected, and fixed. Process control is based upon repeated inspection of a sample of the output of the process that is taken at regular intervals. Inspection, on the other hand, happens before or after the event. If things have gone wrong, resources have been wasted and although the faulty item or service might be repaired or reworked in some circumstances, this is often costly.

Statistical process control

When a process is running, there will always be a certain amount of variation. We need to know when to leave the process alone and when we need to take some action. In other words, we need to be able to distinguish between common causes and special causes of variation as described earlier. Statistical process control (SPC) is a methodology for monitoring the output of a process so that we can distinguish between the causes of variation. When the special causes of variation exist, the process is said to be out of control. However, if the variation in the process is due to common causes, the natural variation of the system, then the process is said to be in statistical control. Figure 9.4(a) and Figure 9.4(b) demonstrate graphically the behaviour of a process over time. Assuming the performance measure is normally distributed; in Figure 9.4(a) is a process where there are only common causes of variation present, and so the process is in control. In Figure 9.4(b), there are special causes of variation present, and so the process is not in control.

SPC is an effective tool for monitoring the output of processes, but it is not sufficient to ensure quality at the source. A process can be in statistical control yet still be producing defective output. An example of a control chart is shown in Figure 9.5 (page 273).

All control charts have three important features: the centre line which is the average of all the results, the upper control limit (UCL) and the lower control limit (LCL). The values for these UCL and LCL lines are three standard deviations (σ) above and below the average. The lines represent the limits of expected variability in the process, that is, variation within these limits

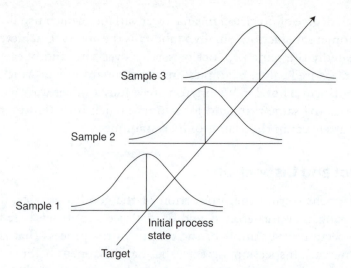

Sample 3

Sample 2

Sample 1

Initial process state

Target

(a) Common causes of variation present (process is in control)

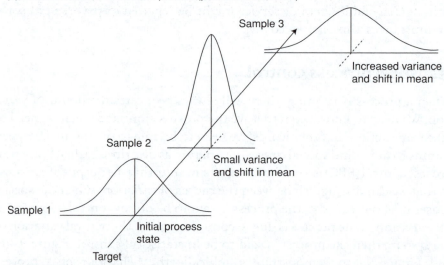

Sample 3

Increased variance and shift in mean

Sample 2

Small variance and shift in mean

Sample 1

Initial process state

Target

(b) Special causes of variation present (process is not in control)

Figure 9.4 (a): Common causes of variation present (process is in control)
(b): Special causes of variation present (process is not in control)
Source: Foster (2007)

generally shows only common cause variation. If we were to find a value outside the limits, it is equivalent to the process telling us that something has changed and we should go and investigate. The reason is that the chance of a value falling outside the UCL or LCL is very small, about 1.5 in 1000.

This method for monitoring the performance of processes was popularised in Japan as they rapidly industrialised after World War II. At that time, workers were not highly educated and advanced data capturing and analysis tools were

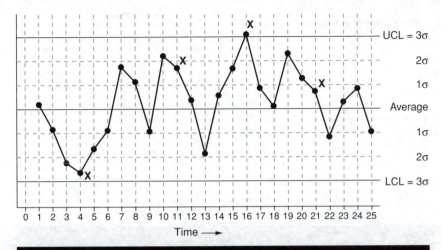

Figure 9.5 An example of a statistical control chart.
Source: Nancy (2004)

not widely available. As a result, the SPC procedures were simplified whereby the behaviour of processes could be measured and analysed manually by examining the average and dispersion patterns of data over time. This led to mean and range charts being used. However, today, with the advent of cheap electronic sensors, data loggers, and computers and display units, much of the statistical process control procedures are highly automated. Based on data patterns in the SPC charts, even the decision to stop processes are automated.

Box 9.5: Combining automatic data capture with statistical process control

Monroe Australia's factory in South Australia is where they manufacture shock absorbers and struts to suit the vast majority of the vehicles on Australian and New Zealand roads. Monroe is also the original equipment supplier for Holden, Ford, Mitsubishi and Toyota, and exports ride control products to a number of other countries. On many of their machine tools, they have installed vision systems that can automatically check the dimensions of the part that has just been made and use that data to plot a statistical process control chart.

Process capability

Process capability analysis is a tool used to determine whether or not, with high probability, a particular process is able to produce output within design specifications. There is always some variation associated with a production process – inherent or natural variation. This assumes that the output of the process can be measured on some continuous scale.

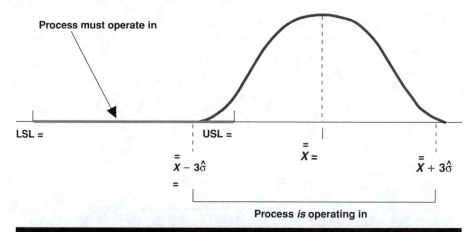

Process must operate in

LSL =

USL =

$$\bar{\bar{X}} - 3\hat{\sigma}$$

$$\bar{\bar{X}} =$$

$$\bar{\bar{X}} + 3\hat{\sigma}$$

=

Process *is* operating in

Figure 9.6 Process capability analysis

The goal of process capability analysis is to determine whether or not a process is able to meet the tolerances defined by the design specifications. By meeting the tolerances, we mean that given the standard operating characteristics of the machine or process there is only a small chance that a unit of output will not conform to specifications. Design specifications are usually given as some target measure plus or minus some tolerance.

For example, a piece of steel may have a specification such as a diameter of 13 mm +/−0.05 mm. Here 13 mm is the target, +/−0.05 mm is the tolerance and double the general tolerance (0.1 mm) is the tolerance range. Process capability is determined by comparing the standard deviation of the process's performance to the tolerance limits of the design specification. It attempts to compare the range of natural or inherent variability in the process with the tolerance limits. If the range of natural variability, given by six standard deviations is greater than the tolerance range, then we can say that in the normal course of events the process will produce some defective output. In the illustration above (Figure 9.6), the curve shows the natural variability in the process with a lower natural tolerance limit (LNTL) of 13.01 and an upper natural tolerance limit (UNTL) of 13.19. These are calculated from the mean +/−3 standard deviations. Process capability analysis requires us to compare this range of natural variation (or process spread 13.01–13.19) with the tolerance range, the distance between the lower specification limit LSL (12.95) and the upper specification limit USL (13.05). In this case, the process is not capable as the process is operating well outside where it should be operating.

Generally, a process must be in statistical control before a process capability analysis is carried out.

Quality improvement tools

While there have been many quality improvement tools developed over the years, the most well-known are the 14 *statistical and management tools*. These are generally split into two groups: the seven *quality control tools* and the seven *management and planning tools*.

As Richard Greene (1993, p. 49) points out, the basic business functions that the 14 tools enable include moving companies:

1. from simply making products to developing systems capable of continually competing in world markets
2. from fighting fires to dealing with root causes before problems occur
3. from measuring good functioning just by profit to measuring it by process comprehensiveness and capability
4. from making hosts of improvement to eliminating most improvements in favour of focusing on a few critical ones, using impact on customer satisfaction to achieve that focus
5. from perfecting departments, divisions, and functions to perfecting cross-functional linkages from customers to products provided for customers.

The seven QC tools are briefly described and illustrated diagrammatically in Figure 9.7 (page 276).

Generally quality programs begin with the use of the seven QC tools because they get the workforce to be scientific and methodical in the way they conduct ordinary work processes. This first seven are quantitative, with the exception of cause and effect diagrams.

The seven management and planning tools are qualitative for the most part and they are usually employed when the company has some years of experience with quality programs. The first seven will allow the company to deal with the easier problems, which are tactical and process related, and then it will have learned how to act in response to data emerging from their processes. In later years, when the harder problems arise, the company will need ways to be more creative and handle qualitative data. Hence, the second seven involve mapping relations among the various system components.

The seven management and planning tools are briefly described and illustrated diagrammatically in Figure 9.8 (page 278).

Implementation issues

Over the years, there have been hundreds of books written about how to implement quality management. Many of these authors became very wealthy on the basis of their books and several have become legends in the field.

Quality management has also spawned a huge industry for management consultants, giving advice to business managers about how to make these sensible and rich ideas and tools work effectively. However, the success rate of quality management improvement initiatives has generally been less than desired.

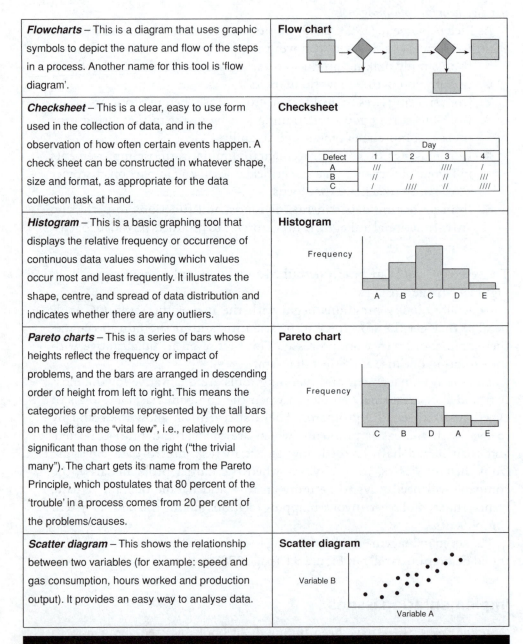

Flowcharts – This is a diagram that uses graphic symbols to depict the nature and flow of the steps in a process. Another name for this tool is 'flow diagram'.	**Flow chart**
Checksheet – This is a clear, easy to use form used in the collection of data, and in the observation of how often certain events happen. A check sheet can be constructed in whatever shape, size and format, as appropriate for the data collection task at hand.	**Checksheet**
Histogram – This is a basic graphing tool that displays the relative frequency or occurrence of continuous data values showing which values occur most and least frequently. It illustrates the shape, centre, and spread of data distribution and indicates whether there are any outliers.	**Histogram**
Pareto charts – This is a series of bars whose heights reflect the frequency or impact of problems, and the bars are arranged in descending order of height from left to right. This means the categories or problems represented by the tall bars on the left are the "vital few", i.e., relatively more significant than those on the right ("the trivial many"). The chart gets its name from the Pareto Principle, which postulates that 80 percent of the 'trouble' in a process comes from 20 per cent of the problems/causes.	**Pareto chart**
Scatter diagram – This shows the relationship between two variables (for example: speed and gas consumption, hours worked and production output). It provides an easy way to analyse data.	**Scatter diagram**

Figure 9.7 Seven quality control tools.

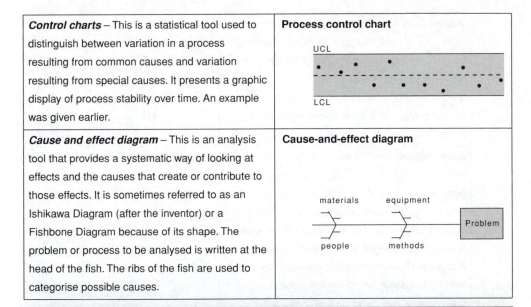

Control charts – This is a statistical tool used to distinguish between variation in a process resulting from common causes and variation resulting from special causes. It presents a graphic display of process stability over time. An example was given earlier.	**Process control chart**
Cause and effect diagram – This is an analysis tool that provides a systematic way of looking at effects and the causes that create or contribute to those effects. It is sometimes referred to as an Ishikawa Diagram (after the inventor) or a Fishbone Diagram because of its shape. The problem or process to be analysed is written at the head of the fish. The ribs of the fish are used to categorise possible causes.	**Cause-and-effect diagram**

Figure 9.7 (*Cont.*)

In what follows, we will discuss the main ideas and issues around implementation of quality management. The most fundamental point is that the process must start at the top of the organisation. Top management must understand the quality ideas, models and tools, have tested them and confirmed their validity. Top management should be involved and receive the initial training and carry out the first trial projects. In many successful organisations such as Xerox Kodak, Marriott and Toyota, the training in quality management is cascaded down from top management.

Another important point is that quality management must be introduced in a climate of trust. This recalls one of Deming's 14 points about driving out fear from the organisation. If there is no climate of trust and people are worried about their jobs, then there are likely to be few volunteers for any quality improvement projects. If there is not a sincere desire and motivation to go forward on quality in the majority of a management team and workforce, the quality management project will likely fail.

Next, top management must devote considerable resources to communication within the organisation to increase awareness of why quality management is important. Typical comments that occur in organisations which show there is inadequate awareness or understanding would be things like:

Affinity Diagram – This is a tool that gathers large amounts of language data (ideas, opinions, issues) and organises them into groupings based on their natural relationships. An affinity process is often used to group ideas generated by brainstorming. Often this is conveniently done using "Post-It" notes on a whiteboard.	**Affinity diagram**
Interrelationship diagram – This is an analysis tool that allows a team to identify, analyse, and classify systematically the cause and effect relationships that exist among all issues. The analysis helps a team distinguish between issues that serve as drivers and those that are outcomes. A driver will have more arrows coming in than going out. A barrier to solving the problem will have more arrows going out than coming in.	**Interrelationship diagram**
Prioritisation matrix – This is a useful technique that can be used with team members or with customers to achieve consensus about an issue. The matrix helps to rank problems or issues (usually generated through brainstorming) by a particular criterion that is important to the organisation. Then, the problems that should be solved first can be more clearly seen.	**Prioritisation matrix**
Tree diagram – This diagram presents a map of the tasks that are needed to solve a problem, achieve a goal or resolve an issue. It is used when broad objectives must be broken down into specific implementation detail and all of the implementation options must be explored. Assignable tasks for team members can be created.	**Tree diagram**

Figure 9.8 Seven management and planning tools.
Source: wikipedia

Activity network diagram – This diagram is a schedule for the completion of a complex project. It is analogous to the critical path or PERT charts produced in project management, using task durations, earliest start, earliest finish dates, etc.	**Activity network diagram**
Matrix diagram – This is a planning tool that can help organise large groups of tasks and responsibilities. This could be used when there are definable and assignable tasks that must be deployed within the organisation. It can also be used when the chosen activities must be tested against other current activities as it may be necessary to prioritise present activities against new objectives.	**Matrix diagram**
Process Decision Program chart – This is a good tool to use for contingency planning. It helps to realize what could go wrong or problems associated with the implementation of programs and improvements. It attempts to map out every conceivable event or contingency that could occur when moving from a problem statement to the possible solutions.	**Process decision program chart**

Figure 9.8 (*Cont.*)

'We can't be doing that badly if we sell everything we can produce and there are not that many complaints'.
'If Department Y did their job properly, we could provide decent quality products.'
'This statistical stuff is too sophisticated for our processes.'
'Our process is different. It does not apply to us. All our staff are artists in their own way.'

Communication must also be aimed at the concern many people in an organisation might feel, that is that the task or the amount of change required is too great. It is therefore important for top management not to be too ambitious in trying to bite off a bigger problem than can be handled at one time. Remember that the answer to the question: 'How do you eat an elephant?' is 'One bite at a time!' In other words, the learning that takes place and the results achieved are likely to be much more effective if the animal is cut up into bite-sized pieces that can be easily digested by the quality or process improvement team.

The experience of the leading quality gurus or implementers is that the program follows an evolutionary path. Initially, the effort must focus on successful control and stabilisation of daily work practices. This calls for clear specification, standards, and operating procedures. At this stage, the workforce would be using the first seven quality tools. Then, gradually the company will move upstream. The next step would be to gain better control and understanding of the processes. And so process capability analysis would gradually be implemented and extended from one project to the next. What happens at this stage is that processes become simplified, improved, and optimised which leads to better control of the total company performance. The final stage is the investment in quality improvement in the product and process design activities. This leads to quality being built into the product and services, and the delivery processes right from the start.

Teams

Management at Toyota has the expression: 'the people who do the job every day know most about it, and therefore they should be the ones given the responsibility to improve it.' Among shopfloor workers and to front-line staff, the best way to improve quality is through the use of quality circles or quality improvement teams or process improvement teams. Some companies find it better to invent their own titles for these teams. There are some differences between quality circles and quality improvement teams. For example, the former tend to come from a single department and participation is voluntarily. Also the quality circle is unchanged from project to project. The quality improvement team, on the other hand, consists of people from more than one department, a cross-functional team, and the participation is mandatory. These teams tend to focus on one of the vital few problems and the team only stays together until project is completed.

The term 'quality circles' has, to all intents and purposes, disappeared from usage nowadays. This is partly because organisations realise that most processes are cross-functional, but it is also due to the way quality circles were treated in many organisations. This particularly relates to the quality circles not being allowed or encouraged to implement the solution they designed. They tended to thrive better in those cultures that had a deeper tradition of autonomous work teams and workplace democracy.

Another issue with quality circles and quality improvement teams is they are or have been seen as a threat to some levels of the supervisory structure. Because members of these teams are encouraged to think and do research on their own work processes, and to track parts of the overall system that might make many local processes less effective or less efficient than they might be, these quality teams eliminate what have been called authority buffers that were present in the pre-quality decision-making and management systems.

The management must provide sufficient resources to provide training for members of the quality improvement teams. This must include training in group processes such as how to run meetings, as well as problem solving skills and use of the quality improvement tools. Many improvement teams often use a facilitator to help with the meetings and with any technical issues regarding the new concepts and methods, or with the implementation phase of the solution. It is important that the facilitators do not replace the chain of command that exists, or that teams do not become so reliant on facilitators that they will not make decisions in their absence.

Quality improvement at the most mature of quality-focused organisations such as Toyota has become a very powerful driver of competitive advantage. On a recent visit to Toyota city in Japan, one of the authors was provided with the astonishing statistic that the average number of improvement suggestions per worker per year is eleven! At this rate, of nearly one suggestion per employee per month, every part of every process at Toyota is moving the quality of its output forward like an inexorable wave that never stops or reduces in intensity. And most of the suggestions for improvement are worth implementing, after careful screening and analysis is conducted. It is no wonder that Toyota has opened up a sizable gap in its efficiency and process quality with other major car companies like Ford and GM chasing it, and it is equally obvious that Toyota is not standing still waiting for its competitors to catch up. Indeed, it must seem at times to Toyota's competitors that is moving away into the distance as far as quality and productivity-based competitive advantage is concerned.

Problems with implementation

There has been much written about the problems with implementing quality management. In the discussion above, we have mentioned lack of awareness and understanding and particularly the lack of commitment and leadership from top management. This can lead to what is known as the *BOHICA effect* – 'bend over, here it comes again' – where a new program such as quality management is seen as a management fad or a flavour of the month. Other common problems include:

1. too much training and not enough action
2. an 'us versus them' syndrome where not enough projects are cross functional or cross departmental
3. losing sight of the customer requirement.

A long-term study of implementation of statistical process control in an American manufacturing organisation uncovered cultural barriers to the introduction of this tool (Bushe, 1988). These are outlined below.

Learning versus performing

Because quality management involves learning new tools and techniques and learning about processes, this contradicted the performance-based norms in the organisation. Managers were more interested in the results rather than what was learned about the process and how to improve it. Improving processes takes time and unfortunately many organisations have a culture that values performance over learning.

The meaning of information

The use of SPC and other quality tools results in displays of performance in public areas within the organisation. This is information that highlights problems and is very useful for fixing them. Senior managers tended to discount the powerful information arising from SPC because of the status of the person giving the information. SPC works against a culture with strong status hierarchies where who is 'right' is often determined by the position of the person giving the information.

Wholism versus segmentalism

Many organisations tend to be highly segmented into structural and cultural dimensions. There may be strong lines of demarcation in many dimensions: workers/managers, plant/division, etc. Work in itself may be broken up into tiny segments to be carried out by individual operators in the units as in an assembly line. In such organisations, there is a tendency to compartmentalise problems and information. On the other hand, some companies are mature enough to take a wholistic approach. This requires multi-level and lateral thinking and works by managing interdependencies among all variables in a process.

Summary

In this chapter, we have examined why quality has become a key business driver and how it has developed from a simple focus on inspection to a company wide improvement activity. We have touched on some of the main ideas of the people and frameworks that have led the development of quality management over the last 50 years. One theme that exists through all these theories and frameworks is the importance of the system, understanding the system, and management's important responsibility in managing the system of operations.

The different definitions of quality were explained. We reported on how different definitions may exist at different points in the system as the product or service is designed, manufactured, marketed, and delivered. We have described the seven quality control tools, mainly quantitative, and the seven management and planning tools, mainly for qualitative data.

Finally, we discussed the implementation issues around a quality management program. The overwhelming evidence points to the importance of the role of top management to demonstrate commitment and leadership in order to raise awareness, understanding, and provide resources to develop the new ways of working, and in-depth knowledge of the company's processes by those who work with them. Quality must become part of the landscape within the company and part of every person's daily work and not seen as an add-on. In all this it is important to remember we must aim for maximum customer satisfaction and minimum variation.

As Zemke and Albrecht (1995, p. 5) said in their book on service quality, staff need to get past any beliefs such as: 'This would be a great business, if it were not for all the damned customers.'

Referring to the management challenge posed at the start of this chapter, at the Intercontinental Hotel in Wellington, New Zealand, in order to minimise the chance that any or every customer will experience dissatisfaction, managers created a plan. They drew up specifications for the standards that must be achieved by every person and process step involved. This had a lot of detail in it, such as the regular and routine inspection and cleaning of door handles and windows, etc. Staff uniforms had to be standardised and worn in the standard way. Processes for greeting customers and handling their registration and baggage delivery to rooms were established and ensured as capable and within tolerances of timeliness. And this was supported by the senior managers who championed the whole initiative and trained the staff on the WHY, the WHAT and the HOW of all these aspects of service quality. Most staff were enthused and wholeheartedly came along on the journey. After all, it's the only way to operate a good business, whether it's in the services sector or any other!

We ask the reader to remember that the only other option to having business processes in control and consistently capable of meeting customers' requirements, is to literally have processes out of control and incapable of meeting their requirements, which is a recipe for disaster.

DISCUSSION QUESTIONS

1. One aspect of the aim for continuous improvement is to set so-called stretch objectives. Think about this situation. If it took 40 minutes to drive to work

today, and you wanted to make a 5 per cent improvement, what would you do? If you wanted to get to work in four minutes, what would you do? (Hint: It is clear you have to do something dramatically different to achieve this stretch objective.)

2. Think about what the names of some companies you associate with high quality goods or services. Attempt to relate the definitions discussed in this chapter to these companies. Which definitions seem most appropriate to the way these companies compete?

3. Discuss how common causes and the special causes are similar to chronic and sporadic waste.

4. If you were throwing three darts at a dart board, what would accuracy, precision, and stability look like with the pattern of darts?

5. As a manager, should you be more concerned with achieving accuracy or with achieving precision in your processes?

6. Think about a time when you are working in a team. Why did it work well or not work well? What role did you take in the team? What would have improved the team's performance?

7. If you were appointed as quality manager in an airline, what would you do to ensure effective service and operational quality? How would you define quality and what would your plan for assurance and improvement consist of?

8. As the corporate quality manager for Toyota, you recognise that your company has achieved so much over the past 40 years in quality improvement, and have been asked the question about whether there is much more improvement possible, or whether Toyota's quality journey has come to a natural end, because it has almost all been achieved. Does the benefit available from improving quality eventually diminish? What should Toyota be doing about quality over the next decade?

9. What key measures of operational quality would you put in place in:
   - a major bank?
   - an airline?
   - a restaurant?
   - a pharmaceutical factory?

References

Bushe, G. R. 1988. 'Cultural contradictions of statistical process control in American manufacturing organisations.' *Journal of Management*, 14(1): 19–31.

Cavana, R. Y., Corbett, L. M. and Lo, G. 2007. 'Extending the SERVQUAL model to link service quality and customer satisfaction in passenger rail services.' *International Journal of Quality and Reliability Management*, 24(1): 7–31.

Deming, W. E. 1986. *Out of the Crisis*. Cambridge, MA: Massachusetts Institute of Technology, Center for Advanced Engineering Study.

Foster, S. T. 2007. *Managing Quality: Integrating the supply chain*. 3rd edn. New Jersey: Pearson.

Garvin, D. 1987. 'Competing on the eight dimensions of quality.' *Harvard Business Review, 65*(6): 202–209.

Greene, R. T. 1993. *Global Quality: A synthesis of the world's best management methods.* Milwaukee: ASQC Quality Press/Business One Irwin.

Juran, J. and Godfrey, A. B. 1998. *Juran's Quality Handbook.* 5th edn. New York: McGraw-Hill.

Kano, N., Saraku, T. and Tsuji, A. 1984. 'Attractive quality and must-be quality.' *Hinshitsu,* 14(2): 1–14.

Pirsig, R. M. 1974. *Zen and the Art of Motorcycle Maintenance: An enquiry into values.* New York: William Morrow & Co.

Price, F. 1984. *Right First Time: Using quality control for profit.* Eldershot: Wildwood House.

Reeves, C. A. and Bednar, D. A. 1994. 'Defining quality: alternatives and implications.' *Academy of Management Review,* 19(3): 419–45.

Sasser, W. E., Olsen, R. P. and Wyckoff, D. D. 1978. *Management of Service Operations: Text, cases and readings.* Boston MA: Allyn and Bacon.

Tague, N. R. 2004 *The Quality Toolbox.* 2nd edn. Milwaukee, WI: ASQ Quality Press.

Terziovski, M., Samson, D. and Dow, D. (1997). 'The business value of quality management systems certification – Evidence from Australia and New Zealand.' *Journal of Operations Management,* 15(1): 1–18.

Zeithaml, V. A., Parasuraman, A. and Berry, L. L. 1990. *Delivering Quality Service: Balancing customer perceptions and expectations.* New York: The Free Press.

Zemke, K. and Albrecht, R. 1995. *Service America: Doing business in the new economy.* New York: Warner Books Inc.

Internet resources

http://www.asq.org
http://quality.dlsu.edu.ph/tools/index.html
www.Deming.org
www.freequality.org
www.mazur.net
http://www.umich.edu/~itdtq/2.10.Quality.tools.html www.superfactory. com

Notes

1 www.mazur.net
2 http://www.iso.org/iso/en/commcentre/pressreleases/2006/Ref1021.html accessed Aug 1 2007

Operations Excellence

Ross Chapman, Terry Sloan and Ron Beckett

Learning objectives

After reading this chapter you should be able to:
- discuss the characteristics of high performing organisations
- describe an excellence framework for operations
- explain the role of standards in the development of models of excellence
- compare differing excellence models
- analyse an organisation using a model for excellence such as the Australian Business Excellence Framework
- describe the different types of organisational performance measurements
- describe some of the tools that can be used for driving transformation of organisations towards becoming better performers.

Box 10.1: Management challenge: what is operations excellence?

Coca-Cola, IKEA, Toyota. These world famous corporations have one common feature – they have all achieved operations excellence. So, what is operations excellence? What are the dimensions of operations excellence? How might organisations strive to go beyond operations excellence? These challenges presented here are concerned with the ability of organisations to develop and balance a number of characteristics of high performing organisations in order to achieve operations excellence. For example, senior managers within the Toyota Corporation in both Australia and Japan have told one of the editors of this book that Toyota's quality of cars built in Australia is the best in the world, including even the 'parent' plants in Japan. Does this constitute operations excellence? How can it be measured? How do we know when we have achieved it? What do we do next? Is it worth striving for operations excellence? What are the costs and benefits of doing so? Even the best of companies in any industry have significant room for improvement, and Toyota executives are the first to admit that about their businesses and operations. In other words, there's no such thing as being perfect. Indeed, no organisation is even close to being perfect, so by definition there is always substantial opportunity for operational and business improvements.

Introduction

We claim in the management challenge above that very successful international firms such as Coca-Cola, IKEA and Toyota are practitioners of operations excellence. These organisations are different in some ways, and similar in others. Amongst their differences, they are headquartered in different parts of the world, have very different histories, operate in very different industries, have different outlooks to the world as corporate citizens, and have distinct management systems in place. Based on these differences, one could conclude that there are few common elements from which one could generalise, and that operations excellence is inherently dependent on context. Developing an understanding of operations excellence would therefore require closely examining the unique circumstances and practices of individual organisations. Such an approach has been popular, but risky. As Tom Peters and Robert Waterman (authors of *In Search of Excellence*, arguably the most popular book on business excellence) have found out, excellence is not a static concept. In the twenty years since the publication of this book, many of the individual organisations that they identified as being excellent have struggled to perform.

So, we will not take such as approach in this chapter. Instead, we plan to look at operations excellence from a slightly higher level of analysis, such that 'generalisable' principles can emerge. Companies are all different in the intricate details of their operating practices and their products and processes, but at a higher and more general level, excellence in operations and organisation can be identified, described and pursued. Applying this level and type of analysis to organisations such as Coca-Cola, IKEA and Toyota, we discover that there are many similarities between them. To varying degrees, all these organisations have been able to successfully compete on all the key dimensions of operations strategy – cost, quality, speed of delivery, flexibility, innovation, etc. This convergence is what we intend to focus on this chapter.

Operations link with a number of business functions to deliver stakeholder value. We start this chapter by considering some broad views of excellence and linkages with operations aspects. Multi-faceted models of excellence are discussed, as are some commonly used measures of operations performance. It might be observed that being judged as excellent today is very satisfying, but there must be a continuing search for improvement. Earlier chapters have discussed the need for innovation and the benefits of operationalising quality. In this chapter we discuss some transformational tools that may facilitate improvement within several facets of operations excellence.

Operations excellence and its context

Characteristics of high performing organisations

There are many studies that have attempted to identify the characteristics of high performing organisations. Peter Drucker's classic works – *Concept of the Corporation* (1946), *The Practice of Management* (1954), *Managing for Results* (1964) all deal with the concept of business excellence. Tom Peters and Robert Waterman's *In Search of Excellence* (1982) and *Built to Last: Successful habits of visionary companies* (1994) by James Collins and Jerry Porras were both international best sellers. In *Patterns of Excellence: The new principles of corporate success* (1999), Danny Samson and David Challis provide descriptions of some Australian organisations that could be considered as business exemplars.

It is not our intention to simply repeat findings from these studies here. This would not be a good idea because we want to focus on operations led excellence. So, in this section, we provide what we think are the key characteristics of high performing organisation. These characteristics are:

1. There is good fit with the operating environment.
2. All operations are viewed as providing a service.
3. Excellent operations deliver great customer value.
4. A mix of measures is used to judge performance.
5. Operations deliver value in concert with other organisational functions.
6. There is a continuous search for ways to improve in excellent operations.

Each of these characteristics is discussed fully in the following sections.

A good fit with the operating environment

High performing organisations come in many shapes and sizes, but all are characterised by a good fit with their operating environment and some uniqueness in the way they deliver value to their customers. Some of today's environmental operating conditions, and organisations' responses, are discussed below.

In broad terms, these environmental conditions lead to the need to manage both tasks and relationships within and between organisations and other partner organisations. There is a merging of product and service offerings. The balance between what is done internally and what is outsourced may change rapidly. Consequently, operations excellence may be judged in terms of how well the whole supply chain is managed, not just in terms of internal operations effectiveness.

Globalisation of markets

Globalisation is changing the nature of competition in a number of ways. A large proportion of world output is produced and consumed in global markets. Thus, even if an organisation does not export itself, it still must operate to globally competitive standards to compete effectively, and it must be competent in global supply chain management.

Fragmentation of demand

There is a trend towards a demand for more customised products and customised services. This has resulted in broader operations skill set being required. Organisations are expected to develop multiple competencies to deal with this, but at the same time, this cannot be done in an uneconomical manner.

Rapid technological change

Information and communication technologies, ongoing improvement in the science behind traditional manufacturing and business processes, and the emergence of new technology areas (e.g., mechatronics and nanotechnology) are all seen to drive continuous change. Low cost and rapid transfer of information can make distributed operations more effective, and networks of specialist operations can broaden the scope of products and services offered by a particular organisation.

Changes in the labour market

Demographic changes such as ageing of the workforce, changing workforce education levels and expectations, and the need for new skill sets all impact upon the nature of operations within and between regions within and between countries. In combination with advances in technology, the outsourcing of services is now as common as the outsourcing of production.

All operations are viewed as a service

As was described in Chapter 1, traditionally, authors have separated organisations and their operations into *manufacturing* and *service* categories, with operations management considered mainly applicable to manufacturing, or the production of tangible goods. However, the essential nature of customer service means that all organisations need to consider service operations as part of their overall activity. This view is by no means recent. As Theodore Levitt wrote in 1972:

> There are no such things as service industries. There are only industries whose service components are greater or less than those of other industries. **Everybody** is in service.

Therefore, as was described in Chapter 1, rather than consider manufacturing, merchandising and service businesses as clearly defined separate entities, it is useful to view all organisations as being in the business of producing outputs generically called *bundles of benefits*. If a tangible and physical product is associated with the bundles of benefits, then it would be a *facilitating good*. Otherwise, the output would be a *pure service*.

Service operations have become a driving force of competitive advantage in many industries traditionally viewed as manufacturing-driven, particularly in industries where only minor distinctions remain between the physical production capabilities of competing organisations. An excellent example of this is the auto industry, now dominated globally by four or five major players. Service-based aspects of customer value such as vehicle warranty, financing, after-sales service and road-side assistance have become key drivers of competitive advantage.

Excellent operations deliver great customer value

As indicated earlier, excellent organisations have some uniqueness in the way they deliver value to customers. But what do customers value? Quality, price and delivery have always been important, but today's customer is seeking more.

Good quality is a necessary entry ticket in the global market. Customers are seeking high levels, if not absolute reliability in all aspects of operations – order-taking, order fulfilment, financial transactions and after-sales support. They also want to work with organisations that are financially stable and sustainable, and increasingly, with organisations that pursue environmentally sustainable practices.

Being price-competitive has always been a market necessity. However, value propositions that enhance a customers' market position and/or reduce their internal costs are also expected. Exactly where, how and when something is delivered can be important (e.g., Just-in-time to a customers' operating line). In a business-to-business relationship, helping a customer economically launch a new product by suggesting product improvements or defraying some up-front costs can also be important. In a business environment where a product can be quickly imitated, and where product life cycles are short, flexibility, responsiveness and short time-to-market lead times are essential operations attributes.

A mix of measures is used to judge performance

When organisations are surveyed in respect to their operations performance, indicators like overall quality (of product and service), inventory turnover, on-time delivery, speed of new product development, unit cost of production and delivery lead time are used – a mix of things important in meeting both customer and shareholder expectations. The relative importance of each of these measures will depend on the type of workflow that is the norm. All three types may be observed in a particular organisation.

> ### Box 10.2: The notion of runners, repeaters and strangers
>
> The dominant practice in operations management depends on the extent to which operations are repetitive or are unique one-off activities. For the purposes of operations excellence, these practices can be defined as:
> * Runners are continuous activities that require a focus on process control (e.g., continuous chemical processing).
> * Repeaters are regular but discontinuous activities that require frequent production changeovers (e.g., batch production).
> * Strangers are one-off activities that require a focus on project management (e.g., building design and construction).

Managing 'runners' often involves standardising procedures, the use of six-sigma ideas (see later in this chapter) to support process control, and an emphasis on continuously reducing waste in all forms. In highly automated operations, there may be a strong emphasis on effective maintenance management. Managing 'repeaters' often involves the development of batch 'recipes' and the use of fast changeover ideas to support excellence in mass customisation or low volume production, with an emphasis on maximising value-adding time. Managing 'strangers' often involves skilful project management using stage-gate and milestone event management, with simultaneous engineering ideas supporting faster project implementation.

These simple differentiators allow us to understand why organisations with different process characteristics need to have different selections of performance measures and improvement strategies, an aspect that will be discussed at length later in this chapter.

Operations deliver value with other organisational functions

In establishing long-term relationships with excellent suppliers, sophisticated customers are looking beyond operations, and considering other organisational functions. The experience of companies such as Lockheed-Martin and Boeing demonstrate this.

Box 10.3: Supplier excellence at Lockheed-Martin

Beginning in the 1990s, global aerospace firms such as Airbus, Boeing and Lockheed-Martin sought to reduce their internal costs by reducing the number of suppliers they engaged with, working only with the best ones. They wanted reliability of quality and delivery, good value deals and agility to meet changing demands in the short term. But their longer-term ambitions were to work with financially sound firms that could invest in new technologies and opportunities, firms that embraced new technology and pro-actively developed proposals for better products and practices. Supplier firms were involved in audit and benchmarking studies that showed how the internal practices of a potential long-term partner firm met all of these requirements. Such firms would be given some form of preferred supplier status. For example, Lockheed-Martin had a scheme where the capabilities of a firm achieving STAR supplier status would be broadcast across all Divisions of the Company. One Australian firm, Hawker de Havilland was, for a number of years, the only firm achieving STAR supplier status in the area of aero-structures design and production.

Box 10.4: Boeing's supplier-related practices

The Boeing Commercial Airplane Group buys components all around the world. Their experience has shown that product price is not the only measure of cost efficiency. Boeing's internal costs in working with a particular supplier have to be considered. In some cases, Boeing has had to deploy its own staff to work with a supplier. Late deliveries and quality problems cause production disruptions within Boeing. There are a variety of costs associated with transportation, unpacking and disposal of packaging material. All costs are collected and the total costs from different suppliers compared.

Box 10.5: Shop-to-shop interactions

In the 1990s, the Boeing Commercial Airplane Group invited component suppliers to send Operations employees to visit their Airplane Assembly 'clients'. The aim was to encourage a better understanding of client needs and identify opportunities for improvement. Two example outcomes were: (i) assembly mechanics suggested that if certain parts could be made consistently within engineering tolerances, but with dimensions towards one end of the tolerance band, assembly would be easier; and (ii) fragile components were shipped encased in foam mouldings. Getting rid of these mouldings after receipt was a non-value-adding nuisance. The subsequent use of cardboard that could be re-cycled, or re-usable containers improved the situation significantly, with reduced environmental impact.

There is a continuous search for ways to improve

Even when things seem to be running smoothly, good managers always look for ways to further improve. It is not uncommon to focus on the three operations excellence capabilities: process control, smart operations and reduced lead times. Thus an understanding of the linkages (or capabilities) between internal attributes and sources of competitive advantage allow organisations to identify specific actions and management interventions to deliver continuous performance improvement in operations.

Some common practices associated with these three capabilities are:

1. To continuously improve reliability and process control
   - Focus on key processes and systems and the role of people within these systems to understand potential sources of variation.
   - Understand the current nature of variation within operations processes and systems, setting a goal to minimise such variation and eliminate waste.
2. To strategically develop the context of smart operations
   - Focus on supply chain development and a willingness to work with suppliers and customers for cooperative improvement. This is particularly important as internal efficiency improves, as what is purchased becomes a larger proportion of cost.
   - Link company-wide mechanisms for continuous innovation and develop mechanisms to identify possible sources of discontinuous or disruptive innovation, for example, finding creative ways to finance operations.
3. To continually strive for shorter lead times
   - Aim at reducing customer queue times.
   - Focus on reducing set-up times for new jobs.
   - Enhance the operational ability to rapidly introduce product or process change.

We will now turn our attention to the broader models of excellence available for organisations seeking to integrate their operations improvement activities across all areas of the organisation.

Models of excellence

Development of the models

ISO 9000 quality management system standards are briefly discussed in this section. These standards were introduced in Chapter 9, where technical aspects were described. Here, we provide a historical account of the development of these standards and discuss how the development, application and extension of these standards have contributed to the development of operations excellence frameworks.

Following the development of statistical process control methods in the 1930s, the military/defence requirements for supplier quality assurance of the 1940s were the beginnings of the quality system standards that are in use today. These US and British standards represented the early attempts to provide models for ensuring product quality through organisational system design and maintenance. While these standards initially focused purely on quality assurance through control of key processes within the organisation, they gradually evolved to encompass a much wider range of functions and activities, such that they became reasonable models for organisational efficiency and quality. We now not only have quality system standards (ISO 9000:2000), but also several others similar to ISO 9000 covering other areas, for example, the environmental system standards labelled the ISO 14000 series standards.

Recognition and adoption of the ISO 9000 series standards grew dramatically during the 1980s and 1990s, driven primarily by supply chain pressures and market penetration issues. In Australia, growth in the interest in quality system standards from organisations was also fuelled by an increasing number of state and federal government departments requiring certification of suppliers to a relevant standard. While the ISO 9000 standards were initially developed for manufacturing-based organisations, considerable efforts were made in the 1990s to provide guidance and assistance for service-based organisations in developing appropriate systems to meet the standard requirements.

To date, the ISO 9000 standards have been adopted by over 70 countries, and, coupled with ISO 14000 standards, continue to provide an excellent mechanism for companies just beginning their excellence journey to assess and improve their systems and key processes. Particular industries and even individual large companies also developed their own quality system standards around this time. These were developed primarily to ensure the quality of supplied products without expensive inbound material quality inspection. The best recognised of these standard were the automotive supplier quality system standards. These standards incorporated most of the criteria found in the more generic ISO 9000 standards but also included a range of automotive-specific technical criteria. The QS-9000 standard was developed primarily for

Ford and Daimler-Chrysler corporations (but is used by many other auto-motive makers). Ford have developed their Q1 accreditation system around this standard and recently the International Automotive Task Force (IATF) has developed the ISO/TS16949 Technical Specification to be used in con-junction with the ISO 9000 standard for generic automotive quality system accreditation.

Box 10.6: ISO 9000 Quality System Standards and SMEs

Dramatic growth in the numbers of organisations seeking third party quality system certification in the 1980s and 1990s spurred the development of large numbers of national and international agreements on auditing standards and protocols, as well as large numbers of consulting organisations offering assistance to organisations looking to develop quality systems suitable to meet the ISO 9000 standards. While many large organisations already had well-established quality systems, many small organisations struggled with the demands of larger customers for systems that met ISO 9000 standards. Once such systems were established, however, smaller organisations often found that these systems provided an excellent foundation for implementing broader cultural changes in their organisations.

While the recognition and adoption of the ISO 9000 standards continued throughout the 1970s, 1980s and 1990s, leading organisations were consid-ering what was required to move beyond the standards. Standards can be complied with, but forward-thinking managers and leading organisations wanted to go further in their performance. Over these years, the total quality management (TQM) approach also grew rapidly, advocating an organisation-wide approach to quality improvement, really requiring a cultural change in most organisations. In progressing from quality system standards to a TQM approach to business, organisations were required to make great many changes in the way they approached their businesses. Some of these changes are listed below:

1. Measure customer satisfaction and ensure such measures were applied to improve operations efficiency.
2. Improve leadership in all areas of the business.
3. Move planning to a longer term, quality basis, rather than the short term cost driven basis.
4. Increased efforts to make better use of skilled personnel through teams and workgroups focusing on waste reduction in all areas.
5. Improve communication channels and information systems through-out the organisation to ensure timely and efficient provision of required data to operations areas.
6. Build a culture where continuous quality and customer satisfaction improvement takes place.

As the TQM approach to business management gained popularity, a number of groups sought to develop models that would assist organisations in developing the systems and actions required for such approaches. The earliest of these was the Deming Prize in Japan. Instituted in the 1950s it is open to companies worldwide, however, very few non-Japanese companies have ever been considered worthy of competing for the Prize. Other schemes developed in a similar vein (but many years later, mostly in the 1980s or 1990s) include the US-based Malcolm Baldrige Award, the Australian Quality Awards and Quality Prize, the New Zealand Quality Award, the Singapore Quality Award, and the European Quality Award. The development of these national awards prompted a host of other nations to develop similar quality award frameworks. Regional and industry-based schemes also proliferated. With the decline in the 'quality industry' in the late 1990s, a number of these schemes changed their nomenclature to provide a stronger focus on 'business excellence', although their basic structure and criteria changed very little. One important addition that was incorporated in most of the schemes (with the exception of the Deming Prize), was criteria on overall organisation performance and success into the full list of organisational criteria. This followed a number of high-profile company failures who had recently been winners of quality awards or prizes.

In the following sub-sections, we describe the key elements of the Australian, Singaporean and New Zealand business excellence awards systems.

The Australian Business Excellence Framework

The Australian business excellence model is based upon twelve 'principles of business excellence' that provide guidance to organisations seeking operations and business excellence (Table 10.1).

The framework itself (see Figure 10.1) is described as 'an integrated leadership and management system that describes the essential features, characteristics and approaches of organisational systems that promote sustainable, excellent performance' (SAI Global Website). In addition to the underpinning principles described above, the framework identifies seven key categories for sustained overall success, each with a number of items used for detailed organisational implementation and assessment purposes (see Table 10.2). Application of the principles, through analysis, review and improvement guided by the categories and items of the framework, has been shown to generate substantial organisational improvement and success.

Assessment of an organisation's performance is undertaken on four key dimensions:

1. Approach (how the organisation puts plans and structures into place);
2. Deployment (how it deploys these plans and structures);
3. Results (how it measures and analyses the outcomes of deployment);
4. Improvement (how it learns from its experiences).

Table 10.1 Principles underpinning the Australian Business Excellence Framework

The Twelve Principles of Business Excellence

1. Clear direction	Clear direction allows organisational alignment and a focus on the achievement of goals
2. Agreed plans	Mutually agreed plans translate organisational direction into actions
3. Customer focus	Understanding what clients value, now and in the future, influences organisational direction, strategy and action
4. Improve processes	To improve the outcome, improve the system and its associated processes
5. Involve people	The potential of an organisation is realised through its people's enthusiasm, resourcefulness and participation
6. Continual learning	Continual improvement and innovation depend on continual learning
7. Systems thinking	All people work in a system; outcomes are improved when people work on the system
8. Use data effectively	Effective use of facts, data and knowledge leads to improved decisions
9. Understand variation	All systems and processes exhibit variability, which impacts on predictability and performance
10. Community impact	Organisations provide value to the community through their actions to ensure a clean, safe, fair and prosperous society
11. Stakeholders value	Sustainability is determined by an organisation's ability to create and deliver value for all their stakeholders
12. Role-model leadership	Senior Leadership's constant re-modelling of these principles and their creation of a supportive environment to live these principles, are necessary for the organisation to reach its true potential

From the Business Excellence Framework, reproduced with permission from SAI Global Ltd. The Business Excellence Framework may be purchased online at http://www.saiglobal.com

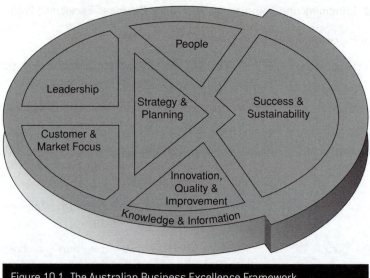

Figure 10.1 The Australian Business Excellence Framework

This is called the ADRI approach to assessment, and it represents a widely adopted approach to the assessment of organisational achievement against the various business excellence models utilised in many countries.

In practical terms, an organisation that applies formally for the award would produce documentation that addresses the criteria of the Australian Business Excellence Award. This organisational profile provides an overview of the organisation, its environment, relationships and challenges, and how it addresses the criteria of the framework. Applicants for the awards have their organisational systems evaluated by a team of trained evaluators. At the end of the evaluation process, the applicant organisation receives a comprehensive feedback report, which includes their current strengths and opportunities for improvement. In addition, they are provided with a score of their current performance, which is able to be benchmarked with organisations nationally and internationally.

The Australian Business Excellence Awards are open to all organisations operating in Australasia. Companies can apply at Award, Category, System or SME levels. At the Award level, Gold, Silver, Bronze awards are available plus the ultimate Excellence Medal is occasionally awarded to outstanding overall performance at the Gold level.

1. Award level – the evaluation is against all Categories and Items in the Australian Business Excellence Framework.
2. Category level – the evaluation is against one nominated Category (from those shown in Table 10.2) and its Items. Applicants may apply in up to three (3) Categories.

Table 10.2 Categories and associated items in the Australian Business Excellence Framework

Category	Item
1.0 Leadership	1.1 Strategic direction 1.2 Organisational culture 1.3 Leadership through the organisation 1.4 Environmental community contribution
2.0 Strategy and Planning	2.1 Understanding the business environment 2.2 The planning process 2.3 Development and application of resources
3.0 Knowledge and Information	3.1 Collection and interpretation of data and information 3.2 Integration and commitment 3.3 Creation and management of knowledge
4.0 People	4.1 Involvement and commitment 4.2 Effectiveness and development 4.3 Health, safety and well-being
5.0 Customer and Market Focus	5.1 Knowledge of customers and markets 5.2 Customer relationship management 5.3 Customer perception of value
6.0 Innovation, Quality and Improvement	6.1 Innovation process 6.2 Supplier and partner processes 6.3 Management and improvement of processes 6.4 Quality of products and services
7.0 Success and Sustainability	7.1 Indicators of success 7.2 Indicators of sustainability

From the Business Excellence Framework, reproduced with permission from SAI Global Ltd. The Business Excellence Framework may be purchased online at http://www.saiglobal.com

3. Systems level – the evaluation is against a nominated business system. Applicants may apply in one or more of seven (7) systems: Customer Service; Quality Systems; Occupational Health and Safety; Corporate Social Responsibility; Governance; Risk Management; and Environmental Management.

4. SME level – applicants must have annual revenue of less than $5 million or fewer than 100 employees.

Like the quality system accreditation history, the initial interest and enthusiasm for the Australian National Quality Awards (or, Australian Business

Excellence Awards, as they are now known) came from manufacturing companies. However, service industry organisations quickly started to utilise the award criteria to assist their business improvement efforts. As the lists of award winners demonstrates, a wide range of organisations are using the award criteria for self diagnosis, and then going on to apply for the various awards available each year. Business Excellence Award winners in 2007 were: Excellence Medal – Fremantle Ports; Gold – Tasmanian Alkaloids and Fremantle Ports; Bronze – City of Marion and the Catholic Education Office. No Silver Awards were given. Thus, in 2007, a service-based business in Western Australia was awarded the Excellence Award, a technology-driven primary producer and manufacturer in Tasmania won a Gold Award, and a city council in South Australia and an education board shared the Bronze Award. This diversity of sectors, regions and organisations was also found in the various Category and System level prizes awarded in 2007.

Box 10.7: Do business and operational excellence pay off?

A study of all past Australian Business Excellence Award Winners (1990–2006) using historical Australian Stock Exchange (ASX) data from between 1990 and 2006, found that a hypothetical investment in all Australian Quality Award winning companies generated a 169 per cent return rate versus a 113 per cent return rate on the Standard and Poor's All Ordinaries Accumulated Index. That is, the Business Excellence Award winning companies performed one and half times better than the average return for all companies included in the All Ordinaries index.

Study
'Business Excellence Pays', *Business Improvement Solutions*, 2006, pp. 16–17. Available from SAI Global
www.saiglobal.com

The Singapore business excellence awards

Launched in 1994 with the Singaporean Prime Minister as its patron, the Singapore Quality Award (SQA) is the equivalent of the Australian Excellence Award. The SQA aims to establish Singapore as a country committed to world-class business excellence and is conferred upon the 'best of the best' in recognition of their attainment of world-class standard of performance. The SQA, along with most other national quality awards has been extended and incorporated into a wider framework of business excellence in recent years.

The Singaporean Standards, Productivity and Innovation Board (commonly known as SPRING) coordinates and manages this overall business excellence initiative. This provides a framework for organisations to develop

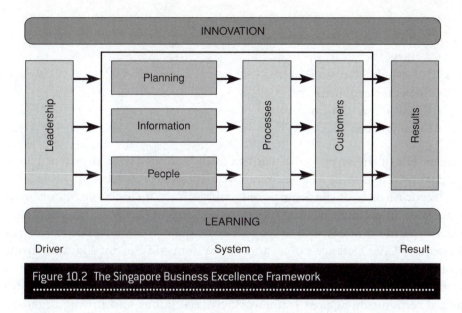

INNOVATION

Leadership

Planning

Information

People

Processes

Customers

Results

LEARNING

Driver   System   Result

and strengthen their management systems and processes to achieve high performance and be more competitive. SPRING is a member of the Global Excellence Model (GEM) Council, which also includes administrators of the US Malcolm Baldrige National Quality Award, the European Quality Award, the Australian Business Excellence Award, the Japan Quality Award and the South African Excellence Award.

The SPRING Business Excellence Framework is very much aligned with those of the other GEM Council members. It has seven categories, namely, Leadership, Planning, Information, People, Processes, Customers and Results, as shown in Figure 10.2.

There are four business excellence standards based on the framework: an overall business excellence standard based on all the requirements of the framework; and three business excellence niche standards for people, innovation and service. Each of these standards focus on management capabilities required for key enablers of business excellence, i. e., people, innovation or service. Organisations can receive certification for attaining a commendable level of performance, or an award for attaining outstanding performance in any of these four standards. The Singapore Quality Award (SQA) is a pinnacle award presented to organisations for achieving world-class standards of business excellence.

The award criteria are built upon the following set of values and concepts providing the foundation for integrating the various performance requirements and criteria in the framework:

- Visionary Leadership
- Customer-Driven Quality
- Innovation Focus

- Organisational and Personal Learning
- Valuing People and Partners
- Agility
- Knowledge-Driven System
- Societal Responsibility
- Results Orientation
- Systems Perspective

The details of the seven key categories of the framework as shown in Figure 10.2, and their associated assessment weightings are described in Table 10.3.

Recent winners of the Singapore Quality Award include: the Subordinate Courts of Singapore; the Singapore Prison Service; Teckwah Industrial Corporation Ltd (in 2006); and Singapore Institute of Technical Education; the Singapore Civil Defence Force; and the Systems on Silicon Manufacturing Company Pty Ltd (in 2005). This list again highlights the broad range of organisations using the Business Excellence Initiative and being assessed for award recognition against framework criteria. Public and private organisations, manufacturing and service based, have all benefited from the guidance provided within the framework and the benchmarking of their key systems and processes against international standards of excellence available through assessment against the framework criteria.

The New Zealand criteria for performance excellence

The Criteria for Performance Excellence that are incorporated into the New Zealand Best Practice Framework are modelled directly upon the US Malcolm Baldrige Award criteria, and are managed by the New Zealand Business Excellence Foundation (NZBEF), a not-for-profit charitable trust set up by private and public enterprise to help improve the overall performance of New Zealand organisations. NZBEF was established in 1992 and its present membership comprises academia, government, small, medium and large companies and associate members from all over New Zealand. The Best Practice Framework developed by the NZBEF is designed to improve organisational performance practices, capabilities and results.

Interestingly, the NZBEF use New Zealand Ministry of Economic Development research to position their Framework against other international business improvement models as shown in Figure 10.3. While this is an interesting comparison at first glance, proponents of the other improvement models (particularly the balanced scorecard and six-sigma approaches – see later in this chapter) would argue that their models are considerably broader than depicted in this comparison.

The New Zealand Best Practice Framework criteria and assessment weightings match exactly those used for the US Malcolm Baldrige Award. The

Table 10.3 The Singapore Business Excellence Framework Criteria and Assessment Weightings

Preface: Organisational Profile

1.	Organisation Description	
2.	Organisation Challenges	

Categories/Items		Point Values
1	Leadership – examines the organisation's leadership system, purpose, vision and values, and its responsibility to the community and the environment.	120
1.1	Senior Executive Leadership	50
1.2	Organisational Culture	50
1.3	Responsibility to Community and the Environment	20
2	Planning – focuses on the organisation's planning process, how key requirements are integrated into the organisation's plans and how these plans are deployed, as well as how performance is tracked	80
2.1	Strategy Development & Deployment	80
3	Information – focuses on the management of information and the use of comparative benchmarking information to support decision-making at all levels of the organisation	80
3.1	Management of Information	55
3.2	Comparison & Benchmarking	25
4	People – focuses on how the organisation taps the full potential of the workforce to create a high performance organisation, emphasising on the workforce training needs and career development, health and satisfaction, and performance and recognition, as aligned with the organisation's objectives.	110
4.1	Human Resource Planning	20
4.2	Employee Involvement & Commitment	20
4.3	Employee Education, Training & Development	30
4.4	Employee Health & Satisfaction	20
4.5	Employee Performance & Recognition	20
5	Process – focuses on the key processes the organisation uses to pursue its objectives and goals, including the innovation processes, production and delivery processes, and supplier and partnering management processes	100
5.1	Innovation Process	40
5.2	Process Management and Improvement	40
5.3	Supplier and Partnering Process	20

(Cont.)

Table 10.3 [*Cont.*]

....

Preface: Organisational Profile

....

6	Customers – focuses on how the organisation determines customer and market requirements, builds relationships with customers, and determines their satisfaction	110

....

6.1	Customer Requirements	40
6.2	Customer Relationship	40
6.3	Customer Satisfaction	30

....

7	Results – examines the organisation's performance and improvements in areas of importance to the organisation, as well as the organisation's performance levels relative to those of competitors and/or benchmarks	400
7.1	Customer Results	140
7.2	Financial and Market Results	90
7.3	People Results	80
7.4	Operational Results	90
TOTAL		1000

....

Reproduced with permission from SPRING Singapore from its website at: http//www.spring.gov.sg

The Business Excellence Framework (Covers organisation-wide activities)						
Leadership	Strategic Planning	Business Results	Measurement and Analysis	Process Management	Customer and Market Focus	Human Resource Focus
		ISO 9000 (Focus on Process and Quality)				**Investors in People** (Focus on HR)
		Balanced Scorecard (Focus on Measurement)				
			Six Sigma (Focus on Process Variation Reduction)			

Figure 10.3 Comparison between business improvement models as presented by the NZBEF

Framework is shown in Figure 10.4 and the individual criteria and assessment weightings are listed in Table 10.4. As for the other national excellence frameworks discussed, the NZBEF places considerable emphasis on the ability of individual organisations to understand the relationships between the various criteria, and assessment of the alignment between business functions is an integral aspect of organisational assessment, thus providing a true systems perspective of the organisational functions.

The NZBEF has prepared different booklets explaining the award criteria (using slightly different terminology for some criteria, but the same assessment weightings) for five different sectors: business, health, education, local

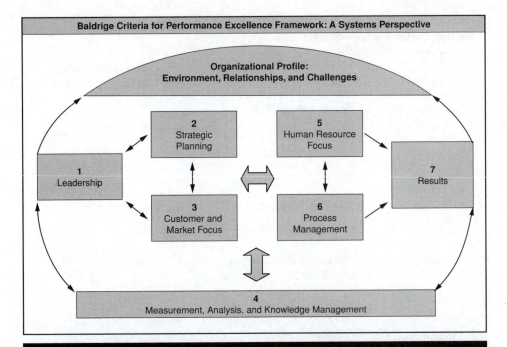

Figure 10.4 New Zealand Criteria for Performance Excellence

authorities and not-for-profit. The booklets provide tailored explanation of how to interpret the criteria for the different approaches and terminology used for each of these sectors.

Organisations can be recognised at four levels: Progress; Achievement (Bronze); Commendation (Silver); and the Award (Gold). In 2006, two organisations received Achievement Awards (Silver) – the Royal New Zealand Navy and Hutt City Council, and three organisations received Commendation Awards (Bronze) – Metso Minerals, City Care Ltd, and Kerridge & Partners. In 2005 only one Silver Award (to Livestock Improvement) and one Bronze Award (to the New Zealand Fire Service) were awarded. Only two Gold Awards have been made in the 13 years of operation of the Business Excellence Framework – to Telecom Directors Ltd in 1995 and to the Toyota Thames Assembly Plant in 1993. This list demonstrates that organisations need to reach truly international levels of excellence for the top awards and, as demonstrated in the Australian and Singapore awards, that companies from a great diversity of industries and sectors are finding value in the application of the framework and in the award assessment process.

Summary of models of excellence

Table 10.5 shows a comparison of several quality system standards and excellence models in terms of their evaluation criteria. The table clearly

Table 10.4 Categories and associated items in the 2007 New Zealand Criteria for Performance Excellence – Business Category

Category	Item	Item point value	Category point value
1. Leadership	Senior Leadership	70	
	Governance and Social Responsibilities	50	120
2. Strategic Planning	Strategy Development	40	
	Strategy Deployment	45	85
3. Customer and Market Focus	Customer and Market Knowledge	40	
	Customer Relationships and Satisfaction	45	85
4. Measurement, Analysis and Knowledge Mgt	Measurement, Analysis and Review of Organisational Performance	45	
	Management of Information, Information Technology and Knowledge	45	90
5. Workforce Focus	Workforce Engagement	45	
	Workforce Environment	40	85
6. Process Management	Work systems design	35	
	Work process management and improvement	50	85
7. Results	Product and Service Outcomes	100	
	Customer Focused Outcomes	70	
	Financial and Market Outcomes	70	
	Workforce Focused Outcomes	70	
	Process Effectiveness Outcomes	70	
	Leadership Outcomes	70	450
	TOTAL POINTS		1000

Table 10.5 Comparison of Quality System Standards and Business Excellence Models against evaluation criteria

Evaluation Criteria	US Military Standards	ISO 9000	Ford Q1 Standard	Deming Prize	Malcolm Baldrige Award	Australian Business Excellence Award
Leadership and organisational Mgt.			◆	◆	◆	◆
Information and analysis	◆	◆	◆	◆	◆	◆
Strategic planning			◆	◆	◆	◆
People involvement				◆	◆	◆
Quality assurance	◆	◆	◆	◆	◆	◆
Quality results		◆	◆	◆	◆	◆
Customer satisfaction		◆	◆		◆	◆
Overall business performance					◆	◆

demonstrates the increasing scope of the coverage of such models as they moved from military supplier standards through to the sophisticated business excellence models available today.

All of the Business Excellence Models examined here share a reasonably common set of main criteria. While there are differences in the details of the scoring frameworks and in some of the terminology and relationships between various criteria, given their relatively independent development, there is remarkably strong similarity between these models of excellence. The controlling body for each scheme recommends its model as a self-assessment tool, and it is clear that this is by far the greatest usage of each framework, as opposed to their use by companies actually seeking independent assessment against the criteria for business excellence award recognition.

In using any of these models, it is recommended that companies use an on-going self assessment approach to assist their progression from a reactive operational mindset with little or no clear strategic alignment, to an effective, integrated approach where operations goals are clearly aligned with organisation strategy and regularly reviewed and updated to accommodate a rapidly changing business and market environment.

Measures of performance

Linking operations performance with financial performance

In the previous section, we discussed models of overall organisational excellence. One way to measure performance is to audit operations against each major theme of one of these models, comparing the outcome with similar audits from other organisations. This will indicate the relative strengths and weaknesses of each organisation which can assist in developing organisational positioning strategies. However, such audits are carried out infrequently and other more frequent measurements are needed to give feedback on potential operations problems. Traditionally, financial measures have dominated, which makes sense, as without financial viability, operations may be unsustainable. Some financial measures are absolute (e.g., sales turnover) and some are ratios (e.g., return on investment). Trends in both can be used to assess the fiscal health of an organisation. The fiscal health of an organisation is often referred to colloquially, being its profit or return on invested funds, as 'the bottom line'.

To highlight some of the operations impacts on financial measures:

1. Faster cycle times can reduce inventory needed in the pipeline, thereby reducing current assets, and can reduce cost per unit by defraying infrastructure costs over more units. Faster cycle times may also reduce delivery time, and on that basis lead to more sales.
2. Reduced inventory can release funds to help make parts of the operation more efficient and can reduce capital interest charges, leading to reduced costs.
3. Schedule attainment both minimises disruption in the supply chain and satisfies customer expectations.
4. Maintaining high quality levels reduces the costs due to scrap, rework and disruption, and supports higher levels of customer satisfaction.
5. Reducing the cost of operations helps maintain competitive selling prices and increased profits.

Keeping score

In some ways, operations are like sporting events where the nature of the environment and the competition influences the way the game is played out. There needs to be coherent performance data collection, analysis and feedback systems with arrangements for follow-up action as needed.

Box 10.8: Kicking goals and keeping score

In sports such as football, the game would be very strange indeed if the goalposts kept on moving, if the scoring system kept on changing, and if there were no score-keepers. The score in a particular game tells us how we are currently performing compared with the opposing team. Player statistics tell us how each team member is contributing. Remarkable events are noted and celebrated. Performance in a number of games over a season provides information about progress towards some broader ambition (such as winning the finals). Players get feedback about how well they are doing as individuals, and how we are doing as a team. People within operations and people managing operations want the same kind of feedback, but there are many more ways that points can be scored to satisfy shareholders, customers and the broader community, and these must be balanced, making performance measurement more complex.

Some typical operations performance measures are flow-oriented and some are event-oriented. Some relate to time, some relate to quality, some relate to productivity, and some relate to cost. Specifically, these measures include:

1 Time and timing: response time (call response time, queue time), schedule compliance (milestone achievement, rate achievement), cycle time (individual operations, overall order fulfilment), changeover time (planning time, setup time).

2 Quality: defect rates (internal rates, customer complaints), waste management arrangements (waste minimisation, pollution rates), customer satisfaction.

3 Productivity: throughput, sales per employee, value added by operations, productive or 'billable' hours compared with paid hours, supplier performance.

4 Cost: cost of labour, cost of materials, unit costs, inventory, capital asset financing and maintenance.

Some of these measures are absolutes and some of them are ratios. The advantage of ratios (e.g., defects per million process steps) is that they allow comparison of some quite different kinds of operation over long periods of time. Some of the measures are based on tangible things, and some on intangibles. Some argue (e.g., Bacon (2005)) that the proliferation of global competitors and the emergence of technologies that support rapid imitation of a successful product or service make it difficult for companies to maintain traditional sources of differentiation. They argue that less tangible factors such as the nature of customer interaction and relationships, how something is delivered, are an important source of differentiation, and need to be measured.

What to measure

What to measure will depend to a large degree on the nature of the operations function and its organisational and environmental context. In some cases, things related to throughput will be important, while in other cases events such as milestones will be important. Taking a broader view, Kaplan and Norton (1996) have suggested a 'Balanced Scorecard' approach that considers measures from a financial, customer, internal business, and from an innovation and learning perspective. The Balanced Scorecard approach aims to align strategic direction and operations focus. Typical questions considered in developing a balanced set of measures for a particular organisation are:

1. What is our vision of the future?
2. If we achieve our vision, how will we look different to our stakeholders– to our shareholders, to our customers, in our internal practices, in our ability to innovate and grow, and to the community at large?
3. What are the critical success factors from each stakeholder perspective, and how will we measure each factor?

A general template for the balanced scorecard, following Kaplan and Norton's (1996) approach, is presented in Figure 10.5.

A systemic view of operations performance management

The 'balanced scorecard' approach links measurements to strategy and will result in some operations conditions to be met and some measurements to be made. In Chapter 6, the use of systems models was described. In Figure 10.6, we present a view of operations using one systems modelling approach – the IDEF approach (see IDEF (1993) for more details).

Excellent operations have coherent input and output interfaces, satisfy imposed conditions of operation, use resources effectively and are internally efficient in adding value. In Table 10.6, we have mapped the main types of measure (time-based, quality-based, productivity-based, and cost-based) against the components of an operation as represented in the systems model of Figure 10.6.

Discussion of each element of this map may help a particular organisation decide what should be measured. For example: what kinds of inputs are appropriate to a particular service operation. What knowledge and materials are required? When are they required? How accurate do these inputs need to be? How do we know if these input requirements are being met? What opportunities are there to learn from suppliers?

Transformation tools

Before commencing to transform an organisation, clear goals must be set for the desired nature of the organisation after the transformation. These goals

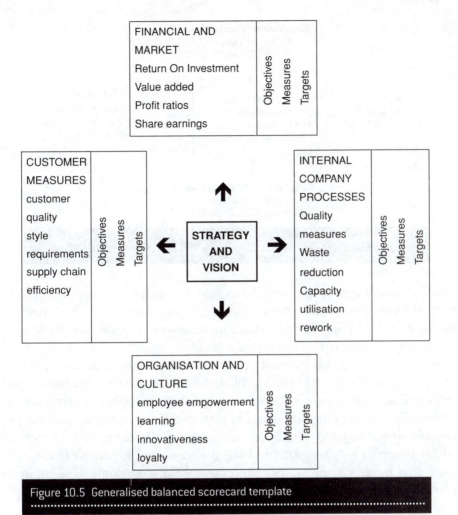

FINANCIAL AND
MARKET
Return On Investment
Value added
Profit ratios
Share earnings

Objectives Measures Targets

CUSTOMER
MEASURES
customer
quality
style
requirements
supply chain
efficiency

Objectives Measures Targets

STRATEGY
AND
VISION

INTERNAL
COMPANY
PROCESSES
Quality
measures
Waste
reduction
Capacity
utilisation
rework

Objectives Measures Targets

ORGANISATION AND
CULTURE
employee empowerment
learning
innovativeness
loyalty

Objectives Measures Targets

Figure 10.5 Generalised balanced scorecard template

will usually be taken from the initial motivations for undertaking the transformation – inefficient or costly operations, a declining market share, a change in organisational strategy or direction, or as the outcome of cross-industry comparisons with competitors' operations (often known as benchmarking). Most of these scenarios view the organisation in terms of its resources to understand its current and future position – resources needed for its operation or available for its operations – and as such, the transformational tools employed often emphasise the measurement and control of processes. It is very much a rational and functionalist view of the world.

In order to be successful, however, it must be remembered that all operations within organisations contain interactions between the technical specifications of the process to be conducted and the social system established within the workplace. Without this understanding of culture of the

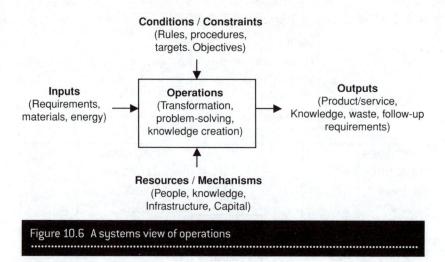

Figure 10.6 A systems view of operations

workplace, and appropriate actions to gain the necessary support for change from the workforce, most attempts at organisational transformation will be unsuccessful, and may actually result in *decreases* in the pre-existing levels of productivity, efficiency or competitiveness.

Bearing in mind this necessity for the involvement of the workforce, we will now examine some of the established tools that have been used as aids in organisational transformation. Some of these tools have been discussed previously in other chapters (such as just-in-time operations, business process re-engineering, TQM, QC/QA and supply chain management practices), whilst others (e.g., six-sigma method) is introduced for the first time. For tools that have been previously presented, we discuss some of these in the context of a transformation tool.

Six-sigma method

Six-sigma method is a well-established organisational improvement methodology that has been adopted by leading global organisations including Sony, ABB, General Electric, Motorola, Ford, Honeywell, and American Express. Six-sigma was originally developed at Motorola in the 1980s as a quality control tool and has since been developed into an overall business improvement methodology.

It is named after the symbol for population variation, sigma (σ), and uses a multiple of six to emphasise the difference of this method from the commonly used $+/-3\sigma$ limits used in control charting. The concept is that if the variation of a process is within $+/-6\sigma$ control chart limits, then there will be very few instances where the process can be declared to be out of control (less than 4 in every 1,000,000 instances on average). On most measures, this would be considered to be very high level of performance.

Table 10.6 Classification of operations measures

System Component	Type of Measure			
	Time	Quality	Productivity	Cost
Inputs	Timeliness of inputs	Input data and materials quality	Opportunities to leverage supplier initiatives, get ideas from customers	Total cost to operations (cost of product, cost of logistics and supplier management)
Outputs	Timeliness of outputs	Output data and materials quality	Opportunities to enhance customer position through the way things are delivered.	Total cost (production, logistics, service) to the customer
Conditions/ Constraints	Achievement of strategic milestones and benchmarks	Compliance with quality and environmental objectives	Evidence of continuous improvement	Meeting cash flow, profit and return on investment objectives
Resources/ Mecha- nism	Timely resource maintenance and renewal	Capability maintenance	Minimisation of resources required	
Operation	Internal process times	Internal quality and waste measures	Optimisation of resource allocation and use	Maintaining competitive operations cost structures

Many organisations are finding it necessary to perform at this very high level. For example, banks process millions of transactions everyday, and all stakeholders would find it intolerable if there were high proportions of errors in the transactions. Similarly, telecommunications companies route billions of data packets and phone calls – misdirected data will cause chaos. Hospitals, utility companies, government departments, etc. all also process large volumes of transactions and activities that need to be done reliably and accurately. Hence, many of these organisations are hoping to get their performance up to $+/-6\sigma$ levels.

Six-Sigma Control Chart

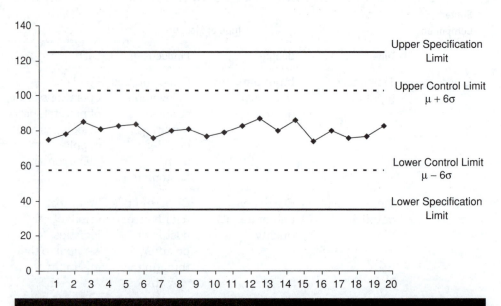

Figure 10.7 A six sigma control chart

The desired operating performance level, as measured by performance specification conformance of an organisation that had successfully implemented a six-sigma improvement program would be as illustrated in Figure 10.7.

From its original emphasis on defect control, the six-sigma methodology has been extended as a method for process improvement. The characteristic of the six-sigma methodology that makes it more than just a new application of quality control methodologies sourced from the works of Deming and others is its explicit linking of the tactical control techniques with strategic operations actions. The six-sigma process employs two key methodologies for its implementation: DMAIC (for process control) and DMADV (for process design). These methodologies are outlined in Table 10.7.

In order to successfully implement the six-sigma methodology, it is essential that leadership is provided by senior management at the highest levels. Senior management is required to generate enthusiasm for six-sigma implementation within the organisation and to empower employees with the necessary decision making abilities and resources. Members of the executive management team should identify champions who will be responsible for the implementation of six-sigma projects across the departments of the organisation.

The sigma approach works best to solve specific problems that may currently exist or may emerge in the future. For example, a bank may develop a

Table 10.7 DMIAC and DMADV methodologies

DMAIC – for process control		DMADV – for process design	
Define	Use Customer information and Organisational strategy to set process improvement goals.	**D**efine	Use Customer information and Organisational strategy to set the goals of the design activity
Measure	Collect relevant data from the current process	**M**easure	Identify product and production capabilities, risks and critical qualities and measure these.
Analyse	Determine the relationships of the causative factors that have been identified and look for other factors that may not have been identified	**A**nalyse	Use measurements to design alternate processes. Evaluate their capabilities and select the design to be implemented
Improve	Use the results of the analysis to optimise the process	**D**esign	Optimise the design and set measures for design verification
Control	Institute control measures to continuously measure and limit variation	**V**erify	Use pilot runs to verify design then implement and handover the process to process owners

six sigma project to solve problems associated with excessive errors in cheque processing activities. Another example: a car manufacturing may decide to use this method to come up with a new design so that door opening and closing would require less effort. So, this methodology is best suited to a limited set of problems, one that requires a team effort and a project management approach to resolve.

Usually, a team would be put together to tackle these problems instead of the whole organisation being galvanised. This team would consist of a range of technical specialists who have also received training in the six-sigma methodology. Descriptors for key roles in these teams have been borrowed from martial arts. For example, black belts are used for those who have high levels of expertise in the six-sigma methodology, and green belts for those who work under their direction on six-sigma projects. These teams would use the DMAIC or DMADV procedures to systematically define, measure, analyse and ultimately resolve the problems that they are tasked with resolving.

As with many other initiatives that have gained attention in the management literature, six-sigma has been criticised. It has been found that many of the companies that announced the introduction of six-sigma programs failed to generate much success from these. Further, controlled studies have shown that companies that have extensive six-sigma programs have not outperformed those who do not have programs in existence. A careful examination of these cases reveals that many of the affected organisations attempted to introduce their programs without first gaining the acceptance and commitment of their employees. Without this, it is highly unlikely that the expected benefits would be achieved.

Just-in-time (JIT) methodology

The just-in-time (JIT) methodology was introduced earlier in Chapter 2. Here, it is discussed in the context of a transformation tool. In this context, JIT is an operations strategy aimed at eliminating waste through the reduction of inventory stock – both of component parts and finished goods – through the smoothing of production and ordering processes. The key elements required for the introduction of JIT are:

1. Levelling of the manufacturing production schedule
2. Greatly reduce set-up times
3. Reduce lead times
4. Reduce batch sizes
5. Institute a rigorous preventative maintenance regime
6. Train a flexible, multi-skilled workforce
7. Require zero defect supply of components by suppliers
8. Small lot, preferably single unit, transfer of work in progress.

Apart from savings in inventory costs, other benefits to the organisation of JIT have been found to include: reduced work in progress, scrap, and obsolete items; higher employee motivation and involvement through a more varied work regime; and smoother production flows. JIT methods also make visible the previous inefficiencies in the production process – problems can no longer be covered up through the drawing down of inventory stocks.

One downside of the full adoption of JIT is that an organisation places great reliance on the performance of all of its suppliers and leaves it vulnerable to supply shocks. Late supply of any component parts will halt the entire production operation as, ideally, no safety stocks are maintained to overcome this eventuality. This situation has been recently illustrated several times in the Australian automotive manufacturing industry where business failures of key component suppliers have led to the temporary closure of the majority of major automotive assemblers, and subsequently, other players in the industry.

Business process re-engineering

Business process re-engineering (BPR) was introduced in an earlier chapter. As indicated then, it is a management approach developed in the 1990s that, through a thorough examination and redesign of work processes, aims at improving business efficiency by removing non-value adding activities. Prior to the emergence of BPR, it was frequently observed that technology was being used to simply automate existing work practices, even if those practices and their processes were ineffective. While this may have increased production rates and brought with it cost efficiencies, it did little to change the nature of the operations being performed.

A better solution is to examine the necessity for each stage of the operation and redesign or eliminate those stages that did not add value to the end product or service. This is the stated aim of BPR. As such, BPR encompasses both product and process innovations – re-engineering the product to better suit the consumer's needs and redesigning operating processes to eliminate those wasteful activities that do not add value. The methodology for implementing BPR as described by Guha et al. (1993) is presented in Table 10.8.

One of the early criticisms of the BPR methodology was that it simply consisted of a return to a 'Taylorist' or scientific management approach. This criticism addressed the failure of BPR to recognise the necessity to include social factors in the realignment of operations processes. As with all other transformation or intervention tools, a failure to allow for socio-technical considerations has resulted in many of the redesigned processes not optimising the process output, nor the overall business system.

Other transformation tools

One of the aims of most business transformation activities is to create greater linkages and interactions between an organisation's operations and its business strategy. Along with those detailed above, there are numerous other transformation methodologies that have been implemented by organisations, studied by theorists, and advertised by management consultants. Most of these tools are used as part of larger improvement efforts, and in most instances, one would find many of these being implemented together. Some of the more common one are: ABC – activity based costing; QFD – quality function deployment; QC/QA – quality control/quality assurance; SCM – supply chain management; and, TQM – total quality management. Since most of

Table 10.8 A business process re-engineering methodology

Implementation step	Required actions
1. Envision new process(es)	Secure management support Identify reengineering possibilities Identify suitable technologies Align change to corporate strategy
2. Initiate Change	Establish reengineering team Agree on performance goals
3. Diagnose	Describe existing process Uncover non value adding steps in existing processes
4. Redesign Processes	Develop alternate processes Develop new process design Design HR configuration Select IT platform Develop overall blueprint and gather feedback
5. Reconstruct	Develop/ install solution Establish process changes
6. Monitor	Establish performance measurement, including time, quality, cost and IT performance Link to continuous improvement

(From Guha et al.)

these have been discussed extensively in other chapters, detailed descriptions of these are not necessary here.

Summary

This chapter has outlined the key characteristics required for organisations to achieve operations excellence. These characteristics may be summarised as: a clear understanding of the organisation's operating environment and a continual process of checking the organisation's 'fit' with its environment; a view of service operations as a driving force of competitive advantage; recognition of the strategic importance of the supply pipeline; regular assessment of operations performance using a business excellence framework; recognition of the linkages between operations and financial performance; utilisation of a 'balanced scorecard' type approach to performance measurement; and, the use of transformational tools to continually renew the organisational drive for operations excellence.

We started this chapter asking three questions as part of the management challenge: What is excellence?; How might we measure it?; and, How might we strive for continuous improvement?

We have noted that excellence has an absolute aspect – offering something unique; has a relative aspect – improving on past performance or better than competitors; and may be measured differently by different stakeholders and customers. We have also noted that customer (both internal and external) expectations may change over time, leading to a need for continuous improvement in a strategic business context.

Various frameworks of excellence have been discussed that list assessment criteria and linkages between them. The point is that operations excellence viewed from one perspective may be necessary but not sufficient. For example, making quality products that are not delivered on time or are excessively expensive may compromise the financial viability of the whole organisation. On the other hand, offering sub-standard products or services will certainly lead to financial failure. Balance is needed, and this is indicated in the nature of measurements – some relate to enabling attributes and some relate to outcome attributes. By using one of the management techniques presented in this chapter to measure progress towards operations excellence, we gain an insight into the strengths and weaknesses of a particular organisation. Areas of relative weakness may be improved by using one or more of the transformational tools discussed above, recognising that some tools are only appropriate for particular types of operations.

In summary, operations excellence can be typified and measured, and this provides a database to pursue continuous improvement/innovation within operations. One of the examples in this chapter, of Toyota, is a case in point. This company clearly strives for operations and indeed, whole-of-business excellence, recognising the never ending journey it is on and that it must continue to pursue. Toyota's quality, delivery and cost management is in general superb, compared to its competitors, however, each year it finds new ways to take these even further forward. Although Toyota has achieved operational excellence in Australia, it is constantly striving to improve its performance. Quality in its local operations is high, yet the challenge of cost competitiveness with low cost countries remains a big issue, as is capacity management and technological change. Companies such as Toyota, IKEA and Coca-Cola do not just measure their performance and strive to beat their external competitors in the market place, but they also conduct detailed benchmarking and measurement exercises within their own companies, from operation to operation and over time. This knowledge gives them a huge lift in their ability to learn and hence to improve.

DISCUSSION QUESTIONS

1. 'The move from mass production in the 1960s to the present trend toward consumer specific production represents a need for labour requirements to move away from the deskilled base, resulting from the standardisation of work routines back to a flexible, multi-skilled workforce reminiscent of the highly skilled artisans of craft guilds of the middle ages'. Discuss this statement with reference to the operating environment of today's organisations.

2. One way to classify varying operations types is as runners, repeaters and strangers. Give an example of each of these types of operations that may be found in a bakery.

3. Describe the ways in which an organisation's technical excellence can generate for it sources of competitive advantage. Use an example.

4. What advantages did companies gain by moving from quality control and adherence to international standards to a total quality management approach to their operations? What changes to their approach to their business were necessary to make this change?

5. Match each of the 12 principles of business excellence to the categories of the Australian business excellence framework. Assume your role is to organise the cake stall for the local primary school fete. Describe one action you would undertake in an attempt to fulfil each of the categories of the Australian business excellence framework.

6. Compare the scoring of the Singapore Quality Award criteria with that of the New Zealand Business Excellence Foundation framework. Is there a difference in the emphasis on the similar categories of the two schemes? Would you expect companies scoring highly on these awards to also be successful financially? – Why or why not?

7. Financial measures dominate business reporting. What operations measures could be used to give a more balanced view of a manufacturing company's competitiveness?

8. Can there be too many performance measures? Discuss with reference to the way in which operations performance measures may be linked to employee pay.

9. One of the key operations of a university is the delivery and assessment of teaching modules. Use the operations measure map in Table 6 and allocate possible performance measures to this operation.

10. What is meant by the term 'socio-technical system'?

11. How would you apply the six-sigma philosophy to an organisation such as a hairdressing salon that individually customised each service it delivered? What performance measures could be used in this situation?

12. 'All effective organisational transformation methodologies are based upon insights gained from statistical analysis of performance data. It is the rigour

of this data collection and analysis that determines the success of any attempt at organisational change'. Give reasons as to why you agree or disagree with this statement.

....

Further readings and references

Bacon, T. 2005. 'Superior products and services confer only a fleeting advantage.' *Handbook of Business Strategy*. Bradford: Emerald Group Publishing, pp. 61–6.

Collins, J. and Porras, J. I. 1994. *Built to Last: Successful habits of visionary companies*. City: Harper Business.

Drucker, P. F. 1946. *Concept of the Corporation*. New York: Transaction Publishers.

Drucker, P. F. 1954. *The Practice of Management*. New York: Harper and Row.

Drucker, P. F. 1964. *Managing for Results*. New York: Harper and Row.

Guha, S., Kettinger, W. J. and Teng, T. C. 1993. 'Business process reengineering: building a comprehensive methodology.' *Information Systems Management*, (Summer): xx–xx.

IDEF 1993. 'Integration Definition for function modelling' *Federal Information Processing Standard183*, National Institute of Standards and Technology, USA.

Kaplan, R. S. and Norton, D. P. 1996. 'Using the balanced scorecard as a strategic management tool.' *Harvard Business Review*, (Jan–Feb): 75–85.

Levitt, T. 1972. 'A production line approach to services.' *Harvard Business Review*, (Sept–Oct): xx–xx.

Peters, T. and Waterman, R. H. 1982. *In Search of Excellence: Lessons from America's best-run companies*. New York: Harper Collins.

Samson, D. and Challis, D. 1999. *Pattern of Excellence: The New Principles of Corporate Success*. City: Financial Times/Prentice-Hall.

Internet resources

The following sites provide useful information on the topics covered in this chapter:

Honeywell Six-Sigma: http://www.honeywell.com/sixsigma/index.html

Motorola University: http://www.motorola.com/motorolauniversity.jsp

SAI Global: http://www.saiglobal.com

Wikipedia Six-Sigma: http://en.wikipedia.org/wiki/Six_sigma

The Australian Business Excellence Framework – overview diagrams sourced from the SAI Global website http://www.sai-global.com/professionalservices/Business Excellence/} – accessed on 25 October 2006.

The European Foundation for Quality Management (EFQM) Excellence Model – information available from the EFQM website http://www.efqm.org/ – accessed on 9 November 2006.

The Malcolm Baldrige Award – information available from the US National Institute of Standards and Technology http://www.quality.nist.gov/ – accessed on 22 November 2006.

The New Zealand Business Excellence Foundation (NZBEF) – information available on the Criteria for Performance Excellence and Award categories from the NZBEF website http://www.nzbef.org.nz/ – accessed on 31 July 2007.

The Singapore Quality Award and Business Excellence Framework – information available from the SPRING website http://www.spring.gov.sg/ – accessed on 25 July 2007.

PART IV

Challenges and Opportunities in Operations

Managing Risk in Operations

Damien Power and Danny Samson

Learning objectives

After reading this chapter, you should be able to:

- appreciate that operations management decisions involve not just costs and benefits, but also risk factors
- understand risk and its management frameworks
- know how to identify and take risks into account in operational decision-making
- incorporate risk factors into major decision areas such as technology choices, capacity choices, and other areas of operations
- identify the key risks and be able to evaluate them and account for them in supply chains, not just in-house operations.

Box 11.1: Management challenge: PETRONAS

Consider the risks faced by the Malaysian oil and gas company PETRONAS. This company explores for oil and gas and then develops these assets into operating refineries and downstream petrochemical plants. In addition it operates pipelines all over the world and a large fleet of ships. Some of the risks this company faces include:

- When PETRONAS explores by drilling for oil and gas, up to $100 million can be spent in any location, with a relatively low probability of success in finding significant deposits (only about one in eight developments is successful overall).

- There is technical risk in operations, such as with new technology and plant reliability.
- Marketing risk involves concerns about the future prices and demand for oil, gas and other petroleum and chemical products and related services.
- PETRONAS operates in many countries where there is political uncertainty. PETRONAS has had to do business with 'warlords' and hence faces risk of asset nationalisation, sabotage etc.
- Economic risk such as associated with currency fluctuation pervades the income stream of this company, which employs and pays most of its staff in Malaysian currency, but sells its products in US dollars.
- As a major shipping company, piracy and other forms of risk are inherent in PETRONAS's transport operations.
- In PETRONAS's plants there are safety-related risks particularly because of the flammable nature of the materials it is processing.

How should PETRONAS executives deal with these risks? Can they be avoided? Should they be minimised?

Introduction

Operations managers need to make their decisions about the strategy they are pursuing, operations system design, and day-to-day running of the operations, bearing in mind not just the estimated benefits and costs, but also the risk factors inherent in their decisions and outcomes. And this also applies to the improvement initiatives that operations managers oversee, for example the introduction of Lean Management (see Chapter 2), or quality management (see Chapter 9) or indeed any other initiative. Because operations managers make decisions that have impacts out into the future, and the future cannot be known with perfect certainty, there is always a degree of 'riskiness' in such decisions.

In designing and operating their production systems, operations managers must do more than just consider the net benefits of the various decisions they make. We live and work in a world in which there are many unforeseen events occurring in the business environment. These can be from any and every source or aspect of the operation. Here are just some examples that have major operational implications of what can and does happen to organisations:

1. A key person in your operations system is sick, retires, resigns, or dies.
2. A supplier experiences a problem within its operation and on very short notice lets you know that you will not be receiving a key input to your operation, without which you can not produce your output.
3. Your key machinery or computer system breaks down unexpectedly, just when you are running 'flat out' to meet important customer requirements.

4. An important customer cancels a big order that you have been gearing up for and have committed resources to.
5. The government changes some laws or regulations necessitating major changes in your operations.
6. An environmental or indigenous or community group pressures your business to change how it operates.
7. A price rise occurs in a key input to your production system, such as fuel oil, dramatically changing your operation's profitability.
8. A new massively efficient global competitor comes to 'town' and targets your customers.
9. Your board of directors changes the overall company strategy, requiring major changes to the operation.
10. New products or services from competitors make your primary product obsolete, or at least reduce your demand or price significantly.
11. New materials of construction become available causing you to need to reconfigure your production system.
12. Global warming or unpredictable weather events massively shift demand for your services in one direction or other.
13. Political events such as war, free trade agreements or other shifts in the world change the competitive dynamics of your marketplace.
14. A disgruntled employee either deliberately or carelessly gives poor service to customers or at worst, sabotages your processes, products or services.
15. A terrorism event or natural catastrophe substantially shifts demand or supply in your industry.
16. Significant changes in currency valuations shift your operation's cost base and hence your profitability.

The list of the causes of volatility or risk facing any and every business could go on almost for ever. Operations managers must cope with the need to be competitive at world-class levels in all that they do: meet customers' requirements, deliver the market requirements, meet the business strategy requirements, provide a profit margin to the business, eliminate waste through lean thinking and management, develop their people, etc.; and they must increasingly do all this in a world full of uncertainty! So, in a nutshell, when making decisions about technology, process choice, selecting suppliers, scheduling work rosters or jobs through an operation, operations managers must consider all these possible sources of uncertainty.

Risk management and its processes are not aimed at reducing the risks facing the firm to zero: zero risk is neither possible nor desirable. Risk must be balanced against return. A business should explicitly decide on what risks it wants to run, and then manage those risks very carefully. It is impossible to eliminate every aspect of risk facing a business and its operations. Usually, most businesses prefer less risk to more, other things being equal; so operations managers do wish to reduce risk, at least up to the point where the risk they keep is commensurate with the expected returns.

Some elements of risk, known as pure risk do not come with profit and these are generally to be avoided or reduced when it makes economic sense to do so; while other risks are inherent to the firm's revenue and profit stream. As illustrations, consider the following two aspects of risk.

Box 11.2: Risk in a hazardous waste business

A business that handles hazardous waste has an inherent operating risk of a spill of such materials, which would pollute the local environment. This risk comes with doing this type of business and cannot be completely eliminated; however, the firm should make sensible and responsible decisions to manage both the likelihood and severity factors of such an operation. It cannot completely eliminate the core process of having hazardous chemicals on its site because it could not operate as such. So it should examine how to reduce the likelihood of a spill, by ensuring that the right processes are in place and adhered to, equipment is maintained and capable, training is done, and that the culture and discipline in the workplace is correct. A further use of both common sense and discharge of legal and moral duties for this firm is to work to reduce the severity of such a spill, should an adverse event occur. Note that the risk cannot be eliminated: however, it can be effectively managed, to bring the likelihood and severity factors down to 'acceptable' levels.

Box 11.3: Risk in a business dependent on imports subject to currency fluctuations

A business that imports a lot of its components from overseas into New Zealand and Australia is naturally exposed in its forward orders to fluctuations in currency levels. It can choose to 'ride' these fluctuations and hope for the best and see its input costs vary as various currencies move up and down, or it can fully or partially lock in to fixed currency exchange rates through purchasing futures contracts or options. These financial instruments come at a cost, so it really is a case of trading in some aspect of the firm's natural uncertainty or risk factors for some larger amount of certainty, at a market price. There is no right or wrong here, as it is clearly a case of what the businesses owners want to do about risk exposure and returns. Certainty can be traded for uncertainty in this case.

These matters are relevant to operations managers because the implementation will be within the company's operations, hence the risk management policy must be developed and understood inclusively, because nobody understands the operational level risks as well as those who built and run the operations.

Another example is that of risk associated with the design of products and services being offered to the market. Operations managers usually do not have full responsibility for product design specifications, although they may hopefully have been involved, but they usually do have full responsibility for manufacturing the goods and services to meet the design specifications. So whether the problem comes from poor design or poor production control, operations management and managers are centrally involved in ensuring that products do not cause harm because of faults or any other aspect of defect. This is both a legal and moral obligation acting on operations managers.

Concepts and frameworks of risk management

The management of risk in business generally has become a strategic focal point for organisations in all sectors. As a result, there have been a number of frameworks and standards developed to help managers formulate a credible and robust response to the problem of balancing risk and opportunity in a dynamic business environment.

COSO enterprise risk management

This framework dates back to the early 1990s, and was articulated by Price-WaterhouseCoopers as a result of a commission from the Committee of Sponsoring Organisations of the Treadway Commission (Briggs, 2006). In this framework, enterprise risk management is defined as:

> a process, effected by an enterprises board of directors, management and other personnel, applied in (a) strategy setting and across the enterprise, designed to identify potential events that may affect the entity, and manage risk to be within its risk appetite, to provide reasonable assurance regarding the achievement of entity objectives (Steinberg et al., 2004, p. 2).

This wordy definition illustrates one of the areas in which this framework has been criticised, with one commentator stating that it 'fails to give adequate advice, is poorly written, and can be confusing' (Briggs, 2006 p. 1). Notwithstanding, this framework is most widely cited, adopted and utilised methodology for identification, assessment and mitigation of risk. The focus of this framework is focused in four areas:

1. strategic – goals and mission of the organisation;
2. operations – allocation and use of resources;
3. reporting – particular focus on reliability; and
4. compliance – laws and regulations (Steinberg et al., 2004)

Within each of these four sets of objectives, the framework also identifies eight interrelated components:

1. internal environment – includes philosophical approach to risk management and 'risk appetite', values and cultural integrity;
2. objective setting – existence of a formal objective setting process;
3. event identification – identification of risks and opportunities in a firms environment;
4. risk assessment – management of risk by determining their likelihood and impact;
5. risk response – tolerance for risk is matched against possible responses such as avoidance, acceptance, reduction or sharing;
6. control activities – policies and standard operating procedures to ensure appropriate action is taken;
7. information and communication – access to and diffusion of required information;
8. monitoring – ongoing monitoring of the above processes (Steinberg et al., 2004).

Other criticisms of this approach have included that it is subjective and too simplistic, overly focused on internal risk, and that it does not address risk pro-actively (Briggs, 2006).

Risk Standard AS/NZ 4360

This Australasian standard is being used as the basis for an ISO standard for the management of risk. This standard has been identified as being more flexible and mature than longer established standards such as COSO (Rasmussen, 2007). It has also been identified as having the following strengths: takes a flexible and holistic view of risk and can be applied in any organisation in any industry; has as strong a focus on external factors as internal issue; stakeholder communication is given a high priority; highlights the importance of opportunity identification as part of the risk management process; uses an extensive set of handbooks for implementation (Rasmussen, 2007).

M-o-R: Management of Risk Framework

This framework has originated in the UK and diverges from the approach of COSO by approaching risk at four different organisational levels: strategic, program, project and operational. It is also built around four concepts: corporate governance, continuous measurement and improvement, six clearly defined processes for identifying, assessing and controlling risk, and inbuilt flexibility allowing individual organisations to adapt the framework to their needs (Briggs, 2006). Within this framework the definition of the management of risk bears stark contrast to the over complicated and confusing one provided by COSO:

> The term 'management of risk' incorporates all the activities required to identify and control the exposure to risk which may have an impact on the achievement of an organisation's business objectives (MoR, 2007).

Risk in the key decision areas of operations

Inventory management

The management of inventory represents both a significant source of risk for operations managers, and an opportunity for the pursuit of operational excellence. Holding inventory is traditionally proposed to be a risk mitigation strategy, with the argument being that safety stocks provide both a method for managing forecast error, and a means for decoupling supply and demand. It is, however, also true that inventory represents a major source of risk for organisations whose business model depends on investment in working capital. The dilemma facing the operations manager, therefore, is that on the one hand you can't live with inventory, and on the other you can't live without it. It is a common maxim amongst practitioners that there are only two mistakes you can make as an operations manager – to be holding too much inventory, or not to be holding enough. The complexities of global operations further amplify this problem, with the extra dimensions of timing (delays in getting inventory to where there is demand), location (placing inventory strategically), and mix (having the right proportion or mix of products within families) coming into play. Against this background of both needing and not wanting inventory, and of having to have it to service customers whilst at the same time needing to minimise it to ensure an acceptable return on investment, effective strategies for managing inventory represent a cornerstone of risk management in operations.

Box 11.4: The hidden cost of inventory at Hewlett-Packard

Hewlett-Packard was confronted with paper thin margins in the late 1990s and was struggling to show a profit despite having replaced IBM as the third largest PC manufacturer based on revenue. The Strategic Planning and Modelling Group at HP conducted a review of operations and concluded (not surprisingly) that excess inventory created by a mismatch between supply and demand was the primary driver of PC costs (equal to the PC businesses total operating margin in 1995). However, what was surprising was that the 'holding cost of inventory' (opportunity cost of capital tied up, warehousing, insurance, taxes etc.) was found to represent less than 10 per cent of total inventory-driven costs. What the Strategic Planning Group at HP found was that there were four other 'hidden costs' that were the primary contributors to spiralling costs placing the viability of the PC division at risk:

1 *Component Devaluation Costs*: This category was found to be the greatest contributor to the problem. In simple terms many of the base components of a PC rapidly lose value over a very short life span (e. g. the price of a CPU, central processing unit, can fall 40 per cent over a 9-month life-cycle). Coupled with this was the common practice of holding inventory in many locations (e. g. manufacturing facilities, distribution centres, in transit) meaning that losses were being incurred at many points in the chain simultaneously. HP had until this point been unaware of the risks it was incurring as a result of its component inventory holding practices – it was effectively holding perishable goods.

2 *Price Protection Costs*: Coupled with the problem of component devaluation was the common practice of reimbursing distributors for potential losses due to price reductions. With the value of the PC being eroded by component devaluation, this practice exposed HP to significant price protection risk, and this was being further compounded by some distributors holding excess inventories themselves. In this sense HP was exposed to significant inventory holding risk even after they had on-sold the PC to a re-seller or channel partner.

3 *Product Return Costs*: In some product categories, returns from re-sellers for a full refund constituted up to 10 per cent of revenue. The majority of these returns were purely due to excess inventory. HP was not only incurring the risk of further devaluation as goods were being moved about in the supply chain (and therefore not available for sale), but was also incurring much of the reverse logistics costs.

4 *Obsolescence Costs*: Short product life-cycles will always increase the risk of obsolescence, but in this case HP found that there were other less obvious risks related to obsolescence. The practice of discounting soon-to-be discontinued lines, whilst a common practice to mitigate obsolescence risk, was identified to in fact be the source of significant extra cost. In particular, the resources consumed in the extra marketing effort required to facilitate this process was found to be an area that was not readily measured, identified nor properly accounted for.

Adapted from Callioni et al., 2005.

The most effective strategies for managing inventory risk can often originate from areas traditionally not seen to be within the realm of operations, or are counter-intuitive in nature. A sample of strategies operations managers may employ to mitigate such risks is outlined below.

Holding safety stock

Holding safety stock is often used to decrease the risk of poor service performance (as captured by metrics such as DIFOTIS, an acronym meaning delivery in full on time in specification). In fact, there is evidence suggesting that there is often an association between high levels of inventory and low levels of service performance (Lee et al., 1997). This is particularly the case for firms with wide product lines that face difficulties in accurately measuring forecast error. Promoting collaboration between functions within an organisation is an effective first step toward reducing risk in this area. The development of a sales and operations planning (S&OP) process in companies facing these problems is a positive move towards both reducing error in forecasts and for the development of a coordinated operations strategy. The operations manager can play a pivotal role in both initiating and facilitating such a process.

Implementing lean manufacturing practices

The implementation of lean manufacturing practices is another means by which an operations manager can reduce risks related to holding excessive inventories. The difficulty, however, is that lean methods, though simple in concept, can be difficult to both implement and maintain. They require high levels of commitment, not just within operations but across an organisation, and more often than not, mean a shift in culture, mindset, and the questioning of underlying assumptions. If this does not occur, the operations manager is exposed to the other form of inventory related risk – running out of inventory. If lean is to be pursued, there are definitely substantial potential benefits as organisations that have been successful in using lean methods often report higher levels of customer service with lower levels of inventory (Bruce et al., 2004; Lamming, 1996).

Lead time reduction

Counter-intuitive strategies that can be employed to reduce inventory risk often revolve around the more effective use of time in operations. In simple terms, if lead times can be reduced in operations, inventory-related risk will also be reduced. Methods for reducing lead times can be applied at a local level in operations by reducing set-up, queue and wait times to increase the proportion of value-adding time in a manufacturing process. Lead time reduction in sourcing of purchased inputs also represents an opportunity for the reduction of safety stocks, and of the subsequent risks associated with high levels of inventory. In this case a vendor managed inventory (VMI) program can be used to link supply with demand more closely, and to reduce both quantities delivered and the gap in time between deliveries (Disney and Towill, 2003). Distribution lead times also affect levels of finished goods inventory that may need to be held to support service level targets. Closer coordination of forecasts and collaborative management of replenishment between a manufacturer, distributors and retailer can also reduce the need for inventory. Collaborative Planning Forecasting and Replenishment (CPFR) provides a framework against which trading partners can develop such an arrangement (Ellinger, 2000; Stank et al., 2001). It is strategies of this nature that have led to the commonly used maxim that 'in modern supply chains information replaces inventory' (Christopher, 2000).

Product design

Product design also has an important role to play in the mitigation of inventory related risk. Strategies such as the use of product platforms, standardisation of components and sub-assemblies, design for manufacture and design for logistics all can play a part in creating a product architecture conducive to minimising inventory risk. Manufacturing postponement can be facilitated by the creative application of such methods such that the design of products and production facilities are coordinated. As a result, opportunities can be created including:

- combining both push and pull manufacturing methods allowing inventory to be held at lower levels of value and at lower risk due to the inter-changeability of components
- use of work cells to reduce batch sizes, queues and total cycle times whilst also increasing yield
- pursuit of 'mass customisation' whereby high product variety can be offered at reasonable volume without incurring unsustainable levels of inventory risk
- traditional make-to-stock manufacturers can pursue a business model closer to that of make-to-order.

Operations managers can play a critical role in both the adoption and use of these methods by building capability in problem solving and process analysis. The development and promotion of a continuous improvement culture within operations does not need to be limited in scope to just local process improvement, but can create the conditions for application more broadly to the coordination of products and value chain design.

Information technology

Growth over recent times in the adoption and use of information technologies within the operations function has been both rapid and broad in scope. It is hard to imagine an operating facility nowadays not being managed with the aid of some form of productivity software, whether it is a single PC running a spreadsheet for planning and scheduling, or a fully operational ERP system coordinating multiple cross-functional processes, and at the same time integrated with similar trading partners systems. The widespread adoption and use of such systems within operations could be taken to mean that investment in information technology leads to higher levels of operational performance. The reality, however, is quite the opposite, with much of the evidence indicating that such investments carry substantial risks. Some are related to the nature of the technologies themselves, their limitations and underlying assumptions. Some are based in the systems, culture and capabilities of the organisation itself. And others exist because of the speed of technological change, the total cost of ownership, and strategic nature of ongoing investment in IT.

Box 11.5: Cisco Systems: high-tech fortune-tellers are still fortune-tellers

By the late 1990s, Cisco Systems had enjoyed more than a decade of stellar success as the market leader in switching technologies. Over a period of 11 years since becoming a public company, revenues moved into the multiple billions, the stock split 12 times, and the number of people employed had grown to 44,000. At one point, market capitalisation was at the half trillion dollar mark.

During this time the company had developed a web-based forecast, order and inventory management system called 'Virtual Close'. This system was quoted by many to be not only at the cutting edge of web-based IT applications, but to provide Cisco managers with near to real-time access to operating and order-based data that could be fed into forecasts, substantially reducing error. The performance of the system up until this time provided ample evidence to support this level of confidence, with predicted growth rates being matched and often exceeded by actual demand. During late 1999 and 2000, however, industry-wide confidence in the ongoing growth of demand for switches and related products started to reduce. Many major players in the industry saw a flattening in demand as being inevitable due largely to the reliance of demand for switches on the growth of investment in what had become unsustainable Internet-based business models. The Internet bubble was about to burst and the majority of players were adjusting forecasts, inventories and capacity plans in anticipation. That is, all except Cisco, who at the same time was predicting a sustained rate of growth through its 'Virtual Close' system.

The experience of Cisco's management with this system had never been other than positive, and it was telling Cisco to invest in more inventories rather than to cut back. In fact, at this time, when the rest of the industry was pulling in its horns, Cisco decided to invest in inventory due to a projected widening gap between supply and demand, and the fear of subsequent loss of market share. By late 2001, Cisco's earnings had plummeted 30 per cent, 8500 people had been laid off and the company was forced to write off $US2.2 billion in dead stock. Ironically a proportion of this stock write-off was 'virtual' stock, in that payments and commitments to suppliers had been made but no stock was actually received. In other cases, near new equipment was being sold on a 'grey market' yielding

15 cents in the dollar, meaning essentially that Cisco was losing money with every sale of this type.

There are many factors that can contribute to a dramatic turnaround in the fortunes of a firm of this magnitude, but there is substantial consensus that the following factors made a significant contribution:

- Cisco's management was following the forecast generated by the 'Virtual Close' system despite warnings from suppliers and other trading partners to the contrary. The faith shown in this system-generated forecast seems to have been based in a belief that ongoing growth was a given. There appears to have been little appreciation of the risk associated with dependence on system-generated forecasts. In particular, the assumptions underpinning historical data seem to have not been questioned, and this was compounded by a naïve assumption that all orders are real orders in a growth market. Many of these orders were at best inflated due to an expectation of rationing.

- The 'Virtual Close' system did not have many key macro-economic variables built into its model. These included levels of debt, interest rates, spending trends, bond markets, etc. The lack of key economic data was exacerbated by the bias toward growth built into estimates. In large part this was due to over-reliance on historical data combined with an acceptance of all orders in the system on face value. In simple terms, Cisco management did not question the forecast or even entertain the idea that growth rates may not be sustainable. The lesson for operations managers is that it is prudent to assume nothing, to be willing to question assumptions that modelling systems rely on, and to balance quantitative forecasts with qualitative assessments. Relying on outputs from systems without being cognisant of the limitations inherent in the assumptions built into their modelling logic represents one of the major sources of risk for operations managers today. Often, the most effective strategy is balance such data with a rich array of qualitative inputs from as many internal and external sources as is practicable. In this way, a forecast can be developed through critical consensus rather than blind acceptance.

Adapted from Berinato, 2001.

While the application of technology within the operations function can be a source of risk requiring managers to develop strategies for mitigation, the appropriate use of technology also has the potential to reduce operating risk. This is particularly the case where technology is applied to the cross-functional coordination of activities that have a direct bearing on the efficiency and effectiveness of operations.

Box 11.6: Dassault Aviation: reducing manufacturing risk through virtual NPD

Dassault Aviation is a 3.4 billion Euro business designing and manufacturing executive jets and military aircraft. The executive jet sector represents 50 per cent of

Dassault's revenue and has a high focus on flexibility, customisation and innovation as order-winning criteria. Coupled with this are the complexity of the product and the diversity of partners involved in developing and making an aircraft. The product also has a long operating life of up to 30 years, meaning that the design phase is critical for determining ongoing maintenance and servicing costs. Dassault has 27 partners involved in the development of new products spread across Europe and North America further complicating the management of design and development. To control and coordinate this process Dassault (in concert with IBM) developed a 'virtual collaborative workspace' where a complete digital prototype could be shared, modified and configured by multiple Dassault engineers and trading partner consultants in next to real time. This workspace combined 3D CAD with software specifically developed to optimise product life-cycle management and maintenance specification. In the words of a senior aerospace engineer at Dassault:

'Thanks to the virtual platform, we were able to work together right from the start from the conception stage, sharing the same database and the same tools, which is something that we could not do in the past' (Anonymous, 2006).

The impact of this technological innovation on the operations function was manifold. The integration of this virtual workspace with existing IT systems meant that product development could be integrated with both the manufacturing and maintenance functions. As a result the following operational benefits were realised:

- Rapid ramp-up of production with no loss of product quality. The combination of technologies allowed the specification of the aircraft to be achieved at a high degree of accuracy. This had always been problematic in the past due to the complexity of the product incorporating 40,000+ parts, 200,000 fasteners and many complex avionic and related systems. As a result, the normal quality learning curve experienced with the development of an aircraft was almost entirely eliminated. In this case, a level of quality was achieved with the first aircraft that would previously have taken dozens of aircraft to attain.
- Assembly time was cut from 16 months to 7 months due to the accuracy of component assembly definition using the virtual workspace allowing 'first-time' fit of assembled parts.
- The ability of upstream partners to share and refine design in the 'co-development' environment created the ability to test for and eliminate assembly problems in a virtual environment. By the time of physical assembly this meant that unforeseen problems had already been addressed and eliminated.
- Tooling costs were also reduced due to the accuracy of component interfaces. Many tools designed to facilitate alignment between sections of the aircraft therefore became redundant.
- The need for physical prototypes was entirely eliminated reducing cost further and eliminating an awkward and time consuming physical mock-up being constructed within the operations function.
- Waste has been significantly impacted as only what is required to build a saleable aircraft is used in its production.

Adapted from Anonymous, 2006.

Process technology

The investment in and implementation of new process technologies represents a major source of risk for the operations management function. This has always been the case as changing systems, incorporating new processes and investing in new technology combines both capital investment with the need for change in human systems, methods, capabilities and many times cultural factors. As such, risk levels are high due to this difficult combination of financial and human factors interacting. Add to this the fact that in recent times, global competitive forces have combined with the lowering of trade barriers to create more pressure for change, and that 'best practice' is underpinned by either a focus on continuous improvement, process reengineering, or some combination of both. Nowadays, a manufacturing or service firm not thinking along these lines would be seen to well behind the pack in competitive potential. Against this background it is critical that the operations function can incorporate effective risk management strategies into planning processes and into the implementation of new processes, methods and technologies.

> ### Box 11.7: Lean manufacturing at Siemens Magnet Technology
>
> Siemens Magnetic Technology division had been at the forefront of design and manufacture of Magnetic Resonance Imaging (MRI) systems since the early 1980s. Siemens superconducting magnets used in such scanners are contained in 30 per cent of such scanners worldwide. This technology has wide medical application particularly in the area of imaging soft tissue for the diagnosis of cancers and related problems. Siemens manufacturing process in the Magnet Technology division had for many years used batch 'push' methods, and this had been identified to lack the flexibility required to meet the needs of the modern market. This system assumed standard lead times and used a linear production flow resulting in the potential for work in process inventory to build up at bottleneck work centres. The size and weight of the magnets made this situation more critical due to the stress this placed on storage space within the manufacturing facilities. Further, this system created long lead times in manufacturing, further compounding the lack of flexibility and poor time competitiveness of the division.
>
> It was decided to move to a 'pull' type manufacturing system controlled by kanban at key points in the process. Although, on paper, systems of this type can appear to be simple and uncomplicated, in reality the change to the new 'pull' method was fraught with risk. There are five stages in manufacturing – coil winding, resin impregnation, coil preparation and termination, assembly, and test. At each point, there can be two separate streams based on different components and work required. There is equipment sharing between types of magnet, but there are also dedicated processes for some combinations of magnet and component type.

Further complexity results from a combination of labour-intensive and capital-intensive operations each with their own local management requirements and systems. As such, it was decided the best way to manage such risk was to commission a simulation of the new system to assess the intended and unintended consequences of the change. An interesting side effect of the initial data gathering phase for the development of the simulation model was that in some areas, the data gathering process led to changes in methods locally (independent of the impact of the new 'pull' system. As a result the risk management process (simulation) had a side effect of challenging the thinking of work centre managers and altering some long established processes. Another important outcome at this early stage was the identification of a lack of consensus on how a 'pull' system would work in each work centre.

It was apparent that process managers at different points had very different ideas as to what the new method was, how it would work, and even why the change was necessary. The identification of this issue alone created an important understanding of a source of risk that had up until now not been anticipated – a fragmented understanding of the why, how and what of the 'pull' system. Had this not been identified it is highly likely that this problem alone could have substantially reduced the effectiveness of the transition. The model developed used Siemens' forecast, planning and capacity data, and was also designed to be similar to interfaces currently used within Siemens. The modelling interface was developed with the user in mind, such that anyone with some basic spreadsheet skills could simulate flows of goods by altering key variables such as number of kanban, volumes, quality yields, etc. As a result of modelling, it was identified at an early stage that the initial planned number of kanban in the system was inadequate. If the system had been implemented 'on-line' with this planned number of kanban, un-anticipated bottlenecks would have materialised dramatically, slowing throughput and causing lead time blowouts. The system was also able to be used to highlight the implications of using at multiple points of the system of local changes in kanban policies. As a result of this process Siemens Magnet Technology division not only managed the risk of adoption and implementation more effectively, but broadened the understanding within the workforce of the dynamics of systems, and their role in maintaining system stability.

Adapted from Anonymous, 2007.

Operating planning and capacity management

The risk associated with capacity planning for operations managers is strongly associated with the difficulties inherent in forecasting demand. All forecasts carry an error, and that error represents risk as it is an estimate that impacts on decisions and resource allocation processes. Models used for the planning of capital investment (i.e. investment in manufacturing capacity), therefore, will only offer assistance to an operations manager if that model adequately addresses and incorporates realistic assessment of potential error.

Box 11.8: Capacity investment in bio-tech: NPV or 'real options' approach?

The complexities and uncertainties inherent in bio-tech manufacturing start-ups amplify the risks already present in decisions relating to manufacturing capacity investment. When such decisions have to be made for products still in development, the choice of in-house manufacture or outsourced capacity becomes vital. Often, these companies face substantial capital investments when they need cash to finance the ongoing refinement of the end product. Insourcing is typically capital intensive in this sector, while outsourcing is subject to risks of loss of IP, lack of control of key assets, mis-alignment of objectives and priorities between trading partners, higher than expected costs, and inflexibility in addition or repositioning of capacity. Added to this is the risk associated with trialling of new products as the probability of (say) a new drug making it through this process and out into the marketplace is less than 20 per cent. As well, the forecasting of demand is likely to be subject to rapid change during this process based on the performance of the product and related factors.

The risk is essentially one of opportunity cost – either you build too much capacity and incur costs associated with redundant investment, or you build too little and suffer from loss of potential revenue. Traditionally, managers would use alternate investment scenarios to make a comparison using the net present value (NPV) method to determine the relative economic value of a capacity decision at current value. The problem with this approach is in the underlying assumptions required to make the model work. These include accepting that future demand can be known at a high degree of certainty, and that once a decision is made it will not change. Unfortunately, in this industry, these two assumptions are at best questionable, and at worst, fundamentally flawed.

An alternate approach is to improve the accuracy of an estimate of the value of an investment decision by incorporating uncertainty and flexibility into the model. Uncertainty can be built in by using multiple simulations and comparing them based on a range of probabilities using a random simulation technique. This provides an expected NPV (based on the median of the simulated models) with an associated probability. To further refine the model, flexibility can be built in to accommodate the need for managers to be able to alter course as better information becomes available. The underlying principle here is that in the real world, managers do not have to commit as a traditional NPV model would suggest, and that they always have other options for developing investment strategies that allow them to take a modular rather than integral approach. Such options include:

- investing in a pilot plant to develop process technologies but then outsourcing when volume is required;
- buying options to expand or reduce capacity if the business environment changes;
- build capacity with contract capacity as a back-up;
- abandoning or delaying investment should the product not take-off or pass clinical trialling; and
- investing in process improvement to free up capacity.

The real value of this approach lies in the fact that it more closely approximates real world conditions and that it incorporates both qualitative and quantitative data to reduce the risk inherent in capacity decisions in this industry.

Adapted from Kusiatan, 2005.

Maintenance and servicing

Maintenance is a critical activity for the operations function as a poorly maintained facility will carry high levels of risk in areas such as health and safety, environmental risk, be incurring higher than expected operating costs, and be exposed to costly replacement of capital equipment before the expiry of it's useful life. Balanced against this is the reality that operations managers are rewarded for high utilisation rates of equipment, and can find themselves under pressure not to shut a facility down when the market is demanding more product. This has led to the development of formalised methodologies for the management of maintenance that will allow a balance to be struck between these competing pressures, and for an optimised approach to planned maintenance.

Box 11.9: Maintenance risk management in electricity transmission

Risk associated with the maintenance of electricity transmission networks is high, and takes many forms dependant on the perspective taken. The nature of the service being provided creates significant risks when interventions are carried out on infrastructure incorporating high voltage systems. These risks can relate to the operators conducting the maintenance, the integrity of the system itself, or the continuity of supply. There are also risks associated with external factors such environmental conditions and geography, as well as changing regulatory requirements. In order to manage this situation effectively, it is prudent to adopt a formal methodology for the management of risk. This is particularly the case for the operations and maintenance function within which such responsibilities would normally be held. A typical formal framework of this type used within this sector would contain five basic elements or phases:

- *Identification of potential risks*: Activities typical to this phase would include examining records of equipment faults and associations between fault rates and sources of equipment (e. g., by manufacturer). This process may also include examination of supplier's specifications and recommendations as well as mode of failure and effect of a failure. The outputs of this process would include a tabular representation of individual component failures, mode of failure, causes and symptoms, consequences and recommendations for mitigation of the risk of re-occurrence in future. As well as providing a plan for avoidance of future failures, this also provides a data source tracking progress in risk avoidance over time.

- *Detailed listing of consequences and impacts*: This phase involves detailing (as distinct from identifying in the previous phase) the specific consequences of each failure, as well as the severity of impact. Severity can be measured many ways but a common classification borrowed from the US Military Standards would include catastrophic, critical, marginal and negligible, with the unit of measure being in a currency of choice.
- *Risk assessment*: In this phase, probabilities associated with the consequences associated with a risk factor are calculated. An important input to this phase would be the reliabilities estimated for pieces of equipment based on the collection in phase one of historical data related to fault rates. Equipment assessed to have a low level of reliability would be assessed to have a higher probability.
- *Risk evaluation*: This phase will often use a method for assessing the acceptability of risk factor such as ALARP ('as low as reasonably practical'). This way, risk factors can be classified as unacceptable, tolerable or acceptable. As well, this stage will use the models developed in earlier stages to develop risk control action plans. These plans can be focused on either accepting, reducing, avoiding, spreading or transferring risk. The outcomes of this process will include schedules for condition monitoring of equipment, implementation of preventative maintenance activities, and procurement of strategic spares.
- *Risk control and monitoring*: The risk control plans developed in the previous phase are monitored and communicated to relevant management areas to identify and communicate any variation from acceptable parameter values. When there is an unacceptable deviation observed, corrective action is initiated which will return the cycle of activity back to the evaluation phase. During this phase, additional areas of activity that will be monitored include audit plans and checklists, emergency preparations, and ongoing training plans.

Adapted from Tummala and Mak, 2001.

Risk in service operations

Queues and throughput represent a significant challenge in the area of service operations. As services cannot be inventoried, the service provider and receiver will often be involved together in the delivery of the service. This means that in simple terms, many service operations problems become queue management problems, with the major risks for the operations manager revolving around either having redundant resources (too many service providers) or lengthy queues (too few service providers). The mitigation of these risks often lies in the coordination of information, and building processes that more effectively respond to variations in supply and demand.

Box 11.10: Understanding capacity requirements in a hospital emergency department

Rush North Shore Medical Centre, located in Skokie Illinois, acts as a teaching hospital as well as providing a high level of care to the local community. This hospital is ranked in the top 50 in the US for cardiology and heart surgery and offers a full range of cardiac care services.

Problems were identified in the Emergency Department with patients spending longer than expected periods of time undergoing treatment, prompting concerns for both the patients and the rating of the department as a Level 2 trauma centre. An important factor in determining the efficiency and effectiveness of the department was the coordination between the Medical Telemetry Unit and the Emergency Department. This unit is responsible for the testing of patients when they enter and assessing the patient's requirements for treatment, medication etc. In essence the risk this created for the Emergency Department was the over-utilisation of resources (both staff and physical assets such as beds/rooms etc.), slow patient throughput and long queues. This risk was not just restricted to the poor utilisation of hospital resources, but also reduced the number of beds available for trauma victims, and the staff's ability to access care when it was needed.

In order to model the impact of a set of alternate processes being proposed that would optimise patient throughput without impacting on service levels, a process mapping exercise was undertaken. The initial inputs into this process came from an extensive range of interview covering the Emergency Department, the Telemetry Unit, housekeeping staff, the Director of Patient Care as well as registration and bed control functions. From these interviews, flow charts of a number of key processes were able to be developed, as well as critical parameters being identified and quantified. These data were then used to create a simulated model of flows through the system, and of the interaction between both the Emergency and Telemetry departments. As a result, hospital staff have been able to test a range of options for new process configurations, additional staff to relieve bottlenecks and re-allocation of or investment in other physical resources in order to optimise throughput.

The use of this off-line simulation model substantially reduced the risks associated with investing in process change, and enabled staff to identify possible unforeseen consequences of process change. The result was that one solution that had been promoted for some time to improve throughput, the hiring of an additional triage nurse, would actually be counter-productive as it would create a new bottleneck in the process whilst increasing overall costs. Additionally, it was found that the best solution lay in either reducing the number of patients being admitted to the Medical Telemetry Unit, or increasing the capacity (i.e., number of beds) in this unit. As well as providing management with a tool that can be used to model, test and optimise processes, this simulation tool substantially reduced the risks associated with process improvement and reengineering in a services environment.

Adapted from Blasak et al., 2003.

Occupational health and safety

Risk in this area of operations manifests itself primarily at the human level in the extent to which employees and/or visitors to a facility may be exposed to the risk of injury whilst on a manufacturing premises. Beyond the traditional approach of managing workplace safety as a separate set of initiatives and investments, a more modern approach is to incorporate such health and safety initiatives into wider programs such as six-sigma and lean manaufacturing.

Box 11.11: Honeywell: increasing productivity and improving safety

Honeywell International Inc. Aerospace manufacturing divisions' facility in Torrance California was facing significant challenges in reducing the risk of musculoskeletal disorder (MSD) due to increased volume, overtime and general expansion within the production function. Ergonomics-related injuries represented a significant proportion of lost time injuries (50 per cent), and this was seen to be at risk of increasing.

In response, a plan to train employees in the identification, assessment and control of MSD risk was put into place. The plan approached this problem at two separate levels, awareness training for operators and problem solving for engineers and technicians. A work cell that up until now had been identified as a high risk MSD area (high volume turbocharger assembly) was selected for the testing and application of an ergonomic re-design project.

This new process involved high levels of operator participation, brainstorming of possible improvements, evaluation of purchased equipment, and a set-up time improvement program. In this sense, the ergonomic re-design of this process was incorporated into the re-design of a work cell using lean manufacturing principles. As such, the benefits realised included better ergonomic design of the work cell as well as better productivity. Some high-risk activities were designed out of the process completely, and two years on productivity had increased 37 per cent while workers compensation costs had been reduced across the plant by $US2 million per year. This return was based on a one off investment in process re-design of $US355,000. Importantly, the benefit of incorporating ergonomic work practices to reduce risk related to workplace injuries was found to complement and reinforce lean manufacturing practice.

Adapted from Wynn, 2004.

Environmental risk

The operations function is becoming increasingly exposed to risks associated with the environmental effects of products, the sustainability of processes over time, and risks incurred by stakeholders such as local communities, employees and the local environment as a result of operational processing.

While once there was a time when the operations manager could focus internally on maximising efficiency and utilisation of resources, nowadays these objectives need to be balanced against the wider environmental risks associated with transformational processes. The operations manager needs to be aware of factors such as: the environmental practices of trading partners; the environmental impact of inputs being used at multiple tiers of the supply chain; the pollution risk associated with internal processes and disposal of used materials; the pollution risk of storage of toxic materials; the needs, requirements and sensitivities of local communities on environmental issues; and the environmental impact of process design (e. g., a lean operating system may require deliveries of small quantities from suppliers many times a day – in Japan this was found to have a significant impact on greenhouse gas emissions and road congestion).

Box 11.12: Environmental compliance in the high-tech industry

The rapid growth in demand for high-tech products, their low cost and short product life cycles combine to expose both the industry and society in general to significant environmental risk. For example, sales of cell phones alone globally have reached 1 billion plus units in 2006 (Wolinsky, 2007). At the same time, it is estimated that only between 5 and 10 per cent of these phones will be re-cycled whilst they contain significant quantities of lead, cadmium, mercury and arsenic-related materials. Given that a cell phone has an estimated life-cycle of around two years, this product group alone represents significant environmental risk for society.

At the same time, the European Union recently passed regulations aimed directly at manufacturers of high-tech products, the RoHS (Restriction on the Use of hazardous Substances) and the WEEE (Waste Electrical and Electronic Equipment). In essence, both these regulations place responsibility on manufacturers for the cost of collection/recycling processes, and re-design to reduce use of hazardous materials across the full life cycle of high-tech products (i.e., from design through to recovery at end of life). Similar initiatives are under way in China, Japan and the US.

In order to meet this challenge manufacturers will have to adopt a combination of strategic and tactical responses to comply with the regulations and mitigate their ongoing exposure to risk in this area. Such responses will include:

- conducting high level assessment of the integrity of business processes;
- developing a sustainability blueprint at the corporate level;
- investigating outsourcing options for the collation and reporting of data critical to meeting reporting guidelines;
- establishing communications linkages with re-cyclers and dis-assemblers;
- developing systems for tracking of recycling processes;
- providing documentation bills of material breakdown similar to those required in food products;

- developing vendor selection criteria balancing traditional factors such as cost, flexibility, reliability and quality with compliance capability;
- considering design parameters such as ease of dis-assembly and recycling (DfE or design for environment);
- developing systems enabling effective End of Life (EOL) processing particularly for long life-cycle products;
- ensuring the compliance of spare parts and service processes;
- managing reverse logistics processes for short life cycle products;
- ensuring compliance of production processes and systems; and
- researching opportunities created by turning re-cycling into a value-adding process.

Adapted from Krishna et al., 2005.

Operations and corporate risk: managerial implications

Clearly, operations managers need to work closely with corporate risk managers on issues identified in the previous sections. The reasons are clearly because many of the company's natural risks come from its operations, generated from and related to the operations systems designs, and also the risk management strategies that come from any risk analysis are going to be implemented by operations managers.

Risk manifests in a company's operations, via the designs of products, the process technologies, quality controls, material input and product output process, human actions etc. Hence operations managers should be principally involved in creating company wide awareness of a firm's natural risks and actions concerning these.

Technological risk is a key part of the risk picture facing managers of firms in every sector. Once again, operations managers, who are those people that must run the companies major value creating processes, would usually be centrally involved in decisions about risk and return concerning technology and innovation. Operations managers who are considering new technology would be asking:

1. Should our new technology be at or near the leading edge of technology, where returns may be higher and risk almost certainly is?
2. How innovative is too innovative, meaning too risky and not worth the projected return?
3. Are we so near the leading edge with a product design or process choice that its actually the 'bleeding' edge?
4. How can we reduce the risk while maintaining the expected return?

5. How can we raise the expected return for a given level of innovation risk?

Operations managers should also note that not all losses are predictable, because no-one has a crystal ball that works! For example, what will be the price of fuel be in five years, or for that matter even five weeks? Techniques for assessing probabilities of outcomes for uncertain factors in an operation can involve using decision trees or risk analysis methods.

Operations managers are often under pressure to achieve performance targets, which may be related to cost, output volumes, productivity, or related measures. These pressures often come directly from General Managers or CEOs to whom those operations managers directly report. Hence the temptation is always present to 'cut corners', which usually results in compromising quality in order to bolster quantity. Sometimes, it even leads to pressure to compromise safety in the workplace. Experience shows that in most instances, such apparent gains in productivity from cutting corners or trading off on quality or safety procedures usually come back to 'bite' the organisation and, indeed increasingly, its managers personally. So operations managers need to be skilled in influencing and negotiating to resist the performance pressures (which may come from high up in the business or from outside analysts or investors) and to shape the culture to do things 'right', meaning by the book, and normally without taking senseless shortcuts that might provide a short term gain but may lead to major losses later.

Many companies have suffered direct monetary and major long-term reputation damage as a result of short-term corner cutting. This is not an argument about running operations as lean (see Chapter 2), but it is an approach to find the right balance between the benefits of running sensibly lean and running unsafely too lean (unsafely can apply to products, or processes and in-business operating procedures and technologies).

Risk analysis process

The methods for analysing and deciding what to do about an operations risks range from simple to complex. The most straightforward way to identify risks is to examine all risk sources and classify them as to whether they are high or low in probability, and separately high or low in severity of outcome. Clearly, potential risk events that are low in both likelihood and severity are of limited concern, relative to events that are high in one or both of these risk dimensions. Once risks are identified, assessed as to likelihood and severity, then an action plan can be prepared as to whether risks can be reduced, transferred to another party, or kept.

Summary

Risk is pervasive to operations. Operations managers need to take many aspects of operating and strategic riskiness into account when designing, conducting and improving their operations. For PETRONAS as described in the opening section of this chapter, the aim is not to eliminate risk, as it is integral to exploration, operations such as refining and transport, and marketing. Rather, this company carefully and deliberately identifies its risks, reduces risks where it is economically sensible to do so, and engages in a number of risk sharing and risk transfer activities. This company, like all others, must retain some risk, which means that it is subject to 'downside' events that will negatively impact on its cash flow. PETRONAS puts a lot of effort into managing risks actively, for example through pursuing excellence in its safety procedures, hedging some of its currency exposures, avoiding high-risk shipping lanes and regions, and by licensing in proven technologies.

DISCUSSION QUESTIONS

1. What is the meaning of risk in operations management?
2. In decisions regarding the management of risk such as in capacity planning, how can risk be accounted for and traded off against cost and benefit?
3. A professor once commented that in planning how many items to produce in a batch: 'You have to choose between being wrong on the high side versus wrong on the low side'. Discuss this statement, and its implications for production decisions.
4. Outline a set of steps for risk identification and mitigation in operational planning.
5. It is sometimes said that 'prevention is the best form of cure'. How does this apply to risk management in operational decisions?
6. What specific risk factors would you consider when potentially locating a call centre in a low cost country? Give specific examples.
7. How can technological risk be measured and taken into account in the process of buying new machinery? What risk reduction strategies might be employed?

References

Anonymous 2006. Dassault Aviation revolutionises aircraft development with the virtual platform and PLM, IBM Corporation, http://www.ibm.com/ondemand

Anonymous 2007. Implementing lean manufacturing at Siemens Magnet Technology, Eynsham, Oxfordshire, UK., Lanner Group Limited, www.lanner.com/en/our_customers/casestudies/Siemens_Magnet_Technology.pdf

Berinato, S. 2001. In CIO Magazine. Framingham, MA: CXO Media Inc.

Blasak, R. E., Armel, W. E., Starks, D. W. and Hayduk, M. C. 2003. 'The use of simulation to evaluate hospital operationsbetween the emergency department and a medical telemetry unit.' In Chick, S., Sanchez, P. J., Ferrin, D. and Morrice, D. J. (eds), *Proceedings of the 2003 Winter Simulation Conference.*

Briggs, L. L. 2006. Framing your choices: weighing three risk management frameworks, ITC Institute, http://www.itcinstitute. com/print.aspx

Bruce, M., Daly, L. and Towers, N. 2004. 'Lean or agile: A solution for supply chain management in the textiles and clothing industry?' *International Journal of Operations and Production Management*, 24(2): 151–70.

Callioni, G., de Montgros, X., Slagmulder, R., Van Wassenhove, L. N. and Wright, L. 2005. 'Inventory driven costs.' *Harvard Business Review*, (March).

Christopher, M. 2000. 'The agile supply chain – competing in volatile markets.' *Industrial Marketing Management*, 29(1): 37–44.

Disney, S. M. and Towill, D. R. 2003. 'The effect of vendor managed inventory (VMI) dynamics on the bullwhip effect in supply chains.' *International Journal of Production Economics*, 85(2): 199–215.

Ellinger, A. E. 2000. 'Improving marketing / logistics cross-functional collaboration in the supply chain.' *Industrial Marketing Management*, 29(1): 85–96.

Krishna, V. N., Kumar, S. and Karra, R. 2005. 'The "green" challenge: Complying with the impending environmental regulations in the Hi-Tech industry.' Infosys White Paper, http://www.infosys.com/industries/high-technology/white-papers/viewpoint-RoHS.pdf

Kusiatan, U. 2005. Investing in Biotech manufacturing capacity – valuing strategic flexibility, Maxiom Consulting Group Inc., www.maxiomgroup.com

Lamming, R. 1996. 'Squaring lean supply with supply chain management.' *International Journal of Operations & Production Management*, 16(2): 183–96.

Lee, H. L., Padmanabhan, V. and Whang, S. J. 1997. 'Information distortion in a supply chain: The bullwhip effect.' *Management Science*, 43(4) 546–58.

MoR 2007. M o R Website, http://www.m-o-r.org/web/site/home/home.asp

Rasmussen, M. 2007. Global View with Forrester's Michael Rasmussen, Reed Business Information, http://www.riskmanagementmagazine.com.au/articles/5B/0C04A75B.asp?Type=125&Category=1241

Stank, T. P., Keller, S. B. and Daugherty, P. J. 2001. 'Supply chain collaboration and logistical service performance.' *Journal of Business Logistics*, 22(1): 29–48.

Steinberg, R. M., Everson, M. E. A., Martens, F. J. and Nottingham, L. E. 2004. 'Enterprise Risk Management – Integrated Framework – Executive Summary.' Committee of the Sponsoring Organizations of the Treadway Commission – COSO http://www.coso.org/Publications/ERM/COSO_ERM_ExecutiveSummary.pdf

Tummala, V. M. R. and Mak, C. L. 2001. 'A risk management modle for improving operation and maintenance activities in electricity transmission networks.' *The Journal of the Operational Research Society*, 52(2): 125–34.

Waller, A. P. and Ladbrook, J. 2006. Experiencing virtual factories of the future, http://www.lanner. com/products/whitepapers/virtualfactories.pdf

Wolinsky, H. 2007. In Chicago Sun-Times, Chicago.
Wynn, M. 2004. In ErgoSolutions, Humantech, Inc.

Internet resources

http://en.wikipedia.org/wiki/Risk_management (Wikipedia)
http://www.riskmanagement. com.au/ (The risk management Standards site)
http://www.rmia.org.au/ (Risk Management Institute of Australia)

Sustainability in Operations Management

Suzy Goldsmith and Danny Samson

Learning objectives

After reading this chapter you should be able to:

- define what sustainability is, and how it applies in the context of an organisation and its operations
- explain why organisations are taking greater account of sustainability
- describe how sustainability initiatives and long-term organisational performance are connected
- describe organisations' approach to sustainability and the important role that operations management can play
- describe how new capabilities in operations management can contribute to sustainability and gain unique strategic advantages for the organisation
- appreciate how concepts of sustainability can and should be integrated into all operations managers' decisions and actions.

Box 12.1: Management challenge: sustainability lessons for BHP

In 1999, Broken Hill Proprietary Ltd (BHP) reported a massive A\$2.3 billion dollar loss. Only four years earlier, the company's profit had been A\$1.2 billion. The huge downward slide resulted from a number of poor decisions including failed development projects, over-priced acquisitions and a chronic environmental problem at the Ok Tedi copper and gold mine in Papua New Guinea.

BHP's shareholders were outraged and the company quickly learned some hard lessons. Perhaps the most profound of these was that the company's access to exploration and mining sites – its 'licence to operate' – could be threatened if it failed to nurture the support of the communities and governments of the countries in which it operates.

Tailings and overburden from the Ok Tedi mine operation contaminated the Fly and Ok Tedi rivers, affecting 43,000 people whose main source of food had been fish – now wiped out. BHP had not faced the problem fully, but comforted itself that it had brought benefits – hospitals, schools, malaria eradication programs – to the region and believed that a technical solution to the tailings problem would be developed. That solution never eventuated, and the environmental damage and its flow-on effects became chronic. The result was a class action in the Victorian Supreme Court; the company's retreat from its 52 per cent stake in the mining operation and donation of any further proceeds to the local community; and significantly, a lot of bad press.

How did one of Australia's leading companies get 'caught on the back foot' in such a big way? And how has it turned this disastrous performance around to a profit of US$10 billion in 2006, and to receive top billing internationally for its efforts on social and environmental performance – an improvement across the triple bottom line?

Introduction: What is sustainability?

How ideas of sustainability have developed

The basic ideas of sustainability are not new. Traditional cultures, such as the Aboriginal peoples of Australia and Maori of New Zealand, developed principles of stewardship that enabled them to depend on the land without degrading it or diminishing its capacity to continue to meet their needs in the long term. A long record of local practices and conditions informed these culturally embedded principles. However, in some communities, the pace of change outstripped the experiential learning process. The Sumerians were arguably the first 'environmental refugees' in history. Their success with irrigated agriculture in the difficult conditions of southern Mesopotamia was short-lived, as farming and irrigation practices brought huge quantities of salt to the surface and destroyed the land's capacity to support plant growth.

Principles for sustainability have continued to emerge in modern society; for example, the cause of cholera outbreaks in London in the mid-19th century was eventually identified as sewage, running in streets and surface drains, contaminating the wells used for drinking and domestic purposes. The principle of ensuring that water supplies and untreated and partially treated sewage should be kept physically separate, has been the cornerstone of public health engineering practice for 150 years. However, in the last few decades, the combined pressures of population growth and increased competition for water have led to this principle being relaxed. Large cities are recycling sewage, for irrigation, industrial purposes and for potable supply. This provides a good example of the trade-offs involved in sustainability decisions: as water supplies become more limited, the goal of protecting human health must be met without compromising other goals such as the equitable supply of water to all citizens, protecting the environment, and ensuring society continues to benefit from industrial and agricultural production.

As globalisation of production, industry and trade has developed, the decisions made in one geographical location have had increasing influence over the conditions in another. Globalisation has also brought improved communication, and the better-off communities have become more aware of the difficulties and inequities suffered in poorer areas. The *ecological footprint* is an attempt to describe the area of the earth's surface required to support a particular individual, group or activity, in terms of the resources consumed and impacts generated. According to a 2006 study (Redefining Progress, 2006), humanity's ecological footprint is nearly 40 per cent greater than the Earth's biological capacity. While the ecological footprint is an approximation involving considerable assumptions, it does illustrate the point that closing the gap between rich and poor nations cannot be done simply by lifting the living standards of the poor; the Earth would be unable to support the demands made on it for production and waste assimilation. The inequities between rich and poor nations, and the limits to continued growth, were the backdrop for the report of the World Commission on Environment and Development, commonly referred to as the Brundtland Commission, *Our Common Future* (World Commission on Environment and Development, 1987). This report is widely acknowledged to be the foundation text for the sustainability movement of the past twenty years.

Accepted definitions

The generally accepted definition of sustainable development is an extract from the Brundtland Commission report:

> Humanity has the ability to make development sustainable – to ensure that it meets the needs of the present without compromising the ability of future generations to meet their own needs.

This goal statement can be made more explicit for practitioners by incorporating some of the other characteristics of sustainability improvements that are described in the Brundtland report. These include:

1. recognising that both technological and social tools may be used to make sustainability improvements

2. clarifying 'needs' as encompassing economic, social and environmental elements, and recognising that some needs may be in conflict, requiring choices and trade-offs to be made

3. assigning the highest priority to those in greatest need, while recognising the equal right of all to determine their needs and have them met

4. establishing sustainability as a relative rather than an absolute goal – thus making continuous improvement a key objective.

A more extensive definition of sustainability practices can be thus derived from the Brundtland report (Goldsmith and Samson, 2005):

> Sustainable development practices manage technology and social organisation to make balanced and equitable progress on economic, environmental and social needs so that meeting these needs in the present does not compromise the ability of future generations to meet their own needs.

The scope of the economic, environmental and social needs addressed by sustainable development practices is described by the *Global Reporting Initiative* (Global Reporting Initiative, 2007).[1] A common reporting framework can assist organisations and their stakeholders in assessing and comparing progress on sustainability. However, perhaps the most significant gain from a common framework is that of efficiency.

Early developments in sustainability reporting in the late 1990s and early 2000s were characterised by a range of sustainability surveys and questionnaires conducted by ethical investment advisors and ranking agencies. These questionnaires and surveys can be time-consuming to complete, as organisations are wary of being caught making misleading or inconsistent claims. Further, organisations wishing to provide evidence of their progress on sustainability through the external investment ranking process found that surveys and questionnaires from different assessment bodies could differ in terms of the scope and relative weighting of the items selected for sustainability assessment. Organisations also spent considerable time in their own right liaising with stakeholders and trying to establish the scope and relative weighting of their sustainability concerns. The advantage of the GRI is that it provides organisations with a consolidated view of stakeholder requirements and with an agreed set of outcome categories and measurement protocols. These are reviewed and updated as the organisational context and stakeholder preferences change. While sustainability investment rankings focus on large, publicly listed companies, the GRI protocols are available free of charge to any organisation seeking guidance and a way of tracking improvements.

The scope of sustainable development concerns, as listed in the *Global Reporting Initiative* (Global Reporting Initiative, 2007) is given in Table 12.1. This list of economic, environmental and social factors shows how

Table 12.1 Economic, environmental and social needs as defined by the global reporting initiative 2002

	Category	Aspect
Economic	Direct economic impacts	Customers Suppliers Employees Providers of capital Public sector
Environmental	Environmental	Materials Energy Water Biodiversity Emissions, effluents and waste Suppliers Products and services Compliance Transport Overall
Social	Labour practices	Employment Labour(management relations Health and safety Training and education Diversity and opportunity
	Human rights	Strategy and management Non-discrimination Freedom of association and collective bargaining Child labour Forced and compulsory labour Disciplinary practices Security practices Indigenous rights
	Society	Community Bribery and corruption Political contributions Competition and pricing
	Product Responsibility	Customer health and safety Products and services Advertising Respect for privacy

wide-ranging the agenda of sustainability are. Many practitioners attend to issues that are individually determined; reflecting their preconceptions, recent events, crises, public relations and self-interest. For example, the economic category is often mistakenly assumed to relate solely to the financial performance of the organisation in the form of profits. Table 12.1 shows that the role of the organisation in providing economic support for a range of stakeholders including customers, suppliers, employees, lenders and the public sector is considered. The opportunities for sustainability improvements can be hard to identify; there is no 'one size fits all'. By providing a list of sustainability issues to consider, the GRI can help practitioners scan their own organisations for a broad range of opportunities for improvement. Selecting the best mix of sustainability improvements, unique to their own organisation, may well provide a competitive advantage.

Sustainability: An organisational context

The considerations of sustainability can be addressed at several levels. The main thrust of the Brundtland Commission report (World Commission on Environment and Development, 1987) was to improve the lot of poorer nations, so it took a global perspective. Sustainability considerations can also be applied to individual countries, states, local communities, government organisations, private and publicly listed companies, not-for-profit organisations, and individual households, schools and workplaces.

What does sustainability mean for an organisation? Perhaps the biggest challenge is that there is no rulebook for sustainability. Although laws and regulations provide guidance on some issues, organisational sustainability is about identifying the optimum mix of strategies and practices to produce sustained, superior performance. This superior performance is measured in both financial and non-financial terms, and needs to be resilient in the face of change and uncertainty. Sustainability is not an absolute concept; an organisation's performance on sustainability will be judged on whether balanced and equitable progress is being made year by year on the full range of issues, and will be compared to the performance of other organisations of similar industry characteristics and size.

Consider the list of sustainability issues provided by the GRI in Table 12.1. For a particular organisation, examples might be:

1. for an economic issue, the level of wages paid to employees
2. for an environmental issue, the total emissions of greenhouse gases generated directly by the organisation's activities, and indirectly throughout the supply chain and product lifecycle
3. for a social issue, the quality control of products for the protection of consumer health and safety.

Box 12.2: Product responsibility

In 2003, the largest recall of medicines in Australia was triggered by the suspension of Pan Pharmaceutical's manufacturing licence. Pan manufactured complementary (or 'natural') medicines. The issue that raised the alarm was the apparent overdose of some consumers using a proprietary tablet for airsickness or seasickness called Travacalm.

When the Therapeutic Goods Administration (TGA), the government body responsible for overseeing the medicines industry, analysed the product to determine the source of the consumer reaction, it found the active ingredients in each tablet to vary from seven times the correct dose to none at all. Further investigation found that results of product-testing conducted by Pan had been falsified. Eventually, the TGA uncovered major quality control problems at the manufacturer, including production, calibration and quality control lapses, poor hygiene, cross-contamination between products, substitution of ingredients, poor practice in analysing the results of tests, and fabrication of some test results.

Given the potential for serious risk to customer health and safety, the TGA moved to recall all Pan Pharmaceutical products from sale and suspended Pan's licence to manufacture. The impact of this on other manufacturers and suppliers in the complementary medicines industry, on consumers, on retailers, on Pan's employees, shareholders and lenders, and on the TGA, the government body responsible for control of the industry, was dramatic.

As well as manufacturing for point of sale, Pan Pharmaceutical was the dominant supplier of ingredients to other complementary medicine manufacturers and packagers. Tracing which products, and often specific batches of products, contained Pan Pharmaceutical manufactures proved extremely difficult. Consumers were made anxious by the lack of clear information about the products they had been taking, after all, to improve their health! Recall information was long and complex involving the publication of long lists of batch and product numbers in the newspapers, and many consumers simply lost faith in the industry as a whole. Retailers also had unclear information, and were forced to provide refunds for recalled products when it was still unclear exactly which products would attract a refund and whether the retailer would be reimbursed by a company that had ceased trading.

Pan's downstream manufacturers and suppliers suffered huge financial losses as well as a loss of consumer confidence in the industry as a whole. Pan Pharmaceuticals employees were laid off, and some were subjected to intense questioning as the TGA and other government agencies sought explanations.

Australia had one of the strictest regulatory regimes in the world. Unlike many countries, where natural health products were regulated as foods, natural health products in Australia were regulated as medicines and referred to as complementary medicines. The TGA attempted to use the Pan Pharmaceuticals case as an example of Australia's superior regulatory system at work. However, consumer concerns led to public demands for stricter regulation of the industry.

Other manufacturers, particularly those who had not used Pan for supplies, were concerned that the Pan incident threatened the particular relationship between the complementary medicines industry and the consumer, which is based on claims backed by evidence and consumers taking responsibility for their own health choices.

Sources
   http://www.abc.net.au/lateline/content/2003/s842086.htm
   http://www.tga.gov.au/recalls/pan.htm
   http://www.tga.gov.au/docs/html/mediarel/mrpan6.htm
   http://www.smh.com.au/specials/panrecall/index.html
   S. K. Goldsmith, 2003. Unpublished research interview, Blackmores P/L.

These examples introduce one of the major challenges in applying sustainability in the organisational context; that of expanding the boundary of organisational responsibility to reduce externalities (costs resulting from organisational activities that are borne by others). For example, a manufacturer that exports its products has economic significance, product responsibility and product end-of-life issues with its overseas customers. A current concern in Australia relates to the export of uranium for nuclear power generation. One approach could be to simply forget the implications of the uranium export once it has left Australian shores. However, a more sustainable approach would expand the view of product responsibility, perhaps to the extent of requiring spent nuclear fuel (radioactive waste) to be returned to Australia for responsible processing and disposal. Similarly, an industry that imports products and raw materials from overseas would include the impacts of the offshore supply chain in its own sustainability assessment, as did the Brotherhood of St Laurence in the following example.

Box 12.3: Labour practices and human rights

The Brotherhood of St Laurence is a 'community organisation with a vision of promoting social justice and a whole of society framework for a poverty free Australia' (Brotherhood of St Laurence, 2007).

In 2000, the organisation acquired a commercial enterprise, Mod-Style, as part of a bequest. Mod-Style was a small company with 17 employees that imported spectacle frames from offshore manufacturers, and supplied them wholesale to retailers. The business had a turnover of around A$5 million, importing 150,000 spectacle frames. Most of the imports were sourced from China, with other suppliers located in Korea, Japan and Italy.

The Brotherhood's board was faced with a dilemma. The business had been bequeathed to the Brotherhood specifically to generate desperately needed ongoing funds to support its charitable work for a better society. But by running the business, could it be supporting the very social and environmental problems in another country that it was working so hard to improve in Australia?

After much deliberation, the board decided it should take a proactive approach. If it sold the business, then any problems would probably remain unchanged, and it would go against the wishes of the benefactor, who wanted the Brotherhood to have a long-term income stream. Since the core activity of the Brotherhood of St Laurence was to improve social conditions, why should it not bring its expertise, and new influence as owner of the business, to bear on identifying and making improvements in the overseas operations?

The Board quarantined the next two years' profits from Mod-Style and employed an Ethical Business Manager to investigate the overseas manufacturers supplying the business, focusing first on the facilities in China.

A major finding from the Brotherhood of St Laurence's supplier ethics exercise was the immense investment of time and resources that was required to gain access, overcome and understand cultural barriers and differences, cope with the large variation in size and practices between suppliers, and understand the social context in which the businesses were operating.

Even with this investment of expertise and effort, the Brotherhood of St Laurence discovered that it could initially have limited influence and penetration in the overseas operations. Some manufacturers were extremely large, and as a relatively insignificant customer, the Brotherhood could not rely on buying power to exert influence. Further, the spectacle frame manufacture involved complex supply chains for the supply of materials and components and some production processes such as electroplating. These were impossible to map and investigate.

The Brotherhood's investigations found that superficial assessments of manufacturing operations did not give a realistic picture of their social performance. Factories could be clean, well-lit and appear to provide a reasonable working environment, while worker conditions such as accommodation, hours and unpaid overtime, oversight, wages and social security and bargaining and dispute resolution, were poor and in some aspects punitive. The Brotherhood realised that although regulations and codes were in place, they were not enforced sufficiently, and the major issue was the lack of ability and capacity of workers to influence their own circumstances. This situation was exacerbated by the high turnover in the workforce as some came from rural areas to undertake this kind of work for only one or two years at a time. At the end of its fact-finding exercise, the Brotherhood had opened up a further dilemma; how should it act on the knowledge it now had about their suppliers?

The Brotherhood of St Laurence chose to engage in stakeholder dialogue, aimed at building a long-term relationship with suppliers around how they might improve the environmental and social performance, particularly in terms of workers' rights. Thinking hard about these issues has resulted in the Brotherhood developing practical suggestions for sustainability improvement. These have informed the organisation's other activities, which have developed to include the provision of advice to other organisations on these issues, and the establishment of a range of 'social enterprises' (self-funding businesses designed primarily for the purpose of social improvement).

Sources
www.bsl.org.au
http://www.bsl.org.au/pdfs/OECD_paper_on_supply_chain.pdf
www.bsl.org.au/main.asp?PageId=66#ethbus
http://www.abc.net.au/rn/nationalinterest/stories/2003/829295.htm

Clearly, expanding the boundary of organisational responsibility introduces additional sustainability considerations. Should a mining company bear the cost of nuclear waste processing and disposal when the activity that has converted the fuel into waste has occurred elsewhere? What about the externalities generated by the transport, processing and disposal activities? Should local communities and workers bear these risks? Can they be compensated adequately? Will a competitor provide fuel at a lower price by failing to consider these factors?

Trading off one sustainability improvement against another is the central problem facing practitioners. For example, when an organisation decides to outsource its information technology division to an organisation in an overseas country, is it placing the interests of its shareholders ahead of those of its employees? Is it fair to deny workers in poorer nations the opportunity to earn better wages and improve their living standards? When an organisation producing asbestos products discovers they may be harmful in the long-term, should they put future, unspecified risks ahead of the economic support of workers who have little prospect of alternative employment? Is there any point in doing this when asbestos products are acceptable according to all laws and regulations, and when the organisation will simply be replaced by a competitor or new entrant if they cease operations?

The flexibility of sustainability approaches allows organisations to tailor their strategies and practices to optimise performance across both financial and non-financial measures. However, this leaves organisations themselves to determine the opportunities for sustainability improvements and debate the trade-offs involved. Many practitioners prefer the old rule-based approach, as it is easier to argue for a particular improvement objectively; 'we have to deliver an outcome of at least X, and by my calculations, our cheapest way of doing that is method Y'. However, while rigid rules make decisions feel more comfortable, they can also lock in poor performance. By working towards a specified outcome, a practitioner might fail to consider an alternative method that could deliver much greater benefits for similar cost.

An example of how poor performance can be encouraged by rules is the disposal of waste solvents from manufacturing in Victoria, Australia. During the 1980s, spent solvents from industrial processes were allowed to be disposed of in hazardous liquid waste landfills, such as the one near the airport at Tullamarine in Melbourne. As the landfill capacity became more limited, the Environment Protection Agency (EPA) tried to encourage companies to seek alternative methods for handling their solvent wastes. Finally, the EPA simply banned waste solvents from the liquid landfill. Faced with no alternative, companies installed solvent recycling units. What is remarkable is that in most cases, the payback period for the recycling units was less than one year, as the companies saved money on the purchase of fresh solvent as well as the disposal of the liquid hazardous waste.[2]

So how can organisations navigate the complex choices and trade-offs involved in improving their performance on sustainability? The next section of this chapter explores why, when and how organisations' strategies and practices can contribute to long-term success across the triple bottom line. Then, we discuss the key role that operations managers can play in identifying and implementing successful sustainability initiatives. Lastly, we discuss some of the key skills and capabilities that operations managers of the future will need to lead a new wave of sustainability and long-term organisational success.

What makes sustainability practices successful?

What is a sustainability practice?

The activities of an organisation can be described as a set of practices. These may be operations practices, such as loading a truck; strategic practices, such as investing in a new business; short-term practices, such as a work-around to cope with an unusual peak demand; long-term practices, such as product quality control; one-off practices, such as the launch of a new product; repeated; structured; informal; and so on. Put simply, practices are tasks or activities that may be required to satisfy a range of objectives. Practices are things that people and their organisations do.

Take the example of the practice that describes the transfer of fuel from a petrol tanker to a storage tank at a service station. The tanker driver is given specific procedures to meet a number of objectives as detailed in Table 12.2.

For the tanker driver, the tasks he undertakes when delivering fuel are part of a single operation. He cannot approach the task in six different ways, to meet six separate objectives. Such an approach would be extremely inefficient, and would require the driver to resolve conflicts between the different objectives 'on the run'. For example, major spillages would be dealt with differently from the point of view of safety and the environment. Safety concerns

Table 12.2 Multiple practice objectives: fuel delivery example

Objective	Procedure
Accurate delivery	The amount of fuel delivered is measured and noted, including adjustments for ambient temperature, to ensure the service station owner is invoiced the correct amount, to guard against fraud and theft, and to check for unplanned losses, for example, a leaky underground tank.
Safe delivery	Strict procedures are followed to guard against fire or explosion; the tanker is earthed before unloading to prevent a build-up of static electricity, bollards keep people and possible sources of sparks away from the delivery area, and spillages are covered quickly to limit the generation of flammable vapours. Tanker compartments are unloaded in order so that the vehicle is as stable as possible on the road. The driver must take personal safety into account when climbing onto the vehicle, handling hoses, inhaling vapours, etc. Emergency procedures are planned and practiced.
Environment protection	Apart from checking for unplanned losses or leaks, strict procedures are followed to prevent spillages (tanks are dipped to check the amount for delivery, valves are opened in order and tagged, and cut-off and dead-man devices are in place). Methods and equipment ensure leaks and spillages are contained, for safe disposal.
Quality control	Tanks are dipped prior to delivery to check for contamination, particularly the presence of water. Samples may be taken for analysis. If contamination is present, or there are unplanned losses, the delivery may not take place.
Customer service	The tanker driver is required to liaise with the service station owner to ensure timely, efficient and friendly service, and to minimize disruption to their business during delivery.
Public relations	The tanker driver is required to maintain a professional image to the public, for example through cleanliness and presentation, driver behaviour, etc.

alone would suggest the spillage should be dispersed as quickly as possible – deluge systems would be deployed to dilute the spill and move the flammable material away from the fuel storage area. Unfortunately, such action would result in fuel entering stormwater systems and natural waterways, causing environmental damage. Environmental concerns alone would suggest the spillage should be contained on-site where it would pose a fire risk. Clearly, procedures need to be developed that satisfy both objectives – protection of the environment and prevention of explosion and fire. The set of procedures that best resolves the multiple objectives of the practice becomes the accepted 'fuel delivery practice'.

Table 12.2 illustrates the complex interdependency and overlap between sustainability objectives and other business objectives for a particular organisational practice. While some practices can be uniquely ascribed to a particular sustainability objective, most satisfy a range of objectives, and trade-offs may need to be resolved. Thus, there can be no common sustainability practice design that will work for any organisation. Rather, sustainability objectives need to be placed alongside other business objectives in designing practices that optimise performance against the complete set of objectives. Sustainability practices, embedded within the full set of organisation practices, depend on the detail of an organisation's strategy, environment, and operations.

Saying that there is no single recipe for sustainability practices that works for every organisation implies that in each situation, some sustainability practices will perform better than others. What characteristics distinguish high performing sustainability practices from the rest? Can an understanding of these characteristics help us to design better practices? We explored these questions in a research project examining the features of the successful sustainability practices of leading organisations (Goldsmith and Samson, 2005). We found that high performing practices could be distinguished on two major sets of characteristics; first, the quality and excellence of the practices themselves; and second, the extent to which the practices supported the strategic objectives of the organisation.

Quality and excellence

Earlier in this section we discussed the importance of specifying the full set of sustainability and other business objectives when designing any organisational practice to meet them. This delivers three clear advantages to leading organisations.

First, by being explicit about all the objectives of a specific practice, including those that may be in conflict, leading organisations can ensure that the sustainability aspects of their practices are integrated with all their business practices. This integration promotes efficiency and consistency in objectives and practices across the organisation. It also encourages innovation, as resolving one objective can often lead to gains in others. For example, an Australian manufacturer and distributor of fresh and ready-to-eat herbs and vegetables, OneHarvest (see www.oneharvest.com.au), introduced nursery-grown product to satisfy year-round demand. A range of substantial benefits emerged from this innovation, including waist-high working (a health and safety benefit); elimination of pests and diseases and associated chemical use (a production, product quality, cost and consumer benefit); and increased nutritional value and *organic* status (a marketing benefit). Consideration of the full range of benefits involved helped underpin OneHarvest's decision to invest in the nursery facilities. This case illustrates the difficulty faced by many organisations in separating out *sustainability practices*, as aspects of sustainability may indeed comprise, or be closely related to, their core business. However, some forms of external monitoring (for example, the assessments of ethical investment funds) rely on separately identifiable sustainability practices for their assessment. Organisations that integrate sustainability considerations with all their business practices run the risk of being ranked lower by such superficial assessments.

Second, by establishing desired outcomes for their practices, leading organisations can develop their own specific outcome-based measures against which they can assess their performance on sustainability. Measurable outcomes provide more objective forms of assessment than the 'process exists' methods of some ethical investment funds, criticised in the previous paragraph. Measurable outcomes allow organisations to track their progress (or lapses) on the broad range of sustainability issues.

Third, an explicit understanding of the desired outcome of a particular practice enables leading organisations to review the effectiveness of the practice itself. In many cases, our research has shown that leading organisations take a 'learning by doing' approach to practice design. They subject their practices to critical review, and where necessary, revise them until the planned outcomes are achieved or surpassed. A willingness to review and revise practices also ensures that practices are introduced, updated, revised or discontinued in response to changes over time.

So leading organisations know what they want to achieve, plan efficient and effective ways of getting there, and monitor their progress and adapt their approaches to ensure that they do. Yet, so far, we have 'glossed over' the specification of sustainability objectives. Understanding the scope of sustainability considerations is not the same as knowing how to address each issue. How do organisations decide what is really appropriate and necessary in each case? How can the complex territory between mandatory compliance and altruism be navigated? When have organisations done enough, and when is doing more simply eroding their business prospects?

In the first section of this chapter, we introduced the Global Reporting Initiative (GRI) as a useful resource for organisations seeking to ensure that their understanding of sustainability issues is up to date with current stakeholder concerns. Climate change provides a prominent[3] example of how stakeholder concerns can shift over time. Although the 'greenhouse effect' was already being discussed in the 1970s, the thrust of aid for developing nations was based on the premise that increased gross domestic product (GDP), and therefore improved living standards for these countries, depended on increased

Table 12.3 Corporate posture towards social responsiveness (Clarkson, 1995)

Reactive	Fight all the way
Defensive	Do only what is required
Accommodative	Be progressive
Proactive	Lead the industry

energy generation capacity per capita. Now, in 2007, the links between energy generation, other primary and secondary production activities, and climate change are widely accepted, along with the threats they pose to the health and prosperity of communities and environments around the globe. Yet, simply understanding the current set of sustainability issues is not enough. Organisations, industries and governments still have to decide on the position they will adopt. Climate change provides a current example of how some can mount a campaign of resistance to change,[4] while others can use it as the catalyst for new opportunities.

Stakeholder theorists categorise *corporate strategy or posture towards social responsiveness* using the RDAP (reactive, defensive, accommodative and proactive) scale (Clarkson, 1995) as shown in Table 12.3.

While this describes the response of different organisations to the issue of climate change, for example, it does not suggest how organisations might explore their optimum position on this scale. Research (Goldsmith and Samson, 2002) identified that this optimum position should be explored and determined practice by practice, as it is at this level that organisations can vary their actions.

Sustainability practices can be distinguished according to their contribution to the goals of sustainability according to the chart in Figure 12.1. Practices are categorised according to whether they comply, conform, perform or transform organisational sustainability performance (see Table 12.4). The optimum (most proactive) position for each sustainability practice maximises: 'Stakeholder Reach', by addressing an expanded set of stakeholder issues to a significant extent; and 'time-to-reap' by delivering benefits over a longer weighted average timeframe. The opportunity for sustainability gains varies for each practice. However, by establishing the optimum position for each practice, organisations can reflect on the resources available for practice improvements and select the set of practices that represents the optimum (most cost-effective) 'mix' for their particular circumstances.

Returning to the climate change example, an organisational practice could: comply, for example by meeting government emission standards; conform,

Table 12.4 Sustainability practices – contribution to organisational performance

Practice Category	Description
Comply	Meets the requirements of laws and regulations
Conform	Satisfies accepted 'norms' for the industry, e.g. codes of practice, standards
Perform	Improves financial and(or non-financial performance by modifying practices, e.g., waste minimisation
Transform	Strategic or operational changes that redesign activities and deliver major sustainability benefits, e.g., using robotic machinery in hazardous working conditions

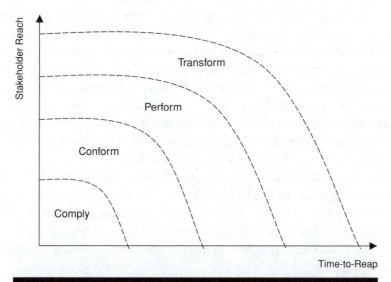

Figure 12.1 Mapping the contribution of sustainability practices (Goldsmith and Samson, 2005)

by installing emission control equipment considered state-of-the-art in that industry; perform, by altering the process to generate fewer emissions; and transform, by introducing a new product using the emissions as a substrate for its manufacture.

It is important to note that more proactive sustainability practices do not necessarily cost more. The advantage of the approach suggested by Figure 12.1 is that it extends the possible set of objectives being addressed by each practice, which in turn encourages more options, including innovations, to be generated. Returning to the waste industrial solvent example earlier this chapter, the opportunity to save costs of solvent purchase and disposal was always present for organisations that were prepared to explore 'perform' options. However, most organisations restricted their thinking to the current landfill disposal option and the costs associated with it. The benefits of the 'perform' solvent recycling option only became apparent to them once it became a condition of compliance.

In this section, we have discussed how organisational practices can be designed to maximise their contribution to the goals of sustainability by attending to their relevance, efficiency and effectiveness over time. However, organisations exist for specific purposes; to make profits, to provide public infrastructure and services, and so on. While some of these purposes may include aspects of sustainability, contributing to sustainability is certainly not the sole purpose of most organisations. So how can organisations identify, design and select practices that will *both* contribute to sustainability and also complement their business?

Strategic connection

As well as having a tactical impact, practices must support the strategic objectives of the organisation. The strategic relevance of sustainability to an organisation can be considered at the industry and enterprise levels, and also at the levels of particular practices and groups of practices.

Various industry characteristics influence the degree to which sustainability issues are core to the strategic objectives of industry members. Mature industries are focused on performance improvement through efficiency gains and reduced costs. For some, such as toy manufacturers and printers, cost competition is fierce and sustainability issues have limited strategic relevance. For others, such as mining and infrastructure, the large upfront investment and extended life of projects means that future sustainability issues need to be planned and provided for to bolster long-term income streams. In these cases, sustainability issues are part of the strategic positioning of each investment.

Sustainability issues may take a stronger strategic position for some emerging industries, for example renewable energy, where not only are investments associated with long-term returns, but they are also capturing specific new markets and premiums catalysed by sustainability concerns. However, other emerging industries, such as biotechnology, can be constrained by sustainability issues. Biotechnology is an interesting example as it highlights the contradictions (trade-offs) involved in sustainability assessments. Consider the development of genetically modified wheat for example. On the plus side, genetically modified wheat may have greater yield, require fewer chemicals and it may be suited to a wider range of growing conditions. With food shortages and environmental pollution major concerns throughout the world, these are attractive benefits. On the minus side, the impacts of genetically modified wheat on the environment and consumers are unknown. Will resistant strains become major weed pests? How will insects be affected, will biodiversity be reduced? What are the implications for human health from eating genetically modified foods?

Within each industry, individual organisations can also make strategic choices about how their prospects align with sustainability goals. For example, OneHarvest has based its strategy on what it views as an emerging market in socially responsible horticulture products. It seeks to position itself as a sustainability leader in tis industry. Whereas, a small business, with no clear succession plan, may take a short-term view and seek to minimise investments as the business will be sold or closed down when the owner retires. For this type of business, sustainability concerns are not front-of-mind and can be viewed as an unnecessary erosion of retirement capital.

Establishing the relevance of sustainability to the organisation's strategy provides a useful guiding framework; however, it is at the level of individual practices that organisations design approaches to deliver strategic benefits.[5] Research (Goldsmith and Samson, 2005) identified three generic strategic requirements that explain the alignment of sustainability practices with strategic advantage, namely, stakeholder support, efficiency and market edge.

Stakeholder support recognises the interdependence between the prospects of the organisation and its stakeholders. Stakeholders include employees, suppliers, customers, regulators, debt-holders, local communities, environment as well as owners and managers. While some theorists have argued that managers can assign priorities to different stakeholder requirements (Agle et al., 1999), the *stakeholder reach* concept introduced earlier this chapter recommends scanning a wide range of stakeholder requirements and seeking initiatives that are as far reaching as possible. Davis' *iron law* states that 'when stakeholders are disadvantaged, they will eventually gather sufficient pressure by direct and indirect means to force a change in behaviour' (Davis, 1973). By attending to stakeholder requirements before being forced to, organisations can gain advantage. Expanding stakeholder support can also help organisations develop new opportunities. For example, OneHarvest has established grower and transport networks so that these stakeholders can collaborate in suggesting new business arrangements to improve sustainability and make savings through the supply chain. In turn, OneHarvest is open to new forms of investment support, for example longer-term supply contracts, to provide sufficient incentive for their stakeholders to invest in improvements.

Efficiency results from practices that directly or indirectly save resources. The waste solvent recycling example described earlier in this chapter is an excellent example of efficiency. By recycling waste solvents rather than sending them to landfill, organisations made efficiency gains: reduced solvent purchase; reduced storage and handling of waste solvent; reduced risk of spillage, fire and personnel exposure to hazardous chemicals; eliminated transport and disposal, reporting and payment processing costs for waste solvent; and reduced dependency on solvent suppliers. The costs of the solvent recycling process itself were much less than these savings, resulting in a typical payback period of one year. However, opportunities for efficiency through sustainability practices are not limited to waste minimisation. Staffing arrangements, such as multi-skilling, training local workers rather than paying relocation costs, and extended product lifecycle arrangements, such as return of used products for remanufacture, are types of efficiency gain.

Market edge results from practices that may increase market share or develop new market opportunities. For example, electricity companies that offer a reduced tariff for off-peak power are developing a product that appeals to customers seeking to reduce their costs, as well as smoothing demand and improving the return on power-generation assets. *Dolphin-free* tuna, and organic fruit and vegetables, are examples of the use of sustainability practices to develop specific new customer appeal.

So, organisations seeking to introduce sustainability practices should:

1. Decide how sustainability might support the overall strategy of the organisation.
2. Review the full range of sustainability issues, and for each, consider how the organisation might impact on them, and in turn, the potential for such action to result in strategic advantage, through stakeholder support, efficiency or market edge. Establish objectives for action, as a first step to developing practices.
3. Evaluate and rank potential practices in terms of their strategic impact, quality and excellence.
4. Map the practices identified so far according to stakeholder reach and time to reap; ensure each practice is optimal in terms of its contribution, and select the most cost-effective set for the organisation.
5. Monitor and review practices to ensure they are achieving their objectives sufficiently and efficiently, and to review overall performance. Repeat steps 1–5 as part of a process of continuous improvement and to maintain relevance and balance of effort.

Business case for sustainability

Figure 12.2 illustrates the business case for sustainability. The combination of industry influence and organisation strategy governs the selection of organisation practices, including sustainability practices, as described in an earlier section. Each practice is optimised in terms of its contribution to sustainability, and the most cost-effective set of practices is selected for implementation and refined, as described in earlier. By aligning practices, strategy and culture (or sustainability orientation, further described later), organisations seek to increase their likelihood of long-term success across the triple bottom line.

The argument for increased opportunity for success rests on the organisation-specific nature of sustainability benefits. If one size were to fit all

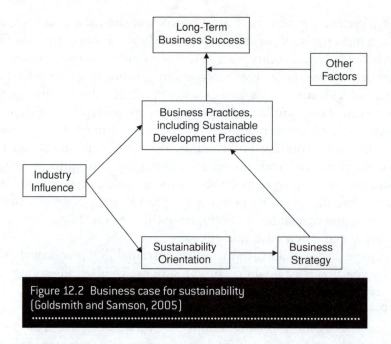

Figure 12.2 Business case for sustainability
(Goldsmith and Samson, 2005)

in organisational sustainability terms, then each organisation could simply follow a recipe for sustainability practices to gain similar advantage to its competitors. However, organisations have specific opportunities available to them through sustainability practices that support their strategy and make a cost-effective sustainability contribution.

The specific nature of these opportunities is increased by trends in regulation and policy to shift the role of determining specific sustainability targets to the organisation through self-regulation. By leading stakeholder preferences, organisations hope to minimise the downside and maximise the upside of their activities over the long-term. For example, rather than carrying potential long-tail liabilities, such as in the case of asbestos goods manufacturers, organisations can act early to avoid these liabilities being developed. On the upside, by creating mutual benefits for key stakeholders, such as supervision agencies, organisations can reduce their barriers in bidding for future contracts.

Building sustainability: the role of operations

Operations managers in all industries make decisions about the design, conduct and improvement of operating systems. These systems have outcomes and impacts which are not just financial; they affect many stakeholders, including customers, employees, those impacted by the local environment, suppliers, and the communities in which their businesses operate.

If a factory produces pollution, the impact is on all who work and live in the vicinity, and if the pollution is bad enough, this may impact regionally or globally. If a ship discharges toxic waste, or if safety standards are low in any work place, employees and many other stakeholders are negatively impacted. If a farm is 'over-farmed' meaning that the land as a core asset is degraded then environmental damage occurs and sustainability is compromised. If a service business takes unfair advantage of a local community or of its employees, then ultimately its working position will not be sustainable.

These decisions are taken by operating managers of those businesses. In the short run, it may cost more to pollute less, or to pay fair wages in emerging economies and provide safe and reasonable working conditions, but the question is not just of what the short run impact is, but more importantly of the long run sustainability of such decisions.

Box 12.4: Emissions, effluents and waste

A manufacturer of dairy products including various types of fresh and powdered milk, yoghurts and dairy desserts was in dispute with the water authorities providing sewerage services to two of its factories; Factory A, located in a major metropolitan area and Factory B, located in a small rural town. The company contacted a consulting firm for advice.

In both cases, the water authorities were concerned that the biological load of the dairy company's wastewater exceeded the capacity of their systems, causing the water authorities to incur additional treatment costs and threatening their own ability to meet strict effluent discharge performance standards. The dairy company had already invested heavily in pre-treatment plants designed to reduce the biological load of its waste before it reached the water authorities' sewers. The dairy company wanted the consultant to investigate why these expensive pretreatment systems were failing.

The bulk of the dairy company's wastewater derived from processes for washing and sterilising the plant and equipment used for food storage, manufacturing and packaging. The consultant knew that there was a direct relationship between the food value (calories) in the dairy company's products and the biological load of its waste streams. Put simply, the more of the dairy company's products that ended up in the waste stream, the greater the biological load. So the consultant undertook a detailed inventory of activities in each factory to work out how the dairy company's waste was generated in each case.

Factory A – major metropolitan location
The factory manager told the consultant there was no point in talking to the factory staff as they were stupid. 'What you need to do,' he said, 'is come up with something to treat the waste that monkeys can operate.' The consultant quietly walked around the factory floor talking to the staff and having them explain the

dairy manufacturing processes, the tasks involved, and how they did them. The consultant knew it was important to talk to the night shift staff separately, as they often did things a different way and were subject to less supervision.

The consultant then managed to estimate the amount of different types of product that were lost to the waste stream in each process. Using the factory price, excluding packaging, the consultant could work out the value of product being wasted. In the previous financial year, Factory A had made a profit of A$600,000. The consultant's calculations showed that A$600,000 of dairy products were ending up in the waste stream. The factory could have *doubled* its profits if it saved all that waste.

The staff of Factory A had many sensible suggestions as to how the waste could be reduced. They told the consultant they had made these recommendations frequently to their managers, but no changes had been made. The factory manager told the consultant that the only reason the staff suggested changes was so they could demand a pay increase.

Factory B – small rural town
Factory B did not even have a factory manager. It was effectively run by a team, led by the chief engineer and chief production manager. The amount of product ending up in the waste stream at Factory B had already been limited as far as possible by the staff, but their efforts were hampered by the age and design of the plant.

Factory B was due for a major upgrade, and the dairy company was planning a major investment in wastewater pre-treatment plus a substantial contribution to the water authority's own treatment capacity expansion. The consultant explained to the Chief Engineer that if the design of the new plant could reduce the amount of product wasted, the wastewater pre-treatment plant could be made much simpler and cheaper, and the contribution to the water authority could be avoided altogether. The consultant explained the relationship between the product food value and the biological load of the waste.

The staff at Factory B were delighted to have a new understanding of how their plans could be improved. When the consultant visited again a month later, the team had made a model of the factory upgrade. Using pins and coloured wool they had worked together to make the product lines as short as possible. This way, much less water and chemicals would be required to clean the lines, hygiene would be improved and there would be less wasted product.

Source
S. K. Goldsmith, 1985–1989. Range of consulting projects, Sinclair Knight P/L.

Role of culture, strategy and operations

Figure 12.2 introduces a culture for sustainability, described as *sustainability orientation*, that describes the culture of the organisation in terms of the goals of sustainability, specifically breadth of vision, stakeholder empowerment and being progressive. Breadth of vision describes leadership in terms of integrity, trust and community service. Stakeholder empowerment describes a concern for mutual benefits and relationship building. Being progressive describes excellence, innovation and being proactive.

Perhaps the most interesting finding from our research was that this culture for sustainability, or sustainability orientation, is developed and reinforced through practices (or 'learning by doing') and strategic choices as well as through the adoption of specific values for sustainability at senior management level. In other words, the development of a sustainability orientation is just as likely to occur 'bottom up', through action, as 'top down' through direction.

Figure 12.2 shows that regardless of how they are initiated, practices are the mainstay of organisational action for sustainability; practices translate intentions into action.

This finding means that operations managers are often best placed to determine and direct sustainability improvements for their organisation. Rather than restricting themselves to following broad policy statements from the executive, operations managers have an unparalleled view of specific opportunities and possibilities for sustainability in the business. It is the operations manager who can see how a job can be redesigned to accommodate a disabled employee, or how suppliers could collaborate on transport arrangements, or how waste could be avoided in a particular process. Operations managers are in a position to decide on and take action.

Operations management – a key role

We have established that successful sustainability practices are:

1. unique to an organisation and its circumstances including changes over time
2. designed for maximum effectiveness and to integrate with other practices and objectives
3. subject to continual review and improvement
4. strategically relevant.

Since the bulk of organisational practices are operations practices, operations managers are best positioned to design, implement and review them. While in theory, senior management can scan the business for the full set of sustainability opportunities, in practice, opportunities may arise at any time for a range of reasons, and the operations manager is best placed to identify and follow them through. Indeed, we argue that the development of relevant and effective sustainability practices depends heavily on the contribution of operations managers and their staff.

In developing sustainability practices, the operations manager makes decisions and draws on their toolkit of approaches, including:

1. planning
2. decision making and analysis
3. coordinating complex activities related to production
4. considerations of risk as well as cost and benefits
5. coordinating product design with marketing colleagues
6. choosing equipment
7. choosing locations for their facilities
8. deciding the operations capacity/ size
9. making choices concerning technology
10. scheduling work through the operations and scheduling people's work patterns in the operations
11. deciding on the materials being used as inputs to the operations

New capabilities in operations management to support sustainability

As organisations place increasing priority on their sustainability performance, operations managers will require new skills to extend the contribution they can make to develop their organisations' sustainability orientation.

New sensitivity

Operations managers will need to develop and maintain an awareness of the broad range of sustainability issues, for example, as described by the GRI (Global Reporting Initiative, 2007). This awareness will need to extend to a more specific understanding of the principles of measurement of each issue, for example, how emissions are accounted for, and which have a greater weighting in greenhouse gas calculations. Awareness of sustainability issues should assist operations managers in identifying relevant stakeholders and their possible concerns and opportunities resulting from the organisations' activities. Further, operations managers will need to practice applying the principles of sustainability and considering the implications of reducing the externalities of operations by expanding the boundary of stakeholders and issues that might be addressed.

New dialogue

Stakeholder values and preferences cannot necessarily be inferred at arm's length. Operations managers will need to develop skills in developing a fruitful two-way dialogue with stakeholders, to understand their views and to develop a wider perspective on the trade-offs and new options that may be possible. This will require a major investment in stakeholder relationships, to develop open communication and trust. Operations managers will require high-level interpersonal skills to surface stakeholder opinions without seeking to control them, and to develop stakeholder capacity to understand and participate effectively in the dialogue process.

Innovation

The scope for innovation is expanded when the objectives of sustainability are added to the mix. Operations managers will need to deal with longer time-frames. New models may need to be developed for option evaluation, to deal with longer timeframes, increased uncertainty, and to explore a wider range of objective functions. For example, operations investments have traditionally been made based on a three to five year payback, and using financial consider-ations as the first-cut approach. Sustainability considerations might trial say, minimum power consumption as an objective over a twenty-year timeframe, yielding a different set of options for evaluation. There may also be scope for innovation in gain-sharing. As operations managers explore options that deliver benefits to stakeholders as well as financial returns to the organisa-tion, they may also need to develop new models for sharing the investment in line with the gains that result.

Putting it into practice

Operations managers in all industries are increasingly going to be immersed in ensuring that their decisions and practices conform to sustainable devel-opment principles. It is not just farms and mines and factories that produce tangible goods.

Do insurance companies and their operations managers make decisions and implement practices with sustainability implications? How about banks, gymnasiums, schools and government departments, universities and a host of other service organisations? The answer is a decided 'Yes', there are indeed strong implications and impacts of and from all these sectors on a variety of stakeholders, on the environment and on resource allocation and efficiency. Not only are these effects direct as a result of the practices and strategies of these organisations, but they also influence organisations across the economy in other primary and secondary industry sectors such as mining, manufac-turing, and farming. So we can conclude that operations managers in any and every industry impact on sustainability outcomes.

Through their lending policies, banks impact on almost every other indus-try. Those operating service businesses can purchase recycled paper, green electricity, etc., or not. Government departments, which operate hundreds or indeed thousands of buildings, can get better at conserving water. Hospitals can attempt to give their nurses better work rosters so as to be more fam-ily friendly. The list of specific possibilities is endless. Operations managers make these types of decisions, and the main intent is that through making these decisions with more than just short term cost reduction in mind, it is possible to improve overall outcomes going forward.

Of course, it is easier for an operations manager to pursue sustainability improvements if the senior executive of their organisation is amenable to such suggestions. However, it is the operations manager who is in the best position to pick up on new opportunities for sustainability. As we have discussed, these opportunities are often unique to an organisation and specific situation, and may arise when pursuing a quite different purpose. It is the responsibility of the operations manager to generate a business case for each investment or practice change. This chapter has provided you with some important guidance for preparing business cases for sustainability, wherever you may work in the future.

Summary

It took a crisis in the late 1990s to force BHP to accept that a more proactive approach to the effects of its operations on the full range of its stakeholders was needed. The organisation learnt the hard way how their 'licence to operate' in Ok Tedi, Papua New Guinea, could be effectively revoked, and their whole investment in the project written off. The adverse press that BHP received over this incident means that the company continues to be subject to intense scrutiny of its environmental and community responsibilities by shareholders and activists, even a decade later.

Now known as BHPBilliton, and the World's largest diversified resources company, the organisation cites 'an overriding commitment to sustainable development' as one of its six strategic foci. It has worked hard to integrate sustainability into its efforts at strategy, planning and design and operations levels. These efforts have been underpinned by increased dialogue with investors and other stakeholders.

One example of how BHPBilliton has taken a more proactive approach to sustainability issues is its joint venture initiative, RightShip P/L (with Rio Tinto). Sub-standard shipping operations pose considerable risks to their crew, cargo and the environment. BHP had a high profile incident in 1995 when its ship, the Iron Baron, ran aground on a reef in the Bass Strait off Tasmania, Australia. The ship leaked oil, causing damage to birds and the environment. RightShip is a ship vetting specialist, established by the two resources companies to evaluate and inspect every ship they use to move their cargoes. In the first six years of operation, the new vetting arrangement has removed 180 ships (about 1 per cent) from the companies' shipping operations.

BHPBilliton has implemented many of the ideas described in this chapter. The company encourages suggestions on how sustainability can be improved, and communicates its own business case for sustainability to all employees. While engaging with a limited number of external assessment exercises, the organisation places trust in its internal knowledge of operations and how they can be improved. It provides simple methods for assessment and comparison benchmarking between similar sites and activities.

It also provides awards and sustainability project descriptions to motivate employees.

While BHPBilliton is now committed to sustainable development across its activities, challenges remain. Placing its share of earnings from the Ok Tedi mine in a community trust has drawn a corporate veil over the environmental damage caused, but it cannot reverse it. Just as it was hard to predict the impact of a tailings dam failure on the company's future prospects in the 1980s, it is difficult for organisations like BHPBilliton to assess trade-offs for current decisions. For example, how can resource and energy conservation, greenhouse gases and other wastes, be weighed against increased global demand for resources, price and supply? If mitigation of adverse impacts does not exceed the effects of production increases, should production be curtailed?

BHPBilliton's immense capacity for investment and expertise can be used to help address such challenges, and the company is already taking steps in this direction. However, there are significant constraints to be overcome, including the pressure for high returns in the short-term, countervailing sustainability objectives of economic progress and equal access, along with other business constraints such as availability of skilled labour, competition in global markets, and so on.

There is no seeming endpoint for efforts in sustainability, but the skills and organisational attributes can be developed for continued well-placed effort and improvement.

DISCUSSION QUESTIONS

1. Research a traditional culture such as the Maori peoples of New Zealand. What principles of sustainability have they established? Can we learn from these in the modern, mainstream sustainability discussion?
2. Choose two sustainable investment ranking schemes, such as the Global Reporting Initiative and the Dow Jones Sustainability Index (Sustainable Asset Management). Compare the two schemes you have chosen in terms of the approach taken to assessing and influencing sustainability.
3. Review the list of sustainability issues identified by the Global Reporting Initiative (Table 12.1). Carefully identify (express your answers in a table) which operations management practices could influence one or more of these issues.
4. You are employed as an operations manager for a multi-national chemicals manufacturer. You work at a pesticides manufacturing operation in Thailand. Choose three items on the Global Reporting Initiative – one economic, one environmental, and one social. For each of the items you have chosen, explain what practices you might introduce or improve to make a sustainability improvement?

5. Why might reducing the externalities (costs resulting from organisational activities that are borne by others) be harder for a small private company to do than for a large multi-national? Give some examples.

6. The Brotherhood of St Laurence had extensive board discussions about the ethics of continuing to run a business that relied on supplies from factories in China that had poor working conditions and environmental performance. Construct a debate between two board members to illustrate the arguments that were probably debated.

7. You are the operations manager for a major dairy products manufacturer in New Zealand. Your general manager has been given a new company target – 'all our operations will be sustainable'. Your general manager understands that this target is open-ended and cannot be achieved immediately and within existing budgets and has asked you to design a table to be used to evaluate alternative practices and determine which should be introduced or adapted first. The rows of your table will be the alternative practices. What columns will you suggest?

8. Following on from Question 7, your general manager has been told that the company will be introducing a new annual declaration, to be signed by each general manager, giving their commitment that the new target 'all our operations will be sustainable' has been met. Given the open-ended nature of this statement, your general manager has asked you to develop a format for this declaration that speaks to progress on the target, but does not force him or her into making unrealistic commitments. What do you suggest this annual declaration should include?

9. Research the chemical explosion that occurred at a Union Carbide factory in Bhopal, India in December 1984. What was different about the regulatory context, country environment, organisation decisions and operations decisions that might have made this event more likely in the company's Indian plant than in one of its plants in the US?

10. You are the operations manager in charge of the IT operations of a major Australian bank. Your general manager has proposed that a large section of IT operations should be outsourced to a company located in India. The bank is a signatory to the UN Global Compact and reports against the Global Reporting Initiative. It has best of sector status in the Dow Jones Sustainability Index. Your general manager has asked you to consider the proposal in terms of the bank's sustainability goals and commitments. Explore three aspects: the Australian bank employees, the employees of the Indian company, and what interventions could have been made, when and by whom, that might alter the choices available now and in the future.

11. Research the issues in the 'Doctor Death' case in Bundaberg, Queensland. Was this an issue of sustainability, customer service or compliance? As the person responsible for hospital operations, what practices and procedures would you put in place to guard against cases of this kind in the future?

12. Is there a difference between 'ethical' operations and 'sustainable' operations?

13. Research a major listed Australian company that produces a Sustainability Report. List out the areas of operations and operations management practices that are referred to by this report. Given the activities of the

company, and the issues covered by the GRI, can you spot any important gaps or mis-emphases in the report's coverage? Why might these occur?

References

Agle, B. R., Mitchell, R. K. and Sonnenfeld, J. A. 1999. 'Who matters to CEOs? An investigation of stakeholder attributes and salience, corporate performance and CEO values.' *The Academy of Management Journal*, 42(5): 507–25.

Brotherhood of St Laurence. Website address: www.bstl.org.au, accessed: 15 July 2007.

Clarkson, M. B. 1995 'A stakeholder framework for analyzing and evaluating corporate social performance.' *The Academy of Management Review*, 20(1): 92–117.

Davis, K. 1973. 'The case for and against business assumption of social responsibilities.' *Academy of Management Journal*, 16: 312–22.

Global Reporting Initiative. Website address: http://www.globalreporting.org/NR/rdonlyres/A1FB5501-B0DE-4B69-A900-27DD8A4C2839/0/G3_GuidelinesENG.pdf, accessed: 15 April 2007.

Goldsmith, S. and Samson, D. 2002. *Sustainable Development – State of the Art: Asking the questions*. Sydney: Australian Business Foundation.

Goldsmith, S. and Samson, D. 2005. *Sustainable Development and Business Success: Reaching beyond the rhetoric to superior performance*. Sydney: Australian Business Foundation.

http://www.ecologicalfootprint.org/pressrelease.html, accessed: 15 April 2007.

World Commission on Environment and Development 1987. *Our Common Future*. G. H. Brundtland. New York: Oxford University Press.

Internet resources

Agenda21, see http://www.un.org/documents/ga/conf151/aconf15126-1annex1.htm

Australian Student Environment Network, see www.asen.org.au

Australian Sustainable Asset Management Index, see http/:://www.aussi.net.au/default.html

European Commission, see http://europe.eu.int

Institute for Social and Ethical Accountability, see http://www.accountability.org.uk

International Labour Organisation, see http://www.ilo.org

International Organisation for Standardisation, see http://www.iso.org

Organisation for Economic Cooperation and Development, see http://www.oecd.org

Pew Center, see www.pewclimate.org

Sustainable Asset Management, see http://www.sam-group.com/htmle/main.cfm

United Nations Environment Program, see http://www.unep.org

Web pages for major companies in the Asia-Pacific Region, try www.bhpbilliton.com (resources), www.westpac.com.au (banking), www.fonterra.com (food manufacture), and other companies you may be interested in.

World Business Council for Sustainable Development, see http://www.wbcsd.org

Notes

1 See www.globalreporting.org
2 'and yet the true creator is necessity, who is the mother of our invention.' Plato, *The Republic*, written 360BC.
3 At the time of writing this chapter, 2007, the problems associated with climate change receive daily attention in global media and politics.
4 See Clive Hamilton 2007. *Scorcher: The dirty politics of climate change*. Melbourne: Black Inc.
5 'I have always thought the actions of men the best interpreters of their thoughts.' John Locke (1632–1704)

Operations Management in Different Settings

Victoria Hanna

Learning objectives

After reading this chapter you should be able to:

- identify the operations function in any kind of organisation or industry
- identify the roles and responsibilities of operations managers in different organisational settings
- identify the operations management aspects of your own career choice
- describe any operation in terms of its transforming resources, transformed resources, operations processes and products and services
- understand the similarities and differences between operations in different industries
- discuss the roles and priorities of operations managers in different industries.

Box 13.1: Management challenge: transferring operations knowledge

The theories, techniques and models of the operations management field mostly originated in the manufacturing sector but have migrated into a variety of other industries and organisations. When managers study successful operations management in other organisations which could be in totally different industry sectors, a key challenge they face is identifying what lessons can be transferred to their own organisation. They also need to work out how the concepts can be translated so their employees can comprehend and deploy these new ideas. How do managers balance the trade-off between lessons from their own industry sector where concepts are easily understood and quickly deployed and novel input from other industries? How can you tell if new operations ideas are relevant for your organisation? Can they be immediately adopted or do they need to be adapted, or would some ideas that might well work in, say Toyota, not work or apply at all in, say a hospital?

Introduction

All types of organisations or enterprises, large or small, profit making or not-for-profit need some form of operations management. An operation is the process by which an organisation converts raw materials, labour and capital into a final product, service or experience. The ultimate challenge is to customise what you offer to meet your target market needs and synchronise their demand with your ability to fulfil it. All types of organisations must engage in operations management (whether they realise it or not) because all organisations produce some mixture of products, services or experiences. Operations usually represent the core business of an organisation: it is the part of the organisation that directly produces and delivers what the customer wants. There are of course always notable exceptions to the rule, for example, Nike contracts factories globally to produce the Nike branded finished product; they do not own manufacturing sites. So while it is true that you do not have to make everything you sell, it is important to exercise control over the production processes that are contracted out. Nike does this effectively, by ensuring that the materials and quality processes in its subcontracting firms all comply with the strict specifications that it lays down.

This final chapter presents a quick recap of the fundamental premise of operations management and then goes on to illustrate how operations management principles have been successfully deployed in a number of different settings, both in services and manufacturing, and in profit and not-for-profit organisations. To do this, two aspects that were initially presented in the very first chapter – transformation process and the five laws of operations management – are used. These illustrate the depth and breadth of the role and responsibilities of operations managers in various industries. In totality, this chapter shows the strong theoretical precepts upon which practices within the field of operations management are based.

Operations management and organisational type

Role of operations managers in different industries

The operations function sometimes has different names in different industries, but it is always concerned with managing the core productive purpose of

Table 13.1 Operations managers in different organisations

Industry	Title of Operations Manager
Logistics	Fleet manager
Insurance	Business Manager
Banking	Branch Manager
Retail	Store Manager
Hospital	Administrative Manager
Government Agencies	Executive Officer
Manufacturing	Production Manager/ Shift Manager
Process	Plant Manager, Lead Engineer
Events & Projects	Project Manager
Distributor	Facilities Manager

the business, to satisfy customer demand. Table 13.1 provides some examples of the various titles of operations in different industries:

The decisions that operations managers make have a major impact on both the cost of producing products and services, and how successfully these offerings are delivered, which in turn has a major impact on the revenue coming into the organisation. In addition, operations often form the main component of an organisation's costs through its use and consumption of resources. Operations is the area of the firm including much of the firm's capital investment. Given it's bearing on both revenue and cost and therefore profits, it is unsurprising that operations have been quoted as accounting for 60–80 per cent of the direct expenses that burden a firm's profit!

Revenue and costs are also a concern for not-for-profit organisations, for example in a local government council, effective operations management will deliver services that both meet the needs of the community and are produced efficiently, ensuring 'value' for all. Similarly, a hospital or charity would be concerned with its margins; consider this quote from the CEO of a hospital, 12 months prior to liquidation:

> You don't have to worry about profits because if you run a good hospital, and look after your doctors and look after your staff, the profits will take care of themselves.

Not-for-profit organisations need to ensure their operations are managed in such a fashion that they can reinvest in equipment and facilities, and like private sectors organisations, renew their competencies. Competencies, those an organisation has now and the ones they will need in the future, allow an organisation to remain competitive and derive an income.

Analysing organisations from an operations view is also important to investors, since the comparative cost of providing a good or service is essential to high earnings growth. As a consequence, financial and market analysts monitor how efficient companies are from an operations view. Companies that are strong operationally are able to generate more profit for each dollar of sales, thus making them attractive investments.

Box 13.2: Fisher & Paykel: successful because of how it manages its operations

Fisher & Paykel Appliances designs, manufactures and markets a range of household appliances developed with a commitment to technology, design, user friendliness and environmental awareness. The company was founded in New Zealand in 1934 and has manufacturing sites located in New Zealand, Australia, USA and Italy. Initially it was an importer of fridges and washing machines to New Zealand but it saw the potential in the household appliance market and in 1939 began to manufacture designs made under licence.

The ambitious and creative founders understood by making appliances under licence they were producing a more expensive version of others' products, so in 1956 they patented their first design and looked for new technologies to integrate into their designs. They continually encouraged an organisational culture that confronted traditional appliance design and production systems. They were the first in the world to commercialise the use of polyurethane foam as plastic liners and insulation for products.

Another major breakthrough came in the late 1960s when the firm found a way of producing short runs of various models through common manufacturing machinery. The ability to make every model every day, just in time, became reality and export opportunities opened up. The firm understood the potential of flexible machinery and how the control of production lines provided them with a competitive advantage. In 1972 it opened a new refrigeration plant that used only advanced flexible manufacturing techniques. The plant continues to evolve and is still in operation today. It has been joined by efficient new warehousing facilities.

Effective operations management is integral to Fisher and Paykel's accomplishments. The firm has successfully generated and adopted technology innovations in both product and processes. Its ability to apply benefits across all product ranges and manufacturing sites has ensured it remains one of New Zealand's most enduring and successful businesses. Chairman Gary Paykel says:

'Everyone who has been involved in the business should be proud of their contribution . . . they have all been part of its success.'

So what is it that operations managers do? They coordinate processes such as shipping and receiving, purchasing, facilities maintenance, production, personnel scheduling, and inventory control. They are 'line' managers too in that they manage people within processes, equipment breakdowns, rush orders from key customers, indeed changes of all kinds, and they solve real problems occurring within the operation, as they occur in real time. They negotiate with suppliers and customers, equipment suppliers and subcontractors. They work with marketing people from their organisation to make sure the operation is able to meet the marketing requirements.

The specific areas handled by individual operations managers vary by industry. For instance

1. In the airline industry, they might coordinate flight and maintenance scheduling, ground support, fuel consumption, and safety monitoring.
2. In a hospital, they may focus on managing patient flow; coordination of the pharmacy, laboratory and pathology services; nurse rostering and the transportation of patients and equipment.
3. In a manufacturing organisation, the role includes production and inventory control, scheduling, product design, industrial engineering and process analysis.
4. In a bank, operations would include teller scheduling, business and personal transaction processing, facilities design and layout, vault operations, technological investments and developments, and maintenance and security.
5. In retail store operations, the role encompasses not only sales and service delivery but security and loss prevention, inbound logistics of the goods to be sold, equipment management and maintenance, merchandise and store presentation, facilities management, people management and financial reconciliation.

As these organisations face mounting pressures to increase revenue, while managing costs and meeting ever-evolving and expanding customer demands, they have looked to the operations management field to provide solutions. There are many improvement methodologies available, some of which have remaining entrenched in manufacturing best practice but others have diffused across a range of industries. Three examples of manufacturing initiatives that have been successfully applied in service organisations would be total quality management, six-sigma and lean thinking. Consider this quote from Womack et al. (1990):

> We have become convinced that the principles of lean production can be applied equally in every industry across the globe and that the conversion to lean production will have a profound effect on human society – it will change the world.

While the principles of operations management may not have achieved world domination quite yet, they have helped organisations in a variety of industries transform their processes and achieve performance levels that were once considered impossible. The examples below are provided by the Lean Enterprise Institute (www.lean.org) and illustrate the types of improvement one particular methodology has delivered:

1. Lean applied in a healthcare provider: Cardiovascular Unit at the Mayo Clinic
   - Cancellation and no shows at physician appointments dropped from 30 to 10 per cent
   - Appointments were given on 90 per cent of occasions on first time contact to the unit
   - Clinical care time (face time with doctor) rose by 45 minutes
   - Wait time from request for appointment to finishing pre-care consultation fell from 33 to 3 days
2. Lean applied in a manufacturing organisation: Thomas & Betts Corporation
   - Lead time reduced from 16 to 6 days
   - Cycle time reduced by 60 per cent
   - Changeover time reduced by 85 per cent
   - Finished good inventory turns increased from 4 to 11
   - Productivity increased 38.6 per cent
   - Space 7,5000 square feet freed up
3. Lean applied in a materials handling organisation: Canada Post (Publications & Advertising Mail Cell)
   - Space used dropped from 17,000 to 9500 square feet
   - Productivity increased from 19 to 25 bags per hour
   - Bag travel distance reduced to 1580 feet
   - Bags double handled reduced from 46 to 11 per cent
   - Ergonomic risk reduced from medium to low

Relevance and setting

In this section we consider which aspects of operations management are relevant to any situation, or to any industry, not just manufacturers. Operations management is commonly defined as the design, operation, and improvement of the systems that create and deliver the organisation's primary products and services. To be able to manage an operation, you need to be able to analyse it – this is done by studying the transformation process. The transformation process was introduced in Chapter 1 in a very generic way. Here, it is used in a much larger array of contexts.

The management of the transformation process is fundamental to operations, in both manufacturing and service organisations and in both the private and not-for-profit sectors. The transformation process is represented by three elements, namely inputs, transformation processes and outputs and

Table 13.2 The inputs to the transformation process

Types of input resource that may be TRANSFORMED:

Materials, the physical inputs to the process
Information that is being processed or used in the process
Customers who are transformed in some way.

What do these resources have in common?
These resources are 'changed' in some way to create the goods or services the
   customer wants.

Types of input that are TRANSFORMING resources:

Facilities. This includes land, buildings, machines and equipment and is often
   described as capital.

Staff. This includes the people directly involved in the transformation process or
   who some how support it. This type of resource is often described as labour.
   These personnel are usually directly employed by the organisation but may be
   contractors who supply services to it.

What do these resources have in common?
These are the resources that 'perform' the transformation, they are not
   consumed.
Operations vary greatly in the mix of labour and capital that make up their
   transforming resources. Highly automated operations depend largely on
   capital; others rely mainly on labour.

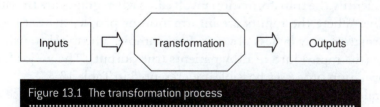

Figure 13.1 The transformation process

is illustrated in Figure 13.1. Managers are responsible for the systematic direction and control of the various processes that transform resources (inputs)
into finished goods or services for customers or clients (outputs). Operations managers have their hands on the 'control levers' that govern how the
inputs are transformed onto outputs, and this occurs in both the design
of the transformation processes, and in the real-time conduct of the daily
operations, which is known as 'line' management.

Some inputs are consumed in the process of producing goods or services;
while others have a role in the transformation process but are not consumed. These two kinds of input resources are described in more detail in
Table 13.2.

Table 13.3 Major types of transformation process

Type of transformation	Example	Explanation
Physical	Manufacturing	Changes in the physical characteristics of materials or customers
Locational	Transportation	Changes in the location of materials, information or customers
Exchange	Retailing	Changes in the ownership of materials or information
Storage	Warehousing	Storage or accommodation of materials, information or customers
Physiological	Healthcare	Changes in the physiological or psychological state of customers.
Informational	Telecommunications	Changes in the purpose or form of information

A transformation process is any activity or group of activities that takes one or more inputs, transforms and adds value to them, and provides outputs for customers or clients. Where the inputs are raw materials, it is relatively easy to identify the transformation involved, as when grapes are transformed into wine. Where the inputs are information or people, the nature of the transformation may be less obvious. For example, a hospital transforms ill patients (the input) into healthy patients (the output). The major forms of transformation processes possible are presented in Table 13.3.

Several different transformations are usually required to produce a good or service. The overall transformation can be described as the 'operation' and the constituent elements can be considered processes. Transformation processes may result in some unwanted outputs as well as the goods and services they are designed to deliver; for example, the outputs of a water treatment plant include clean recycled water to be returned to reservoirs as well as waste (sludge) that requires incineration or long term storage. Some forms of waste are dangerous, such as the output from nuclear reprocessing industries, and these are highly regulated. However, many organisations today focus on minimising the environmental impact of waste over the entire life cycle of their products, up to the point of final disposal. This can be driven by philosophical or ethical considerations, consumer pressure or even economic profit considerations. It can be cheaper to not produce waste, than to dispose of it.

Box 13.3: Waste not want not!

Example A: URS New Zealand – how managing waste helps you manage costs

URS New Zealand is an engineering and environmental consulting firm providing expertise to projects in Zealand, Australia and Asia Pacific. It employs a team of 250 staff to provide technically excellent, cost-effective, innovative and environmentally sustainable solutions for many challenges including bridges, roads, dams, wastewater treatment plants, land remediation, ports, pipelines, telecommunications networks and rapid transit systems. They focus on managing all aspects of major infrastructure projects including concept development, site selection and consultation, consents and regulatory approvals, design, construction management and commissioning. To gauge the success of their in-house waste minimisation system, URS New Zealand is committed to performing regular office waste audits. An initial audit was conducted prior to system implementation, and a second audit was completed several months later. The results of the audits showed a 40 per cent reduction in waste, by volume, due largely to an improved paper recycling programme and the use of council kerbside collection bins for recycling glass, plastic bottles, and cans. More specifically, 52 per cent less paper and 86 per cent less glass was being sent to landfill. The audits have also highlighted that office rubbish bins no longer need to be cleared daily by cleaners. The reduction in the number of times rubbish bins were emptied by cleaners has also provided cost savings.

Example B: Trashbags – an Australian company that transforms waste and lives

Trash Bags is a unique business venture not simply for its unusual products – beautiful bags made from what was once garbage – but also for the fact its structure is based around the core concerns of community responsibility and environmental sustainability. It was not created to satisfy a section of the market, although it does, and it was not created as a purely profit-making venture, although it has made profit. It was created because the owners wanted to be part of a more equitable and sustainable future. It shows a business model that was profitable while also fulfilling these aims as the core beliefs of its business operations and founders. Trash Bags was established in March 2005 by Amber Rowe, after her return from a year working with a small environmental NGO (non-government organisation) in the Philippines. She saw, first hand, the environmental and social devastation of many of the Philippines' economically disadvantaged communities. Many of these communities were trying to create a more prosperous future for themselves and their children by engaging in craft using the most readily available resource, garbage. Garbage, in the developed world, is seen as a problem to get rid of but in many of the poverty stricken communities of the world it is seen as a resource to utilise.

Amber was both in awe of and inspired by these communities and upon her return to Australia she started Trash Bags. This was to show that garbage is a resource to be utilised, not a problem to be wasted, and that each material and product has a life cycle, a story, involving not only what it is made of but who made it and at what cost. Trash Bags started with two community organisations from the Philippines; it has expanded to include organisations from Delhi and Cambodia

Table 13.4 The facilities and staff transforming resources of three operations

	Container ship	Biotech firm	TV station
Types of facilities/ systems	On-board navigation system Steam-generating boilers Gantries for container movement	Pressure vessels Distillation units Process control systems Hazard management systems	Broadcasting equipment Studios and studio equipment Transmitters Outside broadcast vehicles
Types of staff	Sailors Navigation and technical officers Catering staff Maintenance engineers	Operators Chemists and chemical engineers Process plant engineers	Presenters Technicians Researchers

and will shortly bring on further organisations from Malaysia and Bolivia. They all have two things in common, they are wholly or partly owned and operated by the community and directly benefit the community as well as being made from majority recycled materials.

An important aspect of the transformation model shown in Figure 13.1 is feedback and learning. Given the primary purpose of this chapter is to reflect on operations management in different settings, we will not consider these factors in depth. However, it is important for us all to understand that feedback is essential for operations managers. It can come from both internal and external sources. Internal sources include the testing and evaluation of goods and services; external sources include those who supply raw materials or support services as well as feedback from customers themselves.

The simple transformation model in Figure 13.1 provides a powerful tool for looking at operations in many different contexts. It helps us to analyse and design operations in many types of organisation. It is possible to demonstrate that standard categorisations of resources and processes are to be found in any sort of organisation. So for example, Table 13.4 shows what would constitute the facilities and staff transforming resources of three operations.

Box 13.4: When the healthcare system doesn't work

'Operating systems have a huge impact on work climate, staffing, financial results, etc., and yet we are trying to change our health care delivery system without changing its core operations. We are trying to achieve the results we want just by changing the reimbursement system, by asking different parties to collaborate, etc. The cost of health care delivery is inflated because we do not appropriately apply operations management methodologies. And yet we limit the price, so the quality of care is being negatively impacted. Somehow we manage to have both – waste and unsatisfactory quality of care. As long as our total cost, which is clinical cost plus delivery cost, is being limited, and as long as we do not actively employ operations management methods, we will experience this unfortunate scenario.'

Eugene Litvak, PhD, Professor of Healthcare and Operations Management and Director of the Program for Management of Variability in Health Care Delivery, Boston University Health Policy Institute.

By applying operations management principles (focusing on reducing variability) Prof. Eugene Litvak has helped Boston Medical Center reduce its ambulance diversions by 20 per cent, and reduce their last-minute postponement of elective surgeries by 99.5 per cent. (Boston Medical Center, Annual Report 2004).

In Australia, excellent results have been achieved by Prof. Ben-Tovim at Flinders Medical Centre in South Australia. The Flinders Medical Centre is a medium-sized teaching general hospital in Adelaide, the capital city of South Australia. It is well equipped and employs well-trained staff, yet in the winter of 2003 the emergency department was declared systemically unsafe. Initially managers thought the issue was capacity (bed shortage), so they added more capacity, but it only made the problem worse. They consulted the Internet to see what other hospitals were doing, and via the UK NHS Modernisation Agency they were introduced to the concepts of 'process mapping' and 'lean thinking'. They launched the 'Redesigning Care' project, and rather than focusing on business units, clinical diagnoses and professional skills, they concentrated instead on processes and patient flow. The first intervention worked so well, the whole hospital joined the initiative. The benefits were substantial: for example, serious adverse events (events the hospital reported to insurers) were halved in the first 12 months; in the emergency department, serious adverse events related to delays or discharges were virtually nil. The average waiting time the emergency department fell by 25 per cent, while the number of patient presentations rose (an increase of 2.9 per cent from the previous year). The hospital also managed to reduce the length of time patients spent on waiting lists, as elective (planned) surgery cancellations due to lack of beds were reduced by 81 per cent.

Five laws of operations management

To further understand how operations management principles can be deployed in different settings it is useful to consider how we manage the transformation process effectively and efficiently. Professors Schmenner and Swink (1998) identified a set of five laws of operations management that explain an organisation's productivity. These laws are:

1. law of variability
2. law of bottlenecks
3. law of scientific methods
4. law of quality
5. law of factory focus.

Let's consider how each 'Law' is expressed in different organisations.

Law of variability

In operations management terminology 'variability' refers to the random variation in demand an organisation must cope with, the amount of variation inherent in the transformation process and the variation in the final output (be it product or service) delivered. The greater the level of variation, the less output an organisation will deliver per input. In other words if you have to manage a great deal of variation you're unlikely to have highly utilised processes and your productivity will be reduced. Highly effective organisations seek to either minimise variation or accurately forecast the variation (and prepare for it). They will also understand the amount of variation their organisation can tolerate and still retain acceptable productivity. To understand how variation manifests in different organisations consider the examples presented in Table 13.5.

Law of bottlenecks

A bottleneck is one process in a chain of processes that has limited capacity and consequently reduces the capacity of the whole chain. Productivity is improved by eliminating or better managing an organisation's bottlenecks. If you can not add capacity to a bottleneck, you can improve productivity by ensuring the bottleneck process is never idle. Organisations in the manufacturing and process industries have typically achieved this through having long production runs with few changeovers. Bottlenecks are usually easy to find, just look for where large amounts of work in progress is waiting or where people are queuing. Bottlenecks can be 'fixed' (as in they do not move) or they may 'float' depending of what mix of products or services is being delivered.

In a service environment bottlenecks are often managed rather than eradicated. Consider the example of an airport, where bottlenecks often appear at check-in, security checkpoints, immigration and baggage handling points. While additional resource is added at peak times, airports often prioritise activity at bottlenecks to ensure key personnel and passengers paying a premium are not delayed. For instance, airline crew have express access through immigration, business class passengers have separate queues and express

Table 13.5 Variation in different types of organisation

Organisation	How variation can present . . .
School	Variation could present in high or low enrolment numbers, or in the understanding and ability of students and teachers. Schools benefit from a fairly uniform goal for their output: delivering a learning experience in a secure and stimulating environment, and ensuring all students reach their full potential.
Large public hospital	General hospitals must cope with several types of variation. Demand can be scheduled for elective surgeries, but emergency cases must still be processed. Illness itself also presents randomly. The range of specialities can be large, patients can be young or old, there can be differences in the patients' degree of illness, choice of treatment etc. and the ability of the doctors and healthcare delivery systems to provide treatment will also vary.
New biotech start-up	All new firms have to rely on forecasts of the demand that do not have the benefit of past experience. Biotech firms also have to deal with the vagaries of biological processes, which can be difficult to control – especially when trying to increase yields. However, as these firm's are still developing their initial products, many do not have a wide range of items to produce.
Airport terminal	Demand varies according to holidays, sporting events, etc. For example, flights to Melbourne on and just before the Australian Football League Grand Final weekend are fully booked weeks in advance. Demand also varies according to the time of day: there is of course a peak but all airports arrange times when terminals have no flights scheduled to allow for maintenance on support systems like baggage handling and system back ups etc. Given the regulated nature of the industry with respect to safety, processing is fixed but can still be influenced by security changes and adverse weather conditions.
Confectionery manufacturer	Demand is seasonal but it is also dependent on marketing and event sponsorship, for example when KitKat sponsored Big Brother UK in 2006 (in the style of a Willy Wonka Golden Ticket Competition no less!) sales of KitKats increased rapidly. Nestlé's (KitKats' manufacturer) Customer Service Centre was inundated with calls from customers wanting more details and both KitKats and 'golden tickets' appeared for sale on EBay. The confectionery transformation process is well understood in terms of recipe but variation is introduced through the introduction of new technology, novel packaging formats and new products.

Table 13.5 [*Cont.*]

Organisation	How variation can present . . .
Project	A project is a unique interrelated set of tasks with a beginning, an end and a defined outcome. Some projects are well understood but others are novel and become increasingly subject to variation in the sequencing of activities, accurate estimation of costs and definition of the final output. Technical risks also bring variation that can not be accurately forecast.

baggage handling, and travellers with young families or disabilities are often given precedence as they have potential to slow down processing at bottlenecks. Another example of managing rather than removing bottlenecks would be theme parks – queuing theory defines how queues are structured to speed up flow and people are entertained while they wait!

In a multi-project environment, organisations face special challenges with respect to bottlenecks. Depending on the phase or nature of a project, managers will often compete for similar resources creating temporary bottlenecks. Scheduling projects and allocating resources to avoid delays in projects due to bottlenecks gets more difficult as the number of projects being simultaneously managed increases.

Box 13.5: Managing bottlenecks in professional services

Given that bottlenecks are often revealed by stockpiles of incomplete assets (work in progress) how do you identify a problem when your assets are invisible, for example when your asset is knowledge? Professional services organisations have two core assets: the intellectual capital of their people and the client relationships they build. These assets are knowledge-based and essentially intangible and it can be a challenge for an operations manager to ensure they are efficiently and effectively deployed. In these circumstances a realistic understanding of the results you expect from employees is essential, because it is only when these results are not achieved that you have any opportunity to investigate the root cause of the problem, and find the bottleneck.

Operations managers in knowledge-based organisations must focus not only on ensuring that people know how to do a particular job but how to deploy people in their operations to make the best use of their talents, how to make decisions that help build a strong client base, and how to guide change as markets and conditions change. The role encompasses:

1. Developing specific human capital (this refers to skills or knowledge that is useful to the employer or industry, general human capital refers to skills like literacy that are beneficial to all) because it's the key to productivity and the basis for making the best use of both brand capital and client-relationships.

2. Building brand capital because that helps organisations maintain margins under competitive pricing pressure.
3. Finding new ways to measure strategic performance and gain real-time visibility into operations. Employees in these industries cannot compete without access to relevant information and without real time information how can you accurately ascertain the bottleneck?
4. Ensuring retention of relevant knowledge in times of transition from one market to another, (for example when activities are showing diminishing returns) or when employees move on. Professional service organisations utilise formal knowledge management systems which aim to capture and make available the collective knowledge of the organisation's knowledge assets. Of course it is never possible to explicitly capture all of the employees' knowledge, because some of it, known as tacit knowledge simply cannot be articulated and written down. However many organisations have benefited greatly from making the information that exists *anywhere* in the organisation, available *everywhere* in the organisation. Professional service organisations such as Deloitte, Accenture, PwC, KPMG have made major investments in knowledge management systems and approaches.

Taken together, these areas of focus can help knowledge based services organisations manage bottlenecks and enhance performance. Successful bottleneck management in this industry leads to stronger margins and the ability to adjust quickly to a changing market.

Law of scientific methods

Scientific Method is founded in the principles of industrial engineering and focuses on 'improvements to processes that have withstood the test of time in countless situations' (Schmenner and Swink, 1998).

These principles focus on improving quality and productivity by eliminating or reducing the waste of time, money, materials, energy and other resources. They have the most impact when targeted at bottleneck operations. Scientific method integrates the technological aspects of the transformation process and decision making capabilities of operators. Problems range from the operational to the strategic. For example:

1. design of a work method and work station to manufacture bicycles
2. optimisation of factory layout and control of material flow for a confectionary manufacturer
3. design of the layout and the checkout counters in a department store
4. organisation of an office and planning of the work flow for a bank
5. design of the baggage handling system at an airport

6. creation of an overall corporate plan involving materials procurement, production, inventory and distribution

7. development of the rapid response protocol to empty a hospital of non-urgent patients when responding to a disaster.

While the origins of scientific methods are in 'factories', they have delivered excellent results when targeted to services. Healthcare in particular has successfully adopted and adapted these principles; for example, scientific method has led to the development of patient pathways. A 'patient pathway' is the route that patients will take from their first contact with their primary care provider (usually their general practitioner or family doctor), through referral, entry into a hospital and the completion of their treatment. It is often expressed as a timeline, on which every event relating to treatment is entered. Events such as consultations, diagnosis, treatment, medication, diet, assessment, teaching and preparing for discharge from the hospital can all be mapped on this timeline. The pathway gives an outline of what is likely to happen on the patient's journey and can be used both for patient information and for planning of services capacity offered. Pathways are based on expected clinical outcomes, and they also have been used to highlight when a patient is not progressing as normal and may require additional treatment.

The boxed example illustrates how scientific methods have been applied in the project management profession. It introduces the *Project Management Book of Knowledge*, which is an encyclopaedia of the knowledge and processes accumulated by the Project Management Institute (www.pmi.org) through which they share best practice.

Box 13.6: Scientific method in action: the project management body of knowledge

The project management body of knowledge (PMBOK) is a collection of processes and knowledge areas generally accepted as best practice within the project management discipline. As an internationally recognised standard (IEEE Std 1490–2003) it provides the fundamentals of project management, irrespective of the type of project be it construction, software, engineering, automotive etc. PMBOK recognises five basic process groups and nine knowledge areas typical of almost all projects. The basic concepts are applicable to projects, programs and operations. The five basic process groups are: initiating, planning, executing, controlling and closing. Processes overlap and interact throughout a project or phase of a project.

Processes are described in terms of:
- inputs (documents, plans, designs, etc.)
- tools and techniques (transformation mechanisms applied to inputs)
- outputs (documents, products, etc.)

The nine knowledge areas are:
1. project integration management
2. project scope management
3. project time management
4. project cost management
5. project quality management
6. project human resource management
7. project communications management
8. project risk management
9. project procurement management

Law of quality

Productivity is also improved when quality (conformance to a design valued by customers) is improved. Increased conformance leads to fewer incidences of waste.

> 'Quality is never an accident; it is always the result of intelligent effort.'
> John Ruskin (English writer and critic of art, architecture, and society, 1819–1900)

The Law of Quality is about improving processes, products and services. Whether you are an advocate of the approaches of Deming or Juran, whether you follow the principles of TQM or Six Sigma, all quality methodologies are focused on eliminating defects and the root causes of those defects. Quality involves designing products and services that satisfy customers, running processes at greater efficiencies, producing less waste and increasing business productivity. The challenge for operations managers encompasses correctly ascertaining their customer's definition of quality, identifying the processes to deliver the product or service in a defect free manner and last but not least locating the tools that will enable their employees to continuously improve operations. While quality is a conditional and somewhat subjective attribute, manufacturing and engineering firms benefit from a long history of individuals, firms and industries creating and deploying quality management techniques in their field. The concept of quality has evolved from inspection, measurement, and testing, to a profession which focuses on the continual improvement of processes, products and services. There are many resources available, and plentiful case studies of both successful and failed improvement initiatives to assist any manager wishing to improve quality in their organisation.

To increase the value they can extract from limited budgets many not-for-profit organisations are also turning to the quality concepts found in business improvement programmes. To provide the best possible service and continuous improvement initiatives, schools, hospitals, nursing homes and

Table 13.6 Activities and tools that can assist

Activities	Tools that can assist
Gathering information	Walk-throughs
Analysing processes	Cause and effect diagrams, Pareto diagrams, run charts and flowcharts
Gathering data	Sampling
Working in groups and decision making	Affinity grouping and multi-voting to prioritise choices
Documenting work	Project Planning Forms, Plan-Do-Study-Act Worksheets and Storyboards

local governments have begun to apply business-based quality methodologies such as TQM, Six Sigma and Lean Thinking. While these initiatives are 'tried and tested' in the industrial arena, their application in other sectors is not without challenges. Consider these questions:

1. Six-sigma can be used in the manufacturing environment to significantly reduce variability and produce efficient schedules – but how do you use Six Sigma to solve scheduling problems in the labour and delivery wards of a women's hospital? How could you use the same tool to analyse patient falls, spot trends, and develop a proactive approach to preventing injuries? How can Six Sigma be used to release the bottlenecks commonly found in emergency departments?

2. Lean thinking has streamlined processes in manufacturing, but how do you apply it to retail store planning? How do you remove the non-value added steps from the receiving and billing procedures in a department store or to improve stocking procedures in a supermarket?

3. How can the theories of TQM aid the tourism industry? How can continuous improvement tools and techniques be deployed to counteract growing competition, lack of willingness to provide a service, the increasing loss of individuality by standardisation of products or adverse price-performance ratios, etc.?

Managers in the not-for-profit sector need to both understand quality concepts and apply them specifically to their situation. To aid their efforts they also need definitions and explanations that will help them translate the litany of quality related terms and techniques, into a terminology that is understood in their industry. In this last decade these needs have been recognised by service providers, consultants and academics alike. Organisations like the Juran Institute not only produce pithy, easy to understand toolkits for manufacturing industries but work hard to translate and document the application of quality fundamentals in every industry. Some industries have proactively created resources for themselves. The Institute for Healthcare Improvement, for example, has developed and adapted the basics quality toolkit to help their industry accelerate improvement; this toolkit is presented in Table 13.6.

The following boxed example presents a traditional manufacturing checklist to identify waste adapted to fit the healthcare context.

Box 13.7: Ohno's (1988) wastes in manufacturing, adapted to healthcare context

1. Over-servicing
This identifies situations where patients are being processed at a stage earlier or faster than their actual need. This is a symptom of patients being pushed through the system, and while such an approach appears logical and cost effective, it often creates great congestion and large queues. For instance, in many hospitals patients scheduled to have surgery in the morning are requested to arrive between 6.45am and 7.15am. As a consequence you have a glut of patients undergoing preoperative assessment much ahead of their scheduled need, overburdening the subsequent stages resulting in chaotic movement of patients, staff and information, and long wait times. Another example of over-servicing is when diagnostic tests are performed much ahead of their actual need, leading to wasted resources when lost or obsolete test results must be repeated.

2. Waiting
In hospitals, one can observe two kinds of waits – one experienced by patients and another by staff and doctors in the system. Patient waits correspond to poor service and are undesirable. Resource waits result in reduced utilisation and increased costs for the hospital. The hospital practices focus on minimising the wait for doctors and its staff and resort to batching strategies, which result in higher wait for patients. Lack of coordination across stages in the process also results in excessive patient waits and doctor waits. Patient waits have other costs that are not normally recognised by hospitals, for instance, you need more room to hold patients, more resources to engage and monitor them, more resources to progress them through system, etc.

3. Unnecessary transport or conveyance
Hospitals have been historically designed by specialty rather than around the patient. As a result, patients in the middle of their treatment are moved long distances, creating unnecessary transport requirements. Also, they are moved in and out of waiting bay or post operative wards to accommodate capacity restrictions elsewhere. To prevent such redundant transport, a coordinated approach to patient process flow is a must. Specialty hospitals such as Shouldice Hospital (Heskett, 1983) in Toronto have streamlined their process flow around patient needs, minimising movement of the patients through the system.

4. Unnecessary movement

Unnecessary motion is caused by poor workflow, poor layout, and inconsistent or undocumented work methods. Any wasted motion that nurses, surgeons or orderlies have to perform during the course of their work, such as looking for or even reaching for reports and patients can be classified as unnecessary movement. Also any unnecessary walking that they perform will fall under this category.

5. Over processing or incorrect processing

In hospitals, processes evolve over time and are typically not optimised in a holistic manner. Each specialty focuses its effort on enhancing patient care from its own perspective. As a result, you have unnecessary or over processing and sometimes incorrect processing. Unnecessary surgeries and diagnostic tests are well known examples of this type of waste. From a clinical perspective, the development of pathways has enhanced the quality of care and has facilitated earlier detection of deviation from expected treatment paths.

6. Excess inventory

This waste is easily identifiable in hospitals. A typical example would be excess stock of medical supplies, pharmacy stock, and other medical equipment resulting from uncoordinated purchasing policies. In a hospital environment, patients also represent a form of inventory.

7. Defects

Medical service errors such as wrong medication or wrong procedures performed on a patient constitute defects in a hospital context. These errors can be life threatening and the costs of such errors cannot only be measured in terms of money, but of the health outcomes themselves. They also waste resources in at least four ways: the materials (medical supplies and other inputs) that were consumed to provide the service can not be recovered; the labour (doctor and other personnel time) used to provide this service is wasted; labour is required to perform the rework; and lastly, labour is required to address any forthcoming patient complaints (litigation, etc.) and adverse publicity.

Law of factory focus

This law indicates that factories that focus on a limited set of tasks will be more productive than similar factories with a broader array of tasks. The term 'focused factory' was first coined by Skinner (1974), a Harvard Business School Professor, when he argued that complex and overly ambitious factories were at the heart of the American productivity crisis in the late 1960s and early 1970s. He concluded that 'simplicity and repetition breed competence.'

For a simple analogy, consider the decathlon. The decathlon is an athletic competition consisting of ten different track and field contests and won by the participant amassing the highest total points score across the full set of events. The decathlon is a two-day miniature track meet designed to ascertain the sport's best all-around athlete. On the first day each athlete must complete the 100 metres sprint, long jump, shot-put, high jump and the 400 metres sprint. On the second day the athletes must complete the following events: 110 metres hurdles, discus, pole vault, javelin and then they finally run a 1500 metres race. The decathlete does not have to be outstanding in any one event to be the overall champion. Decathletes must range from being at least adequate in their weak events to being exceptional in their stronger events. As they must do well in three running, one hurdling, three jumping and three throwing events, they may not have enough time to perfect performance in any single event. To win therefore, athletes must compromise, and identify where they should focus their preparation to maximise the total score. Athletes must improve technique and gain strength without sacrificing speed or spring, (and vice versa) and develop the endurance that will enable them to compete in a two-day competition. Now, consider the impact that focus has on performance: a professional 100 metres sprinter who specialises in only this event will easily beat even the best decathlete, but could they compete in all 10 events? Given this analogy it is easy to see that the fewer the tasks a factory has to 'focus' on, the easier it will be to achieve excellence.

It is similar with products too. Is there a single vehicle that can be designed and built that handles as well as a superb sports car, has the petrol consumption efficiency of a Toyota Prius, the passenger carrying capability of a family van, the off road capability of a good 4WD, and the ride comfort of a luxury vehicle? The answer is no. But you can buy a vehicle that can very effectively do one or maybe two of these tasks. Similarly, is there a single airplane that can fly at twice the speed of sound, manoeuvre very tight corners, takeoff vertically, hover in the same spot, fly 12,000 km without refuelling, reach heights of 20,000 metres and comfortably carry over 400 people? The answer is again, you can definitely have any one of these things or maybe two of these things in a plane, but not all. It is about specialisation.

Similarly, markets exist in segments and we must consider designing and operating our productive systems to be excellent at a few things not a 'jack of all trades', otherwise our production system will lose in all segments of the market. It's just like what would happen if a decathlete went in any single specialty event at the Olympics: they would not be competitive.

In many industries, the twin challenges of improving operational efficiency and integrating technological advances into product and service offerings are pushing organisations to narrow their focus. Manufacturers have long endured the pressure for increased precision, flexibility, complexity, reliability and environmental awareness, while simultaneously meeting market demand for smaller, lighter and cheaper products. Many leading organisations no longer rely on large aggregated supply chains to manufacture products but view themselves as system builders. They focus on core competencies and devolve component design and manufacture to their suppliers. Others have focused on the type of manufacturing they do, and have organised manufacturing into centres of excellence. For example many confectionery manufacturers separate their production facilities by raw material ingredient, as the skills to effectively and efficiently produce sugar products (starburst, jelly babies, mints, toffees, etc.) are fundamentally different to the skills required to produce cocoa-based products such as chocolate bars or boxed chocolates. Even within chocolate manufacture it is possible to further delineate between grades of chocolate, treatment it will tolerate and various product styles. Confectionery brands such as Cadbury, Nestlé and Mars may be global, but the manufacture of particular products is limited to surprisingly few sites across the globe. Specialist products like Cadbury's Crème Egg or Nestlé's Walnut Whip are only produced at a single site.

Focus is a very important idea in operations management, and indeed in all aspects of management!

Similar situations exist in the process industries. If we consider a small pharmaceutical firm, there are a variety of ways in which it can achieve focus. For example, if we consider production capabilities, firms may need to be able to manufacture and package capsules, tablets, gels, creams, tube products, and suspensions. A factory might be liquid-focused, solids-focused or topical-focused. (Topical products are those that are applied externally.) A research-orientated biotechnology firm would be a little different, such that while it may be involved in several areas of research, a substantial proportion of its budget is often dedicated to one area, and only one area will likely have dedicated commercialisation expertise and effort. The supporting areas of research are often spun out into new companies, or sold off to large pharmaceutical companies to generate income.

To a certain extent service organisations have always understood the benefits of focus. For example, schools have often selected on academic capability, or have created specialist units to develop particular skills, for example drama schools for budding actors. Healthcare too has always understood the advantages of focus. There is a steep learning curve for most medical interventions and hospitals that have a higher volume of cases generally report better clinical outcomes at a lower cost than do centres with a lower volume of cases. This has lead to the creation of hospitals dedicated to women and to children, as well as hospitals focusing on specialties such as orthopaedics. The cost and performance benefits delivered by focus have been shown to hold true for nearly all medical interventions, irrespective of their technological sophistication. More recently there are examples of hospitals focusing on only one single type of surgery; for instance, Shouldice Hospital in Canada (Hestkett, 1983) performs only abdominal hernia repair. Its excellent outcomes, low relapse rates, and relatively low costs have prompted many to reconsider established norms for this type of surgery. Another example of a hospital concentrating on a narrow range of services would be the Aravind Eye Hospital in India.

Aravind started in 1976 as a modest 11-bed eye clinic; by 1992 it had grown to a 1,400-bed hospital complex and today it is the largest and most productive eye care facility in the world. Managed with both compassion and efficiency, it has developed a self-sustaining business and treatment model that now cares for over 1.7 million patients each year, two-thirds of them, for free. The Aravind Eye Care Organisation encompasses five hospitals, a manufacturing centre for ophthalmic products, an international research foundation and a resource and training centre that has revolutionised eye surgery across the developing world.

Successful management of focused factories relies on correctly identifying a limited and manageable set of services that will still be competitive, or still represent value for money for your clients. It is not an easy transition and it will mean losing some skills while learning new ones. It also relies on organisations learning to structure policies and supporting services so that they focus on a few explicit objectives instead of the broad array of goals they may be familiar with.

In summary, the specialist usually beats the generalist!

Summary

Operations management is concerned with the design, management, and improvement of the systems that create an organisation's goods and services. The majority of most organisations' financial and human resources are invested in the activities involved in making products or delivering services. Operations management is therefore critical to organisational success.

In this chapter we have discussed the fundamental aspects of operations that are relevant for any organisation – the concept of the transformation process, and the inherent inputs and outputs. We have also discussed the aspects of operations management that a professional in the field must be able to understand and adapt to ensure they discharge their responsibilities both efficiently and effectively, namely the five laws of operations management. These laws explain the effects of variability, bottlenecks, scientific method, product and process quality improvement and focus, and provide us with insights into an organisation's capabilities and the trade-offs required to achieve acceptable performance.

The management challenge presented at the start of the chapter was: How can you tell if new operational ideas are relevant to your organisation? Answer: Look not for ideas from similar organisations, but organisations that compete on similar characteristics. It is not the obvious similarities in terms of product or service that are significant but close approximations of intrinsic characteristics such as process flow, demand variation etc. that will give you insights into the potential value of operational changes.

DISCUSSION QUESTIONS

1. Look up 'Toyota and hospital' on Google or a similar search engine. Write a summary of your findings about how the principles of the Toyota production system are being applied in hospitals.
2. Port of Melbourne is Australia's largest container and general cargo port, handling 39 per cent of the nation's container trade. Forty-two container shipping lines, as well as a number of other general cargo carriers make around 3200 ship calls a year to Melbourne, providing services to ports in all major parts of the world. List the transformation processes which you think the port's operations managers have to run, and identify their inputs and outputs. What would the port's competitive priorities be?
3. What do you think would be the main design, planning and control, and improvement activities in a large airport such as Singapore's Changi Airport?
4. What factors and tradeoffs do you need to consider in designing a production system? Are service systems different?
5. Why do financial analysts examine the operations function of an organisation when setting its market value?
6. What are the sources of variability in production and service systems? How would you approach managing them?
7. Why is a strong interface between operations management and marketing essential for a profitable organisation?
8. How do you translate concepts that began in a manufacturing environment into a language that service providers can understand and apply?

References

Heskett, J. L. 1983. Shouldice Hospital Limited. Case 9-683-068, Boston, MA: Harvard Business School.

Ohno, T. 1988. Toyota *Production System: Beyond large-scale production. Portland*. OR: Productivity Press.

Schmenner, R. W. and Swink, M. 1998. 'On Theory in Operations Management.' *Journal of Operations Management*, 17: 97–113.

Skinner W. 1974. 'The focused factory.' *Harvard Business Review*, May–Jun:113–22.

Womack, J. P., Jones, D. T. and Roos, D. 1990. *The Machine that Changed the World*. New York: Harper Perennial.

Internet resources

A resource from the Institute of Healthcare Improvement: http://www.ihi.org/ihi
Alliance for Innovative Manufacturing at Stanford, virtual factory tours explaining how every day things are made. http://manufacturing.stanford.edu/

SOMA is a network of faculty, students, and practitioners with interest in Services Management: http://soma.byu.edu/soma

The Association for Operations Management: http://www.apics.org

The UK Office of Government Commerce (OGC) provides a wide range of resources here to help you manage your programmes and projects more effectively. http://www.ogc.gov.uk/programmes_and_projects.asp

PART V

Case Studies

Innovation in the Biotechnology Sector: The Case of IDT Australia

John Morgan

Introduction

The Institute of Drug Technology was a university-owned not-for-profit organisation which operated as part of the College of Pharmacy in Victoria since 1975. It primarily gave academics and industry the chance to conduct research and development together. In 1986, then a professor, Dr Graeme L. Blackman led a management buy-out of the assets of this consulting business. The company was listed on the Australian Stock Exchange in 1988 as IDT.

From 1988 to the early 1990s, there was a move away from an academic orientation and towards a manufacturing focus. This was because the company was commissioned to make active pharmaceutical ingredients (APIs) under long-term manufacturing contracts. As a result, the company integrated forward from a licensor of technology to a production oriented company.

The company has a number of modern manufacturing facilities and laboratories in Melbourne and is licensed by the Australian Therapeutic Goods Administration (TGA) and the United States Food and Drug Administration (FDA) for the production of active pharmaceutical ingredients. IDT is one of the few Australian-owned biotechnology companies that have secured FDA approval, which gives it access to the large and lucrative pharmaceutical market in the United States.

IDT has grown to become a highly successful company with strong international standing. It has built up an international reputation of excellence in the development and manufacture of anti-cancer drugs. Back in 1996,

Dr Blackman described his company as: 'a small, yet ambitious player in the high-risk business of developing the capacity for manufacturing active drug substances in the pharmaceutical industry.' In just over 15 years, IDT has become a highly profitable company with total annual revenue of $25.8 million and a before tax profit exceeding $6 million in 2002/2003. In the five years to 2004, the company achieved 47 per cent compound annual growth in after tax profits.

The corporate mission of IDT, as stated in its Annual Report 2000/2001, is: 'to be a leading internationally recognised pharmaceutical development and manufacturing company, specialising in active pharmaceutical ingredients (APIs).'

Manufacturing capabilities and core competencies of IDT

IDT is now recognised internationally as having world-class expertise and facilities in the specialised area of anti-cancer and potent drug syntheses. The accumulation of this expertise and the development of its core competencies in the manufacture of APIs have strongly positioned IDT in this market niche. Over the five years to 2003, IDT developed strong relationships with major international pharmaceutical companies such as Pfizer, AstraZeneca, Wyeth and Johnson & Johnson. Additional projects commenced in 2000/2001 and 2001/2002 have further secured IDT's long-term development as IDT expanded its manufacturing capacity to capitalise on market opportunities.

Increasingly, IDT is working in collaboration with both multi-national pharmaceutical and small innovator companies in order to develop new drugs to treat serious diseases. These drug development programs investigate the safety and efficacy of new drugs and are aimed at meeting the international regulatory requirements for successful drug commercialisation. These development works frequently lead to phase I and phase II clinical trials. Such projects not only contribute revenue to IDT in the development phase, but also represent significant potential benefits for the growth of IDT's business.

The company's expertise includes process scale up and validation, formulation work, small-scale finished product development and manufacture, stability testing, and other technical and regulatory requirements. IDT also has considerable expertise in documentation and filing requirements for Australian and overseas regulatory agencies to support clinical trial and marketing approvals.

Corporate structure and strategy of IDT

IDT employs over 130 qualified and experienced scientists and engineers. With the leadership of the CEO and the Board of Directors, IDT has managed to capitalise on its scientific expertise by recognising commercial opportunities for its research while, at the same time, meeting the needs of customers and the market for its products.

IDT has two organisational 'arms' which work together synergistically. The Pharmaceutical Research and Development arm has 'fee for business' arrangements with major Australian clients such as Amrad and Starpharma and Meditech Research. This arm also conducts development work on new products and drugs where the validation process is critical. This is in line with IDT's emphasis on developing new chemical entities that will lead to the development of new products, particularly in its core competency area of developing APIs for anti-cancer drugs.

The other arm of IDT is its manufacturing activities and processes that are based on commercial supply agreements. In contrast to most biotechnology firms that are highly vertically integrated, IDT works on the philosophy of forming strategic alliances with companies such as Biota and Amrad or working with smaller biotechnology firms such as Prana on a 'fee for business' basis.

The pharmaceutical business is driven by outsourcing research and development. IDT has benefited from other biotechnology companies outsourcing their research to IDT. Traditionally, pharmaceutical companies have been highly vertically integrated with most firms holding on to the early stages of development right through to the marketing of product. In the past 15 years, this situation has changed and pharmaceutical companies now outsource their research in the clinical development stage. In the past 10 years, manufacturing development has also been outsourced by some companies.

Organisational climate

Numerous scientists with PhDs employed at IDT conduct research and carry out development and testing work requiring a high level of expertise. There is a very low turnover of staff. 'They know we rely on them so they feel valuable to the company.' According to Blackman, 'IDT finds skilled scientists and then 'grafts on' the commercial skills so that they can value add to the business'. This forms the basis of staff selection, recruitment and development that is aligned with the corporate strategy of IDT. Cultural and technical knowledge were both connected throughout the organisation. There is a strong cultural drive underpinning the recruitment process that involves ensuring that employees were recruited on the basis that they fit within the organisation.

Innovation is dependent on highly skilled and motivated staff who are well rewarded for their efforts. Recognising that there is a relationship between culture and a supportive management style, Blackman has created a 'commercial campus-type culture' at IDT. The campus culture is important because it is conducive to scientific enquiry in a relaxed organisational setting. Further, there is a free team-based culture that is conducive to sharing knowledge and ideas. At that same time, there is the realisation that the company is commercially driven. 'People like working at IDT in a non bureaucratic culture', said Dr Blackman.

Leadership style and vision of the CEO

The IDT organisational climate is significantly influenced and moulded by demonstrable leadership inside and outside the organisation. The CEO is both a leader and a mentor to the talented young scientists at IDT. He can communicate with scientists in their language. In 2001, Blackman was awarded 'Australian Entrepreneur of the year – Southern Region.' Criteria for this award included growth in turnover, profit and employee numbers together with such factors as degree of innovation development of creative and ingenious production, marketing and selling techniques and the extent of expansion into national and international markets.

Commercial orientation and commercialisation of research

In addition to being a leading manufacturer of APIs for local and international markets, IDT also provides a comprehensive range of consultancy, research and development, and analytical services to the pharmaceutical, chemical, biotechnology and allied industries. Further, as was explained earlier, IDT is increasingly working in collaboration with large multi-national and small innovator pharmaceutical companies to develop new drugs to treat serious diseases.

Innovation intensity

Biotechnology companies using their intellectual assets to form alliances, networks and to gain access to information flows and formal and informal networks. This enables biotechnology SME's to develop their 'innovation intensity' from which they can leverage to develop products and treatments for global markets.

Intellectual property is not a major issue for IDT as it conducts research on a 'fee for service' basis. The firms for whom IDT performs research services retain ownership of the intellectual property. Similarly, IDT has a 'fee for service' approach to its strategic alliance partners with whom it has long-term (10 year) supply agreements. This enables IDT to remain focused on its core competencies which underpin its innovative capabilities and 'innovation intensity'.

While ownership of patentable intellectual property developed by IDT is assigned to its fee-paying clients, the knowledge from leading-edge scientific research projects accumulates within the company, thereby adding value and capability to do more of the same type of work, better. This equips IDT to address the challenges of its clients and to find solutions that add value to their clients and shorten the duration of the innovation cycle without compromising quality. This provides clients with cost effective solutions, increasing their returns on investment while maintaining the efficacy of the processes.

Intellectual capital is different from intellectual property. As indicated, IDT does not take a position on formal intellectual property. However, intellectual capital is the vast accumulation of knowledge over the years that will lead to new knowledge and to increasing the company's innovation intensity. Staff at IDT acquire knowledge through experience with in-house work and contract 'fee-for-service' work. Skilled scientists retain that knowledge in the form of accumulated knowledge capital. New people come into the organisation and are taken care of by the culture. The low staff turnover of less than 5 per cent in the past ten years has enabled IDT to accumulate knowledge capital.

Major challenges to innovation management

Some major challenges to innovation management at IDT are outlined below.

Accessing large markets through commercial orientation

In the early 1990s, the corporate focus of IDT was on gaining entry to the US market and its potential clients. This was, and continues to be, an enormous challenge to any small Australian biotech company. But Blackman did not 'pursue' potential clients such as the big pharmaceutical companies in the United States. Instead, IDT's CEO spent millions of dollars seeking accreditation from their supreme regulatory Authority, namely the Food and Drug Administration (FDA). In 1998, the FDA gave IDT the rare accolade of an unqualified audit of its processes. This high-order accreditation from the 'tough-by-reputation' FDA was like 'a gold master-key'. FDA approval allowed IDT – a relatively insignificant and young company – to initiate enduring relationships with some of the world's largest pharmaceutical companies such as Pfizer, AstraZeneca, Wyeth and Johnson & Johnson (Lyons, 2002).

Overcoming the 'not invented here' syndrome

The FDA approval was a 'break-through', or watershed, in IDT's corporate development. Blackman was aware of the attitudes that pervaded some companies, such as innovations were 'not invented here' or 'heard it all before'. However, according to Blackman, the FDA accreditation and IDT's expertise in anti-cancer active ingredients caused most cynical global pharmaceutical executives 'to move to the edge of their chairs'.

Taxation system in Australia

IDT felt that the taxation system in Australia is not conducive to large capital investments in R&D compared with the 'zero' tax regimes of countries like Singapore. During the early years of the company, wholesale sales tax was another area of concern to Blackman – although the costs of raw materials for manufacturing or export products were exempt from sales tax, Australian manufactured goods contained sales tax in goods and services provided to other manufacturers in the supply chain. However, when manufacturers exported the semi-processed or finished product, there were no tax refunds available to them.

Distance from major markets

Most pharmaceutical research is done overseas because it makes sense to site bulk activities and manufacturing close to where the R&D takes place. However, IDT's active pharmaceutical ingredients are high value products compared with their weight and are 'cargo light'. Distance from major markets, such as the United States and Europe, is not a problem to IDT. Nevertheless, Dr Blackman said that establishing research and manufacturing operations in a country such as Singapore could not be entirely ruled out 'at some point in the future'. In the short-term, IDT's focus would continue to be on major markets in the United States and Europe.

Expanding the revenue base

IDT could expand its revenue base to fuel corporate growth by growing its existing business or capitalising on new opportunities closely related to its core competencies. Another avenue was through the integration of other businesses which were 'a good strategic fit' with IDT's operations. Achieving the right balance and mix of activities to enhance its innovation performance is an ongoing challenge for IDT. This involves assessing risks and making the right decisions. IDT's acquisition of CMAX from Mayne Health in 2002 provided an opportunity of integration. IDT's long-established pharmaceutical development expertise could now be coupled with the CMAX clinical trial services. This placed IDT in a strong position to achieve an immediate profit contribution from the CMAX business in the 2002/03 financial year.[1]

Enhancing innovation intensity and performance

Management strategies and practices that were identified as enhancing innovation intensity and performance are outlined below.

Quality standards and compliance

At all times and at every stage of a process, there is a high emphasis on *standardised* operating systems to achieve the highest possible quality standards of IDT's processes and products. ISO 9000 quality standards are 'the base line' for meeting very high quality standards at IDT. Staff are trained in compliance standards so they are aware of what is expected.

Disciplined research practices

Blackman maintains there is a strong connection between innovation and discipline: 'Our practiced philosophy is that innovation and science can be driven by disciplined documentation.' IDT is a highly documented but innovative organisation. Details of all experiments and communications are accurately recorded. This develops scientific discipline coupled with a business approach. It is Blackman's opinion that: 'Generally, scientists in the pharmaceutical industry are not disciplined enough to maintain accurate and comprehensive records.' IDT's experience is that maintaining high standards of documentation produces innovation intensity through discipline and thought, especially by its R&D people.

Maintaining documentation and clear 'audit trail'

Innovation and novelty go together with disciplined thought. PhDs at IDT maintain disciplined notebooks that provide a clear record. Blackman maintains that thorough and accurate documentation is essential to provide 'a clear audit trail of the decision-making process' to the FDA. According to Blackman, 'The FDA insists that whenever you make a decision, you have to be able to justify it. The FDA can ask. Why was this done? What was the decision or outcome? What was the justification for making such a decision?' These questions are particularly important in relation to the regulations and laws of the United States governing intellectual property that can date back to the day ideas and concepts were formally documented and not to the day that the patent was filed as is the case under Australian law. The importance of technological audits has been highlighted in the literature (Chiesa et al., 1996; Silverman, 2000).

Staff recruitment and development

Firms are intensely competitive for skilled knowledge workers. Skilled biotech employees have considerable opportunity to move from one company to another, making loyalty a key concern of employers and a critical factor in organisational and management practices (Eaton, 2001). Firms need to retain their skilled knowledge workers and to grow their intellectual capital if they are to become more innovative. Consequently, firms such as IDT pay significant attention to the human side of their organisations.

Retention of valuable employees

Blackman is mindful of attracting and retaining skilled employees. He comments: 'We pay our people pretty well'. Remuneration packages are set at levels that are intended to attract and retain first class executives capable of managing the entity's diverse operations and achieving the company's strategic objectives. The IDT remuneration committee reviews transactions between the organisation and its directors, or any interest associated with the directors, to ensure the structure and the terms of reference comply with the Corporations Laws and are appropriately disclosed. The committee also assumes responsibility for management succession planning, including the implementation of appropriate executive development programs and ensuring adequate arrangements are in place, so that appropriate candidates are recruited for later promotion and senior positions. The executive team also receives executive share options.

Project management and continuous improvement

Autonomous work teams manage projects. There is collaboration with the scientists who work in various project teams. Blackman places great emphasis on the importance of project management in managing the innovation process: 'Project management is very important at IDT'. There are milestones and objectives for every project. Performance and quality measures are in place at all stages of the continuum of each project from idea to implementation. 'Every project has milestones. Using a review process, we highlight what we did well and identify where we can improve', said Blackman. This highlights

IDT's attention to continuous improvement so that its processes and practices remain 'world class'. This approach is consistent with recent literature (Thieme et al., 2003).

Innovation intensity and performance at IDT

The key determinants that enhance innovation intensity and innovation performance at IDT are outlined below.

Core competencies of IDT's staff

IDT would not have been able to achieve commercially viable new products without the expertise and experience of its knowledge workers, particularly R&D staff. The growth of the company's intellectual capital – acquired from providing diagnostic services to clients – is also a key determinant of developing its innovative intensity, capabilities and performance.

Modern state-of-the-art laboratories, plant and facilities

Blackman and the top management team planned ahead so that the company had the processes and capacity to meet the growing demand for its existing products while, at the same time, it continued to develop innovative new products. This commercially oriented strategy also enabled IDT to maintain the highest possible quality standards.

Quality standards and continuous improvement

A key determinant of IDT's innovation performance has been its ability to achieve and maintain 'world class best practice' on quality control of its products and processes. These strategies and practices helped IDT to have six products approved by the FDA and will continue to attract more business from existing and new clients.

Access to the large markets in the United States and Europe

FDA approval of many of IDT's products enabled IDT to access large global markets. This generated cash flows and profitability which enabled IDT to expand its manufacturing plant and laboratories which, in turn, increased its innovative capabilities to drive its performance. IDT developed 'innovation intensity' and capabilities prior to gaining access to large markets. This also required a commercially oriented strategy.

Leadership and vision of the CEO

Blackman has demonstrated leadership and entrepreneurship. He possesses the rare combination of both scientific skills and business acumen. Blackman also has the vision and knowledge to recognise further opportunities for developing and manufacturing active pharmaceutical ingredients (APIs).

DISCUSSION QUESTIONS

1. What are IDT's core capabilities?
2. Does IDT have a sound strategic focus, given its range of activities?
3. How can IDT's capabilities be financially evaluated?
4. To what extent is IDT's future revenue stream dependent on continued outsourcing by mainstream players, and is this a concern?
5. What would happen if Dr Blackman suddenly left the company?
6. How would you further grow the company?
7. Is this company limiting its prospects by being located in Australia?

References

Chiesa, V. 1996. 'Separating research from development: evidence from the pharmaceutical industry'. *European Management Journal*, 14(6): 638–47.

Eaton, S. 2001. 'If you can use them: flexibility policies, organisational commitment, and perceived productivity.' *Working paper RWP01–009*, MA: Harvard University.

Lyons, J. 2002. 'Making the most of active ingredients.' *Australian Financial Review*, 29 January, 2002: 39.

Silverman, A. B. 2000. 'The importance of an intellectual property audit.' Book review in *Journal of Operations Management*, 52(8): 56.

Thieme, R. J., Song, M., and Shin, G. C. 2003. 'Project management characteristics and new product survival.' *Journal of Product Innovation Management*, 20(2): 104–19.

Note

1 The CMAX division of IDT operates a 48-bed clinical trials unit and bio-analytical laboratory within the Royal Adelaide Hospital. This unit provides Phase I and later phase clinical trial services. In the 2002/03 IDT Annual Report, Blackman commented: 'A significant contribution to increased revenue was the acquisition last year of the Adelaide based CMAX clinical trials unit. The unit was acquired in June 2002 and its operations are now fully integrated into the company's operating business.'

New Zealand King Salmon: Value-Chain Innovation

Jay Sankaran

Introduction

Driving to work alongside the scenic and sprawling Tahunanui beach, Paul Steere, Chief Executive of New Zealand King Salmon (NZKS), had reason to smile at the holidaymakers who bathed in the glorious Nelson sun. A recent industry report had revealed NZKS to be in the top 1–2 per cent of salmon farming companies around the world in terms of profitability. It was a far cry from the trying times the company had gone through some years previously. Paul and others in the executive team had the firm conviction that the turnaround was due in no small measure to NZKS's concerted attempts to engage in R&D even in financially troubled periods.

In actual fact, Paul had convened a strategy meeting for that morning, following the three-day Waitangi weekend of 2004. The executive team of NZKS comprised, besides Paul, Don Everitt, GM (Sales & Marketing) who also oversaw new product development (NPD), Bryce Gilchrist, who was GM (Corporate Services & Finance), Paul McHugh, who was GM (Manufacturing), and Stewart Hawthorn, the GM (Aquaculture). The agenda was the budgeting and allocation of investment in R&D; a vertically integrated company such as NZKS naturally offered several avenues for such investment, thereby invariably calling for tradeoffs.

Strategic focus

NZKS was formed in 1996 with the privatisation and merger of New Zealand's two largest salmon companies: Southern Ocean Seafoods Ltd and Regal

Salmon Ltd. It was a wholly-owned subsidiary of Oregon Group Ltd, which was ultimately owned by the Tiong Group. NZKS had an annual turnover of more than $50 million and employed more than 330 staff. It accounted for 80 per cent of New Zealand's total production of farmed king salmon, also known as Chinook, and 40 per cent of the world production of the king salmon species. The company had four salmon farms, two hatcheries and processing facilities (at Nelson) including a ready-to-eat factory. It also had a broodstock research facility at Kaituna, about 60km from Nelson.

Strategically, NZKS had to focus on one species, king salmon, it being the viable introduced species to NZ, while many of the large salmon producers worldwide farmed Atlantic salmon, which was easier to manage (for instance, Atlantic salmon tended to be faster growing and was a more efficient converter of feed into flesh). NZKS avoided farming other species of fish (e.g., shellfish), restricting itself to the processing of such seafood, even if it might encounter difficulties in meeting market demand for by-product derivatives.

The focus on one product-species was related to NZKS's approach of vertical integration. Besides retaining the benefits from value-creation, the company was able to guarantee quality and reliability by owning and controlling every stage of production. Everitt believed the strategy of vertical integration was

> deliberate from day one, for the reason there were no other suppliers. So we had to grow our own fish in a hatchery that we owned, we had to take those fish to a sea-cage farm that we owned, and we had to harvest them using our own harvesting team because there wasn't anybody else.

NZKS also bought out a company, McCure Seafoods, which used to do a lot of contract packing. NZKS had become McCure's major client by the time of the acquisition. While NZKS appeared to have choices for third-party logistics services, it opted to use their own distribution 'because nobody quite understands to the extent that we do'. Further, vertical integration at NZKS appeared to snowball to other aspects of its operation. Everitt noted:

> We had to have our own seafood processing facility. Although there were many other choices, we realised that we had everything else, so we might as well do it ourselves.

However, NZKS had not pursued vertical integration when economies of scale couldn't be realised, an example being the production of highly specific salmon feed, which was presently imported from Chile and to a lesser extent, Tasmania.

The focus on king salmon enabled NZKS to maintain a point of difference in the market. Everitt remarked:

> King salmon is a highly regarded, well-reputed species to go to the market with. It's in scarce supply so we get a premium for our product. You can grow

Atlantic salmon anywhere in the world at low cost, so those producers fight it out for the low prices that they can get for it. We have some comparative disadvantages in resource space, productivity, feed costs, and transport, which force us into growing a premium product. King salmon suits that niche.[1] Further, over time, we have developed intellectual property about vertically integrating the hatching, production, harvesting, processing, sales, distribution, and marketing of king salmon in a profitable manner.

Consequently, NZKS looked to create and operate in niche markets for its species in the markets in which it competed against Atlantic salmon, such as Australia, Japan, and North America. Since NZKS accounted for 40 per cent of world production of farmed king salmon, it was able to set its own price depending on how much it wanted to sell. NZKS was able to command a sizeable premium over Atlantic salmon in overseas markets (e.g., Japan). The premium increased with the extent of value-addition, which provided incentive to NZKS to strive for differentiation of products right to the end of the supply chain.

Commitment to value-addition

Value-added product at NZKS, as Everitt explained, is 'something which has had more value-added than a whole fish'. NZKS realised somewhere between 30 and 50 per cent of its sales by value beyond a whole salmon. As one would expect, there were varying degrees of value-addition at NZKS depending on the number of stages that product flowed through in the processing facility. Highest forms of value-addition were represented by products such as smoked salmon and salmon dips (which were currently being made by another manufacturer under contract to NZKS). A lower level of value-addition was portions or pieces of salmon (e.g., salmon kebabs). Salmon fillets and cuts represented, as Everitt described, 'more intermediate-type products because they are somewhere between a value-added product and a raw commodity. But they have had more work done on them. They have been transformed.' The benefits, from a marketing perspective, of downstream processing were the ability to realise greater premiums through packaging and branding of product.

To pursue differentiation from Atlantic salmon, NZKS had also deliberately stayed away from the low-cost, frozen-food, commodity market; fresh chilled and farmed king salmon accounted for about 75 per cent of NZKS's exports to Japan by tonnage. Everitt explained:

> When you're competing with the frozen product typically for an industrial processor, you are competing against Norway and Chile with the cheapest possible salmon. Most often, they just lump together Chinook and Atlantic salmon. So it's not easy for us to be in a frozen market.

The differentiation strategy had been facilitated by increasing quality discernment on the part of end-consumers in Japan and latterly, Australia. Everitt expressed that end-consumers 'appreciated the quality difference' between the two forms of salmon. In NZ, consumers were already familiar with quality product, as witnessed in the poor reception accorded to imported Canadian salmon products. In Japan, the emergence of labelling laws was working to NZKS's favour. Everitt explained that under the laws, 'If Japanese supermarket chains want to have kings on their retail shelves, they have to come to us or to one of our small number of competitors.'

Another element of NZKS's differentiation strategy was related to commodity markets and the reduction of its exposure to commodity cycles. NZKS accordingly attempted to make its supply chain more demand-driven (growing more fish 'in response to a potential perceived demand as opposed to growing more fish so that we can go out and sell it somewhere'). As a result, harvest volumes had been relatively static for some years now. Instead, NZKS had sought to focus on bottom-line/revenue growth rather than volume growth, while also ensuring reasonable tonnage. In turn, such growth necessitated a 'reasonable amount of investment in the development of new products and new processes in the factory, new distribution, market development, etc.' (The percentage of sales that was invested by NZKS in R&D was more than that for most firms in the New Zealand aquaculture sector. Further, NZKS's investment, as a percentage of sales, in the development of new products and new processes [in both manufacturing and distribution] as well as the development of new markets was comparable to that invested by larger aquaculture companies overseas.)

Research and development at NZKS

Everitt distinguished between 'pure R,' which refers to production research, and 'D,' which includes new product development (NPD). Thus, the research conducted at Kaituna would be 'pure R'.

Production research

Production research at NZKS referred broadly to developing better ways of growing fish ('raw material') in terms of increasing volume, achieving consistency of supply, and/or lowering production costs to enhance bottom-line profitability. One strand of production research entailed the design of fish to meet particular business/market needs. Market needs could be quality attributes (colour, oil, texture, etc.) that were fed back to the aquaculture team by Sales & Marketing. Business imperatives would include the faster growth of fish, better conversion of feed into flesh, and the ability to 'fill the pipeline in the off-season from about mid-February to about mid-June'.

This consistency of supply of raw materials could also be enabled by influencing the maturation of salmon through, for instance, hatchery technology or broodstock selection. Everitt explained that NZKS 'selects fish for rapid maturation by searching through the breed stock'. Likewise, NZKS could opt to deploy fish in different farms that had varying biological characteristics. Feeding regimes were another lever for influencing maturation, as Everitt explained:

> If you feed them more often, they will grow faster, or grow bigger. They may grow inefficiently if you force them, but at least you have that choice. Alternatively, if you want to slow down their growth, you feed them less feed so you have got some influence on the farms.

The techniques cited above may not have been unique to NZKS and hence may not have constituted IP (intellectual property) for NZKS. However, as noted earlier, NZKS had found a unique means of 'putting all the bits together which are already patented by other people'.

Development of new products

One strand of NPD at NZKS was the development of new products that met market needs. Examples of these needs included simplicity (e.g., use by children) and convenience. Corporate clients (e.g., airline caterers) could have specific needs with regard to functionality (e.g., for the NZ food/quick-service market) or size, as Everitt explained: 'In the catering industry in New Zealand, there are some particular dimensions of sliced smoked salmon that some food-service operators need to have.' In cases where the needs of specific corporate clients were being met, NZKS attempted to redeploy its developmental work for other prospective non-competing clients. That way, it increased sales volumes and achieved a better return on its investment in developmental work.

From the perspective of value creation, an important class of new products derived from the innovative use of by-products. McHugh observed that 'an idea was to smoke and pack fins from fish as cocktail nibbles and it has been a very successful by-product utilisation'. Likewise, salmon tails were also now processed into smoked products. Mince made from fish frames was another example of by-product utilisation.

Finally, a more minor form of NPD would be range extensions and/or development of variants (e.g., new pack-sizes).

Development of new processes

At NZKS, the development of new products was often accompanied by the development of new processes; indeed, the split of the developmental work across products and processes was 'about 50/50'. An example of this was gravalax, wherein the salmon is marinated in the traditional Scandinavian manner in sugar, salt, and spices and then flavoured with finely chopped green dill leaf. However, NZKS had developed its own variants over the years, whereby there wasn't as strong a need to disguise the flavour with dill. Everitt explained that in the context of developing new processes to support new products, in lieu of

> strategic alliances with machinery suppliers or equipment suppliers or anything like that, . . . we go on overseas trips to have a look at different products that come through different processes and keep our eyes open using the Net, do specific research . . .

While process development was often driven by product development, the introduction of new process technologies could also in turn enable NPD. An example at NZKS was the deployment of automated cutting and slicing machines that were purpose-built by a local manufacturer for the company. Besides increasing product quality, labour efficiency, and yield, the machines 'opened doors to different sliced configurations for customers,' as McHugh described it.

Tom McKay, Process Systems Engineer, cited this technology as an example of process innovation:

> We took something, modified it, and made something in the top of the South Island that no one else was quite doing and that was a step change in our view, in the quality of our slices . . . The innovation there was to change the actual cutting process.

Process innovation could also arise independently of the development of new products. A good example was steam pasteurisation, for which NZKS had filed patents. The benefits from steam pasteurisation compared to the earlier practice of chlorinating fish in water baths included: labour efficiency; reduced input costs (i.e. no need for chlorine); improved health and safety; improved wholesomeness and food acceptability; increased naturalness of the process; and the elimination of risks that are associated with biological outbreaks as well as the resources that are needed to manage those risks.

Such innovations represented 'step changes' that the company's process systems engineer Tom McKay explained, 'NZKS couldn't have achieved . . . with continuous improvement, with operators concentrating more.'

Everitt described the continuous improvement program at NZKS as finding 'new ways of making the same product but in a more efficient or safer or more profitable manner'. Several other more minor process developments were subsumed under the continuous improvement program, such as in packaging or material-handling. For instance, NZKS had begun to use cardboard boxes in lieu of polystyrene bins to service some of its larger wholesalers partly because, as Paul Gurr, the Market Services Manager, noted, such boxes entail 'less damage to a certain extent because fish get layered properly into the carton so they don't get thrown around whereas with the poly-bin, the noses of fish can get squashed'. Another example of a process development that could be subsumed under the umbrella of the continuous improvement program was the use of electric forklifts in lieu of gas forklifts. The benefits from electric forklifts included a lower cost of operation, improved safety (no fumes), greater compactness, and greater versatility on site.

Developments that McHugh cited included the use of sophisticated laminate preparations to laminate bags for the ready-to-eat market, the improvement of 'microns on our plastic,' and the improvement of 'flute strengths of our cardboard'. Other developments included the use of sliding racks to enable efficiencies in order-picking and packing, as well as modifications in the packaging such as the avoidance of Ezi-Peel to minimise vacuum loss while maintaining user convenience. (However, Paul Gurr clarified that, instead of emerging as a minor development project, the redesign of packaging was part of 'a whole re-branding exercise of the products where they came out with totally new packaging, totally new design, and worked from there'.)

'Pure R' versus 'D'

As already noted, NZKS expended a significant portion of its annual sales on developmental work. However, other salmon companies around the world appeared to do quite a bit more on production research than NZKS. Everitt acknowledged that could be partly because of the natural advantages enjoyed by NZKS in NZ, but noted that 'as the industry has globalised and corporatised overseas, you are getting economies of scale allowing those larger corporates to spend more on research, not necessarily on product development, but more on production research'.

The relative expenditure on production research as opposed to developmental research was an interesting and strategic variable at NZKS. In the first instance, this issue could be observed in light of NZKS's vertically integrated structure, namely, its ownership of both production and processing arms. Further, the two strands of research had somewhat (but not entirely) different drivers. Thus, one driver of production research at NZKS was the slow maturation of king salmon. In this context, Everitt cited the more extreme example of Paua farming in which slowness of maturation was even more problematic:

Paua farming uses recirculation tanks to grow paua or abalone at a faster rate. Their issue is that abalone or paua grows quite slowly, it takes like seven years, I believe, to mature a shell big enough to harvest. What they do is speed that up. There is a distinct advantage.

The seasonality of maturation cycles, when contrasted with the business imperative of year-round supply of immediate fresh chilled salmon, was another driver for production research. Everitt further explained:

Unfortunately salmon being the biological organisms that they are, they want to mature, they have a season, you know, like any other organism. What we are trying to do is either suppress the maturation so that we can harvest for a longer period of time or accelerate the maturation so that we can bring them into a time of the year when they wouldn't normally be big enough or ready enough to harvest.

Another interesting driver for production research was the very location at which such research added value in the value chain: the fish farm. As Everitt clarified:

If the guys on farms can do some research . . . to get their costs down, it will benefit the rest of the supply chain. So if we start with a lower cost for material from which we want to develop new products, we are all better off. So we have tended to start at the farm end rather than the value end.

This push towards production research was also reinforced by the manner in which NZKS evaluated financial performance. Everitt explained:

We convert everything back to gross margin generated per kilo of raw material fish input to the process. It is easier to add value to a lower-cost product than a higher-cost product; you tend again to want to concentrate on getting your fish cost down.

Interestingly, the very difficulty of producing raw material was also an impetus for developmental research at NZKS. While contrasting NZKS with other seafood companies that had easier access to raw material (e.g., by hunting and gathering), Gilchrist observed:

The reason we invest so much in growing our product is there is quite a long cycle time involved – 18 months, 2 years, $2\frac{1}{2}$ years – depending on which strategy your fish is coming out of the water. Then once it is out of the water, within a few hours you can destroy the value of that product. So we have needed to be quite smart in what we have done and the way we have developed the processes. And also there isn't really anybody else doing what we are doing in the way that we are doing it for us to look to and say, 'Who is the leader and who should we follow.' We have had to be quite creative ourselves. So, yield is very important to us because of the cost of getting the fish out of the water in the first place. There's quite a significant dollar amount per kilo being invested into it and somebody can just lose 5 per cent by slicing it the wrong way.

As a result of the high cost of the raw material, McHugh observed,

> There has been quite a push for looking at the by-product streams and trying to add value to those. . . . An A-grade whole gilled and gutted fish is so expensive that it is very hard to add additional value to that . . . excluding the fillets and steaks of course.

The high marginal returns of by-product derivatives (e.g., cocktail nibbles) were another incentive for increased utilisation of by-products; McHugh explained that the input costs of these by-products 'are carried by the A-grade product stream and you can get gains there'.

Gilchrist explained that the high cost of producing king salmon was also the driver for kebabs:

> We were looking at how we could utilise the lower grade of fish, the fish that either had scale damage or a seal bite. So if we cut them up into kebabs we were getting a better return out of that lower grade fish than you would otherwise have, but kebabs themselves are now quite a volume-item.

As already noted, a general thrust for developmental research at NZKS was its focus on revenue/bottom-line growth in lieu of volume growth, reflecting, as Paul Gurr put it, the recognition that value-addition was the long-term 'means to survival . . . in this kind of industry.' While Everitt remarked that NZKS 'have always had the same view and vision' with regard to the imperative and importance of developmental research, the realisation of the vision could, in reality, be tempered by extraneous factors, such as industry recession. He clarified, 'When you are faced with poor cash flows and low profitability, you tend to concentrate on costs before value because there is less risk. Any production cost savings go directly to the bottom-line.' On the other hand, 'as the profit goes up then there's more cash for new product development . . . When any industry is under financial pressure, if anything they may tend to cut their development budgets; they may retain their research budgets for getting out of trouble, but they will be driven towards doing more cost-based research.' Nevertheless, the longer-term trend at NZKS was to invest more 'towards value-added products rather than production cost-driven research'.

Innovation and development processes at NZKS

Sources of product and process ideas

At NZKS, innovations were part of the company-wide ethos and philosophy. McHugh explained that the company had all 170 people employed in the processing plants involved in R&D in some way or another, including those at the operator level. Consequently, several noteworthy ideas for both product and process innovation emerged from the coalface. Gilchrist cited the pasteurisation process, which had 'come from one of our own people'. The use of fins to make cocktail nibbles was described by McHugh as another example. While noting there was 'nothing formal' by way of incentives to employees for idea-generation, Everitt explained, 'We have found the culture of our company motivates staff and managers in taking an interest in new ideas and improvements which may be taken up.'

Besides employees and corporate clients with specific needs, another source of product and process ideas was overseas distributors (e.g., Nissui) who had staff in Nelson. Everitt clarified that the company met regularly with overseas distributors in offshore locations and potential new products were constantly discussed. In the domestic market, the NZ Marketing Manager, who was based in Auckland, was a source of product ideas. He had largely been employed on account of his background in the FMCG (fast-moving-consumer-goods) sector.

NZKS also used overseas trends as a source of ideas for products or packaging. McHugh observed, 'We hear about [particular trends] and think maybe we should get more into those; it is just an osmosis event, really keeping our eyes open.' McHugh cited an example in the context of packaging:

> Recently one of our guys saw a product presented differently. He just saw it in a market, so he ripped the label off the container and found out the name of the company.

Tom McKay elaborated:

> The fish came in a cardboard box, beautifully printed and full of ice—but still transported by airplanes. So we found out how they achieved that. It's all based on different layers of packaging, and absorption and insulation.

Criteria for screening product ideas

All product ideas were vetted through a screening process that employed various criteria, including their potential contribution and viability. The most direct measure of economic value was the gross margin generated per kilo of raw material fish input to the process. Everitt explained: 'We can look at the proposed product and compare its value with its unprocessed form as a commodity.'

The volumes needed to breakeven were a related economic consideration. For range-extensions whose launch results tended to be predictable, Everitt explained that NZKS would do 'simple testing in-house, using informal and formal focus groups consisting of experienced staff'. For innovative products, NZKS supplemented internal focus groups with 'additional external qualitative research provided by external researchers' that would generally involve 'a blind-test of either randomly selected or targeted individuals' (e.g., children for kebabs). Omnibus quantitative studies and exit interviews were an additional recourse to mitigate risk. In cases of high risk, NZKS had 'developed prototype samples in limited quantity and tested specially selected stores or regions'. Key accounts, especially food service accounts and professional caterers, also furnished inputs in terms of projected sales volumes. Likewise, supermarket buyers were sounded out by NZKS for their ideas and agreement about market acceptance.

However, Gilchrist clarified there were several benefits 'outside of just the straight economic costing' of a product idea. He used the example of kebabs:

> Kebabs give us a lot more profile in the market than any other salmon company. Nobody else does kebabs so there are benefits.

Steere noted:

> There is also a corporate advantage: our kebabs were the only NZ product sold at the Sydney Olympics – some 60,000 of them to caterers in the athletes' village. So, we were able to publicise this coup.

In a related vein, Everitt described NZKS's push for differentiation in the domestic market:

> We will actually create a whole new product that we think will sell, one that is discernibly different and differentiated in the market. Not 'me toos'. So we will be truly innovative in the New Zealand market.

Gilchrist explained that such product-ideas lead the market (as opposed to being driven by the marketplace):

> You are actually developing the product, the concept and the idea and the people are latching on to it, and that creates the market. So it is really quite innovative. You are actually creating the opportunity and then developing the need, because it is not like there are people out there saying . . . or thinking, 'Where can I get kebabs?' The object of developments such as kebabs is to gain a foothold into a new area which can then expand further for us, as opposed to just trying to drive more of the same product out there.

The economic gains of new product ideas have also to be gauged in terms of their potential to enhance opportunities for cross-selling. As Gilchrist explained:

> We also evaluate how many of the customers are there because they can get salmon kebabs from us, for example. If they are getting kebabs from us then they are probably going to get their fillets from us as well. They could have got their fillets from another supplier, who couldn't provide kebabs. So it is providing a whole mix into the market.

In this context, McHugh cited the example of caviar:

> The product has very low volume sales, but the barriers to entry for
> competitors are very high. So through adding caviar to part of the range, you
> know, that allows us to leverage existing products over and above competitors
> into certain customers.

Longevity of the product idea and corresponding potential for long-term
stable growth was another consideration, as Gilchrist explained:

> NPD is a strategic move. It is not like putting a new product out there
> expecting to make a big win for 6 months, 18 months, then it's dead. We are
> looking for longer-term stable products that just keep growing the use of our
> core product [fresh chilled farm salmon].

As far as product ideas for exports are concerned, Everitt explained:

> We don't want to take the risk of taking a new product to the market when we
> don't have a customer base for it . . . That's a very expensive process for an
> exporter to do . . . Export new product development projects will emphasise
> customisation for known demand. We tend to work with customers in Japan to
> develop what they want. [This could be a product that someone else supplied
> to the market.]

Organisational structures and management systems

NZKS had cross-functional teams in at least two levels, management and
project level. The NPD management team screened new ideas and reviewed
progress on projects, meeting regularly for these purposes. Project teams comprised of a project champion who belonged to the management team, besides
the relevant marketing and sales managers (whether domestic or export), the
food technologist, various factory supervisors, the process engineer, the technical manager, and if needed, the logistics manager. Everitt noted the cross-
functional constitution of the team minimised the likelihood of 'all those
things that trip you up at the end of the day, you know' (e.g., odd-shaped
product).

The rationale for having the champion from the management team was to
expedite project progress. Everitt explained, 'We cannot afford to wait between
meetings for progress to be made. The champion will push that along.' The
champion, in turn, typically comes from marketing or sales because, as he
described, 'they seem to have the most vested interests with the customer
relationship that they want to get out there'. For the same reason, NPD at
NZKS fell under the purview of the GM (Sales & Marketing).

Nevertheless, in keeping with the cross-functionality of the NPD effort
at NZKS, project champions were also appointed from outside of Sales &
Marketing, e.g., from processing. Everitt explained their role:

They can get quite passionate about a new product idea. 'This is a great new product, I want you guys to go out there and sell it.' And we [in Sales & Marketing] will get challenged by that; we will have to go do something about it.

As the number of NPD projects had increased, a greater number of individuals had become involved. In turn, NZKS had sought to diffuse the heightened workload. This had enhanced the cross-functionality of the NPD effort.

In the course of the project, the NPD team also consulted with personnel within and outside NZKS. They included the IT manager and the financial accountant, in addition to aquaculture staff. If the NPD project had been initiated on behalf of a key account, then that account was also consulted in the course of the project. NZKS did not have representatives from key accounts sit on the project teams, but they had regular meetings with the companies. Various members of the team might go and visit with Air NZ, for example, especially the technical person, the NPD technologist, the GM (Sales & Marketing), or the key account manager.

The NPD effort at NZKS was also facilitated by the relatively small and flat structure. The geographic proximity of the management team and the workforce was another enabler, as was the absence of formality, as described by Everitt:

I, my boss and the other general managers here don't stand for any sort of bureaucratic nonsense about who says what and when and who uses which form to report it by.

With regard to costing the NPD effort in general and projects in particular, Gilchrist observed:

At this stage we have had much bigger issues to be dealing with than trying to isolate costs, because there are much bigger gains in dealing with other areas of business information.

Besides salary budgets, some corporate marketing overhead was also entailed. Other resources that were involved in trials included whole cages of fish and processing plant capacity, though pilot plant work could be done on weekends.

In terms of measuring the effectiveness of the NPD effort, NZKS monitored the percentage of sales realised from products that had been developed in the previous 12 months, for which a challenging target was explicitly stated in the company's strategic plan. NZKS also had a target time-to-market for each new product idea. At any one time, NZKS had about 15 ongoing developmental projects with a 'pretty good' success rate.

The executive meeting

Paul Steere, who chaired the meeting, opened it thus:

> Bryce's 2004/05 business forecast has indicated the available outlay for investment in the next financial year. As you all know, there is always room at the margin if we can make a good case with the owners [the Tiong group]. But we do need to identify priorities for R&D at this meeting.

Looking up from the various agenda papers and turning to Don, Stewart noted:

> Don, I note some swell ideas for new products tabulated by you. Certainly the ones concerning reformed products rather like our salmon dips, are a shoo-in – too good to pass.

Don responded:

> Yeah, I know. Several of those listed were actually from a compilation e-mailed to me by Paul M. Some have come from our NZ marketing manager up in Auckland as well.

Paul McHugh noted:

> Well, Don, I can assure you some of the folks at manufacturing are quite passionate about their suggestions! They would love nothing better than for Sales & Marketing to take up the challenge of going out there and selling such products!

Don replied, 'And they can rest assured that we are just as keen to take up the challenge! My concern though is with regard to the ideas that I had had with regard to production research.' Turning to Stewart, he continued:

> Stu, you will recall that we at Sales & Marketing recently sat down with your guys up Picton way, and specified market needs for fish based on inputs from Japanese distributors. I am keen that we at King Salmon pursue the strategy of differentiating fish for different markets, not just Japan, but Australia as well (and possibly others), because Australia is becoming an increasingly important export destination for us. What is your take on that research?

Stewart paused for a moment before replying:

> Well, as we are all aware, it will take a while for such research to bear fruit given how long it takes us to grow king salmon in the first instance. That said, I suppose that given our present financial health, we can be a bit more relaxed about taking a longer-term perspective on R&D investment than we might have some years back. Do you agree, Paul [Steere]?

Paul Steere responded:

That would be a fair comment, yes. It would be easier for us to argue for more funding given that research and development has played a big part getting us to where we are, and remains a key strategic plank of our business platform.

Paul McHugh noted:

But returning to the point that Stewart was making, we should not forget that fish in several cages are coming to maturity and would be ripe for harvest in the next year and a bit. Our cycle time for NPD is just a few months long. So it might make sense to head in the direction of NPD at least initially so that we can develop new products (besides new markets) and transform the raw material instead of merely gilling and gutting fish and shipping them away – and complete the NPD projects in time for processing some of the increased harvest. Maybe we can defer some of the longer-term production research later in the year? But then cash-flows and ROI come into the picture as well, Bryce, don't they?

Bryce responded:

That is correct. We must also not forget that efficiency gains in processing and distribution are also relatively easy to realise. I guess you guys have had a look at the shortlist of project-ideas that the continuous improvement folks have developed. I have always felt that one key point of difference between other players in the industry and us is that we pay that much more attention to processing and distribution given we are farming the equivalent of deer while the others are farming cattle, so to speak. Moreover, the cycle times for continuous improvement projects tend to be short as well.

At this stage, Paul Steere interposed:

Well, that analogy with deer farming cuts both ways, doesn't it? I.e., it also makes sense for us to continue our investment in research on the production side notwithstanding the progressive development of value-added products and the continuous improvement programs – simply because of the acute sensitivity of ensuring that we optimise the right salmon size and harvest quantity, while keeping costs minimal. Given how much we spend on salmon feed, the multiplier in terms of production cost savings associated with a marginal improvement in the commercial feed conversion ratio is huge! Moreover, the larger the fish, the greater the return we get per kilo in most export markets.

Swivelling his chair and rising, Paul Steere continued:

Well guys, I think we have rather summed up the broad issues that we face. Let's break for coffee and when we return, we will review the benefit vs. investment cost analysis for the various segments so that we can quantify the pie in terms of value and priorities.

DISCUSSION QUESTIONS

1. Four attributes of innovation that have been cited in the literature include: 'innovation quality' (number of successfully marketed new products, new product sales as a percentage of total sales, contribution of new product sales to cash-flow or profits); 'innovation capacity' (R&D expenditure as a percentage of total sales, complemented by evaluations of the organisation of innovation in the company, such as the relationship between marketing and R&D and other aspects of market-orientation); 'willingness to innovate' (an element of the corporate culture that can be related to general management's stimulation of innovativeness by fostering flexible organisation and avoiding bureaucracy in the company and by stimulating and adequately rewarding innovative employees), and 'innovation speed', which refers to the speed of the NPD process. For each attribute, organise the relevant evidence for NZKS from the case.

2. Explain how each of the following inferences may be drawn from the NZKS case study.
   - Greater a firm's strategic focus on differentiation away from commodity markets, greater its investment in new product development.
   - Greater a firm's strategic focus on differentiation through quality, greater its investment in new process development and continuous improvement.
   - Greater the cost of harvesting a unit of raw material, greater the investment in R&D in by-product utilisation.
   - Greater the cost of harvesting a unit of raw material, greater the effort involved in continuous improvement and innovation in processing and distribution.
   - Longer the maturation cycle of the species being farmed, greater the investment in production research for that species.
   - Greater the seasonality in the maturation cycle of the species being farmed, greater the investment in production research for that species.

3. In pictorial form, show how at NZKS, innovation and development ultimately proceed from the competitive strategies of the firm, and how they enhance the bottom-line performance of the firm.

4. What lessons can other NZ seafood firms in general, and aquaculture companies in particular, learn from NZKS's experience?

5. How would you systematically analyse the benefits and investment costs for the various segments of R&D at NZKS?

Note

1 NZKS's overall production by tonnage was about 1 per cent of the size of the Japanese market for salmon.

Pilila Clothing Company Goes Lean

David Parker

The textile industry has all but evaporated from Australia and New Zealand over recent decades. How might it be possible to counter the low wages and huge scale of operations in countries such as China, and remain viable in this industry in Australia or New Zealand?

Box cs3.1: Productivity Commission review report excerpt

The Textiles, Clothing and Footwear (TCF) sector in Australia today is very different from that in the past. Traditionally, local activity was characterised by a series of manufacturing processes, with firms along the supply chain purchasing inputs from (mainly local) upstream suppliers and selling outputs to (mainly local) downstream customers. High tariffs and quota protection ensured the continued viability of firms along the chain, restricted the ability to source from competing offshore suppliers and reduced the incentive to find new (export) markets. Retailers played a largely passive role in selling final products designed and supplied by manufacturers with limited direct contribution to purchasing or production decisions . . .

In recent years, however, competition from emerging low-wage production centres, slowing growth in domestic consumer demand, large reductions in domestic assistance and increased concentration in retailing have collectively placed new pressures on local TCF manufacturers. Many firms have left the sector, while others have rationalised, merged, and pursued new sourcing strategies to survive. As a result, aggregate domestic TCF manufacturing activity has contracted and import penetration has risen sharply.

Industry restructuring and rationalisation, in combination with a sharp rise in import penetration to more than 50 per cent of the total TCF market, have resulted in contractions in overall TCF manufacturing output and employment. . . . The

---

sector's aggregate value added fell by more than 30 per cent in real terms between 1990–01 and 2001–02, while employment was approximately 35 per cent lower. At the TCF industry level, clothing and footwear production has contracted the most with employment losses in these two industries accounting for 60 per cent of the decline in total sectoral employment since 1991 (although there may have been some offsetting increase in the number of outworkers . . .).

This experience has coincided with a surge in imports of clothing and footwear, with China the main source. It supplied nearly 70 per cent of all Australia's imports of clothing and footwear in 2002–03.

Despite these findings set out above, the Productivity Commission concludes that there is a future to the TCF industry in Australia. Contrary to perceptions in some quarters, it is inappropriate to categorise the TCF sector as being in terminal decline. Prospects in particular activities are quite strong and some firms and industry associations are optimistic about their future, even though they face increasing global competition and lower protection.

Source
Productivity Commission, *Review of TCF Assistance Inquiry Report*, Report no 26, 31 July 2003, p. 9.

An example of a clothing manufacturing company that has taken up the challenge from economic pressures as well as tremendous competition from cheap foreign imports has been Pilila Clothing, which is based in Toowoomba, Queensland. When first established in the 1970s, the company was a traditional 'cut-make-and-trim' operation. In other words, it would receive orders from large clothing design companies, cut the garment shapes from the rolls of fabric, sew the parts together, press, finish the garments, and pack for distribution to the retail outlets. Pilila was typical of hundreds of factories throughout Australia. The highly repetitive nature of the work meant that the production layout lent itself to a flow-system. Several hundred machinists were employed on a piecework payment-by-results basis to carry out the highly skilled, labour-intensive operations.

With the massive influx of overseas garments, however, Pilila (as well as most other clothing manufacturing companies) found that that it could not compete on price. This was particularly evident in the mass market where margins are small and the largest cost element is the labour content during production. In the late 1990s, Pilila was considering closing due to lack of orders. Even after considerable efforts to reduce operational costs had been carried out, its comparative final costs still favoured the low-labour-cost imports. It was then that the company came to learn about just-in-time methods of working. As a result, it refocused its product specialisation from the mass market to niche opportunities. Such niche, high-value markets, however, required low-volume, high-variety products. The corporate sector, for example, was initially targeted. Garments included uniforms, corporate-customised sets (for example, banks, petrol stations needing corporate shirts, and trousers), government agencies, school clothing, and similar unique clothing needs. High-performance clothing was also targeted, e.g., local football team shirts. All these products had a common theme, namely that their quantities were small but they attracted premium prices. However, customer satisfaction was of paramount importance to gain return orders. The method of manufacture as well as the way Pilila had done business in the past needed radical change. Lean systems and just-in-time operations appeared to be a solution.

In Pilila's conventional batch or 'push type' manufacturing process, the two time components of the production line were: (1) the working time; and (2) the handling time. Handling time between operations because of the size of the batches accounted for up to 40 per cent of the total production time. Some 40 per cent of total manufacturing time was therefore wasted. With the pressure of large batches and the repetitive nature of the work process, it follows that an operator is more likely to suffer from low levels of job satisfaction and lapses in quality control. Production time from start to finish of any article was often counted in weeks. Invariably, defective items were only detected by an inspector when the batches were finally completed.

Ron Smith, owner of Pilila Clothing, is one manufacturer who has seen the difficulties facing Australian companies as a result of traditional methods of production. His experience both in Victoria and Queensland in garment manufacture indicated an urgent need for change. Many of these problems will take years to solve but a significant number can be eliminated by the implementation of a principle called 'Unit Production'. With a redesigned workspace, significant benefits, including an increase of up to 40 per cent in productivity, have been achieved – much of it from the more efficient use of eliminated handling time.

Contrary to standard practices of batch production with separate functions performed by an operator on large batches, the unit production principle involves a team fabricating a single item from the beginning to the finished product. The production line has several significant differences. Its layout is carefully designed to allow for an uninterrupted flow of the item to and from each working station. Each function is carefully timed and operators may perform up to two or three separate functions before passing the item on to the next workstation. To allow for variations in operator working speed, an over lapping area occurs at the very beginning and end of each operator's workstation. Operators may share a particular operation in this area to maintain a set operation time and can often maintain a faster production rate by frame. This overlapping area allows differences in the function time-frame to be absorbed. The function-time or pitch time is now able to be carefully determined; any component of it can be adjusted to accurately predict the time required to complete a single unit, and therefore an entire order. Operators enjoy job variation and as a result are able to monitor the quality of the product more accurately.

Marion, a skilled machinist, said 'Our work goes through much quicker and tidier; whereas in the other production system you have the work all piled around you'. Sue went on to say:

> I find that in the past, if some other girl does two or three hundred a day and in the old system it takes roughly five days to go through the whole factory. And by the time they get to the end of the factory they have made some little silly mistake and by the time it gets to the end there may be a thousand or so garments. Whereas here, at the most, you have half a dozen. And the mistakes can be picked up straight away.

All sewing functions are performed standing (in conventional sewing factories, sewing machines require operators to be seated) to allow for more operator flexibility, and machinery and benches are designed to allow for the optimum working height. The unified nature of the production line provides a physically closer working environment and the reality of a team effort.

Marion said, 'The others [machinists] sort of tend to help each other, whereas we didn't get that on the old line.'

Sue agreed, 'Yeah, you have to do your own work on the old line: whereas here, you get the help that you want. The environment is much nicer and if you have a good team, then you are OK.' She went on to say, 'Well, even with the machinery, we have fewer problems. Everything being turned [speed] down you have less hassle'.

A significant aspect of the unit production process is the flexibility that it offers for Australian manufacturers to produce short runs of any product. Because the machines are on castors, alterations to the production line are made easier. The relevant staff training can ensure multi-skilling, problem-solving and the setting of work-standards. Machine flexibility allows a breakdown to be replaced quickly with little disruption to the production line and no unnecessary build-up of half-completed articles. As only the required amount of raw material necessary to complete the order is delivered to the factory, unnecessary raw material stocks are eliminated. Moreover, the storage facilities for the competed articles are reduced as each batch is shipped on completion. Any new manufacturing process has to have the full backing of the management, supervisors, team leaders and operators. It also requires the consent of the unions and the full support of the staff who will implement it. New procedures are often met with initial resistance but the immediate short-term benefits coupled with the long-term benefits of the more productive manufacturing industry are a vital, and a telling argument for the changes Ron Smith has made at Pilila Clothing. Management and staff are confident and motivated but the last word belongs to the customer.

The manager of Can't tear Em, a major customer of Pilila, said:

'Concern over the past three years has increased significantly in the industrial clothing field. Our only delays in achieving greater growth are to be able to supply what the customer wants on time. Previously to us this has meant having stock on the shelf – at approximately two months stock against known orders. Now with the introduction of JIT at Pilila, we are now able to obtain greater speeds in deliveries because Pilila can give is up to five days delivery time. On top of this, it has allowed us to reduce our stock-on-hand by a further four weeks. Stock means money tied-up; therefore we have been able to release a great amount or working capital'.

Pilila has introduced lean principles with great success. Customers' needs are what have driven all the changes that have been introduced. The relationships between management and machine workers has changed; as has relationships between workers. Of significance has been the changes introduced throughout the business to quickly adapt and adopt to customers' needs.

DISCUSSION QUESTIONS

1. What do you envisage were the greatest challenges that management and machinists encountered when moving from a flow push system to a pull unit system?
2. What do think are the present and foreseeable challenges for Pilila?
    Does Pilila have a potential future and what advances should it be focused on?

From Singapore to the World: Port Management in Singapore

Sum Chee Chuong

Introduction

PSA was previously called Port of Singapore Authority. Its mission and values statement is shown in Table cs4.1. Starting in 1964, PSA has now become much more than a giant Singapore-based shipping hub entity. In 2007, PSA handled tens of millions of TEUs,[1] with volumes growing some 15 per cent from the previous year.[2]

The signing of the contract to build and operate a major container port at the Panama Canal in March 2007 marked another milestone for PSA International (PSA) – it extends its global reach to yet another continent, the Americas. The new container port at the Panama Canal, the world's third busiest waterway, is slated to double Panama's port capacity and enhances PSA's position in the fast-growing trade between China and East Coast of America.[3]

'I am pleased that we have taken this important step to develop a major port facility on the Pacific coast, in tandem with the widening and expansion of the Panama Canal, which is currently underway', said PSA chief executive Eddie Teh.

Within a few years of its globalisation plan, PSA has extended its reach to 25 ports in 14 countries[4] in Asia, Europe and now the Americas. For the first time in the group's history, its overseas terminals handled more container boxes (27.3 million) than the 24.0 million through-put at Singapore.

Table cs4.1 PSA vision and values

Our Mission

To be the port operator of choice in the world's gateway hubs, renowned for best-in-class services and successful partnerships.

Our Values
Committed to Excellence

We set new standards by continuously improving results and innovating in every aspect of our business.

Dedicated to Customers

We help our customers, external and internal, succeed by anticipating and meeting their needs

Focused on People

We win as a team by respecting, nurturing and supporting one another.

Integrated Globally

We build our strength globally by embracing diversity and optimising operations locally.

However, not all deals were smooth sailing. In March 2006, PSA bowed out of a bidding war with Dubai's DP World to acquire Britain's Peninsular & Oriental Steam Navigation Co (P & O) after accumulating a 4.1 per cent stake in the British company. In another recent development, the 25-year contract with Brunei's government in the setup of Muara Container Terminal (MCT) came to a premature end just six years into its operation. PSA Muara has transferred its port operations knowledge and trained MCT's port managers in the state-of-the-art equipment.[5]

History

PSA was formerly the Port of Singapore Authority, a governmental body responsible for regulating, developing, operating and promoting the port of Singapore's terminals. In 1996, the Singapore government passed a bill to set up a new statutory board called the Maritime and Port Authority of Singapore (MPA) to take over the port development and regulatory functions. PSA Corporation Limited was incorporated in 1997 to concentrate on container terminal operations.

As container volumes grew in the 1970s and 1980s, PSA Singapore Terminals had handled more than five million TEUs, making Singapore one of the world's largest container ports. At present, PSA Singapore Terminals is the world's largest container transshipment hub, handling about one-fifth of the world's total container transshipment throughput, and 6 per cent of the global container throughput.

With an established brand name in the provision of highly efficient and reliable container handling services, PSA expanded its global reach by setting up its first overseas venture in Dalian, China. Today, PSA participates in 25 port projects in 14 countries, and handled a total of 51.3 million TEUs globally in 2006. PSA currently has a network of 200 shipping lines with connections to 600 ports in 123 countries, spanning half the globe across Asia and Europe.[6]

PSA was also perceived to be a 'neutral' operator that enjoys good relations with many countries, including United States, India and China. In 2006, Pakistan announced that it had picked PSA to run its deep-water port of Gwadar. The port was constructed with aid from China, and tagged by Western and Indian analysts as an attempt by Beijing to tap on the alliance to extend its reach to the Arabian Sea.[7] With its neutrality and expertise in port management, PSA was seen as a perfect fit for the contract.

PSA's success is demonstrated in yet another year of record gain: PSA posted a 14.3 per cent rise, or $1.21 billion, in profit for the year 2006, beating the records for the previous two years. Besides strong world economic growth which fuelled robust global trade expansion, PSA has continually strengthened its leadership in 2006. This is achieved through both capacity expansion of existing terminals and investments in new port projects around the world.[8] Over the years, PSA has won many internationally acclaimed awards both in operation excellence and IT innovation (see Figure cs4.1 for the list of awards).

As a reflection of its international orientation, PSA adopted a new corporate structure in December 2003, changing its name from PSA Corporation Ltd to PSA International Pte Ltd and became the main holding company for the PSA Group of companies, including PSA Singapore.

Operational excellence and capabilities

The bulk of the containers that flow through PSA Singapore are transshipment cargo. Transshipment refers to the situation where containers are transported by a vessel to an intermediate port, and then sorted and transferred to other ships according to their final destination.

At the container terminal in Singapore, the containers from arriving vessels are offloaded to prime movers by cranes and transported to other berthed ships or to the yard for storage according to their size, weight, category and destination. This way, the containers from different ports

Awarding Organisation	Award	Year of Achievement
Lloyd's List Maritime Asia Awards	Best Container Terminal	2005, 2004, 2003, 2000, 1999
Asian Freight & Supply Chain Awards	Best Global Container Terminal Operator	2006, 2005
		Won award for
	Best Container Terminal Operator in Asia	17 years
		Won award for
	Best Seaport in Asia	18 years
Lloyd's Freight Transport Buyer: Asia Logistics Awards	Cargo Terminal of the Year	2003, 2002
	Container Terminal of the Year	2006, 2005
National Infocomms Awards	Most Innovative Use of Infocomm Technology in the Private Sector	2006
Computerworld Honors, USA	Computerworld Honors Laureate	2002
		2000
Computerworld Smithsonian Program, USA	Computerword Smithsonian Laureate	2000
	CIO (ASEAN & HONG KONG) Award Winner	2001
	Singapore Innovation Award	2001
Seatrade Organization, UK	Seatrade Awards	2001, 2000, 1999, 1888
Syracuse University, USA	Salzberg Concept Medallion Award	1994
The American Association for Artificial Intelligence, Stanford University, USA	Innovative Application of IT Award 1989	1989
The Singapore Productivity and Standards Board	Singapore Quality Award	1999

Figure cs4.1 List of awards for PSA Singapore

bound for the same destination can be loaded onto one ship, reducing the number of trips the vessel needs to make. Similarly, goods from one port bound for multiple different ports can be sorted and transshipped from Singapore.

Due to the high fixed cost of infrastructure and equipment, the volume handled is crucial to achieve economies of scale and profitability. This is

	1999	2000	2001	2002	2003	2004	2005	2006
Total container throughput (in '000 TEUs)	15,945	17,087	15,571	16,941	18,410	21,329	23,192	24,792

Figure cs4.2 Total container throughput for Singapore
Source: Maritime Port Authority of Singapore http://www.mpa.gov.sg/infocentre/pdfs/countainer-throughput.pdf

where the operational efficiency and high connectivity of PSA comes in as a key competitive element. Due to Singapore's strategic geographical location, PSA provides about 200 shipping lines with connections to 600 ports in 123 countries. This means that shippers will easily find a 'connecting' service to a destination port from Singapore rather than to locate a direct service from the port of loading.

Since 1999, the container throughput in Singapore grew steadily from 15.9 million TEUs to 24.8 million TEUs in 2006 (see Figure cs4.2), making Singapore one of the busiest ports in the world in 2005 (see Figure cs4.3). Equally impressive is the overseas operations of PSA in Europe, China and other parts of Asia. Their combined throughput of 27.3 million TEUs in 2006 is a year-on-year increase of 30.2 per cent.

Technology and systems

PSA is known for its operational excellence. To stay competitive and trans-ship goods in the shortest time possible, PSA continuously upgrades its technology and container-handling infrastructure to ensure the highest quality of services are provided to its customers. In-house software was developed to manage and track more than 60000 TEUs per day and ensure that all aspects of its operations run efficiently and reliably, 24 hours a day, 365 days a year.

At the heart of PSA's operations is two real-time e-commerce and computer-integrated terminal operations systems: PORTNET® and CITOS® (Computer Integrated Terminal Operations Systems).

PORTNET® system

Developed in 1984, PORTNET® is a port community system that integrates services to shipping lines, hauliers, freight forwarders, shippers and local government agencies. The web-based system enables 100 per cent end-to-end information workflow and enables the customers to book berths, order

Port	Calls	Percent of total
Singapore	1463,050	5.4
Hong Kong	744,086	2.7
Rotterdam	521,195	1.9
Kaohsiung	356,949	1.3
Busan	327,182	1.2
LA/Long Beach	289,015	1.1
Gibraltar	260,665	1.0
Houston	250,824	0.9
Antwerp	247,967	0.9
Juaymah Term.	221,588	0.8
New York	221,033	0.8
Shanghai	212,143	0.8
Nagoya	204,128	0.8
San Francisco	202,746	0.7
Yokohama	201,936	0.7
Hamburg	198,436	0.7
Ras Tanura	195,282	0.7
Ningbo	184,449	0.7
New Orleans	177,678	0.7
Philadephia	177,614	0.7
Total, top 20 ports	6657,964	24.6
Total, all ports	27086,664	100.0

Figure cs4.3 Top 20 world ports of call (all vessel types), 2005 capacity, thousand DWT/TEU

marine services, transact bills and receive alerts, and track their vessels and cargo on a real time basis. Its 8000 users generate 90 million transactions on average annually.[9] To serve its various customers better, Portnet.com Pty Ltd was created as a subsidiary company to PSA in 2000.

Other solutions are offered by Portnet.com are outlined below.

EZShip

This is a transshipment facilitation system for both main line operators (MLOs) and feeders. It is an Internet-based system that provides a synergistic linkage with the PORTNET system and is customisable to shipping lines' in-house systems, thus eliminating the need for data re-keying and maintaining data integrity and timeliness. Using a personal computer, customers can log in to EZShip and view details like containers assignment to vessels, vessel space management, receive automated event alerts, process inter-shipping line billing and customise their reports.

Global equipment management system (GEMS)

This is an e-business solution for container owners. It maintains information of a shipping line's container stock at container terminals, on-dock depots, external depots, inland depots and offshore sites, providing real time tracking of container or equipment stock and movement globally to the shipping lines, allowing them to plan ahead and assist in reducing repositioning of the containers. The system provides online submission of repair estimates by depots and online approval of repair. It also manages contracts with leasing companies and shipping lines, and generates overdue and overstaying reports for containers in depots, transit, port, and shippers or consignees premises.

Throughput analysis and vessel information system (TRAVIS)

This is a web-enabled management reporting tool to help shipping lines and shipping agents to track their throughput, transshipment volume, dwell time and vessel performance. The system automates the tedious data collection and entry and generates reports that can be used to analyse transshipment of vessel voyage and connection patterns. Dwell time and vessel performance reports can also be generated for shipping lines to check the container dwell times and connection rebates, vessel rates and crane intensity rates. Throughput reports can also be customised to provide customers with throughput information of their containers, slots and vessels.

ALLIES

This is a suite of modules that facilitate co-ordination and collaboration among shipping alliance partners. ALLIES include modules for load tracking and reporting, re-selling and subletting of slots, online approval for loading of special containers and online exchanges of slots and containers. This value added service enhances the shipping network, which in turns provides added incentives for the shippers to transship their cargo through PSA Singapore.

CargoD2D[10]

This is a one-stop Internet-based global freight reservations system for the shipping community. It facilitates the matching of shippers' cargo transportation requirements to offers from various logistics players in the entire end-to-end supply chain such as warehouse operators, trucking companies, inter-modal operators, shipping lines and terminal handling agents.

CITOS® System

With about 60 vessels of different sizes calling on any given day and 90 per cent of them arriving out of schedule due to weather conditions or delays from other port operations, PSA is able to ensure 'berth on arrival' with its CITOS® (Computer Integrated Terminal Operations) System. This is an Enterprise Resource Planning (ERP) system that manages container handling during loading, unloading and storage.

Besides optimising the allocation of resources, CITOS® also generates ship stowage plans and yard layout plans for container stacking based on factors such as ship stability, weight and destination of container and other special requirements such as refrigeration and handling of flammable or dangerous goods. The system tracks the location of each container and facilitates efficient retrieval. The CITOS® System helped PSA Singapore handle some 24 million TEUs of containers in 2006.

Flow-through gate system

The paperless Flow-Through Gate system processes a haulier in 25 seconds, which is the world's fastest time. This is done through Container Number Recognition System and Auto-Paging. The Flow-Through Gate system handles an average traffic flow of 700 prime movers per peak hour, and 8000 prime movers per day.

The fully automated and paperless process clears prime movers going into the port within 25 seconds through the use of highly automated and streamlined processes. When a truck arrives at the gate, the system automatically picks up the signal from the transponder on the truck's cabin. The container number is captured by the Container Number Recognition System via the CCTVs at the gate. The weight of the truck (taken at the weighbridge), driver's identity, truck's identity and the container number are verified against the system and cleared. The automatic paging system then informs the driver the exact position in the yard where the container will be stacked.

Moving forward

Leveraging its expertise in terminal operations, PSA has successfully emerged as one of the busiest ports in the world and the world's port of call. However, competition in port operations has heated up over the years, notably from neighbouring Malaysia's Port of Tanjung Pelepas (PTP) and the threat from Hong Kong and Shanghai ports. PTP, being in close proximity to Singapore, had in particular diverted some cargo volume when PSA's major customers Maersk Sealand and Evergreen Marine Corporation moved their operations there. As an indication of its success, PTP posted a record throughput of 2.24 million TEUs in the first six months of 2006. In addition, Malaysia is also promoting PTP as the preferred port for customers by integrating PTP to the Port Free Zone which houses logistics and manufacturing industrial centres.

Besides competition in the area of lower costs, more and more shippers are also working on vertically integrating their operations by requesting for a stake in the port and operating their own terminals. PSA had been reluctant to negotiate as this directly impacts its core business of terminal operation.

Yet another challenge lies in the ever increasing vessel capacity. While normal Panamax vessels carry between 3000 and 5000 TEUs, bigger post-Panamax vessels (named as they can no longer pass through the Panama Canal) carry between 4500 and 9800 TEUs. Super post-Panamax vessels like Emma Maersk, which at 397 m length and 56 m width, can carry 11000 standard containers or 15 per cent more than its closest rival, China Shipping Container Lines' Xin Los Angeles. With such big capacities, these ships can potentially bypass transshipment hubs like PSA and ship the cargoes directly to the destinations.

The global shipping landscape has changed significantly with the increasing privatisation of ports by many countries. While PSA has performed well thus far, aided in part by the booming China trade, the task of managing a global corporation amid growing competition becomes more and more challenging and complex.

Looking ahead, how can PSA further leverage on its operation expertise and technology to compete in the competitive and volatile global sea trade business? Is PSA helping to turn its partners into formidable competitors? Can suitable and qualified managers be recruited fast enough to run its rapidly expanding global operations, and what can be done to retain human talent within PSA? Can PSA sustain long-term growth and perhaps launch an IPO?

Note: DWT – Deadweight Ton is the displacement at any loaded condition minus the lightship weight. It includes the crew, passengers, cargo, fuel, water, and stores.

Source: US Department of Transportation Maritime Administration, http://www.marad.dot.gov/

Notes

1 'TEU' is a standard shipping container measure. It is a 'twenty foot equivalent unit'. This is a measure of cargo volume of 20 ft (length), 8 ft (width) and 9 ft (height).

2 http://www.singaporepsa.com/corporate/ourmission.html
3 *The Straits Times*, 14 March 2007.
4 http://www.internationalpsa.com/home/default.html, accessed on 28 March 2007.
5 *The Straits Times*, 25 January 2007.
6 www.internationalpsa.com
7 *The Straits Times*, 25 January 2007.
8 *The Straits Times*, 6 March 2007.
9 www.portnet.com
10 http://www.cargod2d.com/

Striving for Operations Excellence within Queensland Rail Supply Division

Kevin Burgess

Queensland Rail (QR)

Queensland Rail (QR) is a $A3 billion a year business, being one of Australia's largest and most modern transport providers operating on more than 20,000 kilometres of track across Australia. With the acquisition of Australian Rail-road Group (ARG) – the largest freight haulier on the western seaboard and currently holds approximately 39 per cent of the national grain freight market and 45 per cent of the minerals rail freight market – it now has a national footprint.

QR is a government-owned corporation (GOC) accountable to its share-holding ministers, the Queensland Treasurer and the Queensland Minister for Transport. The Board is responsible for ensuring the corporation acts in a commercial manner. QR employs over 14,000 people, including those in QR's three subsidiaries. In today's competitive environment, QR, like any other corporation, is being driven by market and social forces, which demand greater services and better value for money.

Shared Services Group – Supply Division

The Supply Division is a part of the Shared Services Group in QR. It provides procurement, contracting, reclamations and disposals, inventory management, business support, accounts payable and fleet management services. Supply deals with approximately 9000 active suppliers who do business with

QR each year, spending some $1.15 billion annually for the goods and services they provide.

The Supply Division strategy, which was implemented to enable Supply to move forward, was guided by several influences, but, in the interest of structuring what happened over the five years of the strategy, the Australian Business Excellence Framework (BEF) will be used. The BEF is a system which can be used to assess and improve any aspect of an organisation and consists of seven, interconnected categories: leadership, strategy and planning process, data information and knowledge, people, customer and market focus, process management, improvement and innovation, and success and sustainability. What follows is a description of what happened in each of the seven categories.

Leadership

Leadership was one of the categories Supply identified as deficient in its concepts, culture, business processes and management systems. Up until 2000, Supply had operated under a strong hierarchical command control structure which tended to centralise power. The management culture was exclusively male and so strongly focused on generating and maintaining internal processes that customers increasingly experienced the services offered as inflexible and non responsive to their needs.

In 2000, a new General Manager Supply, was appointed. He set about altering the composition and structure of the team in order to bring about cultural change in line with supply chain management principles. Half of the new management team members came from outside the Supply branch. They were selected for their ability to fill some perceived gaps and on their demonstrated ability to live values associated with the culture shift that was perceived as required. The team, which was expanded to eight, had a far wider skill set, gender diversity and age distribution. The new skills in the group included operations management, project management, human resources management and change management. Three were females, two (one male and one female) were of ethnic origin, the age spread was widened from the range of forty to sixty to a range from those in their late twenties through to fifties. This new management team set about creating a more egalitarian culture supported by a flatter organisational structure.

Vision and culture were developed through a series of intensive off site management workshops. Some of these workshops involved key customers and suppliers. The vision statement developed was: 'Supply Division strives to offer total supply chain management for its customers, resulting in optimal procurement and inventory practices.'

It was soon realised that achieving the vision would involve systematically aligning strategy, structure and culture. Creating a culture built on values such as trust and collaboration was seen as having the best alignment to strategy and the overall principles of effective supply chain management. The structure was then designed with the intent of moving away from a formal hierarchical arrangement to one of self-directed work teams that depended upon a much more personal relationship between workers, supervisors and managers. The greater diversity in the senior management structure provided several immediate benefits that helped align with culture change. First, the greater diversity in the management team around skill sets, ethnicity and age modelled to staff that people from very different backgrounds could work together as an effective team. Second, it aligned well with modelling a culture of collaboration and equality which were seen as key values needed to work not only effectively within the Division but also with a diverse range of suppliers. Third, the diversity of the team made it easier for Supply staff to identify with individual team members based on their personal identity. This in turn helped reduce the management-worker division that had existed. All of these initiatives helped the Division reposition itself from a hierarchical, behaviourally rigid bureaucracy to a values-driven organisation that was flexible and responsive to meeting customer needs.

Values were seen to be transmitted primarily through relationships. The management team therefore set about deliberately modelling its espoused values in all its dealings. Within the first two years, the management team went off site every three months to attend two-day workshops. Being away from their day-to-day operations permitted participants the opportunity to not only set and review strategic priorities, but to get to know each other as people and explore how to work more effectively with each other through values. There were two reasons for creating such discipline and feedback around exploring and understanding team values. First, it was felt if the management team could not genuinely live and model unity and cooperation then it would be difficult to ask staff to do so. Second, it was believed that using a relationship approach to model respect for individuals would in turn make it easier for staff to use the same relationship principles with customers and suppliers. In 2003, all staff underwent a two-day training course in communication. This was not an off-the-shelf course. The tools and techniques used in the course had been specifically designed to give behavioural expression to the Division's values. Such was the importance placed on living the values that the management team set aside weekly meetings to review how staff felt and lived the espoused values as they went about their work and what they could do to increase consistency and generally improve on living these values in all their affairs.

A range of systems were set up to encourage staff to comment on the culture and what could be improved. These included areas where suggestions could be logged, either in hard or electronic form, team briefings, survey instruments and ad hoc assessments by independent consultants. By year three, the corporation developed a culture survey that provided a base line measure for progress against culture change. The two survey results, taken at eighteen month intervals, so far have shown a steady improvement trend.

The major obstacles faced by the management around effective leadership to date include: ensuring consistency of messages in all forms of communication, modelling values and behaviours in a stable and predictable manner and being able to measure the effectiveness of such a nebulous concept as leadership. All this had to happen in a background where the wider corporation, which is operating in an ever more rapidly changing environment due to forces such as volatile and more demanding markets, changes in regulatory regimes and technology. Such pace of change means that a multi-business corporation such as QR sends a wide variety of complex messages that can at times appear at odds with previous messages. Sending consistent messages from the Supply management team in this wider context of communication overload has been and remains a challenge. The overall results suggest communication is perceived to have generally improved. While there is still considerable room for improvement, the evidence to date is that the consistency of leadership style has helped reduce much of the fear and suspicion that originally existed among staff as a result of the past, ongoing and proposed changes.

Because of the increasingly turbulent environment that QR faces, and the rapidly changing role around Supply chain management (SCM), leadership around change will involve dealing with even greater levels of uncertainty and ambiguity in the future. For instance, as Supply's strategy has moved forward, it was discovered there were more 'unknowns' as the Division moved into different contracts, strategic alliances and joint ventures with its customers and suppliers to enable greater speed, agility and flexibility. With Supply moving towards a higher risk model for greater benefits, it has been identified that staff require a deeper level of knowledge to be able to make decisions, than offered by the present code of behaviour and code of conduct which have been developed by the corporation. Supply deliberately set about creating a learning environment in order to generate innovative solutions to old problems. This has involved working in new ways and in less structured contexts. It has also involved building upon the codes of conduct and behaviour to a code of ethics. The latter is seen as both superior to the other two codes. The limitation of the other two codes are behaviour-based and while useful in highly structured environments, they are not as well suited to providing guidance on how to act in less structured and more dynamic contexts. Yet, for Supply to continue to deliver value to the corporation, it will be required to take more risks in order to work, learn and innovate in an environment where fewer variables are known and controlled. Culture change is always slow and complex and developing a code of ethics which staff understand and operate in remains a daunting challenge, but one which Supply cannot ignore if it wants to be effective at SCM.

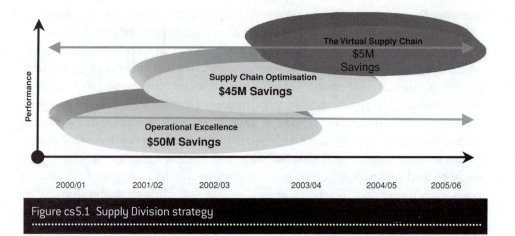

Figure cs5.1 Supply Division strategy

Strategy and planning

Background

In early 2000, there was a recognised need for a common and corporate wide direction to assist staff to make purchasing decisions and to ensure QR achieved value for money. In 2001, Supply initiated the Supply Chain Initiative (SCI) with the long-term potential savings opportunity for the project identified at $100 million. This was the quantum change in Supply with the key business drivers for this project initiation being the need to reduce costs of procurement and inventory, better manage the supply chain to derive strategic competitive advantage and improve flexibility and responsiveness to meet rapidly changing customer and regulatory requirements. It also intended to transform the way the whole of QR procured goods and services through strategic sourcing, inventory optimisation and technology, and aimed to change work practices and transform the culture of Supply. Figure cs5.1 provides a summary of the strategy plan which guided Supply Division for five years, including the financial targets for each of the three main strategies which make up the plan. All three targets were met within the five year period.

It should be noted that the three ovals in Figure cs5.1 are overlayed in a deliberate sequence for the five years. The logic being that the quickest wins would come from operational excellence and these wins would in turn create results, credibility and time to move onto the next level of supply chain optimisation. As supply chain optimisation involved reviewing and improving business processes, it was a deliberate choice to do this prior to moving into the virtual supply chain as the effective use of technology presupposed it supported robust well developed management processes.

Table cs5.1 provides a summary of strategic intent of each of the three major strategies represented in Figure cs5.1.

Table cs5.1 Five year strategies and targets

Strategies	Targets
Operational Excellence Ensuring all possible savings and improvements which can be delivered by the market are found.	$50 m
Supply Chain Optimisation Finding ways to work more collaboratively with suppliers in order to drive out both duplication and unnecessary cost in common supply chains.	$45 m
Virtual Supply Chain Automation of the 'procure to pay' process, improved monitoring and reporting capabilities to all key stakeholders, and the use of technology to make all sourcing activities far easier to perform. This is achieved by reducing complexity and embedding governance requirements into the processes.	$5 m

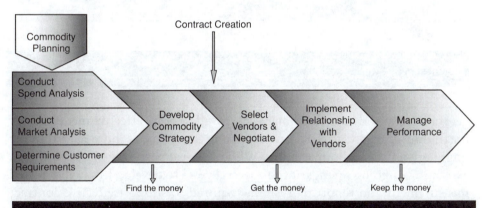

Figure cs5.2 Strategic sourcing methodology

Operational excellence

At the time of commencing this plan, it was acknowledge that Supply Division would need external assistance to help achieve its ambitious targets. The consulting firm PriceWaterhouseCoopers (PwC) were commissioned to provide assistance with above plan. After several months' investigation, PwC confirmed that the targets set in the plan were viable. While they sought to provide assistance with all three strategies, it was in the area of strategic sourcing under the operational excellence strategy that their methodologies proved to be effective. For reasons to be discussed under the other two strategies, they had far less impact. PwC provided a sourcing methodology shown in Figure cs5.2. This methodology was built around three ideas – 'find the money,

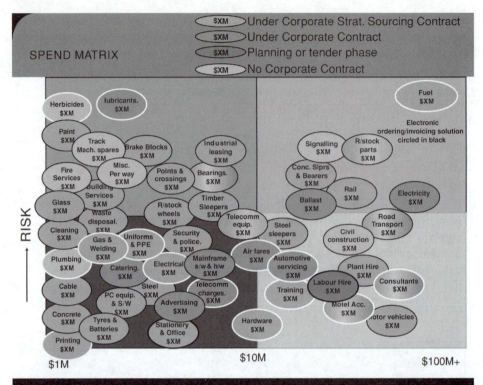

Figure cs5.3 QR spend matrix

get the money and keep the money'. It proved to be an effective methodology for finding and getting the money. Keeping the money is more related to the ongoing contract administration. While QR has been largely successful in extracting ongoing savings, it took several years to develop the sophisticated measurement and reporting systems required to support effective contract administration. While QR still uses the basic concepts outlined in Figure cs5.2, it has modified it over time as it was found that different commodity types require variations on the basic methodology.

Figure cs5.3 provides an illustration of how the various commodities were sorted in order identify priorities. Exact figures are not shown as they vary from year to year, however, to give an example, in 2006/07, fuel is estimated to account for $333 m of spend and the total spend for the year will most likely exceed $1.5 billion. This diagram has proven to be a highly effective tool not only for internal planning purposes but also for communicating with key stakeholders on how important sourcing is and the present state of each commodity procurement strategy.

Despite the success of the Operational Excellence strategy in delivering $50 million in savings, Supply's strategy needs to remain flexible in order to be able to cope with the dynamic changes to corporate strategy. Supply Division's strategic plan was initially based on the assumption of a largely geographically state-based organisation. During the life of Supply's five year plan, QR became a national land-based freight and logistics organisation through a series of acquisitions such Interrail (NSW), CRT (Victoria) and ARG (WA). These changes involved a change in the business model for the corporation including the creation of 'stand up verticals'. Basically these verticals are discrete businesses in their own right and have been given very large autonomy in order to be far more flexible and agile in order to respond to increasingly demanding markets. Under this business model, the business groups that interact with external paying customers are free to choose what services they want and from which providers. This has impacted on Supply Division as customers are no longer mandated to use their services and has pushed Supply to use value add propositions – a clear statement of the tangible results a customer will receive from using their products or services. With all these changes, unit prices may not be as good and scale and volume cost reductions are not viable for the customer. This has seen Supply place even greater importance on working out the customer's needs, what is best for their business and how they can value add to the customer's business.

The emerging challenge for Supply Division is to move from an Operational Excellence strategy based on reducing cost and risk to one that can add demonstrated value. The difficulties associated with this change include: organisational inertia as it has been remarkably successful to date having delivered $50 million in bottom line savings; the absence of proven alternatives (it is still the dominant model pushed by many of the large consulting firms who because of their access to senior managers tend to present this approach as the one true way); and, finally the present financial models used by most corporations are very effective at measuring input costs from suppliers but far less effective at determining how cost drivers lead to different value propositions.

While the present Operational Excellence strategy will continue to deliver some minor benefits, it cannot continue to generate more large step improvements within its present structure. The reasons include: there is only so much that suppliers can give up before the strategy reaches it outer limits, QR's primary strategic imperative as an asset intensive industry is around increasing the availability and utilisation of wealth producing assets as distinct to just reducing cost inputs, and finally, under the new business model, the Supply Division no longer has any governance and policy powers that can compel the business units to use their contracts. This means Supply must now use innovation rather than demand compliance in order to demonstrate unique value propositions for each business.

This challenge requires financial reengineering of accounting practices to support the business model. The choice of financial models used has profound implications for how procurement measures success. While it is widely recognised that financial measures around asset management is the way of the future, developing the sophisticated measures required for such a position remains a difficult task. As will be shown in the next section under data, information and knowledge, there has been some sound progress in financial asset management measures around inventory management measures. However, there is still a need to move these measures toward opportunity costs associated with poor forecasting, tracking and holding relative to asset availability, reliability and total cost.

Moving into a new Operational Excellence strategy involves creating greater dependency upon suppliers which in turn alters the corporations risk profile. The supplier base of capital intensive industries such railway has involved ongoing consolidation of fewer suppliers over the past decade, resulting in power shifting to the suppliers. The purchase of goods and services from these suppliers needed to support QR's prime wealth producing assets account for over 90 per cent of total purchases in dollar terms. QR's approach to these emerging market conditions is to work within an extended enterprise model that uses relationships rather than power. There are several reasons for adopting such an approach, including the lack of market power over, and absence of choice with, key suppliers combined with long life assets requiring OEM parts leave little option for anything but long-term single supplier relationships. As these suppliers possess considerable technical innovative capacity, QR is also eager to influence the research and development agenda of the suppliers to support its own strategic interests. Maintaining open relationships are seen as the most effective way to encourage and support the types of information flows needed to enhance innovation. Finally, working closely with such suppliers provides opportunities to develop SCM capabilities around costs such as those associated with inventory management.

QR has commenced moving from traditional contracts into new forms such as strategic alliances and joint ventures. So far these have been restricted to few very high value contracts associated with key assets (such as track and rollingstock) where a very limited competitive market existed. However, as shown in Figure cs5.4 it is anticipated that these types of contract will continue to become more common in the future. Moving to a relationship strategy has created many challenges which Supply Division is presently working through. These include an understanding that while relationship management works through intangible assets such as trust and collaboration, it is far more difficult to locate, measure and sweat these intangible assets in order to create greater value. Strategic planning for the next five years involves not developing new forms of contracts but developing new competencies and capabilities to work with these new approaches to operational excellence.

Supply chain optimisation

Supply chain optimisation had the strategic intent of working more collaboratively with QR's suppliers in order to drive out both duplication and unnecessary cost in common supply chains. Common costs included

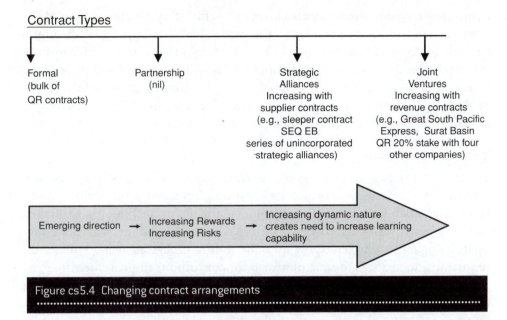

Figure cs5.4 Changing contract arrangements

duplication, technology and excess inventory holdings across the entire chain. The term 'optimisation' was deliberately chosen over terms such as inventory reduction to reflect that risk levels were to be determined by end users who had ultimate responsibility for asset availability. While the strategic intent was to work across the extended supply chain in the first five years, the focus was on getting internal inventory controls and measures under control before going wider.

In 2000, QR's inventory turn ratio was at 0.8 per annum, with approximately $250 million in inventory holdings. Trend data analysis suggested inventory holding would reach $300 million by 2003/04 if nothing was done to change practices. PwC were not able to be of as much help in this area due to a range of issues including data integrity, cataloguing and units of measure. Also, at the time, their expertise was largely in retail as opposed to a maintenance environment. However, the greatest difficulty faced was found to be linked to cultural practices that had developed over the past 130 years, such as keeping 'grass stocks' – a euphemism for those inventory items not recorded on the Enterprise Resource System (ERP) and known only to local managers who kept them as emergency spares.

Progress was initially slow and took almost three years to get real momentum. The cultural practices were at odds with the formal system requirements of the ERP and corporate governance framework. The breakthrough came when it realised it was not a technical but rather a socio-cultural problem. An inventory forum known as the Inventory Optimisation Advisory Group (IOAG) was set up with representatives from different business groups and geographical locations. Four years on, this committee is still operating and continues to ensure that where feasible, the technical system is configured in a way which supports operators in the field. The other large breakthrough came from developing a measurement methodology that could cascade inventory measures from the most senior management level to the local storeman. The measures developed are discussed in more depth in section 4. As a result of these initiatives, the corporation increased its inventory turn ratio to 3.2 (a 400% improvement) and has so far saved $45 million.

Virtual Supply Chain

The virtual supply chain strategy concentrated on automating where possible, activities within the 'procure to pay' process, improving monitoring and reporting capabilities to key stakeholders, and using technology to make sourcing activities easier to perform. A saving of $5 million was achieved by utilising electronic tendering and auctioning processes, using enhanced reporting and analysis to set a platform for continuous improvement.

The corporation was on a SAP R2 platform and as this technology was to be replaced by a more advanced R3 platform, it was considered best to delay progressing this strategy until the new technological infrastructure was in place. An investigation of the software solutions available in 2001 that could assist QR's supply chains found most applications were expensive and limited in capability. It was felt that an additional benefit in delaying moving too fast on this front was that technology would make advances which both reduced costs and increased functionality. Despite these delays it should be noted that starting from a zero base in 2000, over one-third of the 500,000 purchasing transactions are now done electronically. An uptake in the use of bank card combined with merchants also offering e-commerce solutions including vendor managed catalogues, has also assisted with this strategy.

Despite the considerable hype around e-commerce, the results to date have been mixed. While vendor systems are good at the front end around orders, Supply Division has often had to dedicate additional resources to sort out the complexity generated by back end financial processes. It has also been found that once QR locks into a vendor's technology they are completely at the mercy of that system. As many of these systems lack the capabilities needed, they do not deliver the savings initially promised. The journey has therefore been delayed by factors other than those under QR's control.

It was soon realised from several experiences over the first few years that processes had to be refined before automating them. If a process works inefficiently, technology only makes processes faster, not better, and can possibly emphasise the problem. However, if the technology does not work correctly, a lot of time and resources can be expended to fix a technological 'glitch'.

The Procure to Pay Project (P2P) is part of the Virtual Supply Chain initiative. P2P's objective is to streamline procurement processes from the point a decision is made to procure goods or services, through to the point where

QR pays for them, to ensure the lowest unit cost of procurement administration. Supply is constantly looking at streamlining processes, and P2P will endeavour to improve the procurement processes and systems. The P2P project is anticipated to require another change in culture, as occurred with the SCI Project. This is because the evidence to date strongly suggests that unless changes in technology are supported by parallel changes in job roles and cultural practices, it is difficult to sustain large step improvements.

Through P2P, QR is part of a benchmarking study with sixteen major Australian companies benchmarking against each other. Typically, it has been difficult to find an Australian organisation to benchmark against. Through the benchmarking process, Supply has found they are performing well at some things, average for others, and have found some areas needing closer attention.

Information and knowledge

While it took two years to develop a comprehensive set of measures, the benefits have been considerable and include:
1. provision of good systems for analysis and interpretation of data
2. enhanced capability around the integration and use of knowledge in decision making
3. feedback to management teams across the corporation which enhances learning and more timely decision making
4. provision of information and analysis tools for business groups to make their own decisions around spending and inventory management.

The procurement measures needed for the Operational Excellence were the easier set to generate, largely because many were already within the capability of the ERP upgrade. Monthly reports were developed by Supply and made available to the entire corporation. After some time, refinements were made to the variables that were reported Table cs5.2 details the range of measures provided in standard reports currently.

The development of robust inventory measures to support the supply chain optimisation strategy took over two years, primarily because none were available in the market and so QR had to develop its own. Supply Division was recognised by the Logistics Association of Australia for its efforts in 2006 by becoming a finalist under the award category of Scorecard Reporting. The development of these measures represented a major turning point in implementing the supply chain optimisation strategy. Not only did Supply provide reports to all levels of the corporation using these measures, it also detailed recommendations on what could be done by way of improvement initiatives. Figure cs5.5 provides an example of the inventory dashboard which was

Table cs5.2 Current measures reported

....

Description
Displays a snapshot of inventory performance measures for QR at a Corporate, Business Group, Plant and Storage level. The scorecard includes comments on performance and improvement recommendations and is updated at the end of each month.

....

Measures
Stock on Hand

....

Inventory Turnover Ratio

....

Slow Moving Stock

....

Stock Write-Off to Scrap

....

Goods in Transit (over 1 month old)

....

Stocktake Progress

....

Stocktake Line errors

....

Stocktake Write-on/Write-Offs

....

Stocktake Variation by absolute $ value

....

initially developed and subsequently superseded by a less complex representation system.

Figure cs5.6 illustrates how these measures are no longer presented in the dash board format, but rather are in line with the presentation style of the procurement measures.

What is not immediately obvious from Figures cs5.5 and cs5.6 is the enormous effort that went into developing this reporting capability. For example, the Supply cataloguing team was an integral part of this development, as they had to continuously work in consultation and collaboration with QR's business groups to ensure QR had an optimal material master catalogue by 2005. The cataloguing team was successful in removing 130,000 duplicated, unnecessary and incorrectly classified materials.

A material master creation methodology and spreadsheet upload process provided a more efficient method for the business groups in the direct creation of all new materials. It enabled the catalogue master data to be more accurately maintained, materials to be correctly classified and the data integrity of inventory reporting to be preserved.

In addition, information systems and processes had to be developed and put in place to identify what data should be collected and how the

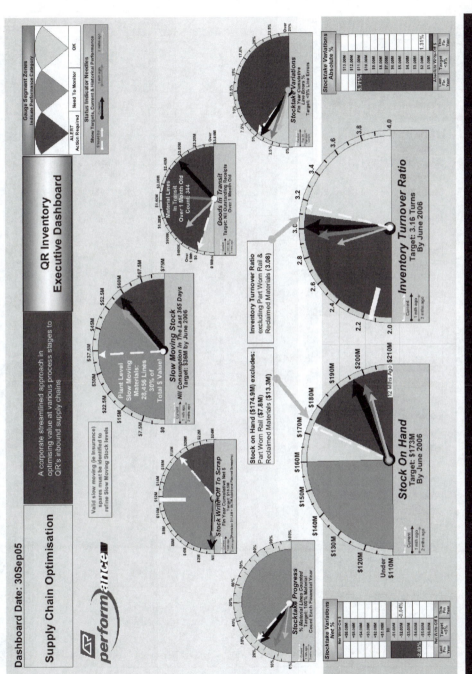

Figure cs5.5 QR inventory dashboard

Figure cs5.6 Inventory balanced scorecard

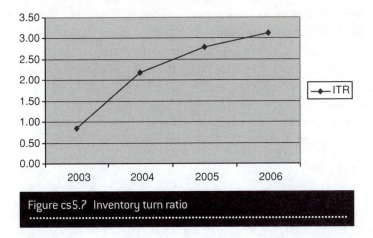

Figure cs5.7 Inventory turn ratio

information should be handled, stored, analysed and interpreted to create information and knowledge. This was followed by a considerable educational effort with all levels of the organisation to help them understand how to interpret and use the dashboard. For example, following an educational session to the senior executive team, information on inventory was generated, collated and analysed by Supply and presented in a detailed quarterly report. These reports not only increased the senior executive team's understanding of the environment in which the project was operating, but also allowed them to continually review and take actions as required.

The increased functionality of software used in the virtual supply chain has made it far easier to collect and distribute reports and trend analysis. However, it was the application of these tools which lead to the large improvements as best shown in Figure cs5.7, which shows a 400 per cent increase in the inventory turn ratio. Research suggests world's best practice in railways is 4 and at this rate of improvement it is highly probable that QR will reach this target.

Despite the progress made to date there are still many challenges being faced by Supply Division. These include:

1. the need to be clearer about what data we need to collect and how it is going to be used and add value to processes
2. using data in decision-making in a more systematic way
3. applying statistical thinking (understanding when systems are out of control), understanding variation (over and under reacting) and the amount of variation in processes in order to better manage risk and reduce forecasting error
4. adopting a more structured approach in training staff to use and interpret these reports
5. identifying and managing the value of intangible assets (knowledge, relationships)

6. gaining better decision support – develop processes that provide data that feed into decision support
7. developing better process measures
8. developing interactive measures around the complex interplay of risk management levels, cost of inventory holding and associated opportunity costs
9. developing measures which more seamlessly interact with suppliers' measurement systems.

People

Supply's approach to the ongoing development of staff was given great consideration because the strategy involved getting rid of all assets and placing them back into the ownership of the business groups who managed them to ensure greater alignment and accountability. This meant that all staff had left to offer was knowledge. The HR strategy was therefore based on increasing and working harder its most valuable and largely intangible asset – knowledge. While there has been considerable progress in codifying and automating explicit knowledge, the most valuable knowledge is still tacit and therefore not easily identified or managed.

The five-year strategic plan was supported by a comprehensive HR plan which focused on developing human capability to meet present and emerging requirements. In the first year, the contract set with PwC specifically stated one of the terms was proof of a transfer of skill to Supply staff. PwC commented at the time that this was not a common practice and it took some time to agree on a methodology by which to measure success. The staff chosen to work with PwC were primarily managers and supervisors as it was felt they would be best placed to cascade skill to other staff. They were also taken off line to ensure that their learning was not distracted by operational requirements.

In the first year, the organisational structure was also rearranged from top to bottom to create roles in line with the new strategic direction. These jobs were then called and this allowed the introduction of staff new to the Division to blend with some of the older more established staff. In 2000, out of staff of over 100, only one had a tertiary qualification. Opening up positions to all comers allowed the rapid introduction of staff with tertiary qualifications as well as different attitudes and values. Calling all jobs initially created a lot of tension among existing staff who were fearful they would either lose their jobs, or status or be excluded from going for higher jobs in the Division. The situation settled down after a year when over half the positions were filled with staff from the original Supply Division.

Staff who did not have tertiary qualifications have been offered training in Queensland State Purchasing Policy. This course has eight levels, with

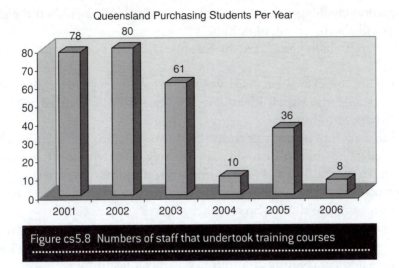

Queensland Purchasing Students Per Year

Figure cs5.8 Numbers of staff that undertook training courses

the first being elementary through to level eight, which is a Masters level qualification. QR pays for all courses and up to level four is offered to staff during work hours. Above that level, staff are required to complete study outside of work hours. Figure cs5.8 below shows the number of staff who have availed themselves of this opportunity so far.

In addition to the aforementioned initiatives, QR has a development program which involves recruiting trainees and graduates, a structured development path for long serving staff, as well as a deliberate strategy aimed at smoothing the age profile across the board in order to avoid the baby boomer bubble and years of skills walking out the door. One of difficulties of the graduate recruitment program is that after a year, graduates become attractive to wider markets who can offer far more in wages. The solution has been to accept high attritions rates and develop a graduate pipeline to meet the challenge of the higher churn. In 2007, QR supported Griffith University in developing a course in Supply Chain Management (SCM) by offering two scholarships valued at $10,000 each as well as vacation placements. In the first year of the course (2007), there were 53 students enrolled, which exceeded even the most optimistic forecasts of the University.

Finally, Supply Division has commissioned research around how to accelerate skill development and application on the job. This project is in large part a demonstration of the Division's commitment to the fact that the only asset the Division controls is the intangible asset of knowledge. As such it needs to grow and use it more frequently and within shorter cycle times to meet present and emerging challenges. It is also a pragmatic response to changing work patterns, especially in generation Y staff who are not attracted to the concept of a job for life that was once offered by QR. Developing and growing the necessary intellectual capital has been and will remain one of the most fundamental challenges faced by the Division and if it fails, then the global strategy will also be at risk of failing.

The overall challenges faced by Supply Division going into the future include:

1. finding quicker formalised ways of responding to ideas/suggestions so people know their ideas have been heard and evaluated in order to enhance innovation
2. influencing HR policies formulation to generate the industrial tools needed be able to deal with an entirely different workforce (higher churn rate, different expectations around promotion, career)
3. capturing the knowledge of those who leave and ensuring it is effectively transferred to those who remain
4. being able to cope with volatile market conditions, which have resulted in experienced workers being made generous offers to leave, which in turn adds to creating an internal critical skill shortage.

Customer and market focus

The contracts developed by Supply staff are done in consultation with representatives from the business groups who will be affected by the changes. Supply therefore takes a facilitation role with customers to ensure their needs are met. As Supply no longer has a governance role under the new business model, it can no longer coerce customers into accepting its solutions and proposals. The SCM focus is and the comments made in Section 2 on measuring value from the customers' perspectives have added to a strong sense of serving customers. Supply has also undertaken extensive, highly detailed benchmarking studies to demonstrate the services offered are comparable to market rates.

A good example of continually trying to improve customer service is the Procure to Pay project (P2P), which has sought to remove as much complexity as possible. A total of 244 key users were interviewed in focus groups across the state using open-ended questions in order to find out the issues and frustrations they faced. The main findings from the research were: first, that financial delegations did not match the spending patterns and needed to be moved upward to reduce a lot of complexity; second, while the ERP technology worked well with certain commodities it created unnecessary complexity for other commodities; and finally, global contracts did not always satisfy local regional requirements. As a result of this research, a proposal went forward to change the financial delegations as did a recommendation to not use one type of purchasing technology for all commodities and finally all future contracts developed will involve regional representatives to ensure all user needs are better understood.

The single greatest challenge for Supply, which it has not, as yet, been able to successfully address, is around benefits realisation. Supply creates benefits for the corporation, but others cash those benefits. The challenge poised by the new business model makes it even more urgent to be able to better show value propositions to the lines of business.

Process management, improvement and innovation

As already demonstrated by the results under each of the three strategies, Supply Division has made significant process improvements such as improved inventory management, automation of one third of ordering and improved reporting on processes resulting in better control. The challenge has not so much been around technology but rather around in being able to better understand the requirements of operators and to develop the systems in line with these requirements. The tendency of large systems to impose a singular solution has been and remains a source of great difficulty in generating business process improvements. Indeed, much of the SCM literature praises the virtues of integration – the very feature ERP so proudly boast of. While not disputing the importance of integration, QR's experience seeking integration through a single technology needs to be questioned. Supply is developing a business process methodology which can translate user requirements firstly into process requirements and then into system requirements. This is a slow process and in the short term at least, the system requirements tend to determine the process requirements.

There are no silver bullets around the interplay of process and technology. QR has tended to get caught into the ERP sales rhetoric around scale and volume and that the more you can get into one system the more efficient you will become. Figure cs5.9 shows what Supply is proposing as a means of getting out of this one shoe fits all purchasing problem.

What Figure cs5.10 seeks to highlight is that the time has come to challenge the scale and volume arguments of ERP vendors which leads to a simplistic logic of placing every type of transaction in the ERP system. There are limits to ERPs which work well with large volume transactions with other large corporations. Business Process management works well with large volume transactions that are unique to a specific industry but unlike the transactions found in QR, ERPs are not generic to all organisations. Finally there are many small vendors of low value that an organisation must deal with, but to integrate them into ERP systems is both costly and possibly creates ill-will with smaller suppliers due to the complexity with getting paid in a timely manner. For this last group, which are high in numbers but low in value, credit cards are a far more effective means of interaction as it offers instant cash flow which is a feature highly valued by small vendors. Such a purchasing

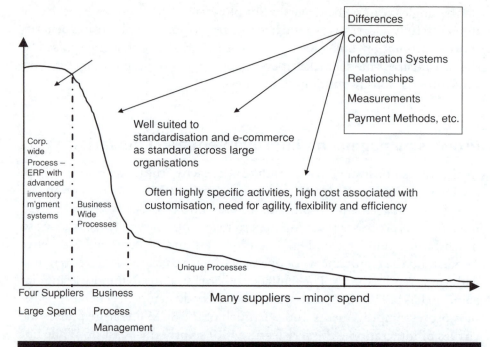

Differences
Contracts
Information Systems
Relationships
Measurements
Payment Methods, etc.

Corp. wide Process – ERP with advanced inventory m'gment systems

Business Wide Processes

Well suited to standardisation and e-commerce as standard across large organisations

Often highly specific activities, high cost associated with customisation, need for agility, flexibility and efficiency

Unique Processes

Four Suppliers
Large Spend

Business Process Management

Many suppliers – minor spend

Figure cs5.9 Challenges – corporate strategy, procurement process and technology

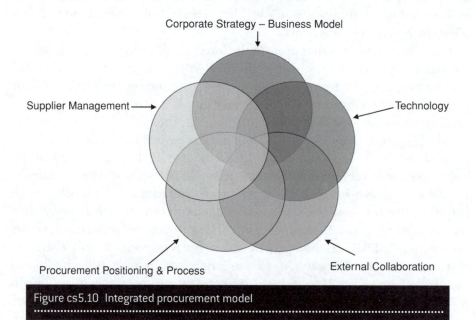

Corporate Strategy – Business Model

Supplier Management

Technology

Procurement Positioning & Process

External Collaboration

Figure cs5.10 Integrated procurement model

and payment method is also cheaper than ERP processes for these limited volume items.

Success and sustainability

The rail industry typically works on a three to five per cent profit margin. To deliver $100 million to the bottom line would require an increase in revenue of between $ 2 to $ 3 billion dollars. Yet because savings in Supply equate as a one to one saving, the $100 million generated in savings has had the same bottom line impact to $2 billion in revenue. On this basis the results of the five year plan are impressive.

For the Supply Division to play an important role in the long-term sustainability of the corporation, the following challenges must be met.

Integration

At present, there is still a tendency to do things in separate silos, which in turn creates many disconnects and complexities. The three major strategies which underpinned the strategic plan shown in Figure cs5.1 tended to be implemented by different staff, with different skill sets working to different priorities. It therefore took another piece of work to bring these strategies together in order to better exploit the value-adding synergies. The level of complexity increased further when Supply Division's overall strategy sought to align with the various lines of business. The evidence to date is that complexity increases exponentially when trying to align QR priorities with those of external suppliers in a fully integrated supply chain. Figure cs5.10 outlines the sort of integration that Supply Division will be pursuing over the next five years. While some integration already exists there is a considerable challenge to get this much tighter in order to deliver on going sustainable improvements. The simplicity of the diagram belies the complexity and effort that will be required to bring about the desired integration at the speed required.

Alignment with corporate strategy

While it is important to work on all the circles shown in Figure cs5.10, the logical starting point is around how to get the Supply strategy aligned with the corporate strategy in a way which maintains the ongoing attention and engagement of senior managers. If any Business Group achieved a $2 to $3 billion increase in revenue, they would doubtless receive considerable senior management attention. Yet Supply in saving $100 million has delivered the same bottom line result. Despite such impressive results, backend functions such as Supply struggle to maintain ongoing discussion and debate in anything comparable to the time and effort given to front end customer focused activities. Traditional ways of thinking around what is important to a corporation continue to dominate and while procurement can get on the strategic radar in rare moments, it cannot stay there for long periods (at least in industrial markets). The strategic sourcing profession generally needs to find more effective ways of engaging Boards and Senior Executives in order to be able to give the respect and resources needed to deliver the value it can add to most modern, large corporations.

DISCUSSION QUESTIONS

1. Outline the key operational and supply capabilities that QR must get right in order to achieve high levels of performance.
2. Describe the key operating systems at QR, and evaluate their performance and capability in supporting the QR Supply vision.
3. What are the most important specific measures of operating performance used at QR, and are these the right ones? Can you suggest any improvements in what and how they measure?
4. Discuss and evaluate the relationships between supply and operations functions and managers at QR and those in the rest of the business.
5. Critique the balanced scorecard approach as used at QR.
6. What are the key operational risks facing QR? Evaluate and suggest potential improvements to the QR risk management approach.
7. Is QR's approach to procurement in line with best practices? What further improvements are possible?
8. How might the Business Excellence Framework help QR?

Should I Stay or Should I Go? Shiraishi Garments Company

Bin Jiang and Patrick J. Murphy

Introduction

Takashi Shiraishi gazed out his office window watching reflections of the afternoon sun on Tokyo Bay. It was 9 February 2005. Since early last year, Shiraishi Garments Co. (SGC) had begun outsourcing whole production to China to increase profit margins. As President, Takashi saw the immediate benefit of outsourcing to his bottom line. But he also saw moral issues with buying low-cost Chinese goods at the expense of worker health and safety. It concerned him for personal and business reasons. As a consumer goods company dealing in clothing and apparel, SGC needed to maintain a positive reputation: market success depended on its brand.

Japanese companies had been wrestling with public trust for several years, ever since the Snow Brand milk poisoning episode in 2000, in which over 13,000 people became seriously ill. Usage of cheap overseas labour was reported widely as the reason Japanese companies were moving operations out of Japan and increasing domestic unemployment. Many Japanese companies outsourcing businesses overseas were taking steps to demonstrate concern for all employees and a strong commitment to corporate citizenship. SGC worked hard to improve labour conditions in its Chinese supply chain. For instance, when Takashi found local suppliers were reluctant to make the initial financial investments for first aid training in factories, SGC paid for the initial sessions. Soon thereafter, Chinese partners saw less time lost due to injuries and began to embrace first aid training. Later, two major suppliers began to use the same first aid training when they noted the same benefits.

Although the costs were absorbed by SGC's bottom line, Takashi undertook additional similar initiatives, such as the production of a first aid handbook and posters with information about hazardous substances.

Takashi wondered personally about similar initiatives designed to boost healthier workplace practices, such as reducing the long working hours and increasing worker compensation, throughout its Chinese operations. But such initiatives would seriously affect the SGC's bottom line: outputs would reduce drastically because fewer hours were worked per employee. Although focusing on employee health and safety might help SGC's reputation, the lower revenues did not make business sense, especially in the short term. Accepting the status quo was not necessarily less risky either: SGC's supply chain was beginning to show cracks due to Chinese labour force dynamics. The Chinese workers who churned out bras for Ginza (famous shopping district in Tokyo) and toys to go under the Christmas tree were no longer happy to work in factories where security guards kept them behind locked gates or where taking a lavatory break of more than a minute could mean a fine. For example, the workers' turnover rates of two SGC's Chinese suppliers were over 100 per cent and they could not recruit enough workers to maintain production. As a result, SGC's orders were frequently not filled on time. Takashi found it unbelievable that a labor shortage had emerged in the world's most populous country. Another option, suggested by SGC's Board of Directors, was to withdraw operations entirely from China and enter other Southeast Asian countries such as Vietnam and Laos, where cheap labour was available and there was not a focus on labour conditions.

Takashi resolved to make a strategic decision before the end of the month but did not know where to start. He did not want to lose the competitive advantage of outsourcing to China and would forgo improving labour conditions if it meant keeping SGC alive. But he deplored exploiting the labour force and knew neighbouring countries had looser interpretations of employee health and safety. All the same, he wanted SGC to maintain the reputation of a company that cared about its employees. Thus, whether to leave China or continue to invest in employee wellness programs was more than just a straightforward question about the bottom line. This puzzle had ethical aspects. Takashi knew he was not going to solve it by looking out the window. He believed it was possible to make a strategic decision optimally positive for SGC and the Chinese workforce. But how? He believed he would figure it out and he knew it might entail leaving China.

Background: Shiraishi Garments Company

Japan currently has one of the biggest and most sophisticated apparel industries in the world. When it comes to fashion, the Japanese are very particular.

For centuries, a woman's most cherished possessions were not silver, gold or precious stones, but her kimonos. Much more than other cultures, clothes in Japan signify worldviews, personal tastes, and sensibilities. Although many modern-day Japanese live in nondescript and plain apartments, most have a strong willingness to spend considerable sums of money on fashionable, stylish, and modish clothing.

Takashi Shiraishi established his Shiraishi Garments Co. in 1978, after watching a news report on television that interested him. The oil crisis was biting hard that year, leaving the Japanese government to announce an 'energy suit.' The suit was a short-sleeved safari outfit designed to allow companies to save expenses on air conditioning. The idea was a failure because, although a few ministers wore the suits for a week or two, nobody thought they were appropriate for the office. The TV reporter said:

> The businessman puts on the darkest suit he owns, white shirt, sober tie, and *that is what he wears* in Japan, no matter what the temperature is outside. The Japanese find such rigidity comforting as it eliminates the sometimes nerve-racking necessity of making choices.

A recent art school graduate, Takashi believed the conservative dressing habit created an entrepreneurial opportunity: introducing customisation into the drab business attire market. He believed differences in taste, preference, and lifestyle mattered significantly to customers, even those in the same age demographic. Thus, the purchasing patterns should be diversified. He eventually opened a men's clothing shop in a Tokyo department store. Even though the small shop offered products in conservative colours such blue, grey, brown and black, there was variety; options besides drab suits and neckties. Based on skin colour, hairstyle, and other characteristics, Takashi helped customers select colours, accessories, styles, and shapes for tie knots. He became a master at making his customers feel special and important. Such personal attention made all the difference. Customers absolutely enjoyed that SGC took such interest in their appearance.

Designs were transferred to SGC's sewing subcontractors in the Tokyo suburbs. SGC usually ordered smaller quantities with more designs whereas other retailers ordered larger quantities and fewer designs. Although easier to fill orders for other retailers, the subcontractors were interested in SGC. As all the other retailers wanted low prices and high quality from sewers, price wars ensued and business relationships between retailers and sewers changed frequently. Yet, the relationship between SGC and its sewing subcontractors was very strong. SGC made detailed reports on defects and gave advice for how to improve quality and production. SGC shared customer comments and fashion forecasts with them, too, so subcontractors and suppliers could keep pace with the market.

Within two weeks of an order, customers would receive customised garments from SGC. Clothes arrived at the customer's home, and delivery personnel even showed customers how to wear the clothing correctly. They would visit the customer ten days later to see if everything was going well. Customers felt a sense of obligation to SGC and felt it would always be there should the clothing require service or repair.

The customer-oriented strategy and supplier relationship strategy were successful. SGC's garments were only 15 per cent higher in cost than ready-made ones, but consumers were able to choose from more than 10,000 unique style permutations. SGC quickly became synonymous with quality and prestige. In the Japanese economy's boom days of the 1980s, SGC was a medium-sized but prestigious brand. By 1991, total annual sales of its eleven retail outlets in department stores exceeded 22 billion yen.

Cutting costs

As the 1990s progressed, economic globalisation and an aging Japanese population dramatically changed the Japanese apparel industry. Rather than purchasing complete designed garments, the new generation purchased items at several different shops, mixing them freely to match their sensitivities. Young shoppers displayed a strong tendency to buy clothes at select shops near railway stations and fashion-specific commercial districts rather than conventional department stores, which were more sophisticated.

There was also a new casual style trend for males. Perhaps general disillusionment with life as 'salary men' made a more laid-back attitude attractive. Simultaneously, the economy entered the 'ten lost years' once the real estate and stock market bubbles burst in 1990. Japanese consumers lowered spending on clothing by making fewer purchases and preferring lower-priced items. From 1991 to 2004, the percentage of household expenditures going to clothing decreased for 13 straight years in a row.

The Japanese male clothing market was becoming fashion-oriented but commodity-driven. SGC's customised business attire did not meet this trend well. Since the late 1990 s they struggled with shrinking sales and profit margins, as shown in Table cs6.1. Takashi knew he had to cut costs to survive. So, in 2004, Takashi outsourced SGC's sewing tasks to Chinese companies.

China: allures and challenges

By 2004 the eyes of the business world were watching the Chinese economy. The reality of 1.3 billion potential consumers and low labour costs were attractive to American, European, and Japanese companies. Shelves around the world were stacked with low-cost goods churned out by 'the world's workshop': clothes, sporting goods, toys, computers, and DVD players.

Table cs6.1 Shiraishi Garments Company – financial highlights (yen, in millions)

March 31 year-end	2000	2001	2002	2003	2004
Sales	236,225	232,819	221,781	215,822	189,313
Operating income	17,661	14,032	15,275	12,910	12,872
Net income	7,266	6,026	5,049	4,567	4,347

Source: SGC internal documents

Table cs6.2 Hourly rates for sewing labourers in Asian urban regions

Country	Rate($/hr)
Laos	0.04
China (mainland / inner)	0.12
Vietnam	0.12
Sri Lanka	0.14
Bangladesh	0.19
Pakistan	0.23
India	0.25
Indonesia	0.42
China (coastal)	0.48
Japan	10.5

Source: Cal Safety Compliance Corporation (CSCC)

Following China's accession to the World Trade Organization (WTO) in 2001, the attractiveness of China as a manufacturing location increased further. The World Bank estimated that by 2010 China could account for half of the world's textile manufacturing.

After some research (Table cs6.2), SGC found China was not actually the cheapest place to outsource. Takashi had always believed that, all things considered, there was a 'best place' for manufacturing goods at any given time. And right now China was it because of low labour costs and the tremendous foreign direct investment in textile and apparel operations. The productivity of Chinese high-tech sewing facilities outpaced anything in the world. Takashi visited several 'supply chain cities' and was impressed by everything needed to manufacture garments existing in a single location. Many Chinese vendors were located within the supply chain cities. Factories were located near textile mills and other suppliers of various components. When considering the factories, political climate, time, fabric availability, human resources, infrastructure and speed to the Japanese market, Takashi was sure China was preferable to other Asian countries.

Cheap labour

Takashi noticed the salary rate in Chinese coastal areas was four times higher than in China's western regions. Many labourers thus had left rural poverty in the countryside for the new factories along the coast. As the 2004 Chinese New Year approached, Takashi was surprised to see that up to 120 million migrant labourers filled roads and railways to reunite with families in countryside. This large migration helped keep wages low. Migrant labourers were a cheap and compliant work force who had attracted much foreign direct investment and ensured the viability of millions of domestic businesses. However, Chinese prosperity had been achieved through their exploitation. In the Pearl River Delta, for example, one local vendor in SGC's new supply chain told Takashi, 'There are many girls with good eyes and strong hands. If we run out of workers who will accept our current wages, we will go deeper into the hinterland and recruit new workers.' In that vendor's factory workers were earning basic monthly wages of $37 and worked 16 hours per day, seven days per week. These realities troubled Takashi.

Low wages and poor labour conditions were the dark side of cheap labour costs. Domestic Chinese policy did not address them. Takashi saw that state-owned enterprises, although not productive or profitable, treated workers fairly well. At the same time, private sector companies were exploiting migrant labour, mostly young females. At the very root of the problem was the failure of local government to address the issue. He recounted in his journal:

> The local authority's priority is to attract foreign direct investment, and labour law enforcement is a selling point when trying to attract foreign inward investment. But the big problem is that local authorities are flexible in interpreting the law and have scarce resources.

Clothing companies had been a focus of non-governmental organisation (NGO) campaigns criticising low pay, overtime, safety problems and child labour in Chinese supply chains. NGO criticisms could lead to significant damages to a company's reputation. Thus, to operate in China, SGC had to face the problem of labour conditions. Other risks associated with poor labour conditions included quality problems, low productivity, and high employee turnover. Takashi summarised two principal risks associated with operating in China. Reputation, as poor labour conditions created negative publicity damaged the brand value. Also, operational risks were important and stemmed from poor productivity and high employee turnover (due to poor labour conditions).

Foreign companies with factories in China were less exposed to those risks than companies outsourcing production. Control was limited when outsourcing. Companies' actual factories in China had implemented occupational health and safety programs. They paid basic wages above the legal minimum. Their social security payments and working hours complied with regulations. Some provided extra benefits, such as housing subsidies and holidays. These factories required a minimum volume of business and had to reinvest continually to update their technology. The overhead costs of an outsourced vendor, on the other hand, were spread over a couple hundred clients. Takashi thought it would take years for a new factory to achieve the best practices, platforms, and intellectual property on par with a third party. So he decided to use Chinese suppliers instead of establishing an SGC factory in China.

Chinese suppliers

In China, Shiraishi Garments Company had two major suppliers. The first one produced accessory goods (supplier 1) and the second one sewed garments (supplier 2). Located on the outskirts of the city of Wenzhou in Zhejiang province, supplier 1 employed 1500 labourers. Its number of overtime hours were problematic, as 78 per cent of employees worked at least 132 hours of overtime per month. Most workers arrived at this factory unskilled. Because they were often paid piecemeal, and never for overtime, there was no incentive for the factory to cut back hours. Workers built skills on the job. The factory did not pay for training, carrying hidden costs of low productivity and quality and factory overhead.

Supplier 1

Although the factory incurred warnings and fines, supplier 1 did not provide any sort of bonus to employees at all. A rule book issued to workers instructed them on every aspect of factory life. The harsh penalty system included fines for any violation of the rules, including (a) arriving late, (b) talking during work, (c) leaving the workplace, or (d) spitting. Supervisors and middle managers spoke rudely and shouted at workers when production goals were not met.

Employees were despondent about the long hours and low pay. The fines and poor quality food exacerbated their unhappiness. Workers reported that there were few ways to communicate at all with managers. Most had no desire to do so. Relationships between workers and supervisors were strained. Employees frequently suspected supervisors of not accurately recording the number of pieces they produced and of extending working hours further than what management had scheduled.

It seemed health and safety management was good. Accidents were recorded by the medical centre and minor injuries were dealt with in the first aid room in each production unit. Takashi still had concerns about ergonomic issues such as congested facility layouts, bad lighting, and poor ventilation. Problems also included inappropriate storage and handling of toxic chemicals, improper protection equipment for workers, and the lack of chemical safety training. Supplier 1 had headaches managing its own suppliers. Low quality and late delivery of raw materials delayed production and squeezed the window of time for jobs and orders. It undertook purchasing from multiple sources, buying from a list of potential suppliers to avoid getting locked into a sole source.

Supplier 2

A small factory in the city of Dongguan in Guangdong province, employing around 400 workers, sewed garments for SGC and a few other foreign retailers. The managers described relations with foreign purchasers as uncomfortable in terms of tight lead times, late sample approval, and last minute changes to product specifications. All these problems put increased pressure on supplier 2 to deliver orders, which were sometimes not filled. It also led poor communication between merchandisers, factory management, and production.

Insufficient communication about changes to product specification led to more reworking and, therefore, overtime. The reworking time averaged 7 per cent during production and 10 per cent after final inspection. On some production lines with particularly difficult styles, reworking could reach levels of more than 50 per cent. As the piece rate compensation system did not cover reworking, a significant proportion of time was not only utterly unproductive, it was also unpaid. Very few workers knew there was a legal minimum wage. But all were aware they were not compensated for overtime and believed their wages were unfair. Two-way communication between workers and management was poor, so changes in pay or hours were not understood and on occasion resented by workers. There were few effective channels for workers to raise concerns with management, and managers usually did not respond to worker concerns or suggestions. Although the factory levied fines for 18 different kinds of offences, workers did not receive any training.

Supplier 2 had other areas of concern. Takaishi saw there were inadequate escape routes and locked or blocked emergency exits. Systems for tracking and improving productivity and quality were poor or nonexistent. There was no formal production line quality control system and there were no records of reworking rates during the production process. The piecemeal workers were given daily productivity targets and supervisors made daily estimates of how many pieces each worker made. Those records were not kept for more than a few days.

Supplier 2 estimated that 70 per cent of its fabric supplies necessary for production were delivered at least one week late. Worker annual turnover at supplier 2 was extremely high, 140 per cent. Most workers left because of the overtime hours and management had no apparent concern for their well-being.

Auditing

Factory auditing by the government was not the best tool for tackling the problem of Chinese labour standards in supply chains but, at the time, it was the only way. Auditing alone was not sufficient to drive positive change. It was easy to audit financial conditions, but difficult to audit a supplier for social conditions related to labour, community, and the environment. Health and safety audits were also difficult. For instance, Takaishi noted one audit checklist item, which stated, 'The supplier has a fire alarm.' Further questions not considered were, 'does it work?' 'Do workers know what it is?' 'Do workers have the right or the will to use it?' 'Would they know what to do in an emergency?' 'Can everyone in the factory hear it?'

A black-and-white audit approach could not solve these kinds of problems. Even if short timeframes to prepare and improve to pass an audit were granted, the fundamental problem was still poor labour conditions. Post-audit follow-up from the auditors was poor and resulted in few improvements actually being implemented.

Audits even could drive dishonesty, lack of openness, and fraud. Suppliers felt forced to provide the 'right' answer or face penalties. Chinese factory managers were becoming skilful faking records and coaching workers to give acceptable responses during interviews. This trend towards concealment was a barrier to improving labour conditions because it wasted time and money without making any change in the workplace.

Whereas workers did not want to work the excessive hours demanded of them, they were willing to work more than the low limits set by Chinese law to increase their pay. They knew that if a factory reduced hours to legal limits as a result of an audit, without some commensurate effort to increase productivity, wages would decrease dramatically.

Should I stay or should I go?

The sun was low and darkness was now descending over the Tokyo Bay's man-made islands. Takashi walked away from the window and turned on the light on his desk. He believed that the current approach, dependent on compliance-focused audits, had made little progress in tackling poor labour conditions in SGC's Chinese operations. The days of sweatshop labour might be numbered because the business environment was changing in China. Workers had mobile telephones and word of worker mistreatment spread fast. International purchasers could no longer rely on profits earned by exploiting Chinese workers.

Takashi thought he needed to focus more on continuous improvement and capacity building activity. But a new approach to finding a sustainable solution was needed. If such an approach was impossible, he was prepared to seriously consider getting out of China.

DISCUSSION QUESTIONS

1. What are the principal drivers of SGC's problems in China? Why did SGC likely not incur such problems in its previous supply chain in Japan?
2. Set out the cost, quality, delivery, flexibility and other operational reasons for and against staying in as against going from China.
3. What are the ethical issues involved in the go/stay decision?
4. If SGC moves out of China and into other developing countries, what are the potential benefits?
5. How can the frameworks of 'sustainable development' be used to assist in the challenges and decisions facing Takashi?
6. What problems is SGC facing in its supply chain?
7. Why are these problems critical to SGC?
8. What is the current approach to dealing with these problems and why it is not effective?

Towards a Green Supply Chain: Toyota Australia

Dayna Simpson

Introduction

Attaining environmental excellence through operations is a well established element of many successful production systems. Organisations have learnt much from establishing a connection between improving processes and operational efficiency and the subsequent benefits in environmental performance. Greener operations management provides benefits to the firm such as waste reduction, improved processes, fewer quality issues, less packaging, removal of toxic materials and environmentally sound innovations to name a few.

Combining environmental performance goals with the goals of the operations function has been borne out as providing a legitimate competitive advantage for the modern corporation. Manufacturers that are able to reduce pollution or waste in-process, avoid the costly re-management of wastes or having to invest in pollution control technology. Thoughtful consideration of environmental goals at the operations level has also led to successful new product innovation examples such as the recyclable disposable camera (Kodak), a 100 per cent recyclability of the automobile (BMW), and the use of hybrid technology to reduce fuel consumption (the Toyota Prius).

As raw material costs increase and environmental protection legislation becomes increasingly stringent, a focus on green operational excellence is becoming the norm in organisations. To attain even greater cost savings from waste reduction, meet comprehensive social and environmental responsibility targets and find new products with smaller ecological footprints, firms are now extending their goals for environmental performance into their suppliers' operations. This type of activity is known as 'green-supply' and is an effective mechanism for firms to improve their record on corporate social responsibility, lower reputational risks, reduce wastes and improve supply chain response-time to new environmental regulations.

Background

The Toyota Motor Corporation Australia Limited (Toyota Australia) consolidated its Australian operations in 1988 with its two manufacturing and assembly plants in Altona and Port Melbourne. Toyota Australia exports around 66,000 vehicles each year mainly into the markets of the Middle East, SE Asia, South Africa and Oceania. Toyota's international operations (Toyota Global) comprise one of the three largest selling automotive brands in the world. The brand is the number one automotive brand position in global sales and profit. Operationally, Toyota is known for the excellence inherent in its manufacturing and supplier management model. It deploys the Toyota Production System model throughout its global operations and expects its suppliers to invest heavily in adapting to its unique production system (including suppliers to Toyota Australia). This adaptation process is assisted by the use of a lengthy process of relationship building, knowledge exchange and information sharing between Toyota and its suppliers. Throughout the mid to late 1990s, Toyota Australia commenced a supplier development program aimed at upgrading its supply base to be able to meet its high standards of manufacturing performance.

Toyota Global sets an equally high standard for the environmental performance of each of its international operations. As with the Toyota Production System, each Toyota Global plant is provided with a comprehensive set of environmental performance metrics and is required to report this performance regularly back to Toyota Global. The global company sets environmental performance targets for waste reduction, energy efficiency, and reducing air emissions and water use that are well above international standards. Toyota Global has been previously recognised internationally with a United Nations Environment Program Global 500 Award (in 1999) and the Global Climate Protection Award from the USEPA (in 1998). Toyota Global was the first vehicle manufacturer in the world to commercially produce an environmentally friendly hybrid-fuel vehicle (the Prius). After a slow start to sales globally of the Prius vehicle, demand for the latest model currently exceeds supply.

Locally, Toyota Australia has been recognised for its environmental excellence with the Banksia Environmental Award (in the years 2003 to 2005); Victorian Premier's Business Sustainability Award (in 2004); a United Nations Association of Australia (UNAA) Environmental Best Practice award (in 2004) and Excellence in Water Management award (in 2003) among others. In

2002, Toyota Australia introduced its own Supplier Environmental Excellence Award and developed and an evaluation criteria for the environmental performance of its suppliers during 2003 and 2004. Toyota's Australian operations work to deliver the same levels of operational excellence as for Toyota Global. This requirement is extended into the operations of its key suppliers that provide first and second tier level of supply into Toyota Australia's assembly plants. The extension by Toyota Australia of its global standards of environmental performance into the operations of its local suppliers however has not experienced the same level of successful uptake by suppliers as that experienced in the uptake by suppliers of its just-in-time operational techniques.

Environmental performance management within Toyota Australia

To attain its high levels of environmental performance at its plants, Toyota Australia uses structure, collaboration between functions, extensive data collection and display, and a clear commitment to its alignment of operational and environmental goals at the operations level. Its overall program of environmental performance management is tied to the program deployed by Toyota Global. The company combines the principles of the Toyota Production System with a goal of continuous environmental improvement. Environmental performance at Toyota is tied to operations through a focus on continuous waste reduction and discovering value while reducing costs.

Environmental performance targets and objectives are initially established by Toyota Global which are then deployed through the CEO at Toyota Australia and managed by a specialised team of environmental staff based at both Altona and Port Melbourne. The environmental team coordinates employee training, data collection, analysis and reporting for the Australian operations and for input into the global operations. The environment team distributes its expertise through another team comprised of production staff who meet regularly to discuss environmental projects. These production personnel act as shop-floor environmental representatives in each of Toyota's main production areas and shops. More recently, the environmental team and the production team have begun to meet with a similar group of purchasing staff who were working on the extension of environmental performance into its existing activities with suppliers.

Interaction between the environmental team and the production team leaders was frequent and collaborative. This allowed the distribution of environmental performance information to production areas as well as the coordination of the collection, analysis and return of environmentally-relevant information from the production areas. Toyota's commitment to the environment could be seen easily in all areas of its Altona plant and all production notice-boards contained a section dedicated to the display of environmental performance data. This activity has led to significant reductions in water and energy usage and overall solid waste between the years 2000 and 2004. It has also allowed the development of a number of shop-floor-inspired environmentally innovations such as the removal of hazardous chemicals used in processes, and changes in the paint spraying technique to reduce paint sludge waste and the use of hazardous solvents.

The operating environment at Toyota Australia presented an exemplary case of how a successful and global manufacturing company can manage high levels of environmental performance whilst still meeting its operational and cost reduction targets.

Environmental performance management by Toyota with its suppliers

Toyota's supplier environmental management policy was based around initially identifying those suppliers most 'at-risk' of environmental incident, i.e., the supplier demonstrated high usage of chemicals, water or energy within its operations or produced a large waste load. Other vehicle assemblers in the Australian market (Ford and GM) had instead chosen to require all suppliers to certify to the internationally recognised environmental management standard ISO14001. Toyota's approach away from 'compliance' and more towards 'management' of the issue was intended to assist its suppliers and hopefully generate innovation. Toyota had also arrived at the conclusion that Ford's cascading of an ISO14001 requirement in the Australian industry during the years prior had ensured that most of Toyota's suppliers were already on the path to ISO14001. Toyota also perceived there to be a strong sense of antagonism between Ford and its suppliers because of the ISO14001 certification requirement and the cost burden these suppliers were forced to bear in an industry struggling to lower its costs.

The Toyota supplier management policy categorised suppliers on the basis of their potential for low, medium or high environmental impact and then specified levels of performance for each of these suppliers to achieve depending on their risk ranking. Level 1 (lowest) required a supplier to maintain a 'written environment policy endorsed by management'. Level 5 (highest) required a supplier to be 'independently audited, maintain a mature environmental management system and to be resourcing research and development for environmental improvement'. The policy aimed to initially provide an industry benchmark for all suppliers to be ranked against and further gave each supplier a target for improvement. The highest level of performance was intended to bring a supplier close to the level of environmental performance found within Toyota's own operations.

The supplier environmental management policy was managed almost entirely by Toyota's Purchasing staff. During 2004, Toyota Australia commenced its program to rank and benchmark each of its suppliers according to the system described above by distributing a compliance survey for suppliers to complete and return. Surveys were to be completed by each supplier; however, Toyota Purchasing did not attempt to visit any of the Toyota suppliers to verify the information provided by each supplier in their surveys. Initially, very few of the suppliers bothered to complete the environmental performance survey as requested by Toyota. Purchasing was eventually forced to actively follow up on each supplier that did not respond to their survey and expend significant effort obtaining a completed survey from each supplier. In parallel to its environmental performance survey, Toyota also conducted a process whereby each year it would call for nominations from suppliers to be considered for the Toyota Supplier Environmental Excellence Award. The supplier that receives the award is later actively promoted by Toyota as an environmental leader within Toyota's local and global reporting programs. The Award process included a site visit by a team of purchasing and environmental staff to six of the finalists. Paradoxically, the response from suppliers to Toyota's call for nominations for their Environmental Excellence Award was much greater than the response from suppliers to its environmental performance survey.

Toyota Purchasing's role in green supply

When Toyota wants its suppliers to work toward its objectives of operational improvement – most frequently the development of suppliers toward just-in-time delivery and leaner manufacturing – it deploys a sophisticated style of relationship management. Its style departs substantially from its major competitors (Ford, GM, Chrysler) through its use of high involvement tactics that attract substantial time and management costs. Its underlying principle is simple – respect for our suppliers requires detailed knowledge of our suppliers and the willingness to assist them toward successfully meeting our own operational objectives. This is created through extensive information sharing, visits to suppliers by Toyota's engineering and purchasing staff and often the investment of Toyota equipment and personnel in the suppliers' plant. The approach used by Toyota is known for its capacity to generate long term trust between customer and supplier, align goals toward mutually beneficial outcomes and deliver superior operational performance. The other assemblers tend to manage their supply bases with the use of more arms-length and antagonistic tactics spread across a far larger supply base. Competition amongst suppliers is the preferred way for these assemblers to drive down prices. The 'relationship' style of management at Toyota does not mean that Toyota is 'soft' in its requirements. Toyota is tough and demanding in the standards that it sets, including and beginning with its own operations, on key aspects impacting performance such as cost reduction. Simultaneous to its demands for outstanding performance, Toyota also provides substantial assistance with process, managerial and technical expertise in its supply base.

In the case of environmental performance management for suppliers in the Australian industry, GM and Ford remained true to their predominant relationship management form and simply cascaded down a mandatory requirement to suppliers – 'certify or you're out'. For Toyota, the situation was a little less clear. While on the one hand the company continued to maintain close relationships with key suppliers in order to ensure operational requirements were being met, it departed from this predominant management style when managing environmental performance requirements with suppliers. Toyota appeared to become decidedly arms-length or hands-off with its suppliers when attempting to pass on environmental performance requirements to suppliers. The outcome of this departure could be witnessed by the lack of will amongst suppliers to complete the environmental performance survey. A clue to this mis-match between the normal mode of Toyota relationship management and the abrupt departure toward an arms-length approach could be found inside Toyota at the purchasing–operations interface.

One of the internal failures occurring at Toyota Australia with its environmental performance management system was a lack of inter-functional collaboration between purchasing and production. Essentially, environmental performance goals were certainly an important part of the Toyota organisation; however, a consistent message being communicated by Toyota purchasing staff to Toyota production staff was the over-riding importance of cost reductions. As long as an environmental performance improvement project did not interfere with cost reductions or production, then it would be approved for funding by Toyota purchasing. This failure occurred through a lack of leadership by senior management at Toyota to step in and resolve these conflicts occurring at the Purchasing-Production interface. Where production or cost became critical, environmental objectives were consistently either left out or delayed during decision making. Environmental performance at the production level was supported by many of the elements that are an integral part of the Toyota Production System – teamwork, excellent data management, group problem solving, cost accounting, and the use of team-dedicated environmental specialists. Failures occurred when there was a lack of senior management support for environmental projects or an overriding emphasis on the importance of cost-downs when making decisions regarding an environmental project. Purchasing personnel, because of their only recent inclusion in the environmental program teams with Environment and Purchasing staff, also displayed an string cost focus and limited knowledge of Toyota's internal environmental performance program.

The management of the supplier environmental performance policy by purchasing staff at Toyota was also considered something that purchasing staff did not have the time to properly deliver. Internally, Toyota largely maintained a high level of environmental awareness and commitment at all levels of the organisation. Its commitment to environmental performance improvement was highly visible. This commitment failed internally however, when Toyota's environmental objectives clashed with the organisation's objectives to meet cost reductions or production targets.

DISCUSSION QUESTIONS

1. Suggest some reasons as to why Toyota may be experiencing difficulties in obtaining supplier collaboration with its supplier environmental management policy.
2. Examine Toyota's policy on green production, from published (including web) sources and compare these to its competitors' approaches.
3. Discuss the pros and cons of Toyota's relationship management style with respect to that used by GM and Ford when ensuring uptake of environmental performance requirements by suppliers.
4. Recommend some solutions to Toyota's problems with delivering fully green supply. Discuss the potential tradeoffs between cost excellence and green excellence in automotive production. Do these arguments apply more generally?

Process Analyses and Improvement at Bartter Enterprises

Tom Bevington, Phillip Irvine and Danny Samson[1]

Phillip Irvine, Operations Director of Bartter Enterprises (Australia's second largest chicken and poultry processor) was sitting in his office in North Ryde, Sydney in June 2006 reflecting on the meeting which had just ended with Geoff Frost, Group CEO, on the strategy for extending the BBX initiative group wide. Without any doubt, the work which Geoff and he had initiated in the Beresfield plant had been extraordinarily successful. Since launch in 2005, it had already delivered verified savings of over $3 m, which would be annualised at over $5 m. The key questions he now had to address were:

How to get this level of change implemented throughout the group?
How to ensure sustainability of this initiative?
How to go beyond this, and embed a culture of continual improvement for the future?

Phillip was not underestimating the challenge of the task ahead. He had just finished reviewing the detailed diagnostic data from the Hanwood, NSW site which had shown that while most of the key *themes* for change were consistent with Beresfield, the differences in such things as plant layout, skills and work practises suggested that less than 30 per cent of the Beresfield change *initiatives* would be applicable group wide. He mused therefore that a simple roll out of implemented changes from Beresfield across the whole group was definitely not an option. However, he had not been counting on such a roll out as he believed passionately in the adage – change imposed is change opposed.

Ticking off the positives in his mind, he reasoned on the motivational side that Bartter had put in place the key elements for a change program described by Kanter and her colleagues (1992).[2] First, he was guaranteed exceptional top management support as Bartter demonstrably had the benefit of a fully committed CEO. Second, the Beresfield work would provide an excellent in-house reference site on what was achievable, something which he knew would be critical to building understanding and motivation within the wider business. Third, the last year had seen the raising of awareness for the urgency and the need for change at the management level across the company. There was now at least some understanding of the industry 'burning platform' which had led Geoff to focus on a process based, operations excellence strategy, and indeed to recruit Phillip in the first place. Phillip also gave Geoff much credit for establishing a powerful change language in Bartter as argued to be necessary by Marshak.[3] As a result, a number of key phrases were in everyday use. These included: 'our burning platform', signalling understanding of the threats to the business and therefore the urgent need for change; 'being on the bus', describing those who were actively supporting, believing in and working towards the challenging strategic outcomes; and, perhaps a little too descriptive for some 'being in the departure lounge'.

Phillip also felt comfortable that there had been real progress on the building of an enabling change infrastructure and capability with the establishment of an organisational unit equipped with appropriate change and measurement tools. He had been able to use the last year to build a functioning, in house, process measurement and change team now with demonstrable delivery capability. He mused that he had successfully recruited Greg Searson, like himself, an ex-GE six-sigma black belt, who now occupied the role of National Manager of Operations Excellence, and who, in turn, then had some six staff. He was also pleased with the outcomes from his decision to acquire the XeP3 process measurement and management tool. He had first come across the tool in GE and had subsequently used it with good effect in Unisys Payment Systems. He liked its precision, delivery consistency and flexibility and was delighted by the way that all levels of staff, the union and management had engaged with it and had committed to the changes identified by using it. The approach had provided the critical group-wide engagement, understanding, quantification and wide acceptance of the large change potential. He also recognised the value of the relatively high staff turnover which allowed productivity gains to be achieved without any redundancies. Finally, high on his list of positives was the change supportive management structure which was now in place, in the form of a new, leaner, centralised, top management structure which would help enormously in addressing state cultural diversity.

The only negative in his mind was the feeling that he needed to get more in-house support capability for XeP3. This was being provided by external consultants.

He let his mind turn to the challenges. He was acutely conscious of the two edged sword nature of the success from Beresfield. It had enabled Phillip to confirm with the CEO that the opportunities promised were realisable, but it had also raised expectations for the size of the business contribution from the change! Even with Phillip's experience of change, there was always room for doubt in his mind on questions such as: does the same level of opportunity exist in the other sites?

He already knew that while the changes might be similar in nature they would differ significantly in their form from site to site. He was also conscious of the pressure to deliver similar results in all sites and the difficulties of running change programs and locking in the benefits across the multiple sites in the large, geographically dispersed business. There was also a downside from the high turnover of staff, could he be confident that the work done would ensure that the improvements in Beresford itself would be sustained, and did this need further work?

He let his mind roam further. What sort of framework would be best fitted to managing multiple site change programs? He recognised that he could not run the risk of waiting until the end of any individual site program to assess impact, but how could he ensure that each stage of the change program would be successful? He also remembered all too vividly the initial reaction from management when his first proposals for Beresfield were presented, typified by comments such as: 'we fully appreciate the need for change Phillip – but . . . the numbers you are talking about just aren't achievable' and 'look Phillip, we have already tried everything which you are suggesting before including Lean and TQM. Each program looked great to start with but they all took up a lot of our management time, disrupted the business, delivered little and then died'. Inevitably these thoughts would be in the minds of the managers and staff in the other plants and would surface as soon as the first potential problem arose. How could he ensure that he got to know quickly when these started to crop up and how would he head them off?

He also thought about the different cultures from state to state and the comments such as 'we do things differently here' and the other site diagnostic which had confirmed this to be the case. What did he need to do to ensure that issues were efficiently dealt with as they would inevitably crop up in many places? Other questions also raced through his mind. Should he aim to standardise procedures and practices across sites? If so how would they identify 'best practice' and how to get agreement on it without overburdening the project with administration?

Company and industry history

Bartter Enterprises had been set up in the mid 1950s by Peter Bartter. He was joined by his brother David some two years later and they built, by the early

70s, the largest chicken egg production business in Australia. The first major challenge to their growth which led to a strategic directional change occurred in the 70s as a result of industry regulation. This regulation manifested itself in the form of needed standards (which Bartter welcomed) and quotas. The quotas, which were destined to cap Bartter's growth, were designed to deal with overcapacity from new entrants and the doubling bird egg production productivity, through genetics, which had progressively occurred. The Bartter brothers took the strategic decision to move into the fast growing chicken meat sector, a move which would ultimately lead them to exiting the egg business.

This fresh meat strategy led to the development of the Griffith facility. By the end of the 1990s, as a result of their tremendous effort and enthusiasm and the dramatic market growth, Bartter had become the third largest player in this fragmented, predominantly family owned industry. The Griffith site was operating pretty much at full capacity and was processing some 600,000 chickens per week for key customers such as Coles, Woolworths and KFC.

At this time, the industry pressures, termed by Geoff as 'the burning platform', were becoming very evident. The retail majors (i.e., Coles and Woolworths) had driven the chicken producers to generic, own label branding, thus reducing the ability of the producers to differentiate their fresh products. The market was suffering from over capacity as the growth in the consumption of fresh chicken meat had slowed after its meteoric rise. There was extreme price competition largely from the twin forces of the buying behaviour of the retail majors, and the family decision making processes in competitors who were pursuing gaining market share at the expense of profitability. Bartter still wanted to continue with its aggressive growth strategy but it also knew that the route of adding expensive new capacity in an already oversupplied market was not the way to go.

A major strategic decision was taken by Bartter to expand through acquisition. This ultimately led to the acquisition of Steggles from Goodman Fielder. Steggles was then the ailing, but much larger competitor, sitting in the number two slot in the industry. This had the immediate and dramatic effect of moving Bartter from number three to number two in the industry and set the management the task, as Geoff says, of 'swallowing an elephant'.

In the event, the resultant high financial leverage necessary to acquire Steggles meant that capital became scarce and the management focus shifted to day to day operations.

The industry and market in 2006

The fresh chicken market in Australia grew five fold between 1964 and 2004. Per capita consumption rose from 4.9 kg/person in 1964 to 32.8 kg/person in 2004, a similar consumption to that of red meat. Average growth in per capita consumption in the decade from 1964 and 1974 was 17.8 per cent per annum. By 2004, the market growth had slowed markedly, growing some 2.48 per cent per annum in the decade to this date. This slowing was more marked towards the end of the period with growth now virtually static.

The industry was made up of three key players with about 80 per cent of the market, 7 substantial players with 1–3 per cent of the market each and many niche operators. Bartter's key competitors were Inghams, the largest supplier in the industry with 30–35 per cent of the market and Baiada who were in the number three position with a 10–15 per cent market share.

Bartter Enterprises in 2005/6

In 2005/6, Bartter was number two in the industry with national representation. The business processed some 2.5 million chickens and 50 thousand turkeys per week. It had 4500 employees and some 3500 customers including the majors such as Coles, Woolworths, Franklins, Lenards, Red Rooster and KFC. Turnover was about $800 million per annum. It operated from 15 locations with chicken processing plants in Beresfield (NSW), Hanwood (NSW, the Griffith site), Ipswich (Queensland), Mareeba (Far North Queensland), Geelong (Victoria) and Osborne Park (WA).

The features of Geoff's 'burning platform' were evident:

customer power (98 per cent unbranded or private label for fresh meat);
flat growth;
industry overcapacity; and
inevitable cost rises (energy, inflation, Union EBA agreements; etc.).

In addition, the market was increasingly volatile because of the major retailers buying approaches and the industry-related issues which affected consumer behaviour; these issues being the bird flu, hormones and antibiotics, genetics, food borne illnesses, etc.

All the above factors led to underlining the key elements of the strategy that the company decided to pursue: improve customer service while reducing costs and increasing flexibility.

It is probably also worth repeating how Geoff characterised the 2005 Bartter internal culture – pushback on targets, quick fix mentality, no improvement structure or tools, no recognition of the need to improve and significantly different cultures and facilities from state to state and plant to plant.

Foundations for operations excellence strategy

Geoff had joined the business in 1987 as management accountant and had become a director in 1990. He became CEO in 1999. Geoff recognised that the day-to-day focus had to change and began to concentrate on the factors where he believed that he could make a difference. He knew that there was limited ability to influence price. This was because costs – wages, transport and energy for example – were increasing for all the market players. The outcome of this thinking was the operations excellence strategy – to improve customer service and reduce cost. A first and necessary enabling step was to restructures the debt. This ultimately led to Bartter exiting the egg business which both enabled some reduction in debt and achieved clearer focus on the new strategy.

Having decided on a strategy based on operational excellence, Geoff concentrated most of 2004 on deciding how he wanted to approach the work and obtain agreement to this direction from within the top management team. He looked for support for this largely internal marketing exercise and found GE's Steve Sergeant (CEO of Bartter's financial services provider) a willing, experienced and effective operations excellence advocate.

Having received support, albeit lukewarm, from his top team, Geoff set about acquiring the expertise to drive the new strategy's execution. Phillip Irvine was recruited in early 2005. Discussion then followed on both the selection of the pilot site and then on the stretch targets which should be set.

The Beresfield pilot

The Beresfield plant is located in NSW some 150 kilometres north of Sydney. In 2005, the plant processed some 600,000 chickens and 50,000 turkeys per week using two shifts and employed some 700 staff.

It had proved to be a relatively straightforward, if somewhat drawn out decision to select the Beresfield plant for the pilot. The plant was not performing well and the management and unions were supportive of any initiative to make the plant viable in the long term. The issue at the front of management's mind was therefore not the need to improve the plant but their profound doubt that any further opportunities existed. Previous projects had been well embraced but the expected outcomes had never materialised.

The first step committed to was therefore to prove that the opportunity existed to achieve Phillip's stretch targets. This involved measurement of exactly what was going on in the Beresfield business processes using Phillip's preferred process measurement tool, XeP3. Figure cs8.1 provides a summary of how this tool operates. This tool was used to both pinpoint, and critically gain full agreement (top to bottom) to all of the gaps and weaknesses in the plant's business processes. The staff, with the support of management, therefore participated in a thorough documentation of *what* tasks were undertaken (the conventional approach), and then more importantly, (and less conventionally), precisely *how* each task was carried out. This detailed documentation

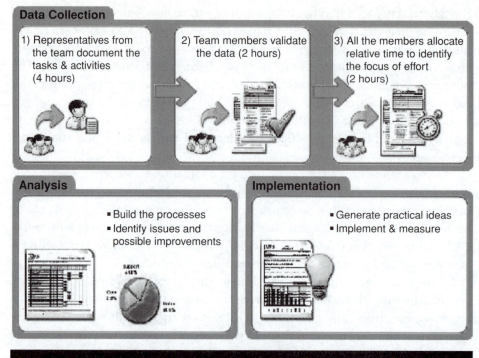

Data Collection

1) Representatives from the team document the tasks & activities (4 hours)

2) Team members validate the data (2 hours)

3) All the members allocate relative time to identify the focus of effort (2 hours)

Analysis

- Build the processes
- Identify issues and possible improvements

Implementation

- Generate practical ideas
- Implement & measure

Figure cs8.1 The basic XeP3 toolkit

was developed for each of the 33 discrete organisational teams operating on the site using the first three steps in the XeP3 tool kit.

The data development was undertaken in three steps. The first was a map of *what* each team did and then in detail how they did it. Some 8 to 30 tasks were identified by representatives from each of the 33 teams. These tasks are shown in the upper box in Figure cs8.2. The staff then described in detail *how* each of these tasks was undertaken. This included the steps virtually always documented in up-to-date and accurate procedure manuals, and, much more importantly, the other tasks which they had to do including routinely occurring rework and correction – termed in XeP3 to be the process *noise*. The lower part of Figure cs8.2 illustrates this level of detail for *some* of activities needed to achieve the first of the eight tasks. In total, this resulted in some 8000 detailed activities being catalogued in the XeP3 data base. This equates to about 300 detailed activities per team.

The second step was to work with each team as a whole, first to verify that in everyones' view, all of the detailed activities had been written down and described adequately. In this same session, the team also conducted step 3, quantifying the relative time, and therefore cost, spent on each of each team's activities. Finally, the each activity was categorised.

XeP3   FOOD 1°   *Tasks and Activities*

Status:	AU27 - Distr: Dock Dayshift
Completed by: Team Member Check: ☐	Date: Tuesday, 27 September 2005

Quantified Tasks	Quantified Services
Picking, Scanning & Staging	
Rework	
Load Trucks	
Unload Trucks	
Pallet De-Hire	
Lines Relief / Cover	
Pre Start Check / End of Shift	
General Admin / Other	

Main and Sub-Activities

A) Picking, Scanning & Staging

1   **Planning and allocating Pickers**

   1.1 Log on to system

   1.2 Get printed picking sheet of transport coordinator

   1.3 Allocate run to pickers

2   **Linehaul Picking (Other Plants)**

   2.1 Get a pick sheet from team leader (Sheet is based on estimate)

   2.2 Go and find the product

   2.3 If you can't find it, go into another product

   2.4 If you can't find it, go and look on lines

   2.5 If you can't find it, go to transport coordinator to contact logistics to find out if produced

   2.6 If produced go and look for it again

   2.7 If you can't find it, look later in the shift

   2.8 Pick carton and place it on pallet

   2.9 If required, move product to pick oldest product first

   2.10 (often not a significant issue as product is reasonably well arranged in morning)

   2.11 If the pallet jack breaks down tow it to battery charger room and tag it and report to office personnel

   2.12 If the pallet jack has flat battery tow it to battery charger room and put on charger and use what is available. (May have to use a walkie Jack instead)

   2.13 If carton or crate has no label, take to QA area

   2.14 Wait, If another picker is picking the same product

   2.15 Take full pallet to scanning area

   2.16 If update order volume at mid morning is less than picked, remove extra (total of received orders at time of print)

   2.17 If update order volume at 11 am update is less than picked, remove extra (total of floor count and received orders at the time of print)

   2.18 (2 updates given in morning)

   2.19 If update order volume at final is less than picked, remove the extra

   2.20 If order volume is more than what has been picked, pick extra product

3   **Linehaul Picking (Interstate)**

   3.1 Get a pick sheet from team leader

   3.2 Go and find the product

   3.3 If you can't find it, go into other products for the rest of the sheet

   3.4 If you can't find it, go to transport coordinator to get information from logistics

   3.5 Call computer room to confirm production.

   3.6 If apparent excess of product contact logistics (Sometimes error in sheets from logistics)

Figure cs8.2 Example of the data developed by each team

The categorisation of each of the 8000 detailed activities began the transformation of an indigestible volume of process data into a meaningful and understandable business system. All of the detailed activities were categorised using the definitions presented in Figure cs8.3.

As a result of this step about 40 per cent of the 8000 detailed activities, some 3000 activities in all, were defined and coded by Beresfield staff as Noise. This step alone achieved much in overcoming the initial reservations. The analysis showed that routine process failure, the Noise, absorbed 32 per cent of the total time[4] of employees confirming that a large opportunity existed. A relatively low 1 per cent Core activity also suggested that there

Noise	Non-value adding activities. Waste within the business	• Rework/recovery from error • Delays
Discretionary	Activities at management's discretion	• Training • Approvals • Audits
Support	Activities that generate current revenue	• Processing • Data entry (the first time!)
Core/Value Driving	Activities that increase revenue, reduce cost or enhance capability.	• New Sales development • Cost reduction activities

Figure cs8.3 Categories for processes

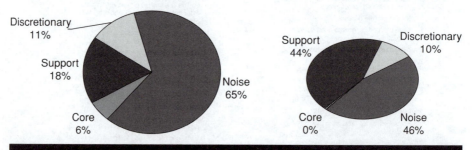

Figure cs8.4 Distribution of activity types for two teams

were real opportunities to increase the focus on value driving activities. It demonstrated that there were more than sufficient opportunities, as well as building understanding in staff and management on where these opportunities were located! Noise levels, as might be expected, varied by team. Examples are included in Figure cs8.4.

Analysis by process enables a strategic perspective to be taken. Clearly, sequencing the data across the whole organisation would reveal all task duplication and overlaps as well as process failures. It would also allow the business performance driving core activities to be assessed against strategic goals such as particular customer service achievement and utilisation and waste management.

Using the XeP3 software features, this data was therefore assigned to particular strategically defined business processes with the help of the Bartter teams. It was sequenced logically so that the processes could be read step by step from, for example, the receipt of an order to the despatch of the product.

Beresfield BBX

Solution Analysis Report

8 *Process 2 – Pick & Despatch*

Solution Analysis Report by Process

Activity Unit:	All Activity Units
CSDN:	Core, Support, Discretionary, Noise, (Unassigned)
Process:	2 - Distribution: Pick and Despatch

		Total Hours	(130 Hrs/Mth=1FTE)
Activity Driver	12 - Formal warehouse management/storage process is inefficient	297.45	
Activity Driver	51 - Specific product required not available to pick	130.19	
Activity Driver	76 - Logistics do not have final orders and/or production data	110.72	
Activity Driver	21 - Labelling Problem	100.37	
Activity Driver	164 - Handle Credit Claim	44.2	
Activity Driver	60 - Handle Shortages	39.82	
Activity Driver	48 - Cedar Creek not accessible	30.02	
Activity Driver	71 - Marsden Park staff unfamiliar with Cedar Creek	29.9	
Activity Driver	146 - Lack of timely communication and complete information	28.45	
Activity Driver	42 - Insufficient scanners	27.07	
Activity Driver	152 - Production process failure	24.32	
Activity Driver	74 - No system for manual orders	21.65	
Activity Driver	73 - DSM and Bartlercus interface is manually initiated	19.79	
Activity Driver	155 - Transfer procedure (TI/TO) not followed	16.8	
Activity Driver	15 - Change of colour code during shift/Forward production	16.45	
Activity Driver	59 - Underproduction of product	16.34	
Activity Driver	56 - CCS doesn't calculate pallet requirements	15.52	
Activity Driver	61 - Insufficient trucks	14.1	
Activity Driver	79 - Cedar Creek system is slow	12.55	
Activity Driver	75 - Live production data not available	12.53	
Activity Driver	40 - Damaged scanner	12.5	
Activity Driver	90 - Logistics subs sheet not aligned with stock situation when picking	12.29	
Activity Driver	46 - Incorrect charging of pallet jack	11.67	
Activity Driver	66 - Pallet jack problem	10.51	
Activity Driver	148 - Insufficient export planning and procedure	10.26	
Activity Driver	62 - Distribution managing trucks directly by phone	9.36	
Activity Driver	149 - Failure to comply with safety procedure	8.52	
Activity Driver	72 - DSM only processes by depot	8.3	

15 / 06 / 2005

© Bevington Process Management Tools

11

August 13, 2007

Figure cs8.5 Example print of individual initiatives

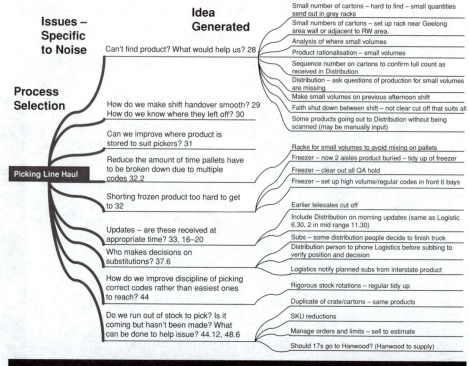

Figure cs8.6   How the software maintains the linkage between the ideas and the business process

Using this feature, Bartter could also be confident that *all* detailed activities had been allocated to one of its processes. None could be overlooked and this obviated the common problem of traditional mapping where only what is believed to be in a process is mapped and thus management is unaware of the other detailed activities.[5]

The various causes of the noise, and its impact in the various teams in the process, could then be seen and quantified. Driving causes were thus established for both Noise and Core and the benefit of addressing each driver costed and organisationally positioned. The high level drivers of noise in ranked order included:

1. warehouse traceability
2. production schedule and sequence
3. plant inefficiency
4. pallet and crate management
5. plant consumables
6. mobile plant availability.

FOOD 1*

Implementation Planning

Idea: 1166	AU7 - CPP Line and Merge (Day)
Completed by: Team Member Check: ☐	Date: Tuesday, 27 September 2005

Idea Description: **Idea:1166**

When packing frozen at high levels leave fitter at cryovacs to provide immediate maintenance response

Affected Activities:

AU	Act.	CSDN	Tot. Hours	Hours Saved	Hours Added	Activity Description	Sub-Activity Description
✓ 7	37.8	N	14.57	14.57		Bag and Pack items	If machine is broken and not flat out, pass bag to next machine
7	37.9	N	116.36	50.0		Bag and Pack items	If cryovac machine breaks down or all positions busy (usually jams on clips), wait for a fitter
7	37.10	N	14.67	13.78		Bag and Pack items	Notify leading hand of a breakdown
11	37.1	N	28.16	11.25		Pack Items	If machine is broken and not flat out, pass bag to next machine
11	37.2	N	28.16	11.25		Pack Items	If cryovac machine breaks down or all positions busy (usually jams on clips), wait for a fitter

Total Hours Saved: 100.85
Total Hours Added:
Total Investment ($000s):

Comments from Review Meeting:

Stategic:
- ○ Low
- ● **Medium**
- ○ High

Behavioural:
- ● **Low**
- ○ Medium
- ○ High

Planned Implementation Stages			
Description	**Accountability**	**Start Date**	**Finish Date**
Establish, when this service is required (if at all) and implement procedure for notifying maintenance when this occurs during the week. Create cryovac downtime book to establish measure prior to implementing			2/09/2005
Notify staff via toolbox of recording cryovac downtime			9/09/2005
Get maintenance to man during frozen			16/09/2005
Assess measure with maintenance on hand whilst packing frozen			23/09/2005
Overall Accountability	PROJ13:CryoSeal	Planned Finish Date:	

Figure cs8.7 Planning a change initiative

High level driver summaries provide a useful guide to management of the nature of the changes which needed to be made. However, each process failure element or performance driver needs to be addressed at its change initiative level. Examples of the change initiatives are included as Figure cs8.5. The quantified hours saving per month is shown on the right hand column.

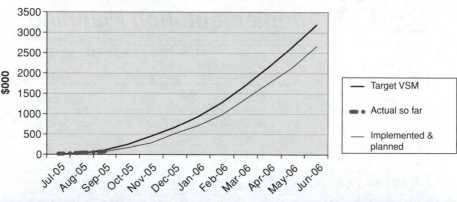

Beresfield VSM Project Savings

Figure cs8.8   Project outcomes

The analysis of this data by business process thus established the key areas for change. The Bartter team analysed the business process data and identified some 300 drivers of noise. The same team then proposed, and costed, broad solutions to the 'no brainers'[6] and selected those towards the top of a Pareto listing. The outcome from this work was a list of prioritised, costed initiatives for the staff and management to focus on.

These prioritised initiatives were then used to re-engage with the staff through the mechanism of idea generation sessions. The input to these idea generation sessions was the data for that particular part of the business process for the selected initiatives. The core invitees were those people who were actually doing the work under discussion and who had provided the process documentation for that segment of the business process. The thesis behind this was that those actually doing the work were the ones who needed to understand and carry through the change.

The outcomes consisted of 1500 pragmatic changes which related to each change initiative to specific elements of each business process as illustrated in Figure cs8.6. The ideas were reviewed by management and the resultant 1000 changes accepted.

At this stage the ideas were grouped into 4 waves and then each was carefully planned out (Figure cs8.7) by the relevant manager and staff. This enabled a project office to monitor that appropriate actions were being taken and that they were on schedule, and, provide help where needed.

The final step was then to sign off on each change and verify the saving.

The outcomes of the project (so far realised and projected) is shown in Figure cs8.8.

DISCUSSION QUESTIONS

1. Why was top management team initially reluctant to engage in the much needed change program to improve productivity and customer service in the Beresfield plant?
2. Using material from the case study, illustrate how the Kanter et al. (1992) change factors apply to the Beresfield plant?
3. What were the key features which made the Beresfield plant change program so successful?
4. Why was it not possible to implement the Beresfield plant initiatives 'top down' across the business in the way that say new warehouse racking could be installed everywhere?
5. What are the key issues Phillip has to address in spreading the program across to the whole group?
6. How should Phillip go about replicating the results across the business?
7. How could Phillip ensure that the changes would endure?

Notes

1 The authors wish to record their grateful thanks for key inputs from Geoff Frost, CEO, Bartter Enterprises and David Piddington, Continuous Improvement Manager at the Beresfield plant of Bartter Enterprises.
2 R. M. Kanter, B. A. Stein and T. D. Jick 1992. *The Challenge of Organizational Change*. Toronto: The Free Press. Kanter et al.'s ten important elements for effecting organisational change are: analyse organisation and need for change; create a shared vision; separate from the past; create a sense of urgency; support a strong leader role; line up political sponsorship; craft an implementation plan; develop enabling structure; communicate; involve people; and, be honest and reinforce and institutionalise change.
3 R. J. Marshak. 2004. 'Morphing: The Leading Edge of Organizational Change in the Twenty-first Century.' *Organization Development Journal*, 22(3): 8–22.
4 Note: a 32 per cent noise activity level, while indicating considerable scope for improvement, is not a characteristic of a poorly managed organisation. Noise levels of 50 to 60 per cent are routinely measured using XeP3 in large organisations. Similarly 1 per cent core is normal to good for a manufacturing plant.
5 XeP3 application has demonstrated that up to 50 per cent of detailed activities undertaken in organisations are never recorded in traditional mapping exercises.
6 Refers to simple changes requiring minimal or no investment and with clearly established saving.

Operations Challenges at Firth Industries Limited, Wellington Division[1]

Lawrie Corbett and D. Clay Whybark

The gray day in the region matched his mood as Dave Newland, Area Team Leader for the Wellington Division of Firth Industries, Limited, contemplated what to do about delivery vehicle productivity. Even the Hutt River seemed darker than usual as he mulled over the problem of simultaneously satisfying customers and satisfying headquarters. He had recently been notified by the corporate office that the trucks he used to deliver ready-mix concrete to his customers were not as productive as those used by some of the sister divisions nor were they as productive as they had been in the past. Over the past several months, construction activity had declined substantially and the demand for concrete had been shrinking. Facing this kind of market, it was very clear that responding to customer needs was critical. Although truck efficiency was important, he was concerned that focusing on efficiency might detract from customer service thereby leading to more order cancellations. Dave already had more of those than he wanted.

Company background

Firth Industries Limited, a fully-owned subsidiary of Fletcher Challenge Limited, is a major supplier of concrete and concrete products through-out New Zealand. The company traces its beginnings back to Josiah Clifton Firth who arrived in New Zealand in 1856. He decided that Auckland needed a modern flourmill, but chose to first build a brick-making factory to provide the bricks. The company's logo 'Leading by Design' stems

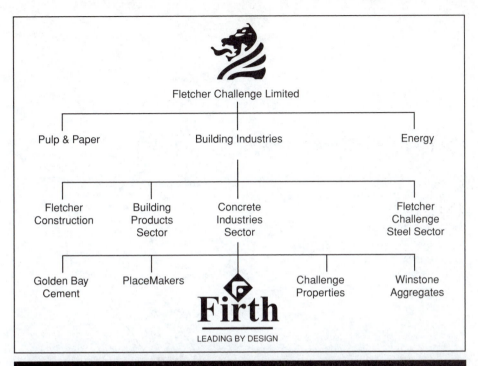

Fletcher Challenge Limited

Pulp & Paper   Building Industries   Energy

Fletcher
Construction   Building
Products
Sector   Concrete
Industries
Sector   Fletcher
Challenge
Steel Sector

Golden Bay
Cement   PlaceMakers   **Firth**
LEADING BY DESIGN   Challenge
Properties   Winstone
Aggregates

Figure cs9.1 Fletcher Challenge company structure

from this entrepreneurial approach to problem solving. Grandsons Ted and Tony Firth formally founded Firth Concrete Ltd in 1925. Over the next 50 years, through product innovation, process improvements and successive building booms, the company grew into a diverse, national organisation.

Fletcher Challenge became involved with Firth in 1973 and by 1979 had acquired the company. In 1993, the company, by then known as Firth Certified Concrete Ltd, was combined with two other Fletcher Challenge companies, Stresscrete Industries Ltd. and Firth Industries Limited. The combination provided a broad range of concrete products and expertise with which to serve the entire New Zealand market. Currently the company operates as an autonomous business unit headquartered in Auckland and headed by a general manager. It is a part of the concrete products sector of the Fletcher Challenge building materials group (Figure cs9.1 shows the corporate relationships). In combination with other group companies Firth Industries is vertically integrated. Everything is taken care of, from the aggregate and cement used in making the concrete products, to the sales and distribution through a national building products retail chain (Placemakers). Firth currently has more than 70 plant facilities throughout the country (see Figure cs9.2 for

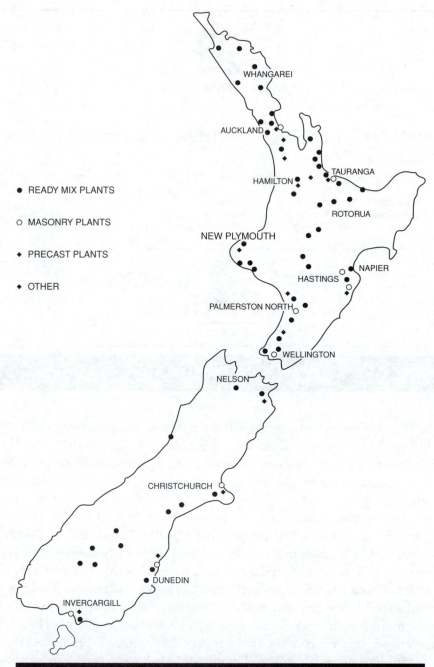

locations) and does some manufacturing and product licensing overseas. Among the New Zealand facilities there are some 50 ready-mix concrete plants, all of which are pursuing ISO 9001 certification to support their domestic and overseas markets.

A key reason for the large number of facilities is that the delivery distances are quite limited for Firth's products due to their high weight, low value combination. For ready-mix products, delivery distances are also limited because concrete can only remain in the delivery trucks for about two hours before becoming unusable. A natural result of this limitation is that management of local operations is highly decentralised. Firth has five facilities in the Wellington area. Three of these, a ready-mix concrete plant, a block making plant and a small retail outlet, are in Lower Hutt, a community about 20 kilometres east of downtown Wellington. The other two facilities, a pre-stress products plant and a ready-mix concrete plant, are located in Porirua some 25 kilometres north of Wellington. Local sales and deliveries of ready-mix concrete for the area are all handled out of the Lower Hutt facility. This enables them to coordinate deliveries in the area by filling delivery trucks at the facility closest to the customer.

The market

Ready-mix concrete is made up of cement, sand, aggregate, water and selected additives that are combined to meet the specifications prescribed by the use of the product (e.g., building construction, roadways, airport runways, and so forth). There are roughly 200 standard mixes of which some 20 comprise well over 90 per cent of the demand and one mix alone accounts for nearly 50 per cent. The demand for ready-mix concrete is related to construction activity that is closely tied to the general state of the economy. When the economy is good, money is available for major public projects like highways, dams, airports and office buildings, all of which require huge quantities of concrete. Similarly, when confidence is high, private investment in construction increases as well.

The relationship between industrial confidence and the economy means that the market for concrete can change substantially from one quarter to the next. This can be seen in Figure cs9.3, which gives the sales by quarter of ready-mix concrete for New Zealand for Dec. 1994–Dec. 1995. The variability is also present in the individual regions of the country, but may not match the national shifts. In the Wellington area, for example, the changes in sales over the same periods are different from the country as a whole (see Figure cs9.4). In fact, due to differences in the local economies, different regions of the country could be in different stages of the demand cycle at the same time. Moreover, when a facility in one location needs some

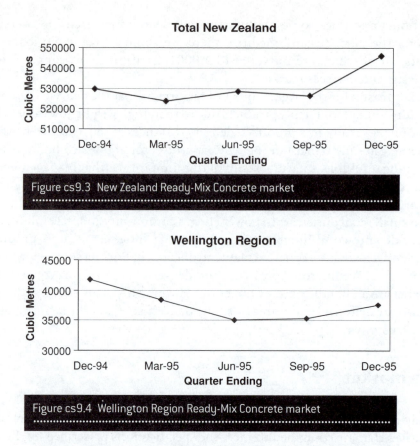

Total New Zealand

Figure cs9.3 New Zealand Ready-Mix Concrete market

Wellington Region

Figure cs9.4 Wellington Region Ready-Mix Concrete market

short-term extra capacity, very little help is available from the facilities outside their region because of the limited delivery distances.

There are other differences in the regions as well. Some are very densely populated, others are in mountainous country and still others have a large industry base. These factors contribute to the difficulties in sharing resources from one part of the country to another and can exaggerate the differences in economic activity from one region to the next. As an example, demand for concrete in the Wellington region has been generally declining for several years while it has been very strong in the Auckland area because of a residential housing boom and considerable major construction. Large-scale projects can lead to big swings in local demand in as well. For instance, Firth had the concrete contract for the construction of the new Museum of New Zealand in Wellington. This is a large building designed to replace a crowded facility housing many nationally important archaeological, zoological and historic exhibits. When the concrete work finished about six months ago, it affected Firth's volumes substantially. (See Figure cs9.5 for Firth's sales for Dec. 1994 – Dec. 1995 by quarters.)

Commercial construction is one of the two major market segments for ready-mix concrete. The other is residential construction. Both of these

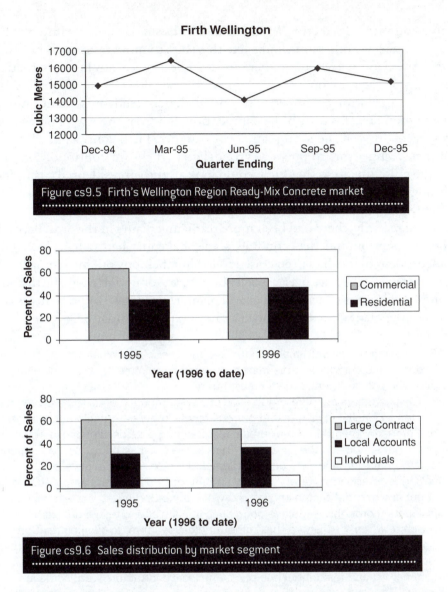

Figure cs9.5 Firth's Wellington Region Ready-Mix Concrete market

Figure cs9.6 Sales distribution by market segment

segments, however, can have large projects that require tendering bids for the business. The new museum in Wellington is an example of a large commercial contract while a retirement village or an apartment building would be examples of residential contracts. The local offices are involved in preparing the bids for very large projects, with support from Firth's national offices in Auckland when requested. Local sales representatives actively seeking opportunities in their area primarily serve the residential market. This includes business coming from local contractors, homebuilders and individual do-it-yourselfers. The composition of the customer base has shifted over the last few years, however. As seen in Figure cs9.6, the percentage of business coming from the commercial segment has decreased as has the portion coming from large contracts. 'Predicting anything in this business is nearly impossible,' said Dave Newland, 'but it looks like this shift to more residential business will be with us for a while and there are no indications of any big construction projects on the horizon.'

There was strong competition among the six ready-mix plants in the Wellington area. Even with the competition, however, there were occasional contracts between the local plants. For instance, Firth contracted with one of their competitors to provide three delivery trucks for continuous service on the museum job so that Firth could look after their residential customers during that time. Firth's strategy was to protect this market for the period after the museum contract was completed.

Until recently, there had been more ready-mix plants in the area. Between the competition and the economy, some shakeouts had taken place. Two independent plants had been closed following their buy out by a competitor. In an attempt to reduce over-capacity in the area somewhat more, Firth and a competitor recently each closed a local plant. How long it would be necessary to keep the plant closed was not clear, however. According to Dave,

> Forecasting the overall local demand is difficult enough. When we get to trying to determine our share of the market or when large projects will come along and who will get them, it gets really murky.
>
> The customers are different in each of the segments. For us to be involved in the tender business means that our customers know our quality and that we can produce the product that they need. Landing a tender depends largely on price, but service on the job is important as well. It may be the service aspect of our reputation that gets us invited back the next time. We have built a strong reputation for variety, quality and integrity. The plant can produce about any mixture that is known and we're inventing more. We test our products thoroughly and have gone back to a job site to take out cured concrete when we learned that something caused it to go off specification. That is very rare, obviously, but there are no arguments when it does occur. Our customers appreciate that. Our reputation is important in both the commercial and residential business. The local contractors want someone who will get the right product to them when they need it. They really don't want to worry about concrete at all. Also all of our contractors appreciate that we can put together a package that includes concrete, blocks, and other products they need on the construction site. On the other hand, they tell us that you can't differentiate ready-mix concrete so we better have the best price in town.
>
> These conflicting signals from our customers make it difficult to decide how to focus our attention on the truck efficiency issue. We might be able to reduce price a little with better efficiency, but if we have to turn down business because we don't have enough capacity or are late on deliveries and lose customers, I'm not sure it is the right trade off. It also turns out that our truck drivers are the face of the company to the customer. His/her actions on the job site can make a big difference in the reputation of the company and our ability

to do repeat business. Moreover, they are in a good position to learn about potential future business.

Local operations

Graeme Lucinsky, operations manager for the Wellington Division, pointed out that the change in demand had already affected operations.

The shift to more residential demand has increased the distances that we drive to reach the customer. Our average delivery now takes about 130 minutes as compared to six months ago when it was 80 and we're making more trips each day. The average order size has decreased as well. Where we had loads that averaged 4.2 cubic meters last year, in April it was down to about 3.1, even though we delivered 2125 cubic meters total. (See Figure cs9.7 for statistics on truck deliveries.) We're trying to cope with the market changes, but it is not clear how. Over the last few months we've reduced the number of trucks and drivers in our fleet from 14 to 10. However, that was debated and some of our people are now saying we don't have enough trucks left to do the job. In fact, the drivers are working between 52 and 58 hours per week, and that's about the same as it was six months ago.

The changes in performance are showing up in the statistics that Auckland uses to compare the regional divisions and we don't look so good. In an effort to increase our driver's awareness of what is going on, we now post the cubic meters delivered by each truck. There is a lot of variability. The figures for April ranged from 122 to 278 cubic meters. But here is what we are up against. In 1995, when we had more trucks, we averaged about 280 cubic meters per truck per month. So far this year we are at less than 250, lagging behind the group's average of about 275. What's more, some of the plants in other parts of the country are at nearly 350 cubic meters per truck per month and some achieved that last year. The market changes don't look favourable to making improvements in these measures in the near future, but we still have to try.

With rare exceptions, each customer's order is filled individually at the plant. The process involves adding all the ingredients for an order in a large container according to the correct recipe, and mixing them until they are thoroughly combined. Once the order is mixed it is dumped into the drum on a delivery truck that is positioned under the mixer. When the mixer is empty, the next order can be started. As soon as the truck pulls out from under the mixer, the next truck can be positioned to receive a load. Although there is only a single mixer in the plant, it can mix up to 6 cubic meters at a time and can operate as long as there are delivery trucks to be filled. Regardless of the number of cubic meters in the load, it only takes about five minutes to charge the mixer, mix the batch, dump the mix into the truck and prepare for the next load.

The truck then heads off to the customer to make the delivery. At the site, the driver checks on where the concrete is to be unloaded, empties the

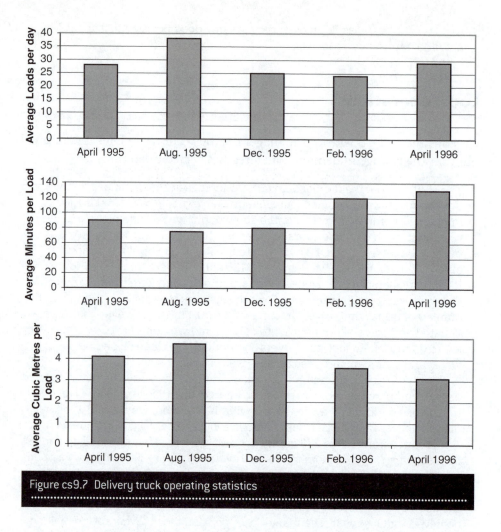

Figure cs9.7 Delivery truck operating statistics

truck, and washes the delivery chutes to avoid any spillage on the way back to the plant. After the paperwork is completed the driver returns to the plant, washes the outside of the truck, wheels, etc., and drives under the mixer or waits in the office for the next delivery assigned to the truck. Although the time to load, complete a delivery and clean up is currently averaging about 130 minutes, there is considerable variation from load-to-load. There are potential delays due to traffic, unclear delivery instructions or road conditions. At the site, the customer might not be completely prepared and driver is sometimes required to wait for the job foreman, additional workers or some special equipment to help with the unloading. Such delays can cause more problems than just the productivity of the truck. Since there is a limit to how long the concrete can stay in the mixer on the truck before beginning to cure, there are quality implications. The plant can add inhibitors (for very hot dry days, for example) or accelerators (for cold, wet days), but predicting when

Sales	100.00%
Costs	
Material	67.77%
Truck/Driver*	5.92%
Admin/Ovhd	24.80%
Profit	1.51%
* 4.06% Driver Wages & 1.86% Truck Variable	

Figure cs9.8 Cost structure of Ready-Mix Concrete

traffic or job site conditions would require their use is very difficult. In one instance the company had to remove a very large section of concrete from a job when they discovered that a traffic delay had caused the concrete to be drier than it should have been when it was poured at the site.

Firth currently has ten trucks in the Wellington delivery fleet all based at the Lower Hutt plant. The majority of the fleet consists of trucks of five cubic meter capacities, each leased at a cost of about $15,000 per year. There is one truck that has a six cubic meter capacity and one with 4.8. One of the five cubic meter trucks has a long delivery conveyor attached which increases the flexibility to deliver in hard to reach places. The weight of the conveyor reduces the effective capacity of the truck to about 4.5 cubic meters, however. There was some concern about the size of the trucks, given the decreasing size of orders. Some residential customers had expressed surprise at the size of the truck that was used to deliver a rather small order and commented on the difficulty of manoeuvring the vehicle around the neighbourhood. On the other hand, the cost of the driver was the same and operating costs didn't decrease much with the use of smaller capacity trucks. (The plant cost structure is shown in Figure cs9.8.)

The drivers are each assigned a particular truck. Depending on the orders that have been pre-booked for a particular day, the first driver is scheduled to start work as early as 5:30 in the morning. The first load is assigned on a rotational basis among the drivers. Although the drivers are scheduled to come in on a staggered basis, often several of them will arrive at the same time. While queuing for their first delivery or when between deliveries during the day, they wait in the office near the dispatcher. The plant usually works a five and one half-day week, with Sunday work occasionally scheduled to help out a customer. In April the drivers averaged about 56 hours of work a week. They are paid regular time for an eight-hour day, receive overtime at time and one-half for the first three additional hours and then double time. With weather, delivery time differences and order volumes all having an influence on the timing of deliveries, it is very difficult to match driver availability with the timing of demand. The day-to-day responsibility for doing so lies with the dispatcher, Allen Drysdale.

Allen schedules the delivery of customer orders throughout the day. Working with a daily dispatch sheet he determines when each order will be mixed and the trucks will be dispatched. The day starts with a list pre-booked orders to meet. If the weather is okay and there are no cancellations, Allen starts by filling some of those orders, taking special care to ensure he has capacity to meet the requirements for any large projects or customers who placed orders some time ago. During the day additional orders come in and some are cancelled or changed. He makes delivery commitments for these new orders, balancing all of these demands with those already on the daily dispatch sheet, the trucks that are in the yard, those that will be returning for another delivery and the driver availability. It is a dynamic and challenging task. Figure cs9.9 provides frequency diagrams of the variation per day in loads (trips), time per trip, cubic meters per load and the truck minutes of capacity requested.

Allen stated:

> There are many factors that I consider every time I tell a customer when he or she can expect their order. I take into account who the customer is, what the daily dispatch sheet looks like, what the weather might do and what I think may happen later in the day. It's important to try to get the order to the customer when they want it so they don't go to someone else. When it's busy for us, though, it's probably busy for the other guys too. Even at that we might lose 4 or 5 customer orders over a really busy day. I try to clean up the orders each day. If the weather has been bad, then I may need to move some orders forward, but when that happens we work real hard to clean up everything before the start of the next week. We can use overtime to help us over some of the humps, like we are doing now. I need to be careful, though because it is expensive and there is a limit as to how much we can use. I try to assign the drivers on a first come, first served basis but it is not always possible. Lunch breaks, truck problems or some mismatch between a customer and a driver get in the way. We try to load out of the other plant up in Porirua when the customer is closer to that facility, so I have to keep track of that as well. Something always seems to come up, though. It is all a great juggling act.
>
> I know that we are under pressure to improve the productivity of the trucks, but I don't see an easy way to do it. The size of the average order is going down and the delivery times are getting longer. It's theoretically possible to combine orders for two customers on a single truck, but practically it is difficult. Even if we could get the customer to agree to a later delivery so we could make the combination, we only have one truck that has a load cell that is used for dispersing a metered in the drum specifically for making multiple deliveries. If we can't use that, what will prevent the first customer from taking too much concrete, shorting the second customer and making us deliver again? We just wouldn't gain anything from that. The do-it-yourselfers are notorious for underestimating how much concrete they need, and some

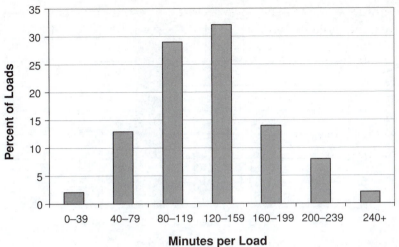

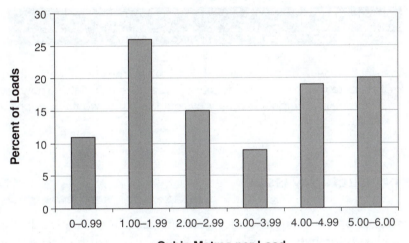

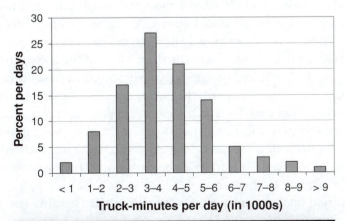

Figure cs9.9 Truck delivery statistics

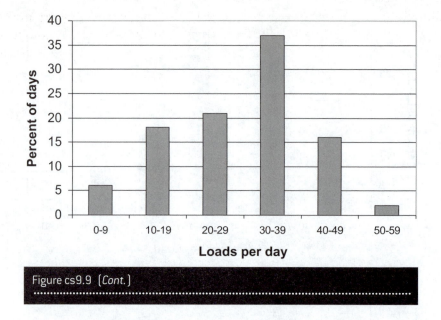

Figure cs9.9 *(Cont.)*

builders are prone to error as well. Besides, I talk to the customers every day. Asking them to wait for an order for our convenience wouldn't go down well. After all, there are a number of other guys out there that would be happy to get that customer's phone call.

The productivity issue

The issue of operational efficiency was very real, but complex. It seemed that truck productivity was important, but so was customer service. As he had learned in the evening program he was taking at Victoria University, the customers were not concerned with his truck efficiency but in how well Firth could serve them. There had already been significant discussions about the number of trucks that should be in the fleet. More of the leased trucks could be returned to the Firth national pool for redistribution to some of the other regions. Dave was reluctant to do this, however, since he had heard some of the drivers complain that the cut backs already left too few trucks. Still, he had the memo from headquarters pointing out that the Wellington Division was not doing as well as some of the other plants. They wanted to know what he was going to do to improve the situation. The memo needed to be answered by the end of the week.

As he turned back to his desk, Dave realised that he only had four days in which to present his answer to the memo from headquarters. His initial instinct was to be a bit rude and invite some of the office types to come out from behind their desks and join him in trying to make a sale in the

Wellington area. On the other hand, he reasoned that he didn't want any of those people talking with any of his customers. Life was difficult enough as it was. He was left with the task of preparing a response. He let out a sigh, sat down at his desk and picked up a pencil.

DISCUSSION QUESTIONS

1. Define the key issues that Dave and Firth faced in this case.
2. How was truck delivery capacity related to customer demand?
3. Were the efficiency measures the ones Dave should be most concerned with or were there others?
4. What was *really* important to the customers in each market? For example, Graeme had been working with the drivers in a program to improve their awareness of the importance of their contacts with the customers. He felt that measures that incorporated some feedback from customers on the drivers' behaviour should be used.
5. How should Dave plan, analyse and then implement a solution to the operational challenges he faced?

Note

1   This case was written by Professors Lawrence M. Corbett and D. Clay Whybark of the University of North Carolina as a basis for classroom discussion. It is part of the CIBER Case Collection, sponsored by Indiana University CIBER and distributed by the ECCH @ Babson. Copyright © 1999 by Lawrence M. Corbett and D. Clay Whybark.

Ford Motor Company: Moving Forward in Australia

Brett Allen

Ford Motor Company – the beginning

The true beginning of the Ford Motor Company will probably never be known as it was born from Henry Ford's relentless efforts to develop a technology that would rapidly replace the horse-drawn carriages of the time and supply motor vehicles to the world. One of the most pivotal points in the history is the first recorded vehicle Henry Ford ever built. Named the Quadricycle, it was constructed at the rear of his and wife Clara's home at 58 Bagley Avenue, Detroit in 1896 (Banham and Newman, 2002).

The Ford Motor Company formally began when the articles of incorporation were signed in Detroit, Michigan on 16 June 1903. At this time Henry Ford and eleven other modern industrialists had a total capitalised sum of $28,000 USD. These funds would lead to the growth and development one of the largest and most successful automotive companies in the world today. Persistence during the early days of incorporation paid off for the Ford Motor Company and the first record of sale was to a Detroit Physician on 20 July 1903, thus the Ford Motor Company began (Brinkley 2003).

From humble beginnings behind his family home, a key differentiating strength of the Ford Motor Company has been its ability to continue to develop new ways of doing things. This pursuit of excellence and continued ability to re-invent itself and move with the times, has helped the Ford Motor Company become a global leader in today's automotive industry. One of the most well-known developments Henry Ford is credited with is the introduction of the Mass Production System into the automotive industry (Womack et al. 1990). In 1913, at Henry Ford's Highland Park Assembly plant, he pioneered the very first mass produced automobiles (Womack et al., 1990). It is this innovative thinking and disciplined approach that has allowed the Ford Motor Company to evolve over the past 100 years into one of the most successful automobile companies in the world today having operations in every major part of the globe covering 129 countries (www.ford.com, accessed 12 November 2006).

Ford Australia

Ford Motor Company of Australia is one of the many subsidiaries of the parent US based Ford Motor Company. Ford cars have been sold in Australia since 1904 but a growing consumer demand for the products led to the establishment of an assembly plant in Australia. Hence the Ford Motor Company of Australia (henceforth called Ford Australia) was commissioned on 31 March 1925. This plant was situated in Geelong, Victoria. In the first year of production, the plant built more than 4000 Model TT trucks, 665 Fordson Tractors and a handful of Lincolns (Banham and Newman, 2002). Approximately three years later in 1928 more than 100,000 model A's were sold.

Nowadays one of the most significant models for Ford Australia is the Ford Falcon which began production in 1960, a nameplate which continues to this day. Ford Australia now employs over 5000 people in design, development, purchasing, sales, administration, manufacturing and assembly facilities across Australia. The Australian headquarters is located in Broadmeadows, on the northern outskirts of Melbourne, and the assembly line there is one of the most diverse in the Ford world. All Falcon sedan and wagon, Falcon Ute, Fairlane, LTD and Territory variants are built on the one assembly line.

Ford Australia's Stamping, Casting and Engine plants still remain in Geelong 70 km southwest of Melbourne. Much of this operation has recently been slated for closing down in 2010 due to global rationalisation strategies. The Ford Proving Ground, located at You Yangs near Geelong, comprises a state-of-the-art vehicle testing and durability facility, complete with an Emissions Laboratory and test-track simulator.

Ford Australia supports the local customer demands in other vehicle segments by importing the European Fiesta and Focus small cars and the Mazda-sourced Escape. Light commercial vehicle imports include the Mazda-sourced Courier and Econovan ranges, the Transit from Britain and the heavy-duty F-Series from Brazil.

The purchasing function

Ford Australia is run and managed by an independent team of people, based in Australia, that have direct reporting relationships back to the global parent in Detroit and regionally into Bangkok. The roles of the people at Ford Australia are many and varied but include the key functions of any multinational enterprise examples include business strategy, design, product development, purchasing, assembly and marketing and sales, human resources, information technology and finance.

One of the key functions within Ford Australia that has had to respond to many current operational business issues is that of the Purchasing Department. There are many roles the purchasing function of an organisation has. Essentially though, the key roles of the function are to:

1. source components at affordable prices, meet quality levels, meet delivery schedules and engineering requirements
2. develop and execute cost reduction strategies
3. continue to develop new operational and strategic process to keep ahead of the ever changing market conditions
4. monitor the supplier manufacturing sites in terms of quality systems adherence and performance.

Since the early 1980s it has been recognised that the purchasing function, if managed well, can contribute to the success of a firm (Carr and Pearson, 2002; Chen et al., 2004). This contribution is seen in the form of revenue generation through access to new technologies, profit increases through cost management and lean supplier chains through supplier development.

Challenges to purchasing at Ford Australia

There are a range of current issues that the Ford Australia needs to face up to in order to continue to compete and remain a world class manufacturer. These issues are summarised below in Table cs10.1, with a discussion of each theme to follow.

Transactional purchasing versus strategic purchasing

Traditional purchasing practices view the purchasing function as a department of clerks, there to simply process various commercial agreements between suppliers and the firm. No consideration is given to the task of strategy, negotiation, or supplier development. Research suggests that this view is now considered a short sighted concept (Ellram and Carr, 1994; Chen

Table cs10.1 Summary of issues facing Ford Australia

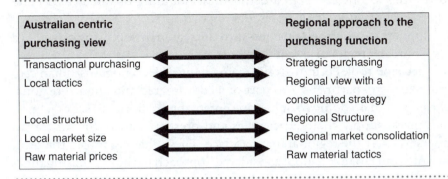

Australian centric purchasing view	Regional approach to the purchasing function
Transactional purchasing	Strategic purchasing
Local tactics	Regional view with a consolidated strategy
Local structure	Regional Structure
Local market size	Regional market consolidation
Raw material prices	Raw material tactics

et al., 2004). To understand the short-sightedness of the traditional view of purchasing one must consider the impact that the purchasing department can have on the profitability of the firm. Simply put, purchasing procure or buy the various raw materials used by the production teams. If these materials can be purchased at more cost competitive rates, this results in lower operating costs for the firm and more profitability, all else being equal. In an automotive business such as Ford Australia and considering the value of purchased components it uses to make the Falcon and Territory range of products, it would be unwise to not follow up on opportunities in the area of cost reduction with the suppliers. So, as a result, Ford Australia began to take a strategic view of the purchasing function.

The purchasing function within Ford Australia took the view that strategic consideration of purchasing would benefit the organisation. In taking this view, the purchasing function became one of the core elements of the company strategy and business plan, with direct and accountable links to the company profit and loss statements. From these strategic plans, targets are defined and operational tasks are identified. This view is consistent with the body of research conducted since the 1980s and into the 21st century. Researchers have identified that there are direct links or positive correlations between a firm that views purchasing as a strategic function and the success of the firm (Carr and Pearson, 1999; Dubois, 2003; Mol 2003; Chen et al., 2004).

Local tactics versus a regional view

After consideration was given to the strategic nature of purchasing at Ford Australia, the next opportunity was to develop this concept on a broader geographic scale, i.e., into the region of Asia Pacific and Africa.

In November 2005, Ford Motor Company restructured the Ford purchasing offices in Asia Pacific and Africa to align on a regional level. This consolidated the purchasing strategies from several local tactical approaches, into a fully coordinated and regionally managed view. This regional view presents opportunities as one can gain a better understanding of value chains and suppliers in the region. It also presents opportunities for current Ford Australia suppliers to grow their business into the region by supplying other Ford Motor Company regional assembly plants.

This decision took Ford Australia from an inward looking Australian centric purchasing department into part of a coordinated and aligned regional purchasing team. In doing so, it has presented opportunities to seek technology advances, supply chain efficiencies and present chances for Australian suppliers to enter the regional market place. These changes forced the team at Ford Australia to take a more considered approach to the purchasing function. Instead of having an internal local tactical approach to purchasing, the department needed to view things from a regional stance. Decisions were no longer made in isolation without consideration of the broader regional impact. For example, the awarding of contracts was more considered. Managers ask themselves questions such as: 'Was this decision a good decision for the region? Did the supplier offer best in class quality/product/price?' Many additional factors need to be considered. The final link in this movement of the firm is to link the various local strategies into one central and coordinated approach. This has been achieved by setting up a management structure to develop regional strategies and deploy them into the countries.

Local structure versus regional structure

With any strategic change, there needs to be an appropriate structure to support the execution of the strategic plan. The regional strategy required several major structural modifications to support the regional purchasing department. Essentially, the fragmented operating business units for the region were consolidated into one business group, albeit in different countries. This brought about new functional management and salary grade roles within each of the countries. Each of these key countries was assigned regional leads for commodities groups as shown in Table cs10.2.

The regional structure also required a redefinition of roles and responsibilities. The key element of change was to allocate all future model purchasing responsibilities to the regional countries. For example, the China sourcing office would develop the strategies and complete the sourcing negotiations for all vehicle programs throughout the region (not only China as in the past). Once the sourcing decisions had been awarded to suppliers, the country purchasing groups would execute the contracts and purchase the parts for their local vehicle programs.

Table cs10.2 Regional commodity lead by country

Group	Commodity Lead	Country
1	Electrical	Ford of Australia
2	Chassis	China Sourcing Office
3	Powertrain (Engine)	Ford of India
4	Powertrain accessories and electronics	Ford of South Africa
5	Interior/Trim	Ford of Taiwan
6	Exterior/Body	Thailand
7	Raw Materials	Thailand

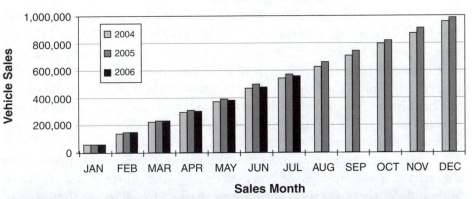

Full Year Sales 2004 v 2005 v 2006
Total Vehicle Market

Figure cs10.1 Market sales by month 2004 – 2006YTD
(www.fcai.com.au)

Market and volume challenges

The Australian automotive market looks very sound with record vehicle sales in 2005 totalling 988,269 units. This surpassed the previous year 2004 by 3.5 per cent at 955,229 units (www.industry.gov.au, accessed 9 September 2006). However, while the total market is buoyant, the domestic manufacturers only contributed to sales of 248,912 vehicles, or 25.2 per cent of the total Australian motor vehicle market. The rest of the market was captured by imported vehicles.

The problem facing the automotive market in Australia is not that the market volume is at an all time high, but there is a decrease in the size of the market for the locally produced vehicles. To further explore this thought, the Australian automotive industry is segmented into several vehicle categories

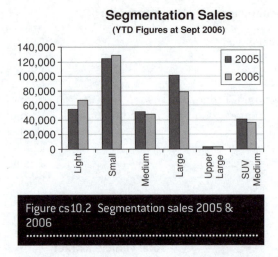

Segmentation Sales
(YTD Figures at Sept 2006)

Figure cs10.2 Segmentation sales 2005 & 2006

ranging from 'light', at the smaller car end of the market, to 'upper large'. The Ford Falcon and Territory, the two vehicles produced locally by Ford, compete in the 'large' vehicle segment. Figure cs10.2 shows how the year over year segments have changed, even in a buoyant market place. Note on this chart the decline in the 'large' and the increase in 'small' market segment cars

This change in customer decision making creates two compounding effects. First, a smaller volume in the market for sellers like Ford; and, second, a more competitive market for the volume that is available.

Another factor that has impacted the volume and competition within the market is the number of competitors. In 2005, there was a choice of 36 brands in the Australian automotive market. Considering that each of these brands has several product offerings, the choice becomes many and varied, thus leading to even greater competition driven by the full range of product offerings to the consumer. Ford Motor Company and Holden brands alone account for 32 products in the market for buyers to select from (www.ford.com.au, www.holden.com.au, accessed 9 September 2006).

Raw material and commodity prices

In the 12 months ending August 2006 we saw unprecedented rises in commodity prices driven by the economic development and growth of other countries in the Asia Pacific region and globally. This was also compounded by a lack of facilities to process raw materials into useable commodities. The effect that raw material price increases have on the business is that it drives up costs of products. These costs need to be offset by seeking alternate strategies. Examples of steep price rises on the commodity market can be seen in Figure cs10.3. These two charts show the price per ton increase recorded on the London Metals Exchange for Aluminium which is used in wheels and suspension components and Copper which is primarily used in wiring.

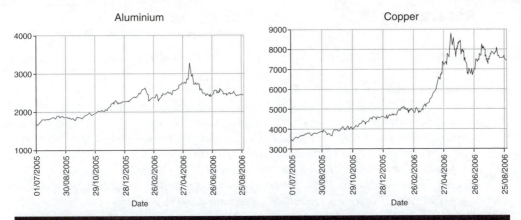

Figure cs10.3 London Metal Exchange cash buyer trend data July 05 – August 06 (USD/T)

In considering these charts, it can be seen that there are many pressures being placed on both suppliers and Ford Australia. These pressures come in the form of increased cost of raw material. Consider an example of a wiring harness that uses 2 kg of copper. On the 3 January 2006, the cash rate for copper was $4537 USD/tonne the price rose steadily during the year to the cash rate of $7410USD/tonne on the 31 October 2006, an increase of $2873USD/tonne or 63 per cent. So the additional cost to the 2 kg copper wiring harness would be from an original price of $9.07 to $14.82 an increase in cost of $5.75.

DISCUSSION QUESTIONS

1. How can and should Ford approach purchasing and rationalise its local ambitions in Australia with its regional and global approach? What factors will determine the long term viability of Ford's operations in Australia and the region?
2. Can the Australian supply base remain viable over say 30 years with the expansion of lower cost operations in countries such as China and Thailand? How do financial strategies integrate with purchasing strategies at Ford?
3. What are the key required skills and capabilities of purchasing functional managers at Ford in Australia?
4. Outline the benefits from changing from a tactical to a strategic approach to purchasing.
5. Will Ford Australia be able to further improve its product cost and quality through better purchasing, and if so, how?
6. Forecast the future of operations and purchasing activities, 5 and 10 years out, for Ford Australia.

References

Banham, R. and Newman, P. 2002. *The Ford Century 100 Years*. Korea: Ford Motor Company.

Brinkley, D. 2003. *Wheels for the World*. New York: Viking.

Carr, A. S. and Pearson, J. N. 1999. 'Strategically managed buyer-supplier relationships and performance outcomes.' *Journal of Operations Management*, 17(5): 497–519.

Carr, A. S. and Pearson, J. N. 2002. 'The impact of purchasing and supplier involvement on strategic purchasing and its impact on firm performance.' *International Journal of Operations & Production Management*, 22(9): 1032–53.

Chen, I. J., Paulraj, A. et al. 2004. 'Strategic purchasing, supply management, and firm performance.' *Journal of Operations Management*, 22(5): 505–23.

Dubois, A. 2003. 'Strategic cost management across boundaries of firms.' *Industrial Marketing Management*, 32(5): 365–74.

Ellram, L. M. and Carr, A. 1994. 'Strategic purchasing: A history and review of the literature.' *International Journal of Purchasing and Materials Management*, 30(2): 10.

Mol, M. J. (2003). 'Purchasing's strategic relevance.' *Journal of Purchasing and Supply Management*, 9(1): 43–50.

Womack, J. P., Jones, D. T. et al. 1990. *The Machine that Changed the World*. New York: Harper Perennial – Harper Collins.

Internet resources

www.fcai.com.au, accessed 19th November, 2006, Federal Chamber of Automotive Industry

www.ford.com.au, accessed 9th September, 2006, Ford Australia website

www.ford.com accessed 11th August, 2006, Global Ford Motor Company website

www.industry.gov.au, accessed 9 September, 2006, Federal Government website for the Department of Industry, Tourism and Resources.

www.holden.com.au, accessed 9th September, 2006, Holden Australia website.

www.lme.com, accessed 19 November, 2006, London Metals Exchange website.

Technology Transfer at Hero Honda

R. D. Pathak, Z. Husain, Sushil and Danny Samson

This case is of the partnership and the technology transfer between a leading Japanese company (Honda) with leading edge automotive technology, and an Indian company (Hero Motors) with a sound domestic market share and solid local reputation. Each had the potential to add significant value to the other, conditional upon their core value systems being compatible. One company, Hero, had the local market presence and the other Honda, had the right technology, in other markets.

The key question is how to make optimal use, in terms of value creation, of technological leadership, in a foreign market that is relatively less sophisticated than that of the technology source. Such matters are strategic issues, not tactical for both the international source and the local host company. The degree to which the technology is appropriate is measured in both technical terms, and most importantly in business, market and financial terms. Strategic technology management for stakeholders engaged in a major international technology transfer refers to the decisions of resource-base, design, technical specifications, organisational arrangements and fees, incentives, financials and contracts, marketing, manufacturing, branding and supply chain, and finally, leadership and cultural and philosophical fit of those stakeholders.

In the early 1980s the Indian economy was opening up and foreign companies and technologies were allowed to come into the sectors of strategic importance. Many automobile manufacturing firms were finding their way to the Indian market. TVS-Suzuki, Maruti Udyog Ltd, Birla Yamaha Limited, Escorts Yamaha Motors Limited, and many others came into existence in the automobile sector and Honda Motors of Japan (Honda) was also looking for partners with whom to venture into the Indian market. Before Honda started looking for business partners in India, they assessed the transportation requirements of the Indian population masses and anticipated a growing market for two wheelers.

A team of experts from Honda visited more than 50 destinations in India, including major cities, small and big towns, hilly and rocky terrain's of the country. They gathered the data for technologies, i.e., a scooter based on two stroke and motor bicycle based on four stroke technology. The reason for this was that India was predominantly a scooter market, besides there was non-availability of a four-stroke motorbike in 100 cc engine capacity category in the domestic market. Honda saw great market potential in 100 cc four-stroke technology in India. Fuel efficiency, environment friendliness (in comparison to two stroke vehicles), and load conditions in urban and rural parts of the country were important reasons that contributed to their decision of bringing out a radically innovative vehicle. The vehicles designed for the other three countries in the neighboring region were not a great deal different. But of course modifying an existing vehicle or designing a new vehicle needs massive investments in terms of money and efforts with the other business risks associated with the technology development. These developments happened before Honda entered into joint venture partnership or technological collaboration with any firm in India. After having done this they started looking for a business partner for a four-stroke motorbike venture.

On the other hand, the local Hero Group also undertook a market survey project, almost on similar lines, and the finding of both the studies delivered comparable results.

The Hero Group made a humble beginning in 1956 in India with bicycle manufacturing. The founding father, late Mr. Dayanand Munjal, laid the foundation of the Hero group with a dream of providing technologically advanced and affordable transportation solutions. Becoming the Number 1 bicycle manufacturer in the world was the first step in the process. The first group company is known world over as Hero Cycles Limited. It manufactures 14,500 bicycles every day, delivered to the customers through a network of nearly 3750 dealers in India and 250 dealers abroad. The second group company was Rockman Cycle Industries Limited, which came into existence in 1961 as a part of indigenisation and backward integration. Continuing with the same process, Highway Cycle Industries Limited was floated in the year 1971. Hero group promoted Majestic Auto Limited in 1978 and Munjal Castings in 1981 to manufacture mopeds and health care equipment and non-ferrous castings respectively. This was followed by a rapid growth phase of promoting Hero Honda Motors Limited (HHML-a joint venture with Honda Motors of Japan) in 1983, Munjal Showa Limited (a joint venture with Showa of Japan) in 1985, Sunbeam Castings in 1987, Hero Motors (a division of Majestic Auto in collaboration with Steyr Daimler Puch, Austria, which recently entered into collaboration with BMW of Germany), Hero Cycles Limited (Unit II), and Gujrat Cycles Limited (a joint venture with Gujrat Industrial Development Corporation) in 1988; and Hero Cold Rolling division in 1990. Starting with bicycles and progressively moving to moped to 100 cc 4 stroke motorbikes, to 650 cc prestigious BMW solutions, the group has 13 companies and 15 manufacturing units to manufacture a full range of two-wheeler transportation options and world class auto components.

Today Hero is a popular name in bicycles not only in India but in 60 countries including in Europe and North America. HHML is an undisputed market leader in the four-stroke 100 cc category. It is also popular with the name and reputation of a: 'Fill It, Shut It, and Forget It' vehicle because of its fuel efficiency and environment friendliness, which are of utmost concern to automotive vehicle producers and users all over the world. The group had also developed two more companies, Hero Exports in 1993, which deals in trading of Basmati rice, garments, bicycle components, steel, and wheat in the international market; and Hero Corporate Service established in 1995, which deals in management services related to strategic business plans, information technology, and project management.

Technology history of the Hero Group

The Hero Group of companies has an impressive track record for indigenisation, exploring economies of scale and scope, and product innovation. Their bicycle business has provided them with an opportunity to learn about the changing choices and preferences of customers in different parts of the world. The group's corporate management has a tradition of keeping in touch with the state-of-art technology in their field of interest. They have also learned to innovate on the existing products to attract the customers who have also helped the group in developing a sound customer base not only in India but also in other countries. In the process of indigenisation and product innovations, the company has strived for developing technology-based products in-house or in the group companies.

What impressed Honda about the Hero Group?

Honda Motors had received 150 applications and short-listed nearly 20 companies in India for a joint venture partnership. The Honda team visited the existing plants and manufacturing facilities of their potential joint venture partners. When the Honda team of experts visited the Hero Group of companies, they were surprised to learn that the management practices were quite at par with the management paradigms taking shape in Japan.

> The chief executive officer of Honda said:

> The team was quite impressed with the Indian version of Just In Time (JIT) inventory system then practiced in Hero Cycles and other Hero companies. The overall interpersonal relationship between workers and management was another bright spot in the managerial practices. The team was particularly impressed with the open door policy of then group Managing Director Late Raman Kant Munjal, who knew many of his workmen by their first names and also knew a lot about their families. The same was valid for dealers in the marketing set up. The Honda team was also impressed with the productivity of the Ludhiana factory and unprecedented record of quality.

Honda experts found the Hero companies practicing the state-of-art Japanese management principles and hence found the group most appropriate for a long-term business relationship.

Technology management at HHML

Hero Group believed in the effectiveness of the Honda technology, particularly the 4-stroke option, and entered into a joint venture partnership after assessing it carefully.

'Honda had undertaken a massive exercise to know customer preferences and had concluded that a fuel efficient and cost effective motorbike could be the solution,' said the Hero Chief Technology Officer (CTO).

As regards the technology assessment, the group thought that Honda was way ahead in automobile technology particularly in four-stroke, and had established its credentials all over the globe. Hero found Honda solutions to be better than other potential technology providers on fuel consumption, emission and durability of the product technology.

As to technological leadership, Honda is the undisputed world leader in four stroke motorbikes. The leadership is visible in the market share, customer preference, in meeting the environmental norms, and investment in technology. The firm believes that its high market share is largely because of better technology and aggressive, but well thought out marketing strategy. The top management has set the agenda for HHML as continued effort for the development of the motorbike industry through new product development, technological innovation, investment in equipment and facilities, and efficient management. HHML sees its core competence in absorbing process technologies. 'HHML is a manufacturing unit which has absorbed the technology very effectively and has modified several process technologies to save cost and also to realise product differentiation. The group management thinks that their core competence lies in effective indigenisation and absorption of technology' said the HHML CTO. The innovations in process technologies, cost reduction in indigenised components, and value addition to the product without extra cost are clear indications of its technology absorption capabilities.

HHML spends nearly 1 per cent of its total revenue on in-house R&D, which is significantly low by world standards, but reasonably high by local (Indian) industry standards. The chief technology officer (CTO) does not feel that they are starving for resources, but thinks that they get enough resources as needed. At present they are not in a position to absorb more resources because the technology agenda, which the firm has laid down for itself, does not ask for more. A firm needs a solid foundation for absorbing the investments made and yielding the desired results.

Capital investment in technological projects involving imports of equipments is discussed in the joint consultative committee, which has given good suggestions on many occasions in the past. Honda experts help in choosing the state-of-art solutions. As far as indigenous equipment is concerned, HHML has enough expertise available. HHML had identified certain leverage points where little investment (or other resources) yielded fabulous benefits in the long run. These included testing of all the components that had helped in smooth indigenisation and suiting the product to meet the changing preferences of the local customers.

A larger part of the manufacturing process technology has been supplied to HHML by Honda Motors exclusively. Many precision and intricate parts are manufactured on these machines. Many other machines have been bought from other manufacturers as suggested by Honda. The Production Engineering Department (PED) has evolved processes that are more cost effective and quality as well as operator friendly. It has been a case of active technology transfer in which HHML is banking on Honda for prompt and effective technological solutions.

'The 'CD100' vehicle after its launch has had many problems but solutions to them have been generated in record time without even letting the customer know about the problem', said the HHML Chief Executive Officer. All design and material aspects are taken care of by Honda while manufacturing is looked after by HHML.

Technology borrowers always needs sound state-of-art testing facilities for analyzing the product performance and process characteristics. It is an important step in technology absorption. HHML has developed testing facilities in which 90 per cent of the testing is done locally. They need to depend on Honda for critical tests for which Honda has developed testing technology, which is scarcely available with other manufacturers in the world.

At the new plant, most of the machines are computer numerically controlled (CNC) and changing of a setting from one model to another takes just minutes. Anticipating the increasing effect of market pull and customers becoming more demanding, small batches of many models will be required in the future. HHML management is technology savvy, having evolved systems to adopt and adapt to new technologies. The chaos occurring because of new technology implementation is reduced to the minimum because of this approach. They form teams and task forces; and then implement very meticulously the structured programs designed by HHML technologists. Their Japanese counterparts also actively support them in these ventures.

Since HHML is the market leader in this category of vehicles, and technological capabilities are utilised to sustain this position, increasing component/material cost is carefully looked into. Serious thought is always given to accommodate the increased cost by better capacity utilisation, product and manufacturing innovations, and rigorous value engineering exercises. Vendors are also motivated to take up innovative ideas for implementation to bring down or maintain the cost and to improve the quality. Raw material conservation, energy conservation, and cost reduction in bought out components are also tried. HHML is an extremely environmentally friendly firm, inside with the process technologies and outside with the product technology.

The Honda and Hero groups' strategic alliance believes in promoting its corporate image in Indian as well as world markets. They undertake a lot of image building exercises, which are based mainly on technological breakthroughs. They cannot afford to compromise with the technology management function in their respective territories in order to stay as market leaders in the two-wheeler segment of the automobile industry.

As far as product technology is concerned, Honda's approval is a must for any innovation. The HHML Research and Development (R&D) and Production Engineering Department (PED) have implemented many innovations in manufacturing technology like induction brazing in place of gas-based operations. In manufacturing technology, HHML enjoys full freedom of innovations and can apply its creativity for making it more efficient and cost effective and for maintaining the quality of the end product.

As to technology waste, there has been almost no incidence in which the technology was developed but could not be utilised. HHML has developed four models so far in the past 13 years of its existence, and all of them have been received well by Indian customers, albeit with different degrees of success. As regards the product technology, plastics are used extensively in many parts of the world in Honda bikes. Through looking to the usage conditions of the vehicles and environmental concerns, plastic components have been used to improve the overall benefit to the customers. Technology waste has been avoided by carefully and proactively selecting the product and process technologies.

In respect of clarity in technology acquisition, the Production Engineering Department (PED) and Research and Development (R&D) group prepare the plans to be implemented in consultation with the Projects division. They work out several options and the advantages and disadvantages of each one of them. The technical director chooses one of them depending upon the firm's long-term business objectives. The choice of option may or may not be divulged to the planners. The decisions related to technology are not transparent to even top management executives.

The definition of state-of-art is different for different people and countries. For example, HHML took a technology that was nearly 10 years old and adapted it to the Indian conditions. Now they have developed a capability wherein changing to any new technology or adopting incremental innovations would not be difficult.

The HHML Chief Technology Officer (CTO) says:

> Every time when the MOU with Honda is renewed, new clauses are added to the benefit of both the partners. Similarly old clauses that become irrelevant over a period of time are excluded. For example, earlier only 100 cc motorbikes were open to HHML, but now they can manufacture any bike that Honda manufactures. This is a measure of technology absorption capability that the firm has developed over time and the confidence that Honda has shown in their joint venture partner (JVP).

Levels of technology absorption

When HHML began to absorb Honda technology, they decided to design an altogether new engine. Honda persuaded them to revise their agenda of technology absorption. The automobile technology is divided into four distinct categories, which are design, product testing, manufacturing, and marketing after sales. The first and last categories are classified as soft technologies, and second and third as hard technologies. 'Honda made a point to HHML, that if you start developing an engine now, you will take two years time and even after that you will not be sure whether you will be able to do that or not; whereas Honda can do it in three months time with a high probability of success. Similar things were told about the testing technology. HHML was convinced about their strengths in manufacturing, marketing and after sales. However, in design and testing, HHML was assured of full support from Honda. This revision, Honda suggested, was based on their experience in Nigeria, Brazil, Argentina, and other places. HHML did very well on these two fronts and absorbed the manufacturing and after sales technologies quite effectively. In after sales, Honda trained people of HHML for maintenance and repair of the motorbikes. As the four-stroke is a sensitive engine, such that if it is maintained well with proper tooling and adequate training, it gives wonderful performance, otherwise it is not able to deliver desired results. HHML, following the advice of Honda, revised its priorities and concentrated on training of roadside mechanics, dealers, and authorised service stations. For rural markets, mobile workshops were introduced. Japanese personnel were not available for after-sales service and manufacturing, and therefore, this was a field left open only to Indians. Manufacturing technology was also included, making the product in the same way as has been described in the design and thereby assuring its performance.

Next on the agenda was vendor development and development of testing facilities. HHML does work out design modifications but does not develop original designs. In technology management and particularly transfer, there are two parts, one is 'know-how' and the second is 'know-why'. No technology provider will disclose to its collaborator or joint venture partner the know-why part and Honda does the same. Most of 'know-why' is held with Honda Research and Development (R&D), which is a separate firm altogether and it sells its intellectual information to Honda companies and joint venture partners the world over. Honda pays Honda R&D for intellectual information and joint venture partners pay Honda. Hence Honda partners do not have a direct dialogue with Honda R&D. Honda is a fairly open global player but some of the technologies are very closely held.

Indigenisation: a significant challenge

HHML imports 14 per cent of the components (value wise) from Japan for two reasons. First, the cost effectiveness of those components, i.e., HHML's consumption level of these components, doesn't justify a separate plant for them in India. Second, there are some key components whose quality cannot be compromised. When the volume grows further, vendors may be asked to bring technology from Japan to India and start manufacturing in India. In that case the imports are likely to go down further.

The Hero Group has a fascinating history of indigenisation right from its beginning. Hero Cycles Ltd., the first group company, indigenised the imported components quite early and took over the leadership of this industry. The same philosophy prevails in HHML too, as far as indigenisation is concerned.

The HHML Chief Technology Officer says:

> Vendors, who have already brought in the technology from other firms abroad and are meeting quality and performance standards; HHML goes ahead and sources components from them. But in case a particular vendor needs improvement in technology then HHML not only suggests but plays a mediator role in getting the technology from the firm which is supplying the same component(s) to Honda in Japan.

HHML is the world number one plant in Honda joint ventures all over the world in level and speed of indigenisation. It is also the world's number 1 plant in manufacturing the base model 'CD100' in such a large volume (approximately 1000 motorbikes per day). The local Research and Development (R&D) team has proved itself to be highly productive in terms of developing new models. It developed the 'CD100 SS' model on its own which is a grand success in the Indian rural market. Similarly 'Splendor' is another model, which is a roaring success in high-income clientele. Together with Honda R&D, it takes up Value Engineering (VE) exercises, which improve the quality and performance of the products without increasing the cost, so it can also be termed as cost savings in a sense. The Chief Technology Officer (CTO) of the firm is an international authority in VE and makes use of VE techniques quite effectively and innovatively.

Expected performance outcomes

Dependence on imported components was expected to reduce over time. Building core competencies in technology acquisition and subsequent indigenisation in the shortest period of time would allow for HHML to stay ahead of its competition and emerge as the technology leader in the Indian motorbike market.

Dependence on other firms would potentially only be for acquiring radical innovations in technology. The smaller step improvements would be totally generated from within HHML, giving it a competitive advantage that would be difficult to replicate in the region. The overall result would be a thorough and complete strategy delivering wealth maximisation through effective technology management.

DISCUSSION QUESTIONS

1. From the perspective of Hero Motors, what choices did it have going forward, and why was Honda an attractive partner?
2. From the perspective of Honda Motors, what was the attraction of Hero Motors, and what value was available to be added?
   How would the synergy be created through such a joint venture, and how would such value be shared?
3. What key success factors need to be in place to ensure success of two such different companies from such culturally different countries?
4. What key risks existed at the time that the j.v. was being set up? For Hero? For Honda?
5. How is HHML faring currently in business, financial and strategic terms? (Hint look on the Internet.)

Why Is the Patient Resident Time so Long?: The Case of St Martin's and Charity Private Hospital

Victoria Hanna and Kannan Sethuraman

Introduction

In mid March 2006, Mr William Lovejoy, CEO of St Martin's and Charity Private Hospital was concerned about the performance deterioration in the day surgery unit at the Charity campus. The unit had witnessed (i) a steady erosion in its theatre throughput (shorter lists planned by surgeons), (ii) greater use of overtime nurses and technicians (resulting in increased costs) and (iii) frustration from all quarters (patients, surgeons, anaesthetists, nurses, technicians and orderlies). Patients were constantly complaining about the excessive wait they experienced. The inability to start surgeries on time had caused considerable dissatisfaction among the practising surgeons and was inhibiting Charity's ability to attract and retain high performing surgeons. Sixty to seventy per cent of the theatre sessions were experiencing delayed starts.

Hospital background

St Martin's and Charity Private Hospital is a not-for-profit Catholic hospital in Melbourne with 430 registered beds, and it is located across two campuses. In total they handle about 22,000 overnight cases and a further 13,700 day cases annually. The hospital does not employ any doctors or anaesthetists. Instead, it has arrangements with a large group of consultant surgeons who hold privileges to use the hospital facilities for treatment of their patients. The times they are allocated for surgery are commonly referred to as sessions and the surgeons are free to select their anaesthetists to assist them in their surgeries. The hospital derives its revenues from the fees levied to the patients for the use of its facilities, for example operating rooms (OR), hospital beds and other services. In most cases, hospital charges are borne by health insurance providers (the billing system is well established) and the hospital's revenue is based on negotiated rates with these firms.

Day surgery unit at Charity campus

The day surgery unit on the Charity Campus handles only elective surgeries and annually processes about 10,000 overnight admissions and 7400 day surgeries. They offer a range of specialties including orthopaedics, neurosurgery, urology, plastics, breast surgery and dental surgery. The hospital provides facilities, equipment and nursing staff. The hospital facilities consist of nine operating rooms (OR) with state-of-the-art equipment and hospital wards for in-patients. The management team faces the challenge of managing and allocating staff and equipment so that surgeries can be performed efficiently, cost effectively and safely. The OR staff is comprised of registered nurses, nursing assistants, scrub technicians and administrators. OR equipment may either be owned by the hospital or be procured from outside on a loan or hire basis. The equipment that is owned by the hospital will usually be shared across theatres. Once the assignment of suitable theatres for the scheduled surgery has been completed, the Director of Nursing is responsible for ensuring the availability of staff when needed.

Regulatory requirements specify threshold levels for nurse-patient ratios and inability to provide adequate number of qualified nurses to meet the ratio requirements can result in 'unused' beds and consequent underutilisation of available capacity. The decisions about the size and mix of nursing staff are critical areas for the Director of Nursing. Overstaffed, undermanned, and unbalanced nursing teams have implications for the quality and cost of patient care. St Martin's and Charity hospital has adopted a hybrid strategy to meet its nurse requirements in both wards and ORs. The hospital employs a core group of permanent nursing staff, complemented by a bank of casual nurses available at short notice. In addition, the hospital also has arrangements with several private agencies that provide qualified nurses for short periods, on a temporary basis. Historically, 80 per cent of the hospital's requirements (in terms of nurse hours) have been met by permanent staff and 20 per cent from casual or agency staff. But more recently, the need for hiring agency staff has been escalating.

Schedule of surgeries

Prior to interacting with Charity the patient consults with his or her primary care physician. Upon receiving a referral from the general practitioner to visit a medical specialist, the patient then be assessed by the specialist. This stage does not involve the hospital and may consist of several visits to the specialist's office and diagnostic laboratories. Once the need for surgery is established, the patient's name is added to the surgeon's list of patients requiring surgery or hospitalisation. Typically, specialist doctors have privileges at several hospitals in the area, and the choice of hospital for surgery is determined by a number of factors that include cost, patient preference, case complexity, wait involved, facilities and other services provided by the hospital. St Martin's and Charity competes on location, range of services offered and its reputation for quality and patient care. It is not uncommon for elective surgeries to be scheduled several weeks (even a few months) in advance. Charity receives information of surgeon lists as late as 24 hours prior to surgery. The surgeon's operating list is dynamic; with additions possible just a few hours ahead of surgery session start time. The hospital is expected to be responsive and be able to provide the requisite support of staff, equipment and supplies.

How does the hospital plan for its resources?

Planning and scheduling at both campuses is similar to other hospitals in Australia with annual theatre plans forming the basis for hospital's activities. Advanced IT solutions are rare in Australia, with schedules predominantly being planned manually. The theatre plan involves assignment of theatre sessions to consultant surgeons and essentially defines the demand for hospital's services. A half-day slot is considered the basic unit for this purpose and surgeons expect hospitals to provide complete flexibility in organising the activities within their sessions. The assignment of a theatre session to a surgeon commits the hospital for providing the necessary staff and equipment for surgery and post-operative care, and hence the hospital workload is a direct consequence of the theatre plan. The theatre plan is developed in consultation with the surgeons and varies little from year to year, except for changes to accommodate vacation periods of surgeons and other planned absences. Often surgeons do not provide this information in a timely manner, and hospitals rely on word-of-mouth intelligence from theatre nurses for advance knowledge of surgeon absences. Surgeons can lose their allocated sessions if they do not utilise it enough, but in practice this is rare.

The labour cost of nurses and technicians is perhaps the most significant controllable operating cost at the hospital and directly impacts the hospital's financial viability. A staffing plan for nurses in the OR theatres is prepared on a monthly basis, two weeks in advance to conform to regulatory requirements. The initial plan is developed on the basis of the session plan. The nurse schedule is revised and frozen only a day in advance, at which time the requirements are assessed based on surgery lists available in the hospital. Besides adjustments for providing the required number of qualified nurses, the final schedule takes into account deviations from the initial plan (for example, absence due to sickness, or inability to schedule the nurse due to excess overtime on the previous day etc.) At this stage there is only very limited flexibility in respect of permanent, full time staff and the nurse scheduler relies on external sources to meet the requirements.

Typical patient flow at Charity

Figure cs12.1 illustrates a typical patient flow at Charity for day surgery cases. When patients arrive they first go to hospital reception. At this stage they handover any test results or medical notes they have brought with them, and complete the necessary information regarding private health insurance. They are also be advised of any additional payment necessary. Patients are seen on a first come first serve basis, rather than the order their name appears on the surgeons list. All of the patients having surgery in the morning session (across all of the 9 ORs) are requested to arrive between 6.45 and 7 a.m. There can be between 30 and 50 people attempting to access the reception desk at this time. Once the business office (behind reception) has completed all the necessary paperwork, the patient is released and proceeds to the Surgical Admission Unit (SAU) reception. When patients are admitted to SAU their medical records are checked again and any discrepancies are followed up. The patients can then change out of their clothes and proceed to the SAU Waiting Room. Most patients are accompanied by family members, and there is a small waiting room area adjoining SAU where they can stay. Unless they are accompanying a child they cannot enter the SAU itself.

All patients are required to complete nurse education before being transferred to OR and the majority of cases also require preoperative assessment by their anaesthetist. Nurse education involves meeting with one of the SAU nurses who will explain how their day will proceed, this could be done at the same time as admission but when there are large numbers of patients waiting, it is often delayed to a later stage. Due to the congestion in SAU, these meetings occur on an ad hoc basis. Both anaesthetists and nurses can be seen frantically searching for their patients, trying to ensure the first patients on the surgeons' lists are ready to enter OR on time. The anaesthetists are under

Table cs12.1 Typical patient wait times for day surgery cases at Charity

Description	Min Time (minutes)	Max Time (minutes)	Average (minutes)
Patient waiting at reception	1	54	13
Patient waiting for admission into the Surgical Unit	1	154	25
Pre-operative interview with anaesthetists	1	18	4
Surgery duration	10	180	30
Time from entering SAU to entering OR	11	273	128
Total time in system	64	584	374

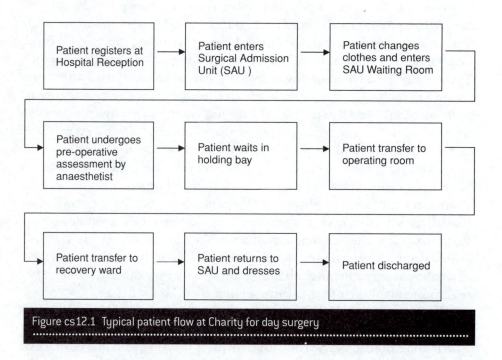

Figure cs12.1 Typical patient flow at Charity for day surgery

even more time duress because they want to see all their patients for the session before surgery begins on the first patient. The reason for this practice is that the anaesthetists want to be physically present in the theatre for the complete duration of surgery, and they are also under pressure from surgeons to ensure fast turnaround between surgical cases. Another contributing factor is the physical layout of the theatres, which are not in proximity to the preoperative assessment rooms.

Once the surgery is complete, the patient transfers to a recovery ward. Once fully recovered, they walk back to SAU and get dressed. If no further payment is required they are then discharged via SAU. If additional payment is required they are directed back to the hospital reception; whereupon they will make final payment to the hospital and are discharged by the business office. The patients for the afternoon session all arrive between 10.30 a.m. and 11 a.m., repeating the chaos of the morning. Table cs12.1 illustrates how long patients usually wait at various stages of their day. Some patients move rapidly through the system, but others can spend long periods of time waiting to enter both the SAU and the OR. But on an average, a patient resides more than six hours in the system where the actual value added time is less than an hour in duration.

DISCUSSION QUESTIONS

1. What are the operational problems and their key drivers at this hospital?
2. What are the strategies you would use to improve the responsiveness of the day surgery unit?
3. What are the strategies you would use to improve the efficiency of the day surgery unit?
4. Are responsiveness and efficiency goals in conflict, and if so, how can these aspects of operations best be resolved?
5. Would obtaining and allocating more resources be the best way forward, and if so, what resources and how much would you suggest?
6. How could better planning and scheduling improve the operational outcomes?

Index